Records of the Grand Historian of China

TRANSLATED FROM THE *Shih chi* OF SSU-MA CH'IEN

IN TWO VOLUMES

PREPARED FOR THE COLUMBIA COLLEGE PROGRAM
OF TRANSLATIONS FROM THE ORIENTAL CLASSICS
WM. THEODORE DE BARY, EDITOR

NUMBER LXV OF THE
RECORDS OF CIVILIZATION: SOURCES AND STUDIES
EDITED UNDER THE AUSPICES OF THE
DEPARTMENT OF HISTORY, COLUMBIA UNIVERSITY

DS748
S7453
v.2

Records of the Grand Historian of China TRANSLATED FROM THE Shih chi OF ṢSU-MA CH'IEN BY BURTON WATSON

VOLUME II:

THE AGE OF EMPEROR WU

140 TO CIRCA 100 B.C.

COLUMBIA UNIVERSITY PRESS

NEW YORK AND LONDON

NOV 12 1970

155397

Copyright © 1961 Columbia University Press
First printing 1961
Third printing 1968
Library of Congress Catalog Card Number: 60-13348
Printed in the United States of America

The addition to the "Records of Civilization:
Sources and Studies" of a group of translations
of Oriental historical materials, of which this
volume is one, was made possible by funds granted
by Carnegie Corporation of New York. That Corporation
is not, however, the author, owner, publisher, or
proprietor of this publication, and is not to be
understood as approving by virtue of its grant
any of the statements made or views expressed therein.

UNESCO COLLECTION OF REPRESENTATIVE WORKS
CHINESE SERIES
This work has been accepted in the Chinese Translations
Series of the United Nations Educational, Scientific
and Cultural Organization (UNESCO).

RECORDS OF CIVILIZATION
SOURCES AND STUDIES

EDITED UNDER THE AUSPICES OF THE
DEPARTMENT OF HISTORY, COLUMBIA UNIVERSITY

GENERAL EDITOR

JACQUES BARZUN, *Seth Low Professor of History*

EDITORS EMERITI

JAMES T. SHOTWELL, *Bryce Professor Emeritus of the History of International Relations*

AUSTIN P. EVANS, *Professor Emeritus of History*

EDITOR: EUROPEAN RECORDS

JOHN H. MUNDY, *Associate Professor of History*

EDITORS: ORIENTAL RECORDS

C. MARTIN WILBUR, *Professor of Chinese History*

WM. THEODORE DE BARY, *Professor of Chinese and Japanese*

CONSULTING EDITORS

SALO W. BARON, *Professor of Jewish History, Literature, and Institutions on the Miller Foundation*

GILBERT HIGHET, *Anthon Professor of the Latin Language and Literature*

DONALD KEENE, *Professor of Japanese*

PAUL O. KRISTELLER, *Professor of Philosophy*

GARRETT MATTINGLY, *William R. Shepherd Professor of European History*

CONTENTS

MAP

VOLUME II

The Age of Emperor Wu

140 *to circa* 100 B.C.

INTRODUCTION

The chapters of the *Shih chi* translated in this volume deal principally with the reign of Emperor Wu, the period of Ssu-ma Ch'ien's own lifetime. The historian is here no longer copying and systematizing the written accounts of ancient China, as he had done in the chapters on pre-Ch'in history, nor relating the somewhat romanticized tales of the founding and early days of the Han that had been handed down to him. He is writing about "the present emperor," the ruler at whose court he spent his adult life, about the nobles and ministers he knew there, about his friends, and about his enemies.

Ssu-ma Ch'ien was in an excellent position to gather material for a history of his age. Undoubtedly he heard the speeches of many of the men he describes, listened to the deliberations of the courtiers, consulted files of official documents kept in the palace, and observed the effects of various government policies when he accompanied the emperor on tours through the provinces. He had personally visited some of the barbarian lands that were being brought under Han rule by Emperor Wu's foreign conquests, and in other cases he no doubt heard from the generals themselves the accounts of their wars and hardships. Even his description of penal conditions under Emperor Wu is based, we may be sure, upon personal experience, since he himself was imprisoned for a time.

Regarding this last it may be well to review here the facts of Ssu-ma Ch'ien's melancholy brush with the law. In 108 B.C. Ssu-ma Ch'ien succeeded his father, who had died two years earlier, in the post of grand historian at the court of Emperor Wu. During the years immediately following, he was engaged in revising and correcting the calendar. At the same time he seems to have been busily at work writing his history of China's past, a task which his father had begun and had charged him to complete. In 99 B.C., however, his fortunes, like those of so many of the officials he describes, took an unexpected and disastrous turn.

This year a large force of Chinese cavalry and infantry was sent to attack the Hsiung-nu, one of a long series of expeditions launched by Emperor Wu in an attempt to break the power of these troublesome northern tribes. One of the commanders, Li Ling, won a brilliant initial success against the enemy, news of which was received with rejoicing at the court. Later, however, when reinforcements failed to arrive and his troops had been decimated by a running battle, he was surrounded by the enemy and persuaded to surrender. Emperor Wu expected his unsuccessful generals to die with their men, and when word of Li Ling's capitulation reached him he was sick with rage. The other courtiers united in condemning Li Ling's action, but Ssu-ma Ch'ien, who had known Li Ling personally, attempted to speak on his behalf, pointing out the glory which the general had won before he was overwhelmed by superior numbers, and suggesting that he had surrendered only in hopes of finding some opportunity to escape and return to China.

But the emperor was in no mood to listen to palliative arguments and summarily had Ssu-ma Ch'ien handed over to the law officials for "investigation." Knowing what was expected of them, they found him guilty of attempting "to deceive the emperor," a crime punishable by death. With a sufficient amount of money Ssu-ma Ch'ien might have bought commutation of the sentence, but this he did not possess. No one raised a hand to help him. According to Han custom, a gentleman of honor was expected to commit suicide before allowing himself to be dragged off to prison for investigation—which meant torture until the victim confessed. But Ssu-ma Ch'ien declined to take this drastic step because, as he himself states, he hoped at all cost to finish writing his history. In the end he was sentenced to undergo castration, the severest penalty next to death and one which carried with it a peculiar aura of shame. Whether the emperor considered him too learned and valuable a man to execute, or whether Ssu-ma Ch'ien himself requested to undergo this disgrace in preference to death and the end of his hopes for literary fame, we do not know.

After his punishment the emperor made him a palace secretary, a position of great honor and trust that could be filled only by a eunuch, since it involved waiting upon the emperor when the latter was at leisure in the women's quarters. At this time Ssu-ma Ch'ien seems to have completed his history. We do not know when he died, though it was probably around 90 B.C., a few years before the death of his sovereign.[1]

Obviously a man who had suffered such a punishment would have every reason to hate the ruler who inflicted it and to despise his fellow courtiers who had been too timid or callous to come to his aid. For this reason many critics have eyed the sections of the *Shih chi* relating to Emperor Wu and his court with suspicion and have suggested that the historian may have deliberately distorted the facts out of motives of spite and revenge. In the Latter Han Emperor Ming (A.D. 58–75), who did not like Ssu-ma Ch'ien's unflattering portrait of his predecessor, accused the historian of "using veiled words to criticize and slander, attacking his own times." [2] From very early times all but the opening paragraph of "The Basic Annals of Emperor Wu" has been missing, either lost or never written. Some writers have asserted that the chapter as Ssu-ma Ch'ien wrote it was so derogatory that when it was shown to the emperor he scraped the writing off the tablets.

Unfortunately we have almost no other accounts of Emperor Wu with which to check the fairness of Ssu-ma Ch'ien's version. No reports by Ssu-ma Ch'ien's contemporaries, if they were ever written, have survived, and posterity must forever view Emperor Wu and his age solely through the eyes of a man whom the emperor, in a fit of petty rage, condemned to the most humiliating punishment conceivable. It is difficult to image a more striking and ironical example of the awesome power wielded by historians.

Ssu-ma Ch'ien's portrait of Emperor Wu is a complex one: in this respect at least we may be sure that it does justice to its original. The personality of the emperor impresses one first and foremost by its tremendous energy. That the energy was often misdirected, guided

---

[1] For a more detailed account of the Li Ling affair and Ssu-ma Ch'ien's life, see Watson, *Ssu-ma Ch'ien: Grand Historian of China* (New York, Columbia University Press, 1958).
[2] *Ibid.,* p. 150.

by stubbornness and severity, or led astray by blatant charlatanism, we cannot deny. Yet not since the First Emperor of the Ch'in, whom Emperor Wu at times disturbingly resembles, had China had such a vigorous and strong-willed ruler, nor was she to have another one for many centuries to come. Much that he did was of undeniable benefit to the nation. Abroad he drove back the Hsiung-nu in the north and brought the Han into contact with the states of Central Asia and the tribes of the southwest, southeast, and Korea. At home he greatly strengthened the authority of the central government, built roads, constructed canals, and controlled the ravages of the Yellow River. He brought to the Han a power and splendor it had never known before—a splendor perhaps most vividly conveyed in the rich and exuberant language of his court poet, Ssu-ma Hsiang-ju.

But it was a costly glory. Though Ssu-ma Ch'ien never attempts to belittle the military triumphs and material benefits of the emperor's reign, he carefully notes the fearful price of each, in loss of fighting men and animals, in expenditures of gold, in labor and hardship to the people. And besides these material losses he notes, more subtly but no less positively, the spiritual losses of the empire—the growing timidity and sycophancy of the court ministers, the increasing harshness of the provincial officials, the callousness of the generals, the wiliness and ugly sophistication that were spreading among the once simple and law-abiding commoners, the slow death of freedom in all areas of life. It is not a pretty picture.

But were things really this bad? Or is this merely the biased view of a disillusioned scholar, steeped in the idealized tales of antiquity and embittered by the experiences of his lifetime? All we can say is that no historian writing in the centuries immediately after Ssu-ma Ch'ien's death, when there was still time to correct distortions if they existed, ever attempted to ameliorate this somber portrayal of the reign of Emperor Wu.

Emperor Ming's assertion that the *Shih chi* is written in "veiled words" introduces another problem. In Han times it was widely believed that Confucius had used "veiled words" in composing the *Spring and Autumn Annals* in order to convey his judgments of contemporary events and persons. And at the end of his account of the Hsiung-nu,

Ssu-ma Ch'ien makes a seemingly irrelevant reference to this tradition, by which he evidently wishes to warn the reader that he too is obliged to use such veiled and indirect language when writing about his own times. In view of this we are presumably justified in looking for irony and covert criticism in the pages that follow. But where are we to draw the line? Is no utterance of the historian to be taken at face value? Are even his infrequent praises suspect?

Such are the problems which confront the reader in understanding and assessing Ssu-ma Ch'ien's narrative. They are problems which have never been settled, and there is no prospect that they ever will be. If there is irony in Ssu-ma Ch'ien's writing, it is in many cases so subtle as to defy positive identification. If there is prejudice, it is not the kind which betrays itself through gross distortion or stoops to caricature. No man can be expected to give a completely unbiased account of his own age. That Ssu-ma Ch'ien's description of the era of Emperor Wu, for all its somberness, never exceeds the bounds of verisimilitude is probably the best indication we have of his integrity as a historian.

Ssu-ma Ch'ien begins his history with an account of the ancient sage rulers, the Yellow Emperor, Emperors Yao and Shun, and Emperor Yü, the founder of the Hsia dynasty. He traces the rise and decline of the Hsia, of its successor, the Shang or Yin dynasty, and of the Chou whose glories are described so profusely in the Confucian Classics. He surveys the decay of the Chou court and the division of the empire into a number of rival feudal states engaged in a protracted struggle for supremacy. He describes the steady rise to power of the state of Ch'in, the changes brought about by the First Emperor of the Ch'in, and the sudden collapse of his regime shortly after his death. Finally, in the part of his history translated in these volumes, he relates the story of the founding of the Han and the fortunes of the dynasty under the succeeding rulers.

This is the entire span of Chinese history—indeed of all human history—as Ssu-ma Ch'ien knew it. Writing in the cold light of "to-day"—for him, around 100 B.C.—reviewing such a past, comparing it with his own time, was he filled with exhilaration, one wonders, or with despair? Did he see human history as a process of evolution, of devolution, or of endlessly repeating cycles? And if as the last, had they any meaning in his eyes?

These questions, like those I have mentioned above, the reader should keep in mind when reading the *Shih chi,* though I cannot guarantee that he will find any answers. Ssu-ma Ch'ien is not a philosopher but a historian. Like most Chinese historians, he indulges in a minimum of personal comment, and such scattered opinions as he states cannot be made to conform to any recognizable school of thought. Somewhere behind the vast, sprawling array of facts and anecdotes we sense the personality of the historian, manipulating the figures of his drama, aligning cause and effect as he would like us to see them. But the more we seek to discover and define that personality, the more it eludes us. Like Tacitus, the historian of Western antiquity whom he most resembles, his interests are so broad and his sympathies so complex that it is never possible to say with certainty, "This is the *real* Ssu-ma Ch'ien."

Yet, elusive as it may be, the personality of Ssu-ma Ch'ien lights up for us the period of human experience known as the early Han. As the Persian Wars live only through Herodotus, the Peloponnesian War through Thucydides, so the early Han, and more especially the era of Emperor Wu, is illumined almost entirely through the writing of this one man. Had he not lived there would probably be only darkness there.

TRANSLATOR'S NOTE

As I have said, no text exists for "The Basic Annals of Emperor Wu." Most likely Ssu-ma Ch'ien never wrote the chapter but merely prepared the summary and first paragraph (translated in Volume I), and laid the work aside while he waited to see how the reign of Emperor Wu would turn out. The tale that Emperor Wu read the chapter and angrily destroyed it seems very dubious. As Ssu-ma Ch'ien drew nearer to his own time in his narrative, he tended to use the Basic Annals section of his history for mere summaries of the official acts of the emperors, quoting at length from memorials and imperial edicts. Emperor Wu could hardly have objected to such material. Moreover, it was always Ssu-ma Ch'ien's practice to present the most favorable picture of a person in the chapter devoted to that person, revealing the man's less pleasant aspects in other chapters. This is the way, for example, that he treats Emperor Wen in the chapters translated in Volume I. If he actually wrote a "Basic Annals of Emperor Wu," therefore, it is unlikely that it contained anything as derogatory to the emperor's reputation as the information found in the chapters which follow and which have survived without damage.

The first large section of the *Shih chi,* the "Basic Annals," is therefore not represented in this volume.[1] The reader must construct the biography of Emperor Wu for himself from the information contained in other chapters.

The second section, the "Chronological Tables," is represented by the brief introduction to Chapter 20, "The Chronological Table of Marquises Enfeoffed from the *Chien-yüan* Era on." The last two chronological tables, Chapters 21 and 22, have only the tersest headings and have therefore not been included.

---

[1] For a complete list of the chapters translated and where they are to be found, see the Finding List of Chapters Translated in Volumes I and II at the end of this volume.

Of the third section, the "Treatises," I have presented here the last three chapters. The other five treatises, dealing with rites, music, the pitch pipes, the calendar, and astronomy, are either in fragmentary condition or too specialized for inclusion here.

Of the fourth section, the "Hereditary Houses," those chapters dealing with Han times, namely, Chapters 48 to 59, have been translated in Volume I. Chapter 60, "The Hereditary Houses of the Three Kings," contains no narrative, but simply the texts of memorials and edicts dealing with the enfeoffment of three of Emperor Wu's sons. Apparently Ssu-ma Ch'ien never got around to working up the material into biographical form, and the chapter has accordingly been omitted.

The last and longest section of the *Shih chi,* comprising Chapters 61 to 130, consists of biographies of famous men and accounts of foreign peoples. In Volume I, I have translated or summarized all those dealing with the early Han, namely Chapter 84, Chapters 89 to 104, and Chapter 106. Chapter 105, the biographies of famous doctors, contains a great deal of specialized information on early Chinese medical lore. Unfortunately, it would require an expert in such matters to interpret and translate it adequately, and I have therefore omitted this chapter.

Volume II therefore begins with Chapter 107 and continues to the end with the following omissions. Chapter 126, "The Biographies of Wits and Humorists," deals with courtiers who were famous for their witty reprimands and retorts. Regrettably, they all belong to pre-Ch'in or Ch'in times and hence fall outside the scope of this translation. Chapter 128, "On Divination by the Tortoise Shell and Milfoil Stalks," is a fragment of doubtful authenticity and did not seem to merit inclusion. Chapter 130, "The Postface of the Grand Historian," containing the biographies of Ssu-ma Ch'ien and his father, has already been translated in my study, *Ssu-ma Ch'ien: Grand Historian of China.* I have rearranged the order of the chapters slightly to facilitate reading.

In preparing the material in this part I have been aided by a new Japanese translation of the *Shih chi* by Noguchi Sadao and others, entitled *Shiki,* in the Chûgoku koten bungaku zenshû series (Tokyo, Heibonsha, 1958–59); and by *Food and Money in Ancient China,* by Nancy Lee Swann (Princeton, Princeton University Press, 1950), as well as by the works listed in the textual note in Volume I.

Part I

HEAVEN, EARTH, AND MAN

Shih chi 28: The Treatise on the Feng and Shan Sacrifices [1]

Among those who have received the mandate of Heaven and become rulers, few have been blessed with the auspicious omens telling them that they are worthy to perform the Feng and Shan sacrifices. When these are carried out, there is none among the countless spirits who does not enjoy pure offerings. Thus I have traced the origins of the religious rites appropriate to the various gods, the famous mountains, and the great rivers, and made The Treatise on the Feng and Shan Sacrifices.

Among the emperors and kings who from ancient times have received the mandate of Heaven to rule, why are there some who did not perform the Feng and Shan sacrifices? For all who were blessed with the heavenly omens signifying their worthiness to perform these rites hastened without fail to Mount T'ai to carry them out, and even some who had not received such signs took it upon themselves to perform them. Yet others, though they enjoyed the mandate to rule, felt that their merit was not yet sufficient; or, though their merit was sufficient, they felt that their virtue had not been fully manifested to all creatures; or again, though their virtue had been fully manifested, they felt that they could not spare the time to carry them out. This is the reason that these rites have seldom been performed!

One of the ancient books says, "If for three years rites are not performed, they will fall into disuse. If for three years music is not played,

---

[1] The Feng and Shan were sacrifices of the greatest solemnity, performed by the emperor at Mount T'ai and addressed to Heaven and Earth respectively. Though apparently of fairly late origin, the Han scholars maintained that they had been performed by all the great sage rulers of antiquity. The present chapter has traditionally been interpreted as a veiled attack by Ssu-ma Ch'ien upon Emperor Wu, the first Han ruler to decide that he was worthy to perform these rites.

it will become lost." [2] When each dynasty attains the height of its glory, then the Feng and Shan are celebrated, but when it reaches a period of decline, they are no longer performed. Thus the performances of these have at times been separated by periods of as many as a thousand or more years, and at the least by several hundred years. This is the reason that the details of the ancient ceremony have been completely lost, and it is now impossible to discover with any exactitude just how it was carried out.

In the *Book of Documents* we read:

Emperor Shun, holding the jeweled astronomical instruments, checked the movements of the Seven Ruling Bodies.[3] Then he performed a special sacrifice to the Lord on High, made pure offerings to the Six Honored Ones,[4] sacrificed from afar to the mountains and rivers, and performed his obeisances to all the various spirits. Gathering together the jade tokens of enfeoffment from the five ranks of feudal lords, he selected an auspicious month and day and held audience with the barons of the four directions and the governors of the various provinces, at which time he returned the jade tokens. In the second month of the year he journeyed east on a tour of inspection and made a visit to Tai-tsung. (Tai-tsung is Mount T'ai.) There he made a burnt offering to Heaven and sacrificed from afar to the various mountains and rivers in succession. After that he met with the princes of the east. (The princes of the east are the feudal lords.) He harmonized the seasons and months, corrected the days of the week, and standardized the pitch pipes and the measures of length, capacity, and weight. He attended to the five rites and the five kinds of jewels and received the three kinds of silk, the two living offerings, and the one dead one.[5] In the fifth month he journeyed south

---

[2] The quotation is now found in *Analects* XVII, 21, though Ssu-ma Ch'ien is perhaps quoting from some lost work on ritual.

[3] The sun, the moon, and the planets Jupiter, Mars, Saturn, Venus, and Mercury. The passage is quoted from the first section of the *Book of Documents,* the Canon of Yao and Shun. The phrases in parentheses are Ssu-ma Ch'ien's own glosses on the text. He quotes the passage here no doubt to show that even in the most ancient of the Confucian Classics there is no detailed account of the Feng and Shan sacrifices.

[4] The seasons, cold and heat, the sun, the moon, the stars, and drought.

[5] The five rites are the rites appropriate to each of the five feudal ranks; the five jewels are the jeweled tokens of enfeoffment for each rank. The two live offerings are lambs, presented by the high ministers, and wild geese, presented by the lesser officials. The one dead offering is pheasants, presented by the *shih,* or lesser nobility.

on a tour of inspection and made a visit to the Southern Peak. (The Southern Peak is Mount Heng.) In the eighth month he journeyed west on a tour of inspection and made a visit to the Western Peak. (The Western Peak is Mount Hua.) In the eleventh month he journeyed north on a tour of inspection and made a visit to the Northern Peak. (The Northern Peak is Mount Hengg.) [6] At all of these, he performed the same rites that he had at Tai-tsung. (The Central Peak is Mount Sung-kao.) Once every five years he made these inspection journeys.

Emperor Yü, the founder of the Hsia dynasty, who succeeded Emperor Shun, followed this same procedure. Later, however, the fourteenth ruler of the dynasty, Emperor K'ung-chia, who practiced evil ways and was too fond of supernatural affairs, committed sacrilege before the spirits, and the two dragons, sent to his court from Heaven, took their departure.[7]

Three generations later, T'ang, the founder of the Shang dynasty, attacked and overthrew Chieh, the last ruler of the Hsia. T'ang's followers wished to move the altars of the Hsia rulers to their own territory, but T'ang made the "Altars of Hsia," a declaration proclaiming to them the reasons why this was impossible.[8] Eight generations after T'ang, when Emperor T'ai-wu came to the throne of the Shang dynasty, a mulberry and a paper mulberry sprang up together in the court of his palace and in the space of one night grew so large that a person could not reach around them with his arms. The emperor was frightened, but his minister I Chih said, "Evil omens cannot prevail over virtue!" Then Emperor T'ai-wu strove for greater virtue in his rule and the two mulberries died. I Chih praised the emperor to the shaman Hsien. It was at this time that the shaman Hsien came to power.

[6] Though the two characters are pronounced alike in modern Chinese, this Mount Heng is written with an entirely different character from the southern Mount Heng above. To distinguish them I have written the second "Heng" with two *g*'s.

[7] According to the version of the legend in *Shih chi* 2, "The Basic Annals of the Hsia Dynasty," Heaven sent a pair of dragons to the court of Emperor K'ung-chia, but the emperor, not knowing how to feed them, turned them over to one of his barons to take care of. When the female of the pair died, the dragon keeper gave the emperor its flesh to eat. But here Ssu-ma Ch'ien seems to have some other version of the tale in mind.

[8] Said to have been a section of the *Book of Documents,* now lost.

Fourteen generations later, Emperor Wu-ting succeeded in obtaining Fu Yüeh as his minister and the Shang dynasty was once more restored to glory. In recognition of this Emperor Wu-ting was given the posthumous title of Great Patriarch. Once a pheasant came and climbed up on the ear of the emperor's sacrificial cauldron and crowed. Wu-ting was afraid, but his minister Tsu Chi said, "Only strive for virtue!" Wu-ting, by following this advice, was able to occupy his throne during a long and peaceful reign.

Five generations later, Emperor Wu-i defied the spirits and as a result he was killed by thunder. Three generations later, Emperor Chou gave himself up to licentiousness and evil, until King Wu of the Chou dynasty attacked and overthrew him.

From this we may see that the rulers at the beginning of each new dynasty never failed to conduct themselves with awe and reverence, but that their descendants little by little sank into indolence and vain pride.

The *Offices of Chou* says:[9] "At the winter solstice a sacrifice shall be made to Heaven in the southern suburbs in order to greet the arrival of lengthening days. At the summer solstice a sacrifice shall be made to the Earth God. At both ceremonies music and dances shall be performed. Thus one may pay respect to the spirits."

The Son of Heaven sacrifices to all the famous mountains and great rivers of the empire. He regards the Five Peaks as his high ministers and the four great watercourses as his feudal lords. The feudal lords sacrifice only to the famous mountains and great rivers that are within their respective domains. The four watercourses are the Yangtze, the Yellow River, the Huai, and the Chi. The halls of state of the Son of Heaven are called the Bright Hall and the Water-encircled Hall. Those of the feudal lords are called Proclamation Palaces.

After the duke of Chou became minister to King Ch'eng, the third ruler of the Chou dynasty, he sacrificed to his distant ancestor Hou Chi, the Lord of Grain, in the southern suburb, treating him as the equal of Heaven; and in the Bright Hall he sacrificed to the founder of

[9] Also known as *The Rites of Chou*. But the present text of this work does not contain any passage exactly like this. Perhaps Ssu-ma Ch'ien is summarizing rather than quoting.

the dynasty, his father King Wen, treating him as the equal of the Lord on High. From the time of Emperor Yü on, there had always been sacrifices performed to the altars of the soil and, since Hou Chi taught the people how to grow grain, there were also offerings made to him. Thus the sacrifices to Hou Chi in the southern suburb and the sacrifices to the altars of the soil date from very ancient times.

The Chou kings overthrew the Shang and founded a new dynasty but, during the fourteen generations of rulers which followed, the power of the Chou gradually waned, its rites and music fell into disuse, and the feudal lords conducted themselves in any way they pleased. Finally, after King Yu of the Chou had been defeated by the Ch'üan barbarians, the dynasty moved its capital east to the city of Lo. Duke Hsiang of the state of Ch'in came to the rescue of the Chou by attacking the barbarians and for the first time a ruler of Ch'in was made a feudal lord of the Chou dynasty on an equal footing with the lords of the other states [771 B.C.].

After Duke Hsiang of Ch'in had become a feudal lord, since his domain was on the western border of the empire, he adopted the spirit of Shao-kao as his patron deity and set up the so-called Altar of the West where he offered sacrifices to the White Emperor.[10] For sacrifices he used a red colt with a black mane, a yellow ox, and a ram.

Sixteen years later, when Duke Wen of Ch'in went east to hunt between the Ch'ien and Wei rivers, he consulted his diviners to find out whether he should make his home in the region and was given a favorable answer. Duke Wen dreamed that he saw a yellow serpent dangling down from heaven and touching the ground, and its mouth came to rest in the Vale of Fu. When he consulted the historian Tun about his dream, Tun replied, "This is a sign from the Lord on High. You should offer sacrifices here!" The duke thereupon constructed the Altar of Fu where he conducted the suburban sacrifice to the White Emperor, using the three animals mentioned above. (Before the Altar

---

[10] Shao-kao was one of the mythical rulers of antiquity and was regarded as the guardian deity of the White Emperor, the god of the west. Eventually five of these heavenly emperors were recognized: the Green Emperor of the east, the Red Emperor of the south, the White Emperor of the west, the Black Emperor of the north and the Yellow Emperor of the center, associated with the elements wood, fire, metal, water, and earth respectively.

of Fu had been constructed, there already existed in the region of Yung a Wu Altar on the southern side of Mount Wu and a Hao Altar east of Yung, but both had fallen into disuse and no sacrifices were offered there. Some people claimed that, because the province of Yung occupied a region of highlands and provided a suitable place for spiritual beings to make their home, these altars had from ancient times been established there and suburban sacrifices offered to the Lord on High. Thus the places of worship of all the spirits came to be concentrated in this area. Such sacrifices had been conducted in the time of the Yellow Emperor, people claimed, and therefore, although it was now the declining years of the Chou dynasty, there was no reason why suburban sacrifices should not be carried out in the same places. No evidence for these assertions could be found in the classical texts, however, and for this reason men of learning refused to lend them any credence.)

Nine years after the construction of the Altar of Fu, Duke Wen came into possession of some stone-like objects which he placed in a shrine on the northern slopes of Ch'en-ts'ang and sacrificed to. The spirits of the objects sometimes would not appear for a whole year, while at other times they would come several times in the year. They always appeared at night, shedding a brilliant light like shooting stars, coming from the southeast, and gathering on the wall of the shrine. They looked like roosters and made a screeching sound so that the fowl in the fields about began to crow in answer, although it was the middle of the night. Duke Wen made an offering of one set of sacrificial animals [11] and called the objects "The Treasures of Ch'en."

Seventy-eight years after the construction of the Altar of Fu, Duke Te came to the throne of Ch'in. Consulting the arts of divination as to whether he should go to live in the region of Yung, he was told that "in ages to come your sons and grandsons shall water their horses in the Yellow River." [12] He therefore transferred his capital to Yung, and the various places of worship in Yung began from this time to

[11] A set of sacrificial animals consisted of an ox, a sheep, and a pig.

[12] Yung was the region west of the Yellow River which became the site of the Ch'in dynasty capital, Hsien-yang, and later of the Han capital, Ch'ang-an.

prosper. He offered three hundred sets [13] of sacrificial animals at the Altar of Fu, instituted sacrifices to quell baneful influences, and had dogs sacrificed at the four gates of the capital to prevent the entrance of evil and disaster. Duke Te died two years after he came to the throne. Six years later Duke Hsüan of Ch'in set up the Mi Altar south of the Wei River, where he sacrificed to the Green Emperor.

Fourteen years later Duke Mu came to the throne of Ch'in. Falling ill one time, he lay unconscious for five days, and when he awoke he reported that he had seen the Lord on High in a dream. The Lord on High had ordered him to pacify the revolt in the state of Chin. The historians at his court made a record of the event and stored it away in the treasury. Thus later ages all say, "Duke Mu of Ch'in ascended to Heaven."

Nine years after Duke Mu came to the throne of Ch'in, Duke Huan of Ch'i made himself leader of the feudal states and summoned all the lords to a conference at Sunflower Hill. At this time he proposed to carry out the Feng and Shan sacrifices, but his minister Kuan Chung said: "It is related that in the past the rulers of seventy-two houses performed the Feng sacrifice at Mount T'ai and the Shan sacrifice at Liang-fu, though I can find the names of only twelve of these in the records. In the most ancient times, Wu Huai performed the Feng at Mount T'ai and the Shan at Yün-yün, and the same was done by Fu Hsi, Shen Nung, and the Fire Emperor. The Yellow Emperor performed the Feng at Mount T'ai and the Shan at T'ing-t'ing. Emperors Chuan Hsü, K'u, Yao, and Shun all performed the Feng at Mount T'ai and the Shan at Yün-yün, while Emperor Yü, the founder of the Hsia, performed the Feng at Mount T'ai and the Shan at K'uai-chi. T'ang, the founder of the Shang, performed the Feng at Mount T'ai and the Shan at Yün-yün, while King Ch'eng, the ruler of the Chou, performed the Feng at Mount T'ai and the Shan at She-shou. All of these had first to receive the mandate of Heaven to rule before they could perform these sacrifices."

[13] Three hundred sets is a prodigious number of sacrificial animals and some commentators would amend the text to read "three sets of white animals," since the Altar of Fu was dedicated to the White Emperor.

Duke Huan replied, "I have marched north to attack the mountain barbarians, past the land of Ku-chu. In the west I have attacked the Great Hsia, crossing the drifting sands and, binding tight my horses and strapping together the carriages, have ascended Pi-erh Mountain. In the south I have invaded as far as Shao-ling, and climbed the Bear's Ear Mountain to gaze out over the Yangtze and the Han rivers. Three times I have met with the other lords in war conferences and six times I have met with them in times of peace. Nine times I have called together the other feudal lords to order the affairs of the empire. None of the others lords dares to disobey me. How then am I different from the rulers of the Three Dynasties of antiquity with their mandates of Heaven?"

Kuan Chung saw that he could not dissuade Duke Huan from his intentions by such arguments and so he brought forward the following stipulations: "In ancient times when the Feng and Shan were performed, millet from Ho-shang and grain from Pei-li were used as offerings. A certain kind of reed which grows between the Huai and Yangtze rivers and has three ridges was used to spread the grain offerings on. Fish were brought from the eastern sea having two eyes on one side of their heads, and pairs of birds from the western sea whose wings were grown together. In addition there were fifteen kinds of strange creatures which appeared of their own accord without being summoned. Now the phoenix and the unicorn have not come to our court and the auspicious grain does not spring up, but instead only weeds and brambles, tares and darnel, while kites and owls appear in swarms. Is it not unthinkable at such a time to attempt to perform the Feng and Shan sacrifices?" With this Duke Huan abandoned his proposal.

This same year Duke Mu of Ch'in sent his soldiers to escort Prince I-wu of Chin, who was in exile, back to his state and set him up as duke of Chin. By his support Duke Mu thus made it possible for Prince I-wu, who became Duke Hui of Chin, as well as the two succeeding rulers, Duke Huai and Duke Wen, to secure the throne of Chin. In this way he brought an end to the internal troubles in the state of Chin. Duke Mu of Ch'in died in the thirty-ninth year of his rule.

Some hundred years later, when Confucius was teaching and transmitting the Six Classics, he is reported to have said something to the effect that there had been over seventy rulers in the past who, on assuming new surnames and becoming kings, had performed the Feng at Mount T'ai and the Shan at Liang-fu. He added, however, that the details of the rituals which they followed were far from clear and that it was impossible to say much about them. When someone asked him the meaning of the Great Sacrifice to the ancestors of the ruler, Confucius replied, "I do not know. If anyone knew the meaning of the Great Sacrifice, he would find it as easy to govern the empire as to look at the palm of his hand!" [14]

While Emperor Chou, the last ruler of the Shang dynasty, still occupied the throne, King Wen received the mandate of Heaven to found a new dynasty, but his rule did not extend as far as Mount T'ai. His son, King Wu, finally overthrew the Shang dynasty, but passed away two years later before the empire had been brought to peace. It was his son "King Ch'eng who first manifested the virtue of the house of Chou to the world." [15] King Ch'eng was therefore quite correct in performing the Feng and Shan sacrifices. Later, when the ministerial families of the feudal states came to exercise the power of government in place of their lords, however, the Chi family of the state of Lu sacrificed to Mount T'ai; such impertinence was severely condemned by Confucius.

At about the same time as Confucius there lived a certain Ch'ang Hung who served King Ling of the Chou dynasty with his magical arts. By this time none of the feudal lords troubled to journey to the Chou court to pay their respects and the power of the Chou had waned sadly. Ch'ang Hung therefore lectured the king on matters pertaining to the spirits and persuaded him to hang up the head of a wildcat and use it as a target for archery. The wildcat's head symbolized the fact that the feudal lords did not come to court, and Ch'ang Hung thus hoped by the use of this strange object to induce the lords

[14] The quotation is from *Analects* III, 11.

[15] The passage in quotation marks differs in style from the rest of the narrative and appears to be a quotation. The words "the *Book of Odes* says," which appear erroneously in the text shortly before this, perhaps belong here.

to appear.[16] The lords, however, were not persuaded by this device, and later the men of Chin captured Ch'ang Hung and murdered him. Ch'ang Hung was the first among the men of Chou to expound the use of such magical arts.

Some hundred years later Duke Ling of Ch'in constructed on the southern side of Mount Wu an Upper Altar, where he sacrificed to the Yellow Emperor, and a Lower Altar, where he sacrificed to the Fire Emperor. Forty-eight years later Tan, the grand historian of the Chou court, while visiting Duke Hsien of Ch'in, made the statement: "Ch'in was originally joined with Chou, but later they separated. After five hundred years, however, they shall be joined again, and seventeen years after they are joined, a dictator king shall come forth!" [17]

A rain of metal fell at Li-yang, and Duke Hsien of Ch'in, deciding that this was an auspicious sign of the power of the element metal, set up the Garden Altar at Li-yang, where he offered sacrifices to the White Emperor.

A hundred and twenty years later the state of Ch'in wiped out the Chou dynasty and the nine sacred cauldrons of the Chou were carried off to Ch'in. Some people, however, claim that the cauldrons were sunk in the Ssu River where it flows past the city of P'eng-ch'eng and that this took place at the time of the destruction of the Sung state's altars of the soil at Big Hill, a hundred and fifteen years before the time when Ch'in conquered the empire.

After the First Emperor of the Ch'in had united the world and proclaimed himself emperor, someone advised him, saying, "The Yellow Emperor ruled by the power of the element earth, and therefore a yellow dragon and a great earthworm appeared in his time. The Hsia dynasty ruled by the power of wood, and so a green dragon came to rest in its court and the grasses and trees grew luxuriantly. The Shang dynasty ruled by metal, and silver flowed out of the mountains. The Chou ruled by fire, and therefore it was given a sign in the form of

[16] Commentators disagree as to just why the wildcat's head had this symbolic meaning; some claim it is because another name for the wildcat is *pu-lai,* literally "not-come." In any event there was some kind of sympathetic magic involved in the use of the wildcat's head.

[17] Interpretations of this prophecy vary, but it is obviously intended to refer to the First Emperor of the Chi'n dynasty.

a red bird. Now the Ch'in has replaced the Chou, and the era of the power of water has come. In ancient times when Duke Wen of Ch'in went out hunting, he captured a black dragon. This is an auspicious omen indicating the power of the element water." For this reason the First Emperor of the Ch'in changed the name of the Yellow River to "Powerful Water." He began his year with the tenth month, honored the color black, and used the number six, the number of the element water, as a standard for all his measurements. Among the musical tubes he selected *Ta-kung* for the greatest honor, and in all his government affairs he put laws before everything else.[18]

Three years after he assumed the imperial title the First Emperor made a tour of the eastern provinces and districts. He performed a sacrifice at Mount I in Tsou and there set up a stone marker lauding the achievements of the Ch'in. He then summoned seventy Confucian masters and scholars from Ch'i and Lu to meet with him at the foot of Mount T'ai, where the scholars began to debate the proper procedure for carrying out the Feng and Shan sacrifices. "In ancient times when the Feng and Shan were performed," said some of them, "the wheels of the carriages were wrapped in rushes so as not to do any injury to the earth and grass of the mountain. The ground was swept clean and sacrifices performed, using rushes and peeled stalks of grain for mats. The ceremony, it is said, was very easy to carry out." But as the First Emperor listened to the debates of the scholars, he found that each of them expressed a different opinion and their recommendations were difficult to carry out, and with this he dismissed the whole lot.

Eventually he had a carriage road opened up, ascending from the southern foot of the mountain to the summit, where he set up a stone marker praising his own virtue as First Emperor of the Ch'in. This he did to make clear to all that he had succeeded in performing the Feng sacrifice. From the summit he descended by a road leading down the northern slope and carried out the Shan sacrifice at Liang-fu. In both of these ceremonies he followed on the whole the procedure used

[18] Supposedly because water is associated with the dark power, yin, the force of punishment and death, though actually it was because he was a follower of the Legalist philosophy of government.

by the master of invocations in sacrificing to the Lord on High at Yung, but the directions for the ritual were sealed and stored away, being kept strictly secret, so that none of the men of the time were able to record any description of the ceremonies.

When the First Emperor was ascending Mount T'ai he encountered a violent wind and rain storm halfway up the slope and had to stop for a while under a large tree. The Confucian scholars, who had been dismissed and were not allowed to take part in the ritual of the Feng sacrifice, hearing of the emperor's encounter with the storm, promptly used it as a basis to speak ill of him.

The First Emperor then proceeded east on his journey as far as the borders of the sea, stopping along the way to perform rituals and sacrifices to the various famous mountains and great rivers and to the Eight Spirits, and searching for immortal spirits such as Hsien-men and his companions.

The Eight Spirits appear to have existed from ancient times. Some people say that their worship was begun at the time of the Great Duke, the first lord of the state of Ch'i at the beginning of the Chou dynasty.[19] But since the sacrifices were later discontinued, no one knows exactly when they originated.

Of the Eight Spirits, the first was called the Lord of Heaven; sacrifices to him were offered at the Navel of Heaven. The Navel of Heaven, or *T'ien-ch'i*, is the name of a spring situated at the foot of a mountain in the southern suburbs of the city of Lin-tzu. It is said that the state of Ch'i takes its name from this place.

The second was called Lord of the Land and was sacrificed to at Liang-fu near Mount T'ai. It appears that since Heaven loves the yin, the principle of darkness, it must be worshiped at the foot of a high mountain or on top of a small hill, at a place called an "Altar"; while because Earth honors the yang, the principle of light, the sacrifices to it must always be conducted on a round hill in the midst of a lowland.[20]

[19] The sentence which follows this in the original belongs a little farther on in the text.

[20] That is, Heaven, representing the yang, the principle of light, fire, the male, loves its opposite, the yin, the principle of darkness, water, the female; while Earth, like a good wife, "honors" its opposite, the yang.

The third spirit was called Lord of Arms and was worshiped by offering sacrifices to Ch'ih Yu.[21] The grave of Ch'ih Yu is situated in the Lu-chien district in the province of Tung-p'ing, on the western border of the state of Ch'i.

The fourth was called Lord of the Yin and was worshiped at Three Mountains. The fifth was called Lord of the Yang and was worshiped at Chih-fu. The sixth was called Lord of the Moon and was worshiped at Mount Lai. All these places mentioned above are in the northern part of Ch'i along the Gulf of Pohai.

The seventh spirit was called Lord of the Sun and was worshiped at Mount Ch'eng. Mount Ch'eng juts out into the ocean like the handle of a dipper and is situated in the farthest corner of northeastern Ch'i. The sacrifices were thus held here in order to greet the sun as it rose from the sea. The eighth was called Lord of the Four Seasons and was worshiped at Lang-ya. Lang-ya is in the eastern part of Ch'i. It is said that at the beginning of each year sacrifices were offered at all of these places consisting of one set of sacrificial animals, though the jade and silk offerings presented by the shamans and invocators who directed the ceremonies were of various kinds and number.

From the time of Kings Wei and Hsüan of Ch'i, the disciples of the philosopher Tsou Yen were very active in propounding their master's theory of the succession of the five elements. When the ruler of Ch'in took the title of emperor, the men of Ch'i accordingly explained to him this theory, and hence it was that the First Emperor selected water as the patron element of his reign.

Sung Wu-chi, Cheng-po Ch'iao, Ch'ung Shang, Hsien-men Kao, and Tsui Hou were all men of Yen who practiced magic and followed the way of the immortals, discarding their mortal forms and changing into spiritual beings by means of supernatural aid. Tsou Yen won fame among the feudal lords for his theories of the yin and yang and the succession of the five elements, but the magicians who lived along the seacoast of Ch'i and Yen, though they claimed to transmit his teachings, were unable to understand them. Thus from this time there appeared a host of men, too numerous to mention, who expounded all sorts of weird and fantastic theories and went to any lengths to

[21] A legendary warrior of antiquity.

flatter the rulers of the day and to ingratiate themselves with them.

From the age of Kings Wei and Hsüan of Ch'i and King Chao of Yen, men were sent from time to time to set out to sea and search for the islands of P'eng-lai, Fang-chang, and Ying-chou. These were three spirit mountains which were supposed to exist in the Gulf of Pohai. They were not very far from the land of men, it was said, but the difficulty was that, whenever a boat was about to touch their shores, a wind would always spring up and drive it away. In the past, people said, there had been men who succeeded in reaching them, and found them peopled by fairy spirits who possessed the elixir of immortality. All the plants and birds and animals of the islands were white, and the palaces and gates were made of gold and silver. Seen from afar, the three spirit mountains looked like clouds but, as one drew closer, they seemed instead to be down under the water. In any event, as soon as anyone got near to them, the wind would suddenly come and drag the boat away, so that in the end no one could ever reach them.

The rulers of the time were all roused to envy by such tales, and when the First Emperor of the Ch'in united the empire under his sway and journeyed to the sea, a countless throng of magicians appeared to tell him of these wonders. The First Emperor decided that, even though he were to set out in person on the sea, he would most likely be unable to reach the islands, and so he ordered his men to gather together a number of youths and maidens and send them to sea to search in his stead. The sea was soon full of boats, crisscrossing this way and that, and when the parties returned without success they all used the wind as an excuse. "We were unable to reach the islands," they reported, "but we could see them in the distance!"

The following year the First Emperor again journeyed to the sea, going as far as Lang-ya; then, passing by Mount Hengg, he returned to the capital by way of Shang-tang. Three years later he made a trip to Chieh-shih on the coast, at which time he cross-examined the magicians who were supposed to have gone to sea to look for the islands. He returned to the capital by way of Shang Province.

Five years after this he made a trip south to Mount Hsiang and from there went to climb Mount K'uai-chi. He followed along the sea coast on his way back, hoping to acquire some of the wonderful medicine of immortality brought from the three spirit mountains in the sea. But his hopes were in vain. When he had gone as far as Sandy Hill, he passed away.

The Second Emperor of the Ch'in made a tour east to Chieh-shih in the first year of his reign [209 B.C.] and from there followed the sea coast south past Mount T'ai as far as K'uai-chi. At all these places he performed ceremonies and sacrifices, and had new inscriptions carved on the sides of the stones set up by his father, the First Emperor, in which he lauded his father's glorious achievements. This same autumn the feudal lords rose in revolt against the Ch'in, and in his third year the Second Emperor was assassinated. Thus the Ch'in dynasty fell just twelve years after the First Emperor performed the Feng and Shan sacrifices. The Confucian scholars loathed the Ch'in for having burned the *Book of Odes* and the *Book of Documents* and mercilessly put to death the scholars who expounded them, while the common people hated its harsh laws, so that the whole world rose up in rebellion. At this time everyone began to speak ill of the Ch'in, saying, "When the First Emperor ascended Mount T'ai, he was attacked by violent wind and rain and thus was never really able to carry out the Feng and Shan sacrifices!" This is an example, is it not, of a ruler who, though he did not possess the virtue necessary to perform the sacrifices, yet proceeded to carry them out?

The rulers of the Three Dynasties of antiquity all resided in the region between the Lo and Yellow rivers. Thus Mount Sung, which was nearby, was called the Central Peak, while the other four peaks of North, South, East, and West were situated in those directions respectively. The four watercourses were all east of the mountains. When the Ch'in ruler assumed the title of emperor and fixed his capital at Hsien-yang, however, it meant that all the five peaks and the four watercourses were east of the capital.

From the time of the ancient Five Emperors down to the Ch'in dynasty, periods of strong central government alternated with periods of decay, and the famous mountains and great rivers were sometimes in the possession of the feudal lords and sometimes in the possession of the Son of Heaven. The rituals employed in the worship of these places, therefore, were often changed and varied from age to age. It is consequently impossible to give a detailed description of them all here.

When the First Emperor united the world, he instructed the officials in charge of sacrifices to put into order the worship of Heaven and Earth, the famous mountains, the great rivers, and the other spirits that had customarily been honored in the past. According to this new arrangement, there were five mountains and two rivers east of Yao designated for sacrifice. The mountains were the Great Hall (that is, Mount Sung), Mount Hengg, Mount T'ai, K'uai-chi, and Mount Hsiang. The two rivers were the Chi and the Huai. In the spring offerings of dried meat and wine were made to insure the fruitfulness of the year, and at the same time prayers were offered for the melting of the ice. In the autumn prayers were made for the freezing of the ice, and in the winter prayers and sacrifices were offered to recompense the gods for their favor during the year. A cow and a calf were invariably used as sacrifices, but the sacrificial implements and the offerings of jade and silk differed with the time and place.

From Mount Hua west, seven mountains and four rivers were designated. The former were Mount Hua, Mount Po (that is, Mount Shuai), Mount Yüeh, Mount Ch'i, Wu Peak, Crane Mound, and Mount Tu (that is, Mount Wen in Shu). The rivers were the Yellow River, which was worshiped at Lin-chin; the Mien, worshiped at Han-chung; the Chiao Deep, worshiped at Ch'ao-na; and the Yangtze, worshiped at Shu. Sacrifices were offered in the spring and autumn for the thawing and freezing of the rivers, and in winter prayers of recompense the same as those for the mountains and rivers of the east were made; a cow and a calf were used as sacrifices, but the implements and other offerings all differed. In addition the four great peaks of Hung, Ch'i, Wu, and Yüeh all received offerings of new grain. The Treasures of Ch'en were worshiped at the season when they appeared. The Yellow River was given an additional offering of thick wine. All of these, being in the region of Yung near the capital of the emperor, were also given an offering of a carriage and four red horses with black manes.

The Pa, Ch'an, Ch'ang-shui, Feng, Lao, Ching, and Wei are all small rivers but, since they are in the vicinity of Hsien-yang, they were all accorded the same worship as the great rivers, though without the additions mentioned above. Rivers such as the Ch'ien, Lo, Two Deeps, and Ming-tse, and Mounts P'u and Yüeh-hsü, though small in comparison to the other mountains and rivers, were also accorded ceremonies of recompense, thawing, and freezing each year, though the rituals used were not necessarily the same in all places.

In addition there were over a hundred shrines dedicated to the worship of the sun, the moon, Orion, Antares, the Northern and Southern Dippers, Mars, Venus, Jupiter, Saturn, the twenty-eight constellations, the Lord of the Wind, the Master of the Rain, the Four Seas, the Nine Ministers, the Fourteen Ministers, the Displayers, the Majestic Ones, the Transmitters, etc.[22]

To the west of the capital there were also some twenty or thirty places of worship. In the region of Hu sacrifices were offered to the Son of Heaven of the Chou dynasty; in Hsia-kuei to the Heavenly Spirit; and on the Feng and Hao rivers to the Radiant One and the Round Lake of the Son of Heaven. At Po in Tu there were three places of worship to the Lords of the Soil and the Stars of Long Life, and in the Thatch Shrine of Yung there was also a place for the worship of Lord Tu. Lord Tu was a leading general of the Chou dynasty in ancient times. Even the most insignificant spirits of the region of Ch'in, if they displayed divine powers, were worshiped with offerings at the appropriate seasons of the year, but the Lords on High worshiped at the four Altars of Yung were regarded as the most honorable of the gods. The Treasures of Ch'en were also noteworthy because their gleaming lights had the power to move the common people.

At the four Altars of Yung prayers were offered in the spring for a successful crop and for the thawing of the waters; in the fall for the freezing of the waters; and in the winter to thank the deities for their aid. In the fifth month colts were sacrificed, and in the second month of each of the four seasons a "month" sacrifice was held, similar to that offered at the season when the Treasures of Ch'en appeared.[23]

---

[22] The Majestic Ones and Transmitters were apparently deities of the roads and fields, though their identity is uncertain, as is that of the Ministers. Mercury has probably dropped out of the list of planets and should be included.

[23] Following the reading in *Han shu* 25A.

For this sacrifice red colts were used in spring and summer and red colts with black manes for fall and winter. The colts sacrificed at the Altars were always four in number, along with a belled chariot drawn by four dragons and a regular chariot drawn by four horses, these last two both modeled out of wood and painted the color appropriate to the deity being sacrificed to. Four yellow calves and four lambs were also sacrificed along with a specified number of jades and silks. All the sacrifices were buried alive in the ground and no sacrificial implements such as stands or platters were used.

The suburban sacrifice was performed once every three years. Since the Ch'in dynasty had designated the tenth month as the beginning of its year, it was always in the tenth month that the emperor fasted and journeyed to the suburbs to visit the deity. Beacon fires were raised at the place of worship, and the ruler went to pay his respects outside the city of Hsien-yang. White was used for the vestments, and the procedure followed was the same as that for ordinary sacrifices.

The sacrifices at the Altar of the West and the Garden Altar continued to be observed as before, though the emperor did not go in person to perform them. All of these places of worship were customarily under the jurisdiction of the master of invocations, who saw to it that offerings and sacrifices were made at the appropriate seasons of the year. As for the other famous mountains, great rivers, gods and deities such as the Eight Spirits, if the emperor happened to be passing by their places of worship, he performed sacrifices; otherwise, no ceremonies were carried out. The spirits and holy places of the various provinces and other distant regions were worshiped by the people of their respective localities and were not under the control of the emperor's religious officials. Among the religious officials of the court was one called the private invocator. If any disaster or evil omen appeared, it was his duty to offer sacrifices with all speed and pray that the blame for the mishap might be transferred from the ruler to the officials or the people.

At the time of the founding of the Han, when Kao-tsu was still a commoner, he once killed a great snake, whereupon a spirit appeared and announced, "This snake was the son of the White Emperor and he who killed him is the son of the Red Emperor!" When Kao-tsu first began his uprising, he offered prayers at the altar of the soil at White Elm in the city of Feng, and after he had won control of the district of P'ei and become its governor he sacrificed to the warrior god Ch'ih Yu and anointed his drums and flags with the blood of the sacrifice.

Eventually, in the tenth month of the year, he reached Pa-shang, where he joined with the other feudal lords in bringing order to the capital city of Hsien-yang and was made king of Han. He therefore designated the tenth month as the first month of the year and chose red as his patron color.

In the second year of his reign [205 B.C.] he marched east to attack Hsiang Yü and then returned once more to the area within the Pass. There he inquired what deities the Ch'in rulers had worshiped in their sacrifices to the Lords on High and was told that there had been sacrifices to four deities, the White, the Green, the Yellow, and the Red Emperors.

"But I have heard that there are Five Emperors in Heaven," said Kao-tsu. "Why is it that the Ch'in rulers worshiped only four?"

When no one was able to offer an explanation, Kao-tsu replied, "I know the reason. They were waiting for me to come and complete the five!" He accordingly set up a place of worship for the Black Emperor, called the Altar of the North, with officials appointed to carry out its sacrifices; Kao-tsu did not go in person to perform sacrifices. He then summoned all of the former religious officials of the Ch'in dynasty and restored the posts of master of invocations and grand supervisor, ordering these officials to carry out the rites and ceremonies as they had in the past. He also gave instructions for altars of the dynasty to be erected in all the provinces and issued an edict saying, "I hold the places of worship in highest regard and deeply respect the sacrifices. Whenever the time comes for sacrifices to the Lord on High or for the worship of the mountains, rivers, or other spirits, let the ceremonies be performed in due season as they were in the past!"

Four years later, after peace had been restored to the empire, Kao-tsu issued an edict to the imperial secretary instructing the officials of the city of Feng to tend the altar of the soil at White Elm, performing ceremonies each season, with a sacrifice of a sheep and a pig each spring. He also ordered the religious officials to set up a place of worship to Ch'ih Yu in the capital, Ch'ang-an.

He appointed various officials for sacrifice and invocation in Ch'ang-an, as well as women shamans. The shamans from the region of Liang worshiped such deities as Heaven and Earth, the Heavenly Altar, Heavenly Water, Within the House, and In the Hall. Those from the region of Chin worshiped the Five Emperors, the Lord of the East, the Lord in the Clouds, the Arbiter of Fate, the Altar of the Shamans, the Kinsman of the Shamans, the Bringer of Fire, etc. Those from Ch'in worshiped the Lord of the Altar, the Protector of Shamans, the Family Imprisoned, etc. The shamans of Ching worshiped the deities Below the Hall, Ancestor of Shamans, Arbiter of Fate, and Giver of Gruel.[24] Other shamans appointed especially for that purpose worshiped the Nine Heavens. All of these performed their sacrifices at the appropriate seasons during the year in the palace. The shamans of the Yellow River, however, performed their sacrifices at Lin-chin, while those of the Southern Mountains performed sacrifices to these mountains and to Ch'in-chung. (Ch'in-chung is the spirit of the Second Emperor of the Ch'in.) All these sacrifices were performed at specified months and seasons.

Two years later someone advised the emperor, "At the beginning of the Chou dynasty, in the city of T'ai, a place of worship was set up for Hou Chi, the ancestor of the Chou and god of agriculture, and from that time until today the blood and flesh of the sacrifices have continued to be offered for the benefit of the world." Kao-tsu accordingly issued an edict to the imperial secretary ordering places of worship set up in all the provinces, districts, and feudal kingdoms, called Shrines of the Sacred Star, and dedicated to Hou Chi, where oxen should be sacrificed at the appropriate seasons each year.

In the spring of the tenth year of Kao-tsu's reign [197 B.C.] the officials requested that the emperor order the districts to make offerings of a sheep and a pig to the altars of the soil and grain in the third and twelfth months of each year, the people in each district to raise the

---

[24] The nature of most of these deities is obscure and the translations of their names in many places only tentative.

money for the sacrifices at their respective local shrines. The emperor gave his approval.

Eighteen years later Kao-tsu passed away and Emperor Wen came to the throne. In the thirteenth year of his reign [167 B.C.] Emperor Wen issued an edict saying, "At the present time the private invocator is delegated to pray that the blame for any faults committed by me be transferred to himself or the lower officials. I find this practice wholly unacceptable. From now on, let the post of private invocator be abolished!"

Originally it had been left to the religious officials of the feudal lords to perform sacrifices and offerings to any of the famous mountains or great rivers that happened to be within their domains; the officials of the emperor had no jurisdiction over such affairs. When the kingdoms of Ch'i and Huai were temporarily abolished, however, Emperor Wen ordered his master of invocations to see to it that all the proper ceremonies were carried out in these regions at the proper times as they had been in the past.

In this year the emperor issued a proclamation saying:

It has now been thirteen years since I came to the throne.[25] By the aid of the spirits of the ancestral temples and the blessing of the altars of the soil and grain, the land within the borders is at peace and my people are without distress. Moreover, for the past several years the empire has enjoyed good harvests. How could I, who am of no virtue, be deserving of such fortune? Rather are these gifts, all of them, from the Lord on High and the other spirits.

I have heard that in ancient times when a ruler enjoyed reward for his virtue he invariably returned recompense to the gods for the merits they had bestowed. Therefore I would increase the sacrifices to the spirits. Let the officials open deliberations to increase the offerings at the Five Altars of Yung by the addition of a great chariot for each altar, fitted out with full trappings; and for the Western and Garden altars, one chariot each modeled in wood, with four wooden horses and full trappings. Let the Yellow, Chiao, and Han rivers be granted an addition of two pieces of jade each, and at all the various places of worship let the altars and altar grounds be broadened and the jades,

[25] In "The Basic Annals of Emperor Wen" this proclamation is dated in the fourteenth year and reads, "It has now been fourteen years, etc."

silks, and other sacrificial implements be increased as may be proper to each place.

At present when prayers are offered for blessing, it is asked that all good fortune may come to me in person, while no mention is made of my people. From now on let the invocations be carried out with all reverence, but let there be no more such prayers for myself alone.

A man of Lu named Kung-sun Ch'en submitted a letter to the throne stating, "Formerly the Ch'in dynasty ruled by the power of the element water. Now that the Han has succeeded the Ch'in it is obvious that it must rule by the power of the element earth, since the cycle of the five elements revolves, going back to the beginning when it has once ended. To confirm this, an omen of the power of earth will appear in the form of a yellow dragon. It is proper, then, that the month on which the year begins should be changed and the color of the court vestments altered to pay honor to the color yellow."

The chancellor at this time was Chang Ts'ang, who was very fond of matters of the pitch pipes and the calendar, and it was his contention that the Han belonged to a period in which the power of water was in ascendancy. Proof of this, he said, was to be found in the fact that the Yellow River had burst its dikes at a place called Metal Embankment [i.e., water ascendant over metal]. The Han year should therefore begin with the tenth month, the first month of winter, and the vestments should be black on the outside and red within, thus corresponding to the element water. He declared that Kung-sun Ch'en's opinion was completely false and the matter was allowed to drop.

Three years later [26] a yellow dragon appeared at Ch'eng-chi. Emperor Wen thereupon summoned Kung-sun Ch'en to court, made him an erudit, and set him to work with the other court scholars drawing up plans to change the calendar and the color of the court vestments. In the summer the emperor issued an edict saying, "A supernatural being in the form of a strange creature has appeared at Ch'eng-chi, but no harm will come to the people and the year will be a plentiful one. I wish to perform the suburban sacrifice and offer prayers to the Lord on High and the other spirits. Let the officials in charge of rites

[26] But "The Basic Annals of Emperor Wen" dates this in the fifteenth year, only one year later.

deliberate on the matter and let them not hesitate in their recommendations for fear of putting me to too much trouble."

The officials all replied, "In ancient times the Son of Heaven went in summer to the suburbs to sacrifice in person to the Lord on High. Hence this was called the suburban sacrifice."

In the summer of this year, in the fourth month, Emperor Wen for the first time performed the suburban sacrifice, visiting the Five Altars of Yung and worshiping there. His robes were all designed to honor the color red.

A man of Chao named Hsin-yüan P'ing, appearing before the emperor to report an unusual cloud formation he had seen, asserted that in the sky northeast of Ch'ang-an a supernatural emanation had appeared, made of five colors and shaped like a man's hat.

"The northeast is the dwelling place of the spirits," suggested someone else, "and the western region is where they have their graves. Now, since Heaven has sent down this auspicious sign, it is right that places of worship should be set up to offer sacrifices to the Lord on High in answer to this omen."

Accordingly the Temples of the Five Emperors were constructed north of the Wei River. They were housed under a single roof, but each emperor had his own hall of worship. A separate gate faced each of the five halls, painted in the color appropriate to the deity worshiped there. The animals sacrificed and the ceremonies conducted were the same as those at the Five Altars of Yung.

In the summer, the fourth month, Emperor Wen went in person to pay his respects to the confluence of the Pa and Wei rivers, and at the same time performed the suburban sacrifice to the Five Emperors north of the Wei. The temples of the Five Emperors overlooked the Wei River on the south, and to the north channels had been cut to bring water into the Lake of Rushes. Beacon fires were raised while the sacrifices were performed, their light pouring forth and their flames seeming to reach to the heavens.

The emperor honored Hsin-yüan P'ing with the rank of superior lord and presented him with several thousand pieces of gold. He also ordered the erudits and court scholars to select material from the Six Classics and compose a work on the institutes of the rulers, as well as to begin plans for an inspection tour of the provinces and the performance of the Feng and Shan sacrifices.

As Emperor Wen was leaving the place called Long Gate he saw something that looked like five men standing to the north of the road. Because of this he had an altar to the Five Emperors set up on the spot, where he offered five sets of sacrificial animals.

The following year Hsin-yüan P'ing had a man bring a jade cup and present it at the gate of the palace, along with a letter to the throne. Hsin-yüan P'ing then remarked to the emperor, "There are emanations in the sky which indicate that someone has come to the palace gate with a precious object!" When a man was sent to verify this announcement, it was found that a jade cup bearing the inscription "Long Life to the Lord of Men" had in fact been presented at the gate.

Another time Hsin-yüan P'ing announced that, according to his observations, the setting sun would stop in its course and ascend again to the center of the sky. After a little while the sun began to move backward until it had returned to the meridian. Thereupon the emperor began to number the years of his reign over again, making the seventeenth year the first year of a new period, and ordered great feasting throughout the empire.

Next Hsin-yüan P'ing announced, "The cauldrons of the Chou dynasty were lost in the Ssu River. Now the Yellow River has overflowed and runs into the Ssu. Observing the sky in the northeast, I note that there are certain emanations right over Fen-yin which indicate the presence of precious metal objects. That, I believe, is where the cauldrons will be found. When such an omen appears, however, unless some action is taken in response, nothing will ever come of it!"

The emperor therefore sent envoys to build a temple at Fen-yin, overlooking the Yellow River to the south, and offer sacrifices, hoping to bring the cauldrons to light. At this time someone sent a letter revealing to the emperor that all of the emanations and supernatural occurrences described by Hsin-yüan P'ing were frauds. Hsin-yüan P'ing was handed over to the law officials for trial and was executed, along with his three sets of relatives.

After this Emperor Wen lost interest in changing the calendar and the color of the vestments and in matters concerning the spirits. He ordered his sacrificial officials to see to the upkeep of the temples and altars of the Five Emperors north of the Wei River and at Long Gate and to perform ceremonies at the proper seasons, but he himself no longer visited them.

The following year the Hsiung-nu several times invaded the border and troops were raised to guard against further incursions. During the last years of his reign the harvests were not very plentiful.

A few years later Emperor Ching ascended the throne. During the sixteen years of his reign the officials in charge of sacrifices continued to perform their various duties at the appropriate seasons of the year, but no new forms of worship were instituted. And so we come to the reign of the present emperor.

When the present emperor first came to the throne, he showed the greatest reverence in carrying out the sacrifices to the various spirits and gods. In the first year of his reign [140 B.C.], because it had been over sixty years since the founding of the Han, and the empire was at peace, the gentlemen of the court all hoped that the emperor would perform the Feng and Shan sacrifices and change the calendar and other regulations of the dynasty. The emperor favored the teachings of the Confucians and summoned to court a number of men who were noted for their wisdom and good character. Among these were Chao Wan, Wang Tsang, and others of their group, who were made officials because of their literary accomplishments. These men wished to begin discussions on the establishment of a Bright Hall south of the capital, where the ruler would receive the feudal lords in audience, as had been done in ancient times. They also drew up rough plans for an imperial tour of inspection, the performance of the Feng and Shan, alterations of the calendar and the color of court vestments, etc. Before any of these plans had been put into effect, however, the emperor's grandmother, Empress Dowager Tou, who was a follower of Taoist teachings and had no use for Confucianism, sent men in secret to spy on Chao Wan and the rest and gather evidence to show that they were deriving illegal profit from their posts. Chao Wan and Wang Tsang were summoned to answer these charges, but both men committed suicide and all the projects which they had sponsored were abandoned.

Six years later [135 B.C.] Empress Dowager Tou passed away and the following year the emperor summoned to court a number of literary men such as Kung-sun Hung. The next year [133 B.C.] the emperor journeyed to Yung for the first time to perform the suburban sacrifice at the Five Altars. From this time on he invariably performed the suburban sacrifice once every three years.

At this time the emperor also sought out the Spirit Mistress and housed her in the T'i-shih Tower in the Shang-lin Park. The Spirit Mistress was originally a woman of Ch'ang-ling who died in childbirth. Later her spirit appeared and took possession of her brother's wife, Yüan-jo. Yüan-jo offered sacrifices to the spirit in her house, and many people came to join in the worship. Lady P'ing-yüan, the maternal grandmother of the present emperor, was among those who sacrificed to the spirit, and later her sons and grandsons all became famous and honored. Thus when the present emperor came to the throne he treated the Spirit Mistress with great reverence and transferred her place of worship to his own palace in the Shang-lin Park. It was said that one could hear the words spoken by the spirit but could not see her form.

It was at this time also that Li Shao-chün appeared before the emperor to expound the worship of the god of the fireplace and explain his theories on how to achieve immortality through dietary restrictions. The emperor treated him with great respect. Li Shao-chün had formerly been a retainer of the marquis of Shen-tse and specialized in magical arts. He kept his real age and place of birth a secret, always telling people that he was seventy years old. Claiming that he could make the spirits serve him and prevent old age, he traveled about to the courts of the various feudal lords, expounding his magic. He had no wife or children. When people heard of his power to command the spirits and drive away death they showered him with a constant stream of presents, so that he always had more than enough food and clothing and money. Impressed that he seemed to enjoy such affluence without engaging in any business, and also not knowing where he was from, people put even greater faith in his claims and vied with each other in waiting on him. He relied wholly on his ability to work magic and was clever at making pronouncements that were later found to have been curiously apt.

Once when he was staying with T'ien Fen, the marquis of Wu-an, and was drinking with the marquis and his friends, he told one of the guests, an old man of over ninety, that he had gone with the man's grandfather to such and such a place to practice archery. The old man had in fact, when he was a child, accompanied his grandfather, and remembered visiting the place that Li Shao-chün mentioned. With this the whole party was struck with amazement.

When Li Shao-chün appeared before the emperor, the latter questioned him about an ancient bronze vessel which the emperor had in his possession. "This vessel," replied Li Shao-chün, "was presented at the Cypress Chamber in the tenth year of the reign of Duke Huan of Ch'i [676 B.C.]." When the inscription on the vessel was deciphered, it was found that it had in fact belonged to Duke Huan of Ch'i. Everyone in the palace was filled with astonishment and decided that Li Shao-chün must be a spirit who had lived hundreds of years.

Li Shao-chün then advised the emperor, "If you sacrifice to the fireplace you can call the spirits to you, and if the spirits come you can transform cinnabar into gold. Using this gold, you may make drinking and eating vessels which will prolong the years of your life. With prolonged life you may visit the immortals who live on the island of P'eng-lai in the middle of the sea. If you visit them and perform the Feng and Shan sacrifices, you will never die. This is what the Yellow Emperor did. Once I wandered by the sea and visited Master An-ch'i, and he fed me jujubes as big as melons.[27] Master An-ch'i is an immortal who roams about P'eng-lai. If he takes a liking to someone he will come to meet him, but if not he will hide."

As a result, the emperor for the first time began to sacrifice in person to the fireplace. He dispatched magicians to set out on the sea in search of Master An-ch'i and the immortals of P'eng-lai, and attempted to make gold out of cinnabar sand and various kinds of medicinal ingredients.

After some time, Li Shao-chün fell ill and died. The emperor, however, believed that he was not really dead but had transformed himself into a spirit, and he ordered K'uan Shu, a clerk from Huang-ch'ui, to carry on the magical arts which Li Shao-chün had taught. None of the

[27] Following the reading in *Han shu* 25A.

group sent out to search for Master An-ch'i in the island of P'eng-lai succeeded in finding anything.

After this, any number of strange and dubious magicians from the seacoast of Yen and Ch'i appeared at court to speak to the emperor about supernatural affairs. Among them was a man from Po named Miu Chi who instructed the emperor on how to sacrifice to the Great Unity. "The Great Unity," he explained, "is the most honored of the spirits of Heaven and his helpers are the Five Emperors. In ancient times the Son of Heaven sacrificed to the Great Unity each spring and autumn in the southeastern suburbs, offering one set of sacrificial animals each day for seven days. An altar was constructed for the purpose which was open to the spirit roads of the eight directions."

The emperor accordingly ordered the master of invocations to set up such a place of worship southeast of Ch'ang-an where sacrifices were conducted regularly according to the method described by Miu Chi.

Later someone submitted a letter to the throne stating that in ancient times the Son of Heaven had offered a set of sacrificial beasts once every three years to the spirits called the Three Unities. These were the Heavenly Unity, the Earthly Unity, and the Great Unity. The emperor gave his consent to the ritual and ordered the master of invocations to see to it that such sacrifices were carried out at Miu Chi's altar of the Great Unity in the manner recommended.

Later someone again sent a letter to the throne advising that in ancient times the Son of Heaven had always performed in the spring a ceremony to drive away evil in which he sacrificed an owl and a broken mirror[28] to the Yellow Emperor; a sheep to the god called Dark Ram; a blue stallion to the god Horse Traveler; an ox to the Great Unity, the Lord of Mount Tse, and the Earth Elder; a dried fish to the lords of Wu-i; and an ox to the Messenger of the Yin and Yang. The emperor gave orders to the religious officials to see that such sacrifices were performed in the recommended manner at the side of Miu Chi's altar to the Great Unity.

[28] According to some commentators "broken mirror" is the name of a beast which eats its own father. The owl is infamous in Chinese lore for eating its mother, and these two creatures were therefore offered in order to prevent unfilial behavior.

Some time afterwards white deer appeared in the emperor's park. He had their hides made into a type of currency which he issued in order to make known this auspicious omen, and also had currency minted out of white metal.

The following year [122 B.C.] when the emperor went to Yung to perform the suburban sacrifice he captured a beast with one horn which looked like a unicorn. The officials announced, "Since Your Majesty has performed the suburban sacrifice with such reverence and care, the Lord on High has seen fit to reward you by presenting this one-horned beast. Is this not what is called a unicorn?"

The emperor thereupon visited the Five Altars and presented an additional burnt offering of an ox at each one. He presented the white metal coins, symbolic of the auspicious white deer, to the various feudal lords as a hint to them that he had by now received the necessary omens proving that he had found favor with Heaven.

The king of Chi-pei, assuming from these moves that the emperor was about to perform the Feng and Shan sacrifices, sent a letter to the throne in which he presented to the emperor Mount T'ai and the surrounding cities, which were situated in his domains. The emperor accepted the gift and conferred upon the king a district elsewhere by way of compensation. The king of Ch'ang-shan was accused of some crime and transferred to another region. The emperor enfeoffed the king's younger brother in the region of Chen-ting so that he might carry on there the sacrifices to the former kings of Ch'ang-shan, and made the region of Ch'ang-shan, where Mount Hengg is situated, into a province. Thus it was that, after these two events, all the regions in which the Five Peaks were situated came under the direct jurisdiction of the emperor.

The following year a man of Ch'i named Shao-weng gained the emperor's ear with his tales of ghosts and spirits. The emperor had formerly had a favorite concubine named Madam Wang who had died. It is said that Shao-wang by his magical arts succeeded in summoning forth at night the apparitions of Madam Wang and the god of the fireplace, while the emperor stood within a curtained enclosure and gazed at them from afar. The emperor accordingly honored Shao-weng with the title of General of Peaceful Accomplishment and rewarded him with lavish gifts, treating him with the courtesy due to an imperial guest.

Shao-weng then said to the emperor, "I perceive that Your Majesty wishes to commune with the spirits. But unless your palaces and robes are patterned after the shapes of the spirits, they will not consent to come to you." He fashioned five chariots, symbolizing the five elements and painted with cloud designs, and on the days when each of the five elements was in ascendancy, he would mount the appropriate chariot and ride about, driving away evil demons. He also directed the emperor to build the Palace of Sweet Springs, in which was a terrace chamber painted with pictures of Heaven, Earth, the Great Unity, and all the other gods and spirits. Here Shao-weng set forth sacrificial vessels in an effort to summon the spirits of Heaven.

A year or so passed, however, and Shao-weng's magical arts seemed to grow less and less effective, for no spirits appeared to answer his summons. He then wrote a message on a piece of silk and fed it to an ox and, pretending to know nothing of the matter, announced to the emperor, "There appears to be some strange object in this ox's belly!" The ox was slaughtered and its belly opened, revealing the piece of silk, and the words written on it were exceedingly strange. The emperor, however, recognized the handwriting and, when he cross-examined Shao-weng, discovered that the message was in fact a fraud. He had Shao-weng executed but kept the matter a secret. Following this he built the Terrace of Cypress Beams with the Bronze Pillars, and atop them the Immortals holding in their palms the Pans for Receiving Dew, and similar structures.

The year after Shao-weng's execution [118 B.C.] the emperor was taken gravely ill at Cauldron Lake and, though all the doctors and shamans were summoned to attend him, none could cure his sickness. Earlier, a man of Yu-shui named Fa Ken had advised the emperor that in the province of Shang there lived a shamaness who, when ill, became possessed by spirits. The emperor had accordingly summoned the shamaness to the Palace of Sweet Springs and set up a place of worship for her. When the emperor later fell ill at Cauldron Lake he sent someone to consult the Spirit Mistress through the shamaness, who returned this answer: "The Son of Heaven need not worry about his illness. When he is a little better he should make an effort to come and meet with me at Sweet Springs!"

After this the emperor's illness improved somewhat until he was able to rise from his bed and journey to Sweet Springs. There he recovered completely and proclaimed a general amnesty to the empire. He set up the Temple of Long Life dedicated to the Spirit Mistress. The Spirit Mistress was accorded honor equal to that of the Great Unity.[29] Her helpers were called the Great Forbidden Ones, and it was said that the other deities such as the Arbiter of Fate were all her attendants. It was impossible to catch a glimpse of her form, but her words could be heard, sounding the same as a human voice. At times she went away and at other times returned, and when she came, the wind made a sighing sound. She dwelt within the curtains of the chamber and spoke sometimes during the day, though usually at night. The emperor would always perform rites of ablution before entering her presence and there, through the offices of the shamaness, he would eat and drink with the deity as though she were his host. Whatever the spirit wished to say to him she would relay by way of the shamaness. The emperor also set up another temple north of the Temple of Long Life, where he hung feathered banners and set out the implements of sacrifice to perform ceremonies in honor of the Spirit Mistress. Whenever the Spirit Mistress spoke, the emperor ordered his secretaries to take down the words, calling these messages his "Planning Laws." There was nothing the least bit extraordinary about the words of the deity, which were the sort of thing that anyone at all could say, but the emperor alone took great delight in them. The whole affair, however, was kept secret so that most people at the time knew nothing about it.

Three years later [114 B.C.] the officials advised the emperor, saying, "When a ruler begins the numbering of the years of his reign over again, he should not call the periods merely 'first,' 'second,' etc., but should select names from the auspicious omens that have appeared at the time. Thus the first period of Your Majesty's reign should be called *chien-yüan* or 'Establishment Period'; the second, when the comet appeared, should be called *yüan-kuang,* or 'Period of Light'; and the

---

[29] The text at this point seems to be corrupt and the translation is highly tentative.

third, when the one-horned beast was captured at the time of the suburban sacrifice, should be called *yüan-shou,* or 'Hunting Period.' " [30]

In the winter of the following year [113 B.C.] the emperor performed the suburban sacrifice at Yung. He called his officials into conference and said, "I have now performed the suburban sacrifice in person to the Lord on High. But unless I also sacrifice to the Earth Lord, I fear these ceremonies will have no effect."

The officials debated with the grand historian [31] and the minister in charge of sacrifices, K'uan Shu, and made the following announcement: "In the past, at the sacrifices to Heaven and Earth, oxen with horns as small as silk cocoons or chestnuts were used. Now if Your Majesty wishes to sacrifice in person to the Earth Lord, it is necessary to set up five altars on a round hill in the middle of a swamp. At each altar a yellow calf and a set of three sacrificial animals should be offered, and when the ceremony is completed these should all be buried in the earth. All persons attending the ceremony should wear vestments honoring the color yellow."

The emperor then journeyed east and for the first time set up the altar to the Earth Lord on top of Rump Hill in Fen-yin as K'uan Shu and the others had recommended. There he personally performed worship ceremonies, following the same ritual as that used for the Lord on High. When the ceremony was completed the emperor proceeded to Jung-yang and from there returned to the capital.

When he passed through Lo-yang the emperor issued an edict which read: "The Three Dynasties of antiquity are far removed in time and it is difficult at this day to make provisions for the preservation of their lines. Since Lo-yang was the capital of the Chou dynasty, let thirty *li* of land here be set aside as a fief for the descendant of the Chou rulers so that, with the title of Lord Tzu-nan of Chou, he may carry out sacrifices to his ancestors."

---

[30] Emperors Wen and Ching had both begun the numbering of the years of their reigns over again several times, but no particular titles had been given to the periods of numbering. This was the first time that *nien-hao* or "era names" were used. The practice was continued throughout later Chinese history and was imitated in Japan and Annam.

[31] Ssu-ma T'an, the father of Ssu-ma Ch'ien.

This year the emperor for the first time made a tour of the provinces and districts and visited Mount T'ai.

In the spring the marquis of Lo-ch'eng sent a letter to the throne recommending a man named Luan Ta. Luan Ta was a palace attendant of the king of Chiao-tung. Originally he had studied under the same teacher as Shao-weng, the magician whom the emperor had executed, and later he became the master of magical arts to King K'ang, the king of Chiao-tung. King K'ang's queen was the elder sister of the marquis of Lo-ch'eng. She had no children, however, and when King K'ang died, one of his sons by a concubine was made king to succeed him. The queen was a woman of loose conduct and was on very poor terms with the new king; the two of them were constantly searching for some legal excuse to trip each other up. When the queen heard that the magician Shao-weng had been executed, she hoped to ingratiate herself with the emperor by dispatching Luan Ta to the capital. She therefore enlisted the aid of her brother, the marquis of Lo-ch'eng, to help Luan Ta gain an audience with the emperor so that he could expound his magic. The emperor, after having executed Shao-weng, began to regret that he had been so hasty with the death sentence and had not given the magician an opportunity to finish displaying his powers. He was therefore extremely delighted to see Luan Ta.

Luan Ta was tall and handsome and full of magical schemes and stratagems. He did not hesitate to come out with the most grandiose pronouncements and never betrayed any sign that he doubted the truth of what he was saying. "I once traveled far and wide over the sea," he informed the emperor, "and visited An-ch'i, Hsien-men, and the other immortals. But they all considered me a man of humble station and would not confide in me. Also, because I served King K'ang, who was only one of the feudal lords, they considered that I was not worthy to receive their teachings. I often spoke to King K'ang about the matter, but he would not listen to my suggestions. My teacher had told me that gold could definitely be made from cinnabar, that the break in the dikes of the Yellow River could be repaired, the elixir of immortal life made, and the immortals persuaded to appear. But I was afraid that if I mentioned these things, I would meet the same fate as Shao-weng. This is the reason I and all the other magicians have kept our mouths closed. How could I dare under the circumstances to discuss my magic?"

"As for Shao-weng," said the emperor, "he happened to eat some horse liver and died, that was all.[32] But if you can really carry on his magic arts, what will I not give you?"

Luan Ta replied, "My teacher has no reason to seek for men. It is men who seek for him. If Your Majesty really wishes to summon him, then you must first honor the envoys that you send to him, making them members of the imperial family,[33] and treating them as guests rather than subjects, doing nothing that would humiliate them. If you grant each of the envoys the imperial seals, they may go and speak to the spirit man. Whether or not he will consent to give ear, I do not know, but I believe that if you confer sufficient honors upon the envoys you send, then he may be persuaded to come."

In order to test Luan Ta, the emperor instructed him to give a minor display of his magical powers by making some chessmen fight. When the board was set up, the chessmen were seen to rush against each other of their own accord.

At this time the emperor was very worried about the break in the dikes of the Yellow River and concerned that he had not been able to change cinnabar into gold. He therefore honored Luan Ta with the title of General of the Five Profits. After a few months, Luan Ta was able to wear four seals at his girdle, those of General of the Heavenly Man, General of the Earthly Man, and General of the Great Way having been granted to him in addition to the previous one.

The emperor issued an edict to the imperial secretary which read: "In ancient times Emperor Yü opened up the nine rivers and fixed the courses of the four waterways. In recent years, however, the Yellow River has flowed out over the land and the laborers working on its dikes have been able to find no rest. For twenty-eight years I have watched over the empire, and now it is as though Heaven has sent me this man to open up the great way for me. In the *Book of Changes* we read of 'the

---

[32] Horse liver was believed to be poison.

[33] By seeking to become a member of the imperial family, presumably through a marriage alliance, Luan Ta hoped to preclude the possibility of meeting the same fate as Shao-weng.

flying dragon' and 'the wild swan advancing to the great rock.' [34] Do these oracles not apply to this great man whom Heaven has sent to me? Therefore let a fief of two thousand households be granted to General Luan Ta and let him be given the title of marquis of Lo-t'ung."

In addition the emperor presented Luan Ta with one of the finest mansions of the marquises, a thousand servants, carriages for use on ordinary and special occasions, and hangings, draperies, and vessels of every kind to adorn his house. He also bestowed his daughter Princess Wei, the eldest daughter of Empress Wei, upon Luan Ta to be his wife, along with ten thousand catties of gold, and changed the name of the princess's fief to "Princess Tang-li." The emperor in person went to visit the home of Luan Ta and in addition sent a constant stream of envoys to inquire how he was and supply him with anything he needed. From the emperor's aunt and the highest officials of the government on down, people invited him to their homes to dine and showered him with gifts.

The emperor then had another jade seal carved with the title "General of the Heavenly Way" and sent his envoy to present it to Luan Ta. The presentation ceremony was performed at night, the envoy being dressed in a feather cloak and standing on a spread of white rushes, while Luan Ta, similarly dressed and standing on the rushes, received the seal. This was done to indicate that Luan Ta was not being treated as a subject of the emperor. The words "Heavenly Way" on the seal meant that Luan Ta should open up a way to the heavenly spirits for the emperor.

After this Luan Ta spent every evening offering sacrifices at his home, hoping that he would be able to call down the spirits. No spirits appeared, however, but only a multitude of ghosts who gathered around. These he was able to command. Sometime later he began to make preparations for a journey, announcing that he would travel east and set out upon the sea to search for his teacher.

In no more than a few months from the time he was granted an audience with the emperor, Luan Ta bore at his girdle six seals, those of his five generalships and his marquisate, and his honor awed the empire. After this there was hardly a soul living on the seacoast of Yen

[34] From the *Book of Changes,* the oracles of the hexagrams *ch'ien* and *chien.* Both refer to the finding of a worthy minister by the ruler.

and Ch'i who did not begin waving his arms about excitedly and proclaiming that he possessed secret arts and could command the spirits and immortals.

In the summer, during the sixth month of this year [113 B.C.], the shaman Chin of Fen-yin was performing a sacrifice for the sake of the common people to the Earth Lord at the Rump Hill altar in the region of Wei, when he noticed an object shaped like a hook sticking up out of the ground at the side of the altar. Digging up the soil around it, he unearthed a cauldron. It was much larger than any ordinary cauldron and had a pattern incised on it, but no inscription.[35] Much struck by his find, he reported it to the officials, who in turn informed Sheng, the governor of Ho-tung Province. The governor having relayed intelligence of the affair to the throne, the emperor dispatched an envoy to question the shaman on how he had come into possession of the cauldron. The envoy, finding no evidence of fraud or deceit, sacrificed with full ceremony at the altar and bore the cauldron back with him to the Palace of Sweet Springs, where the emperor determined to take it along with him on one of his journeys and offer it to the spirits of Heaven. For this purpose he made a trip to the mountains, whereupon the sun shone forth with a bright, warm glow and a yellow cloud came and stood over the place where the cauldron was. Just then a large deer passed by the imperial party, which the emperor shot down in person and used as a sacrifice.

When the emperor and his party returned to Ch'ang-an, the ministers and high officials all gathered in conference and requested that due honor be shown to the precious cauldron. The emperor announced, "Recently the Yellow River overflowed its banks and for several years the harvests were poor. Therefore I journeyed about the empire and performed sacrifices to the Earth Lord, praying for the sake of the common people that the grain might grow well. This year, though the

[35] It will be recalled that in the reign of Emperor Wen the charlatan Hsin-yüan P'ing had predicted that the lost cauldrons of Chou would come to light at Fen-yin. As commentators have suggested, Hsin-yüan P'ing had probably had this cauldron buried at Fen-yin so that it could be "discovered" to fulfill his prediction, but death cut short his career before the plan could be carried to completion.

harvest has been rich and plentiful, I have not yet returned thanks for this blessing. Why then should this cauldron appear?"

To this the officials all replied, "We have heard that in ancient times the Great Emperor Fu Hsi made a single sacred cauldron. The number one symbolizes the unification of heaven and earth, showing that all things of creation were brought together. The Yellow Emperor made three precious cauldrons, symbolizing heaven, earth, and man, while Emperor Yü collected metal from the nine ancient provinces and cast nine cauldrons. All of them used the cauldrons to boil offerings and present them to the Lord on High and the other spirits. Only when a sage ruler appeared on the throne were these cauldrons made. The cauldrons were handed down during the successive dynasties of the Hsia and Shang, but later, when the virtue of the Chou rulers declined and the altars of the soil of the state of Sung, ruled by the descendants of the Shang kings, were destroyed, the cauldrons sank into the waters and disappeared from sight. The temple hymn in the *Book of Odes* reads:

> From hall to gatehouse,
> From ram to bull he moves,
> With great cauldron and small; . . .
> Neither contentious nor proud,
> Beautiful shall be the blessing of long life for him! [36]

"Now this cauldron was brought to the Palace of Sweet Springs and a radiance burst forth, shimmering like a dragon. Boundless beauty was received from on high when it was carried among the mountains. A cloud of yellow and white descended to cover it and an omen in the form of a beast appeared. With the great bow and a set of four arrows, the beast was captured and placed at the foot of the altar, a sacrifice of thanksgiving accepted with great favor on high. Only an emperor who has received the mandate of Heaven can understand the meaning of these signs, and he alone possesses the virtue needed to answer them. The cauldron should therefore be presented in the temple of the ancestors and stored away in the imperial court in accordance with these bright omens!"

[36] From the *Book of Odes,* "Temple Hymns of the Chou," "Ssu-i."

The emperor gave his consent to this.

The men who had been sent to sea in search of the island of P'eng-lai reported that it was not far away, but that they had as yet been unable to reach it because they could barely make out the emanations which indicated its location. The emperor therefore dispatched more men whose duty, it was said, was to watch the sky from afar and aid the magicians in locating the emanations.

In the autumn the emperor journeyed to Yung and was preparing to perform the suburban sacrifice when someone advised him, saying, "The Five Emperors are no more than the helpers of the Great Unity. It would be well if Your Majesty were to set up an altar to the Great Unity and perform the suburban sacrifice in person to this spirit." The emperor, however, was in doubt about what to do and came to no decision.

At this point a man of Ch'i named Kung-sun Ch'ing appeared with a letter which he wished to present to the throne, reading as follows:

This year the precious cauldron was found, and this winter the first day of the month, *hsin-ssu,* corresponds with the winter solstice. This is the same conjunction of circumstances that occurred in the time of the Yellow Emperor. I have in my possession a document on wood which states: "When the Yellow Emperor obtained the precious cauldron at Yüan-kou he questioned Kuei-yü Ch'ü, who replied, 'The Yellow Emperor has obtained the precious cauldron and the sacred calculations. This year the first day of the month, *chi-yu,* corresponds to the winter solstice, which indicates that the heavenly reckonings are in order. When the cycles of heaven have come to an end, they shall begin again.' The Yellow Emperor then proceeded to reckon ahead and found that after approximately twenty years the first day of the month would once more fall on the winter solstice. After about twenty such cycles had passed, or three hundred and eighty years, the Yellow Emperor became an immortal and ascended to heaven."

Kung-sun Ch'ing asked one of the officials named So Chung to present this letter to the throne. But when So Chung read over the letter, he saw that it made no sense and, suspecting that Kung-sun Ch'ing had concocted the whole thing out of his own head, he declined, saying, "The matter of the precious cauldron has already been disposed of. Nothing further can be done about it at this time."

Kung-sun Ch'ing then got one of the emperor's favorites to present his letter and the emperor was exceedingly pleased. He immediately summoned Kung-sun Ch'ing and questioned him, whereupon the latter replied, "I was given this letter by Master Shen, but he is dead."

"And who was Master Shen?" asked the emperor.

"Master Shen was a man of Ch'i who was friendly with the immortal, Master An-ch'i, and from him received the words of the Yellow Emperor. He possessed no writings, but only a cauldron inscription which said: 'When the Han dynasty comes to power, the months and days shall fall the same as they did at the time of the Yellow Emperor.' It further said: 'The sage of the Han shall be the grandson or great-grandson of Kao-tsu. A precious cauldron shall appear and he shall commune with the spirits at the Feng and Shan sacrifices. Of all the seventy-two rulers who attempted the Feng and Shan, only the Yellow Emperor was able to ascend Mount T'ai and perform the Feng!' Master Shen told me, 'The ruler of the Han shall also ascend the mountain and perform the Feng, and when he has done this, then he will become an immortal and will climb up to heaven!'

"In the time of the Yellow Emperor there were ten thousand feudal lords, and among these seven thousand lived in fiefs containing the places of worship of the gods. In the world there are eight famous mountains, three of them in the lands of the barbarians and five of them within China. The five in China are Mount Hua, Mount Shou, The Great Room, Mount T'ai, and Mount Tung-lai. The Yellow Emperor often visited these five mountains and met there with the spirits. At times the Yellow Emperor made war, and at times he studied the arts of becoming an immortal, but he was distressed that the common people criticized his ways and so he beheaded anyone who spoke ill of the spirits. After a hundred years or so he was able to commune with the spirits.

"The Yellow Emperor performed the suburban sacrifice to the Lord on High at Yung, camping there for three months. Kuei-yü Ch'ü's other name was Great Crane, and when he died he was buried in Yung. Therefore the mountain is now called Crane Mound. Later the Yellow Emperor communed with the myriad spiritual beings in the Bright

Court. The Bright Court was located at Sweet Springs, and Cold Gate was the name for the mouth of the valley.

"The Yellow Emperor collected copper from Mount Shou and had it melted and cast into a cauldron at the foot of Mount Ching. When the cauldron was completed, a dragon with whiskers hanging from its chin came down from the sky to fetch him. The Yellow Emperor mounted on the dragon's back, followed by his ministers and palace ladies, making a company of over seventy persons. When they had all mounted, the dragon rose from the ground and departed. The lesser ministers, unable to mount the dragon, clung to its whiskers until the whiskers came out and fell to the ground, along with the bow of the Yellow Emperor. The common people gazed up into the sky till the Yellow Emperor had reached heaven and then they clasped the whiskers and the bow and began to wail. Therefore in later ages the spot where all of this took place was named Cauldron Lake and the bow was called The Cry of Sorrow."

When the emperor heard this, he gave a great sigh and said, "Ah! If I could only become like the Yellow Emperor, I would think no more of my wife and children than of a castoff slipper!" He then honored Kung-sun Ch'ing with the position of palace attendant and sent him east to wait upon the spirits at the Great Room, Mount Sung.

The emperor proceeded to carry out the suburban sacrifice at Yung, after which he traveled west as far as Lung-hsi, climbed Mount K'ung-t'ung in the west, and then returned to the Palace of Sweet Springs. There he gave orders to K'uan Shu and the other officials in charge of sacrifices to fit out an altar to the Great Unity. It was modeled after Miu Chi's altar to the Great Unity and had three levels. Surrounding the base of it were the altars of the Five Emperors, each disposed in the direction appropriate to the particular deity, except that the altar to the Yellow Emperor, the deity of the center, was placed on the southwest side. Thus the eight roads by which demons approach were blocked. For the worship of the Great Unity the same offerings were used as at the altars of Yung, with the addition of such things as thick wine, jujubes, and dried meat. A yak was also slaughtered and offered with the appropriate dishes and other sacrificial implements. The Five Emperors were given only offerings of rich wine in the appropriate sacrificial vessels. Wine was poured on the ground at the four corners of the altar for the purpose, it was said, of giving sustenance to the lesser spirits and attendants and to the Big Dipper. When the offerings were completed, the beasts that had been sacrificed were all burned. The ox was white, and inside it was placed a deer, and inside the deer a pig; water was then sprinkled over them while they burned. An ox was offered to the sun and a ram or a pig to the moon. The priest who presented the offerings to the Great Unity wore robes of purple with brocade; those for the Five Emperors wore the color appropriate to the particular deity. The robes of those who performed the sacrifice to the sun were red, and those for the moon white.

On the first day of the eleventh month, the day *hsin-ssu* [Dec. 24, 113 B.C.], which corresponded to the winter solstice, just before daylight, the emperor for the first time performed the suburban sacrifice in honor of the Great Unity. In the morning he made the morning bows to the sun, and in the evening the evening bows to the moon. The ritual used for the Great Unity was the same as that for the suburban sacrifice at Yung. The words of praise employed in the sacrifice read: "Heaven has for the first time granted to the Supreme Emperor the precious cauldron and the sacred calculations. The first day of the month corresponds to the winter solstice: when the cycles have come to an end, they shall begin again. The Supreme Emperor, reverently bowing, appears here."

The vestments used in the ceremony honored the color yellow. At the time of the sacrifice, the altar was covered with rows of torches, and at the side of the altar were set the vessels for boiling and roasting the sacrifices. "During the sacrifices," the officials concerned with the ceremony reported, "a light appeared in the sky over the offerings." The high ministers of the court announced, "The Supreme Emperor has for the first time performed the suburban sacrifice to the Great Unity at Yün-yang. The officials presented large circlets of jade and offerings of the finest sacrificial animals. On the night of the sacrifice a beautiful light appeared, and the following day yellow exhalations rose from the altar and reached to heaven."

The grand historian and K'uan Shu and the other officials in charge of sacrifices advised the emperor, saying, "The spiritual beings in their beauty have come to aid Your Majesty with blessings and show forth auspicious omens. It is right that an Altar of the Great Unity should be permanently established in this region where the light shone, in clear answer to these portents." The emperor ordered the Altar to be placed under the jurisdiction of the master of invocations. The emperor performed the suburban sacrifice here in person once every three years, and during these intervals sacrifices were performed by the officials in the autumn and the last month of the year.

In the autumn, in preparation for the attack on the state of Southern Yüeh, an announcement was made to the Great Unity, along with prayers for success. A banner was made, fixed to a handle of thorn wood, and painted with representations of the sun, the moon, the Big Dipper, and an ascending dragon. These represented the Spear of the Great Unity [that is, the three stars in the mouth of the Big Dipper]. It was called the "spirit banner" and when the announcement and prayers for the soldiers were offered, the grand historian took it in his hand and pointed it at the country that was about to be attacked.

Meanwhile the magician Luan Ta, who had supposedly set off as the emperor's envoy to search for his teacher, had not ventured to set out to sea but had instead gone to Mount T'ai, where he was performing sacrifices. The emperor dispatched men to trail Luan Ta and see whether there were any evidences of his magical powers. They reported that Luan Ta had in fact met with no spiritual beings at all, and that the story of his going to visit his teacher was all nonsense. Since it seemed that Luan Ta's magical powers were exhausted, and since his claims in most cases were not borne out by the facts, the emperor had him executed.

In the winter Kung-sun Ch'ing went to observe the spirits in the region of Ho-nan and reported that he had seen the footprints of an immortal being on top of the city wall of Kou-shih, where a creature like a pheasant had flown back and forth over the wall. The emperor went in person to Kou-shih to examine the footprints. "Are you sure you are not trying the same sort of trick as Shao-weng and Luan Ta?" the emperor asked.

"The immortals do not seek for the ruler of men," replied Kung-sun Ch'ing. "It is the ruler who must seek for them! Unless one sets about the task with a liberal and open-minded attitude, I am afraid that the spirits will never appear. When men discuss spiritual matters, their words are apt to sound wild and irrational, but if these matters are pursued for a sufficient number of years, the spirits can eventually be persuaded to come forth!"

After this all the provinces and feudal kingdoms set about busily cleaning their roads, and repairing their palaces and towers and the places of worship of the spirits and the famous mountains, anticipating a visit from the emperor.

In the spring, after the kingdom of Southern Yüeh had been wiped out, Li Yen-nien, who became one of the emperor's favorite ministers, attracted the ruler's attention because of his knowledge of music. The emperor was much impressed with his views and ordered the high ministers to open discussions on the following question: "At the places of worship among the common people, musical instruments and dances are still in use, yet at present no such music is employed at the sub-urban sacrifice. How can this be right?"

"In ancient times," replied the ministers, "music was used at all the sacrifices to Heaven and Earth, and thus the deities of those two realms were treated with the highest degree of propriety." Others said, "The Great Emperor Fu Hsi ordered the White Maiden to play upon a fifty-stringed zither. The music was exceedingly sad and the Great Emperor tried to stop her from playing, but she would not cease. Therefore he broke the zither in two, making an instrument of only twenty-five strings."

As a result of their deliberations, sacrifices and prayers of thanks-giving for the success of the expedition to Southern Yüeh were offered to the Great Unity and the Earth Lord, and at these music and dances were used for the first time. A number of boys were summoned to sing at the services and twenty-five stringed zithers and lutes of the kind called *k'ung-hou* were made. It was at this time that zithers and lutes first came into use for religious ceremonies.

In the winter of the following year [110 B.C.] the emperor held dis-cussions with his ministers and announced, "In ancient times the troops were brought back from their posts and temporarily disbanded before the Feng and Shan sacrifices were performed." He proceeded to make a tour of the northern border, calling up a force of over a hundred thousand troops to accompany him. He returned and sacrificed at the grave of the Yellow Emperor at Bridge Mountain and then disbanded the troops at Hsü-ju. "I have been told that the Yellow Emperor did not die," said the emperor. "Why is it that we now find his grave here?" To this question someone replied, "After the Yellow Emperor had been transformed into an immortal and had ascended to Heaven, his ministers made a grave here for his robes and hat!"

After the emperor had returned to the Palace of Sweet Springs he began making preparations to perform the sacrifices at Mount T'ai, first offering a special sacrifice to the Great Unity. From the time the precious cauldron was discovered, the emperor had ordered his high ministers and court scholars to discuss the question of the Feng and Shan, but since these sacrifices were so seldom performed and since the last performance had been so long ago, no one knew the proper ceremony to be followed. The Confucian scholars selected material from the *Book of Documents,* the *Offices of Chou,* and the *Institutes of a King* to show that it was a mountain sacrifice in which the ruler in person shot the sacrificial bull with an arrow. However, a certain Master Ting of Ch'i, who was over ninety years old, stated, "The word *feng* indicates the concept of immortality. The First Emperor of the Ch'in did not succeed in ascending the mountain and performing the Feng sacrifice. If Your Majesty wishes to make the ascent, you should do so in gradual stages, and when it is apparent that there is no wind or rain, you may proceed to the top and carry out the sacrifice."

The emperor therefore ordered the Confucian scholars to practice shooting bulls and to draw up rough plans for the performance of the Feng and Shan. Several years had passed since that time, and the emperor felt that the moment had come to perform the sacrifices. He had been told by Kung-sun Ch'ing and the other magicians, however, that when the Yellow Emperor and the rulers before him had performed the Feng and Shan, they had all succeeded in summoning forth supernatural beings and communing with the spirits. He therefore wished to imitate the example of these rulers by getting into touch with the spirits and the immortals of P'eng-lai and achieving fame in the world so that his virtue might be compared to that of the Nine Bright Ones of antiquity. At the same time he wished to follow as much as possible the doctrines of the Confucians in order to lend elegance to the proceedings. The Confucian scholars for their part had been unable to produce any detailed information on the Feng and Shan ceremonies. Furthermore, they insisted upon confining themselves to what was written in the *Odes* and *Documents* and other old works and seemed incapable of coming forward with any worthwhile suggestions. When the emperor had sacrificial vessels made for use in the Feng and Shan and showed them to the Confucian scholars, some of them objected, saying, "These are not the same as the ones used in ancient times!" In addition an erudit named Hsü Yen informed the emperor, "The scholars who are charged with the conducting of ceremonies under the master of ritual are not as skillful as those of Lu!" Another named Chou Pa called all the scholars together and began making his own plans for the ceremony. With this the emperor demoted Hsü Yen and Chou Pa and called a halt to the discussions of the Confucian scholars, making no further use of their suggestions.

In the first month [37] the emperor journeyed east and visited Kou-shih. He stopped at Mount Sung, the Central Peak, and ascended the crest called The Great Room to pay his respects. The attendants who were waiting for him at the foot of the mountain reported that they had heard a voice that seemed to say "Long Life!" The emperor questioned the men who had ascended the mountain with him, but they replied that they had not spoken any such words, and the men at the foot of the mountain gave the same answer. The emperor then set aside a fief of three hundred households to support the sacrifices to The Great Room, calling it The City Which Honors Mount Sung.

He then proceeded east and ascended Mount T'ai. At this time the grass and leaves of the trees had not yet come out and so, without fear of injuring them, he was able to order his men to drag a stone up the mountain and erect it on the summit of Mount T'ai.

From there the emperor journeyed along the seacoast, paying his respects and sacrificing to the Eight Spirits on the way. The men of Ch'i who came to the emperor with tales of supernatural beings and magical powers numbered in the tens of thousands, but none of them

[37] Following the reading in *Han shu 6*.

were able to offer any proofs. The emperor then dispatched a number of boats, ordering several thousand of the men who had brought him tales of the mountain of the gods in the middle of the sea to set out in search of the spiritual beings of P'eng-lai.

Kung-sun Ch'ing in the meantime had been proceeding in advance of the emperor, bearing the seals of an imperial envoy and looking for signs of the spirits at the various famous mountains. When he reached Mount Tung-lai, he reported that he had encountered a giant man at night who measured several *chang* in height.[38] When he approached to speak to the being, it disappeared, but its footprints were still visible, he said, being very large and like those of an animal. One of the emperor's ministers also reported that he had seen an old man leading a dog. The man had said, "I am looking for the Great Lord!" and had then abruptly disappeared. The emperor had in the meantime gone to see the large footprints reported by Kung-sun Ch'ing, but was not yet persuaded that they were genuine. When his ministers told him about the old man with the dog, however, he became firmly convinced that it had actually been an immortal being. He therefore lingered for a while on the seacoast, providing his magicians with post carriages so that they could get about quickly and sending out several thousand men to search in secret for immortal beings.

In the fourth month the emperor started back west, arriving at Feng-kao. He had thought over the various recommendations which the Confucian scholars and the magicians had made concerning the Feng and Shan sacrifices, but he was troubled by the fact that each said something different and that many of their recommendations were absurd or almost impossible to put into practice. When he reached Liang-fu, he sacrificed to the Lord of the Land. On the day *i-mao* [May 17, 110 B.C.] he ordered the Confucians who attended him to don leather caps and wide sashes and to carry out the shooting of the ox, performing the Feng sacrifice at the eastern foot of Mount T'ai. He followed the ceremony used at the suburban sacrifices to the Great Unity. The *feng* or altar mound was one *chang* and two *ch'ih* in breadth and nine *ch'ih* high. Buried beneath it was a jade tablet inscribed with a message, but the contents were kept secret. After this ceremony was completed, the

[38] A *chang* was equal to about 7′ 7″.

emperor alone, accompanied by only one attendant, the carriage server Tzu-hou,[39] ascended Mount T'ai and again performed the Feng sacrifice. This latter ceremony was carried out entirely in secret. The following day the emperor descended the mountain by the northern road.

On the day *ping-ch'en* [May 18] the emperor performed the Shan sacrifice at Mount Su-jan in the northeast foothills of Mount T'ai, following the ceremony used for the sacrifices to the Earth Lord. At all of these ceremonies the emperor made his obeisances and presented himself in person, wearing garments honoring the color yellow, and music was employed throughout. A type of rush having three ridges on one stalk, which grows between the Yangtze and Huai rivers, was used to make the sacred mats for the offerings, and earth of five colors was heaped on top of the sacrificial mound. In addition to the offerings all sorts of strange beasts, flying creatures, white pheasants, and other animals brought from distant regions were set free so that the ritual would be complete. Rhinoceroses, elephants, and such creatures, however, were not set free, but were brought to Mount T'ai and then taken away again. While the Feng and Shan were being performed, something like a light appeared in the sky at night, and during the day white clouds rose from the mounds.

Returning from the Shan sacrifice, the emperor took his seat in the Bright Hall, where all his ministers in turn offered him their congratulations. The emperor issued an edict to the imperial secretary which read:

I, in my humble and insignificant person, have been accorded the position of highest honor; constantly I tremble with fear that I shall not be worthy of it, for my virtue is poor and slight and I have no understanding of rites and music. When I performed the sacrifice to the Great Unity, something which looked like a beam of light was seen faintly from afar. I was filled with awe at this strange occurrence and would have proceeded no farther, but I did not dare to halt. Thus I ascended Mount T'ai to perform the Feng sacrifice, journeyed to Liang-fu, and later performed the Shan sacrifice at Mount Su-jan, thus renewing myself. In recognition of this new beginning which I and my ministers have made, I grant to every hundred households of the common people one ox and ten piculs of wine, and in addition, to all those over eighty

---

[39] Ho Shan, the son of the famous general Ho Ch'ü-ping.

and to orphans and widows, two bolts of silk cloth. Po, Feng-kao, I-ch'iu, and Li-ch'eng shall be exempted from *corvee* labor and need pay no taxes this year. In addition, let a general amnesty be granted to the empire of the same kind as that ordered in the year *i-mao* [120 B.C.]. None of the places which I have passed through in my visit shall be required to send labor forces, and no criminal charges dating from more than two years in the past shall be tried.

He also issued an edict saying,

In ancient times the Son of Heaven journeyed about on an inspection tour once every five years, and at that time he performed sacrifices to Mount T'ai. The feudal lords who came to pay court to him constructed their lodgings there. Let an order therefore be given to the feudal lords to build their own lodges at the foot of Mount T'ai.

The emperor had succeeded in performing the Feng and Shan and had not been troubled by wind or rain, and the magicians now came forward one after the other to assure him that the time had surely come when he would make contact with the spirits of P'eng-lai. The emperor was overjoyed and, convinced that his meeting with the gods was near, he returned east once more to the seacoast, gazing from afar in hopes of sighting the island of P'eng-lai. Instead, however, his carriage server Tzu-hou, who had accompanied him to the top of Mount T'ai, was stricken with a violent sickness and died the same day. The emperor departed and, following the coast, journeyed north as far as Chieh-shih. From there he traveled through Liao-hsi, passed along the northern border to Chiu-yüan, and in the fifth month returned to the Palace of Sweet Springs.

The officials suggested that the era when the precious cauldron was found should be called *yüan-ting* or "Cauldron Period," and that the present year should be designated as the first year of a new era, to be called *yüan-feng,* the "Feng Period."

In the autumn a comet appeared in the constellation of the Eastern Well and some ten or twelve days later it appeared in the constellation of the Three T'ai. Wang So, a man versed in the observation of the skies, reported that he had seen the star [40] swell forth until it was as large as a melon, and after a while disappear again. The officials all

[40] Following the reading in *Shih chi* 12.

assured the emperor, "Since Your Majesty has instituted the Feng and Shan sacrifices for the house of Han, Heaven has sent forth in response this star of virtue!" In the winter of the following year the emperor performed the suburban sacrifice to the Five Emperors at Yung and on his return he worshiped and sacrificed to the Great Unity. The following words of praise were used in the ceremony: "The star of virtue, large and brilliant, has shown us this auspicious omen. The Star of Long Life shines forth as before; deep and glowing is its great light.[41] The starry signs have appeared for all to see. The Supreme Emperor bows in reverence before the offerings of the master of invocation."

In the spring of this year Kung-sun Ch'ing reported that he had met a spiritual being at Mount Tung-lai who had said that he wished to see the Son of Heaven. The emperor therefore paid a visit to Kou-shih, where he honored Kung-sun Ch'ing with the rank of palace counselor, and then proceeded to Tung-lai. He lodged there for several days but did not succeed in meeting the spirit, though he did see what were said to be the footprints of a giant man. He once more dispatched a group of several thousand magicians to search for the spirits and gather the herbs of immortality.

This year there was a drought, and since the emperor had had no official business which could be used as an excuse for a trip to the east, he took this opportunity to journey to the altar of the Ten Thousand Mile Sands and offer prayers for rain. On his way back he sacrificed at Mount T'ai and then returned to Hu-tzu, where he inspected the work which was being done to close the break in the dikes of the Yellow River there. He remained for two days and then, casting offerings into the Yellow River as a sacrifice, departed. He left orders for two of his ministers to bring a force of soldiers and complete the closing of the breach, leading the waters off in two channels so that the river might be restored to the course it had followed in the time of Emperor Yü.

By this time the emperor had completed the conquest of the two barbarian kingdoms of Yüeh. A man of Yüeh named Yung Chih informed the emperor that the spirits of the dead were highly honored

[41] The "star of virtue" is the comet; the Star of Long Life is Canopus, (Alpha Argus), whose shining was said to portend peace and order.

CHINA AND ITS NEIGHBORS IN THE FORMER HAN

Based on Yanai Watari, *Tōyō dokushi chizu* (Tokyo, Fuzambō, 1931), map 7. The dotted line indicates the and therefore probably unknown to him do not appear on this map. There is some doubt as to which part of India among the people of Yüeh and that at their sacrifices these spirits invariably appeared, often giving proofs of their power. In former times, he said, the king of Eastern Ou had honored the spirits and had consequently lived to the age of a hundred and sixty, but later generations had grown careless and indifferent and therefore the power of Yüeh had declined. The emperor then ordered the shamans of Yüeh to set up a place for Yüeh sacrifices in the capital. It had a terrace but no altar. Here sacrifices were also offered to the spirits of Heaven, the Lord on High, and the various spirits of the dead, and a type of divination using chicken bones was employed which the emperor put great faith in. Thus the Yüeh sacrifices and chicken divination began from this time.

Kung-sun Ch'ing advised the emperor, saying, "It is quite possible to meet with the immortals. It is only that Your Majesty always rushes off in great haste to see them and therefore never succeeds. Now if you would only build some turrets like those on the city wall of Kou-shih and set out dried meat and jujubes, I believe the spirits could be induced to come, for they like to live in towers!"

Therefore the emperor gave orders for the construction of the Flying Eaves and Cassia Towers in Ch'ang-an and the Increased Life and Long Life Towers at the Palace of Sweet Springs. He presented Kung-sun Ch'ing with the seals of an imperial envoy and ordered him to set out the necessary offerings and watch for the arrival of the spirits. He also built the Terrace that Reaches to Heaven and had the sacrificial utensils laid out at the foot, hoping to induce the spirits and immortals to visit it. In addition he constructed a Front Hall at the Palace of Sweet Springs and for the first time enlarged the various rooms of the palace.

In the summer the fungus of immortality sprang up in one of the rooms of the palace, and when the Terrace that Reaches to Heaven, which the emperor had built in honor of the closing of the breach in the dikes of the Yellow River, was completed, something that looked like a light in the sky was said to have appeared. The emperor therefore issued an edict saying, "In a room of the Palace of Sweet Springs the fungus of immortality, with its nine stalks, has sprung up. A general amnesty shall be granted to the empire and no more construction labor shall be required."

The following year [108 B.C.] the army attacked Korea. In the summer there was a drought. Kung-sun Ch'ing informed the emperor, "In the time of the Yellow Emperor, whenever the Feng sacrifice was performed, Heaven sent a drought for three years in order to dry out the earth of the *feng* or altar mound." The emperor then issued an edict saying, "Heaven has sent this drought for the purpose of drying out the earth of the *feng*. Let all the empire be ordered to pay honor and sacrifice to the Sacred Star."

The following year the emperor performed the suburban sacrifice at Yung. He opened up a road through Hui-chung and, passing through the region, reached Ming-tse in the spring, from whence he returned to the capital by way of Hsi-ho.

In the winter of the following year [106 B.C.] the emperor visited Nan Province, traveling to Chiang-ling and the east, where he ascended and paid his respects to the Mountain of the Heavenly Pillar in Ch'ien, which he designated the Southern Peak. He embarked on the Yangtze and traveled from Hsün-yang to Ts'ung-yang, passing through Lake P'eng-li and paying his respects to the famous mountains and rivers along the way. From there he proceeded north to Lang-ya, following the seacoast, and in the fourth month reached Feng-kao, where he renewed the Feng sacrifice.

When the emperor first performed the Feng sacrifice at Mount T'ai a spot was pointed out to him at the northeast foot of the mountain which was said to be the site of the Bright Hall in ancient times. The place was steep and narrow, however, and the emperor wished to build his own Bright Hall in the vicinity of Feng-kao, but he did not know what sort of plan to follow for the building. Then a man of Chi-nan named Kung-yü Tai presented to the emperor a plan of the Bright Hall used in the time of the Yellow Emperor. According to this design, there was a hall in the center, wallless on all four sides and roofed with rushes. Streams flowed beside the fence which surrounded the building, and a two-story walk, topped by towers, led into it from the southwest. The Son of Heaven entered by the walk, which was called *K'un-lun*, and performed sacrifices here to the Lord on High. The emperor accordingly gave orders for a Bright Hall to be constructed beside the Wen River at Feng-kao following the plan submitted by Kung-yü Tai.

In the fifth year of *yüan-feng* [106 B.C.] when the emperor renewed the Feng sacrifice, he sacrificed to the Great Unity and the Five Emperors at the Bright Hall, placing them in the highest seats and placing the seat of Emperor Kao-tsu facing them. In the lower room he sacrificed to the Earth Lord. Twenty sets of animals were used for these sacrifices. The emperor entered from the K'un-lun Walk and for the first time paid his respects at the Bright Hall, following the ceremony used at the suburban sacrifice. When the ceremony was completed the sacrifices were burned outside the hall.

The emperor then once more ascended Mount T'ai and performed a secret sacrifice at the summit, while at the foot of the mountain the officials performed sacrifices to the Five Emperors, each place of sacrifice being situated in the appropriate direction, except that that for the Yellow Emperor, the ruler of the center, was combined with that for the Red Emperor of the south. When torches were lit on top of the mountain the officials at the foot all lit their torches in answer.

Two years later those who were in charge of reforming the calendar announced that it would be appropriate to carry out their changes on the day *chia-tzu* of the eleventh month [Dec. 25, 105 B.C.], on which the first day of the month would correspond with the winter solstice. The emperor therefore went in person to Mount T'ai and on that day sacrificed in the Bright Hall to the Lord on High, but he did not renew the Feng and Shan. The words of praise used in the ceremony were as follows: "Heaven has once more granted to the Supreme Emperor the sacred calculations of the Great Beginning. When the cycles of the heavens have been completed, they shall in this way begin again. The Supreme Emperor respectfully bows to the Great Unity."

The emperor then proceeded east to the sea, where he examined those who had gone to sea and the magicians he had dispatched to seek for the gods, but none of them were able to report any success. He sent a large party of them out again, however, still hoping to accomplish some meeting with the spirits.

In the eleventh month, the day *i-yu* [Jan. 15, 104 B.C.], a fire broke out at the Terrace of Cypress Beams.

On the first day of the twelfth month, the day *chia-wu* [Jan. 24], the emperor in person performed the Shan sacrifice at Mount Kao-li and offered sacrifices to the Earth Lord. He then went on to the Gulf of Pohai, where he performed sacrifices from afar to the island of P'eng-lai and such places, hoping always to reach their wonderful halls.

The emperor then returned to the capital area and, because the Terrace of Cypress Beams had been destroyed by fire, held his court at the Palace of Sweet Springs and received the yearly accounts from the provinces and kingdoms there. Kung-sun Ch'ing informed him, "The Yellow Emperor constructed the Blue Spirit Terrace, but twelve days later it burned down. He then built the Bright Court, which was located at the site of the present Palace of Sweet Springs." Many of the other magicians likewise assured the emperor that there had been rulers in ancient times who had had their capital at Sweet Springs. The emperor therefore decided that in the future he would also hold court with the feudal lords at Sweet Springs, where mansions would be built to house the lords during their visits.

Yung Chih of Yüeh informed the emperor, "According to the custom of Yüeh, when there has been a fire and the buildings are rebuilt, they must always be larger than before in order to overcome the evil influences." The emperor then constructed the Chien-chang Palace or Palace for Establishing the Statutes. It had a countless number of gates and doors, and the front hall was larger than that of the Eternal Palace. On the east side was the Phoenix Tower, measuring over twenty *chang* in height. On the west were the walks, with a garden measuring twenty or thirty *li* in which tigers were kept. North of the palace was built a large lake called the Great Fluid, with the Terrace of the Lapping Water rising over twenty *chang* from it. In the middle of the lake were P'eng-lai, Fang-chang, Ying-chou, and Hu-liang, islands built to represent the spirit isles of the sea or such things as turtles and fish. On the south were the Jeweled Hall, the Jade Gate, the Great Bird, and similar constructions, as well as the Terrace of the Spirits and the Railing Tower, measuring fifty *chang,* all connected by walks for the imperial palanquin.

In the summer the calendar of the Han dynasty was changed so that the official year began with the first month. Yellow, the color of earth, was chosen as the color of the dynasty, and the titles of the officials were recarved on seals so that they all consisted of five characters, five being the number appropriate to the element earth. This year was designated as the first year of the era *t'ai-ch'u* or "Great Beginning."

This year the armies marched west to attack Ferghana. Swarms of locusts appeared. Ting Fu-jen, Yü Ch'u of Lo-yang, and others used their magical arts and sacrifices to put a curse upon the leaders of the Hsiung-nu and Ferghana.

The following year the officials informed the emperor that there were no proper vessels for use in boiling the sacrificial animals at the Five Altars of Yung, and for this reason the fragrance of the offerings was not being properly presented. The emperor therefore ordered the sacrificial officials to present vessels to the altars for use in the calf offerings. The color of the sacrificial animals was to be that appropriate to whichever of the Five Emperors was being sacrificed to. He ordered, however, that wooden models of horses be substituted for the former offerings of colts.[42] Real colts were to be used only when the emperor in person performed the suburban sacrifice. Likewise all of the sacrifices to famous mountains and rivers which had previously used colts were to substitute wooden horses except when the emperor visited the region to perform the sacrifice himself. In all other respects the ceremonies were to be carried out in the same way as before.

The following year [102 B.C.] the emperor journeyed east to the sea to examine the men who had been sent to search for the immortals, but none of them had any success to report. The magicians then informed him that in the time of the Yellow Emperor there had been five city walls and twelve towers at Chih-ch'i from which the spirits were observed, which were called "Prolonged Life." The emperor gave permission for the construction of similar walls and towers according to the directions of the magicians, to be called "Bright Life." The emperor sacrificed there in person to the Lord on High.

Kung-yü Tai advised the emperor, saying, "When the Yellow Em-

[42] The Han was chronically short of horses, and particularly at this time when large armies were needed for the campaigns against Ferghana and the Hsiung-nu. The five characters which follow this in the text appear to be a later addition and have not been translated.

peror was alive, although he performed the Feng sacrifice at Mount T'ai, his ministers Feng-hou, Feng-chü, and Ch'i-po instructed him to perform the Feng at the Eastern Mount T'ai and the Shan at Mount Fan as well. Only when he had thus obeyed the omens sent from Heaven was he able to obtain immortal life!"

The emperor accordingly ordered the sacrificial utensils prepared and journeyed to the Eastern Mount T'ai, but he found it to be a small hill of no great height, in no way measuring up to the exalted name it bore. He therefore ordered the sacrificial officials to conduct ceremonies there, but he did not perform the Feng or Shan sacrifices. He later ordered Kung-yü Tai to perform sacrifices and watch for spiritual beings.

In the summer the emperor proceeded to Mount T'ai to renew the Feng sacrifice, as was appropriate every five years, using the same ceremony he had used before except that he also performed the Shan sacrifice at Stone Gate. Stone Gate is located at the southern foot of Mount T'ai. According to a number of the magicians, it is the gateway to the village of the immortals and for this reason the emperor performed the Shan in person there.

Five years later [98 B.C.] he once more went to Mount T'ai to renew the Feng sacrifice, and on his way back to the capital he sacrificed at Mount Hengg.

The sacrifices instituted by the present emperor, then, are those to the Great Unity and the Earth Lord, as well as the suburban sacrifices performed by the ruler in person every three years. He has established the Feng and Shan sacrifices for the Han dynasty, which are renewed every five years, as well as the five sacrifices to the Great Unity recommended by Miu Chi, the Three Unities, the Dark Ram, the Horse Traveler, the Red Star, and those at the altars recommended by K'uan Shu, with officials to perform the ceremonies to them at the appropriate seasons. All of the last six groups of sacrifices are under the jurisdiction of the master of invocations.

As for the Eight Spirits and the other deities, Bright Life, Mount Fan, and similar sacrificial places mentioned, if the emperor happens to be passing by, then sacrifices are performed to them, and when he has departed, they are discontinued. Any places of sacrifice instituted by the magicians themselves are left to their own charge; they continue as long as the particular man is living, and are discontinued at his death, the sacrificial officials of the government having nothing to do with them. All other sacrifices are carried on as they were in previous reigns.

The present emperor, after performing the Feng and Shan, made another tour twelve years later [98 B.C.], visiting all the Five Peaks and the Four Watercourses. The magicians who had been instructed to watch for spirit beings, and those who had been sent to search for the island of P'eng-lai in the sea, failed completely during that time to produce any evidence of success. Kung-sun Ch'ing was supposed to be observing the spirits, but he too had nothing to show for his efforts and could only make excuses by pointing out the footprints of giant men. Thus the emperor grew increasingly weary and disgusted with the inane tales of the magicians, and yet he was bound and snared by them and could not free himself, for always he hoped to find one who spoke the truth. From this time on, the magicians who came to him recommending sacrifices to this or that deity grew even more numerous, but the results of all this are as you can see.

The Grand Historian remarks: I accompanied the emperor when he journeyed about to sacrifice to Heaven and Earth, the other deities, and the famous mountains and rivers, and when he went to perform the Feng and Shan. I entered the Temple of Long Life and assisted at the sacrifices there when the deity spoke, and I thus had an opportunity to study and examine the ways of the magicians and the sacrificial officials. Later I retired and wrote down in order all that I knew about the worship of the spirits from ancient times on, setting forth both the outside and the inside stories of these affairs. Gentlemen in later ages will thus be able to peruse what I have written. As for the details of sacrificial plates and utensils, the types of jades and silks offered, or the exact ritual to be followed in presenting them—these I have left to the officials who handle such matters.

Shih chi 29: The Treatise on the Yellow River and Canals

In ancient times Emperor Yü deepened the rivers and saved the empire from flood, bringing relief and security to the nine provinces. Concerning the waterways that were opened or diked, the river courses that were fixed, and the canals that were constructed, I made The Treatise on the Yellow River and Canals.

The documents on the Hsia dynasty tell us that Emperor Yü spent thirteen years controlling and bringing an end to the floods, and during that period, though he passed by the very gate of his own house, he did not take the time to enter. On land he traveled in a cart and on water in a boat; he rode a sledge to cross the mud and wore cleated shoes in climbing the mountains. In this way he marked out the nine provinces, led the rivers along the bases of the mountains, decided what tribute was appropriate for each region in accordance with the quality of its soil, opened up the nine roads, built embankments around the nine marshes, and made a survey of the nine mountains.

Of all the rivers, the Yellow River caused the greatest damage to China by overflowing its banks and inundating the land, and therefore he turned all his attention to controlling it. Thus he led the Yellow River in a course from Chi-shih past Lung-men and south to the northern side of Mount Hua; from there eastward along the foot of Ti-chu Mountain, past the Meng Ford and the confluence of the Lo River to Ta-p'ei. At this point Emperor Yü decided that, since the river was descending from high ground and the flow of the water was rapid and fierce, it would be difficult to guide it over level ground without danger of frequent disastrous break-throughs. He therefore divided the flow into two channels, leading it along the higher ground to the north, past the Chiang River and so to Ta-lu. There he spread it out to form the Nine Rivers, brought it together again to make the

Backward-flowing River [i.e., tidal river], and thence led it into the Gulf of Pohai.[1] When he had thus opened up the rivers of the nine provinces and fixed the outlets of the nine marshes, peace and order were brought to the lands of the Hsia and his achievements continued to benefit the Three Dynasties which followed.

Sometime later the Hung Canal was constructed, leading off from the lower reaches of the Yellow River at Jung-yang, passing through the states of Sung, Cheng, Ch'en, Ts'ai, Ts'ao, and Wei, and joining up with the Chi, Ju, Huai, and Ssu rivers. In Ch'u two canals were built, one in the west from the Han River through the plains of Yün-meng, and one in the east to connect the Yangtze and Huai rivers.[2] In Wu a canal was dug to connect the three mouths of the Yangtze and the Five Lakes, and in Ch'i one between the Tzu and Chi rivers. In Shu, Li Ping, the governor of Shu, cut back the Li Escarpment to control the ravages of the Mo River and also opened up channels for the Two Rivers through the region of the Ch'eng-tu.

All of these canals were navigable by boat, and whenever there was an overflow of water it was used for irrigation purposes, so that the people gained great benefit from them. In addition there were literally millions of smaller canals which led off from the larger ones at numerous points along their courses and were employed to irrigate an increasingly large area of land, but none of these are worth mentioning here.

Hsi-men Pao built a canal to lead off the waters of the Chang River and irrigate Yeh, and as a result the region of Ho-nei in the state of Wei became rich.

Another time the state of Hann, learning that the state of Ch'in was fond of undertaking large projects, dispatched a water engineer named Cheng Kuo to go to Ch'in and persuade the ruler to construct a canal from a point on the Ching River west of Mount Chung to the pass at Hu-k'ou, and from there along the Northern Mountains east into the the Lo River, a distance of over three hundred *li*. Ostensibly the pur-

---

[1] Needless to say, this is simply a description of the course of the Yellow River in ancient times. The passage, though not a direct quotation, is based upon the "Tribute of Yü" section of the *Book of Documents*.

[2] Following the reading in *Han shu* 29.

pose of the project was to provide irrigation for the fields, though in fact Cheng Kuo and the rulers of Hann hoped thereby to wear out the energies of the state of Ch'in so that it would not march east to attack Hann. Cheng Kuo succeeded in getting the project started, but halfway through the real nature of his mission came to light. The Ch'in ruler was about to kill him, but Cheng Kuo said, "It is true that I came here originally with underhanded intentions. But if the canal is completed, it will profit the state of Ch'in as well!"

The Ch'in ruler, deciding that this was sensible, in the end allowed him to go ahead with the canal. When it was finished, it was used to spread muddy, silt-laden water over more than forty thousand *ch'ing* of land in the area which up until this time had been very brackish, bringing the yield of the land up to one *chung* per acre [*mou*].³ As a result the area within the Pass was converted into fertile fields and no longer suffered from lean years; Ch'in became rich and powerful and eventually was able to conquer all the other feudal lords and unite the empire. In honor of its builder the canal was named Cheng Kuo Canal.

Thirty-nine years after the founding of the Han [168 B.C.], in the reign of Emperor Wen, the Yellow River overflowed its banks at Suan-tsao and destroyed the Metal Embankment east of there. Accordingly a large force of laborers was called up in Tung Province to repair the break.

Some forty years later,⁴ during the era *yüan-kuang* [134–129 B.C.] of the present emperor, the Yellow River broke its banks at Hu-tzu, flowing southeast into the marsh of Chü-yeh and joining up with the Huai and Ssu rivers. The emperor accordingly ordered Chi An and Cheng Tang-shih to raise a force of laborers and repair the breach, but no sooner had they done so than the river broke through again. At this time T'ien Fen, the marquis of Wu-an, was serving as chancellor and his income came from an estate in Shu. Shu is located north of the Yellow River, and since the break was on the southern side, suffered no damage from floods; on the contrary the revenue from the estate

---

³ One *ch'ing* was equal to about 57 English acres, and there were 500 *mou* in a *ch'ing*. One *chung* was equal to ten *hu*, or about five and a half bushels.

⁴ Ssu-ma Ch'ien's figure is misleading; the break took place in 132 B.C., only thirty-six years after the earlier break.

actually increased. T'ien Fen said to the emperor, "Breaks in the banks of the Yangtze and the Yellow River are all the work of Heaven. It is no easy task to stop up such breaks forcibly by human labor, and indeed to do so would hardly be in accord with the will of Heaven!" The numerologists and those who interpret the emanations in the sky supported him in this view and the emperor therefore hesitated and for a long time made no further attempts to repair the break.

At this time Cheng Tang-shih, who was serving as minister of agriculture, said to the emperor, "Up to now grain from east of the Pass has been brought to the capital by being transported up the Wei River. The operation requires six months to complete and the course is over nine hundred *li* and beset with dangerous places. Now if we were to dig a canal from the Wei River, beginning at Ch'ang-an and following along the Southern Mountains to the Yellow River, the distance could be reduced to something over three hundred *li*. We would have a much easier route for transporting grain, and the trip could be accomplished in three months. Moreover, the people living along the canal could utilize the water to irrigate over ten thousand *ch'ing* of farmland. Thus we could reduce the time and labor required to haul grain and at the same time increase the fertility of the lands within the Pass and obtain a higher yield."

Approving the plan, the emperor ordered Hsü Po, a water engineer from Ch'i, to plot the course of the transport canal and called up a force of twenty or thirty thousand laborers to do the digging. After three years of labor, it was opened for use in hauling grain and proved extremely beneficial. From this time on grain transport to the capital gradually increased, while the people living along the canal were able to make considerable use of the water to irrigate their fields.

After this, P'an Hsi, the governor of Ho-tung, said to the emperor, "Every year over a million piculs of grain are transported to the capital from the area east of the mountains. Since it is brought up the Yellow River, it must be shipped through the dangerous narrows at Ti-chu Mountain, where much of it is lost, and in addition the cost of transportation is very high. Now if we were to dig canals from the Fen River to irrigate the region of P'i-shih and parts of Fen-yin, and other canals from the Yellow River to irrigate P'u-p'o and the rest of Fen-yin,

I believe we could bring five thousand *ch'ing* of land under cultivation. At present this region is nothing more than a strip of uncultivated land along the Yellow River where the people graze their flocks but, if it were turned into irrigated fields, I think it could be made to yield over two million piculs of grain. This could be transported up the Wei River to the capital and would be no more expensive than grain produced in the area within the Pass. It would then no longer be necessary to haul grain from the east past the dangerous part of the river at Ti-chu."

The emperor considered this a sound idea and called up a force of twenty or thirty thousand laborers who worked for several years digging canals and opening up the fields. But the Yellow River changed its course so that the water did not flow into the canals properly and the farmers who worked the newly opened fields were unable to produce enough to repay the cost of planting. After some time, therefore, the newly opened canals and fields in Ho-tung were abandoned and the area was turned over to settlers from the state of Yüeh. What little revenue it produced was allotted to the privy treasury.

Following this, someone sent a letter to the throne proposing that a road be opened up between the Pao and Yeh rivers, and that they be used to transport grain. The emperor referred the proposal to the imperial secretary Chang T'ang who, after conducting an inquiry, reported as follows: "At present anyone wishing to travel to the province of Shu must go over the Old Road, a very long and roundabout route beset with steep places. Now if the Pao and Yeh rivers were dredged and a road opened between them, it would provide a much more level route and the distance could be reduced to four hundred *li*. The Pao River runs into the Mien River and the Yeh River runs into the Wei, both of which can be used to transport grain. Therefore grain could be brought from Nan-yang up the Mien River and into the Pao, and where the Pao ends it could be transported overland by carts for a distance of a hundred *li* or so to where the Yeh begins, and from there down the Wei to Ch'ang-an. Thus grain from Han-chung could be brought to the capital. At the same time, by making use of the Mien River, grain could be transported from east of the mountains in unlimited quantities and the route would be much more convenient than the present one up the Yellow River and through the narrows at Ti-chu. Moreover, the region of the Pao and Yeh is as rich in timber and bamboo as the provinces of Pa and Shu."

The emperor approved the proposal and appointed Chang T'ang's son Chang Ang as governor of Han-chung, calling up a force of twenty or thirty thousand laborers and setting them to work constructing the Pao and Yeh road and waterway which extended more than five hundred *li*. When the road was finished it did in fact prove to be much shorter and more convenient than the old route, but the rivers were too full of rapids and boulders to be used for transporting grain.

Following this, a man named Chuang Hsiung-p'i reported to the emperor that the people of Lin-chin wished to dig a canal from the Lo River to be used to irrigate some ten thousand *ch'ing* of land east of Ch'ung-chüan. The land in this area was brackish, but the people believed that if it could be irrigated with water led in from the Lo River, it could be made to produce ten piculs per acre. The emperor therefore called up a labor force of over ten thousand men and set them to work digging a canal leading off from the Lo River at Cheng and extending to the foot of Mount Shang-yen. There, however, it was found that the banks of the canal kept collapsing, so the men dug wells, some of them over forty *chang* deep, at various points along the course and induced the water to flow from one well to another. Thus the water disappeared from sight at Mount Shang-yen and flowed underground to the eastern side of the mountain, a distance of over ten *li*. This was the beginning of the so-called well-canals. In the course of the digging a dragon bone was discovered and the canal was therefore named Dragon Head Canal. It has been over ten years now since it was constructed but, although the water flows through it fairly well, the land has not yet shown much improvement.

More than twenty years had passed since the Yellow River broke through its banks at Hu-tzu. The break had not been repaired and the harvests were frequently poor, the damage being particularly severe in Liang and Ch'u. The emperor, having gone east to perform the Feng and Shan sacrifices [110 B.C.], made a tour through the empire, sacrificing to various mountains and rivers. The following year [109 B.C.] there was a drought (the purpose of which, it was said, was to dry out the earth of the altar mound constructed for the Feng sacrifice), and very little rain fell. The emperor ordered Chi Jen and Kuo Ch'ang to raise a force of twenty or thirty thousand men and close the break in the banks of the Yellow River at Hu-tzu, while he himself went east to pray for rain at the Altar of the Ten Thousand Mile Sands. On his way back to the capital he stopped to inspect the break in person and cast offerings of jade and a white horse into the river. He ordered all the courtiers and ministers who were accompanying him, from the generals on down, to carry bundles of brushwood and help close the break in the embankment. As it happened, the people of Tung Province had just burned off all their grasslands, so there was very little brushwood to be found in the area. The workmen were therefore obliged to sink lengths of bamboo from the Ch'i Park to form a weir across the opening. As the emperor surveyed the break, he was filled with despair at the difficulty of the task and composed this song:

> The river broke through at Hu-tzu;
> What could we do?
> Beneath its rushing waves,
> Villages all became rivers.
> The villages have all become rivers
> And there is no safety for the land.
> Our labors know no rest,
> Our mountains crumble.
> Our mountains crumble
> And the marsh of Chü-yeh overflows.
> Even the fish lament
> As the winter days press near.
> The river raged from its boundaries,
> It has left its constant course.
> Dragons and water monsters leap forth,
> Free to wander afar.
> Let it return to the old channel
> And we will truly bless the gods.
> But for my journey to the Feng and Shan,
> How would I have known what it was like?
> Ask the Lord of the River for me,
> "Why are you so cruel?

Your surging inundations will not cease;
You grieve my people!
The city of Nieh-sang is awash;
The Huai and Ssu brim over.
So long, and yet you will not return—
You break the laws of nature!"

The river rages on,
Its wild waters tossing.
It swirls back to the north,
A swift and dangerous torrent.
We bring the long stakes
And cast the precious jade.
The Lord of the River hears our plea
But there is not enough brushwood.
There is not enough brushwood—
The fault of the people of Wei.
They have wasted the land with fire—
What can we use to check the waters?
We sink the forest bamboo
And ballast the weir with stones.
We will stem the break at Hsüan-fang
And bring ten thousand blessings!

Thus they finally succeeded in closing the gap at Hu-tzu and built a temple on top of the embankment called the Temple of Hsüan-fang. They led the waters of the river off to the north in two channels so that it returned to the course it had followed in the time of Emperor Yü. Safety was restored to the regions of Liang and Ch'u, and they no longer suffered any damage from flood waters.

After this the men who were concerned with such affairs all rushed to the emperor with proposals for utilizing the rivers to greater advantage. As a result canals were dug in So-fang, Hsi-ho, Ho-hsi, and Chiu-ch'üan to draw off water from the Yellow River or smaller rivers in the valleys and use it to irrigate the fields. Within the Pass the Fu and Ling-chih canals were constructed, making use of the water of various rivers in the region; in Ju-nan and Chiu-chiang water was drawn off from the Huai River; in Tung-hai from the marsh of

Chü-ting; and at the foot of Mount T'ai from the Wen River. In all these places canals were dug to water the fields, providing irrigation for over ten thousand *ch'ing* of land in each area. In addition many other small canals and waterways through the mountains were opened up, but they are too numerous to describe here. Of all these exploits, however, the most outstanding was the closing of the break in the Yellow River at Hsüan-fang.

The Grand Historian remarks: I have climbed Mount Lu in the south to observe the courses which Emperor Yü opened up for the nine tributaries of the Yangtze. From there I journeyed to K'uai-chi and T'ai-huang and, ascending the heights of Ku-su, looked out over the Five Lakes. In the east I have visited the confluence of the Yellow and Lo rivers, Ta-p'ei, and the Backward-flowing River, and have traveled along the waterways of the Huai, Ssu, Chi, T'a, and Lo rivers. In the west I have seen Mount Min and the Li Escarpment in the province of Shu, and I have journeyed through the north from Lung-men to So-fang. How tremendous are the benefits brought by these bodies of water, and how terrible the damages! I was among those who carried bundles of brushwood on their backs to stem the break at Hsüan-fang and, deeply moved by the song of Hu-tzu, I made this treatise on the Yellow River and the canals.

Shih chi 30: The Treatise on the Balanced Standard

The purpose of currency is to provide a medium of exchange between farmers and merchants, but in extreme cases it is subject to all kinds of clever manipulation. As a result, the great landholders increase their power and men compete for the opportunity to turn a neat profit, abandoning the pursuit of agriculture, which is basic, to follow the secondary occupations of commerce. Thus I made The Treatise on the Balanced Standard, showing how these changes come about.

When the Han dynasty came to power, it inherited the evils left by the Ch'in. The able-bodied men were all away with the army, while the old and underaged busily transported supplies for them. There was much hard work and little wealth. The Son of Heaven himself could not find four horses of the same color to draw his carriage, many of his generals and ministers were reduced to riding about in ox carts, and the common people had nothing to lay away in their storehouses.

Because the currency of the Ch'in was heavy and cumbersome to use, the Han ordered the people to mint new coins. The unit for gold was one catty. The laws and prohibitions of the Ch'in having been simplified or done away with, people who were intent upon making a profit by underhanded means began to hoard their wealth, buying up the commodities on the market, so that the price of goods shot up. Grain put up for sale brought as much as ten thousand cash [1] a picul, and a horse fetched a hundred catties of gold.

After peace had been restored to the empire, Kao-tsu issued an order forbidding merchants to wear silk or ride in carriages, and increased the taxes that they were obliged to pay in order to hamper and humiliate them. [2] During the reigns of Emperor Hui and Empress Lü, because the empire had only just begun to recover from the period of war and

[1] Ten thousand copper cash were equal in value to one catty of gold.
[2] The traditional Chinese practice of making life difficult for the merchants in order to encourage agriculture.

confusion, the laws concerning the merchants were relaxed, though the sons and grandsons of merchant families were prohibited from holding government office.

The salaries of officials and the costs of the administration were estimated, and the necessary funds collected from the people in the form of a poll tax. Revenues from the natural resources of mountains, rivers, parks, and lakes, as well as those from the government market places and from other kinds of taxes, were all used for the private maintenance of the Son of Heaven or the feudal lords and princesses from whose lands they were collected, and were not entered in the budget for the empire as a whole. The amount of grain transported from east of the mountains each year to supply the officials of the capital did not exceed two or three hundred thousand piculs.

In the time of Emperor Wen, because the "elm-pod" coins, minted earlier, had grown too numerous and light in weight, new coins were cast weighing four *shu* and inscribed with the words *han-liang* or "half-tael." The people were allowed to mint them at will.[3] As a result the king of Wu, though only a feudal lord, was able, by extracting ore from the mountains in his domain and minting coins, to rival the wealth of the Son of Heaven. It was this wealth which he eventually used to start his revolt. Similarly, Teng T'ung, who was only a high official, succeeded in becoming richer than a vassal king by minting coins. The coins of the king of Wu and Teng T'ung were soon circulating all over the empire, and as a result the private minting of coinage was finally prohibited.

At this time the Hsiung-nu were making frequent raids across the northern border, and farming garrisons had to be set up along the frontier to stop them. The grain produced by these garrisons alone, however, was not sufficient to feed all the border troops. The government then called upon the people to supply grain, offering honorary ranks to those who were prepared to send grain to the frontier. The ranks varied with the amount of grain but reached as high as the eighteenth rank, called *ta-shu-ch'ang*. Later, during Emperor Ching's reign, because of the drought which prevailed in Shang Province and

---

[3] Though Kao-tsu had allowed the people to mint the "elm-pod" shaped coins, there is evidence that Empress Lü put a stop to the practice of private minting.

the west, the order concerning the sale of ranks was revived, but the price of the ranks was reduced in order to attract more people. In addition men who had been condemned to duty on the frontier for a year, together with the women of their families who were sentenced to menial service in the government workshops, were permitted to buy off their sentences by transporting grain to the district officials. More pastures for raising horses were opened up in order to supply the needs of the nation, and the number of palaces and pleasure towers, carriages and horses at the disposal of the emperor was increased.

By the time the present emperor had been on the throne a few years, a period of over seventy years had passed since the founding of the Han. During that time the nation had met with no major disturbances so that, except in times of flood or drought, every person was well supplied and every family had enough to get along on. The granaries in the cities and the countryside were full and the government treasuries were running over with wealth. In the capital the strings of cash had been stacked up by the hundreds of millions until the cords that bound them had rotted away and they could no longer be counted. In the central granary of the government, new grain was heaped on top of the old until the building was full and the grain overflowed and piled up outside, where it spoiled and became unfit to eat. Horses were to be seen even in the streets and lanes of the common people or plodding in great numbers along the paths between the fields, and anyone so poor as to have to ride a mare was disdained by his neighbors and not allowed to join the gatherings of the villagers. Even the keepers of the community gates ate fine grain and meat. The local officials remained at the same posts long enough to see their sons and grandsons grow to manhood, and the higher officials occupied the same positions so long that they adopted their official titles as surnames. As a result, men had a sense of self-respect and regarded it as a serious matter to break the law. Their first concern was to act in accordance with what was right and to avoid shame and dishonor.

At this time, however, because the net of the law was slack and the people rich, it was possible for men to use their wealth to exploit others and to accumulate huge fortunes. Some, such as the great landowners and powerful families, were able to do anything they pleased in the countryside, while the members of the imperial house and the nobility, the high officials and the lesser government officers, strove to outdo each other in luxurious living; there was no limit to how far each would go in aping the houses, carriages, and dress of his social superiors.

But it has ever been the law of change that when things reach their period of greatest flourishing, they must begin to decay. Shortly after this time Chuang Chu, Chu Mai-ch'en, and others invited the people of the region of Eastern Ou to move to China, intervening in the war between the two kingdoms of Yüeh, and the area between the Huai and Yangtze rivers, to which they were transferred, was put to great trouble and expense. T'ang Meng and Ssu-ma Hsiang-ju opened up a road to the land of the barbarians in the southwest, cutting a passage over a thousand *li* long through the mountains in order to broaden the provinces of Pa and Shu, but the undertaking exhausted the people of these regions. P'eng Wu established relations with the peoples of Wei-mo and Ch'ao-hsien and set up the province of Ts'ang-hai on the Korean Peninsula, but the move caused great unrest among the inhabitants of the neighboring states of Yen and Ch'i.[4]

After Wang Hui made his unsuccessful attempt to ambush the Hsiung-nu at Ma-i, peaceful relations with the Hsiung-nu came to an end and they began to invade and plunder the northern border. Armies had to be dispatched time and again and could not be disbanded, causing extreme hardship to the empire. As the conflicts became fiercer day by day, men set off to war carrying their packs of provisions, while those left behind at home had to send more and more goods to keep them supplied. Those at home and those on the frontier were kept busy guarding the empire and supplying rations until the common people were exhausted and began to look for some clever way to evade the laws. The funds of the government were soon used up and, in order to supply the deficiencies, it was agreed that men who presented goods would be appointed to official positions, and those who made appropriate contributions would be pardoned for their crimes. The old system of selecting officials on the basis of merit fell into disuse, and modesty and a sense of shame became rare qualities. Military achievement was

---

[4] Following the reading in *Han shu* 24B. Detailed accounts of these events will be found in the chapters dealing with foreign peoples later on in this volume.

now the key to advancement. The laws were made stricter and more detailed, and officials whose main job was to make a profit for the government for the first time appeared in office.

After this the Han generals every year led forces of twenty or thirty thousand cavalry in attacks on the barbarians and the general of carriage and cavalry Wei Ch'ing seized the region south of the bend of the Yellow River from the Hsiung-nu and fortified So-fang.

At the same time the Han government was building the road through the region of the southwestern barbarians, employing a force of twenty or thirty thousand laborers. Provisions for them had to be carried on back for a distance of a thousand *li,* and of ten or more *chung* sent out, only one picul, or less than one tenth of the original amount, reached its destination. In addition gifts of money were distributed to the inhabitants of Ch'iung and P'o in order to win their support. Several years passed, however, and the road was still not completed. In the meantime, the barbarians several times attacked the laborers, and the Han officials were forced to call out troops to control them. All the taxes from the region of Pa and Shu were insufficient to cover the expenses of the road, and it was decided to invite wealthy families to open up farms in the region of the southern barbarians; for any grain which they turned over to the district officials, they would be reimbursed in cash by the financial officers of the ministry of agriculture in the capital. Again, when the road was opened up to the province of Ts'ang-hai in the east, the expenditures for laborers were just as great. In addition, a force of over a hundred thousand men was conscripted to build the fortifications at So-fang and guard them. Provisions for all these undertakings had to be transported great distances over land and water, and the burden fell upon all the regions east of the mountains. Expenditures ran from two to three to ten billions of cash and the government treasuries became emptier than ever. An order was issued allowing those who presented male or female slaves to the government to be exempted from military and labor services for lifetime or, if the donor was already a palace attendant and therefore exempt, to receive an advancement in rank. It even reached the point where men were made palace attendants because of donations of sheep!

Four years later [124 B.C.] the general in chief Wei Ch'ing, commanding six generals and an army of over a hundred thousand, attacked the Hsiung-nu leader known as the Wise King of the Right, beheading or capturing fifteen thousand of the enemy. The following year Wei Ch'ing again led six generals in another attack on the barbarians, beheading or capturing nine thousand men. Those who had beheaded or captured enemy soldiers were presented with gifts totaling over two hundred thousand catties of gold. Generous gifts were also given to the tens of thousands of enemy captives, and food and clothing were supplied to them by the district officials. The men and horses killed on the Han side amounted to over a hundred thousand. In addition, there were the expenses for weapons and the cost of provisions transported to the armies.

By this time the reserves of cash stored up by the ministry of agriculture from earlier years had been exhausted and the revenue from taxes had likewise been used up, so that there was not enough money left to support the troops. When the officials reported this fact to the emperor, he replied, "I have been told that the Five Emperors of antiquity did not necessarily follow the same policies, and yet they all achieved good government; that the rulers Yü and T'ang did not necessarily use the same kind of laws, though they were both worthy kings. The roads they followed were different, but all led to the same ultimate goal of establishing virtue. Now peace has not yet been retored to the northern frontier, a fact which grieves me deeply. Recently the general in chief attacked the Hsiung-nu and beheaded or captured nineteen thousand of the enemy, and yet the rewards and supplies due him and his men are held back and they have not yet received them. Let deliberations begin on a law to allow the people to purchase honorary ranks and to buy mitigations of punishments or freedom from prohibitions against holding office."

The officials responded by requesting the establishment of honorary official positions, to be known as "ranks of military merit." One grade of the rank was to be priced at one hundred and seventy thousand cash, the total value of the sale amounting to over three hundred thousand catties of gold.[5] Among the purchasers of "ranks of military merit,"

[5] The sentence is obscure, and commentators differ widely in their interpretations.

those of the *kuan-shou* or fifth grade or above were to be accorded the same privileges as regular government officials of the fifth lord class. Those guilty of some crime were to have two grades deducted from the ranks they purchased, but were to be allowed to purchase as high as *lo-ch'ing,* the eighth grade. The purpose of this was to honor military achievements, but where such achievements were particularly numerous, the awards exceeded the limits set for the various grades, so that those with the most distinguished records were enfeoffed as marquises or appointed as high government officials, while even the lesser ones became palace attendants or petty officials. As a result, so many avenues to official position were opened and such confusion reigned that the whole system of government offices broke down in chaos.

After Kung-sun Hung secured the post of chancellor because of his recommendations for correcting the conduct of ministers according to the principles of the *Spring and Autumn Annals,* and after Chang T'ang was made commandant of justice because of his enforcement of decisions on the basis of severe laws, the legal principle that anyone who allows a criminal act to go unreported is as guilty as the criminal himself came into being, and the law officials were busily engaged in conducting investigations of officials who ignored, impeded, or criticized the orders of the government.

The following year [122 B.C.] the plans for revolt laid by the kings of Huai-nan, Heng-shan, and Chiang-tu came to light. The high ministers conducted a thorough investigation of everyone connected with the affair and ferreted out all the conspirators. Twenty or thirty thousand persons were tried and executed. The government authorities became increasingly cruel and exacting and the laws more precise and detailed than ever.

At this time the emperor had sent out a call for men of unusual character and learning to take positions in the government, and some of them had reached the highest offices. Among them Kung-sun Hung, who became chancellor, made a point of using coarse bedding and refusing to eat highly spiced food, hoping to set an example for the empire. His efforts, however, had no effect upon the customs of the time and men only devoted themselves with greater energy to the pursuit of reward and gain.

The following year the general of swift cavalry Ho Ch'ü-ping led another attack on the Hsiung-nu, returning with forty thousand enemy heads. In the fall the Hun-yeh king, leading thirty or forty thousand of his barbarian subjects, came to surrender to the Han. The Han dispatched twenty thousand carriages to fetch them, and when they arrived in the capital, gifts and rewards were bestowed upon them, as well as upon the Han soldiers who had distinguished themselves. This year the total expenditures amounted to over ten billion cash.

Some ten or more years previous to this the Yellow River had broken its banks in the region of Kuan, and during the years that followed, the regions of Liang and Ch'u suffered repeatedly from floods. The provinces bordering the river would no sooner repair the embankments than the water would break through again, so that an incalculable amount of money was spent in vain.

Some time after this P'an Hsi, hoping to avoid the difficulties involved in transporting grain past Mount Ti-chu, on the Yellow River, began work on irrigation canals from the Yellow and Fen rivers which were intended to open up the region between the two rivers for farming, a project requiring a labor force of twenty or thirty thousand men. Cheng Tang-shih, considering the transport of grain via the Wei River to be too lengthy and circuitous, began work on a canal running directly from Ch'ang-an to Hua-yin, a project which required a similar number of laborers. Still other canals were under construction at So-fang, requiring the same number of laborers. Each of these projects had been in progress for two or three years without reaching completion and each necessitated expenditures ranging into billions of cash.

The emperor also turned his attention to the large-scale raising of horses for use in campaigns against the barbarians. Twenty or thirty thousand horses were brought to the region of Ch'ang-an to be pastured, but as there were not enough conscripts in the area within the Pass to train and take care of them, more men were recruited from the neighboring provinces. The Hsiung-nu barbarians who had surrendered were all supposed to be fed and clothed by the district officials, but funds in the district offices proved insufficient, and the emperor was obliged to reduce the expenses of his own table, dispense with his carriage drawn by four horses of matched color, and pay out money from his private reserves in order to make up the deficiency.

The next year [120 B.C.] the lands east of the mountains were troubled by floods and many of the people were reduced to starvation. The emperor dispatched envoys to the provinces and kingdoms to empty the granaries and relieve the sufferings of the poor, but there was not enough food to go around. He then called upon wealthy families to make loans to the needy, but even this did not remedy the situation. At last he ordered some seven hundred thousand of the poor to emigrate and resettle in the lands west of the Pass and the region of New Ch'in south of So-fang. Food and clothing were to be supplied to them for the first few years by the district officials, who were also instructed to lend them what they needed to start a livelihood. Envoys sent to supervise the various groups of emigrants poured out of the capital in such numbers that their carts and carriage covers were constantly in sight of each other on the roads. The expenses of the move were estimated in the billions, the final sum reaching incalculable proportions.

By this time the funds of the district officials were completely exhausted. The rich merchants and big traders, however, were busy accumulating wealth and forcing the poor into their hire, transporting goods back and forth in hundreds of carts, buying up surplus commodities and hoarding them in the villages; even the feudal lords were forced to go to them with bowed heads and beg for what they needed. Others who were engaged in smelting iron and extracting salt from sea water accumulated fortunes amounting to tens of thousands of catties of gold, and yet they did nothing to help the distress of the nation, and the common people were plunged deeper and deeper into misery.

With this the emperor consulted his high ministers on plans to change the coinage and issue a new currency in order to provide for the expenses of the state and to suppress the idle and unscrupulous landlords who were acquiring such huge estates. At this time there were white deer in the imperial park, while the privy treasury was in possession of a considerable amount of silver and tin. It had been over forty years since Emperor Wen changed over to the four-s*hu* copper coins. From the beginning of Emperor Wu's reign, because revenues in coin had been rather scarce, the district officials had from time to time extracted copper from the mountains in their areas and minted new coins, while among the common people there was a good deal of illegal minting of coins, until the number in circulation had grown beyond estimate. As the coins became more numerous and of poorer quality, goods became scarcer and higher in price. The officials therefore advised the emperor, saying, "In ancient times, currency made of hides was used by the feudal lords for gifts and presentations. At present there are three types of metal in use: gold, which is the most precious; silver, which ranks second; and copper, which is third. The 'half-tael' coins now in use are supposed by law to weigh four *shu,* but people have tampered with them to such an extent, illegally filing off bits of copper from the reverse side, that they have become increasingly light and thin and the price of goods has accordingly risen. Such currency is extremely troublesome and expensive to use, especially in distant regions."

The white deer in the imperial park were accordingly killed and their hides cut into one-foot squares, embroidered at the borders with silk thread of different colors, and made into hide currency. Each square was valued at four hundred thousand cash. When members of the imperial house and the nobility appeared at court in the spring and autumn and offered their gifts to the throne, they were required to present their jade insignia upon one of these deerskin squares before they were allowed to proceed with the ceremony.

In addition, "white metal" coins were made from an alloy of silver and tin. Since the dragon is most useful in the heavens, the horse most useful on earth, and the tortoise most useful to mankind,[6] the coins were made in three grades. The first was inscribed "weight eight taels" and was round, with a picture of a dragon on it. It was called a "white *hsüan*" and was valued at three thousand cash. The second was inscribed "less in weight," was square, and bore a picture of a horse. It was worth five hundred cash. The third was inscribed "still less in weight," was oval in shape, and bore a picture of a tortoise. It

6 Because its shell may be used for divination.

was valued at three hundred cash. Orders were sent to the district officials to melt down the old "half-tael" coins and mint new three-*shu* coins, inscribed with their weight. Orders were also given that all persons found guilty of illegally minting any of the new silver or copper coins should be put to death. In spite of this, however, any number of persons in the government and among the people were apprehended for illegally minting silver coins.

At this time Tung-kuo Hsien-yang and K'ung Chin were appointed assistants to the ministry of agriculture and put in charge of the control of salt and iron, while Sang Hung-yang, because of his experience in money matters, was given a post in the palace. Tung-kuo Hsien-yang was a leading salt manufacturer of Ch'i, and K'ung Chin a great iron smelter of Nan-yang; both of them had accumulated fortunes amounting to a thousand catties of gold. Sang Hung-yang was the son of a merchant of Lo-yang who, because of his ability to work sums in his head, had been made a palace attendant at the age of thirteen. When it came to a question of how to make a profit, therefore, the three of them knew their business down to the smallest detail.

By this time the laws had been made much stricter, and many of the lesser officials had been dismissed from office as a result. Military expeditions were frequent, but since many people had bought exemption from military service, purchasing ranks as high as the equivalent of fifth lord, there were fewer and fewer men left who could be called into service. The government therefore decided to demote men of the *ch'ien-fu* or fifth lord rank to the level of petty officials, making them subject to conscription; anyone who wished to avoid service was then obliged to present a horse to the government. The petty officials who had been dismissed were punished by being made to cut underbrush in the Shang-lin Park or work on the construction of the K'un-ming Lake.[7]

The following year [119 B.C.] the general in chief Wei Ch'ing and the general of swift cavalry Ho Ch'ü-ping marched in great force to attack the Hsiung-nu, capturing or killing eighty or ninety thousand of the barbarians. Rewards handed out for the expedition amounted to

[7] The lake was used to practice naval tactics in preparation for an attack on the region of southwest China known at this time as K'un-ming; hence its name.

five hundred thousand catties of gold. The Han armies lost over a hundred thousand horses. In addition, there were the usual costs for transporting provisions and for carriages and weapons. At this time the government treasuries were so depleted that the fighting men received hardly any of their pay.

The officials, complaining that the three-*shu* coins were too light and easy to tamper with, proposed that the provinces and feudal kingdoms be ordered to mint five-*shu* coins with rims around the edge of the reverse side so that it would be impossible to file them down without detection.

The minister of agriculture also brought to the emperor's attention a proposal of his assistants in charge of salt and iron, K'ung Chin and Tung-kuo Hsien-yang, which read:

Mountains and seas are the storehouses of heaven and earth, and it is proper that any revenue from them should go to the privy treasury of the Son of Heaven. Your Majesty, however, being of an unselfish nature, has turned over the control of these natural resources to the ministry of agriculture to supplement the income from taxes. We propose, therefore, that the manufacture of salt be permitted to any of the common people who are willing to supply their own capital and agree to use implements furnished by the government. Evaporating pans will be rented to them by the officials. At present there are people with no fixed residence or occupation who attempt without authority to gain control of the resources of the mountains and seas, accumulating enormous fortunes and exploiting the poor. Countless proposals have already been made on ways to prevent this situation. We suggest that anyone who dares to cast his own iron vessels and engage in the evaporation of salt be condemned to wear fetters on his left foot, and that his vessels and other equipment be confiscated by the government. In provinces which do not produce iron, suboffices for the control of iron goods should be set up, subject for convenience's sake to the jurisdiction of the district in which they are located.

As a result of this proposal, K'ung Chin and Tung-kuo Hsien-yang were sent by post carriage to travel about the empire and put into effect their scheme for salt and iron monopolies, establishing the necessary government bureaus. Wealthy men who had previously been engaged in the salt and iron industries were appointed as officials in the bureaus so that the way to official position became even more confused, depending less and less upon the older methods of selection, and many merchants actually got to be government officials.

The merchants, taking advantage of the frequent changes in currency, had been hoarding goods in order to make a profit. The high officials therefore announced to the emperor:

The provinces and kingdoms have suffered from repeated disasters and many of the poorest people who had no means of livelihood have been moved to broader and more fertile lands. To effect this, Your Majesty has economized on food and other expenses and paid out funds from the privy treasury to relieve the sufferings of your subjects, liberalizing the terms of loans and taxes. And yet there are still some who do not turn to the work of the fields, while merchants grow more numerous than ever. The poor have no stores of provisions left and must look to the district officials for support.

Formerly graded taxes were levied on small carts and on the strings of cash in the possession of merchants. We request that these taxes be levied again in the same way as before. All merchants and those engaged in secondary occupations, all those who lend money for interest, who buy up goods and hoard them in the villages, and who travel about in search of profit, although their names are not listed on the market registers, should be required to make a declaration of their possessions and should be taxed at the rate of one *suan* [one hundred and twenty cash] on each two thousand cash. For all craftsmen and founders who have already paid a tax to carry on their occupation, the rate should be one *suan* on each four thousand cash. All those who are not equal in rank to petty officials, or who are not "elders" [8] or soldiers engaged in the defense of the northern frontier, should be required to pay one *suan* for each cart; but for merchants the rate should be two *suan* per cart. Boats five *chang* or more in length should be taxed one *suan*. Anyone hiding his possessions and failing to report them, or failing to make a complete report, should be sent to a frontier post to serve for a year and his wealth should be confiscated. Anyone who can produce evidence that a false report has been made should receive half of the wealth confiscated as a result. Merchants who are enrolled in the market registers, as well as the members of their families, should be forbidden

[8] Distinguished men over fifty chosen from among the common people to act as consultants to government officials.

to register any farm lands in their names. The purpose of this would be to benefit the farmers. Anyone found guilty of violating this law should have his lands and field laborers confiscated.[9]

The emperor, impressed by the words of a man named Pu Shih, summoned him to court and made him a palace attendant, giving him the honorary rank of *tso-shu-ch'ang* and presenting him with ten *ch'ing* of land. These rewards were announced throughout the empire so that everyone might know of Pu Shih's example.

Pu Shih was a native of Ho-nan, where his family made a living by farming and animal raising. When his parents died, Pu Shih left home, handing over the house, the lands, and all the family wealth to his younger brother, who by this time was full grown. For his own share he took only a hundred or so of the sheep they had been raising, which he led off into the mountains to pasture. In the course of ten years or so, Pu Shih's sheep had increased to over a thousand and he had bought his own house and fields. His younger brother in the meantime had failed completely in the management of the farm, but Pu Shih promptly handed over to him a share of his own wealth. This happened several times. Just at that time the Han was sending its generals at frequent intervals to attack the Hsiung-nu. Pu Shih journeyed to the capital and submitted a letter to the throne, offering to turn over half of his wealth to the district officials to help in the defense of the border. The emperor dispatched an envoy to ask if Pu Shih wanted a post in the government.

"From the time I was a child," Pu Shih replied, "I have been an animal raiser. I have had no experience at government service and would certainly not want such a position."

"Perhaps then your family has suffered some injustice that you would like to report?" inquired the envoy.

But Pu Shih answered, "I have never in my life had a quarrel with anyone. If there are poor men in my village, I lend them what they need, and if there are men who do not behave properly, I guide and counsel them. Where I live, everyone does as I say. Why should I

[9] As in the case of the proposal above for the minting of three-*shu* coins, the text gives only the suggestion of the officials and does not say what action was taken on it. In both cases, however, the proposals were put into effect.

suffer any injustice from others? There is nothing I want to report!"

"If that is the case," said the envoy, "then what *is* your objective in making this offer?"

Pu Shih replied, "The Son of Heaven has set out to punish the Hsiung-nu. In my humble opinion, every worthy man should be willing to fight to the death to defend the borders, and every person with wealth ought to contribute to the expense. If this were done, then the Hsiung-nu could be wiped out!"

The envoy made a complete record of Pu Shih's words and reported them to the emperor. The emperor discussed the matter with the chancellor Kung-sun Hung, but the latter said, "The proposal is simply not in accord with human nature! Such eccentric people are of no use in guiding the populace, but only throw the laws into confusion. I beg Your Majesty not to accept his offer!"

For this reason the emperor put off answering Pu Shih for a long time, and finally, after several years had passed, turned down the offer, whereupon Pu Shih went back to his fields and pastures.

A year or so later the armies marched off on several more expeditions, and the Hun-yeh king and his people surrendered to the Han. As a result the expenditures of the district officials increased greatly and the granaries and treasuries were soon empty. The following year a number of poor people were transferred to other regions, all of them depending upon the district officials for their support, and there were not enough supplies to go around. At this point Pu Shih took two hundred thousand cash of his own and turned the sum over to the governor of Ho-nan to assist the people who were emigrating to other regions. A list of the wealthy men of Ho-nan who had contributed to the aid of the poor was sent to the emperor and he recognized Pu Shih's name. "This is the same man who once offered half his wealth to aid in the defense of the border!" he exclaimed, and presented Pu Shih with a sum of money equivalent to the amount necessary to buy off four hundred men from military duty.[10] Pu Shih once more turned

[10] Men were allowed to purchase exemption from military service on the border for 300 cash. According to the interpretation I have followed, therefore, the emperor returned to Pu Shih the sum of 120,000 cash, though there are other interpretations of the sentence.

the entire sum over to the district officials. At this time the rich families were all scrambling to hide their wealth; only Pu Shih, unlike the others, had offered to contribute to the expenses of the government. The emperor decided that Pu Shih was really a man of exceptional worth after all, and therefore bestowed upon him the honors mentioned above in order to hint to the people that they might well follow his example.

At first Pu Shih was unwilling to become a palace attendant, but the emperor told him, "I have some sheep in the Shang-lin Park which I would like you to take care of." Pu Shih then accepted the post of palace attendant and, wearing a coarse robe and straw sandals, went off to tend the sheep. After a year or so, the sheep had grown fat and were reproducing at a fine rate. The emperor, when he visited the park and saw the flocks, commended Pu Shih on his work. "It is not only with sheep," Pu Shih commented. "Governing people is the same way. Get them up at the right time, let them rest at the right time, and if there are any bad ones, pull them out at once before they have a chance to spoil the flock!"

The emperor, struck by his words, decided to give him a trial as magistrate of the district of Kou-shih. When his administration proved beneficial to the people of Kou-shih, the emperor transferred him to the post of magistrate of Ch'eng-kao and put him in charge of the transportation of supplies, where his record was also outstanding. Because of his simple, unspoiled ways and his deep loyalty, the emperor finally appointed him grand tutor to his son Liu Hung, the king of Ch'i.

Meanwhile K'ung Chin had been sent throughout the empire to establish the government monopoly on the casting of iron vessels, and in the course of three years had reached the position of minister of agriculture, ranking as one of the nine highest officers in the government. Sang Hung-yang acted as his assistant and had charge of all affairs pertaining to accounts. Little by little they set up the offices for equalization of goods through transportation,[11] by which they hoped to

---

[11] These were government offices which bought up goods that were cheap in one part of the country and transported them to regions where they were scarce for resale. The purpose was ostensibly to provide better distribution of goods throughout the nation, though it would seem that the actual object was to make money for the government.

achieve an equal distribution of goods. For the first time an order was issued allowing the petty officials to purchase promotion to higher offices by the presentation of grain; in the case of palace attendants they were allowed to advance as high as posts paying six hundred piculs of grain.

Five years after the minting of the silver coins and the five-*shu* cash some two or three hundred thousand officials and commoners who had been condemned to death for illegal minting of coins were pardoned by a general amnesty, while the number whose crimes were hushed up and never came to light is beyond computing. At the time of the amnesty [in 115 B.C.] over a million persons came forward to confess their crimes, but this can hardly be half of the number who were actually guilty.[12] In effect, the whole empire was engaged in minting silver and copper coins. Those guilty of violations of the laws were so numerous that the officials could not get around to punishing them all. The emperor therefore dispatched the erudits Ch'u Ta, Hsü Yen, and others to journey in groups to the various provinces and feudal kingdoms and apprehend the great landholders and governors or prime ministers who were conniving for their own profit.

At this time the imperial secretary Chang T'ang was at the height of his power, with Chien Hsüan and Tu Chou as his assistants. Men such as I Tsung, Yin Ch'i, and Wang Wen-shu were winning high ministerial posts because of their harsh and stern administration, and the imperial inquisitors such as Hsia Lan appeared for the first time.

Shortly before this, the minister of agriculture Yen I had been put to death. Yen I had originally been a village head in Chi-nan. Because of his honesty and integrity, he was gradually promoted in office until he became one of the nine highest ministers. After the emperor and Chang T'ang had made the "deer money" out of the hides of the white deer, the emperor questioned Yen I on his opinion of the move. Yen I replied, "When the kings and marquises come to court to offer their congratulations, they are expected to present their insignia of green jade, which are worth several thousand cash a piece. Now, however, they will be required to present the insignia on deer hides worth four hundred thousand cash. There seems to be a certain lack of balance

---

[12] The text of this passage appears to be corrupt and the translation is highly tentative.

between the basic elements of the ceremony and those that are only secondary." The emperor was not at all pleased by these words.

In addition, Yen I was on bad terms with Chang T'ang. When someone brought an accusation against Yen I for some other affair, the matter was referred to Chang T'ang for investigation. Earlier Yen I had been talking with one of his guests, when the guest remarked that some new law that had just been put into effect did not seem very practical. Yen I had made no answer, but given only a subtle wry twist of his lips. Chang T'ang sent a memorial to the throne relating this affair and stating, "Yen I, one of the nine highest ministers, having seen that the law was impractical, did not state his opinion to the emperor, but nevertheless disapproved of it in his heart. For this offense he is deserving of death!" From this time on, the crime known as "disapproval at heart" became a part of the law, and most of the high ministers and officials resorted to gross flattery in order to stay in the good graces of the emperor.

The emperor had already issued the order for levies on strings of cash and had also heaped honors on Pu Shih, but it was soon found that no other private citizens were willing to imitate Pu Shih's example by donating wealth to the district officials. The emperor therefore began to listen to as many accusations as could be brought forward against persons attempting to hide their wealth in order to avoid the levy.

In the provinces and kingdoms there was so much illegal minting going on that the cash had become extremely numerous and light in weight. The high officials therefore asked that the officials in the capital who were in charge of casting metal be ordered to mint coins with red rims, each of which would be worth five of the five-*shu* cash presently in circulation. No taxes or other payments to the government were to be accepted unless made in these coins. The silver coins had likewise little by little become debased in value until the people no longer regarded them as worth using. The district officials attempted to halt this tendency by laws, but these had no effect and by the time a year or so had passed, the silver coins had gone completely out of circulation.

This same year [116 B.C.] Chang T'ang died, an occurrence which grieved the common people not at all.

Two years later, the red-rimmed coins had become worthless, the people having managed to use them while cleverly evading the intention of the law. They were declared impractical and withdrawn from circulation.

With this an order was issued forbidding any further minting of coins in the provinces and feudal kingdoms. All minting was to be done by three offices set up in the Shang-lin Park. Since there were already a number of coins in circulation, it was ordered that no cash other than those minted by the three offices should be accepted as legal tender anywhere in the empire. All copper coins previously minted in the provinces and kingdoms were withdrawn from circulation and melted down, the copper being turned over to the three offices. After this there were fewer and fewer people who attempted to mint their own cash, since the cost of making a passable imitation did not repay the effort. Only highly skilled professional criminals continued to produce counterfeit coins.

Pu Shih was transferred to the post of prime minister of Ch'i. At the instigation of Yang K'o, charges were brought forward all over the empire against men who attempted to conceal their wealth from the levy; practically every family of middling means or over found itself under accusation. Tu Chou was put in charge of the investigations and, of those brought to trial, very few got off with a light sentence. The emperor dispatched parties of assistants under the imperial secretary and the commandant of justice to go to the various provinces and kingdoms and examine the charges of concealed wealth. The wealth confiscated from the people as a result of their investigations was calculated in the billions of cash, with male and female slaves numbering in the thousands; the confiscated fields amounted to several hundred *ch'ing* in the larger districts, and over a hundred *ch'ing* in the smaller ones, with a proportionate number of houses. Practically all the merchants of middling or better means were ruined and the people, deciding that they had better indulge in tasty food and fine clothing while they still had the opportunity, made no effort to lay away any wealth for the future. The district officials for their part found themselves with more and more funds at their disposal, due to the salt and iron monopolies and the confiscations of wealth.

The customs barrier at the Han-ku Pass was moved east to enlarge the area within the Pass, and the left and right districts of the capital were established.

Originally the minister of agriculture had charge of the salt and iron monopolies, but the number of government offices and the expenses involved proved so large that an official called the director of waterworks was set up to take charge of the salt and iron monopolies. Later, when the confiscation of concealed wealth was initiated by Yang K'o, the goods and funds stored in the Shang-lin Park became so numerous that the director of waterworks was ordered to take charge of the park. The treasuries of the park were already full by this time and had to be continually enlarged.

At this time the kingdom of Southern Yüeh was preparing to use its ships to attack and drive out the Han forces in its territory. For this reason extensive alterations were made on the K'un-ming Lake, rows of observation towers built along its borders, and ships constructed with superstructures rising ten *chang* or more and topped with banners and flags, forming a most impressive spectacle. The emperor was so stirred by the sight that he ordered the construction of the Terrace of Cypress Beams, which measured twenty or thirty *chang* in height. From this time on the building of imperial palaces proceeded on a more lavish scale day by day.

The wealth confiscated as a result of the accusations was divided among the director of waterworks, the privy treasurer, the minister of agriculture, and the master of carriage. Each of these appointed agricultural officials who traveled from time to time about the provinces and directed the cultivation of the confiscated fields as soon as they were taken over from their former owners. The male and female slaves who had been seized were assigned to the imperial parks to raise dogs, horses, other animals, and birds, or were sent to the various government offices for employment. The government offices became increasingly confused in function and were set up in greater and greater number, while the number of slaves moved from the provinces to the capital was so large that only by transporting four million piculs of grain up from the lower reaches of the Yellow River, and adding it to the grain bought up by the officials, was the capital able to keep itself adequately supplied.

When So Chung informed the emperor that among the sons of the old established families and the rich merchants there were many who engaged in cock fighting, horse racing, hunting, and gambling, thereby setting a bad example for the common people, the emperor ordered the officials to arrest such persons for violation of the laws and regulations. By getting one suspect to implicate his associates as well, they managed to drag in several thousand persons, who were called "rooted-out convicts." If those arrested were willing to pay a sufficient price to the government, however, they were pardoned and even appointed as palace attendants. This marked the ruin of the old system of selecting palace attendants on the basis of merit.

At this time the lands east of the mountains were suffering from floods caused by the Yellow River, and for several years the harvests had been poor. Within an area of one or two thousand *li* square the distress was so great that people were reduced at times to cannibalism. The emperor, taking pity upon the plight of the people, issued an edict which read: "In the region of the Yangtze they burn their fields before plowing and flood them before hoeing. Let the famine victims now be permitted to leave their homes and emigrate to the area between the Huai and the Yangtze rivers in search of food, and if they wish to settle there, let them do so." He dispatched a veritable stream of officials along the roads to look out for the people and had grain sent down from Pa and Shu to relieve the crisis.

The following year [114 B.C.] the emperor for the first time made a tour of the provinces and kingdoms, traveling east across the Yellow River. The governor of Ho-tung Province east of the river, not expecting the emperor to visit his territory, had made no preparations. He committed suicide. [In the following year] the emperor traveled west, crossing the Lung Mountains. The imperial entourage arrived so suddenly that the governor of Lung-hsi was unable to provide food for all of the emperor's attendants, and he too committed suicide. The emperor then journeyed north through the Hsiao Pass and, accompanied by twenty or thirty thousand cavalry, hunted in the region of New Ch'in, where he inspected the disposition of the troops along the border before returning to the capital. He discovered that in New Ch'in stretches of land measuring as much as a thousand *li* or more were being left wide open without guards or patrol posts. To remedy the situation he executed the governor of Pei-ti and his subordinates, who were responsible for this state of affairs, and gave orders that the people were to be allowed to raise horses in the districts along the border. Mares were lent out by the government officials for a period of three years, after which they were to be returned with an interest of one foal for every ten mares. The people of the region were also exempted from the reports and levies on wealth, so that the region of New Ch'in was soon filled with immigrants.

By this time the precious cauldron had been found and altars set up to the Earth Lord and the Great Unity, and the high officials were debating on plans for the performance of the Feng and Shan sacrifices. Throughout the empire the provinces and feudal kingdoms were all busy repairing roads and bridges and putting the old palaces in order, while in the various districts along the imperial highway the district officials laid in provisions and prepared their tableware in anticipation of the imperial visit.

The next year [112 b.c.] the kingdom of Southern Yüeh rebelled and the Ch'iang barbarians of the west invaded the border, pillaging and murdering. Because the region east of the mountains was still suffering from a lack of food, the emperor declared a general amnesty to the empire. With the prisoners thereby released, and the men trained in the south for service on the towered ships—a force of over two hundred thousand in all—an attack was launched on Southern Yüeh. At the same time twenty or thirty thousand cavalry men from the provinces of Ho-nei, Ho-tung, and Ho-nan were sent west to attack the Ch'iang barbarians. Another twenty or thirty thousand were sent across the Yellow River to fortify the western border at Ling-chü. The provinces of Chang-yeh and Chiu-ch'üan were set up, and in the provinces of Shang, So-fang, Hsi-ho, and Ho-hsi, officials in charge of the opening of new lands, as well as soldiers designated to garrison the lands along the border, numbering six hundred thousand men, were set to working the lands in garrison farms. Roads were repaired and provisions sent to the forces from the central part of the empire. All of the men were dependent upon the ministry of agriculture for their supplies, although the distance over which supplies had to be transported was anywhere from a thousand to three thousand *li*.

Since there were not enough arms to supply the men on the border, weapons were dispatched from the imperial armory and workshops to make up the deficiency. There was also a serious lack of horses for carriages and cavalry and, since the district officials had so little money, they found it difficult to buy up enough to keep the troops supplied. The government therefore issued an order to everyone, from the feudal lords down to officials of the three hundred picul class, commanding them to donate a specified number of stallions to the government, depending upon their rank. At village posts throughout the empire men were set to breeding colts, for which they received a certain interest each year.

Pu Shih, at this time the prime minister of Ch'i, sent a letter to the throne saying, "I have always heard that the distresses of the sovereign are a source of shame to his subjects. Now that the kingdom of Southern Yüeh has revolted, I beg that my sons and I be allowed to join the men of Ch'i who are skilled in naval warfare to go and die in battle!"

The emperor responded with an edict saying, "Although Pu Shih in person plowed the fields and pastured his animals, he did not work for private gain. If he had any surplus, he immediately turned it over to the district officials to aid in the expenses of government. Now unhappily the empire faces this threat from abroad, and Pu Shih, roused to action, has volunteered to go with his sons to die in battle. Although he has not actually taken part in combat, it is obvious that he bears in his heart a true sense of duty!" The emperor therefore presented Pu Shih with the rank of a marquis in the area within the Pass, along with sixty catties of gold and ten *ch'ing* of farmland. He had the action widely publicized throughout the empire, but no one responded to the hint. Among all the hundreds of marquises, there was not one who volunteered to join the armies in attacking the Ch'iang and Yüeh barbarians.

In the eighth month, when the feudal lords came to present new wine in the ancestral temples of the dynasty, the officials of the privy treasury made a close examination of the tributes of gold which they brought with them. As a result, over a hundred marquises were tried on charges of having presented insufficient or faulty gold and were deprived of their titles.

Following this, Pu Shih was appointed to the post of imperial secretary. After he took over this position, he discovered that in the provinces and kingdoms the system of government salt and iron monopolies was working to great disadvantage. The utensils supplied by the government were poor in quality and high in price, and yet at times the people were actually being forced by the officials to buy them. In addition, because of the tax on boats, traders had diminished in number and the price of goods gone up. He therefore asked K'ung Chin to speak on his behalf to the emperor, recommending the abolition of the boat tax. From this time on the emperor began to dislike Pu Shih.

After three years of continuous fighting, the Han forces managed to suppress the Ch'iang barbarians and wipe out the kingdom of Southern Yüeh. On the southern border, from P'an-yü [13] on the coast to the south of Shu, seventeen new provinces were set up. These were governed in accordance with the old customs of the inhabitants and were not required to pay taxes. The provinces of Nan-yang, Han-chung, and those farther on, were ordered to supply food and money to the officials and soldiers of the new provinces which adjoined their respective borders, as well as horses and equipment for the relay service. From time to time, however, there were minor uprisings in the new provinces in which Han officials were murdered, so that the central government was obliged to dispatch troops recruited from the south to punish the rebels. In the space of a year over ten thousand men had been dispatched and the expenses for all of this had to be borne by the ministry of agriculture. Because of its system of equitable transport and its levies on salt and iron, which it used to supplement the revenue from taxes, the ministry of agriculture was able to meet these expenses. In the districts through which the troops passed, however, the officials, concerned only that they should have enough funds to supply the armies without running short, did not dare to complain of the inordinate tax burden placed upon them.

[13] The region of the present city of Canton. The line of new provinces ran from here west to present-day Szechwan Province.

The following year, the first year of the era *yüan-feng* [110 B.C.], Pu Shih was degraded to the post of grand tutor to the heir apparent. Sang Hung-yang was made secretary in charge of grain and put in control of the ministry of agriculture, as well as taking over from K'ung Chin complete supervision of the salt and iron monopolies throughout the empire. Sang Hung-yang believed that the reason prices had risen so sharply was that the various government officials were engaging in trade and competing against each other. Furthermore, when goods were transported to the capital as payment for taxes from various parts of the empire, their value often did not equal the cost of transportation. He therefore proposed that some twenty or thirty assistants be appointed to the ministry of agriculture who would be sent out to supervise the various provinces and kingdoms, where they would travel about and set up the necessary transport offices for equalizing prices, as well as salt and iron offices. In the case of distant regions, orders were to be given that local products commanding a high price, such as would ordinarily be carted away and sold by the traders in other regions, should be transported to the capital in lieu of taxes. In the capital a balanced standard office was to be set up which would receive and store these goods brought in from various parts of the empire. The government artisans were to be ordered to make carts and other equipment needed to put the system into effect. All expenses would be borne by the ministry of agriculture, whose officials would then have complete control over all the goods in the empire, selling when prices were high and buying when they were low. In this way the wealthy merchants and large-scale traders, deprived of any prospect of making big profits, would go back to farming, and it would become impossible for any commodity to jump in price. Because the price of goods would thereby be controlled throughout the empire, the system was to be called the "balanced standard."

The emperor agreed with this idea and gave permission for it to be put into effect. Following this, the emperor traveled north as far as So-fang; from there he proceeded to Mount T'ai, journeyed along the seacoast and the northern border, and returned to the capital. He handed out gifts and awards to the places he visited along the way, doling out over a million rolls of silk as well as cash and gold in the hundreds of millions, all of which the ministry of agriculture was able to supply.

Sang Hung-yang proposed that petty officials be allowed to buy office by presenting grain to the government, and that men accused of crimes be permitted to purchase their ransom in the same way. He also suggested that the common people be allowed to present varying quantities of grain to the granary at Sweet Springs in exchange for lifetime exemption from military service and guarantees that they would not be subject to accusations leading to confiscation of their wealth.

Areas that were in need were immediately supplied by shipments of grain from other provinces, and the various officials of the ministry of agriculture all drew grain from east of the mountains, so that the amount transported to the capital increased to six million piculs annually. Within a year the granary at T'ai-tsung in the capital and that at Sweet Springs had been filled, the frontiers enjoyed a surplus of grain and other goods, and the transportation offices had five million rolls of silk. Though taxes on the people had not been increased, there was now more than enough to cover the expenditures of the empire. As a result Sang Hung-yang was rewarded with the rank of *tso-shu-ch'ang* and once more presented with a hundred catties of gold.

This year there was a minor drought and the emperor ordered the officials to pray for rain. Pu Shih remarked to the emperor, "The district officials are supposed to collect what taxes they need for their food and clothing, and that is all! Now Sang Hung-yang has them sitting in the market stalls buying and selling goods and scrambling for a profit. If Your Majesty were to boil Sang Hung-yang alive, then I thing Heaven might send us rain!"

The Grand Historian remarks: When the farmers, the artisans, and the merchants first began to exchange articles among themselves, that was when currency came into being—tortoise shells and sea shells, gold and copper coins, knife-shaped money and spade-shaped money. Thus its origin is very old. Concerning the time of Emperor K'u [14] and the ages before him we can say nothing, for they are too far away. The *Book of Documents,* however, tells us something about the reigns of Emperors

[14] The third of the legendary "Five Emperors" of antiquity.

Yao and Shun, while the *Book of Odes* describes the Shang and Chou dynasties. Thus we know that in times of peace and security, stress was laid upon the system of schools; agricultural pursuits, which are the basis of the nation, were honored; secondary occupations such as trade were disparaged, and the people were taught a sense of propriety and duty in order to discourage them from the search for profit. In periods of war and unrest, however, the opposite situation prevailed. When a thing has reached its height it must begin to decay, and when an age has gone to one extreme it must turn again in the opposite direction; therefore we find periods of rude simplicity and periods of refinement alternating with each other endlessly.

From the description of the nine provinces in the "Tribute of Yü" [15] we learn that, in the time of that ruler, each region submitted as its tribute to the throne whatever goods it was best fitted to produce and whatever the people had the most of. King T'ang, the founder of the Shang dynasty, and King Wu, the founder of the Chou dynasty, both heirs to the chaos of the dynasties which preceded them, worked to put the empire into order, causing the people to be unflagging in their efforts, and both of them, by their diligence and circumspection, succeeded in establishing firm rule. And yet little by little the ages after them sank into weakness and decay.

Duke Huan of Ch'i, following the advice of his minister Kuan Chung, initiated the system of buying up goods when the price was low and selling when it was high, and of exploiting the resources of the mountains and seas, until he had the other feudal lords paying court to him and, with what had up until then been the little and out-of-the-way kingdom of Ch'i, had won for himself the title of dictator. Similarly the king of Wei, by following the theories of Li K'o, was able to secure the maximum yield from his lands and become a powerful ruler.

From the time of these men on, the empire was torn by the strife of the warring kingdoms. Men honored deceit and power and scoffed at benevolence and righteousness; they put wealth and possession first and courtesy and humility last. Thus it happened that commoners grew so

[15] A section of the *Book of Documents*. Emperor Yü was the founder of the Hsia dynasty.

rich that their wealth was counted in the hundreds of millions, while among the poor there were those who could not even get enough dregs and chaff to fill their bellies. The more powerful rulers annexed the smaller fiefs and made subjects of their lords, while in the weaker states the ruling families were wiped out and the sacrifices to their ancestors cut off forever. So it continued until the Ch'in finally united all the land within the four seas under a single rule.

The currency of the times of Emperor Shun and the Hsia dynasty consisted of three types of metal: gold, silver, and copper; while in Chou times there was copper cash, knife-shaped money, cloth-shaped money, and money made of tortoise shells or sea shells. When the Ch'in united the world, only two [16] kinds of currency were used throughout the nation. The more valuable was that made of gold in denominations of twenty taels. The less valuable was the copper cash, inscribed with the words "half-tael" and weighing that amount. (Pearls, jade, tortoise shells, sea shells, silver, tin, and similar materials, though used for utensils or ornaments or stored away as treasures, were not employed as currency.) The currency, however, fluctuated according to the times, having no fixed value. At that time the ruler was busy driving back the barbarians from the borders of the empire, while within the empire he was carrying out various construction works and projects, so that although the men who remained at home worked the fields, they could not supply enough to eat, and though the women wove and spun, they could not produce enough clothing. And so we see that in antiquity there was once a time when the entire wealth and resources of the nation were exhausted in the service of the ruler, and yet he found them insufficient. There was but one reason for this: the stream of circumstances flowed so violently at that time that it made such a situation inevitable. Surely there is nothing strange about this! [17]

[16] Most texts erroneously read "three."

[17] This last is of course a veiled attack on Emperor Wu, whose foreign wars and various other expensive undertakings—the "stream of circumstances," as Ssu-ma Ch'ien euphemistically calls them—had brought the empire to the same state of exhaustion as that which prevailed under the First Emperor of the Ch'in.

Part II
STATESMEN, GENERALS, AND
FOREIGN PEOPLES

Shih chi 107: The Biographies of the Marquises of Wei-ch'i and Wu-an

When Wu and Ch'u rose in revolt, Tou Ying, the marquis of Wei-ch'i, proved to be the wisest leader among the families related to the imperial house by marriage. He appreciated the worth of other men and as a result they all flocked to him. He led his army to Jung-yang east of the mountains and there blocked the advance of the rebel armies. Thus I made The Biographies of the Marquises of Wei-ch'i and Wu-an.

Tou Ying, the marquis of Wei-ch'i, was the son of a cousin of Empress Tou, the consort of Emperor Wen and mother of Emperor Ching. Up until his father's time, his family had been residents of Kuan-chin.[1] He himself was very fond of supporting guests and retainers in his home.

In the reign of Emperor Wen, Tou Ying was appointed prime minister of Wu, but later retired on grounds of ill health. When Emperor Ching first came to the throne, Tou Ying was made steward of the household of the empress and the heir apparent.

King Hsiao of Liang was the younger brother of Emperor Ching and the favorite son of Empress Dowager Tou. Whenever he came to court Emperor Ching would hold a banquet for him, treating him as a brother rather than a vassal. On one such occasion, before Emperor Ching had formally announced his choice for heir apparent, he remarked casually at the height of the drinking, "After my thousand years of life are over, I shall pass the rule of the empire along to the king of Liang!"

Empress Dowager Tou was delighted at this announcement, but Tou Ying, seizing a goblet of wine and hastening forward to offer it to the emperor, said, "The empire is the empire of the founder, Kao-tsu, and

[1] The old home of Empress Tou. After she became empress, she summoned her relatives to the capital.

it is a law of the Han dynasty that the rule must pass from father to son! How could Your Majesty arbitrarily hand it over to the king of Liang?"

Because of this affair Empress Dowager Tou grew to hate Tou Ying, while he in turn came to despise his post of steward and resigned on grounds of illness. The empress dowager then had his name removed from the roster of officials that was kept at the palace gate so that he could no longer come and go at court as he had in the past.

In the third year of Emperor Ching's reign, when the kings of Wu and Ch'u revolted, the emperor began to cast about among the members of the imperial house and the Tou family for able leaders and found that no one could match the wisdom of Tou Ying. He accordingly summoned Tou Ying to an audience, but when the latter appeared before the emperor he adamantly declined to accept any appointment, insisting that he was unfit because of illness to take on the responsibilities of leadership. Empress Dowager Tou likewise was embarrassed by the emperor's proposal to appoint Tou Ying. But the emperor refused to listen. "At a time when the empire is faced with crisis, how can you think of making polite excuses?" he demanded, and proceeded to appoint Tou Ying as general in chief, presenting him with a gift of a thousand catties of gold. Tou Ying in turn recommended Yüan Ang, Lüan Pu, and other distinguished military men and worthy gentlemen who were not at the time employed in the government and succeeded in having them appointed to various posts. The money presented to him by the emperor he stored along the corridors and in the gatehouse of his home, where his junior officers, if they needed any for military expenditures, could help themselves to it without further ado. Not a cent of it went into his own coffers.

Tou Ying marched east to guard Jung-yang and observe the movements of the troops of Ch'i and Chao. After the armies of the seven rebellious kingdoms had been defeated, he was enfeoffed as marquis of Wei-ch'i, and all sorts of gentlemen with no fixed place of employment, guests and retainers, vied with each other in offering him their services. During the reign of Emperor Ching, whenever there was some important matter to be discussed at court, none of the marquises dared to try to stand on an equal footing with Chou Ya-fu, the marquis of T'iao, and Tou Ying, the marquis of Wei-ch'i.

In the fourth year of his reign, when Emperor Ching set up his son Prince Li as heir apparent, he appointed Tou Ying as the boy's tutor. In the seventh year, however, the emperor decided to dismiss Prince Li from the position of heir apparent, and though Tou Ying several times remonstrated with him, he was unable to prevent the move. Pleading illness once more, he retired to Lan-t'ien in the foothills of the Southern Mountains, where he lived in seclusion for several months. Although a number of his retainers and rhetoricians attempted to make him change his mind, he refused to return to the capital. Among them was a man from Liang named Kao Sui who advised him in these words: "The emperor has the power to make you rich and honored and the empress dowager, your relative, can offer you intimate friendship. Now you have been appointed to tutor the heir apparent and, in spite of your protests, he has been dismissed from his position. Yet, though you were unable to argue your case successfully, you have also proved yourself unable to die for your cause. Instead you have taken yourself off on the excuse of illness and sit here, living a life of ease and retirement, dallying with beautiful women and, with your band of followers, passing judgment on the rest of the world. By such conduct you are deliberately attempting, it would seem, to broadcast to everyone the faults of the ruler! But if you should thereby incur the anger of both the emperor and the empress dowager, I fear, General, it would mean extinction for you and your whole family!"

Tou Ying, realizing that what he said was true, eventually returned to the capital and attended court as before.

At this time Liu She, the marquis of T'ao, retired from the post of chancellor, and Empress Dowager Tou several times suggested to Emperor Ching that Tou Ying be appointed as his successor, but the emperor replied, "I hope you do not think, Mother, that I begrudge him the post. It is only that Tou Ying tends to be somewhat self-righteous and fond of having his own way. On numerous occasions he has acted rather thoughtlessly, and I am afraid that it would be difficult to entrust him with the heavy responsibilities of chancellor." In the end Tou Ying did not get the post; instead Wei Wan, the marquis of Chien-ling, was appointed chancellor.

T'ien Fen, the marquis of Wu-an, was a younger brother of Empress Wang, the consort of Emperor Ching and mother of Emperor Wu; he was born after his mother, Tsang Erh, had remarried into the T'ien family and was living in Ch'ang-ling. When Tou Ying had already become general in chief and was at the height of his power, T'ien Fen still held a rather humble post as palace attendant. He used to go to Tou Ying's house from time to time to wait on him and serve him his wine, bowing politely and treating Tou Ying with great courtesy as though he himself were one of Tou Ying's sons. Toward the end of Emperor Ching's reign T'ien Fen began to enjoy increasing favor at court until he had risen to the post of palace counselor.

T'ien Fen was a very skillful talker and studied the "Cauldron Inscriptions" [2] and similar works on statecraft. His sister, Empress Wang, had great respect for his wisdom. When Emperor Ching passed away and the heir apparent, Empress Wang's son, was proclaimed emperor, the empress for a while issued edicts in her son's name, and many of the measures which she took to insure order and stability in the government during the period of change were suggested to her by T'ien Fen's retainers. In the same year, the third year of the latter part of Emperor Ching's reign [141 b.c.], T'ien Fen and his younger brother T'ien Sheng were both enfeoffed, T'ien Fen as marquis of Wu-an and T'ien Sheng as marquis of Chou-yang. This was done because they were both younger brothers of Empress Dowager Wang. [3]

T'ien Fen found himself in a position of new importance at court and decided that he would like to become chancellor. He therefore conducted himself with great humility before his guests and retainers and worked to advance eminent gentlemen who were living in retirement and secure them honorable positions, hoping thereby to outshine Tou Ying and the elder statesmen of the time.

[2] A work in 26 sections, no longer extant, supposedly compiled by K'ung Chia, the official historian at the court of the Yellow Emperor.

[3] Although the year is designated as the third year of the latter period of Emperor Ching's reign, the enfeoffments took place two months after the death of Emperor Ching when Empress Dowager Wang was managing the government for her son, Emperor Wu.

In the first year of the era *chien-yüan* [140 B.C.] Wei Wan retired from the post of chancellor because of ill health, and the emperor began deliberations with the court to decide who should be appointed to fill this position, as well as that of grand commandant. Chi Fu, one of T'ien Fen's retainers, advised him, saying, "Tou Ying has held a position of great honor for a long time and many of the most worthy men of the empire were originally members of his group. Now, although you have begun to come up in the world, you still cannot rival Tou Ying. If the emperor offers to make you chancellor, you should therefore yield the post to Tou Ying. If Tou Ying is made chancellor, you will surely be made grand commandant, a position which is just as distinguished as that of chancellor. In addition you will thereby gain a reputation for humility and wisdom!"

Impressed by this advice, T'ien Fen mentioned the matter in secret to his sister, Empress Dowager Wang, asking her to drop a hint with the emperor to this effect. As a result the emperor appointed Tou Ying as chancellor and T'ien Fen as grand commandant.

Chi Fu went to congratulate Tou Ying on his new appointment but took the opportunity to deliver a grave warning: "It is Your Lordship's nature, I know, to delight in good men and hate evil ones. At the present time it happens that the good men have joined together in praising you and you have thereby been able to reach the position of chancellor. And yet you hate evil, and evil men are numerous. It will not be long before they too join together—to slander you! If you could find some way to get along with both groups, then I believe you could enjoy your present high position for a long time. But if not, their slanders will drive you right out of office!" Tou Ying paid no attention to this advice.

Tou Ying and T'ien Fen were both admirers of Confucian teachings, and they combined their efforts in boosting Chao Wan into the post of imperial secretary and Wang Tsang into that of chief of palace attendants and in bringing the eminent Confucian scholar Master Shen of Lu to court. They also worked for the establishment of a Bright Hall like the great audience halls of antiquity, ordered the marquises to proceed to their territories, abolished the customs barriers, and changed the funeral ceremonies to conform with correct ritual practice, striving to bring about an era of peace and prosperity. In addition, they conducted an inquiry into the members of the various branches of the imperial family and the Tou family and expunged the names of anyone found guilty of misconduct. At this time many of the male members of the families related to the throne by marriage had become marquises and, since a number of them were married to princesses of the blood, they had no desire to leave the capital and proceed to their own territories. They were unanimously opposed to the new order directing them to leave the capital and their criticisms of the law day after day came to the ears of the emperor's grandmother, Empress Dowager Tou.

Empress Dowager Tou was very fond of the teachings of the Yellow Emperor and Lao Tzu, while Tou Ying, T'ien Fen, Chao Wan, Wang Tsang, and the others of their group all did their best to advance the influence of Confucian doctrines and disparage the teachings of the Taoist school. As a result Empress Dowager Tou grew more and more displeased with Tou Ying and his party.

Eventually, in the second year of *chien-yüan* [139 B.C.], when the imperial secretary Chao Wan asked the emperor for permission to dispose of state affairs himself without consulting Empress Dowager Tou, the empress dowager flew into a rage and proceeded to expel Chao Wan, Wang Tsang, and the others from office and to force the resignation of the chancellor Tou Ying and the grand commandant T'ien Fen. She then had Hsü Ch'ang, the marquis of Po-chih, appointed as the new chancellor, and Chuang Ch'ing-ti, the marquis of Wu-ch'iang, as imperial secretary.

As a result of this affair Tou Ying and T'ien Fen were both obliged to retire to their homes to live the life of ordinary marquises. T'ien Fen, however, although holding no position in the government, still enjoyed his usual favor and intimacy with his sister, Empress Dowager Wang, and was therefore able on occasion to express his opinion concerning affairs of state with considerable effect. The officers and gentlemen of the empire and all who sought after profit and position thereupon abandoned Tou Ying and flocked about T'ien Fen, who grew more arrogant in his ways with each passing day.

In the sixth year of the era *chien-yüan* [135 B.C.] Empress Dowager Tou passed away. The chancellor Hsü Ch'ang and the imperial secretary Chuang Ch'ing-ti were accused of delay in arranging the funeral ceremonies and were dismissed from office. T'ien Fen was then appointed chancellor and Han An-kuo, the former minister of agriculture, was made imperial secretary. The gentlemen of the empire, the officials of the provinces, and the other marquises hastened in even greater numbers to ally themselves with T'ien Fen.

T'ien Fen was rather short and unimposing in appearance but, because he was related by birth to the emperor, he conducted himself with a very lordly air. He believed that, since many of the marquises and kings were men of mature years, while the emperor, who had just ascended the throne, was still very young, it was up to him as a close relative of the ruler and chancellor of the central government to force others to submit to his will and treat him with the proper courtesy. Otherwise, he felt, the world would have no respect for the imperial house.

At this time, whenever he would enter the palace to report on some affair connected with his duties as chancellor, he would sit for hours, and sometimes for days, in conference with the emperor, and whatever suggestions he made were always followed. In recommending people for office he succeeded on occasion in having men promoted in one leap from private citizen to official of the two thousand picul rank. His authority in fact outweighed that of the emperor himself, who remarked to him one day, "Have you quite finished making your appointments and dismissals of officials? Because if you have, I think I might like to make a few appointments too!" Another time T'ien Fen asked the emperor for the land used by the government artisans so that he could increase the grounds of his estate, to which the emperor replied angrily, "Why yes! And while you're about it why don't you go ahead and take over the imperial arsenal as well!" After this last remark, T'ien Fen conducted himself with somewhat more discretion in the emperor's presence.

Once when he had invited some guests to his home to drink, he seated his older brother, Wang Hsin, the marquis of Kai, in a place facing south, while he himself took the place of honor facing east. He explained that this arrangement was necessary because of the honor due to himself as chancellor of the Han, which could not be disregarded for the sake of a private family relationship such as that of older and younger brother.

From this time on T'ien Fen lived a life of increasing arrogance and ostentation, building for himself the finest mansions in the capital, laid out with sumptuous grounds and gardens; the merchants with their wares from the distant provinces stood in lines before his door. In his front hall he hung bells and drums, with pennants on curved flagstaffs, while the women's quarters at the back housed wives and maidens in the hundreds. The other nobles flocked about with gifts of gold and jewels, dogs, horses, and trinkets for his amusement, in quantities too great to be reckoned. Tou Ying for his part had grown more and more estranged from the emperor since the death of Empress Dowager Tou. His advice was no longer heeded, his power was gone, and his friends and retainers one by one drifted away, treating him with scorn and indifference. Only General Kuan continued to respect him as before. He spent his days in silent frustration and despair, lavishing his generosity on his one remaining friend, General Kuan.

General Kuan Fu was a native of Ying-yin. His father, whose name was Chang Meng, had originally been a servant of Kuan Ying, the marquis of Ying-yin, and had enjoyed great favor. Eventually, on the strength of the marquis's recommendation he advanced to a post paying two thousand piculs, and out of gratitude he adopted the family name of his patron, being known thereafter as Kuan Meng. At the time of the revolt of Wu and Ch'u, Kuan Ho, who had succeeded to the marquisate after the death of his father, Kuan Ying, was made a general in the command of the grand commandant Chou Ya-fu. He requested that Kuan Meng be made a subordinate commander and his son Kuan Fu be allowed to accompany his father as head of a battalion of a thousand men. Kuan Meng was actually too old for such a post, but the marquis pressed his request until he succeeded in getting permission. Kuan Meng was profoundly embittered by the reluctance with which his appointment had been granted and decided that he would never be allowed to exercise his authority with any freedom; therefore, whenever a battle took place he always plunged into the midst of the enemy's fortifications. Eventually he died a prisoner in the Wu camp.

According to the rules of warfare, when a father and son are both taking part in a campaign and one of them is killed, the other is permitted to accompany the body home for burial. But Kuan Fu refused to take his father's body back home, declaring passionately, "I would far rather seize the head of the king of Wu or one of his generals and thereby avenge my father's death!" Donning his armor and taking up his halberd, he went about the camp, gathering together twenty or thirty stalwart young friends of his who were willing to accompany him. When the group emerged from the gate of the Han camp, however, none of the men dared advance any further. In the end Kuan Fu, with only two companions and ten or twelve mounted attendants, galloped off to the encampment of the Wu army, fighting his way right up to the headquarters of the Wu general and killing or wounding twenty or thirty of the enemy. When he found that he could advance no further, he wheeled about and galloped back to the Han fortifications. His companions had lost almost all of their attendants, only one returning with the party, and Kuan Fu himself bore over ten serious wounds. Fortunately he happened to have some excellent medicine which he applied to his injuries and thus saved his life.

When his wounds had healed a little, he again spoke to his commanding officer, General Kuan Ho. "Now that I know a little more about the ins and outs of the Wu camp, I beg you to let me make another try!" The general admired his bravery and sympathized with his desire, but he was afraid that this time he would surely lose Kuan Fu. He therefore took the matter up with the grand commandant, but the latter absolutely forbade another such foray.

After the armies of Wu had been defeated, the story of Kuan Fu's daring exploit spread all over the empire. General Kuan Ho recommended him to Emperor Ching, who appointed him as a general of palace attendants, but after a few months he was accused of some violation of the law and dismissed. After this he made his home in Ch'ang-an, where he was known and praised by all the gentlemen of the capital. He was later recalled to government service and during the reign of Emperor Ching reached the post of prime minister of the kingdom of Tai.

When Emperor Ching passed away and the present emperor first came to the throne, he was afraid that the province of Huai-yang, being one of the main crossroads of the empire and noted for its military strength, might become a source of trouble and he therefore shifted Kuan Fu to the position of governor of Huai-yang. In the first year of the *chien-yüan* era [140 B.C.] he summoned Kuan Fu to court to take over the post of master of carriage.

In the second year of the same era Kuan Fu was one time drinking with Tou Fu, the colonel of the guard of the Palace of Lasting Joy, when the two men got into an argument over some question of etiquette. Kuan Fu, who was drunk at the time, ended by striking Tou Fu. Tou Fu, it happened, was a close relative of Empress Dowager Tou, and the emperor, fearful that the empress dowager would demand Kuan Fu's life for the insult, hastily transferred him to the post of prime minister of Yen. Several years later Kuan Fu was accused of some violation of the law and removed from office, after which he returned to private life in Ch'ang-an.

Kuan Fu was a very stubborn and outspoken man, especially when he had had something to drink, and despised any kind of flattery. When he was in the company of members of the aristocracy, influential statesmen, or anyone who was socially his superior, he showed great reluctance to treat them with the proper politeness, and indeed was actually insulting; but when it came to men who were socially inferior, the poorer and more humble they were the greater respect he showed them, behaving as though they were his equals. When he was with a large group, he made a point of recommending and showing favor to his inferiors, a trait for which he was much admired by people.

He had no taste for literature but loved feats of honor and daring and was absolutely true to his word. All his friends were rich or influential citizens, local bosses, or gangster leaders. His wealth amounted to almost ten thousand in gold, and every day he had from twenty or thirty to a hundred men eating at his house. He owned a number of lakes and farm lands in Ying-ch'uan Province from which his relatives and the retainers of the family derived great profit, and this permitted the Kuan family to run the affairs of the province in any way they pleased. The children of Ying-ch'uan made up a song about this which went:

> While the waters of the Ying run bright
> It means the Kuans are still all right;
> But when the waters run polluted
> We'll know they've all been executed!

When Kuan Fu returned to private life in Ch'ang-an, although he was still very wealthy, his political influence was gone, and he soon found the ministers and courtiers, the guests and retainers who had frequented his home in the past gradually drifting away. When Tou Ying likewise lost his political power, he was happy to make friends with Kuan Fu and rid himself once and for all of those acquaintances who had avidly sought his company in the old days but later turned their backs upon him. Kuan Fu in turn profited from his friendship with Tou Ying, which allowed him to mingle with the nobles and members of the imperial family and increase his fame. Thus the two men aided and respected each other and their friendship was like that of father and son. They never tired of the pleasures they shared and their only regret was that they had come to know each other so late in life.

Once, while Kuan Fu was in mourning for one of his relatives, he happened to pay a call on the chancellor T'ien Fen. In the course of the visit T'ien Fen remarked casually, "I was thinking that I would like to go with you some time to call on Tou Ying, but of course at the moment you are in mourning." [4]

"If you would really be so kind as to go with me to visit Tou Ying, I would certainly not let the matter of my mourning stand in the way!" replied Kuan Fu. "If I may have your permission, I will speak to Tou Ying about it at once so that he may make preparations to entertain you. I trust he may expect the honor of your presence early tomorrow morning."

T'ien Fen gave his consent, whereupon Kuan Fu went to tell Tou Ying, repeating to him what T'ien Fen had said. Tou Ying and his wife hastily laid in a large supply of beef and wine and spent the night sweeping and cleaning the house, working until dawn to set up the curtains and lay out the dishes. When daybreak came Tou Ying sent

[4] And therefore ought not, according to custom, pay social calls.

his servants to escort T'ien Fen to his house, but noon came and the chancellor had still not appeared.

"You don't think the chancellor has forgotten, do you?" Tou Ying asked Kuan Fu, who replied uneasily, "I was the one who invited him to come, in spite of the fact that I am in mourning. I had better go and see what has happened."

Kuan Fu then rode off in his carriage to fetch the chancellor in person. As it turned out, however, T'ien Fen had only been joking the day before when he consented to the visit and had not the slightest intention of going. When Kuan Fu reached T'ien Fen's house, he found that the chancellor was still in bed. He marched straight into the room and confronted T'ien Fen. "Yesterday you were kind enough to agree to visit Tou Ying, and that gentleman and his wife have made all the preparations! They have been waiting from dawn until now without daring to take a bite to eat!"

T'ien Fen was very startled and began to apologize, saying, "I was a little drunk yesterday and I completely forgot about our conversation." He finally got up and set off in his carriage, but on the way he insisted upon driving very slowly, which made Kuan Fu angrier than ever.

When the party finally got started and the drinking had reached its height, Kuan Fu stood up and performed a dance, requesting the chancellor to follow with a dance of his own, but T'ien Fen merely sat where he was and refused to move. Kuan Fu then began to make insulting remarks from his seat until Tou Ying pulled him to his feet and hurried him out of the room, apologizing to the chancellor for his behavior. T'ien Fen stayed and drank until evening when, having enjoyed himself thoroughly, he took his leave.

Some time later, T'ien Fen sent his retainer Chi Fu to ask Tou Ying if he would mind turning over to him some farm land south of the city which Tou Ying owned. Tou Ying was furious when he heard the request. "Though I am only an old man who has been abandoned by his friends and though the chancellor is a high official, he has absolutely no right to try to seize my possessions from me like this! I refuse to give up the land!"

When Kuan Fu heard of the incident he cursed Chi Fu roundly. Chi Fu for his part was sorry to see enmity develop between Tou Ying and

T'ien Fen and so he did his best to smooth over the affair, returning to T'ien Fen with excuses which he himself had invented. "After all, Tou Ying is an old man and will die soon. Surely you can do without the land for a while. You had better wait a bit," he said.

Later on, however, T'ien Fen chanced to hear that Tou Ying and Kuan Fu had in fact been greatly angered at his request and had refused to hand over the land, whereupon he too became incensed. "Once in the past Tou Ying's son killed a man but I managed to save him from punishment. I have always treated Tou Ying with respect and done everything he has asked me to. Why should he begrudge me a few acres of land? As for Kuan Fu, what does he have to say in the matter? If that is the way they act, I will make no further requests for land!" Because of this T'ien Fen came to bear a deep grudge against Kuan Fu and Tou Ying.

In the spring of the fourth year of *yüan-kuang* [131 B.C.] T'ien Fen reported to the emperor that Kuan Fu's family in Ying-ch'uan were behaving with complete disregard for the law and causing great hardship to the common people. He requested that their conduct be investigated. "It is up to you as chancellor to settle such matters," replied the emperor. "Why ask me about it?" Meanwhile Kuan Fu happened to learn about certain secret dealings of the chancellor involving illegal profits, bribes received from the king of Huai-nan, and agreements made between the king and the chancellor. The retainers of T'ien Fen and Kuan Fu undertook to mediate between the two men and eventually persuaded them to cease their attacks and let each other alone.

In the summer of the same year T'ien Fen married the daughter of Liu Chia, the king of Yen. Empress Dowager Wang issued an edict inviting all of the nobles and members of the imperial family to visit T'ien Fen and offer their congratulations. Tou Ying called on Kuan Fu and asked him to go with him to T'ien Fen's house, but Kuan Fu declined. "I have already gotten into trouble with the chancellor on several occasions by trying to drink with him. And anyway at the moment he and I are not on good terms."

"But that matter has been all settled!" said Tou Ying, and kept insisting until Kuan Fu finally agreed to join him. When the drinking had reached its height, T'ien Fen arose and proposed a toast, whereupon all the guests moved off their mats and bowed.[5] This over, Tou Ying proposed a toast, but only his old friends moved off their mats, the rest of the company simply kneeling where they were.

Kuan Fu, highly displeased at the way things were going, got up with a container of wine and went over to pour a drink for T'ien Fen. "I can't drink a whole cup!" T'ien Fen protested, rising to his knees on the mat.

Kuan Fu was angrier than ever, but he gave a forced laugh and said, "Come, sir, surely a man of your eminence. . . . I insist!" But T'ien Fen refused to drink.

Kuan Fu went next with the wine container to the marquis of Lin-ju. The marquis was at the moment busy whispering in the ear of Ch'eng Pu-shih, and he too failed to get off his mat. Kuan Fu, unable to find any other outlet for his rage, began to curse the marquis. "On ordinary days you go around speaking ill of Ch'eng Pu-shih and telling people he isn't worth a cent, and yet today all of a sudden when one of your elders comes and offers you a drink, you start cooing in Ch'eng Pu-shih's ear like a love-sick maiden!"

T'ien Fen called Kuan Fu aside and said, "Ch'eng Pu-shih and Li Kuang are the commanders of the guards at the Eastern and Western Palaces, you know.[6] If you start insulting General Ch'eng in front of everyone, won't you be casting aspersions on your friend General Li as well?"

"Let them cut off my head or rip open my breast right now!" said Kuan Fu. "What do I care about Ch'eng or Li?"

With this the guests began to excuse themselves and go out to the toilet, one by one drifting away from the party. When Tou Ying was about to leave, he motioned to Kuan Fu to go out with him, but T'ien Fen exclaimed angrily, "I was at fault for ever letting Kuan Fu behave in such an arrogant manner!" and ordered his horsemen to detain Kuan Fu. Thus when Kuan Fu tried to leave the house he found he

[5] As in Japan today, the highest degree of courtesy was expressed by sliding all the way off one's mat and kneeling on the floor. A lesser degree of courtesy was expressed by straightening up on the mat and coming to a kneeling position.

[6] The Eastern Palace, of which Ch'eng Pu-shih was the commander of the guard, was the residence of the empress dowager; the Western Palace was another name for the emperor's palace.

could not get out. Chi Fu jumped up and came forward to apologize, pushing Kuan Fu by the neck and trying to make him kneel down and apologize too, but Kuan Fu only grew angrier than ever and refused to offer any apology.

T'ien Fen then signaled to his horsemen to bind Kuan Fu and take him to the post station. After this he sent for his chief secretary and, explaining that he had invited the members of the imperial family to his house in accordance with an edict from the empress dowager, instructed him to draw up charges against Kuan Fu for insulting the guests and failing to show the proper respect, and to have him put into chains in the Inquiry Room. He then proceeded to investigate the earlier rumors of the misconduct of Kuan Fu's relatives and sent his officers out in parties to arrest all the branches of the Kuan family and charge them with crimes punishable by public execution.

Tou Ying was greatly distressed by this turn of events and, laying out funds from his own resources, sent his retainers to plead on Kuan Fu's behalf, but they were unable to obtain his release. T'ien Fen's officers did their best to carry out their orders but the other members of the Kuan family all succeeded in escaping into hiding. Since Kuan Fu was bound and imprisoned, he had no opportunity to report to the emperor what he knew about T'ien Fen's secret dealings.

Tou Ying tried everything he could to save Kuan Fu. His wife warned him, saying, "Kuan Fu has offended the chancellor and gotten into trouble with Empress Dowager Wang and her whole family. How can you possibly save him?" But Tou Ying replied, "I won the title of marquis by my own efforts and if necessary I will give it up of my own accord and have no regrets. In any event I could not think of leaving Kuan Fu to die while I am still alive!"

Then, without informing his family, he slipped out of the house and sent a letter to the emperor. He was immediately summoned to an audience at which he explained in detail that Kuan Fu's misconduct had been due simply to an excess of wine and did not deserve the death penalty. The emperor expressed his agreement and even invited Tou Ying to dine in the palace. "However," he added, "you will have to go to the Eastern Palace and explain things to the empress dowager."

Proceeding to the court of the empress dowager, Tou Ying began to point out with zeal all of Kuan Fu's good points. He explained that Kuan Fu had behaved rudely when he was in his cups, but that the chancellor was trying to use other charges to build a false case against him. The chancellor, however, who was also present, set out with equal zeal to accuse Kuan Fu of arrogant and unlawful conduct, claiming that he was guilty of rebellion and treason. Tou Ying, judging that no other course would be of any avail, finally began to speak ill of the chancellor himself.

T'ien Fen replied to these charges as follows: "Today the world is blessed with peace and harmony, and I have the special fortune to belong to a family which is related to the imperial house by marriage. I am the sort of man who delights in music, in dogs and horses, gardens and houses; I have a fondness for singers, actors, and clever craftsmen. In this respect I am different from Tou Ying and Kuan Fu, who summon to their homes all the powerful bosses and daring young men of the empire and sit day and night talking with them; whose hearts are set on slander and whose minds are full of deceit; who, when they are not searching the heavens for omens of change, are scanning the earth to plot their campaigns, always with a crafty eye fixed upon the relations between the emperor and the empress dowager, praying that the empire may be convulsed by some strife and that they may thereby win great merit for themselves! To what lengths men like Tou Ying and his party will go, I would not venture to guess!"

The emperor then assembled the ministers of his court and asked them which of the two contestants, Tou Ying or T'ien Fen, they believed was in the right. The imperial secretary Han An-kuo gave his opinion as follows: "As Tou Ying has pointed out, Kuan Fu's father died in the service of the dynasty, while Kuan Fu himself seized his spear and galloped into the midst of the rebel camp of Wu, facing untold danger. He bore on his body a dozen wounds and his fame outshone that of every other soldier in the three armies. Truly he is one of the bravest men of the empire. Now he has committed no serious offense, but only become involved in a petty argument over a cup of wine. There is therefore no reason, as Tou Ying says, to drag in other charges and condemn him to execution. In this respect Tou Ying's opinion is correct.

"On the other hand the chancellor has charged Kuan Fu with associating with evil and lawless men, oppressing the poor, amassing a fortune that runs into millions, running his affairs in Ying-ch'uan in an arbitrary and tyrannical manner, insulting the dignity of the imperial house, and molesting men who are flesh and blood of that family. As the proverb says, 'When the branches grow bigger than the roots, then something must break; when the shins grow mightier than the thighs, then something must give.' Thus the opinion of the chancellor is also correct. It remains only for our enlightened sovereign to decide in the case."

The master of titles chief commandant Chi An expressed himself in agreement with Tou Ying, and the prefect of the capital Cheng Tang-shih also said he thought Tou Ying was right, though in the course of the deliberations he became frightened and did not dare to defend his assertion. (None of the other officials ventured to offer any opinion at all.) The emperor was furious with Cheng Tang-shih and said, "All the time you go around discoursing on the relative merits and faults of Tou Ying and T'ien Fen, and yet today when I summon you to court to give your opinion, you cringe and hang your head like a pony in the shafts! I ought to cut off your head as well!"

With this the emperor dismissed the court and, rising from his seat, retired to the inner palace to wait on his mother, Empress Dowager Wang, while she took her meal. The empress dowager had sent her observers to court and they had already reported to her in detail the discussions which had taken place. She was in a rage and refused to eat. "Even while I am alive, people go about insulting my brother T'ien Fen! After I have passed on, I have no doubt that they will gobble him up like so much fish and flesh! And you—you are no man of stone! You are mortal the same as everyone else! Can't you see that these men are only biding their time and pretending to be docile while you are still alive? After your days are ended, do you think there is one of them who can be trusted?"

The emperor apologized, saying, "It is only because T'ien Fen and Tou Ying are both related to the imperial family by marriage that I brought the matter before the court for discussion. If it were not for that, the affair could be left for any law officer to settle."

At this time the chief of palace attendants Shih Chien drew up for the emperor a list of the opinions presented for and against the two contestants. When the court session was over T'ien Fen left the palace and went to the gate where the carriages were drawn up. Calling to the imperial secretary Han An-kuo to join him in his carriage, he began to berate him angrily. "You and I together are pitted against a single, bald-headed old man, Tou Ying! Why did you have to be so timid in expressing your opinion, like a rat trying to look both ways at once?"

After considering for some time, Han An-kuo replied, "You ought to think a little more highly of yourself. If Tou Ying abuses you, you should remove your cap, undo your seals of office and, handing them over to the emperor, say, 'Because of my family connections I have graciously been permitted to serve Your Majesty, but I am basically unfit for the position. Everything that Tou Ying has said about me is quite correct!' In that case the emperor would be sure to admire your humility and would refuse to accept your resignation. As for Tou Ying, he would be so ashamed of himself that he would retire to his home and, biting his tongue with remorse, take his own life. Instead of that, when someone abuses you, you begin abusing him back until the two of you end up quarreling like a pair of fishwives! This is surely not a very dignified way to behave!"

"I am sorry," said T'ien Fen, acknowledging his fault. "In the heat of the argument I became so carried away that it never occurred to me to do such a thing."

Shortly after, the emperor ordered the imperial secretary Han An-kuo to draw up charges against Tou Ying, accusing him of making statements in Kuan Fu's defense that were wholly false and irresponsible. Tou Ying was impeached and imprisoned in the custody of the head of criminal affairs for the imperial family.

Previously, at the end of Emperor Ching's reign, Tou Ying had received a testamentary edict from the emperor stating, "If you ever find yourself in any difficulty, you should appeal your case directly to the throne." Now Kuan Fu had been arrested and accused of a crime punishable by death for himself and his whole family, and the situation grew more serious each day. Moreover, none of the officials dared make any further attempt to explain Tou Ying's position to the emperor. Tou Ying therefore directed his brother's son to write a letter on his behalf to the emperor requesting that he be granted another audience. The letter was submitted to the throne, but when the master of documents searched the files, he could find no such testamentary edict among the papers dating from the time of Emperor Ching's decease. The only copy of the edict in existence, it appeared, was the one preserved in Tou Ying's house, bearing the seal of Tou Ying's private secretary. Hence Tou Ying was charged with having forged an edict of the former emperor, a crime punishable by execution in the market place.

In the tenth month of the fifth year of *yüan-kuang* [130 B.C.] Kuan Fu and all the members of his family were condemned to execution. After some time, news of this reached Tou Ying in jail. He was deeply embittered and, being afflicted with a swelling in his joints, refused to eat anything in hopes that he would soon die. Someone assured him, however, that the emperor had no intention of executing him, and with this he took heart and began to eat again so that his illness improved. The emperor and his ministers had in fact decided not to sentence Tou Ying to death, but just then rumors began to reach the emperor's ears that Tou Ying was speaking evilly of him, and so on the last day of the twelfth month the emperor ordered the death sentence.[7] Tou Ying was executed in the market place of Wei-ch'eng.

The following spring, T'ien Fen, the marquis of Wu-an, fell ill; he spent all his time crying out "I was at fault!" and begging forgiveness for his crimes. When he summoned sorcerers with the power to discern ghosts and asked them what they saw, they reported that they could see Tou Ying and Kuan Fu standing watch together by his bedside and preparing to kill him. Before long T'ien Fen died and his son T'ien T'ien succeeded to the marquisate. In the third year of the era *yüan-so* [126 B.C.] T'ien T'ien was tried on charges of disrespect for

[7] Since spring is the time when life returns to the earth, it was considered unlucky to perform executions in the spring, and the beginning of spring (the first month) was often accompanied by an amnesty. T'ien Fen therefore had to work quickly to spread his rumors in order to dispose of his enemy before the end of the twelfth month.

the throne because he came to the palace dressed in short robes, and was deprived of his territory.

Sometime afterwards it was discovered that Liu An, the king of Huai-nan, had been plotting a revolt. Liu An and his conspirators were brought to justice, and in the course of the investigations it was found that once in the past, when the king paid a visit to court, T'ien Fen, then grand commandant, had driven out as far as Pa-shang to greet him. "The emperor has not yet designated an heir apparent," T'ien Fen was reported to have said, "while Your Highness is the most worthy among the kings, being a grandson of the founder of the dynasty, Kao-tsu. If there should be a funeral in the imperial palace, I cannot think of anyone but you who would be suitable to succeed to the throne!" The king of Huai-nan, it was said, was greatly pleased with these words and presented T'ien Fen with generous gifts of money and goods.

From the time of the Tou Ying affair the emperor no longer put any trust in T'ien Fen, but merely tolerated him because he was a brother of the empress dowager. When he heard these reports of money presented to T'ien Fen by the king of Huai-nan, he declared, "If T'ien Fen were still around today I would have him and his whole family executed!"

The Grand Historian remarks: Tou Ying and T'ien Fen both commanded great respect because they belonged to families related to the throne by marriage. Kuan Fu became famous as a result of a daring exploit of the moment; Tou Ying won promotion in the Wu and Ch'u rebellion; but T'ien Fen's position of honor was more a matter of time and fortunate circumstance.[8]

Tou Ying, however, did not know how to change with the times, and Kuan Fu, though a man of no learning, refused to be humble. Both men tried to help each other, but they succeeded only in bringing disaster upon themselves.

T'ien Fen enjoyed great honor and loved the feel of power, but because of the resentment occasioned by a single cup of wine, he set

[8] I.e., that Emperor Ching died young and T'ien Fen's sister, Empress Dowager Wang, was able to exercise great power.

about to destroy two men. How pitiful! Those who attempt to vent their anger on innocent persons can never hope to live for long. Those who fail to win the commendation of the mass of lesser men will end by suffering their slanders. Alas, alas! No misfortune ever comes without due cause!

Shih chi 108: The Biography of Han Ch'ang-ju[1]

His wisdom was such that he could respond to the changes of the present age; his kindness enabled him to win over others. Thus I made The Biography of Han Ch'ang-ju.

The imperial secretary Han An-kuo was born in Ch'eng-an in Liang; later he moved to Sui-yang, the capital of Liang. In his youth he studied the theories of the Legalist philosopher Han Fei Tzu and those of the other philosophical schools with Master T'ien of Tsou and served as a palace counselor to King Hsiao of Liang.

When the states of Wu and Ch'u began their rebellion, King Hsiao dispatched Han An-kuo and Chang Yü as generals to block the advance of the Wu army on the eastern border. Chang Yü fell upon the rebels outright, while Han An-kuo proceeded with caution and foresight, and between them they kept the army of Wu from advancing beyond Liang. After the rebellion was put down, both Han An-kuo and Chang Yü became well known for the part they had played in its suppression.

King Hsiao of Liang was a younger brother of Emperor Ching. Their mother, Empress Dowager Tou, loved him dearly and persuaded Emperor Ching to allow him to appoint his own prime minister and officials of the two thousand picul class, though this was contrary to Han custom. In his travels, his hunting expeditions, and his whole way of life, King Hsiao imitated the Son of Heaven, a fact which secretly displeased Emperor Ching when he learned of it. The empress dowager, well aware of the emperor's displeasure, vented her annoyance on the envoys from Liang, refusing to receive them in audience and presenting them with a list of the king's misdemeanors.

Han An-kuo, who came to court as an envoy from Liang, visited

[1] Ch'ang-ju is the polite name of Han An-kuo; Ssu-ma Ch'ien uses it in the title of the biography but in the biography itself refers to him throughout by his familiar name, Han An-kuo.

Emperor Ching's elder sister Princess Ch'ang and, weeping, said, "No one is a more filial son and a more loyal subject than the king of Liang. Why is it that the empress dowager will not recognize this? Some time ago, when Wu, Ch'u, Ch'i, Chao, and the others of the Seven Kingdoms rebelled, all the lands east of the Pass joined together in alliance and began their march westward to the capital. Only Liang remained faithful and shouldered the burden of resistance. The king of Liang, thinking of the empress dowager and the emperor far away in the capital and observing the lawlessness of the other feudal lords, wept floods of tears with each word he spoke. Kneeling and bidding farewell to me and his other six generals, he sent us with a force of men to attack and drive back the armies of Wu and Ch'u. Therefore the rebels did not dare advance westward and were in the end defeated and wiped out. This was all due to the efforts of the king of Liang!

"Now, because of some petty scruple, some fine point of behavior, the empress dowager has become angry with the king of Liang. One must remember, however, that the king's father was an emperor, and his older brother is emperor today; he has been accustomed from youth to the pomp of imperial life. Therefore he has his attendants cry 'Clear the way!' and 'Attention!' when he leaves or returns to his palace, in the manner of an emperor. As for the imperial flags which he flies from his carriage, they were all presented to him by the emperor. If he uses these when he rides about his kingdom, making a show before the country towns and putting on a boastful appearance in the eyes of the other feudal lords, it is because he wishes the whole empire to know that he enjoys the love of the empress dowager and the emperor. And yet now when the Liang envoys come to court they are summarily confronted with a list of the king's misdemeanors. The king is deeply afraid. Day and night he weeps, thinking fondly of his loved ones in the capital but not knowing what to do! How can the empress dowager be so coldhearted toward one who is such a filial son and loyal subject?"

Princess Ch'ang reported to the empress dowager everything that Han An-kuo had said. The empress dowager was pleased and said, "For the king's sake you had better tell the emperor about this." Princess Ch'ang repeated her story to the emperor, whose annoyance was somewhat appeased. When he went to pay his respects to his mother, the empress dowager, he removed his hat and apologized, saying, "I am afraid that, because my brother and I had some difference of opinion, we have caused our mother unnecessary anxiety!"

He then received all the Liang envoys in audience and rewarded them with generous gifts. From this time on the king of Liang enjoyed greater favor and intimacy with the emperor. The empress dowager and Princess Ch'ang also presented gifts to Han An-kuo amounting to over a thousand catties of gold. Because of this incident Han An-kuo grew more famous than ever and came to be on close terms with the imperial family.

Sometime later Han An-kuo was tried for an offense and condemned to punishment. T'ien Something-or-other,[2] the prison official of Meng where Han An-kuo was held for questioning, took the occasion to humiliate him.

"Do you think," said Han An-kuo, referring to his present state of disgrace, "that because the fire has for the moment died out in these ashes, it will never come to life again?"

"If it does," replied T'ien, "I will piss on it!"

Shortly afterwards the post of internal secretary of Liang fell vacant and an envoy was sent from the central government to appoint Han An-kuo to the position. In one stroke he was raised from the status of a convict to that of a two thousand picul official. The prison official T'ien fled into hiding, but Han An-kuo sent word to him: "If you do not return to your post, I will execute all the members of your family!" T'ien finally appeared and, with his arms bared, apologized for his former behavior. "Now is the time to piss on me!" said Han An-kuo with a laugh. "I certainly can't be bothered punishing the likes of you!" In the end he treated T'ien very well.

When the post of internal secretary fell vacant, King Hsiao had just obtained the services of a rhetorician from Ch'i named Kung-sun Kuei and was thinking of asking the emperor for permission to appoint this man as internal secretary. The empress dowager, hearing of his plans, ordered the king to appoint Han An-kuo to the post. Kung-sun Kuei

---

[2] Ssu-ma Ch'ien has been unable to ascertain the personal name of the official and has substituted the word *chia,* or "A."

and another rhetorician named Yang Sheng had been urging the king to try to get himself designated as heir apparent to his brother, Emperor Ching, and to increase his lands, but they were afraid that the high officials of the Han court would never listen to such proposals. They therefore sent men in secret to assassinate the officials of the Han court who were opposing these measures, and succeeded in murdering Yüan Ang, the former prime minister of Wu. Emperor Ching, learning in time that Kung-sun Kuei and Yang Sheng were the authors of the assassination plot, dispatched envoys with orders to arrest the two men without fail. A group of ten Han officials arrived at the court of Liang and, enlisting the services of everyone from the prime minister on down, began a search for the culprits throughout the kingdom, but over a month passed and they had still not succeeded in apprehending them.

Han An-kuo, learning that King Hsiao was concealing them in his own residence, went to the king and, with tears in his eyes, said, "The shame of the lord, it is said, must be paid for by the death of his ministers. It is because Your Highness has no worthy ministers that affairs have reached this wretched state. Now, since Kung-sun Kuei and Yang Sheng have not been arrested, I beg to be relieved of my post and sentenced to death!"

"But why go to this extreme?" the king protested.

Han An-kuo, the tears coursing down his face, replied, "Your Highness is on intimate terms with the emperor. But, though you are his brother, are you as close to him as Emperor Kao-tsu was to his father, the Grand Supreme Emperor, or as the king of Lin-chiang was to the present emperor?"[3]

"Surely not," said the king.

"These men were linked by the closest bond possible—that of father and son. And yet Emperor Kao-tsu boasted that 'It was *I* who won the empire with my three-foot sword' and consequently his father, the Grand Supreme Emperor, never took any part in the governing of

[3] Liu Jung, the eldest son of Emperor Ching, was originally designated as heir apparent but later removed from that position and appointed king of Lin-chiang. See in Volume I his biography, in "Hereditary Houses of the Five Families," and that of his mother, Lady Li, in "Hereditary Houses of the Families Related to the Emperors by Marriage."

the empire but lived in retirement in Li-yang. Similarly the king of Lin-chiang, though the eldest son of the emperor and the rightful heir, was deprived of the title of heir apparent because of one little slip in speech committed by his mother, Lady Li.[4] Later he was accused of having torn down the wall of one of the ancestral temples, and finally he committed suicide in the office of the palace military commander. Why did Emperor Kao-tsu and the present emperor treat their closest kin in this way? Because in governing the empire one must never let private feelings interfere with the public welfare! There is a popular saying, 'Though he's your father, he may still turn out to be a tiger; though he's your older brother, he may still turn out to be a wolf!'

"Now, although you are ranked among the feudal lords, you have been beguiled by the fatuous advice of evil ministers into violating the prohibitions of the emperor and perverting the enlightened laws of the land. For the sake of the empress dowager, the Son of Heaven has forborne to call you to account before the law. The empress dowager herself weeps day and night, praying that you will mend your ways of your own accord, and yet you have failed to wake to your error. But someday if the funeral carriages were to bear the empress dowager away to her final rest, whom would you have left to turn to?"

Before he had finished speaking, the tears began to stream down King Hsiao's face and, apologizing to Han An-kuo, he said, "I will expel Kung-sun Kuei and Yang Sheng from their hiding place!" Kung-sun Kuei and Yang Sheng committed suicide, and the Han envoys returned to the capital to report to the emperor. Thus the settlement of the affair was due solely to the efforts of Han An-kuo. From this time on Emperor Ching and Empress Dowager Tou held Han An-kuo in even higher esteem.

After King Hsiao died and his son, Liu Mai, posthumously known as King Kung, came to the throne, Han An-kuo was tried for some offense and removed from his post, after which he lived at home in retirement.

---

[4] In the biography of Lady Li we are told that, although Emperor Ching asked her to look after his sons in the event of his death, she "had refused to acknowledge his request, and when she did speak her words were lacking in humility." This is probably the "slip in speech" to which Han An-kuo is referring.

During the era *chien-yüan* [140–135 B.C.] T'ien Fen, the marquis of Wu-an, was made grand commandant of the Han court and enjoyed great favor and honor in the exercise of his duties. Han An-kuo presented him with a gift of five hundred catties of gold, in exchange for which T'ien Fen spoke on his behalf to his half-sister, Empress Dowager Wang, the mother of the present emperor. The emperor had also heard of Han An-kuo's reputation for wisdom and summoned him to be chief commandant of Pei-ti. Shortly afterwards he was transferred to the post of minister of agriculture. When the state of Min-yüeh attacked its neighbor, Southern Yüeh, Han An-kuo and the grand messenger Wang Hui were dispatched with troops to put down the trouble. Before they had reached Min-yüeh, however, the people of that state murdered their king and surrendered, whereupon the Han forces withdrew.

In the sixth year of *chien-yüan* [135 B.C.] T'ien Fen was made chancellor and Han An-kuo was made imperial secretary. At this time the Hsiung-nu had come with offers of a peace alliance and the emperor had referred the question to his ministers for debate. The grand messenger Wang Hui, a native of Yen who had several times served as an official on the northern border and was familiar with the ways of the Hsiung-nu, stated his opinion: "Although the Han concludes peace treaties with the Hsiung-nu, it is never more than a couple of years before they violate the agreement. It would be better to refuse their offer and send troops to attack them!"

Han An-kuo, however, replied, "No profit comes to an army that has to fight a thousand miles from home. The Hsiung-nu move on the feet of swift war horses, and in their breasts beat the hearts of beasts. They shift from place to place as fast as a flock of birds, so that it is extremely difficult to corner them and bring them under control. Though we were to win possession of their land, it would be no great addition to the empire, and though we ruled their hosts of warriors, they would do little to strengthen our power. From the most ancient times the Hsiung-nu have never been regarded as a part of humanity. If we march thousands of miles away and try to fight with them, our men and horses will be worn out, and then the wretches will muster all their strength and fall upon us. An arrow from the most powerful crossbow, when it has reached the end of its flight, will not pierce the sheerest Lu gauze; the strongest wind, when its force is spent, will not lift a goose feather—not because both are not strong at the outset, but because their force in time is dispersed. It would not be expedient to attack the Hsiung-nu. Better to make peace with them!"

Many of the other ministers agreed with Han An-kuo's opinion, and the emperor therefore consented to the peace alliance.

The following year, the first year of the era *kuang-yüan* [134 B.C.] Nieh Weng-i, an influential man from the city of Ma-i in Yen-men Province, conveyed word to the emperor via the grand messenger Wang Hui, saying, "Now that peaceful relations have been established with the Hsiung-nu and they are on good terms with us here on the border, it would be an ideal opportunity to entice them with prospects of gain." The emperor therefore ordered Nieh Weng-i to cross the border in secret and, in the guise of a refugee, to enter the territory of the Hsiung-nu. Once there, he had an interview with the *Shan-yü,* the Hsiung-nu leader, and said, "If you wish, I can murder the governor of Ma-i and his officials and turn the city over to you so you can seize all the wealth there!"

The *Shan-yü,* trusting Nieh Weng-i, was attracted by his offer and agreed to cooperate. Nieh Weng-i returned to Ma-i and, putting to death some condemned criminals instead, hung their heads on the city wall as a sign to the *Shan-yü*'s envoys that he had carried out his part of the agreement, telling them at the same time, "The high officials of Ma-i have all been killed. Now is the time to attack with all speed!" The *Shan-yü* then broke through the border defenses and, with a force of over a hundred thousand cavalry, invaded the empire through the barrier at Wu-chou.

At this time the Han had a force of over three hundred thousand infantry, cavalry, and bowmen concealed in the valley around Ma-i, lying in wait for the Hsiung-nu. The colonel of the guard Li Kuang commanded the cavalry; the master of carriage Kung-sun Ho commanded the light carriages; the grand messenger Wang Hui was the garrison commander; the palace counselor Li Hsi was commander of the bowmen; and the imperial secretary Han An-kuo was in command of the supporting army. All the other leaders were under Han

An-kuo's command. An agreement was made that as soon as the *Shan-yü* had entered the city of Ma-i, the Han troops would pour out of hiding to attack him. Wang Hui, Li Hsi, and Li Kuang were to lead a separate force across from the direction of Tai and concentrate on attacking the baggage trains of the enemy.

As already stated, the *Shan-yü* broke through the Great Wall at the Wu-chou barrier and began to march toward Ma-i, plundering as he went along. He was still some hundred *li* from the city when, noticing that there were large numbers of domestic animals in the fields but no people anywhere in sight, he began to grow suspicious. He attacked a beacon warning station and captured one of the defense officials of Wu-chou. He was about to run the official through with his sword, but instead began to question him, whereupon the official told him, "There are twenty or thirty thousand Han troops lying in ambush at Ma-i!"

The *Shan-yü*, turning to those around him, said, "It appears that we have been tricked by the Han!" and began to lead his forces back toward the border. After he got beyond the pass, he said, "Heaven was on my side when I captured this defense official!" and he awarded the man the title of "Heavenly King."

When word came from the border that the *Shan-yü* had turned around and was leading his troops back out of the country, the Han forces set out in pursuit. They followed him as far as the border but, realizing that they could not overtake him, abandoned the pursuit. Meanwhile Wang Hui and the others of his group of thirty thousand, hearing that the *Shan-yü* had not made contact with the Han armies, and considering that if they tried to attack the baggage trains they would be pitted against the finest soldiers of the *Shan-yü* and would surely suffer defeat, likewise abandoned any idea of attack. Thus none of the generals achieved any distinction.

The emperor was furious at Wang Hui for failing to cross the border to attack the *Shan-yü*'s baggage train, but instead leading his troops back to the capital in defiance of orders. Defending himself, Wang Hui said, "If the wretches had gotten as far as Ma-i and the other Han troops had made contact with the *Shan-yü* according to the agreement, then I could have attacked his baggage train with good prospects of success. But when the *Shan-yü* discovered the plot and turned back before reaching the city, I knew that my thirty thousand men could never stand up to his hordes and that we would win nothing but disgrace. I was perfectly aware, of course, that I would be executed as soon as I returned to the capital, but I wished to save the lives of those thirty thousand men of Your Majesty's."

Wang Hui was handed over to the commandant of justice, who recommended that he be executed for cowardly shirking of duty. Wang Hui secretly sent a thousand pieces of gold to the chancellor T'ien Fen to speak on his behalf, but T'ien Fen did not dare to say anything directly to the emperor. Instead he spoke to Empress Dowager Wang: "Wang Hui was the one who engineered the plot to attack the *Shan-yü* at Ma-i. Now if he is to be executed for its failure, this is simply doing the Hsiung-nu the favor of satisfying their anger!"

When the emperor came to pay his morning visit to his mother, Empress Dowager Wang, she repeated to him what T'ien Fen had said, but the emperor replied, "Wang Hui was indeed the one who engineered the Ma-i plot. It was because of him that I called out several hundred thousand troops and disposed them as he recommended. Even if it was impossible to capture the *Shan-yü,* Wang Hui and his group of men could at least have attacked his baggage train and won some sort of gain to repay the soldiers for all their labor. Now if I fail to execute him, I will have no way to apologize to the empire for this failure!"

When Wang Hui heard what the emperor had said, he committed suicide.

Han An-kuo was the sort of man who is full of grand schemes. He was wise enough to know how to get along in the world, but at the same time his actions all sprang from a deep sense of loyalty. Although he himself was greedy in matters of money, those whom he recommended for office were all men of scrupulous integrity and worthier than himself. He worked for the promotion of such men as Hu Sui, Tsang Ku, and Chih T'o from his own state of Liang, all of whom became famous throughout the empire. Everyone admired him for his efforts to promote others and the emperor himself considered him an invaluable asset to the nation.

Han An-kuo had been imperial secretary for some four years when the chancellor T'ien Fen died. Han An-kuo temporarily took over the duties of chancellor but one day, when he was leading the imperial procession, he fell from his carriage and injured his foot. The emperor had begun discussions on a replacement for the post of chancellor and was anxious to appoint Han An-kuo, but when he sent someone to see how Han An-kuo was, the man reported that he was still limping badly as a result of his fall. The emperor therefore appointed Hsieh Tse, the marquis of P'ing-chi, as chancellor instead of Han An-kuo, who declined the post on grounds of his illness.

After a few months Han An-kuo's limp went away and the emperor made him palace military commander; a year or so later he was transferred to the post of colonel of the guard. At this time the carriage and cavalry general Wei Ch'ing attacked the Hsiung-nu, riding north from Shang-ku Province and defeating the barbarians at Lung-ch'eng. General Li Kuang, who took part in the expedition, was captured by the Hsiung-nu but managed to escape, while another of the generals, Kung-sun Ao, lost a large number of his men. Both were condemned to die but were allowed to buy off the death sentence and become commoners instead.

The following year the Hsiung-nu crossed the border in great numbers and murdered the governor of Liao-hsi. From Liao-hsi they advanced to Yen-men, killing and carrying off several thousand men. The carriage and cavalry general Wei Ch'ing marched out of Yen-men to attack them, leaving the colonel of the guard Han An-kuo in command of a force of bowmen to garrison Yü-yang. One of the Hsiung-nu whom Han An-kuo had taken prisoner informed him that the Hsiung-nu hordes had by this time moved on far away from the area, and Han An-kuo therefore sent a letter to the throne requesting that, since it was time for the work in the fields to begin, he be allowed to disband the army at the garrison for a while. Permission was granted, but the garrison army had not been disbanded for more than a month or so when the Hsiung-nu invaded Shang-ku and Yü-yang in great numbers. Han An-kuo had no more than seven hundred some men in the fort where he was stationed and, though they marched out and engaged the enemy, they could win no advantage and were forced to retire into the fort again. The Hsiung-nu meanwhile plundered the region, seizing over a thousand prisoners and all the domestic animals before they left the area.

When word of this reached the emperor he was furious and sent a messenger to reprimand Han An-kuo. He then transferred Han An-kuo far to the east, putting him in charge of the garrison at Yu-pei-p'ing, because one of the Hsiung-nu prisoners had said that the Hsiung-nu were preparing to invade in the east.

Han An-kuo had been imperial secretary early in his career and had commanded the armies at Ma-i, but later he incurred the displeasure of the emperor and was demoted to lesser posts, while the emperor's new favorite, the young general Wei Ch'ing, continued to pile up achievements and rise in importance. Han An-kuo suffered this increasing estrangement from the emperor in gloomy silence. After he was made garrison commander and was tricked by the Hsiung-nu into losing so many of his men, he was filled with the deepest humiliation and requested permission to resign his post and return home. Instead of this, however, he was transferred further east to command another garrison, where he continued to grow more depressed and melancholy than ever. A few months after his transfer, he fell ill and spat blood and died. His death occurred during the second year of the era *yüan-so* [127 B.C.].

The Grand Historian remarks: I worked on the establishment of the new calendar with Hu Sui, whom Han An-kuo had recommended to office, and had an opportunity to observe Han An-kuo's strict sense of duty and Hu Sui's deep and abiding loyalty. It is no wonder people these days say that Liang is rich in worthy men. Hu Sui advanced as high as the post of steward in the household of the empress dowager and the heir apparent. The emperor had great faith in him and was planning to make him chancellor when death ended his career. Had he lived, he would, with his integrity and fine conduct, have been one of the most conscientious and diligent men alive today.

Shih chi 109: The Biography of General Li Kuang

Valorous in the face of the enemy, good to his men, he gave no petty or vexatious orders, and for this reason his subordinates looked up to him with admiration. Thus I made The Biography of General Li.

General Li Kuang was a native of Ch'eng-chi in Lung-hsi Province. Among his ancestors was Li Hsin, a general of the state of Ch'in, who pursued and captured Tan, the crown prince of Yen.[1] The family originally lived in Huai-li but later moved to Ch'eng-chi. The art of archery had been handed down in the family for generations.

In the fourteenth year of Emperor Wen's reign [166 B.C.] the Hsiung-nu entered the Hsiao Pass in great numbers. Li Kuang, as the son of a distinguished family, was allowed to join the army in the attack on the barbarians. He proved himself a skillful horseman and archer, killing and capturing a number of the enemy, and was rewarded with the position of palace attendant at the Han court. His cousin Li Ts'ai was also made a palace attendant. Both men served as mounted guards to the emperor and received a stipend of eight hundred piculs of grain. Li Kuang always accompanied Emperor Wen on his hunting expeditions. The emperor, observing how he charged up to the animal pits, broke through the palisades, and struck down the most ferocious beasts, remarked, "What a pity you were not born at a better time! Had you lived in the age of Emperor Kao-tsu, you would have had no trouble in winning a marquisate of at least ten thousand households!"

When Emperor Ching came to the throne, Li Kuang was made chief commandant of Lung-hsi; later he was transferred to the post of general of palace horsemen. At the time of the revolt of Wu and Ch'u, he served as a cavalry commander under the grand commandant Chou Ya-fu, joining in the attack on the armies of Wu and Ch'u, capturing the enemy pennants, and distinguishing himself at the battle of

---

[1] He had sent a man to the Ch'in court in an unsuccessful attempt to assassinate the king, who later became the First Emperor of the Ch'in.

Ch'ang-i. But because he had accepted the seals of a general from the king of Liang without authorization from the Han government, he was not rewarded for his achievements when he returned to the capital.

Following this he was transferred to the post of governor of Shang-ku Province, where he engaged in almost daily skirmishes with the Hsiung-nu. The director of dependent states Kung-sun K'un-yeh went to the emperor and, with tears in his eyes, said, "There is no one in the empire to match Li Kuang for skill and spirit and yet, trusting to his own ability, he repeatedly engages the enemy in battle. I am afraid one day we will lose him!" The emperor therefore transferred him to the post of governor of Shang Province.[2]

At this time the Hsiung-nu invaded Shang Province in great force. Emperor Ching sent one of his trusted eunuchs to join Li Kuang, ordering him to train the troops and lead them in an attack on the Hsiung-nu. The eunuch, leading a group of twenty or thirty horsemen, was casually riding about the countryside one day when he caught sight of three Hsiung-nu riders and engaged them in a fight. The three Hsiung-nu, however, began circling the party and shooting as they went until they had wounded the eunuch and were near to killing all of his horsemen. The eunuch barely managed to flee back to the place where Li Kuang was. "They must be out hunting eagles!" said Li Kuang, and galloped off with a hundred horsemen in pursuit of the three Hsiung-nu. The Hsiung-nu, having lost their horses, fled on foot. After they had journeyed twenty or thirty *li,* Li Kuang caught up with them and, ordering his horsemen to fan out to the left and right of them, began to shoot at them. He killed two with his arrows and took the third one alive. As he had guessed, they were eagle hunters.

Li Kuang had bound his prisoner and remounted his horse, when he spied several thousand Hsiung-nu horsemen in the distance. The Hsiung-nu, catching sight of Li Kuang and his men, supposed that they were a decoy sent out from the main body of the Han forces to lure them into combat. They made for a nearby hill in alarm and drew up their ranks on its crest.

[2] The thirty-one characters which follow at this point in the text have been shifted in the translation to a point farther along in the narrative, following the reading in the parallel passage in *Han shu* 54.

Li Kuang's horsemen were thoroughly terrified and begged him to flee back to camp as quickly as possible, but he replied, "We are twenty or thirty *li* away from the main army. With only a hundred of us, if we were to try to make a dash for it, the Hsiung-nu would be after us in no time and would shoot down every one of us. But if we stay where we are, they are bound to think we are a decoy from the main army and will not dare to attack!"

Instead of retreating, therefore, Li Kuang gave the order to his men to advance. When they had reached a point some two *li* from the Hsiung-nu ranks, he told his men, "Dismount and undo your saddles!"

"But there are too many of them and they are almost on top of us!" his men protested. "What will we do if they attack?"

"They expect us to run away," said Li Kuang. "But now if we all undo our saddles and show them we have no intention of fleeing, they will be more convinced than ever that there is something afoot."

The Hsiung-nu in fact did not venture to attack, but sent out one of their leaders on a white horse to reconnoitre. Li Kuang mounted again and, with ten or so of his horsemen, galloped after the barbarian leader and shot him down. Then he returned to his group and, undoing his saddle, ordered his men to turn loose their horses and lie down on the ground. By this time night was falling and the Hsiung-nu, thoroughly suspicious of what they had seen, still had not ventured to attack. They concluded that the Han leaders must have concealed soldiers in the area and be planning to fall upon them in the dark, and so during the night the Hsiung-nu chiefs and their men all withdrew. When dawn came Li Kuang finally managed to return with his group to the main army, which, having no idea where he had gone, had been unable to follow him.

After this Li Kuang was assigned to the governorship of several other border provinces in succession, returning finally to Shang Province. In the course of these moves he served as governor of Lung-hsi, Pei-ti, Tai, and Yün-chung Provinces and in each won fame for his fighting.

After some time, Emperor Ching passed away and the present emperor came to the throne. The emperor's advisers informed him of Li Kuang's fame as a general, and he made Li Kuang the colonel of the guard of the Eternal Palace, while allowing him to retain the governorship of Shang Province.

At this time Ch'eng Pu-chih was the colonel of the guard of the Palace of Lasting Joy. Ch'eng Pu-chih had been a governor in the border provinces and a garrison general at the same time as Li Kuang. When Li Kuang went out on expeditions to attack the Hsiung-nu, he never bothered to form his men into battalions and companies. He would make camp wherever he found water and grass, leaving his men to set up their quarters in any way they thought convenient. He never had sentries circling the camp at night and beating on cooking pots, as was the custom, and in his headquarters he kept records and other clerical work down to a minimum. He always sent out scouts some distance around the camp, however, and he had never met with any particular mishap.

Ch'eng Pu-chih, on the other hand, always kept his men in strict battalion and company formation. The sentries banged on the cooking pots, his officers worked over their records and reports until dawn, and no one in his army got any rest. He likewise had never had any mishaps. Ch'eng Pu-chih once expressed the opinion, "Although Li Kuang runs his army in a very simple fashion, if the enemy should ever swoop down on him suddenly he would have no way to hold them off. His men enjoy plenty of idleness and pleasure, and for that reason they are all eager to fight to the death for him. Life in my army may be a good deal more irksome, but at least I know that the enemy will never catch me napping!"

Li Kuang and Ch'eng Pu-chih were both famous generals at this time, but the Hsiung-nu were more afraid of Li Kuang's strategies, while the Han soldiers for the most part preferred to serve under him and disliked being under Ch'eng Pu-chih's command. Ch'eng Pu-chih advanced to the position of palace counselor under Emperor Ching because of the outspoken advice he gave the emperor on several occasions. He was a man of great integrity and very conscientious in matters of form and law.

Sometime later, the Han leaders attempted to entice the *Shan-yü* into entering the city of Ma-i, concealing a large force of men in the valley around the city to ambush the Hsiung-nu. At this time Li Kuang was appointed as cavalry general under the command of Han An-kuo, the leader of the supporting army. As it happened, however, the *Shan-yü* discovered the plot and escaped in time, so that neither Li Kuang nor any of the other generals connected with the plot achieved any merit.

Four years later [129 B.C.] Li Kuang, because of his services as colonel of the guard, was made a general and sent north from Yen-men to attack the Hsiung-nu. But the Hsiung-nu force he was pitted against turned out to be too numerous and succeeded in defeating Li Kuang's army and capturing him alive.

The *Shan-yü* had for a long time heard of Li Kuang's excellence as a fighter and had given orders, "If you get hold of Li Kuang, take him alive and bring him to me!" As it turned out, the barbarian horsemen did manage to capture Li Kuang and, since he was badly wounded, they strung a litter between two horses and, laying him on it, proceeded on their way about ten *li*. Li Kuang pretended to be dead but managed to peer around him and noticed that close by his side was a young Hsiung-nu boy mounted on a fine horse. Suddenly he leaped out of the litter and onto the boy's horse, seizing his bow and pushing him off the horse. Then, whipping the horse to full gallop, he dashed off to the south. After traveling twenty or thirty *li* he succeeded in catching up with what was left of his army and led the men back across the border into Han territory. While he was making his escape, several hundred horsemen from the party that had captured him came in pursuit, but he turned and shot at them with the bow he had snatched from the boy, killing several of his pursuers, and was thus able to escape.

When he got back to the capital, he was turned over to the law officials, who recommended that he be executed for losing so many of his men and being captured alive. He was allowed to ransom his life and was reduced to the status of commoner.

Following this, Li Kuang lived in retirement for several years, spending his time hunting. His home was in Lan-t'ien, among the Southern Mountains, adjoining the estate of Kuan Ch'iang, the grandson of Kuan Ying, the former marquis of Ying-yin.

One evening Li Kuang, having spent the afternoon drinking with some people out in the fields, was on his way back home, accompanied by a rider attendant, when he passed the watch station at Pa-ling. The watchman, who was drunk at the time, yelled at Li Kuang to halt.

"This is the former General Li," said Li Kuang's man.

"Even present generals are not allowed to go wandering around at night, much less former ones!" the watchman retorted, and made Li Kuang halt and spend the night in the watch station.

Shortly after this, the Hsiung-nu invaded Liao-hsi, murdered its governor, and defeated General Han An-kuo. Han An-kuo was transferred to Yu-pei-p'ing, where he died, and the emperor forthwith summoned Li Kuang to be the new governor of Yu-pei-p'ing. When he accepted the post, Li Kuang asked that the watchman of Pa-ling be ordered to accompany him, and as soon as the man reported for duty Li Kuang had him executed.[3]

After Li Kuang took over in Yu-pei-p'ing, the Hsiung-nu, who were familiar with his reputation and called him "The Flying General," stayed away from the region for several years and did not dare to invade Yu-pei-p'ing.

Li Kuang was out hunting one time when he spied a rock in the grass which he mistook for a tiger. He shot an arrow at the rock and hit it with such force that the tip of the arrow embedded itself in the rock. Later, when he discovered that it was a rock, he tried shooting at it again, but he was unable to pierce it a second time.

Whatever province Li Kuang had been in in the past, whenever he heard that there was a tiger in the vicinity he always went out to shoot it in person. When he got to Yu-pei-p'ing he likewise went out one time to hunt a tiger. The beast sprang at him and wounded him, but he finally managed to shoot it dead.

Li Kuang was completely free of avarice. Whenever he received a reward of some kind, he at once divided it among those in his command, and he was content to eat and drink the same things as his men. For over forty years he received a salary of two thousand piculs, but when he died he left no fortune behind. He never discussed matters of

---

[3] The parallel text in *Han shu* 54 records that Li Kuang wrote a letter to the emperor apologizing for this act of personal vengeance, but the emperor replied that he expected his generals to be merciless so that they would inspire awe in their men and terrify the enemy.

family wealth. He was a tall man with long, apelike arms. His skill at archery seems to have been an inborn talent, for none of his descendants or others who studied under him were ever able to equal his prowess. He was a very clumsy speaker and never had much to say. When he was with others he would draw diagrams on the ground to explain his military tactics or set up targets of various widths and shoot at them with his friends, the loser being forced to drink. In fact, archery remained to the end of his life his chief source of amusement.

When he was leading his troops through a barren region and they came upon some water, he would not go near it until all his men had finished drinking. Similarly he would not eat until every one of his men had been fed. He was very lenient with his men and did nothing to vex them, so that they all loved him and were happy to serve under him. Even when the enemy was attacking, it was his custom never to discharge his arrows unless his opponent was within twenty or thirty paces and he believed he could score a hit. When he did discharge an arrow, however, the bowstring had no sooner sounded than his victim would fall to the ground. Because of this peculiar habit he often found himself in considerable difficulty when he was leading his troops against an enemy, and this is also the reason, it is said, that he was occasionally wounded when he went out hunting wild beasts.

Sometime after Li Kuang was made governor of Yu-pei-p'ing, Shih Chien died, and Li Kuang was summoned to take his place as chief of palace attendants.

In the sixth year of *yüan-so* [123 B.C.] Li Kuang was again made a general and sent with the general in chief Wei Ch'ing to proceed north from Ting-hsiang and attack the Hsiung-nu. Most of the other generals who took part in the expedition killed or captured a sufficient number of the enemy to be rewarded for their achievements by being made marquises, but Li Kuang's army won no distinction.

Three years later Li Kuang, as chief of palace attendants, was sent to lead a force of four thousand cavalry north from Yu-pei-p'ing. Chang Ch'ien, the Po-wang marquis, leading ten thousand cavalry, rode out with Li Kuang but took a somewhat different route. When Li Kuang had advanced several hundred *li* into enemy territory, the Hsiung-nu leader known as the Wise King of the Left appeared with forty thousand cavalry and surrounded Li Kuang's army. His men were all terrified, but Li Kuang ordered his son Li Kan to gallop out to meet the enemy. Li Kan, accompanied by only twenty or thirty riders, dashed straight through the Hsiung-nu horsemen, scattering them to left and right, and then returned to his father's side, saying, "These barbarians are easy enough to deal with!" After this Li Kuang's men were somewhat reassured.

Li Kuang ordered his men to draw up in a circle with their ranks facing outward. The enemy charged furiously down on them and the arrows fell like rain. Over half the Han soldiers were killed, and their arrows were almost gone. Li Kuang then ordered the men to load their bows and hold them in readiness, but not to discharge them, while he himself, with his huge yellow crossbow, shot at the sub-commander of the enemy force and killed several of the barbarians. After this the enemy began to fall back a little.

By this time night had begun to fall. Every one of Li Kuang's officers and men had turned white with fear, but Li Kuang, as calm and confident as though nothing had happened, worked to get his ranks into better formation. After this the men knew that they could never match his bravery.

The following day Li Kuang once more fought off the enemy, and in the meantime Chang Ch'ien at last arrived with his army. The Hsiung-nu forces withdrew and the Han armies likewise retreated, being in no condition to pursue them. By this time Li Kuang's army had been practically wiped out. When the two leaders returned to the capital, they were called to account before the law. Chang Ch'ien was condemned to death for failing to keep his rendezvous with Li Kuang at the appointed time, but on payment of a fine he was allowed to become a commoner. In the case of Li Kuang it was decided that his achievements and his failures canceled each other out and he was given no reward.

Li Kuang's cousin Li Ts'ai had begun his career along with Li Kuang as an attendant at the court of Emperor Wen. During the reign of Emperor Ching, Li Ts'ai managed to accumulate sufficient merit to advance to the position of a two thousand picul official, and under the present emperor he became prime minister of Tai. In the fifth year of *yüan-so* [124 B.C.] he was appointed a general of light carriage and accompanied the general in chief Wei Ch'ing in an attack on the Hsiung-nu Wise King of the Right. His achievements in this campaign placed him in the middle group of those who were to receive rewards and he was accordingly enfeoffed as marquis of Lo-an. In the second year of *yüan-shou* [121 B.C.] he replaced Kung-sun Hung as chancellor of the central court. In ability one would be obliged to rank Li Ts'ai very close to the bottom, and his reputation came nowhere near to equaling that of Li Kuang. And yet, although Li Kuang never managed to obtain a fief and never rose higher than one of the nine lower offices of the government, that of colonel of the guard, his cousin Li Ts'ai was enfeoffed as a marquis and eventually reached the position of chancellor, one of the three highest posts. Even some of Li Kuang's own officers and men succeeded in becoming marquises.

Li Kuang was once chatting with Wang So, a diviner who told men's fortunes by the configurations of the sky, and remarked on this fact. "Ever since the Han started attacking the Hsiung-nu, I have never failed to be in the fight. I've had men in my command who were company commanders or even lower and who didn't even have the ability of average men, and yet twenty or thirty of them have won marquisates on the strength of their achievements in attacking the barbarian armies. I have never been behind anyone else in doing my duty. Why is it I have never won an ounce of distinction so that I could be enfeoffed like the others? Is it that I just don't have the kind of face to become a marquis? Or is it all a matter of fate?"

"Think carefully, general," replied Wang So. "Isn't there something in the past that you regret having done?"

"Once, when I was governor of Lung-hsi, the Ch'iang tribes in the west started a revolt. I tried to talk them into surrendering, and in fact persuaded over eight hundred of them to give themselves up. But then I went back on my word and killed them all the very same day. I have never ceased to regret what I did. But that's the only thing I can think of."

"Nothing brings greater misfortune than killing those who have already surrendered to you," said Wang So. "This is the reason, general, that you have never gotten to be a marquis!"

Two years later the general in chief Wei Ch'ing and the general of swift cavalry Ho Ch'ü-ping set off with a large force to attack the Hsiung-nu. Li Kuang several times asked to be allowed to join them, but the emperor considered that he was too old and would not permit him to go. After some time, however, the emperor changed his mind and gave his consent, appointing him as general of the vanguard. The time was the fourth year of *yüan-shou* [119 B.C.].

Li Kuang accordingly joined the general in chief Wei Ch'ing and set off to attack the Hsiung-nu. After the group had crossed the border, Wei Ch'ing captured one of the enemy and learned the whereabouts of the *Shan-yü*. He therefore decided to take his own best troops and make a dash for the spot, ordering Li Kuang to join forces with the general of the right Chao I-chi and ride around by the eastern road. The eastern road was rather long and roundabout and, since there was little water or grass in the region, it presented a difficult route for a large army to pass over. Li Kuang therefore asked Wei Ch'ing to change the order. "I have been appointed as general of the vanguard," he said, "and yet now you have shifted my position and ordered me to go around by the east. I have been fighting the Hsiung-nu ever since I was old enough to wear my hair bound up, and now I would like to have just one chance to get at the *Shan-yü*. I beg you to let me stay in the vanguard and advance and fight to the death with him!"

Wei Ch'ing had been warned in private by the emperor that Li Kuang was an old man and had already had a lot of bad luck in the past. "Don't let him try to get at the *Shan-yü*, or he will probably make a mess of things!" the emperor had said. Also, at this time Kung-sun Ao, who had recently been deprived of his marquisate, was serving as a general under Wei Ch'ing, and Wei Ch'ing wanted to take him along with him in his attack on the *Shan-yü* so that Kung-sun Ao would have a chance to win some distinction. For these reasons he removed Li Kuang from his post of general of the vanguard.

Li Kuang was aware of all this and tried his best to get out of obeying the order, but Wei Ch'ing refused to listen to his arguments. Instead he sent one of his clerks with a sealed letter to Li Kuang's tent and orders to "proceed to your division at once in accordance with the instructions herein!" Li Kuang did not even bother to take leave of Wei Ch'ing but got up and went straight to his division, burning with rage and indignation and, leading his troops to join those of the general of the right Chao I-chi, set out by the eastern road. Lacking proper guides, however, they lost their way and failed to meet up with Wei Ch'ing at the appointed time. Wei Ch'ing in the meantime engaged the *Shan-yü* in battle, but the latter fled and Wei Ch'ing, being unable to capture him, was forced to turn back south again. After crossing the desert, he joined up with the forces of Li Kuang and Chao I-chi.

When Li Kuang had finished making his report to Wei Ch'ing and returned to his own camp, Wei Ch'ing sent over his clerk with the customary gifts of dried rice and thick wine for Li Kuang. While the clerk was there, he began to inquire how it happened that Li Kuang and Chao I-chi had lost their way, since Wei Ch'ing had to make a detailed report to the emperor on what had happened to the armies. Li Kuang, however, refused to answer his questions.

Wei Ch'ing sent his clerk again to reprimand Li Kuang in the strongest terms and order him to report to general headquarters at once and answer a list of charges that had been drawn up against him. Li Kuang replied, "None of my commanders was at fault. I was the one who caused us to lose our way. I will send in a report myself."

Then he went in person to headquarters and, when he got there, said to his officers, "Since I was old enough to wear my hair bound up, I have fought over seventy engagements, large and small, with the Hsiung-nu. This time I was fortunate enough to join the general in chief in a campaign against the soldiers of the *Shan-yü* himself, but he shifted me to another division and sent me riding around by the long way. On top of that, I lost my way. Heaven must have planned it this way! Now I am over sixty—much too old to stand up to a bunch of petty clerks and their list of charges!" Then he drew his sword and cut his throat.

All the officers and men in his army wept at the news of his death, and when word reached the common people, those who had known him and those who had not, old men and young boys alike, were all moved to tears by his fate. Chao I-chi was handed over to the law officials and sentenced to death, but on payment of a fine he was allowed to become a commoner.

Li Kuang had three sons, Tang-hu, Chiao, and Kan, all of whom were palace attendants. One day when the present emperor was amusing himself with his young favorite, Han Yen, the boy behaved so impertinently that Li Tang-hu struck him and drove him from the room. The emperor was much impressed with Tang-hu's courage. Li Tang-hu died young. Li Chiao was made governor of Tai Province. He and Tang-hu both died before their father. Tang-hu had a son named Li Ling who was born shortly after Tang-hu died. Li Kan was serving in the army under the general of light cavalry Ho Ch'ü-ping when Li Kuang committed suicide.

The year after Li Kuang's death his cousin Li Ts'ai, who was serving as chancellor at the time, was accused of appropriating land that belonged to the funerary park of Emperor Ching. He was to be handed over to the law officials for trial, but he too committed suicide rather than face being sent to prison, and his fief was abolished.

Li Kan served as a commander under Ho Ch'ü-ping, taking part in an attack on the Hsiung-nu Wise King of the Left. He fought bravely in the attack, seizing the pennants of the barbarian king and cutting off many heads. He was rewarded by being enfeoffed as a marquis in the area within the Pass, receiving the revenue from a city of two hundred households. In addition he was appointed to replace his father, Li Kuang, as chief of palace attendants.

Sometime afterwards, deeply resentful at the general in chief Wei Ch'ing for having brought about his father's disgrace, he struck and wounded Wei Ch'ing. Wei Ch'ing, however, hushed up the incident and said nothing about it. Shortly afterwards, Li Kan accompanied the emperor on a trip to Yung. When the party reached the Palace of Sweet Springs, an imperial hunt was held. Ho Ch'ü-ping, who was on very close terms with Wei Ch'ing, took the opportunity to shoot and kill Li Kan. At this time Ho Ch'ü-ping enjoyed great favor with the emperor, and the emperor therefore covered up for him, giving out the story that Li Kan had been gored and killed by a stag. A year or so later, Ho Ch'ü-ping died.

Li Kan had a daughter who became a lady in waiting to the heir apparent and was much loved and favored by him. Li Kan's son Li Yü also enjoyed favor with the heir apparent, but he was somewhat too fond of profit. So the fortunes of the Li family gradually waned.

(When Tang-hu's son Li Ling grew up, he was appointed as supervisor of the Chien-chang Palace, being in charge of the cavalry. He was skillful at archery and took good care of his soldiers. The emperor, considering that the Li family had been generals for generations, put Li Ling in charge of a force of eight hundred cavalry. Once he led an expedition that penetrated over two thousand *li* into Hsiung-nu territory, passing Chü-yen and observing the lay of the land, but he returned without having caught sight of the enemy. On his return he was appointed a chief commandant of cavalry and put in command of five thousand men from Tan-yang in the region of Ch'u, and for several years he taught archery and garrisoned the provinces of Chiu-ch'üan and Chang-i to protect them from the Hsiung-nu.

In the autumn of the second year of *t'ien-han* [99 B.C.] the Sutrishna General Li Kuang-li led a force of thirty thousand cavalry in an attack on the Hsiung-nu Wise King of the Right at the Ch'i-lien or Heavenly Mountains. He ordered Li Ling to lead a force of five thousand infantry and archers north from Chü-yen and advance about a thousand *li* into enemy territory. In this way he hoped to split the Hsiung-nu forces so that they would not all race in his direction.

Li Ling had already reached the point he was ordered to proceed to and had begun the march back, when the *Shan-yü* with a force of eighty thousand men surrounded his army and began to attack. Li Ling and his army of five thousand fought a running battle for eight days, retreating as they fought, until all their weapons and arrows were gone and half the men had been killed. In the course of the fighting they managed to kill or wound over ten thousand of the enemy.

When they reached a point only a hundred *li* or so from Chü-yen, the Hsiung-nu cornered them in a narrow valley and cut off their avenue of escape. Li Ling's food supplies were exhausted and no rescue troops were in sight, while the enemy pressed their attack and called on Li Ling to surrender. "I could never face the emperor and report such a disaster," Li Ling told his men, and finally surrendered to the Hsiung-nu. Practically all his soldiers perished in the fight; only some four hundred managed to escape and straggle back to Han territory. The *Shan-yü* had already heard of the fame of Li Ling's family and observed his bravery in battle, and as a result he gave him his own daughter as a wife and treated him with honor. When the emperor received news of this, he executed Li Ling's mother and his wife and children. From this time on the name of the Li family was disgraced and all the retainers of the family in Lung-hsi were ashamed to be associated with it.) [4]

The Grand Historian remarks: One of the old books says, "If he is an upright person, he will act whether he is ordered to or not; if he is not upright, he will not obey even when ordered." [5] It refers, no doubt, to men like General Li.

I myself have seen General Li—a man so plain and unassuming that you would take him for a peasant, and almost incapable of speaking a word. And yet the day he died all the people of the empire, whether they had known him or not, were moved to the profoundest grief, so deeply did men trust his sincerity of purpose. There is a proverb which says, "Though the peach tree does not speak, the world wears a path beneath it." It is a small saying, but one which is capable of conveying a great meaning.

[4] This last section in parentheses is most likely not by Ssu-ma Ch'ien, but a later addition. It differs from the account of Li Ling's life in *Han shu* 54 and deals with events that are later than those described elsewhere in the *Shih chi*. It may be recalled that Ssu-ma Ch'ien was condemned to castration for speaking out in defense of Li Ling to the emperor when the news of Li Ling's surrender reached the court. Ssu-ma Ch'ien's own account of Li Ling's battle and surrender is found in his letter to Jen Shao-ch'ing, translated in *Ssu-ma Ch'ien: Grand Historian of China*, pp. 57–67.

[5] *Analects* XIII, 6.

Shih chi 110: The Account of the Hsiung-nu

From the time of the Three Dynasties on, the Hsiung-nu have been a source of constant worry and harm to China. The Han has attempted to determine the Hsiung-nu's periods of strength and weakness so that it may adopt defensive measures or launch punitive expeditions as the circumstances allow. Thus I made The Account of the Hsiung-nu.

The ancestor of the Hsiung-nu was a descendant of the rulers of the Hsia dynasty by the name of Ch'un-wei. As early as the time of Emperors Yao and Shun and before, we hear of these people, known as Mountain Barbarians, Hsien-yün, or Hun-chu, living in the region of the northern barbarians and wandering from place to place pasturing their animals. The animals they raise consist mainly of horses, cows, and sheep, but include such rare beasts as camels, asses, mules, and the wild horses known as *t'ao-t'u* and *t'o-chi*. They move about in search of water and pasture and have no walled cities or fixed dwellings, nor do they engage in any kind of agriculture. Their lands, however, are divided into regions under the control of various leaders. They have no writing, and even promises and agreements are only verbal. The little boys start out by learning to ride sheep and shoot birds and rats with a bow and arrow, and when they get a little older they shoot foxes and hares, which are used for food. Thus all the young men are able to use a bow and act as armed cavalry in time of war. It is their custom to herd their flocks in times of peace and make their living by hunting, but in periods of crisis they take up arms and go off on plundering and marauding expeditions. This seems to be their inborn nature. For long-range weapons they use bows and arrows, and swords and spears at close range. If the battle is going well for them they will advance, but if not, they will retreat, for they do not consider it a disgrace to run away. Their only concern is self-advantage, and they know nothing of propriety or righteousness.

From the chiefs of the tribe on down, everyone eats the meat of the domestic animals and wears clothes of hide or wraps made of felt or fur. The young men eat the richest and best food, while the old get what is left over, since the tribe honors those who are young and strong and despises the weak and aged. On the death of his father, a son will marry his stepmother, and when brothers die, the remaining brothers will take the widows for their own wives. They have no polite names [1] but only personal names, and they observe no taboos in the use of personal names.

When the power of the Hsia dynasty declined, Kung Liu, the ancestor of the Chou dynasty, having lost his position as minister of grain, went to live among the Western Jung barbarians, adopting their ways and founding a city at Pin. Some three hundred years later the Jung and Ti tribes attacked Kung Liu's descendant, the Great Lord Tan-fu. Tan-fu fled to the foot of Mount Ch'i and the whole population of Pin followed after him, founding a new city there. This was the beginning of the Chou state.

A hundred and some years later Ch'ang, the Chou Earl of the West, attacked the Ch'üan-i-shih tribe, and ten or twelve years later, his son, King Wu, overthrew Emperor Chou, the last ruler of the Shang dynasty, and founded a new capital at Lo. He also occupied the regions of Feng and Hao, drove the barbarians north beyond the Ching and Lo rivers, and obliged them to bring tribute to his court at specified times. Their lands were known as "the submissive wastes."

Some two hundred years later, when the power of the Chou dynasty had declined, King Mu attacked the Ch'üan barbarians and brought back with him four white wolves and four white deer which he had seized. From this time on, the peoples of the "submissive wastes" no longer journeyed to court. (At this time the Chou adopted the penal code of Marquis Fu.) [2]

Some two hundred years after the time of King Mu, King Yu of the Chou, egged on by his beloved concubine Pao-ssu, quarreled with Marquis Shen. In anger, Marquis Shen joined forces with the Ch'üan

[1] The text says "no family names or polite names," but it is obvious later on that the Hsiung-nu did have family names. Polite names are names which are used in place of personal names to avoid the appearance of overfamiliarity.

[2] The penal code now comprises a chapter of the *Book of Documents,* where it is known as the code of Marquis Lü.

barbarians and attacked and killed King Yu at the foot of Mount Li. Eventually the barbarians seized the region of Chiao-huo from the Chou, occupied the area between the Ching and Wei rivers, and invaded and plundered the central region of China. Duke Hsiang of Ch'in came to the rescue of the Chou court, and King Yu's successor King P'ing abandoned the regions of Feng and Hao and moved his capital east to the city of Lo. (At this time Duke Hsiang of Ch'in attacked the barbarians and advanced as far as Mount Ch'i; as a result he was for the first time ranked among the feudal lords of the Chou dynasty.)

Sixty-five years later [704 B.C.] the Mountain Barbarians crossed through the state of Yen and attacked Ch'i. Duke Li of Ch'i fought with them in the suburbs of his capital. Forty-four years later the Mountain Barbarians attacked Yen, but Yen reported its distress to Duke Huan of Ch'i, who rode north and attacked the barbarians, driving them off.

Some twenty years later the barbarians rode as far as the capital city of Lo and attacked King Hsiang of the Chou; King Hsiang fled to the city of Fan in Cheng. Previously King Hsiang had wanted to attack the state of Cheng and had therefore married a daughter of the barbarians and made her his queen; then, with the aid of the barbarian forces, he had made his attack on Cheng. Having accomplished his purpose, however, he cast aside his barbarian queen, much to her resentment. King Hsiang's stepmother, Queen Hui, had a son named Tzu-tai whom she wished to place on the throne, and therefore Queen Hui, her son, and the barbarian queen agreed to cooperate with the barbarian attackers from within the capital by opening the city to them. Thus the barbarians were able to enter, defeat and drive out King Hsiang, and set up Tzu-tai as Son of Heaven in his place.

After this the barbarians occupied the area of Lu-hun, roaming as far east as the state of Wei, ravaging and plundering the lands of central China with fearful cruelty. The empire was deeply troubled, and therefore the poets in the *Book of Odes* wrote:

> We smote the barbarians of the north.

> We struck the Hsien-yün
> And drove them to the great plain.

We sent forth our chariots in majestic array
And walled the northern regions.[3]

After King Hsiang had been driven from his throne and had lived abroad for four years, he sent an envoy to the state of Chin to explain his plight. Duke Wen of Chin, having just come to power, wanted to make a name for himself as dictator and protector of the royal house, and therefore he raised an army and attacked and drove out the barbarians, executing Tzu-tai and restoring King Hsiang to his throne in Lo.

At this time Ch'in and Chin were the most powerful states in China. Duke Wen of Chin expelled the Ti barbarians and drove them into the region west of the Yellow River between the Yün and Lo rivers; there they were known as the Red Ti and the White Ti. Shortly afterwards, Duke Mu of Ch'in, having obtained the services of Yu Yü,[4] succeeded in getting the eight barbarian tribes of the west to submit to his authority.

Thus at this time there lived in the region west of Lung the Mien-chu, the Hun-jung, and the Yüan tribes. North of Mounts Ch'i and Liang and the Ching and Ch'i rivers lived the I-ch'ü, Ta-li, Wu-chih, and Ch'ü-yen tribes. North of Chin were the Forest Barbarians and the Lou-fan, while north of Yen lived the Eastern Barbarians and Mountain Barbarians. All of them were scattered about in their own little valleys, each with their own chieftains. From time to time they would have gatherings of a hundred or more men, but no one tribe was capable of unifying the others under a single rule.

Some hundred years later Duke Tao of Chin sent Wei Chiang to make peace with the barbarians, so that they came to pay their respects to the court of Chin. A hundred or so years after this, Viscount Hsiang

[3] Ssu-ma Ch'ien quotes from three different poems: "Pi-kung" of the "Temple Odes of Lu," and "Liu-yüeh" and "Ch'u-chü" of the "Lesser Odes."
[4] Yu Yü's ancestors came from the state of Chin; he himself had been born among the barbarians but could speak the language of Chin. The barbarian king sent him to the court of Duke Mu of Ch'in, who questioned him closely on the customs, lands, and military strength of the barbarians. Duke Mu later succeeded in arousing enmity between the barbarian ruler and Yu Yü, and the latter finally fled to Ch'in and became the duke's adviser on barbarian affairs. The fuller account is found in *Shih chi* 5, "The Basic Annals of Ch'in."

of the Chao family of Chin crossed Mount Chü-chu, defeated the barbarians, and annexed the region of Tai, bringing his state into contact with the Hu-ho tribe. Shortly afterwards he joined with the viscounts of the Hann and Wei families in wiping out their rival, Chih Po, and dividing up the state of Chin among the three of them. Thus the Chao family held possession of Tai and the lands north of Mount Chü-chu, while the Wei family held the provinces of Ho-hsi [Ordos] and Shang, bordering the lands of the barbarians.

After this the I-ch'ü tribes began to build walls and fortifications to protect themselves, but the state of Ch'in gradually ate into their territory and, under King Hui, finally seized twenty-five of their forts. King Hui also attacked the state of Wei, forcing it to cede to him the provinces of Ho-hsi and Shang.

During the reign of King Chao of Ch'in the ruler of the I-ch'ü barbarians had illicit relations with King Chao's mother, the Queen Dowager Hsüan, by whom he had two sons. Later the queen dowager deceived and murdered him at the Palace of Sweet Springs and eventually raised an army and sent it to attack and ravage the lands of the I-ch'ü. Thus Ch'in came into possession of Lung-hsi, Pei-ti, and Shang Provinces, where it built long walls to act as a defense against the barbarians.

At the same time King Wu-ling of Chao changed the customs of his people, ordering them to adopt barbarian dress and to practice riding and shooting, and then led them north in a successful attack on the Forest Barbarians and the Lou-fan. He constructed a defensive wall stretching from Tai along the foot of the Yin Mountains to Kao-ch'üeh, establishing the three provinces of Yün-chung, Yen-men, and Tai.

A little later a worthy general named Ch'in K'ai appeared in the state of Yen. He had earlier been sent as a hostage to the barbarians and had won their deepest confidence; on returning to his state, he led an attack on the Eastern Barbarians, defeating and driving them over a thousand *li* from the border of the state. (The Ch'in Wu-yang who took part with Ching K'o in the attempted assassination of the king of Ch'in was this man's grandson.) Yen also constructed a long wall from Tsao-yang to Hsiang-p'ing and set up the provinces of Shang-ku,

Yü-yang, Yu-pei-p'ing, Liao-hsi, and Liao-tung to guard against the attacks of the barbarians.[5]

By this time China, the land of caps and girdles, was divided among seven states, three of which bordered the territory of the Hsiung-nu. Later, while the Chao general Li Mu was living, the Hsiung-nu did not dare to cross the border of Chao.

Finally Ch'in overthrew the other six states, and the First Emperor of the Ch'in dispatched Meng T'ien to lead a force of a hundred thousand men north to attack the barbarians. He seized control of all the lands south of the Yellow River and established border defenses along the river, constructing forty-four walled district cities overlooking the river and manning them with convict laborers transported to the border for garrison duty. He also built the Direct Road from Chiu-yüan to Yün-yang. Thus he utilized the natural mountain barriers to establish the border defenses, scooping out the valleys and constructing ramparts and building installations at other points where they were needed. The whole line of defenses stretched over ten thousand *li* from Lin-t'ao to Liao-tung and even extended across the Yellow River and through Yang-shan and Pei-chia.

At this time the Eastern Barbarians were very powerful and the Yüeh-chih were likewise flourishing. The *Shan-yü* or chieftain of the Hsiung-nu was named T'ou-man. T'ou-man, unable to hold out against the Ch'in forces, had withdrawn to the far north, where he lived with his subjects for over ten years. After Meng T'ien died and the feudal lords revolted against the Ch'in, plunging China into a period of strife and turmoil, the convicts which the Ch'in had sent to the northern border to garrison the area all returned to their homes. The Hsiung-nu, the pressure against them relaxed, once again began to infiltrate south of the bend of the Yellow River until they had established themselves along the old border of China.

T'ou-man's oldest son, the heir apparent to his position, was named Mo-tun, but the *Shan-yü* also had a younger son by another consort whom he had taken later and was very fond of. He decided that he

[5] From this it may be seen that the First Emperor of the Ch'in, in building the Great Wall, did not have to begin from scratch, as is often implied, but simply repaired and linked up the older walls of these northern states.

wanted to get rid of Mo-tun and set up his younger son as heir instead, and he therefore sent Mo-tun as a hostage to the Yüeh-chih nation. Then, after Mo-tun had arrived among the Yüeh-chih, T'ou-man made a sudden attack on them. The Yüeh-chih were about to kill Mo-tun in retaliation, but he managed to steal one of their best horses and escape, eventually making his way back home. His father, struck by his bravery, put him in command of a force of ten thousand cavalry.

Mo-tun had some arrows made that whistled in flight and used them to drill his troops in shooting from horseback. "Shoot wherever you see my whistling arrow strike!" he ordered, "and anyone who fails to shoot will be cut down!" Then he went out hunting for birds and animals, and if any of his men failed to shoot at what he himself had shot at, he cut them down on the spot. After this, he shot a whistling arrow at one of his best horses. Some of his men hung back and did not dare shoot at the horse, whereupon Mo-tun at once executed them. A little later he took an arrow and shot at his favorite wife. Again some of his men shrank back in terror and failed to discharge their arrows, and again he executed them on the spot. Finally he went out hunting with his men and shot a whistling arrow at one of his father's finest horses. All his followers promptly discharged their arrows in the same direction, and Mo-tun knew that at last they could be trusted. Accompanying his father, the *Shan-yü* T'ou-man, on a hunting expedition, he shot a whistling arrow at his father and every one of his followers aimed their arrows in the same direction and shot the *Shan-yü* dead. Then Mo-tun executed his stepmother, his younger brother, and all the high officials of the nation who refused to take orders from him, and set himself up as the new *Shan-yü*.

At this time the Eastern Barbarians were very powerful and, hearing that Mo-tun had killed his father and made himself leader, they sent an envoy to ask if they could have T'ou-man's famous horse that could run a thousand *li* in one day. Mo-tun consulted his ministers, but they all replied, "The thousand-*li* horse is one of the treasures of the Hsiung-nu people. You should not give it away!"

"When a neighboring country asks for it, why should I begrudge them one horse?" he said, and sent them the thousand-*li* horse.

After a while the Eastern Barbarians, supposing that Mo-tun was afraid of them, sent an envoy to ask for one of Mo-tun's consorts. Again Mo-tun questioned his ministers, and they replied in a rage, "The Eastern Barbarians are unreasoning beasts to come and request one of the *Shan-yü's* consorts. We beg to attack them!"

But Mo-tun replied, "If it is for a neighboring country, why should I begrudge them one woman?" and he sent his favorite consort to the Eastern Barbarians.

With this the ruler of the Eastern Barbarians grew more and more bold and arrogant, invading the lands to the west. Between his territory and that of the Hsiung-nu was an area of over a thousand *li* of uninhabited land; the two peoples made their homes on either side of this wasteland.[6] The ruler of the Eastern Barbarians sent an envoy to Mo-tun saying, "The Hsiung-nu have no way of using this stretch of wasteland which lies between my border and yours. I would like to take possession of it!"

When Mo-tun consulted his ministers, some of them said, "Since the land is of no use you might as well give it to him," while others said, "No, you must not give it away!"

Mo-tun flew into a rage. "Land is the basis of the nation!" he said. "Why should I give it away?" And he executed all the ministers who had advised him to do so.

Then he mounted his horse and set off to attack the Eastern Barbarians, circulating an order throughout his domain that anyone who was slow to follow would be executed. The Eastern Barbarians had up until this time despised Mo-tun and made no preparations for their defense; when Mo-tun and his soldiers arrived, they inflicted a crushing defeat, killing the ruler of the Eastern Barbarians, taking prisoner his subjects, and seizing their domestic animals. Then he returned and rode west, attacking and routing the Yüeh-chih, and annexed the lands of the ruler of Lou-fan and the ruler of Po-yang south of the Yellow River. Thus he recovered possession of all the lands which the Ch'in general Meng T'ien had taken away from the Hsiung-nu; the border between his territory and that of the Han empire now followed the old line of defenses south of the Yellow River, and from there he marched into the Ch'ao-na and Fu-shih districts and then invaded Yen and Tai.

[6] The Gobi Desert.

At this time the Han forces were stalemated in battle with the armies of Hsiang Yü, and China was exhausted by warfare. Thus Mo-tun was able to strengthen his position, massing a force of over three hundred thousand skilled crossbowmen.

Over a thousand years had elapsed from the time of Ch'un-wei, the ancestor of the Hsiung-nu, to that of Mo-tun, a vast period during which the tribes split up and scattered into various groups, sometimes expanding, sometimes dwindling in size. Thus it is impossible to give any ordered account of the lineage of the Hsiung-nu rulers. When Mo-tun came to power, however, the Hsiung-nu reached their peak of strength and size, subjugating all of the other barbarian tribes of the north and turning south to confront China as an enemy nation. As a result of this, it is possible to give an account here of the later Hsiung-nu rulers and of the offices and titles of the nation.

Under the *Shan-yü* are the Wise Kings of the Left and Right, the left and right Lu-li kings, left and right generals, left and right commandants, left and right household administrators, and left and right Ku-tu marquises. The Hsiung-nu word for "wise" is *"t'u-ch'i,"* so that the heir of the *Shan-yü* is customarily called the *"T'u-ch'i* King of the Left."* Among the other leaders, from the wise kings on down to the household administrators, the more important ones command ten thousand horsemen and the lesser ones several thousand, numbering twenty-four leaders in all, though all are known by the title of "Ten Thousand Horsemen." The high ministerial offices are hereditary, being filled from generation to generation by the members of the Hu-yen and Lan families, and in more recent times by the Hsü-pu family. These three families constitute the aristocracy of the nation. The kings and other leaders of the left live in the eastern sector, the region from Shang-ku east to the lands of the Hui-mo and Ch'ao-hsien peoples. The kings and leaders of the right live in the west, the area from Shang Province west to the territories of the Yüeh-chih and Ch'iang tribes. The *Shan-yü* has his court in the region north of Tai and Yün-chung. Each group has its own area, within which it moves about from place to place looking for water and pasture. The Left and Right Wise Kings and Lu-li kings are the most powerful, while the Ku-tu marquises assist the *Shan-yü* in the administration of the nation. Each of the twenty-four leaders in turn appoints his own "chiefs of a thousand," "chiefs of a hundred," and "chiefs of ten," as well as his subordinate kings, prime ministers, chief commandants, household administrators, *chü-ch'ü*[7] officials, and so forth.

In the first month of the year the various leaders come together in a small meeting at the *Shan-yü*'s court to perform sacrifices, and in the fifth month a great meeting is held at Lung-ch'eng at which sacrifices are conducted to the Hsiung-nu ancestors, Heaven and Earth, and the gods and spirits. In the autumn, when the horses are fat, another great meeting is held at the Tai Forest when a reckoning is made of the number of persons and animals.

According to Hsiung-nu law, anyone who in ordinary times draws his sword a foot from the scabbard is condemned to death. Anyone convicted of theft has his property confiscated. Minor offenses are punished by flogging and major ones by death. No one is kept in jail awaiting sentence longer than ten days, and the number of imprisoned men for the whole nation does not exceed a handful.[8]

At dawn the *Shan-yü* leaves his camp and makes obeisance to the sun as it rises, and in the evening he makes a similar obeisance to the moon. In seating arrangements the left side or the seat facing north is considered the place of honor. The days *wu* and *chi* of the ten-day week are regarded as most auspicious.

In burials the Hsiung-nu use an inner and an outer coffin, with accessories of gold, silver, clothing, and fur, but they do not construct grave mounds or plant trees on the grave, nor do they use mourning garments. When a ruler dies, the ministers and concubines who were favored by him and who are obliged to follow him in death often number in the hundreds or even thousands.

Whenever the Hsiung-nu begin some undertaking, they observe the stars and the moon. They attack when the moon is full and withdraw their troops when it wanes. After a battle those who have cut off the

[7] It is impossible to tell from the name alone what this title means. In later times, when the barbarians invaded and conquered northern China, Chü-ch'ü became a Chinese surname.

[8] Ssu-ma Ch'ien is inviting a comparison with the situation in China in his own day, when the jails were full to overflowing with men awaiting sentence.

heads of the enemy or taken prisoners are presented with a cup of wine and allowed to keep the spoils they have captured. Any prisoners that are taken are made slaves. Therefore, when they fight, each man strives for his own gain. They are very skillful at using decoy troops to lure their opponents to destruction. When they catch sight of the enemy, they swoop down like a flock of birds, eager for booty, but when they find themselves hard pressed and beaten, they scatter and vanish like the mist. Anyone who succeeds in recovering the body of a comrade who has fallen in battle receives all of the dead man's property.

Shortly after the period described above, Mo-tun launched a series of campaigns to the north, conquering the tribes of Hun-yü, Ch'ü-she, Ting-ling, Ko-k'un, and Hsin-li. Thus the nobles and high ministers of the Hsiung-nu were all won over by Mo-tun, considering him a truly worthy leader.

At this time Kao-tsu, the founder of the Han, had just succeeded in winning control of the empire and had transferred Hsin, the former king of Hann, to the rulership of Tai, with his capital at Ma-i. The Hsiung-nu surrounded Ma-i and attacked the city in great force, whereupon Hann Hsin surrendered to them. With Hann Hsin on their side, they then proceeded to lead their troops south across Mount Chü-chu and attack T'ai-yüan, marching as far as the city of Chin-yang. Emperor Kao-tsu led an army in person to attack them, but it was winter and he encountered such cold and heavy snow that two or three out of every ten of his men lost their fingers from frostbite. Mo-tun feigned a retreat to lure the Han soldiers on to an attack. When they came after him in pursuit, he concealed all of his best troops and left only his weakest and puniest men to be observed by the Han scouts. With this the entire Han force, supplemented by three hundred and twenty thousand infantry, rushed north to pursue him; Kao-tsu led the way, advancing as far as the city of P'ing-ch'eng.

Before the infantry had had a chance to arrive, however, Mo-tun swooped down with four hundred thousand of his best cavalry, surrounded Kao-tsu on White Peak, and held him there for seven days. The Han forces within the encirclement had no way of receiving aid or provisions from their comrades outside, since the Hsiung-nu cavalry surrounded them on all sides, with white horses on the west side, greenish horses on the east, black horses on the north, and red ones on the south.[9]

Kao-tsu sent an envoy in secret to Mo-tun's consort, presenting her with generous gifts, whereupon she spoke to Mo-tun, saying, "Why should the rulers of these two nations make such trouble for each other? Even if you gained possession of the Han lands, you could never occupy them. And the ruler of the Han may have his guardian deities as well as you. I beg you to consider the matter well!"

Mo-tun had previously arranged for the troops of Wang Huang and Chao Li, two of Hann Hsin's generals, to meet with him, but though the appointed time had come, they failed to appear and he began to suspect that they were plotting with the Han forces. He therefore decided to listen to his consort's advice and withdrew his forces from one corner of the encirclement. Kao-tsu ordered his men to load their crossbows with arrows and hold them in readiness pointed toward the outside. These preparations completed, they marched straight out of the encirclement and finally joined up with the rest of the army.

Mo-tun eventually withdrew his men and went away, and Kao-tsu likewise retreated and abandoned the campaign, dispatching Liu Ching to conclude a peace treaty with the Hsiung-nu instead.

After this Hann Hsin became a general for the Hsiung-nu, and Chao Li and Wang Huang violated the peace treaty by invading and plundering Tai and Yün-chung. Shortly afterwards, Ch'en Hsi revolted and joined with Hann Hsin in a plot to attack Tai. Kao-tsu dispatched Fan K'uai to go and attack them; he recovered possession of the provinces and districts of Tai, Yen-men, and Yün-chung, but did not venture beyond the frontier.

At this time a number of Han generals had gone over to the side of the Hsiung-nu, and for this reason Mo-tun was constantly plundering the region of Tai and causing the Han great worry. Kao-tsu therefore dispatched Liu Ching to present a princess of the imperial family to the *Shan-yü* to be his consort. The Han agreed to send a gift of specified quantities of silk floss and cloth, grain, and other food stuffs each

[9] These four colors are symbolic of the four directions in Chinese belief and, if the narrative is correct, in Hsiung-nu belief as well.

year, and the two nations were to live in peace and brotherhood. After this Mo-tun raided the frontier less often than before. Later Lu Wan, the king of Yen, revolted and led his party of several thousand followers across the border to surrender to the Hsiung-nu; they roamed back and forth in the region from Shang-ku to the east, causing considerable disturbance.

After Emperor Kao-tsu passed away, Emperor Hui and Empress Lü in turn ruled the country. At this time the Han had just come to power and the Hsiung-nu, unimpressed by its strength, were behaving with great arrogance. Mo-tun even sent an insulting letter to Empress Lü.[10] She wanted to launch a campaign against him, but her generals reminded her that "even Emperor Kao-tsu, with all his wisdom and bravery, encountered great difficulty at P'ing-ch'eng," and she was finally persuaded to give up the idea and resume friendly relations with the Hsiung-nu.

When Emperor Wen came to the throne he renewed the peace treaty with the Hsiung-nu. In the fifth month of the third year of his reign [177 B.C.], however, the Hsiung-nu Wise King of the Right invaded the region south of the Yellow River, plundering the loyal barbarians of Shang Province who had been appointed by the Han to guard the frontier, and murdering and carrying off a number of the inhabitants. Emperor Wen ordered the chancellor Kuan Ying to lead a force of eighty-five thousand carriages and cavalry to Kao-nu, where they attacked the Wise King of the Right. The latter fled beyond the frontier. The emperor in person visited T'ai-yüan, at which time the king of Chi-pei revolted. When the emperor returned to the capital he disbanded the army which Kuan Ying had used in the attack on the barbarians.

The following year the *Shan-yü* sent a letter to the Han court which read:

The great *Shan-yü* whom Heaven has set up respectfully inquires of the emperor's health. Formerly the emperor broached the question of a peace alliance, and I was most happy to comply with the intentions expressed in his letter. Certain of the Han border officials, however, imposed upon and in-

[10] In his letter Mo-tun suggested that, since both he and Empress Lü were old and lonely, they might get together and console each other.

sulted the Wise King of the Right, and as a result he heeded the counsel of Hou-i, Lu-hou, Nan-chih, and others of his generals and, without asking my permission, engaged in a skirmish with the Han officials, thus violating the pact between the rulers of our two nations and rupturing the bonds of brotherhood that joined us. The emperor has twice sent letters complaining of this situation and I have in turn dispatched an envoy with my answer, but my envoy has not been allowed to return, nor has any envoy come from the Han. As a result, the Han has broken off peaceful relations and our two neighboring countries are no longer bound in alliance.

Because of the violation of the pact committed by the petty officials, and the subsequent events, I have punished the Wise King of the Right by sending him west to search out the Yüeh-chih people and attack them. Through the aid of Heaven, the excellence of his fighting men, and the strength of his horses, he has succeeded in wiping out the Yüeh-chih, slaughtering or forcing to submission every member of the tribe. In addition he has conquered the Lou-lan, Wu-sun, and Hu-chieh tribes, as well as the twenty-six states nearby, so that all of them have become a part of the Hsiung-nu nation. All the people who live by drawing the bow are now united into one family and the entire region of the north is at peace.

Thus I wish now to lay down my weapons, rest my soldiers, and turn my horses to pasture; to forget the recent affair and restore our old pact, that the peoples of the border may have peace such as they enjoyed in former times, that the young may grow to manhood, the old live out their lives in security, and generation after generation enjoy peace and comfort.

However, I do not as yet know the intentions of the emperor. Therefore I have dispatched my palace attendant Hsi-hu-ch'ien to bear this letter. At the same time I beg to present one camel, two riding horses, and eight carriage horses. If the emperor does not wish the Hsiung-nu to approach his frontier, then he should order the officials and people along the border to withdraw a good distance back from the frontier. When my envoy has arrived and delivered this, I trust that he will be sent back to me.

The envoy bearing the letter arrived in the region of Hsin-wang during the sixth month. When it was delivered to the emperor, he began deliberations with his ministers as to whether it was better to attack or make peace. The high officials all stated, "Since the *Shan-yü* has just conquered the Yüeh-chih and is riding on a wave of victory, he cannot be attacked. Moreover, even if we were to seize the Hsiung-nu lands, they are all swamps and saline wastes, not fit for habitation. It would be far better to make peace."

The emperor agreed with their opinion and in the sixth year of the former part of his reign [174 B.C.] he sent an envoy to the Hsiung-nu with a letter which read as follows:

The emperor respectfully inquires about the health of the great *Shan-yü*. Your palace attendant Hsi-hu-ch'ien has brought us a letter which states: "The Wise King of the Right, without asking my permission, heeded the counsel of Hou-i, Lu-hou, Nan-chih, and others of his generals, violating the pact between the rulers of our two nations and rupturing the bonds of brotherhood that joined us, and as a result the Han has broken off peaceful relations with me, and our two neighboring countries are no longer bound in alliance. Because of the violation of the pact committed by the petty officials, I have punished the Wise King of the Right by sending him west to attack the Yüeh-chih. Having completed the conquest of the region, I wish to lay down my weapons, rest my soldiers, and turn my horses to pasture; to forget the recent affair and restore our old pact so that the peoples of the border may have peace, the young may grow to manhood, the old live out their lives in security, and generation after generation enjoy peace and comfort."

We heartily approve these words. This indeed is the way the sage rulers of antiquity would have spoken.

The Han has made a pact of brotherhood with the Hsiung-nu, and for this reason we have sent generous gifts to you. Any violations of the pact or ruptures of the bonds of brotherhood have been the work of the Hsiung-nu. However, as there has been an amnesty since the affair of the Wise King of the Right occurred,[11] you need not punish him too severely. If your intentions are really those expressed in your letter, and if you will make them clearly known to your various officials so that they will henceforth act in good faith and commit no more violations of the pact, then we are prepared to honor the terms of your letter.

Your envoy tells us that you have led your troops in person to attack the

---

[11] It is not clear what amnesty this refers to. The *Han shu* "Annals of Emperor Wen" records a general amnesty in the seventh year (173 B.C.), but none for the years between the Hsiung-nu attack and the date of this letter. Perhaps the letter should be dated in the seventh year. The whole statement about the amnesty is of course no more than a cleverly phrased assertion of the Han emperor's sovereignty over the Hsiung-nu.

other barbarian nations and have won merit, suffering great hardship on the field of battle. We therefore send you from our own wardrobe an embroidered robe lined with patterned damask, an embroidered and lined underrobe, and a brocaded coat, one each; one comb; one sash with gold ornaments; one gold-ornamented leather belt; ten rolls of embroidery; thirty roles of brocade; and forty rolls each of heavy red silk and light green silk, which shall be delivered to you by our palace counselor I and master of guests Chien.

Shortly after this, Mo-tun died and his son Chi-chu was set up with the title of Old *Shan-yü*. When Chi-chu became *Shan-yü,* Emperor Wen sent a princess of the imperial family to be his consort, dispatching a eunuch from Yen named Chung-hsing Shuo to accompany her as her tutor. Chung-hsing Shuo did not wish to undertake the mission, but the Han officials forced him to do so. "My going will bring nothing but trouble to the Han!" he warned them.

After Chung-hsing Shuo reached his destination, he went over to the side of the *Shan-yü,* who treated him with the greatest favor.

The Hsiung-nu had always had a liking for Han silks and food stuffs, but Chung-hsing Shuo told them, "All the multitudes of the Hsiung-nu nation would not amount to one province in the Han empire. The strength of the Hsiung-nu lies in the very fact that their food and clothing are different from those of the Chinese, and they are therefore not dependent upon the Han for anything. Now the *Shan-yü* has this fondness for Chinese things and is trying to change the Hsiung-nu customs. Thus, although the Han sends no more than a fifth of its goods here, it will in the end succeed in winning over the whole Hsiung-nu nation. From now on, when you get any of the Han silks, put them on and try riding around on your horses through the brush and brambles! In no time your robes and leggings will be torn to shreds and everyone will be able to see that silks are no match for the utility and excellence of felt or leather garments. Likewise, when you get any of the Han foodstuffs, throw them away so that the people can see that they are not as practical or as tasty as milk and kumiss!"

He also taught the *Shan-yü*'s aides how to make an itemized accounting of the number of persons and domestic animals in the country.

The Han letters addressed to the *Shan-yü* were always written on wooden tablets one foot and one inch in length and began, "The emperor respectfully inquires about the health of the great *Shan-yü* of the Hsiung-nu. We send you the following articles, etc., etc." Chung-hsing Shuo, however, instructed the *Shan-yü* to use in replying to the Han a tablet measuring one foot two inches, decorated with broad stamps and great long seals, and worded in the following extravagant manner: "The great *Shan-yü* of the Hsiung-nu, born of Heaven and Earth and ordained by the sun and moon, respectfully inquires about the health of the Han emperor. We send you the following articles, etc., etc."

When one of the Han envoys to the Hsiung-nu remarked scornfully that Hsiung-nu custom showed no respect for the aged, Chung-hsing Shuo began to berate him. "According to Han custom," he said, "when the young men are called into military service and sent off with the army to garrison the frontier, do not their old parents at home voluntarily give up their warm clothing and tasty food so that there will be enough to provide for the troops?"

"Yes, they do," admitted the Han envoy.

"The Hsiung-nu make it clear that warfare is their business. And since the old and the weak are not capable of fighting, the best food and drink are naturally allotted to the young men in the prime of life. So the young men are willing to fight for the defense of the nation, and both fathers and sons are able to live out their lives in security. How can you say that the Hsiung-nu despise the aged?"

"But among the Hsiung-nu," the envoy continued, "fathers and sons sleep together in the same tent. And when a father dies, the sons marry their own stepmothers, and when brothers die, their remaining brothers marry their widows! These people know nothing of the elegance of hats and girdles, nor of the rituals of the court!"

"According to Hsiung-nu custom," replied Chung-hsing Shuo, "the people eat the flesh of their domestic animals, drink their milk, and wear their hides, while the animals graze from place to place, searching for pasture and water. Therefore, in wartime the men practice riding and shooting, while in times of peace they enjoy themselves and have nothing to do. Their laws are simple and easy to carry out; the relation between ruler and subject is relaxed and intimate, so that the governing of the whole nation is no more complicated than the governing of one person. The reason that sons marry their stepmothers and brothers marry their widowed sisters-in-law is simply that they hate to see the clan die out. Therefore, although the Hsiung-nu encounter times of turmoil, the ruling families always manage to stand firm. In China, on the other hand, though a man would never dream of marrying his stepmother or his brother's widow, yet the members of the same family drift so far apart that they end up murdering each other! This is precisely why so many changes of dynasty have come about in China! Moreover, among the Chinese, as etiquette and the sense of duty decay, enmity arises between the rulers and the ruled, while the excessive building of houses and dwellings exhausts the strength and resources of the nation. Men try to get their food and clothing by farming and raising silkworms and to insure their safety by building walls and fortifications. Therefore, although danger threatens, the Chinese people are given no training in aggressive warfare, while in times of stability they must still wear themselves out trying to make a living. Pooh! You people in your mud huts—you talk too much! Enough of this blabbering and mouthing! Just because you wear hats, what does that make you?"

After this, whenever the Han envoys would try to launch into any sermons or orations, Chung-hsing Shuo would cut them off at once. "Not so much talk from the Han envoys! Just make sure that the silks and grainstuffs you bring to the Hsiung-nu are of the right measure and quality, that's all. What's the need for talking? If the goods you deliver are up to measure and of good quality, all right. But if there is any deficiency or the quality is no good, then when the autumn harvest comes we will take our horses and trample all over your crops!"

Day and night he instructed the *Shan-yü* on how to maneuver into a more advantageous position.

In the fourteenth year of Emperor Wen's reign [166 B.C.] the *Shan-yü* led a force of one hundred and forty thousand horsemen through the Ch'ao-na and Hsiao passes, killing Sun Ang, the chief commandant of Pei-ti Province, and carrying off large numbers of people and animals. Eventually he rode as far as P'eng-yang, sent a surprise force to break into and burn the Hui-chung Palace, and dispatched scouts as far as the Palace of Sweet Springs in Yung.[12]

Emperor Wen appointed the palace military commander Chou She and the chief of palace attendants Chang Wu as generals and put them in command of a force of a thousand chariots and a hundred thousand horsemen to garrison the vicinity of Ch'ang-an and guard the capital from the barbarian invaders. He also appointed Lu Ch'ing, the marquis of Ch'ang, as general of Shang Province; Wei Su, the marquis of Ning, as general of Pei-ti; Chou Tsao, the marquis of Lung-lü, as general of Lung-hsi; Chang Hsiang-ju, the marquis of Tung-yang, as general in chief; and Tung Ch'ih, the marquis of Ch'eng, as general of the vanguard, and sent them with a large force of chariots and cavalry to attack the barbarians. The *Shan-yü* remained within the borders of the empire for a little over a month and then withdrew. The Han forces pursued him beyond the frontier but returned without having been able to kill any of the enemy.

The Hsiung-nu grew more arrogant day by day, crossing the border every year, killing many of the inhabitants, and stealing their animals. Yün-chung and Liao-hsi suffered most severely, while in Tai Province alone over ten thousand persons were killed. The Han court, greatly distressed, sent an envoy with a letter to the Hsiung-nu, and the *Shan-yü* in turn dispatched one of his household administrators to apologize and request a renewal of the peace alliance.

In the second year of the latter part of his reign [162 B.C.] Emperor Wen sent an envoy to the Hsiung-nu with a letter that read:

The emperor respectfully inquires about the health of the great *Shan-yü.* Your envoys, the household administrator and *chü-ch'ü* Tiao Ch'ü-nan and the palace attendant Han Liao, have delivered to us two horses, which we have respectfully accepted.

According to the decree of the former emperor, the land north of the Great Wall, where men wield the bow and arrow, was to receive its commands from the *Shan-yü,* while that within the wall, whose inhabitants dwell in houses and wear hats and girdles, was to be ruled by us; thus might the countless inhabitants of these lands gain their food and clothing by agricul-

---

[12] Bringing them within sight of the capital.

ture, weaving, or hunting; father and son live side by side; ruler and minister enjoy mutual security; and all forsake violence and rebellion. Now we have heard that certain evil and deluded men, succumbing greedily to the lure of gain, have turned their backs upon righteousness and violated the peace alliance, forgetting the fate of the countless inhabitants and disrupting the concord which existed between the rulers of our two states.

This, however, is an affair of the past. In your letter, you say that "since our two countries have been joined again in peace and the two rulers are once more in concord," you desire "to rest your soldiers and turn your horses to pasture, in order that generation after generation may know prosperity and joy and we may make a new beginning in peace and harmony." We heartily approve these words. The sage, it is said, renews himself daily, reforming and making a new beginning in order that the old people may have rest and the young grow to manhood, that each may preserve his own life and fulfill the years which Heaven has granted him. So long as we and the *Shan-yü* join in walking this road, following the will of Heaven and pitying the people, bestowing the blessing of peace on generation after generation without end, then there will be no one in the whole world who will not benefit.

Our two great nations, the Han and the Hsiung-nu, stand side by side. Since the Hsiung-nu dwell in the north, where the land is cold and the killing frosts come early, we have decreed that our officials shall send to the *Shan-yü* each year a fixed quantity of millet, leaven, gold, silk cloth, thread, floss, and other articles.

Now the world enjoys profound peace and the people are at rest. We and the *Shan-yü* must be as parents to them. When we consider past affairs, we realize that it is only because of petty matters and trifling reasons that the plans of our ministers have failed. No such matters are worthy to disrupt the harmony that exists between brothers.

We have heard it said that Heaven shows no partiality in sheltering mankind, and Earth no bias in bearing it up. Let us, then, with the *Shan-yü*, cast aside these trifling matters of the past and walk the great road together, wiping out former evils and planning for the distant future, in order that the peoples of our two states may be joined together like the sons of a single family. Then, from the countless multitudes of the people down to the very fish and turtles, the birds which fly above, all creatures that walk or breathe or move, there will be none that fail to find peace and profit and relief from peril.

To allow men to come and go without hindrance is the way of Heaven.

Let us both forget past affairs. We have pardoned those of our subjects who fled to the Hsiung-nu or were taken prisoner. Let the *Shan-yü* likewise ask no further concerning Chang Ni and the other Hsiung-nu leaders who surrendered to us.

We have heard that the rulers of ancient times made their promises clearly known and that, once they had given their consent, they did not go back on their words. The *Shan-yü* should consider this well, so that all the world may enjoy profound peace. Once the peace alliance has been concluded, the Han shall not be the first to violate it! Let the *Shan-yü* ponder these words!

When the *Shan-yü* expressed his willingness to abide by the peace agreement, Emperor Wen issued an edict to the imperial secretary which read:

The great *Shan-yü* of the Hsiung-nu has sent us a letter signifying that the peace alliance has been concluded. No action need be taken concerning those who have fled from one state to the other, since they are not sufficiently numerous to affect the population or size of our territories. The Hsiung-nu shall not enter within our borders, nor shall the Han forces venture beyond the frontier. Anyone who violates this agreement shall be executed. It is to the advantage of both nations that they should live in lasting friendship without further aggression. We have given our consent to this alliance, and now we wish to publish it abroad to the world so that all may clearly understand it.

Four years later the Old *Shan-yü* Chi-chu died and was succeeded by his son Chün-ch'en. After Chün-ch'en assumed the title of *Shan-yü,* Emperor Wen once more renewed the former peace alliance. Chunghsing Shuo continued to act as adviser to the new *Shan-yü.*

A little over a year after Chün-ch'en became *Shan-yü* [158 B.C.] [13] the Hsiung-nu again violated the peace alliance, invading Shang and Yünchung provinces in great numbers; thirty thousand horsemen attacked each province, killing and carrying off great numbers of the inhabitants before withdrawing. The emperor dispatched three generals with armies to garrison Pei-ti, the Chü-chu Pass in Tai, and the Flying Fox Pass in Chao, at the same time ordering the other garrisons along the border to guard their defenses in order to hold off the barbarians. He also stationed three armies in the vicinity of Ch'ang-an at Hsi-liu, at

[13] Following the reading in *Han shu* 94A.

Chi-men north of the Wei River, and at the Pa River, so as to be prepared for the barbarians in case they entered that area. The Hsiung-nu cavalry poured through the Chü-chu Pass in Tai, and the signal fires along the border flashed the news of their invasion to Ch'ang-an and the Palace of Sweet Springs. After several months the Han troops reached the border, but by that time the Hsiung-nu had already withdrawn far beyond and the Han troops were recalled.

A year or so later Emperor Wen passed away and Emperor Ching came to the throne. At this time Liu Sui, the king of Chao, sent envoys in secret to negotiate with the Hsiung-nu. When Wu, Ch'u, Chao, and the other states revolted, the Hsiung-nu planned to cooperate with Chao and cross the border, but the Han forces besieged and defeated the king of Chao, and the Hsiung-nu called off their plans for an invasion.

After this Emperor Ching once more renewed the peace alliance with the Hsiung-nu, allowing them to buy goods in the markets along the Han border and sending them supplies and a princess of the imperial family, as had been done under the earlier agreements. Thus, throughout Emperor Ching's reign, although the Hsiung-nu from time to time made small plundering raids across the border, they did not carry out any major invasion.

When the present emperor came to the throne he reaffirmed the peace alliance and treated the Hsiung-nu with generosity, allowing them to trade in the markets of the border stations and sending them lavish gifts. From the *Shan-yü* on down, all the Hsiung-nu grew friendly with the Han, coming and going along the Great Wall.

The emperor then dispatched Nieh Weng-i, a native of the city of Ma-i, to carry contraband goods to the Hsiung-nu and begin trading with them. This done, Nieh Weng-i deceived them by offering to hand over the city of Ma-i to the *Shan-yü*, intending by this ruse to lure him into the area. The *Shan-yü* trusted Nieh Weng-i and, greedy for the wealth of Ma-i, set out with a force of a hundred thousand cavalry and crossed the border at the barrier of Wu-chou. The Han in the meantime had concealed three hundred thousand troops in the vicinity of Ma-i, headed by four generals under the imperial secretary Han An-kuo, who was the leader of the expeditionary forces, ready to spring on the *Shan-yü* when he arrived.

The *Shan-yü* crossed the Han border but was still some hundred *li* from Ma-i when he began to notice that, although the fields were full of animals, there was not a single person in sight. Growing suspicious, he attacked one of the beacon warning stations. A defense official of Yen-men who had been patrolling the area but had caught sight of the barbarian invaders had at this time taken refuge in the warning station, for he knew of the plan of the Han forces to ambush them. When the *Shan-yü* attacked and captured the warning station, he was about to put the defense official to death when the latter informed him of the Han troops hiding in the valley. "I suspected as much!" exclaimed the *Shan-yü* in great alarm, and proceeded to lead his forces back to the border. After they had safely crossed the border he remarked, "Heaven was on my side when I captured this defense official. In effect Heaven sent you to warn me!" and he awarded the defense official the title of "Heavenly King."

The Han forces had agreed to wait until the *Shan-yü* had entered Ma-i before launching their attack but, since he never proceeded that far, they had no opportunity to strike. Meanwhile another Han general, Wang Hui, had been ordered to lead a special force from Tai and attack the Hsiung-nu baggage train, but when he heard that the *Shan-yü* had retreated and that his forces were extremely numerous, he did not dare to make an attack. When it was all over the Han officials condemned Wang Hui to execution on the grounds that, though he was the one who had engineered the entire plot, he had failed to advance when the time came.

After this the Hsiung-nu broke off friendly relations with the Han and began to attack the border defenses wherever they happened to be. Time and again they crossed the frontier and carried out innumerable plundering raids. At the same time they continued to be as greedy as ever, delighting in the border markets and longing for Han goods, and the Han for its part continued to allow them to trade in the markets in order to sap their resources.

Five years after the Ma-i campaign, in the autumn [129 B.C.], the

Han government dispatched four generals, each with a force of ten thousand cavalry, to make a surprise attack on the barbarians at the border markets. General Wei Ch'ing rode out of Shang-ku as far as Lung-ch'eng, killing or capturing seven hundred of the enemy. Kung-sun Ho proceeded from Yün-men, but took no captives. Kung-sun Ao rode north from Tai Province, but was defeated by the barbarians and lost over seven thousand of his men. Li Kuang advanced from Yen-men, but was defeated and captured, though he later managed to escape and return to the Han. On their return, Kung-sun Ao and Li Kuang were thrown into prison by the Han officials but were allowed to purchase a pardon for their offenses and were reduced to the status of commoners.

In the winter the Hsiung-nu several times crossed the border on plundering expeditions, hitting hardest at Yü-yang. The emperor dispatched General Han An-kuo to garrison Yü-yang and protect it from the barbarians. In the autumn of the following year twenty thousand Hsiung-nu horsemen invaded the empire, murdered the governor of Liao-hsi, and carried off over two thousand prisoners. They also invaded Yü-yang, defeated the army of over a thousand under the command of the governor of Yü-yang, and surrounded Han An-kuo's camp. Han An-kuo at this time had a force of over a thousand horsemen under his command, but before long even these were on the point of being wiped out. Relief forces arrived from Yen just in time, and the Hsiung-nu withdrew. The Hsiung-nu also invaded Yen-men and killed or carried off over a thousand persons.

The Han then dispatched General Wei Ch'ing with a force of thirty thousand cavalry to ride north from Yen-men, and Li Hsi to ride out from Tai Province to attack the barbarians. They succeeded in killing or capturing several thousand of the enemy.

The following year Wei Ch'ing again rode out of Yün-chung and proceeded west as far as Lung-hsi, attacking the kings of the Lou-fan and Po-yang barbarians south of the Yellow River, capturing or killing several thousand of the enemy, and seizing over a million cattle and sheep. Thus the Han regained control of the area south of the bend of the Yellow River and began to build fortifications at So-fang, repairing the old system of defenses that had been set up by Meng T'ien during the Ch'in dynasty and strengthening the frontier along the Yellow River. The Han also abandoned claims to the district of Shih-pi and the region of Tsao-yang that had formed the extreme northern part of the province of Shang-ku, handing them over to the Hsiung-nu. This took place in the second year of the era *yüan-so* [127 B.C.].

The following winter the *Shan-yü* Chün-ch'en died and his younger brother, the Lu-li King of the Left, I-chih-hsieh, set himself up as *Shan-yü*. He attacked and defeated Chün-ch'en's heir, Yü-tan, who fled and surrendered to the Han. The Han enfeoffed Yü-tan as marquis of She-an, but he died several months later.

The summer after I-chih-hsieh became *Shan-yü* the Hsiung-nu invaded the province of Tai with twenty or thirty thousand cavalry, murdering the governor, Kung Yu, and carrying off over a thousand persons. In the fall the Hsiung-nu struck again, this time at Yen-men, killing or carrying off over a thousand of the inhabitants. The following year they once more invaded Tai, Ting-hsiang, and Shang Provinces with thirty thousand cavalry in each group, killing or carrying off several thousand persons. The Wise King of the Right, angry that the Han had seized the territory south of the Yellow River and built fortifications at So-fang, several times crossed the border on plundering raids; he even went so far as to invade the region south of the river, ravaging So-fang and killing or carrying off a large number of the officials and inhabitants.

In the spring of the following year [124 B.C.] the Han made Wei Ch'ing a general in chief and sent him with an army of over a hundred thousand men and six generals to proceed north from So-fang and Kao-ch'üeh and strike at the barbarians. The Wise King of the Right, convinced that the Han forces could never penetrate far enough north to reach him, had drunk himself into a stupor when the Han army, marching six or seven hundred *li* beyond the border, appeared and surrounded him in the night. The king, greatly alarmed, barely escaped with his life, and his best horsemen managed to break away in small groups and follow after him; the Han, however, succeeded in capturing fifteen thousand of his men and women, including over ten petty kings.

In the autumn a Hsiung-nu force of ten thousand cavalry invaded

Tai Province, killed the chief commandant Chu Ying, and carried off over a thousand men.

In the spring of the following year [123 B.C.] the Han again dispatched the general in chief Wei Ch'ing with six generals and a force of over a hundred thousand cavalry; they rode several hundred *li* north from Ting-hsiang and attacked the Hsiung-nu. All in all they succeeded in killing or capturing over nineteen thousand of the enemy, but in the engagements the Han side lost two generals and over three thousand cavalry. Of the two generals one of them, Su Chien, the general of the right, managed to escape, but the other, Chao Hsin, the marquis of Hsi, who was acting as general of the vanguard, surrendered to the Hsiung-nu when he saw that his men could not win a victory.

Chao Hsin was originally a petty king of the Hsiung-nu who later went over to the side of the Han. The Han enfeoffed him as marquis of Hsi and made him general of the vanguard, sending him to accompany Su Chien, the general of the right, on a different line of advance from that of the rest of the expedition. Chao Hsin and the forces under his command were alone, however, when they encountered the *Shan-yü's* men, and as a result his troops were wiped out. The *Shan-yü,* having accepted Chao Hsin's surrender, appointed him to the rank of *Tzu-tz'u* king, gave him his own sister as a wife, and began to plot with him against the Han. Chao Hsin advised the *Shan-yü* to withdraw farther north beyond the desert instead of maneuvering near the Chinese border. In this way he would be able to lure the Han troops after him and, when they were thoroughly exhausted, take advantage of their weakness to wipe them out. The *Shan-yü* agreed to follow this plan.

The following year ten thousand barbarian horsemen invaded Shang-ku and killed several hundred inhabitants.

In the spring of the next year [121 B.C.] the Han dispatched the general of swift cavalry Ho Ch'ü-ping to lead ten thousand cavalry out of Lung-hsi. They rode more than a thousand *li* beyond Mount Yen-chih and attacked the Hsiung-nu, killing or capturing over eighteen thousand of the enemy cavalry, defeating the Hsiu-t'u king, and seizing the golden man which he used in worshiping Heaven.[14]

---

[14] Scholars have long speculated whether the "golden man" might not have been a Buddhist image. If so, this passage would mark the earliest record of Chinese contact with the Buddhist religion.

In the summer Ho Ch'ü-ping, accompanied by Kung-sun Ao, the Ho-ch'i marquis, led a force of twenty or thirty thousand cavalry some two thousand *li* out of Lung-hsi and Pei-ti to attack the barbarians. They passed Chü-yen, attacked in the region of the Ch'i-lien Mountains, and captured or killed over thirty thousand of the enemy, including seventy or more petty kings and their subordinates.

Meanwhile the Hsiung-nu invaded Yen-men in Tai Province, killing or carrying off several hundred persons. The Han dispatched Chang Ch'ien, the Po-wang marquis, and General Li Kuang to ride out of Yu-pei-p'ing and attack the Hsiung-nu Wise King of the Left. The Wise King of the Left surrounded Li Kuang's army and came near to wiping out his four thousand men, though he managed to inflict extraordinary damage on the enemy. Chang Ch'ien's forces came to the rescue just in time and Li Kuang was able to escape, but the Han losses amounted to several thousand men. When the armies returned to the capital, Kung-sun Ao was accused of having arrived late at a rendezvous with Ho Ch'ü-ping and was condemned to die along with Chang Ch'ien; both men purchased pardons and were reduced to the rank of commoners.

The *Shan-yü* was angry at the Hun-yeh and Hsiu-t'u kings who lived in the western part of his domain because they had allowed the Han to capture or kill twenty or thirty thousand of their men; in the autumn he sent them a summons, intending to execute them. The Hun-yeh and Hsiu-t'u kings, terrified, sent word to the Han that they were willing to surrender. The Han dispatched Ho Ch'ü-ping to go and meet them, but on the way the Hun-yeh king murdered the Hsiu-t'u king and combined the latter's forces with his own. When he surrendered to the Han, he had a force of over forty thousand men, though it was commonly referred to as a force of a hundred thousand. Having gained the allegiance of the Hun-yeh king, the Han found itself far less troubled by barbarian invasions in the regions of Lung-hsi, Pei-ti, and Ho-hsi. It therefore moved a number of poor people from east of the Pass to the region south of the bend of the Yellow River known as New Ch'in, which had been seized from the Hsiung-nu, in order to populate the area, and reduced the number of garrison troops along the border west of Pei-ti to half.

The following year [120 B.C.] the Hsiung-nu invaded Yu-pei-p'ing and Ting-hsiang with a force of twenty or thirty thousand cavalry in each region, killing or carrying off over a thousand persons before withdrawing.

In the spring of the following year [119 B.C.] the Han strategists plotted together, saying, "Chao Hsin, the marquis of Hsi, who is acting as adviser to the *Shan-yü,* is convinced that, since the Hsiung-nu are living north of the desert, the Han forces can never reach them." They agreed therefore to fatten the horses on grain and send out a force of a hundred thousand cavalry, along with a hundred and forty thousand horses to carry baggage and other equipment (this in addition to the horses provided for transporting provisions). They ordered the force to split up into two groups commanded by the general in chief Wei Ch'ing and the general of swift cavalry Ho Ch'ü-ping. The former was to ride out of Ting-hsiang and the latter out of Tai; it was agreed that the entire force would cross the desert and attack the Hsiung-nu.

When the *Shan-yü* received word of the approach of these armies, he ordered his baggage trains to withdraw to a distance and, with his finest soldiers, waited on the northern edge of the desert, where he closed in battle with the army of Wei Ch'ing. The battle continued throughout the day and, as evening fell, a strong wind arose. With this the Han forces swooped out to the left and right and surrounded the *Shan-yü.* The *Shan-yü,* perceiving that he was no match for the Han forces, abandoned his army and, accompanied by only a few hundred of his finest horsemen, broke through the Han encirclement and fled to the northwest. The Han forces set out after him in the night and, though they did not succeed in capturing him, cut down or seized nineteen thousand of the enemy on the way. They proceeded north as far as Chao Hsin's fort at Mount T'ien-yen before turning back.

After the *Shan-yü* had fled, his soldiers, mingling with the Han forces in the confusion, little by little made their way after him. It was therefore a considerable time before the *Shan-yü* was able to reassemble his army again. The Lu-li king of the right, believing that the *Shan-yü* had been killed in battle, declared himself the new *Shan-yü,* but when the real *Shan-yü* gathered his forces together again the Lu-li king renounced the title and resumed his former position.

Ho Ch'ü-ping had meanwhile advanced some two thousand *li* north from Tai and closed in battle with the Hsiung-nu Wise King of the Left. The Han forces killed or captured over seventy thousand of the enemy and the wise king and his generals all fled. Ho Ch'ü-ping performed a Feng sacrifice at Mount Lang-chü-hsü and a Shan sacrifice at Mount Ku-yen, gazing out across the sea of sand before returning. After this the Hsiung-nu withdrew far from the Chinese border, and their leaders no longer established their courts south of the desert.

In the territory beyond the Yellow River from So-fang west to Ling-chü the Han established irrigation works and set up garrison farms here and there, sending fifty or sixty thousand officials and soldiers to man them. Gradually the farms ate up more and more territory until they bordered the lands of the Hsiung-nu to the north.

In the campaign just concluded, when the two Han generals advanced north in great force and surrounded the *Shan-yü,* the Han had succeeded in killing or capturing eighty or ninety thousand of the enemy. At the same time, however, twenty or thirty thousand Han soldiers lost their lives in the expedition and over a hundred thousand horses were killed. Thus, although the Hsiung-nu had withdrawn far to the north to nurse their wounds, the Han, being short of horses, was unable to strike at them again. Following the advice of Chao Hsin, the Hsiung-nu dispatched an envoy to the Han court to use soft words and request a peace alliance. When the emperor referred the proposal to his ministers for deliberation, some of them spoke in favor of a peace pact, while others urged that the Han pursue the Hsiung-nu and force them to submission. Jen Ch'ang, the chief secretary to the chancellor, announced his opinion, "Since the Hsiung-nu have just recently been defeated and their spirits broken, they should be treated as foreign vassals and required to come to the border in the spring and autumn to pay their respects to the Han."

The emperor accordingly sent Jen Ch'ang to the *Shan-yü* with this counterproposal. When the *Shan-yü* heard Jen Ch'ang's suggestion, he flew into a rage and detained him in his camp, refusing to send him back to China. (Earlier, one of the Hsiung-nu envoys had gone over to the side of the Han and remained in China and the *Shan-yü* therefore detained Jen Ch'ang by way of retaliation.)

The Han then began to gather together a force of men and horses in preparation for another campaign, but just at that time the general of swift cavalry Ho Ch'ü-ping died and so for several years the Han made no further attacks on the Hsiung-nu.

The *Shan-yü* I-chih-hsieh, after having ruled for thirteen years, died and was succeeded by his son Wu-wei. This occurred in the third year of the *yüan-ting* era [114 B.C.]. At the time that Wu-wei became *Shan-yü*, the Son of Heaven made his first imperial tour of the various provinces, and after that the Han armies were busy in the south putting down the rebellion in the two kingdoms of Southern and Eastern Yüeh, so no attacks were made on the Hsiung-nu. The Hsiung-nu for their part likewise made no raids across the border.

Three years after Wu-wei became *Shan-yü* the Han, having wiped out the kingdom of Southern Yüeh, dispatched the former master of carriage Kung-sun Ho at the head of a force of fifteen thousand cavalry; they rode more than two thousand *li* north from Chiu-yüan, advancing as far as Fu-chü-ching before turning back, but they did not catch sight of a single Hsiung-nu. The Han also dispatched Chao P'o-nu, the former Ts'ung-p'iao marquis, with over ten thousand cavalry to ride out of Ling-chü; Chao P'o-nu proceeded several thousand *li,* reaching the Hsiung-ho River before turning back, but he too failed to see a single Hsiung-nu.

At this time the emperor was making a tour of the border. When he reached So-fang, he held an inspection of one hundred and eighty thousand cavalry soldiers in order to make a display of military might, at the same time dispatching a man named Kuo Chi to the *Shan-yü* to make sure that the Hsiung-nu were fully informed of the event.

When Kuo Chi reached the Hsiung-nu, the Hsiung-nu master of guests asked him what his business was. Replying in very polite and humble terms, Kuo Chi said, "I would like to wait until I am granted an audience with the *Shan-yü* before stating my business."

When he was shown before the *Shan-yü* he said, "The head of the king of Southern Yüeh hangs above the northern gate of the Han capital. Now, if you are able, advance and engage the Han forces in battle! The Son of Heaven has led his troops in person and is waiting on the border. But if you are not able, then turn your face to the south and acknowledge yourself a subject of the Han! Why this useless running away and hiding far off north of the desert in a cold and bitter land where there is no water or pasture? It will get you nowhere!"

When he had finished speaking, the *Shan-yü,* livid with rage, ordered the master of guests who had ushered him in to be cut down on the spot. He detained Kuo Chi and would not let him return to China; later he moved him to the shore of the Northern Sea [Lake Baikal]. In the end, however, the *Shan-yü* refused to be provoked into invading the Han border but turned his horses to pasture, rested his troops, and practiced archery and hunting instead, sending envoys to the Han from time to time to speak with soft words and honeyed phrases and request a peace alliance.

The Han in turn sent Wang Wu and others as envoys to observe the Hsiung-nu. According to Hsiung-nu law, unless an envoy from the Han surrendered his credentials and allowed his face to be tattooed in black, he would not be admitted to the *Shan-yü's* tent. Wang Wu had been born in the north and was familiar with the barbarian customs, and therefore he readily gave up his credentials, submitted to the tattooing, and was able to gain admittance to the *Shan-yü's* tent. The *Shan-yü* showed a great liking for him and pretended to agree amiably with whatever he said, even with the suggestion that he send his son, the heir apparent to the position of *Shan-yü,* as a hostage to the Han in order to secure a peace alliance. The Han then dispatched Yang Hsin as envoy to the Hsiung-nu.

At this time the Han forces in the east had conquered the barbarian states of Hui-mo and Ch'ao-hsien and made provinces out of them, while in the west the Han had created the province of Chiu-ch'üan in order to drive a wedge between the Hsiung-nu and the Ch'iang barbarians and cut off communications between them. It had also established relations with the Yüeh-chih people and Ta-hsia [Bactria] farther west and had sent an imperial princess to marry the ruler of the Wu-sun people, all in an effort to create a split between the Hsiung-nu and the states to the west which had up to this time aided and supported them. In addition, the Han continued to expand its agricultural lands in the north until the frontier had been pushed out as far as Hsüan-lei. In spite of all these moves, however, the Hsiung-nu did not dare to voice any objections. This year Chao Hsin, the marquis of Hsi, who had been acting as adviser to the *Shan-yü*, died.

The Han administrators believed that the Hsiung-nu had already been sufficiently weakened and could now be made to acknowledge themselves subjects of the Han and submit to Chinese rule, and therefore they had dispatched Yang Hsin as envoy to the *Shan-yü*. But Yang Hsin was by nature very outspoken and unyielding and had never been high in the Han bureaucracy; the *Shan-yü* showed no liking for him. When summoned for an interview in the *Shan-yü's* tent, he refused to surrender his credentials, and so the *Shan-yü* had mats spread outside his tent and received Yang Hsin there. "If you wish to conclude a peace alliance," Yang Hsin announced when he had been shown into the *Shan-yü's* presence, "you must send your heir to the Han court as a hostage!"

"That is not the way things were done under the old alliance!" the *Shan-yü* objected. "Under the old alliance the Han always sent us an imperial princess, as well as allotments of silks, foodstuffs, and other goods, in order to secure peace, while we for our part refrained from making trouble on the border. Now you want to go against the old ways and make me send my son as a hostage. I have no use for such proposals!"

It is the way with the Hsiung-nu that, whenever an envoy from the Han comes who is not a high court official, if he is the scholarly Confucian type, they assume that he has come to lecture them and they do all they can to squelch his rhetoric, while if he is a young man, they assume he has come with assassination in mind and concentrate on destroying his nerve. Every time a Han envoy arrives among the Hsiung-nu, they send an envoy of their own to the Han in exchange. If the Han detains the Hsiung-nu envoy, then the Hsiung-nu detain the Han envoy and will not release him until they have received what they consider just treatment.

After Yang Hsin returned from his mission to the Hsiung-nu, the Han dispatched Wang Wu again, and once more the *Shan-yü* began to talk in a mild and conciliatory way, hoping to be given a sizable grant of Han goods. As part of the deception he told Wang Wu, "I would like to make a trip to the Han and visit the Son of Heaven so that face to face we may swear a pact of brotherhood!"

When Wang Wu returned and reported on his mission, the Han built a residence for the *Shan-yü* in Ch'ang-an. The *Shan-yü*, however, sent word that "unless some important member of the Han government is sent as envoy, I cannot discuss the matter seriously."

Meanwhile the Hsiung-nu dispatched one of their important men as envoy to the Han. When the man reached China, however, he fell ill and, although the Han doctors gave him medicine and tried to cure him, he unfortunately died. The Han then sent Lu Ch'ung-kuo to act as envoy and to accompany the body of the dead Hsiung-nu back to his country, spending several thousand gold pieces on a lavish funeral for him. Lu Ch'ung-kuo was given the seals of a two-thousand picul official to wear at his belt and bore assurances to the Hsiung-nu that "this man is an important official of the Han." The *Shan-yü*, however, was convinced that the Han had murdered the Hsiung-nu envoy and therefore detained Lu Ch'ung-kuo and refused to let him return to China. By this time everyone on the Han side was of the opinion that the *Shan-yü* had only been deceiving Wang Wu with empty talk and in fact had no intention of coming to China or sending his son as a hostage. After this the Hsiung-nu several times sent surprise parties of troops to raid the border, and the Han for its part conferred on Kuo Ch'ang the title of "Barbarian Quelling General" and sent Chao P'o-nu, the marquis of Cho-yeh, to garrison the area from So-fang to the east and defend it against the Hsiung-nu.

Lu Ch'ung-kuo had been detained by the Hsiung-nu for three years when the *Shan-yü* Wu-wei died, having ruled for ten years. He was succeeded by his son, Wu-shih-lu. Wu-shih-lu was still young and was therefore called the Boy *Shan-yü*. The change took place in the sixth year of the *yüan-feng* era [105 B.C.].

After this the *Shan-yü* gradually moved farther to the northwest, so that the soldiers of his left or eastern wing occupied the area north of Yün-chung, while those of his right wing were in the area around Chiu-ch'üan and Tun-huang provinces.

When the Boy *Shan-yü* came to power the Han dispatched two envoys, one to the new *Shan-yü* to convey condolences on the death of his father, and the other to convey condolences to the Wise King of the Right, hoping in this way to cause dissension between the two leaders. When the envoys entered Hsiung-nu territory, however, the Hsiung-nu guides led them both to the *Shan-yü*. The *Shan-yü*, discovering what they were up to, was furious and detained them both. The Hsiung-nu had already detained over ten Han envoys in the past, while the Han had likewise detained a proportionate number of Hsiung-nu envoys. This same year the Han sent the Sutrishna General Li Kuang-li west to attack Ta-yüan [Ferghana] and ordered the Yin-yü General Kung-sun Ao to build a fortified city called Shou-chiang-ch'eng, the "City for Receiving Surrender."

In the winter the Hsiung-nu were afflicted by heavy snowfalls, and many of their animals died of starvation and cold. The *Shan-yü*, still a young boy, had a great fondness for warfare and slaughter, and many of his subjects were restless under his leadership. The Hsiung-nu chief commandant of the left wanted to assassinate the *Shan-yü* and sent a messenger in secret to report to the Han, "I wish to assassinate the *Shan-yü* and surrender to the Han, but the Han is too far away. If the Han will send a party of troops to meet me, however, I will at once carry out the plot."

It was in fact because of this report that the Han had built the fortified City for Receiving Surrender. But the Han still considered that the chief commandant of the left was too far away to carry out his plot successfully.

In the spring of the following year the Han sent Chao P'o-nu, the marquis of Cho-yeh, to lead a force of over twenty thousand cavalry some two thousand *li* northwest from So-fang and make contact with the chief commandant of the left at Mount Chün-chi before returning. Chao P'o-nu arrived at the point of rendezvous but, before the chief commandant of the left could carry out the assassination, his plot was discovered. The *Shan-yü* had him executed and dispatched the forces from his left wing to attack Chao P'o-nu. Chao P'o-nu had by this time begun to withdraw, taking prisoners and killing several thousand Hsiung-nu soldiers on the way. When he was still four hundred *li* from the City for Receiving Surrender, however, eighty thousand Hsiung-nu cavalry swooped down and surrounded him. Chao P'o-nu slipped out of the encirclement during the night and went by himself to look for water, but was captured alive by Hsiung-nu scouts. The main body of the Hsiung-nu then pressed their attack on Chao P'o-nu's army. Kuo Tsung and Wei Wang, two of the high officers in the Han army, plotted together, saying, "All of us, down to the company commanders, are afraid that, having lost our commanding general, we will be executed under military law. Therefore no one is anxious to return home." Eventually the whole army surrendered to the Hsiung-nu. The Boy *Shan-yü* was delighted with his catch and sent a raiding party to attack the City for Receiving Surrender, but the city held fast. The party then plundered the border area and withdrew.

The following year the *Shan-yü* again set out to attack the City for Receiving Surrender, this time in person, but before he reached his destination he fell ill and died. He had been *Shan-yü* only three years. Since his son was still very small, the Hsiung-nu appointed his uncle Kou-li-hu, the former Wise King of the Right and younger brother of the *Shan-yü* Wu-wei, as the new *Shan-yü*. This took place in the third year of the era *t'ai-ch'u* [102 B.C.].

After Kou-li-hu had become *Shan-yü* the Han sent the superintendent of the imperial household Hsü Tzu-wei to ride out of the barrier at Wu-yüan and range through the area from several hundred to a thousand *li* or more north of the border, building forts and watch stations as far as Mount Lu-ch'ü. The Han also dispatched the scouting and attacking general Han Yüeh and the marquis of Ch'ang-p'ing, Wei K'ang, to garrison the region, at the same time sending the chief commandant of strong crossbowmen Lu Po-te to build fortifications along the swamp at Chü-yen.

In the autumn the Hsiung-nu invaded Ting-hsiang and Yün-chung in great force, murdering or carrying off several thousand persons. They also defeated several officials of the two thousand picul rank before withdrawing, and destroyed the forts and watch stations that Hsü Tzu-wei had built as they went along. At the same time the Wise King of the Right invaded Chiu-ch'üan and Chang-i provinces and carried off several thousand persons. The Han general Jen Wen, however, came to the rescue, attacking the Hsiung-nu and forcing them to give up all the spoils and prisoners they had taken.

This year the Sutrishna General Li Kuang-li defeated the kingdom of Ta-yüan, cut off the head of its ruler, and returned. The Hsiung-nu tried to block his return but could not reach him in time. In the winter they planned an attack on the City for Receiving Surrender, but just at that time the *Shan-yü* died. The *Shan-yü* Kou-li-hu had ruled for only a year when he died. The Hsiung-nu set up his younger brother, Chü-ti-hou, the former chief commandant of the left, as *Shan-yü*.

At this time the Han had just conquered the kingdom of Ta-yüan, and its might filled the neighboring states with terror. The emperor had hopes of carrying out the final suppression of the Hsiung-nu and issued an edict which read:

Emperor Kao-tsu has left us the task of avenging the difficulties which he suffered at P'ing-ch'eng. Furthermore, during the reign of Empress Lü the *Shan-yü* sent to the court a most treasonable and insulting letter. In ancient times when Duke Hsiang of Ch'i avenged an insult which one of his ancestors nine generations earlier had suffered, Confucius praised his conduct in the *Spring and Autumn Annals*.

This year was the fourth year of the era *t'ai-ch'u* [101 B.C.].[15]

After Chü-ti-hou became *Shan-yü* he returned all of the Han envoys who had not gone over to his side. Thus Lu Ch'ung-kuo and the others were able to come home. When the new *Shan-yü* assumed the rule, he was afraid that the Han would attack him and so he said, "I consider that I am but a little child. How could I hope to equal the Han Son of Heaven? The Son of Heaven is like a father to me."

The Han dispatched the general of palace attendants Su Wu to present generous gifts to the *Shan-yü*. With this the *Shan-yü* grew increasingly arrogant and behaved with great rudeness, betraying the hopes of the Han.

The following year Chao P'o-nu managed to escape from the

[15] Ssu-ma Ch'ien's narrative probably ends somewhere around this point; the remainder of the chapter down to the closing remarks, a series of rather choppy notes, is most likely the work of Ch'u Shao-sun or one of the other writers who undertook to make additions to the *Shih chi*.

Hsiung-nu and return home. The year after, the Han sent Li Kuang-li with thirty thousand cavalry north from Chiu-ch'üan to attack the Wise King of the Right in the Heavenly Mountains. He killed or captured over ten thousand of the enemy before returning. The Hsiung-nu, however, surrounded him in great force and he was barely able to escape; six or seven out of every ten of his men were killed.

The Han also sent Kung-sun Ao north from Hsi-ho; at Mount Cho-t'u he joined forces with Lu Po-te, but neither of them succeeded in killing or capturing any of the enemy. The Han also sent the cavalry commandant Li Ling with a force of five thousand infantry and cavalry to march north from Chü-yen. After they had proceeded over a thousand *li* they engaged the *Shan-yü* in battle. Li Ling killed or wounded over ten thousand of the enemy, but his provisions soon gave out and his men began to scatter and flee for home. The Hsiung-nu then surrounded Li Ling, who surrendered to them. Most of his men were wiped out, only four hundred of them managing to return to safety. The *Shan-yü* treated Li Ling with great honor and gave him his own daughter for a wife.

Two years later the Han again dispatched Li Kuang-li with sixty thousand cavalry and a hundred thousand infantry to march north from So-fang. Lu Po-te led some ten thousand men to join them, while Han Yüeh advanced with thirty thousand infantry and cavalry from Wu-yüan. Kung-sun Ao proceeded from Yen-men with ten thousand cavalry and thirty thousand infantry. When the *Shan-yü* received word of their advance, he moved all his family and wealth far to the north beyond the Yü-wu River. He himself, with ten thousand cavalry, waited south of the river and engaged Li Kuang-li in battle. Li Kuang-li's lines broke and he began to retreat, fighting a running battle with the *Shan-yü* for over ten days. But when word reached him that his entire family had been wiped out as a result of the witchcraft affair,[16] he and all his men surrendered to the Hsiung-nu. Only one or two out of every thousand men who set out with him managed to return

[16] In 91 B.C. the heir apparent, Prince Li, and his mother, Empress Wei, were accused of attempting to kill the emperor by black magic. Many high officials of the dynasty were implicated in the investigations that followed, among them Li Kuang-li. But the battle referred to above took place in 99 B.C., so the text is obviously out of order.

to China. Han Yüeh did not succeed in killing or capturing any of the enemy, while Kung-sun Ao, though he fought with the Wise King of the Left, was unable to win any advantage and likewise retreated. From all the parties that went out to attack the Hsiung-nu this year, among those who returned there were none to testify as to what degree of success the various generals had achieved and therefore no honors were awarded. An imperial edict had been issued ordering the arrest of the grand physician Sui Tan. He in turn gave out the news that Li Kuang-li's family had been exterminated and thereby caused Li Kuang-li to surrender to the Hsiung-nu.

The Grand Historian remarks: When Confucius wrote the *Spring and Autumn Annals,* he was very open in treating the reigns of the early dukes of Lu, Yin, and Huan; but when he came to the later period of Dukes Ting and Ai, his writing was much more covert. Because in the latter case he was writing about his own times, he did not express his judgments frankly, but used subtle and guarded language.[17]

The trouble with the ordinary run of men these days who discuss Hsiung-nu affairs is that they seek only for some temporary advantage, resorting to any kind of flattery in order to have their own views accepted, without considering what the effect may be on all parties concerned. At the same time the generals and military leaders, relying upon the vastness and might of China, grow increasingly bold, and the ruler follows their advice in making his decisions. Thus no profound achievement is ever reached.

Emperor Yao in ancient times, as wise as he was, was not completely successful as a ruler; the nine provinces of China had to wait until the reign of Emperor Yü before they knew real peace. If one would establish a truly worthy dynasty such as those of old, therefore, nothing is more important than selecting the right generals and ministers! Nothing is more important than selecting the right generals and ministers!

[17] Ssu-ma Ch'ien's purpose in making these seemingly irrelevant remarks about Confucius and the *Spring and Autumn Annals* is of course to warn the reader that he too is obliged to use "guarded language" in his discussion of the Hsiung-nu problem.

Shih chi 111: The Biographies of General Wei Ch'ing and the Swift Cavalry General Ho Ch'ü-ping

They patrolled the winding frontier, broadened our lands south of the bend of the Yellow River, defeated the enemy at Ch'i-lien, opened up contact with the western states, and overpowered the northern barbarians. Thus I made The Biographies of General Wei Ch'ing and the Swift Cavalry General Ho Ch'ü-ping.

The general in chief Wei Ch'ing was a native of P'ing-yang. His father, Cheng Chi, was a clerk in the household of the marquis of P'ing-yang, where he had illicit relations with Dame Wei, a concubine of the marquis. From this union Wei Ch'ing was born. Before this Dame Wei had already given birth to a boy, Wei Ch'ang-tzu, and a girl, Wei Tzu-fu. The latter, because she was employed in the household of the princess of P'ing-yang, the wife of the marquis of P'ing-yang and older sister of Emperor Wu, later managed to obtain favor with the emperor. For this reason Wei Ch'ing also adopted the family name Wei and the polite name Chung-ch'ing, and his brother Ch'ang-tzu changed his name to Ch'ang-chün. The oldest daughter of their mother was named Wei Ju, her second daughter Wei Shao-erh, and her third daughter Wei Tzu-fu. Later she had another son named Pu-kuang. All her children adopted the surname Wei.[1] Wei Ch'ing became a servant in the household of the marquis of P'ing-yang.

When he was young Wei Ch'ing went to live with his father, but his father set him to herding sheep and all his half-brothers, sons of his father's legitimate wife, treated him like a slave and refused to recognize him as a brother.

Once, while Wei Ch'ing was a servant, he had occasion to visit

---

[1] The narrative is remarkably confused. Was Cheng Chi the father of all Dame Wei's children, and was Wei her own family name? Or did she have a husband named Wei? Apparently Ssu-ma Ch'ien was not certain of the facts when he wrote the passage.

the prison at the Palace of Sweet Springs. There one of the convicts in chains examined his face and said, "You will become a great man and will rise to the position of marquis!"

Wei Ch'ing laughed and said, "I was born a slave and if I can get by without being beaten and scolded that will be good enough. How would *I* ever get to be a marquis?"

When he grew to manhood he became a rider in the marquis's household and attended the princess of P'ing-yang.

In the second year of *chien-yüan* [139 B.C.] Wei Ch'ing's elder sister Wei Tzu-fu went to live in the palace and won favor with Emperor Wu. The emperor's consort at this time was Empress Ch'en, the daughter of Princess Ch'ang of T'ang-i, the older sister of Emperor Ching. Empress Ch'en had no children and was of a very jealous nature. When Princess Ch'ang heard that Wei Tzu-fu had won favor with the emperor and was pregnant, she was very envious and sent men to arrest Wei Ch'ing. Wei Ch'ing at this time was serving in the Chien-chang Palace and was little known, so that Princess Ch'ang was able to have him seized without difficulty. She was about to put him to death when Wei Ch'ing's friend Kung-sun Ao, a palace horseman, went with a band of young men to the place where he was being held and managed to snatch Wei Ch'ing up and carry him off to safety. Thus his life was saved.

When the emperor heard of the incident, he summoned Wei Ch'ing and made him superintendent of the guards at the Chien-chang Palace. He also summoned Wei Ch'ing's brothers, the other sons of Dame Wei, and appointed them to high positions, in the course of a few days showering them with gifts amounting to a thousand pieces of gold. Wei Ch'ing's eldest sister Wei Ju was given as a wife to the master of carriage Kung-sun Ho. His next eldest sister, Wei Shao-erh, had previously had an affair with Ch'en Chang and the emperor therefore summoned Ch'en Chang and gave him a high post. Kung-sun Ao won fame because of his part in saving Wei Ch'ing's life, Wei Tzu-fu became a lady of the palace, and Wei Ch'ing was advanced to the rank of palace counselor.

In the fifth year of the *yüan-k̬uang* era [129 B.C.] Wei Ch'ing was appointed general of carriage and cavalry and sent out of Shang-ku to attack the Hsiung-nu; the master of carriage Kung-sun Ho was made general of light carriage and sent out of Yün-chung; the palace counselor Kung-sun Ao was made cavalry general and sent out of Tai Province; and the colonel of the guard Li Kuang was made general of resolute cavalry and sent out of Yen-men. Each commander had a force of ten thousand horsemen. Wei Ch'ing reached Lung-ch'eng and killed or captured several hundred of the enemy. Kung-sun Ao lost seven thousand of his horsemen, and Li Kuang was taken prisoner by the enemy, though he managed to escape. Both Kung-sun Ao and Li Kuang were condemned to execution for their failures, but were allowed to ransom their lives and become commoners. Kung-sun Ho likewise failed to win any distinction in the campaign.

In the spring of the first year of *yüan-so* [128 B.C.] Wei Tzu-fu gave birth to a son and was designated as the new empress. In the autumn Wei Ch'ing as general of carriage and cavalry rode out of Yen-men with a force of thirty thousand horsemen and attacked the Hsiung-nu, killing or capturing several thousand of the enemy.

The following year the Hsiung-nu crossed the border and killed the governor of Liao-hsi, carrying off over two thousand of the inhabitants of Yü-yang and defeating the army of General Han An-kuo. The emperor ordered General Li Hsi to attack them from Tai and Wei Ch'ing to attack from Yün-chung. Wei Ch'ing proceeded west to Kao-ch'üeh and from there invaded the region south of the bend of the Yellow River as far as Lung-hsi. He captured or killed several thousand of the enemy, seized twenty or thirty thousand of their domestic animals, and put to flight the kings of the Po-yang and Lou-fan tribes, thus making it possible to establish the province of So-fang south of the bend of the river. Because of this Wei Ch'ing was enfeoffed as marquis of Ch'ang-p'ing with three thousand eight hundred households. His subordinate commander Su Chien, who had also won distinction in the campaign, was enfeoffed as marquis of P'ing-ling with eleven hundred households and sent to build fortifications in So-fang. Another subordinate commander, Chang Tz'u-kung, was enfeoffed as marquis of An-t'ou because of his achievements.

The imperial edict issued on the occasion read:

The Hsiung-nu have turned their backs on the principles of Heaven and brought disorder to human relations, assaulting and maltreating the aged and dedicating themselves to rapine and plunder. They have tricked the other barbarians into joining their plots and lending them their soldiers, and have repeatedly violated our borders. Therefore we have called out the armies and dispatched the generals to punish their offenses. Does it not say in the *Book of Odes:*

> We struck the Hsien-yün
> And drove them to the great plain.

> We sent forth our chariots in majestic array
> And walled the northern regions.[2]

Now the general of carriage and cavalry Wei Ch'ing has crossed the upper reaches of the Yellow River and marched as far as Kao-ch'üeh, capturing and killing two thousand three hundred of the enemy and seizing all of their baggage and animals. For this he has been enfeoffed as a ranking marquis. After this he proceeded west to win control of the land south of the bend of the Yellow River as far as the old frontier at Elm Valley; he has crossed the Catalpa Ridge, built a bridge across the North River, struck the enemy at P'u-ni, defeated them at Fu-li, and cut down their swiftest soldiers, capturing three thousand seventy-one of their scouts. By questioning the captives, he was able to discover and seize the main body of their force. Then, with over a million horses, oxen, and sheep, and with his entire army still intact, he returned. Therefore we have increased his fief by three thousand households.

The following year the Hsiung-nu invaded Tai Province and killed the governor, Kung Yu; they also crossed into Yen-men and carried off over a thousand of the inhabitants. The year after, they invaded Tai, Ting-hsiang, and Shang Provinces in great force, killing and carrying off several thousand Chinese.

In the spring of the following year, the fifth year of *yüan-so* [124 B.C.], the Han ordered the general of carriage and cavalry Wei Ch'ing to proceed from Kao-ch'üeh with a force of thirty thousand cavalry; the colonel of the guard Su Chien was appointed scouting and attacking general; the left prefect of the capital Li Chü was made general of strong bowmen; the master of carriage Kung-sun Ho was made

[2] From the poems entitled "Liu-yüeh" and "Ch'u-chü" of the "Lesser Odes."

cavalry general; and the prime minister of Tai, Li Ts'ai, was made general of light carriage. All were under the command of Wei Ch'ing and rode north from So-fang. The grand messenger Li Hsi and the marquis of An-t'ou, Chang Tz'u-kung, were appointed as generals and ordered to proceed from Yu-pei-p'ing and join the others in attacking the Hsiung-nu.

The Hsiung-nu Wise King of the Right, whose forces were matched against those of Wei Ch'ing, considered that the Han soldiers would never be able to reach his headquarters and had drunk himself into a stupor. During the night Wei Ch'ing and his men reached the Hsiung-nu encampment and surrounded the Wise King of the Right. He woke in great astonishment and fled in the night, accompanied only by his favorite concubine and a few hundred of his best horsemen, galloping through the Han encirclement and making off to the north. The light cavalry colonel Kuo Ch'eng and several others pursued him for two or three hundred *li,* but were unable to overtake him. In the action, however, Wei Ch'ing managed to capture ten or more petty chiefs under the Wise King of the Right, as well as over fifteen thousand of his men and women and between a hundred thousand and a million domestic animals. Wei Ch'ing then led his forces back to the frontier.

The emperor sent a messenger to meet him and present him with the seals of general in chief, conferring this title upon him. From this time on, all the troops of the other generals were under his command. After assuming his new title, Wei Ch'ing returned to the capital.

The emperor issued an edict saying:

The general in chief Wei Ch'ing has led the troops in person and won a great victory in battle, capturing over ten of the petty chiefs of the Hsiung-nu. Therefore let his fief be increased by six thousand households and let his son Wei K'ang be enfeoffed as marquis of I-ch'un, his son Wei Pu-i as marquis of Yin-an, and his son Wei Teng as marquis of Fa-kan.

Wei Ch'ing firmly declined to accept the honors accorded to his sons, saying, "Unworthy as I am, I have been granted the privilege of riding into battle. Through the divine wisdom of Your Majesty, the army has won a great victory, but the merit is due wholly to the fighting ability of my officers. Your Majesty has graciously increased my own fief, but my sons are still in swaddling clothes and have performed no service. Though Your Majesty kindly wishes to set aside lands and enfeoff them as well, I fear it would do little to encourage the men who have fought under me. How could I dare to accept fiefs for K'ang and my other sons?"

But the emperor replied, "I have not forgotten the achievements of your officers. At this very moment I am considering how to reward them."

Then he issued an edict to the imperial secretary which read:

The chief commandant of the supporting army Kung-sun Ao has three times served under the general in chief in attacking the Hsiung-nu, providing constant protection for the army and joining with the other divisions in capturing a number of the Hsiung-nu leaders. Let him be enfeoffed as Ho-ch'i or "Combined Cavalry" marquis with fifteen hundred households. The chief commandant Han Yüeh followed the general in chief in riding out of Yü-hun, proceeding to the court of the Wise King of the Right, and fighting under the general in chief's command in the capture of the Hsiung-nu leaders. Let him be enfeoffed as marquis of Lung-wo with thirteen hundred households. The cavalry general Kung-sun Ho accompanied the general in chief in capturing the Hsiung-nu leaders, for which he shall be enfeoffed as marquis of Nan-p'ao with thirteen hundred households. The general of light carriage Li Ts'ai twice accompanied the general in chief in capturing groups of Hsiung-nu leaders, for which he shall be enfeoffed as marquis of Lo-an with sixteen hundred households. The subordinate commanders Li So, Chao Pu-yü, and Kung-sun Jung-nu all served three times under the general in chief and took part in the capture of the enemy leaders, for which Li So shall be enfeoffed as marquis of She-chih with thirteen hundred households, Chao Pu-yü as marquis of Sui-ch'eng with thirteen hundred households, and Kung-sun Jung-nu as marquis of Ts'ung-p'ing with the same number. Since the generals Li Chü and Li Hsi and the subordinate commander Tou Ju-i have also won distinction, they shall be awarded the rank of marquis within the Pass and granted the revenue from towns of three hundred households each.

In the fall the Hsiung-nu invaded Tai, killing the chief commandant Chu Ying.

In the spring of the following year the general in chief Wei Ch'ing rode out of Ting-hsiang. The Ho-ch'i marquis Kung-sun Ao acted as his general of the center; the master of carriage Kung-sun Ho as general of the left; the marquis of Hsi, Chao Hsin, as general of the vanguard; the colonel of the guard Su Chien as general of the right; the chief of palace attendants Li Kuang as general of the rear; and the left prefect of the capital Li Chü as general of strong bowmen, all of them under the command of the general in chief. They succeeded in killing or capturing several thousand of the enemy before returning.

A month or so later they rode out of Ting-hsiang again to attack the Hsiung-nu, capturing or killing over ten thousand of the enemy.

The general of the right Su Chien and the general of the vanguard Chao Hsin, with a combined force of three thousand or more cavalry, being separated from the main body of the army, faced the soldiers of the *Shan-yü* alone and fought with them for over a day until most of their own men had been wiped out. Chao Hsin was actually a Hsiung-nu himself, who had later gone over to the Chinese side and been enfeoffed as marquis of Hsi. When his situation became critical, the Hsiung-nu tempted him with promises until he finally fled with the eight hundred or so cavalry that remained of his army and surrendered to the *Shan-yü*. Su Chien lost his entire army and barely managed to escape alone and make his way back to the headquarters of the general in chief.

The general in chief questioned his expert on military law, Hung, his chief secretary An, his adviser Chou Pa, and others as to what punishment they thought Su Chien deserved for his defeat. Chou Pa replied, "Since you took the field as a military commander, you have never had occasion to execute any of your subordinate generals. Now that Su Chien has abandoned his army, it would be well to execute him in order to give a clear demonstration of your might!"

Hung and An objected, however, saying, "That would not be right! According to the laws of military science, a small force that attempts to hold its ground at all cost will end up as the prisoners of a larger force. Now Su Chien, with only a few thousand men, has had to face twenty or thirty thousand of the *Shan-yü*'s soldiers. He fought them for over a day until his men were wiped out and then, not daring to be disloyal, he made his way back of his own accord. If you execute men who return of their own volition, you will only succeed in demonstating that from now on it does not pay to return! He should not be executed!"

Wei Ch'ing then spoke, saying, "Because I am related to the empress, I have graciously been allowed to serve in the field. I am not worried about my might, and Chou Pa's suggestion that I do something to demonstrate it is wholly at variance with my wishes. Moreover, though it might be proper and within my power to execute a general, considering the confidence and favor the emperor has shown me I would hardly dare to carry out the punishment arbitrarily and on my own authority here beyond the frontier. Would it not be better to return, report to the emperor in full, and allow him to make the decision himself? In this way I can show that I do not venture to abuse my authority."

His officers all agreed that this would be the best course and Su Chien was consequently made a prisoner and sent to the place where the emperor was residing. Wei Ch'ing then led his forces back across the border and disbanded them.

This year Ho Ch'ü-ping, the eighteen-year-old son of Wei Ch'ing's elder sister Shao-erh,[3] was favored by being made an attendant of the emperor. He was skillful at riding and shooting, and accompanied his uncle Wei Ch'ing on two campaigns. Wei Ch'ing, acting on imperial order, granted him a force of young fighting men and gave him the title of swift commander. Ho Ch'ü-ping, with eight hundred of the fastest and most daring riders, promptly broke away from the main army and ranged ahead several hundred *li* in search of gain, killing and capturing a disproportionately large number of the enemy. The emperor accordingly issued an edict, saying:

The swift commander Ho Ch'ü-ping has killed and captured two thousand twenty-eight of the enemy, including a prime minister and a household administrator; he has cut down Ch'an, the marquis of Chi-jo, one of the *Shan-yü's* elder relatives, has captured alive the *Shan-yü's* uncle Lo-ku-pi, and has in both campaigns won the highest distinction in the army. He shall therefore be enfeoffed with sixteen hundred households and the title of Kuan-chün or "Highest in the Army" marquis. In addition, Hao Hsien, the gov-

[3] His father, Ho Chung-ju, had had an affair with Wei Shao-erh before her marriage to Ch'en Chang.

ernor of Shang-ku Province, who has served in four campaigns under the general in chief and has killed or captured over two thousand of the enemy, shall be enfeoffed with eleven hundred households and the title of Chung-li or "Manifold Gain" marquis.

In the campaigns this year two armies, those of Su Chien and Chao Hsin, were lost (Chao Hsin deserting to the enemy), and the armies failed to achieve any outstanding accomplishments. Therefore Wei Ch'ing's fief was not increased. When Su Chien was brought back to the capital, the emperor did not execute him but pardoned his offenses and allowed him to ransom his life and become a commoner. After Wei Ch'ing returned, the emperor awarded him a thousand pieces of gold.

At this time Lady Wang had begun to enjoy favor with the emperor. A certain Ning Ch'eng accordingly advised Wei Ch'ing, saying, "Although you have not yet won any extraordinary amount of distinction, you enjoy the revenue from ten thousand households and all three of your sons have become marquises. All this is due merely to the fact that you are a brother of the empress. Now Lady Wang enjoys the emperor's favor, but the members of her family have not yet acquired wealth and honor. I would suggest, general, that you take the thousand gold pieces which you have received and give them to Lady Wang's mother as a birthday present."

Wei Ch'ing followed this advice and presented five hundred of the gold pieces to Lady Wang's mother. When the emperor heard about it, he questioned Wei Ch'ing, who told him exactly how he had come to make the presentation. The emperor then honored Ning Ch'eng with the post of chief commandant of Tung-hai Province.

Chang Ch'ien also served under Wei Ch'ing in the army. Formerly he had been sent as envoy to Ta-hsia [Bactria] and had been detained for a long time by the Hsiung-nu. He therefore knew where the best pastures and watering places in the barbarian territory were situated and guided the army to them; in this way he saved the army from hunger and thirst. Because of the merit he had won on his earlier mission to the distant lands of the west, he was enfeoffed with the title of Po-wang or "Broad Vision" marquis.

After Ho Ch'ü-ping had been a marquis for three years he was appointed general of swift cavalry and sent with a force of ten thousand horsemen out of Lung-hsi in the spring of the second year of the era *yüan-shou* [121 B.C.]. In recognition of his achievements on this campaign the emperor announced:

The general of swift cavalry Ho Ch'ü-ping has led his fighting men across Mount Wu-li and struck at the tribes of Su-p'u; he has crossed the Hu-nu River and marched through the lands of five barbarian rulers with his baggage trains and hosts of followers, sparing only those who submitted in fear before him. Hoping to capture the son of the *Shan-yü,* he fought a running battle for six days, riding a thousand *li* or more beyond Mount Yen-chih, meeting the enemy in close combat, killing the ruler of Lan, slaying the barbarian King Lu, wiping out the entire enemy force and capturing the son of the Hun-yeh king and his ministers and chief commandants. He has killed and captured over eight thousand of the enemy and seized the golden man which the Hsiu-t'u king uses in worshiping Heaven. Therefore let his fief be increased by two thousand households.

In the summer Ho Ch'ü-ping and the Ho-ch'i marquis Kung-sun Ao proceeded north from Pei-ti, taking different routes, while the Po-wang marquis Chang Ch'ien and the chief of palace attendants Li Kuang rode north from Yu-pei-p'ing, also by different routes, all with the objective of attacking the Hsiung-nu. Li Kuang, with a force of four thousand cavalry, made contact with the enemy first, while Chang Ch'ien and his ten thousand horsemen were still on the way. The Hsiung-nu Wise King of the Left, commanding a force of twenty or thirty thousand horsemen, surrounded Li Kuang's army. Li Kuang fought with him for two days until over half of his own men had been killed and a far larger number of the enemy had perished. When Chang Ch'ien arrived with reinforcements, the Hsiung-nu soldiers finally withdrew. On his return to the capital Chang Ch'ien was tried for having been late in arriving and was condemned to execution, but was allowed to ransom his life and become a commoner.

Meanwhile Ho Ch'ü-ping had proceeded north from Pei-ti and penetrated deep into enemy territory, but Kung-sun Ao lost his way and failed to make contact with Ho Ch'ü-ping's army as planned. Ho Ch'ü-ping crossed through Chü-yen and reached the Ch'i-lien Mountains, killing and capturing many of the enemy.

The imperial edict read:

The swift cavalry general Ho Ch'ü-ping has crossed through Chü-yen, passed the land of the Lesser Yüeh-chih, and attacked the enemy at the Ch'i-lien Mountains, capturing the Yu-t'u king and receiving the surrender of twenty-five hundred of his men. He has killed or taken prisoner thirty thousand two hundred of the enemy, captured five kings and their mothers, as well as the consort of the *Shan-yü,* fifty-nine princes and sixty-three high ministers, generals, and chief commandants. Yet only three tenths of his own men were lost in the campaign. Therefore his fief shall be increased by five thousand households. Moreover, the subordinate commanders who followed him to the land of the Lesser Yüeh-chih shall be awarded the rank of junior chiefs of the multitude.

The hawklike attacking marshal Chao P'o-nu has twice accompanied Ho Ch'ü-ping, executing the king of Su-p'u, capturing the king of Chi-chü and his general of a thousand cavalry, seizing a king, the mother of a king, and forty-one princes and lesser leaders, and taking prisoner three thousand three hundred and thirty of the enemy; then, advancing ahead of the rest of the army, he captured another fourteen hundred prisoners. Therefore he shall be granted a fief of fifteen hundred households and the title of Ts'ung-p'iao or "Follower of the Swift Cavalry General" marquis.

The subordinate commander Kou-wang Kao Pu-chih accompanied Ho Ch'ü-ping on his campaign and captured the Hu-yü-t'u king, eleven princes and minor leaders, and seven thousand seven hundred and sixty-eight of the enemy, for which he shall be enfeoffed with eleven hundred households and the title of I-kuan or "Worthy of His Command" marquis. The subordinate commander P'u To has also won distinction and shall be enfeoffed as marquis of Hui-ch'ü.

The Ho-ch'i marquis Kung-sun Ao was tried for having proceeded at too slow a pace and failing to meet with Ho Ch'ü-ping's army at the scheduled rendezvous. He was condemened to execution but on payment of a fine was reduced to the status of commoner.

The soldiers and horses under the command of the older generals were no match for the exploits of Ho Ch'ü-ping. For one thing, Ho Ch'ü-ping always saw to it that he had a select group of soldiers, and in addition he was daring enough to penetrate deep into enemy territory, time and again riding off ahead of the main body of the army with the best cavalry. Moreover, his men seemed to enjoy the favor of

Heaven, for they had never encountered any serious difficulties. The older generals, on the other hand, were constantly being tried for proceeding too slowly and failing to appear on time. As a result of his successes, Ho Ch'ü-ping's favor with the emperor increased day by day until it matched that of his uncle, the general in chief Wei Ch'ing.

In the autumn the *Shan-yü,* angry that the Hun-yeh king, who lived in the western part of the Hsiung-nu realm, had so often been defeated by Ho Ch'ü-ping's soldiers and had lost twenty or thirty thousand of his men, sent a summons to the Hun-yeh king, intending to execute him. The Hun-yeh king, the Hsiu-t'u king, and others of their group plotted together and decided to surrender to the Han; they sent one of their men ahead to the border as envoy to make the arrangements.

At this time the grand messenger Li Hsi was overseeing the construction of fortifications along the Yellow River, and the envoy from the Hun-yeh king was brought to him. He at once hastened off by relay carriage to the capital to report to the emperor. On hearing the report, the emperor, fearing that the surrender offer was only a ruse to launch an attack on the border, dispatched Ho Ch'ü-ping with a force of soldiers to go to the frontier to meet the Hsiung-nu.

Ho Ch'ü-ping crossed the Yellow River and rode to within sight of the army of the Hun-yeh king. Many of the subordinate generals under the Hun-yeh king, however, were opposed to the surrender and when they saw the Han troops advancing, they turned and fled in great numbers. Ho Ch'ü-ping immediately galloped into the midst of the enemy, met with the Hun-yeh king, and cut down eight thousand of the king's men who were attempting to flee. He placed the Hun-yeh king in a relay carriage and sent him on ahead alone to the emperor's residence, and then led all of the king's followers across the river into Han territory. The Hsiung-nu who surrendered numbered thirty or forty thousand, though they were referred to as a force of a hundred thousand. When they reached Ch'ang-an, the emperor handed out rewards and gifts to them amounting to a billion cash. The Hun-yeh king was enfeoffed as marquis of T'a-yin with ten thousand households, the petty king Hu-tu-ni as marquis of Hsia-mo, Ying-pi as marquis of Hui-ch'ü, Ch'in-li as marquis of Ho-ch'i, and the grand household administrator T'ung-li as marquis of Ch'ang-lo.

The emperor issued an edict congratulating Ho Ch'ü-ping on his achievement in these words:

When the general of swift cavalry Ho Ch'ü-ping led his forces to attack the Hsiung-nu, the Hun-yeh king, who is the ruler of the western region, and his multitude of followers all came running to our army to surrender. With the enemy's provisions to feed his army and over ten thousand of their bowmen added to his force, Ho Ch'ü-ping punished the fierce and violent, capturing or killing over eight thousand of the enemy and receiving the surrender of thirty-two rulers of the foreign tribes. His fighting men suffered not a single wound, and yet a host of a hundred thousand of the enemy flocked about him and submitted. Thus has the fame of his numerous military exploits spread to the frontiers along the Yellow River, and we may hope from now on that they will be free from peril and may enjoy lasting peace. He shall therefore be enfeoffed with seventeen hundred additional households, and the number of soldiers garrisoning the provinces of Lung-hsi, Pei-ti, and Shang shall be reduced to half in order to lighten the burden of frontier duty upon the empire.

Shortly afterwards the Hsiung-nu who had surrendered were divided into groups and sent to inhabit the five provinces of Lung-hsi, Pei-ti, Shang, So-fang, and Yün-chung which had been created in the region south of the bend of the Yellow River beyond the old frontier of the empire. There they were allowed to follow the customs of their native land and were treated as a subject nation.

The following year the Hsiung-nu invaded Yu-pei-p'ing and Ting-hsiang, killing or carrying off over a thousand Chinese. The year after, the emperor plotted with his generals, saying, "Since Chao Hsin, the marquis of Hsi, has gone over to the enemy, he is acting as adviser to the *Shan-yü* and is planning his strategy for him. He is convinced that the Han forces can never cross the desert, and therefore he and the *Shan-yü*, despising our might, remain in the same place. Now if we were to dispatch a really large army, we could be sure of accomplishing our aim by force of numbers!" This was in the fourth year of the *yüan-shou* era [119 B.C.].

In the spring of the same year the emperor dispatched the general in chief Wei Ch'ing and the swift cavalry general Ho Ch'ü-ping to lead a force of fifty thousand cavalry each, with several hundred thousand infantry and baggage carriers to follow in their rear. All of the bravest fighters who were daring enough to risk a plunge deep into enemy territory were placed under the command of Ho Ch'ü-ping. Originally Ho Ch'ü-ping was supposed to ride north from Ting-hsiang and attack the *Shan-yü*, but when enemy captives revealed that the *Shan-yü* was farther east, the emperor ordered Ho Ch'ü-ping to ride out of Tai Province. Wei Ch'ing was then ordered to proceed from Ting-hsiang, while the chief of palace attendants Li Kuang led the vanguard, the master of carriage Kung-sun Ho acted as general of the left, the master of titles Chao I-chi acted as general of the right, and the marquis of P'ing-yang, Ts'ao Hsiang, commanded the rear. All were under the command of Wei Ch'ing. When the troops of the various generals had crossed the desert, a force of fifty thousand men and horses in all, they were to join with the men of Ho Ch'ü-ping and all together attack the *Shan-yü*.

Chao Hsin advised the *Shan-yü*, saying, "By the time the Han troops have crossed the desert their men and horses will be worn out and we can make prisoners of them without the slightest difficulty!" The *Shan-yü* therefore ordered his baggage trains to withdraw far to the north, while he waited with his best troops on the northern edge of the desert.

Wei Ch'ing's army, having ridden over a thousand *li* beyond the border, emerged from the desert just at the point where the *Shan-yü* was waiting. Spying the *Shan-yü*'s forces, Wei Ch'ing likewise pitched camp and waited. He ordered the armored wagons to be ranged in a circle about the camp and at the same time sent out five thousand cavalry to attack the Hsiung-nu. The Hsiung-nu dispatched some ten thousand of their own cavalry to meet the attack. Just as the sun was setting, a great wind arose, whirling dust into the faces of the men, until the two armies could no longer see each other. The Chinese then dispatched more men to swoop out to the left and right and surround the *Shan-yü*. When the *Shan-yü* saw how numerous the Han soldiers were and perceived that the men and horses were still in strong fighting condition, he realized that he could win no advantage in battle. In the gathering dusk he mounted a team of six mules and, accompanied by several hundred of his finest horsemen, broke straight through the Han encirclement and fled to the northwest.

By this time night had fallen, and the Han and Hsiung-nu soldiers were jumbled together in complete confusion, both sides suffering an equal number of dead and wounded. One of the Han commanders of the left captured a prisoner who informed him that the *Shan-yü* had already fled before dark, and the Han army accordingly dispatched a party of light cavalry to pursue him in the night. Wei Ch'ing and the rest of his army followed after, while the Hsiung-nu fighters scattered in all directions. By the time dawn came, the Han army had traveled over two hundred *li,* but they were unable to overtake the *Shan-yü.* All in all, Wei Ch'ing killed or captured over ten thousand of the enemy. He then proceeded to Chao Hsin's fort at Mount T'ien-yen, where he seized the Hsiung-nu's supplies of grain and feasted his men. He and his army remained there only a day, however, and then, setting fire to all the remaining grain, began the journey home.

When Wei Ch'ing encountered the forces of the *Shan-yü,* his generals of the vanguard and the right, Li Kuang and Chao I-chi, were making their way around by a separate route to the east, but they lost their way and failed to arrive in time to take part in the attack on the *Shan-yü.* It was not until Wei Ch'ing had led his army back south across the desert that he met up with Li Kuang and Chao I-chi. He sent his chief clerk to question Li Kuang and draw up a list of charges against him, intending to send a full report to the emperor, but Li Kuang committed suicide. When Chao I-chi returned to the capital he was handed over to the prison officials but was allowed to ransom his life and become a commoner. By the time Wei Ch'ing's army re-crossed the border into China he and his men had succeeded in killing or capturing nineteen thousand of the enemy.

The *Shan-yü* in his flight was separated from his forces for over ten days, during which time the Lu-li King of the Right, learning of his disappearance, set himself up as the new *Shan-yü.* When the real *Shan-yü* regained possession of his army, however, the Lu-li king renounced his claim to the title.

Meanwhile, Ho Ch'ü-ping with his fifty thousand cavalry rode more than a thousand *li* north from Tai and Yu-pei-p'ing and attacked the forces of the Wise King of the Left. He was accompanied by a force of carriages and baggage similar to that which traveled with Wei Ch'ing's army, but he had no subordinate generals under his command. Instead he appointed men like Li Kan, Li Kuang's son, and others to act as division commanders in place of subordinate generals. He succeeded in killing and capturing so many of the enemy that his achievements exceeded those of Wei Ch'ing.

When Ho Ch'ü-ping's army returned to the capital, the emperor issued an edict which read:

The general of swift cavalry Ho Ch'ü-ping has led forth the troops and personally commanded a force of barbarians captured in previous campaigns, carrying with him only light provisions and crossing the great desert. Fording the Huo-chang-ch'ü, he executed the enemy leader Pi-chü-ch'i and then turned to strike at the enemy general of the left, cutting down his pennants and seizing his war drums. He crossed over Mount Li-hou, forded the Kung-lü, and captured the T'un-t'ou king, the Han king, and one other, three in all, as well as eighty-three generals, ministers, household administrators, and chief commandants of the enemy. He performed the Feng sacrifice at Mount Lang-chü-hsü and the Shan sacrifice at Mount Ku-yen, ascending the hills and gazing out across the sea of sand. He seized a great multitude of the enemy, taking seventy thousand four hundred and forty-three captives, while only three tenths of his own men were lost in the campaign. He snatched the food supplies of the enemy and penetrated deep into their territory, and his provisions never gave out. Therefore his fief shall be increased by five thousand eight hundred households.

The governor of Yu-pei-p'ing, Lu Po-te, arrived on time at his rendezvous with the general of swift cavalry at Yü-ch'eng and from there accompanied him as far as Mount T'ao-yü, killing or capturing twenty-seven hundred of the enemy, for which he shall be enfeoffed as marquis of Fu-li with six hundred households. The chief commandant of Pei-ti, Hsing Shan, accompanied the general of swift cavalry in capturing the enemy kings, for which he shall be enfeoffed as marquis of I-yang with twelve hundred households. The Yin-ch'un king Fu-lu-chih and the Lou-chuan king I-chi-chien, Hsiung-nu leaders who have come over to the side of the Han, both accompanied the general of swift cavalry and won distinction in the campaign. Therefore Fu-lu-chih shall be enfeoffed as Chuang marquis with thirteen hundred households, and I-chi-chien shall be enfeoffed as Chung-li marquis with eighteen hundred households. The Ts'ung-p'iao marquis Chao P'o-nu and the marquis of Ch'ang-wu, An Chi, both won distinction under the command of the general of swift cavalry and their fiefs shall be increased by three hundred households each. The subordinate commander Li Kan captured the enemy pennants and drums and shall be made a marquis within the Pass with the revenue from two hundred households. The subordinate commander Hsü Tzu-wei shall be awarded the rank of superior chief of the multitude.

In addition, a great many of Ho Ch'ü-ping's officers and men were appointed as officials and presented with rewards. Wei Ch'ing, on the other hand, received no increase in his fief, and not one of the men in his army was made a marquis.

When the armies of the two generals rode out across the border, they had with them a total of one hundred and forty thousand horses, both government-owned and private, but when they recrossed the border they had less than thirty thousand horses left. The emperor created a new rank of grand marshal and appointed both Wei Ch'ing and Ho Ch'ü-ping to it. In this way he made it possible for Ho Ch'ü-ping to enjoy the same rank and salary as Wei Ch'ing. From this time on Wei Ch'ing day by day retired farther into the background, while Ho Ch'ü-ping enjoyed ever-increasing honor. Many of Wei Ch'ing's old friends and followers deserted him and went to serve Ho Ch'ü-ping, where they were immediately awarded offices and titles. Only Jen An refused to follow their example.[4]

Ho Ch'ü-ping was a man of few words and was little given to idle talk, but he possessed great daring and initiative. The emperor once tried to teach him the principles of warfare as expounded by the ancient philosophers Sun Tzu and Wu Tzu, but he replied, "The only thing that matters is how one's own strategies are going to work. There is no need to study the old-fashioned rules of warfare!"

Another time the emperor had a mansion built for Ho Ch'ü-ping and summoned him to look at it, but he only commented, "While the Hsiung-nu have still not been wiped out there is no time to think about houses!" Because of such incidents the emperor regarded him with even greater favor.

[4] Jen An was the friend to whom Ssu-ma Ch'ien wrote his famous letter explaining why he chose to suffer castration rather than commit suicide.

Ho Ch'ü-ping had become an attendant in the palace when he was still young, and after he became honored he took little thought for the men in his command. Whenever he went on a campaign, the emperor would send his own steward along with twenty or thirty carriages full of provisions for Ho Ch'ü-ping's private consumption. When the army returned to the capital, the baggage carts would still be full to overflowing with grain and meat, although the soldiers would be starving. Again, when he was campaigning beyond the border there were times when his men were so short of provisions that many of them did not have the strength to stand up, and yet Ho Ch'ü-ping would make them dig out a playing field for him so he could amuse himself at football. He did many other things of a similar nature.

Wei Ch'ing, on the other hand, was a kindly, retiring man, who attempted to ingratiate himself with the emperor by being mild and compliant. Yet no one in the empire had a good word to say for him.

Ho Ch'ü-ping died in the sixth year of *yüan-shou* [117 B.C.], three years after taking part in the campaign described above. The emperor was deeply grieved and ordered soldiers from the tribes of Hsiung-nu who had submitted to Han rule to be called to the capital and ranged along the road from Ch'ang-an to Mou-ling bearing iron weapons. At Mou-ling he had a grave mound constructed in the shape of the Ch'i-lien Mountains. In recognition of Ho Ch'ü-ping's military achievements and his services in extending the borders of the empire, the emperor awarded him the double posthumous name of Ching-huan or "Righteous and Martial" marquis.

His son Ho Shan or Ho Tzu-hou succeeded to the marquisate. The emperor was very fond of him and wanted to make him a general when he grew up, but six years later, in the first year of *yüan-feng* [110 B.C.], the boy died. He was given the title of Ai or "Pitiful" marquis. He left no heir and the fief was abolished.

Sometime after Ho Ch'ü-ping died, Wei Ch'ing's oldest son, Wei K'ang, the marquis of I-ch'un, was tried for some offense and deprived of his marquisate. Five years later Wei K'ang's two younger brothers, Wei Pu-i, the marquis of Yin-an, and Wei Teng, the marquis of Fa-kan, were accused of having presented faulty tribute money and were likewise deprived of their marquisates. (It was two years after this that

Ho Ch'ü-ping's son died and his marquisate was abolished.) Four years later, the general in chief Wei Ch'ing died and was given the posthumous title of Lieh or "Ardent" marquis. His son Wei K'ang was allowed to succeed his father and become marquis of Ch'ang-p'ing.

Wei Ch'ing died fourteen years after he led the great expedition against the Hsiung-nu and surrounded the *Shan-yü*. The reason he made no further attacks on the Hsiung-nu was that the Han at this time was short of horses and its troops were busy putting down the rebellion in the two kingdoms of Yüeh, attacking Korea in the east and the Ch'iang and other barbarian tribes in the southwest. Therefore the attacks on the Hsiung-nu were suspended for a considerable time.

Wei Ch'ing's wife was Princess P'ing-yang, the younger sister of Emperor Wu, and for this reason their son Wei K'ang, although he had been deprived of his own marquisate, was allowed to succeed to his father's title. (Six years later Wei K'ang was tried for some offense and deprived of the marquisate a second time.) [5]

The following is a brief résumé of the accomplishments of Wei Ch'ing and Ho Ch'ü-ping and the generals who served under them:

General in chief Wei Ch'ing, who achieved the highest distinction. Made seven attacks on the Hsiung-nu, capturing or killing over fifty thousand of the enemy. Fought one encounter with the *Shan-yü*, brought the region south of the bend of the Yellow River under Han control, and established the province of So-fang. Fief increased twice, reaching a final total of 11,800 households. Three sons also enfeoffed as marquises with 1,300 households each, making a grand total of 15,700 households for the family. Nine subordinate commanders and generals who served under him became marquises, and fourteen were made full generals in their own right. Among his subordinate generals were the following men:

Li Kuang. He has his own biography and will not be treated here.

General Kung-sun Ho. A native of I-ch'ü whose ancestors were barbarians. His father, Kung-sun Hun-yeh, became marquis of P'ing-ch'ü during the reign of Emperor Ching but was later tried for some offense and deprived of the title. When Emperor Wu was still heir apparent,

[5] The sentence in parentheses is a later addition.

Kung-sun Ho served in his household. Eight years after Emperor Wu came to the throne, Kung-sun Ho, who held the post of master of carriage, was appointed general of light carriage and sent to garrison Ma-i. Four years later went on a campaign out of Yün-chung. Five years later was made cavalry general and served in an expedition under Wei Ch'ing. Was enfeoffed as marquis of Nan-p'ao because of his achievements. A year later again accompanied Wei Ch'ing as general of the left in an expedition north from Ting-hsiang but failed to win any merit. Four years later was accused of some fault in tribute money and deprived of marquisate. Was appointed Fu-chü General eight years later and rode over two thousand *li* north from Wu-yüan but failed to achieve any distinction. Eight years later was promoted from post of master of carriage to that of chancellor and was enfeoffed as marquis of Ko-i. Served as a general in seven attacks on the Hsiung-nu but never won any outstanding merit. Was twice enfeoffed as a marquis and later became chancellor. (His son Kung-sun Ching-sheng was accused of adultery with Princess Yang-shih and of practicing black magic. The entire family was wiped out and no heir left to succeed to the marquisate.) [6]

General Li Hsi. A native of Yü-chih. Served Emperor Ching and, eight years after Emperor Wu came to the throne, was appointed general of bowmen and sent to garrison Ma-i. Six years later was made a general in a campaign out of Tai and three years later accompanied Wei Ch'ing out of So-fang. Won no merit in any of these actions. Served as a general three times; later acted as grand messenger.

General Kung-sun Ao. A native of I-ch'ü; served as palace attendant to Emperor Wu. In the twelfth year after Emperor Wu's accession to the throne was made general of light cavalry and sent out of Tai. Lost seven thousand men; condemned to death but on payment of fine was made a commoner. Five years later accompanied Wei Ch'ing as subordinate commander and won distinction. Enfeoffed as Ho-ch'i marquis. One year later was appointed general of the center and accompanied Wei Ch'ing on two campaigns out of Ting-hsiang but won no merit. Two years later was appointed general on a campaign out of

[6] This and other passages in parentheses are later additions.

Pei-ti. Failed to reach rendezvous with Ho Ch'ü-ping at appointed time; condemned to death but on payment of fine was made a commoner. Two years later accompanied Wei Ch'ing as subordinate commander; no merit. Fourteen years later appointed Yin-yü General and ordered to build the "City for Receiving Surrender." Seven years later again made two attacks on Hsiung-nu as Yin-yü General. Reached Yü-wu but lost most of his men. Thrown into prison and condemned to death (but managed to escape by feigning death and lived in hiding among the common people for five or six years. Was later discovered and thrown into prison again. Tried on charges that his wife was practicing black magic; he and his entire family executed). Served as a general four times in attacks on the Hsiung-nu; enfeoffed as marquis once.

General Li Chü. Native of Yün-chung; served under Emperor Ching. In seventeenth year after Emperor Wu's accession, while holding post of left prefect of the capital, was appointed general of strong bowmen. One year later he again served as general of strong bowmen.

General Li Ts'ai. Native of Ch'eng-chi; served Emperors Wen, Ching, and Wu. Accompanied Wei Ch'ing as general of light carriage and won distinction. Enfeoffed as marquis of Lo-an. Later became chancellor but was tried for an offense and committed suicide.

General Chang Tz'u-kung. Native of Ho-tung. Served as subordinate commander to Wei Ch'ing and won merit. Enfeoffed as marquis of An-t'ou. After death of Empress Dowager Wang was made general and put in charge of the Northern Garrison. One year later accompanied Wei Ch'ing. Served as general twice but was tried for some offense and deprived of marquisate. His father, Chang Lung, a skillful archer, served as armed archer of the light carriage division and enjoyed favor with Emperor Ching.

General Su Chien. Native of Tu-ling. Served as subordinate commander to Wei Ch'ing and won merit. Enfeoffed as marquis of P'ing-ling. Appointed general and sent to garrison So-fang. Four years later was appointed scouting and attacking general and accompanied Wei Ch'ing out of So-fang. One year later, as general of the right, accompanied Wei Ch'ing on two attacks out of Ting-hsiang. Allowed Chao

Hsin to escape and lost his own army; condemned to death but permitted to pay fine and become a commoner. Later became governor of Tai Province and died in office. Grave situated in Ta-yu County.

General Chao Hsin. Formerly a high minister of the Hsiung-nu but surrendered to the Han and was enfeoffed as marquis of Hsi. In seventeenth year after Emperor Wu's accession was appointed general of vanguard and attacked *Shan-yü;* surrendered to the Hsiung-nu.

General Chang Ch'ien. Sent as envoy to Bactria; on return was appointed subordinate commander in campaign under Wei Ch'ing. Won merit and was enfeoffed as Po-wang marquis. Three years later was made general and went on campaign out of Yu-pei-p'ing. Failed to arrive at rendezvous point on time; condemned to death but allowed to pay fine and become a commoner. Later sent as envoy to Wu-sun barbarians. Became grand messenger and died in office. Grave situated in Han-chung.

General Chao I-chi. Native of Tai-hsü. In twenty-second year after Emperor Wu's accession was made general of right while holding post of master of titles; accompanied Wei Ch'ing out of Ting-hsiang. Lost his way; condemned to death but allowed to pay fine and become a commoner.

General Ts'ao Hsiang. Marquis of P'ing-yang. Appointed general of rear and accompanied Wei Ch'ing on campaign out of Ting-hsiang. He was a grandson of Ts'ao Ts'an, the famous statesman.

General Han Yüeh. Illegitimate grandson of marquis of Kung-kao.[7] Won distinction as a subordinate commander under Wei Ch'ing. Enfeoffed as marquis of Lung-wo but later accused of irregularity in tribute money and deprived of title. In sixth year of *yüan-ting* [112 B.C.] was summoned and appointed General Who Traverses the Sea and sent to attack Eastern Yüeh. Won distinction and was enfeoffed as marquis of An-tao. In third year of *t'ai-ch'u* [102 B.C.] was appointed scouting and attacking general and sent to garrison the string of forts beyond Wu-yüan. (Appointed superintendent of the imperial household. Dug up the palace of Crown Prince Wei and discovered the

---

[7] A Hsiung-nu leader who came over to the side of the Chinese and was enfeoffed as a marquis. He was said to be a descendant of Hann Hsin, the king who rebelled and fled to the Hsiung-nu in the time of Kao-tsu.

charms by which the prince was attempting to bewitch the emperor. Murdered by the crown prince.)

General Kuo Ch'ang. Native of Yün-chung. Served as subordinate commander under Wei Ch'ing. In fourth year of *yüan-feng* [107 B.C.], while serving as palace counselor, was made Barbarian Quelling General and sent to garrison So-fang. Returned and attacked the kingdom of K'un-ming. Failed to achieve any merit and was relieved of post.

General Hsün Chih. Native of Kuang-wu in T'ai-yüan. Won audience with the emperor because of skill as carriage driver and was appointed to serve in the palace. Several times served as subordinate commander under Wei Ch'ing. In third year of *yüan-feng* [108 B.C.] was appointed general of left and sent to attack Korea. No merit. Was tried and executed on charges of having arrested his fellow commander, Yang P'u.

General of Swift Cavalry Ho Ch'ü-ping, who achieved highest distinction. Made six attacks on Hsiung-nu, four as a general. Killed or captured 110,000 of the enemy. When the Hun-yeh king surrendered with thirty or forty thousand followers, he opened up the regions of Ho-hsi and Chiu-ch'üan and greatly decreased the incursions of the western barbarians. Fief was four times increased, reaching total of 15,100 households. Six of his officers won merit and were enfeoffed as marquises, and two later became generals.

General Lu Po-te. Native of P'ing-chou. Governor of Yu-pei-p'ing; served under Ho Ch'ü-ping and won merit. Enfeoffed as marquis of Fu-li. After death of Ho Ch'ü-ping became colonel of the guard and was appointed General Who Calms the Waves, and attacked and defeated Southern Yüeh. Fief increased. Later tried and deprived of marquisate. Appointed chief commandant of strong bowmen and sent to garrison Chü-yen, where he died.

General Chao P'o-nu. Originally from Chiu-yüan but fled to territory of the Hsiung-nu. Later came over to the side of the Han and served as marshal under Ho Ch'ü-ping in campaign out of Pei-ti. Won distinction in this campaign and was enfeoffed as Ts'ung-p'iao marquis. Tried for irregularity in tribute money and deprived of marquisate. One year later appointed Hsiung-ho General and attacked barbarians, advancing as far as Hsiung-ho River. No merit. Two years later attacked and captured king of Lou-lan. Again enfeoffed, this time as marquis of Cho-yeh. Six years later was appointed Chün-chi General and led twenty thousand cavalry in attack on Hsiung-nu Wise King of Left. Fought Wise King and was surrounded by eighty thousand enemy cavalry; taken prisoner and lost his army. (Lived ten years among the Hsiung-nu but fled with An-kuo, the Hsiung-nu crown prince, and returned to the Han. Later tried on charges of witchcraft and executed along with his family.)

When the Wei family rose to power, the general in chief Wei Ch'ing was the first to be enfeoffed. Later five other members of the family were enfeoffed as marquises. In the course of twenty-four years, however, all five were deprived of their titles, so that in the end not a single member of the family was a marquis.

The Grand Historian remarks: Su Chien has told me that he once reprimanded the general in chief Wei Ch'ing for the fact that, although he occupied a position of honor and trust, he enjoyed no praise among the worthy men of the empire. "You should observe how the famous generals of antiquity worked to select and promote men of worth, and strive to imitate their example!" Su Chien told him. But General Wei Ch'ing declined to accept the advice, saying, "Ever since Tou Ying and T'ien Fen by their generosity gathered together their own groups of followers and caused such trouble, the Son of Heaven has been enraged at the thought of anyone doing such a thing. It is the prerogative of the ruler of men to attract others to his service and to decide who is worthy of promotion and who is not. An official's job is simply to obey the laws and fulfill the duties of his post and that is all. What has he to do with the promotion of others?"

Ho Ch'ü-ping was apparently of the same opinion. That is the kind of generals they were.

North they struck at the powerful Hsiung-nu; south they put down the strong forces of Yüeh. In the campaigns against the barbarians they won the merits which are set forth here. Thus I made The Chronological Table of Marquises Enfeoffed from the *Chien-yüan* Era [140–135 B.C.] on.

The Grand Historian remarks: The Hsiung-nu broke off peaceful relations and attacked the northern border where the roads lead across it. The people of Min-yüeh willfully marched against Eastern Ou, which begged to surrender to us and receive assistance. Thus the northern and southern barbarians in turn committed outrages against the glory of the powerful Han, whose subjects won merit in battle against them and received fiefs, proving themselves the equals of their ancestors. For do we not read in the *Odes* and *Documents* how the men of the Three Dynasties

> Smote the northern barbarians
> And punished the tribes of Ching and Shu; [1]

have we not heard how Duke Huan of Ch'i crossed through the state of Yen to strike at the mountain barbarians; how King Wu-ling of Chao, though ruler of a small and unimportant state, brought the *Shan-yü* to his knees; how Duke Mu of Ch'in, by following the advice of Po-li Hsi, became dictator of the western barbarians; and how the rulers of Wu and Ch'u, feudal lords of the Chou, marched against the hundred tribes of Yüeh? How much more so now, therefore, when all China is united under the rule of an enlightened emperor, excelling in both civil and military arts, who has rolled up the land within the four seas like a mat and gathered into his realm a multitude of millions? How could he sit quietly by and not march against those who violate

[1] "Pi-kung," of the "Temple Odes of Lu," *Book of Odes*.

our borders? Therefore he sent forth his armies to strike the powerful Hsiung-nu in the north and to put down the strong forces of Yüeh in the south, and enfeoffed his victorious generals as I have recorded here.

While the high ministers and members of the imperial family were all out-doing each other in luxurious living, Kung-sun Hung, the marquis of P'ing-chin, alone, by his frugality in dress and food, set an example for the other officials. Thus I made The Biographies of the Marquis of P'ing-chin and Chu-fu Yen.

The Marquis of P'ing-chin

The chancellor Kung-sun Hung, whose polite name was Chi, was a native of the district of Hsieh in the state of Tzu-ch'uan, formerly a part of Ch'i. In his youth he served as a prison official of Hsieh but was forced to retire because of some offense. His family was very poor and he made a living by raising pigs on the seacoast. When he was over forty he studied the *Spring and Autumn Annals* and the theories of the various philosophical schools. He took care of his stepmother, treating her with great respect and filial piety.

In the first year of the *chien-yüan* era [140 B.C.], when the present emperor came to the throne, a call was sent out for men of high moral character and literary ability to take service in the government. At this time Kung-sun Hung was sixty, but because of his worth he was summoned and appointed as an erudit. He was sent on a mission to the Hsiung-nu, but when he returned and made his report, his views did not accord with those of the emperor, who grew angry and concluded that he was a man of no ability. Kung-sun Hung thereupon retired from his post on grounds of illness and returned to his home.

In the fifth year of *yüan-kuang* [130 B.C.] a call was again sent out summoning men of literary ability to court. The state of Tzu-ch'uan once more recommended Kung-sun Hung. Kung-sun Hung begged the men of his state not to submit the recommendation, saying, "I have already answered the summons once in the past and journeyed west to the capital, but because of my lack of ability I was dismissed and sent home. I beg you to recommend someone else." But the people of his state insisted upon sending Kung-sun Hung.

When Kung-sun Hung and the other Confucian scholars who had answered the summons, a hundred men or more, arrived at the office of the master of ritual, they were ordered to write answers to some question of government policy. At the examination Kung-sun Hung was seated near the bottom of the group, but when the results were presented to the throne, the emperor selected Kung-sun Hung's answer and gave it the highest mark. The emperor then summoned Kung-sun Hung for an audience and, struck by his handsome and imposing appearance, once more honored him with the post of erudit.

At this time the Han government was busy building a road out of China to the lands of the southwestern barbarians and setting up new provinces in the region, undertakings which were causing great hardship to the people of Pa and Shu Provinces in the west. The emperor ordered Kung-sun Hung to go on a mission to the area to observe what progress had been made. When he returned and made his report, he strongly criticized the project, insisting that there was no benefit to be gained from establishing communication with the southwestern barbarians. The emperor, however, paid no attention to his views.

Kung-sun Hung was a man of broad and unusual ideas and wide learning. He always used to say that the greatest fault in a ruler was lack of breadth and magnanimity, while the greatest failing in ministers was a lack of frugality. Kung-sun Hung himself wore the plainest hemp robes and never ate more than one meat dish at a meal. When his stepmother died he mourned for three years. Whenever debates were held at court he would simply state the pros and cons of the question and leave the emperor to make his own decision; he never ventured to contradict the emperor to his face or argue with the other ministers in court.

The emperor observed that he was sincere in action, that his speeches were full of depth, that he was experienced in legal and bureaucratic affairs and in addition gave a strict Confucian garb and trimming to everything he did, all of which pleased the emperor greatly. In the course of two years at court Kung-sun Hung advanced to the post of left prefect of the capital.

Whenever he made some proposal at court, if the emperor did not approve of it, he would never attempt to argue his case before the other ministers. Instead he and the master of titles chief commandant Chi An would ask to speak to the emperor in private. Chi An would then begin by explaining the proposal and Kung-sun Hung would follow after him and second his opinion. The emperor was invariably pleased by this procedure and would agree to whatever they advised. In this way Kung-sun Hung came to enjoy greater and greater favor with the emperor.

Once he made an agreement with the other high ministers that he would support certain proposals that they were going to make, but when the group appeared before the emperor, Kung-sun Hung broke all of his promises and simply agreed with whatever opinion the emperor expressed. Chi An began to berate him in front of the whole group at court, saying, "The men of Ch'i are full of deceit and have no respect for truth! Originally you agreed to cooperate with the rest of us in supporting these proposals, but now you have gone back on your word in every case. This is downright disloyalty!"

When the emperor asked Kung-sun Hung what he had to say to this, he apologized and replied, "Those who understand me think I am loyal; those who do not understand me think I am disloyal." The emperor approved of his answer and from then on, whenever any of the emperor's favored ministers criticized Kung-sun Hung, the emperor only treated him with greater favor and generosity.

In the third year of *yüan-so* [126 B.C.], when Chang Ou retired, Kung-sun Hung was appointed to succeed him as imperial secretary.

At this time communications were being established with the southwestern barbarians, the province of Ts'ang-hai was being set up in the east, and in the north fortifications were being built in the newly created province of So-fang. Kung-sun Hung several times criticized these moves, saying that the wealth and manpower of China were being exhausted in the service of worthless foreign regions, and begging that the projects be abandoned. The emperor then ordered Chu Mai-ch'en and others of the court ministers to refute Kung-sun Hung's opinion. They drew up a list of ten reasons why the establishment of the province of So-fang would be of advantage to the nation. Kung-sun Hung then professed himself unable to refute a single one of their arguments and apologized, saying, "I am a simple country man from east of the mountains. I had no idea that such advantages as these were entailed. I beg therefore that the projects among the southwestern barbarians and in Ts'ang-hai be abandoned and that the government concentrate upon that in So-fang." The emperor gave his consent.

One day in court Chi An said to the emperor, "Kung-sun Hung occupies one of the three highest offices in the government and enjoys a very large salary, and yet he goes around wearing a plain hemp robe. This is sheer hypocrisy!"

The emperor turned and questioned Kung-sun Hung about this, whereupon the latter apologized and replied, "It is true. Among all my friends in high office, none is closer to me than Chi An, and yet today he has accused me before the whole court. There is no doubt that he has put his finger upon my shortcoming. For me to occupy one of the three highest posts and yet wear a plain hemp robe is indeed no more than a hypocritical show by which I had hoped to fish for fame. In the old days, they say, when Kuan Chung was serving as prime minister to the state of Ch'i, he had a great mansion called the 'Three Returnings'[1] and strove to imitate the luxurious living of his lord, Duke Huan. He helped Duke Huan to become one of the feudal dictators of the time, and yet he tended to usurp to himself the way of living of his lord. On the other hand, when Yen Ying was acting as prime minister to Duke Ching of Ch'i he ate no more than one meat dish at a meal and his wife never wore silk robes, and yet at that time also the state of Ch'i was well governed. In his case he strove to live in the same manner as the common people. Now though I occupy the post of imperial secretary I wear a plain hemp robe so that there will be no difference between myself and any other official down to the

[1] There are various interpretations of the word "three returnings." I have followed the one which regards it as the name of Kuan Chung's mansion, though some commentators take it to mean that he had three wives. Kuan Chung and Yen Ying were famous statesmen of the seventh and sixth centuries B.C. respectively.

lowest clerk in the government. Indeed, it is just as Chi An has said. And if it had not been for his outspoken loyalty, how would Your Majesty have ever become aware of the situation?"

The emperor considered that Kung-sun Hung had replied with exemplary modesty and treated him with even greater favor; eventually he enfeoffed him as marquis of P'ing-chin.

By nature Kung-sun Hung was suspicious and envious of others. On the surface he seemed to be magnanimous, but at heart he was a stern and cold-blooded man. If he ever had a falling out with anyone, although he pretended to be as friendly with the person as before, he would work in secret to bring about his downfall. The execution of Chu-fu Yen and the transfer of Tung Chung-shu to Chiao-hsi were both due to his efforts. He himself ate only unpolished grain and no more than one meat dish at a meal, but if any of his old friends or people he liked came to his house and asked for food and clothing, he would supply them with whatever they needed out of his salary, so that his family never accumulated any wealth. For this he won praise among worthy men.

Just at the time when it was discovered that the kings of Huai-nan and Heng-shan were plotting revolt and the investigations of the conspirators were being pressed with the greatest intensity, Kung-sun Hung became seriously ill. He considered that he had achieved no merit that warranted his being enfeoffed as a marquis. In addition, he held the post of chancellor at this time and by rights ought to have worked to enlighten the ruler, bring order to the nation, and see to it that the inhabitants conducted themselves as loyal subjects and obedient sons. Instead of this, however, there were feudal lords who were actually plotting revolt, all of which proved, he believed, that he had failed in his duties as chief minister of the nation. He was afraid that if his illness grew worse and he should die he would have no way to atone for his failures, and he therefore wrote a letter to the throne which read:

I have heard that there are five abiding duties to be observed throughout the world, and three means by which they are put into practice. The five duties are the hierarchical relationships to be observed between ruler and subject, father and son, older and younger brother, husband and wife, and senior and junior. The three abiding virtues by which these are brought to realization are wisdom, benevolence, and courage. Therefore it is said that to be diligent in action is near to benevolence, to be fond of inquiry is near to wisdom, and to understand dishonor is near to courage. He who knows these three will know how to govern himself, and he who knows how to govern himself will then understand how to govern others. There has never been anyone in the world who could govern others without first being able to govern himself. This principle has remained unchanged for a hundred generations.[2]

Now Your Majesty has in person practiced the greatest filial piety, surveyed the Three Dynasties of antiquity, established the principles of the Chou rulers, and shown yourself proficient in both civil and military affairs, encouraging the worthy and rewarding them with stipends, weighing the abilities of others and selecting them for government office.

I, on the other hand, have no more worth than a tired old horse, nor have I ever won any distinction on the field of battle. Your Majesty, in an act of excessive generosity, has selected me from among the rank and file, enfeoffed me as a marquis, and promoted me to one of the three highest posts in the government. Yet there has been nothing in my actions or ability that is worthy of praise. From the beginning I have been undeserving of these honors, and now that I am ill, if I should drop dead in service like one of the palace dogs or horses, and end tumbled in a ditch, I would never have the opportunity to repay the generosity I have enjoyed or atone for my faults. I therefore beg to return the seals of the marquisate I have received and be allowed to retire as a commoner so that I may clear the way for true men of ability.

The emperor replied to this as follows:

In ancient times merit was rewarded and virtue praised. When the nation was well ordered, civil accomplishments were honored, and only when disaster threatened was warfare accorded a higher place. This principle has never changed. Day and night I have thought how I might fulfill the obligations of my high office, fearing always that I would be unable to bring peace to the nation. You who have shared with me the governing of the empire must know this. It is the duty of a gentleman to love good and hate evil, and this too you must know. Your careful and judicious actions are always before my eyes. Now, although you have unfortunately been afflicted with this ill-

[2] In wording and thought, this passage closely parallels the famous Confucian work, the *Chung-yung* or *Doctrine of the Mean*, XX, 8–11.

ness, brought on by frost and dew, what reason is there to despair of recovery? And yet you have submitted a letter, returning your marquisate and begging for retirement: this is only to make clear to everyone my lack of virtue! Now that you have some leisure from your duties, you must reconsider your decision. Do your best to rally your spirits and take what aid you can from medicines.

At the same time the emperor granted Kung-sun Hung a vacation and presented him with meat, wine, and various silk goods. After a few months Kung-sun Hung recovered his health and was able to resume his duties.

In the second year of *yüan-shou* [121 B.C.], however, he fell ill again and died while holding the office of chancellor. His son Kung-sun Tu succeeded him as marquis of P'ing-chin and became governor of Shan-yang, but some ten years later he was tried for an offense and deprived of the marquisate.

Chu-fu Yen

Chu-fu Yen was a native of Lin-tzu in Ch'i. He studied the diplomatic and military theories of the Warring States period, and in his later years the *Book of Changes,* the *Spring and Autumn Annals,* and the works of the various philosophers. He traveled about among the scholars of Ch'i but could find none who would treat him with any liberality. On the contrary they refused to have anything to do with him, so that he could get nowhere in his native state of Ch'i. His family was very poor and he likewise failed in all attempts to borrow money. Later he traveled north to Yen, Chao, and the region of Chung-shan, but again was unable to find anyone who would employ him. He suffered great hardship on his travels.

He finally decided that it was no use seeking employment among the feudal lords and during the first year of the *yüan-kuang* era [134 B.C.] of the present emperor he journeyed west beyond the Pass to the capital, where he obtained an interview with General Wei Ch'ing.

Wei Ch'ing mentioned him several times to the emperor, but the emperor failed to summon him to court. Although he had very little money, he continued to linger about the capital until many of the officials and their retainers had grown to dislike him. At last he decided to submit a letter directly to the throne. His petition was brought before the emperor in the morning, and that same evening he was summoned for an audience. His memorial dealt with nine items, of which eight were concerned with legal matters. The other item was a criticism of the attacks being made on the Hsiung-nu. This portion of his letter read as follows:

I have heard that an enlightened sovereign does not take offense at remonstrances, no matter how severe, so long as they broaden his understanding; and that a loyal subject does not hesitate for fear of the gravest punishment if he feels that outspoken criticism is needed. Only in this way can all matters of policy be effectively disposed of, and the achievements of the ruler passed on to his heirs for ten thousand generations. Now I have not dared to hide my feelings of loyalty for fear of death and have ventured to state these unworthy opinions. I beg Your Majesty to forgive my shortcomings and to deign to consider these words.

In the *Rules of the Marshal* describing the ancient art of warfare it is said that, no matter how large a nation may be, if it is too fond of fighting it is doomed to perish. It is also said that, no matter how peaceful the world may be, if men forget warfare altogether, danger will ensue.

Now the empire has been brought to peace and the Son of Heaven sings the song of victory, carrying out the great spring and autumn hunts, while the feudal lords review their troops in the spring and train their soldiers in the fall. Thus warfare is not forgotten.

And yet it is said that anger is the thief of virtue, weapons are the tools of evil, and strife is the least noble of actions. In ancient times, if the ruler became truly angry, he did not stop until he had strewn the ground with corpses and loosed a river of blood. Therefore a sage king regards the venting of anger as a grave matter indeed.

No one who has devoted himself to arms and spent all his efforts on military endeavors has ever failed to regret it. In earlier times the First Emperor of the Ch'in, relying upon his might in battle, gobbled up the whole world, seized the other warring states, and united all within the four seas into a single domain, winning as great distinction as the rulers of the Three Dynasties of antiquity. And yet he would not cease his warfare there, but wanted to go on and attack the Hsiung-nu.

His minister Li Ssu reprimanded him, saying, "It is impossible. The Hsiung-nu have no fixed cities or forts and no stores of provisions or grain. They move from place to place like flocks of birds and are just as difficult to catch and control. Now if we send parties of lightly equipped soldiers deep into their territory, our men will soon run out of food, and if we try to send provisions after them, the baggage trains will never reach them in time. Even if we were to seize control of the Hsiung-nu lands, they would bring us no profit, and even if we were to win over their people, we could never administer and keep control of them. And if, after we had won victory, we were to massacre them, this would hardly be a fitting action for a Son of Heaven, who must act as a father and mother to the people. Therefore we would only be wearing out the strength of China in an attempt to have our way with the Hsiung-nu. Surely this is not a wise policy!"

But the First Emperor would not listen to his advice and sent his general Meng T'ien with troops to attack the barbarians. He extended the borders of the empire a thousand *li*, establishing the frontier along the Yellow River, but the land he won over was nothing but brackish swamp, unfit for the cultivation of the five grains.

After this the young men were called up from all over the empire and sent to guard the northern frontier along the river. The troops spent over ten years fighting in the wastes and wildernesses, where they died in untold numbers, and yet they were never able to extend the empire north beyond the Yellow River. Surely this was not because there were not enough fighting men, or because their weapons and equipment were insufficient. Rather it was because the circumstances made any other outcome impossible.

At the same time the whole empire was ordered to rush fodder and grain to the soldiers. Shipments were sent from as far away as the provinces of Huang-chui and Lang-ya along the seacoast, but by the time they had been transported to the northern frontier along the Yellow River, no more than one picul out of an original thirty bushels remained. Though the men worked the fields as hard as they could, they were unable to supply enough provisions, and though the women wove and spun, they could not produce enough tents and hangings for the army. Soon the common people were exhausted; there was no surplus left to feed the orphans and widows, the children and the old people; and the roads were filled with dead and dying. This was why the empire turned in revolt against the Ch'in.

Later, when Emperor Kao-tsu had won control of the empire and was working to bring the border areas under control, he heard that the Hsiung-nu were gathered north of the valley of Tai and decided to attack them. His imperial secretary Ch'eng Chin advised him against this, saying, "It is impossible. It is the nature of the Hsiung-nu to swarm together like so many beasts, and to disperse again like flocks of birds. Trying to catch them is like grabbing at a shadow. In spite of all Your Majesty's noble virtue, I fear that any attempt to attack the Hsiung-nu will only lead to danger!"

But Emperor Kao-tsu did not heed his advice. Instead he rode north to the valley of Tai and, as Ch'eng Chin had feared, was surrounded by the enemy at P'ing-ch'eng. He regretted deeply what he had done and forthwith dispatched Liu Ching to conclude a peace alliance with the Hsiung-nu, and from that time on the empire was able to forget the sorrows of war.

It is said in the *Art of War:* "He who raises an army of a hundred thousand must spend a thousand pieces of gold a day." The Ch'in was forever calling together armies and sending its soldiers into the field, two and three hundred thousand of them. But although they won distinction by overpowering armies, slaying generals, and taking the *Shan-yü* prisoner, such victories served only to insure the hatred of the enemy and deepen their resentment; in no way did they compensate for the expense which they cost the empire. Any policy which empties the treasuries and arsenals and exhausts the strength of the common people merely for the purpose of having one's way with foreign nations is hardly a sound one.

It is not only our generation which finds the Hsiung-nu difficult to conquer and control. They make a business of pillage and plunder, and indeed this would seem to be their inborn nature. Ever since the times of Emperor Shun and the rulers of the Hsia, Shang, and Chou dynasties, no attempt has ever been made to order or control them; rather they have been regarded as beasts to be pastured, not as members of the human race.

Now Your Majesty does not observe how the Hsia, Shang, and Chou dynasties managed to preserve their rules for so long, but imitates only the mistakes of the recent past, which is a source of grave concern to me and of tribulation and trial to the common people.

Moreover, warfare prolonged over a great period often gives rise to rebellion, and the burden of military service is apt to lead to disaffection, for the people along the border are subjected to great strain and hardship until they think only of breaking away, while the generals and officers grow suspicious of each other and begin to bargain with the enemy. It was circumstances such as these which caused Chao T'o to turn against the Ch'in and make himself an independent ruler in Southern Yüeh, and the Ch'in general Chang Han to desert to the army of the rebellious nobles. The rule of the Ch'in ceased to be effective because its authority was weakened by the loss of these two men. Such are the results of an erroneous policy. Therefore it is said in the *Book of Chou:* "The safety of the state depends upon what kind of orders are issued; its preservation depends upon what kind of men are employed."

I beg Your Majesty to examine closely what I have written, to give it some consideration, no matter how slight, and to ponder carefully what steps should be taken!

At this time a man of Chao named Hsü Yüeh and a man of Ch'i named Yen An both submitted memorials to the throne on some aspect of current policy. Hsü Yüeh's memorial read as follows:

I have heard that in the past and present alike the greatest danger to the empire is a landslide, not a few falling tiles. What do I mean by a landslide? The end of the Ch'in dynasty is a good example. Ch'en She commanded no force of a thousand chariots, nor did he possess so much as a foot of territory. He was not the descendant of any ruler or famous man, nor did he enjoy any outstanding reputation in his village. He did not have the wisdom of a Confucius, a Mo Tzu, or a Tseng Tzu, nor the wealth of a T'ao Chu or an I Tun. And yet he rose up from the lanes and alleys, grasped his spear, bared his arm, and raised a mighty cry, and the whole empire followed after him as though driven by the wind.[3] Why did it happen thus? Because the people were in misery and their rulers had no mercy, because the governed were full of hatred and the governors lost in ignorance, and because the customs of the nation had been thrown into complete confusion and the rule of the dynasty had ceased to be effective. These three conditions were the material out of which Ch'en She fashioned success. This is what is called a landslide and therefore I say that it is the greatest danger to the safety of the empire.

What do I mean by a few falling tiles? The armies of Wu, Ch'u, Ch'i, and Chao are an example. When the leaders of the Seven Kingdoms plotted together to overthrow the Han government, everyone of them was what is called a "lord of ten thousand chariots." Their soldiers numbered several hundred thousand, their might was sufficient to insure the strictest obedience within their realms, and their resources plentiful enough to spur their subjects to action. And yet they were unable to advance west and seize a single inch of territory, but instead were taken prisoner on the central plains. Why was this? Surely not because their authority was less than that of Ch'en She, a mere commoner, or because their armies were weaker than his. Rather it was because at that time the virtue and mercy of the early Han emperors

[3] This description of Ch'en She is paraphrased from Chia I's famous essay, "The Faults of Ch'in," part of which is translated in Volume I, at the end of "The Hereditary House of Ch'en She."

still prevailed in the land and the majority of the people lived in peace and contentment with their lot. Therefore the rebellious lords were unable to receive any assistance from the people outside their domains. This is what I call a few falling tiles, and therefore I say it is not a real danger to the empire.

From this we may see that, if the conditions in the empire are really ripe for a landslide, then even the poorest and lowliest man in a coarse robe can become the leader of a rebellion and endanger the safety of the entire land within the four seas. Ch'en She is proof of this, and if he could accomplish so much, how much more could the lords of states such as Hann, Chao, and Wei at that time?

On the other hand, although the empire may not be completely at peace, if the conditions are not yet ripe for a landslide, then even the strongest lords and the most powerful armies, if they venture to rebel, will suffer defeat and capture before they have time to turn around. Under such circumstances, then, how could ordinary officials or commoners succeed in carrying out a revolt?

These two conditions represent the crux of safety or peril for the nation, and any enlightened ruler must give them careful thought and profound consideration.

Recently the grain crops east of the Pass have not been good and the harvests have not yet returned to normal, so that many of the people are poor and starving. On top of this they are burdened by the military campaigns along the border. In view of this, if I were to attempt to predict the future on the basis of reason, I would say that the people will soon become restless in their present habitations. Being restless, they will begin to shift about, and shifting about is what brings on landslides.

The wise ruler is primarily concerned in perceiving the sources from which all changes arise, in understanding the keys to safety and peril, and in incorporating this knowledge in his governing of the nation, in order to forestall danger before it has taken form. The important thing for Your Majesty, therefore, is simply to strive to prevent conditions in the empire that would bring about a landslide. If this is done, then, although powerful states and strong armies were to oppose you, Your Majesty would be free to spend your time pursuing galloping beasts in the chase and shooting at fleeting birds, broadening your pleasure parks, giving yourself up to the most carefree wanderings, and tasting every pleasure of the hunt with complete security and confidence. The sound of bells and chiming stones, strings and flutes, would never cease to soothe your ears, while within the curtains of your private rooms the antics of actors and comic dwarfs would forever delight your eyes, and yet the empire would never know sorrow. Why must your name be King T'ang or King Wu? Why must your rule be that of Kings Ch'eng or K'ang? If I may be so bold, I would say that Your Majesty was a natural born sage, endowed with tolerance and benevolence. If you will only give thought to the governing of the empire, then your name may easily rival those of the sage rulers T'ang and Wu, and you may revive in your own time the glorious rules of Kings Ch'eng and K'ang. Then, when you have achieved these two goals, you may rest in true honor and security, spread your fame abroad to the world of your time, and win the loyalty of the empire and the submission of the barbarian tribes which surround it, and the effects of your virtue and generosity will insure the prosperity of your heirs for generations to come, so that they may face south before their screens of state, fold their garments about them, and receive the feudal lords and high officials in audience. This is what Your Majesty should strive for!

I have heard that, though one does not succeed in becoming a true king, yet his efforts will be sufficient to bring him security. And with peace and security, what could Your Majesty seek for that would not be gained, what could you do that would not meet with success, whom could you attack without winning submission?

Yen An's memorial read as follows:

I have heard that when the house of Chou won control of the empire it was able to rule effectively for over three hundred years. The dynasty reached its height in the time of Kings Ch'eng and K'ang, when such order reigned that punishments could be set aside and were not needed for over forty years. Later, although the power of the dynasty declined, it was still able to maintain nominal rule for another three hundred years and more. During this latter period the five great feudal dictators arose one after the other, seeking always to assist the Son of Heaven, to encourage profitable measures and prevent danger to the empire, to punish violence and prohibit evil, and to bring order and justice to the land within the four seas so that the Son of Heaven might enjoy greater honor.

But after the five dictators had passed away, no more wise men appeared to succeed them. The Son of Heaven was left alone and powerless, his commands ignored, while the feudal lords did as they pleased. The strong tyrannized the weak; the many oppressed the few. T'ien Ch'ang usurped the throne of Ch'i; the six ministers of Chin divided the kingdom of Chin among themselves; and the era of the Warring States ensued. This was the beginning of hardship for the people.

The powerful states devoted themselves to offensive warfare, while the weaker ones strove for self-preservation, some joining the Vertical Alliance, others the Horizontal Alliance. The soldiers dashed into battle in their war chariots, the hubs clashing against each other; they wore their armor day and night until their bodies were covered with lice; and there was no one whom the people could turn to for help.

Then the king of Ch'in rose to power, gobbling up the empire piece by piece until he had united all the warring states under his command. He assumed the title of Supreme Emperor and became lord of the entire land within the four seas. He razed the fortifications of the feudal lords, and seized their weapons and melted them down to make bells, to show the world that they would never again be needed.

The masses of the common people, believing that they would henceforth be spared the hardships of the Warring States period and be ruled by an enlightened sovereign at last, rejoiced as though each man had been born anew. At this time, if the Ch'in had only relaxed its punishments, lightened the burden of taxation, and decreased its demands upon the labor of the people; if it had honored benevolence and righteousness and scorned power and profit; if it had placed more value on sincerity and less on cunning, and had worked to reform the ways and manners of the people and to educate the empire to virtue, then it might have ruled in peace and security for generations. Yet it did none of these, but merely continued to follow its old customs, advancing men who thought only of craft and cunning, power and profit, and pushing aside men of sincerity and good faith. Its laws were stern and its government harsh. A multitude of flatterers and sycophants appeared, day after day singing the praises of the emperor, until his will was blown up and his heart lulled into ease.

Then, vainly desiring to extend his might to foreign lands, he dispatched Meng T'ien with an army to attack the barbarians to the north. He broadened the empire, pushed back the frontier, and sent an army to garrison the area north of the Yellow River, dispatching a stream of porters bearing fodder and grain in the wake of the fighting men to keep them supplied.

At the same time the emperor sent the military commander T'u Sui with a force of men in towered ships to sail south and attack the hundred tribes of Yüeh, and ordered the supervisor Lu to dig a canal to transport supplies for the men so that they could penetrate deep into the region of Yüeh. But the natives of Yüeh fled before the invaders, and the Ch'in soldiers were left to sit idly day after day with no opponent, until their provisions were exhausted. Then the men of Yüeh launched an attack and inflicted a severe defeat on the Ch'in army. Finally the emperor was obliged to dispatch the military commander Chao T'o with another force of soldiers to occupy Yüeh.

At this time the Ch'in was plagued in the north by its involvements with the Hsiung-nu, and in the south by its entanglements in Yüeh. For over ten years the armies were camped in worthless tracts of land, able to advance but never to withdraw. The young men were obliged to don armor and the girls to transport provisions; hardship made life no longer worth living and the people hanged themselves from the roadside trees in such numbers that one corpse dangled within sight of another.

Finally, when the First Emperor of the Ch'in passed away, the whole empire rose up in revolt. Ch'en She and Wu Kuang raised an army in Ch'en, Wu Ch'en and Chang Erh in Chao, Hsiang Liang in Wu, T'ien Tan in Ch'i, Ching Chü in Ying, Chou Shih in Wei, and Han Kuang in Yen. In the farthest mountains and the remotest valleys heroes sprang to action in numbers too great to recount. None of them were the descendants of feudal lords; none were high officials. Without so much as a foot of land in their possession, they rose up from the lanes and alleys, grasped their spears, and marched into battle, answering the call of the times. No plots had been laid, and yet they sprang up on all sides; no agreements had been reached, and yet their armies joined together; bit by bit they broadened the areas under their control and increased their territories until they had become self-appointed kings. It was the state of the times which brought it all about. The Ch'in enjoyed the honor of the imperial title and the wealth of the empire, and yet its heirs were wiped out and its sacrifices cut off, all because of the evil effects of excessive warfare. The Chou dynasty failed because of its weakness, the Ch'in because of its strength; both suffered by not changing with the times.

Now Your Majesty wishes to induce the southern barbarians to come to court and to make the land of Yeh-lang acknowledge your sovereignty, to conquer the Ch'iang and P'o tribes, gain control of Hui-chou, and build fortified cities there, to invade deep into the territory of the Hsiung-nu and burn the headquarters of the Hsiung-nu at Lung-ch'eng. Your advisers all applaud these aims, but they are thinking only of their own profit; these are not wise policies for the empire as a whole. Now, when China is not troubled by so much as the bark of a dog, to become involved in wearisome projects in distant lands that exhaust the wealth of the nation—this is hardly right for a ruler whose duty is to be a father to the people. To seek to fulfill endless ambitions, determining to win revenge and incurring the hatred of the Hsiung-nu—this will not bring peace to the frontier. To incite troubles and leave them unsolved, to disband the armies only to call them up again, bringing sorrow and hardship to those near at hand and alarm to distant lands—this is no way to insure the continuance of the dynasty!

At present the whole empire is engaged in forging armor and sharpening swords, straightening arrows and stringing bows, transporting supplies and hauling provisions without a moment's rest. This is the burden shared by everyone in the empire. But warfare continued too long may give rise to rebellion, and duties which are too burdensome may breed treasonable thoughts. Some of the outlying provinces are almost a thousand *li* in size, with lines of twenty or thirty fortified cities, situated in strategic areas and with tightly controlled populations, posing a threat to the feudal lords whose territories adjoin them. This is not to the advantage of the imperial house.

We have seen that in ancient times the rulers of Ch'i and Chin were overthrown because the royal houses in those states had sunk too low and the great ministers were too powerful, while in more recent times we have observed that the Ch'in was destroyed because its laws were harsh and its ambitions grandiose and endless. Now the power of the governors in the provinces is much greater than that of the high officials of Ch'i and Chin; their territories of a thousand *li* offer a far better basis for revolt than the lanes and alleys from which Ch'en She raised his rebellion; and their weapons and military resources are hardly limited to the homemade spears which Ch'en She fought with. If, by one chance in ten thousand, a revolt should break out, it would end in consequences so fearful I dare not name them.[4]

When these memorials had been presented to the throne, the emperor summoned the three men, Chu-fu Yen, Hsü Yüeh, and Yen An, and said to them, "Gentlemen, where have you been keeping yourselves up till now? Why have we not met sooner?" And he honored them with the rank of palace attendant. Chu-fu Yen continued to appear before the emperor from time to time and submit memorials on government policy. The emperor promoted him four times within a single year until he had advanced him to the post of master of guests. He also promoted Hsü Yüeh to the rank of palace counselor.

On one occasion Chu-fu Yen advised the emperor, saying, "In an-

[4] Yen An's memorial, which is mainly a criticism of Emperor Wu's foreign wars, seems to wander from the point at the end in warning of the danger of revolt in the outlying provinces. It should be remembered, however, that the reason the outlying provinces were strong enough to pose a threat to the central government was that the armies were stationed there for the purpose of launching attacks abroad. Anyone familiar with the history of imperial Rome knows what such a situation could mean.

cient times the territories of the feudal lords did not exceed a hundred
li in breadth, so that it was easy to control them and insure that they
did not become too strong. Now, however, some of the feudal lords
possess lands a thousand *li* square, dotted by twenty or thirty strong
cities. If they are treated with leniency, they may give themselves up
to wayward and luxurious living, which leads easily into lasciviousness
and moral chaos, while if they are pressed to mend their ways, they are
apt to band together and use their might to defy the capital. Any
attempt to deprive them of territory by legal means will only nourish
the seeds of revolt, as we have seen from the case of Ch'ao Ts'o and
the revolt of the Seven Kingdoms in the time of Emperor Ching.

"Now, although some of the feudal lords have as many as ten or
more sons and younger brothers, only one of them, the recognized
heir to the title, receives any inheritance; the others, though of the same
flesh and blood as the heir, do not receive a single foot of territory.
Surely this is not the way to encourage the practice of benevolence and
filial piety.

"I beg Your Majesty, therefore, to issue an order allowing the feudal
lords to extend the blessings of your generosity by dividing their lands
among their sons and younger brothers, enfeoffing each as a marquis
with a grant of territory. In this way each one will rejoice in the
gratification of his desires and Your Majesty, while performing an act
of virtue, will in fact be dividing up the feudal states. Thus, without
your resorting to forced deprivations of territory, the feudal lords will
be gradually weakened."

The emperor approved this plan and put it into effect.

On another occasion Chu-fu Yen said, "Now that Your Majesty's
mausoleum has been established at Mou-ling in the suburbs, it would
be advisable to gather together the wealthy and powerful families and
the troublemakers among the people from all over the empire and resettle them at Mou-ling. In this way you will increase the population
of the capital area and at the same time prevent the spread of evil and
vicious ways in the provinces. This is called preventing danger without
resorting to punishments." The emperor put this suggestion into effect
as well.

Chu-fu Yen also won distinction by the part he played in having

Wei Tzu-fu made empress and in exposing the evil deeds of Liu Ting-kuo, the king of Yen. The other high officials were all terrified of the power of Chu-fu Yen's words and presented him with bribes of thousands of gold pieces to win his favor. One of them cautioned him about his actions, saying, "You are being too headstrong!" But Chu-fu Yen only replied, "After I bound up my hair and entered manhood I spent over forty years wandering from place to place and studying, never able to win success. My father would not treat me as a son, my brothers refused to have anything to do with me, and my friends rejected me. Many were the days when I knew nothing but hardship. Any real man knows that there are only two alternatives in life—to succeed and dine from rich cauldrons, or to fail and end by being boiled alive in them. Now my days are drawing to a close, and I have no time for virtuous ways. So I do anything I please, no matter how unreasonable, and never worry about the consequences!"

Chu-fu Yen spoke strongly in favor of occupying the region of So-fang in the north. It was a very fertile area, bounded by the Yellow River on the north, he argued, and had been fortified by Meng T'ien during the Ch'in and used as a base in driving out the Hsiung-nu. If it were occupied once more, it would help to reduce the transportation of supplies and soldiers from the interior of the empire, broaden the territory of China, and serve as a foundation for wiping out the barbarians. The emperor considered his proposal and referred it to the high ministers for discussion, but all of them opposed it as impractical. Kung-sun Hung pointed out, "Although the Ch'in constantly kept a force of three hundred thousand men in the area to fortify the northern border along the Yellow River, they were never able to accomplish anything and finally had to abandon the project." [5]

But Chu-fu Yen continued to urge the advantages of the project,

[5] It seems odd that Chu-fu Yen would urge expansion into the area of So-fang when his first memorial showed him strongly opposed to Emperor Wu's wars against the Hsiung-nu. It should also be recalled that Kung-sun Hung, though at first opposing the plan to set up fortifications in So-fang, later changed his mind and supported it. Apparently both men were capable of altering their views to conform to the wishes of the emperor, which is no doubt one reason why Ssu-ma Ch'ien chose to treat them both together in this chapter.

and the emperor finally decided to follow his advice and set up the province of So-fang.

In the second year of *yüan-so* [127 B.C.] Chu-fu Yen reported that Liu Tzu-ching, the king of Ch'i, was guilty of lewd and immoral conduct. The emperor appointed him as prime minister of Ch'i and sent him to that kingdom to investigate. When he arrived in Ch'i he summoned all his brothers and friends and scattered gifts amounting to five hundred gold pieces among them. Then he reviled them, saying, "Formerly, when I was poor, my brothers would not clothe or feed me and my friends would not let me inside their gates. Now that I am prime minister of Ch'i, you all come rushing to greet me, some from as far away as a thousand *li*. But I want nothing more to do with any of you! Don't ever enter my gate again!"

Then he sent men to warn the king to mend his ways, telling him that he knew all about the king's incestuous relations with his older sister. The king, concluding that he would never be able to escape punishment, and fearing that he would be condemned to execution in the same way as Liu Ting-kuo, the king of Yen, committed suicide. The officials reported his death to the emperor.

In his early days, when Chu-fu Yen was still a commoner, he had traveled widely in Yen and Chao, and after he won favor with the emperor he had utilized his experience to bring to light the misdoings of the king of Yen. The king of Chao was afraid that he himself might suffer the same fate and wanted to send a letter to the emperor accusing Chu-fu Yen of secret misdeeds, but as long as Chu-fu Yen was serving at the emperor's side he did not dare to make a move. After Chu-fu Yen had been appointed prime minister of Ch'i and had left the capital and gone beyond the Pass, however, the king of Chao sent an envoy with a letter to the emperor reporting that Chu-fu Yen had accepted bribes of money from the feudal lords. "That is why he urged that so many of the sons and brothers of the feudal lords be enfeoffed!"

Sometime afterwards the emperor received word of the death of the king of Ch'i and was extremely angry, believing that Chu-fu Yen had threatened the king and driven him to suicide. He therefore summoned Chu-fu Yen back to the capital and turned him over to the law officials for investigation. Chu-fu Yen admitted having accepted gold from the feudal lords, but denied that he had threatened the king of Ch'i and driven him to suicide.

The emperor was in favor of sparing him the death penalty, but Kung-sun Hung, who was imperial secretary at this time, said, "Since the king of Ch'i has committed suicide and left no heir, his kingdom should be abolished and his territory taken over and made into a province of the central government. As for Chu-fu Yen, he was the one who originally started all the trouble. If Your Majesty does not execute him, there will be no way to make amends to the empire for what has happened!"

Accordingly, the emperor in the end ordered the execution of Chu-fu Yen and all his family. While Chu-fu Yen enjoyed honor and favor, his guests and retainers numbered in the thousands, but when he and his family were executed, none of them was willing to dispose of the corpses. Only one man, K'ung Ch'e of Hsiao, came forward to accept the bodies and bury them. Later on, when the emperor learned of this, he admired K'ung Ch'e as a man of true worth.

The Grand Historian remarks: Although Kung-sun Hung was careful to act according to righteous principles, he was also fortunate in having lived at the right time. It had been over eighty years since the dynasty was founded, and the emperor looked with favor on literary accomplishments and invited men of talent and worth to take service in the government in order to spread the teachings of Confucius and Mo Tzu. Kung-sun Hung won the highest place in the examination.

While Chu-fu Yen was in a position of power, men all united in praising him. But when his good name was gone and he had been condemned to execution—alas, they outdid each other in speaking ill of him! [6]

[6] The remainder of the chapter, dealing with events long after the death of Ssu-ma Ch'ien, is a later addition and has therefore been omitted.

Shih chi 113: The Account of Southern Yüeh

After the Han had brought peace to China, Chao T'o gained control of the region of Yang-yüeh, guarding the south as a vassal of the Han and sending tribute to the court. Thus I made The Account of Southern Yüeh.

The king of Southern Yüeh, formerly known as military commander T'o, was a native of Chen-ting. His family name was Chao. After the Ch'in dynasty had unified the empire, it sent troops to invade and seize control of the region of Yang-yüeh, setting up the provinces of Kuei-lin or Cassia Forest, Nan-hai or Southern Sea, and Hsiang or Elephant, and moving bands of condemned Chinese into the area, where they lived among the natives for the following thirteen years.

Under the First Emperor of the Ch'in, Chao T'o served as magistrate of Dragon River in the province of Nan-hai. After the Second Emperor came to the throne the military commander of Nan-hai, Jen Hsiao, fell ill. Just before he died he summoned Chao T'o, the magistrate of Dragon River, and said to him, "I have received news that Ch'en She and others have started a revolt. The rule of the Ch'in has been cruel and tyrannous and the whole empire is embittered. Hsiang Yü, Liu Chi, Ch'en She, Wu Kuang, and others have gathered bands of men and raised armies in every province, fighting like tigers with each other for the possession of the empire. All of China is in turmoil and no one knows when the fighting will cease, for the powerful leaders have all turned against the Ch'in and set themselves up as independent rulers. Nan-hai is a distant and out-of-the-way region, and yet I am afraid that the rebel soldiers may invade even this far. I had hoped to call out the troops and cut off the new road that connects us with China, fortifying ourselves so that we may be prepared for any move of the feudal leaders. Unfortunately, however, I have contracted this grave illness.

"The region of P'an-yü [1] is rugged and backed by mountains, and

[1] The site of the capital of Southern Yüeh in the region of present-day Canton.

Nan-hai measures several thousand *li* from east to west. Moreover, there are a number of Chinese in the region who can be of assistance. Thus anyone who holds command of this area has in effect a whole prefecture under his control and could easily set it up as an independent kingdom. None of the provincial officials here, however, are worth talking to, and therefore I have summoned you to tell you my ideas."

Jen Hsiao drew up a letter empowering Chao T'o to act as military commander of Nan-hai, and shortly afterwards died.

Chao T'o then circulated a notice to the customs barriers at Heng-p'u, Yang-shan, and Huang-ch'i saying, "The rebel troops will soon be here! Close the roads as fast as you can and call together your troops to defend yourselves!"

On one legal pretext or another he little by little did away with the officials appointed by the Ch'in and filled the posts with temporary appointees belonging to his own party. By the time the Ch'in dynasty fell, Chao T'o had attacked and brought under his command the provinces of Kuei-lin and Hsiang as well and had set himself up as King Wu of Southern Yüeh.

After Kao-tsu won control of the empire he allowed Chao T'o to go unpunished, since China had enough to do to take care of internal troubles, and in the eleventh year of his reign [196 B.C.] he dispatched Lu Chia to recognize Chao T'o as king of Southern Yüeh, presenting him with the split tallies of a feudal lord. He enjoined Chao T'o to unite all the people of Yüeh in peace and not to cause any disturbance along the southern border, which adjoined that of the kingdom of Ch'ang-sha.

In the time of Empress Lü the officials requested that all trade in iron goods between Southern Yüeh and China be prohibited. When Chao T'o received word of this, he protested. "Emperor Kao-tsu set me up as a feudal lord and sent his envoy giving me permission to carry on trade. But now Empress Lü, heeding the advice of slanderous officials, is discriminating against me, treating me as one of the barbarians and breaking off our trade in iron vessels and goods. This must be a plot of Wu Jui, the king of Ch'ang-sha. He thinks he will be able to use the forces of China to attack and destroy Southern Yüeh, and then increase his prestige by making himself king of this region as well!"

Chao T'o thereupon assumed the title of Emperor Wu of Southern Yüeh and sent out his troops to attack the towns along the border of Ch'ang-sha. They succeeded in capturing several district towns before returning to their own territory.

Empress Lü dispatched General Chou Tsao, the marquis of Lung-lü, to attack Southern Yüeh, but he encountered such heat and dampness, and so many of his officers and men fell ill, that his army could not cross the mountains into the region. After a year or so Empress Lü passed away and Chou Tsao's troops were recalled to China.

Chao T'o began once more to threaten the border with his forces. He sent gifts and bribes to the chiefs of Min-yüeh, Western Ou, and Lo-lo, persuading them to submit to his authority, until the region under his control extended over ten thousand *li* from east to west. He then began to ride about in a carriage with a yellow top, decorated with plumes on the left side, and to call his orders "edicts" in imitation of the Han emperor, all of which was intended to show that he was an equal of the ruler of China.

In the first year of Emperor Wen's reign [180 B.C.], because peace had only recently been restored to the empire, the emperor sent an announcement to the feudal lords and the barbarian chiefs, explaining his reasons for leaving his kingdom of Tai and journeying to the capital to take the throne, and informing them of his virtuous intentions. At the same time, learning that Chao T'o's parents were buried in Chen-ting, he set aside one of the towns in that district to take care of their graves and offer sacrifices at certain times each year. He also summoned Chao T'o's cousins to court and appointed them to high offices, treating them with great generosity. He then asked the chancellor Ch'en P'ing and the other high officials to recommend someone to act as envoy to Southern Yüeh. Ch'en P'ing suggested Lu Chia of Hao-chih, who had had experience under the former emperor as envoy to Southern Yüeh. Emperor Wen summoned Lu Chia, made him a palace counselor, and sent him to Southern Yüeh with instructions to reprimand Chao T'o for setting himself up as an "emperor" and at the same time failing to send a single envoy to report the fact to the Han court. When Lu Chia arrived in Southern Yüeh, Chao T'o, thoroughly frightened, wrote a letter of apology. Referring to himself as "Your aged subject T'o, a barbarian chief," Chao T'o explained:

Some time ago, when Empress Lü cut off trade with Southern Yüeh and began to discriminate against me, I suspected that it was due to the slanders of the king of Ch'ang-sha. I also heard rumors that all the members of my clan in China had been executed and the graves of my ancestors dug up and desecrated. Therefore in desperation I dared to violate the borders of the kingdom of Ch'ang-sha. Moreover, this region of the south is low and damp and inhabited only by barbarian tribes. To the east of me is the chief of Min-yüeh who, with no more than a thousand subjects, calls himself a king, while to the west are the lands of Western Ou and Lo-lo, whose rulers likewise call themselves kings. So your aged subject, to gratify a whim, presumed in his delusion to call himself "emperor." Yet how could he dare to report such a fact to the Heavenly King of China?

Chao T'o bowed his head and apologized, begging that he might be allowed to continue to serve the emperor as a feudal lord, rendering his tribute and labor services as before. He then circulated an order throughout his kingdom which read:

I have heard that two great men do not stand side by side, and two wise men never appear in the same age. The emperor is in truth a wise Son of Heaven. From this time onward, I relinquish the use of the words "emperor" and "edict" and the yellow covered carriage with plumes on the left side.

Lu Chia returned and reported the success of his mission, which greatly pleased Emperor Wen. Thus, for the remainder of his reign, as well as for that of Emperor Ching, Chao T'o called himself a subject of the Han and sent envoys with tribute to the court in the spring and fall. As a matter of fact, however, he continued secretly to use the designations "emperor" and "edict" the same as before within his kingdom, and only referred to himself as a "king" and used the other terms appropriate to a feudal lord when he sent envoys to the rulers of China.

Chao T'o died in the fourth year of the era *chien-yüan* [137 B.C.]. His grandson Chao Hu succeeded him as king of Southern Yüeh. At this time Tsou Ying, the king of Min-yüeh, had called out his troops and was attacking the border towns of Southern Yüeh. Chao Hu dispatched a messenger to the Han court with a letter to the emperor saying,

Since the two kings of Southern Yüeh and Min-yüeh are both vassal lords of the Han, it is not right that they should arbitrarily call out their troops and attack each other. Yet now the king of Min-yüeh has raised his troops and is invading my territory. I do not dare call out my own troops unless the Son of Heaven commands me to.

The emperor, much impressed by the fidelity with which the king of Southern Yüeh had abided by his duties as a vassal lord, called up an army for his sake and dispatched it under the command of two generals to attack Min-yüeh. Before the Han troops had crossed the mountains into the south, however, Tsou Yü-shan, the younger brother of Tsou Ying, the king of Min-yüeh, murdered his brother and surrendered to the Han forces. The emperor then recalled his troops and dispatched Chuang Chu to go and explain his intentions to Chao Hu, the king of Southern Yüeh. Chao Hu bowed his head and replied, "For my sake the Son of Heaven has raised an army and attacked Min-yüeh. Death could not repay the debt of gratitude which I owe him." He sent his son, the crown prince Chao Ying-ch'i, to return with Chuang Chu to the capital and serve as an attendant at the imperial court, telling Chuang Chu, "Since my country has suffered recently from these attackers, you had better return at once to the capital, while I for my part will make preparations day and night and follow shortly afterwards to pay my respects in person to the Son of Heaven."

After Chuang Chu had returned to China, however, Chao Hu's high ministers reprimanded him for making such a commitment, saying, "We have just recovered from the excitement caused by the Han armies which came to punish Tsou Ying. Now, if you should leave the kingdom and journey to the Han court, it would cause great alarm and unrest in Southern Yüeh. Moreover the former king used to say that in serving the Son of Heaven, all that was necessary was to avoid a breach of etiquette. The important thing is not to be taken in by friendly words to the point where you commit yourself to a journey to the capital. If you ever go to the capital to visit the Son of Heaven, you will never return again! It will mean the downfall of the kingdom!"

Chao Hu therefore pleaded illness and in the end never went

through with his plans to visit the capital. Some ten or so years later he actually did fall gravely ill, and his son, the crown prince Chao Ying-ch'i, received permission to return home. Chao Hu died and was given the posthumous title of Wen, the "Civil King." Chao Ying-ch'i succeeded to the throne and put away the old seal which Chao T'o had used when he called himself by the title "Emperor Wu."

While Chao Ying-ch'i was at the court in Ch'ang-an he married a daughter of the Chiu family of Han-tan, by whom he had a son named Hsing. After he took the throne he sent a letter to the emperor requesting that his wife be formally declared queen and his son Hsing designated as heir to the throne. The Han envoys who came from time to time hinted to Chao Ying-ch'i that it would be well for him to go to the capital to visit the emperor. But Chao Ying-ch'i was accustomed to doing as he pleased, murdering people and giving free rein to his passions, and he was afraid that if he went to the capital he would be treated the same as the feudal lords of China proper and tried for his offenses under Han law. So he kept insisting that he was too ill to make the journey and never went to the capital, instead sending his second son Chao Tzu-kung to be an attendant at court. Chao Ying-ch'i died and was given the posthumous title of Ming, the "Enlightened King."

The crown prince Chao Hsing succeeded to the throne and his mother became queen dowager. Before the queen dowager married Chao Ying-ch'i she had had an affair with a man of Pa-ling named An-kuo Shao-chi. After Chao Ying-ch'i's death, in the fourth year of the era *yüan-ting* [113 B.C.], this same An-kuo Shao-chi was sent as envoy from the Han court to persuade the king of Southern Yüeh and the queen dowager that they should come to the capital to visit the emperor and conduct themselves the same as the other feudal lords. The admonisher Chung Chün and others skilled at rhetoric were designated to present the arguments in favor of such a move, with Wei Ch'en and other men noted for their daring standing by to help out. The colonel of the guard Lu Po-te was ordered to lead his troops and station them at Kuei-yang, where he would wait for the return of the envoys.

The king was still very young, and his mother, the queen dowager, was a native of China. Moreover, as mentioned before, she had once had an affair with An-kuo Shao-chi, and when he arrived as an envoy from the Han, she resumed the illicit relationship, a fact which was known to quite a number of people of the kingdom. The majority of them therefore had little use for her. The queen dowager, fearing the outbreak of revolt and hoping to use the authority of the Han to strengthen her position, repeatedly urged the king and his ministers to seek closer ties with the Han court. The king asked the Han envoys to forward a letter to the throne requesting that he be treated the same as the feudal lords of China proper and promising to journey to court once every three years to pay his respects. He also asked that the customs barriers on the border between his kingdom and China be removed. The emperor granted his requests and presented the prime minister of Southern Yüeh, Lü Chia, with a silver seal, along with the seals for the internal secretary, the military commander, and the grand tutor. The king was left to appoint the other officials of his court without consulting the emperor. The old punishments of tattooing and cutting off the nose were abolished and the Han laws put into effect, so that the kingdom would be governed the same as those of the other feudal lords. The envoys from the Han court were to remain in the kingdom to see that no trouble occurred. The king and the queen dowager then set about getting their baggage together and selecting a number of rare gifts to be presented to the emperor when they made their trip to the capital.

The prime minister Lü Chia was an old man and had served as prime minister to three kings of Southern Yüeh. Over seventy members of his family held high posts as officials of the state. His sons were all married to princesses and his daughters were all married to men of the royal family. In addition, he was related by marriage to King Ch'in of Ts'ang-wu. He therefore wielded enormous power in the kingdom. The people of Yüeh trusted him, and many of them were happy to act as ears and eyes for him; he had a firmer hold on the hearts of the multitude than the king himself.

When the king was preparing to send his letter to the emperor, Lü Chia several times advised him against the move, but the king would not listen. Lü Chia by this time was already contemplating revolt and repeatedly refused to see the Han envoys, claiming that he was ill. The envoys for their part kept a close watch on Lü Chia, but the situation had not yet reached a point where they could take action against him.

The king and the queen dowager also were afraid that Lü Chia and the others of his party would seize the initiative by making a decisive move. They therefore decided to give a banquet and, relying on the support of the Han envoys, to do away with Lü Chia and his party. At the banquet the envoys were all seated facing east. The queen dowager faced south, the king faced north, and Lü Chia and the other high ministers all faced west. Lü Chia's younger brother, who was a general, led his soldiers and stationed them outside the palace.

When the drinking had reached its height, the queen dowager turned to Lü Chia and said, "Obviously all of Southern Yüeh would profit by being treated as a part of China proper. And yet you as prime minister have bitterly opposed the move. What is the reason?"

She thought in this way she could arouse the envoys to a display of anger, but the envoys hesitated and held back, waiting for each other to make a move, and in the end did not dare do anything. Lü Chia, judging from the faces of those about him that something was afoot, jumped up and started out of the room. The queen dowager in her rage tried to strike him down with a spear, but the king prevented her and Lü Chia succeeded in escaping from the room. Once outside, he got a party of his brother's soldiers to escort him back to his lodging, from which he sent word that he was ill and would not meet with the envoys again. In the meantime he laid plans in secret with the high ministers to start a revolt.

The king had originally had no intention of doing away with Lü Chia. Lü Chia knew this, and so for several months made no move. The queen dowager tried every way she could to get rid of Lü Chia and his group, but because of her immoral conduct and the fact that the people of the kingdom had no use for her, she could not muster enough support to accomplish her aim.

The emperor soon received word that Lü Chia was refusing to obey the king and the queen dowager and that the queen dowager was alone and powerless to remedy the situation, while the Han envoys were too afraid to make a move. He considered, however, that since the king and queen dowager had already declared their loyalty to the Han, and since it was only Lü Chia who was rebellious, there was no need to send an army against Southern Yüeh. He therefore decided to dispatch Chuang Ts'an with two thousand men to act as his envoy. Chuang Ts'an declined to accept the mission, however, declaring that it was impossible. "If the mission is a friendly one, then two or three men will be sufficient. But if it is to be a display of force, two thousand men are not enough to accomplish anything!"

After the emperor had dismissed Chuang Ts'an, Han Ch'ien-ch'iu, a young man of Chia who had formerly been prime minister to the king of Chi-pei, stepped forward and exclaimed, "A little, insignificant country like Yüeh, and in addition we have the support of the queen dowager to count on! The only one who is causing any trouble is the prime minister Lü Chia. Give me two hundred brave men and I will cut off his head and bring it back without fail!"

The emperor thereupon dispatched Han Ch'ien-ch'iu, together with the queen dowager's younger brother Chiu Yüeh, to lead a force of two thousand men. When they crossed the border of Southern Yüeh, Lü Chia and his men finally started their revolt. Lü Chia circulated an order throughout the kingdom which read:

The king is very young and the queen dowager is a Chinese. Moreover she has had immoral relations with one of the Han envoys. Her only thought is to make the kingdom a part of China. She intends to take all of the precious goods and vessels of our former rulers and present them to the Son of Heaven in order to curry favor with him, and as soon as she reaches the capital, the numerous attendants in her party will be seized and sold as slaves. In her haste to snatch a momentary advantage for herself she disregards the sacred altars of the Chao family and gives no thought to the future of the state!

With the assistance of his brother's soldiers Lü Chia then attacked the palace and murdered the queen dowager and the Han envoys. He sent men to report what he had done to King Ch'in of Ts'ang-wu and to the various provinces and districts, and set up Chao Chien-te, the marquis of Shu-yang, the eldest son of Chao Ying-ch'i by a wife of the Yüeh people, as king.

After Han Ch'ien-ch'iu and his soldiers had attacked and defeated several small towns, the people of Yüeh opened up the roads and began to supply food to his soldiers. Then, when Han Ch'ien-ch'iu had marched to within forty *li* of P'an-yü, the Yüeh soldiers fell upon him and his men and wiped them out. Lü Chia ordered men to take the imperial credentials of the Han envoys and, sealing them up, deposit them with the officials at the border, giving some sort of false excuse and apologizing for the action he had taken. He also dispatched troops to guard the vital points of the kingdom.

When the emperor received word of what had happened he announced that, although Han Ch'ien-ch'iu had failed in his mission, he had distinguished himself by leading the attack, and therefore he enfeoffed his son Han Yen-nien as marquis of Ch'eng-an. In addition, because Chiu Yüeh's sister, the queen dowager, had been the leader in the movement to make the kingdom of Southern Yüeh a part of China, he enfeoffed Chiu Yüeh's son Chiu Kuang-te as marquis of Lung-kang. Then he granted a general amnesty to the empire, declaring: "In the *Spring and Autumn Annals* Confucius has expressed his condemnation of a situation in which, the Son of Heaven being weak and the feudal lords engaged in fights among themselves, no one troubles to punish rebels. Now Lü Chia, Chao Chien-te, and the others of their party have revolted and brazenly put themselves in power. Let the convicts who are freed by this amnesty, as well as a hundred thousand sailors of the towered ships who are stationed south of the Huai and Yangtze rivers, be sent to attack them!"

In the autumn of the fifth year of *yüan-ting* [112 B.C.] the colonel of the guard Lu Po-te was appointed General Who Calms the Waves and ordered to leave Kuei-yang and sail down the Hui River. The master of titles chief commandant Yang P'u was made General of the Towered Ships and ordered to sail down the Heng-p'u River from Yü-chang. Two men of Yüeh who had surrendered to the Han and been made marquises were appointed as General of the Daggered Ships and General Who Descends the Torrents respectively and sent out of Ling-ling, one to sail down the Li River and the other to move into Ts'ang-wu. Another native of Yüeh, the Marquis Who Hastens to Duty, was ordered to lead a band of criminals from Pa and Shu and, mobilizing the troops of Yeh-lang, to descend the Tsang-ko River. All were to meet at P'an-yü, the capital of Southern Yüeh.

In the winter of the sixth year of *yüan-ting* [111 B.C.] Yang P'u, leading his best men, advanced ahead of the others, captured Hsün-hsia, and broke through the line at Shih-men. There he seized the Yüeh grain ships and, moving forward again, drove back the vanguard of the Yüeh forces. Then he halted with his twenty or thirty thousand men to await the arrival of Lu Po-te. Lu Po-te had set out with his army of released convicts as scheduled, but because he had such a long distance to travel he did not reach the rendezvous point as soon as planned, and when he finally joined up with Yang P'u, he had no more than a thousand or so men with him.

The two armies then advanced together, but since Yang P'u was in front, he reached P'an-yü first. Chao Chien-te, Lü Chia, and the others of their party were all guarding the city. Yang P'u, selecting the most advantageous site, took up a position facing the southeast side of the city, while Lu Po-te was forced to draw up on the northwest side. By this time night had fallen. Yang P'u attacked and defeated a number of the Yüeh defenders and set fire to the city.

The men of Yüeh had heard before of Lu Po-te's reputation, but since it was already night, they could not tell how many men he had with him. After Lu Po-te had set up his camp he sent envoys inviting the men of Yüeh to surrender and presenting those who did so with the seals of a marquis. Then he sent them back into the city to persuade more of their friends to surrender. In the meantime Yang P'u began attacking the city with force and setting fire to it, which had the un-expected effect of driving the enemy over into Lu Po-te's camp. By the time dawn came, therefore, all the defenders of the city had sur-rendered to Lu Po-te.

Lü Chia and Chao Chien-te had already escaped in the night with several hundred of their followers and, embarking in ships, had fled west. Lu Po-te, however, questioning one of the noblemen who had surrendered to him, discovered Lü Chia's destination and sent men to pursue him. Thus a colonel named Ssu-ma Su-hung succeeded in capturing Chao Chien-te, for which he was enfeoffed as marquis of Hai-ch'ang, and Tu Chi, a palace attendant of Yüeh, captured Lü Chia, for which he was enfeoffed as marquis of Lin-ts'ai.

King Ch'in of Ts'ang-wu, Chao Kuang, bore the same surname as the kings of Southern Yüeh. When he heard that the Han forces had arrived, he sent word through Shih Ting, the magistrate of Chieh-yang, that he was prepared to submit to Han rule. The overseer of Kuei-lin, Chü Weng, also persuaded the chiefs of Western Ou and Lo-lo to submit to the Han. All of them were made marquises. Before the forces of the General of the Daggered Ships, the General Who Descends the Torrents, or the soldiers of Yeh-lang mobilized by the Marquis Who Hastens to Duty had even arrived in the area, peace was restored to Southern Yüeh. The region was eventually divided up into nine provinces. Lu Po-te's fief was increased and Yang P'u, because his soldiers had captured a strongly fortified city, was enfeoffed as marquis of Chiang-liang. Thus five generations, or ninety-three years, after Chao T'o first became king of Southern Yüeh, the state was destroyed.

The Grand Historian remarks: It was through Jen Hsiao that Chao T'o originally got to be a king, and when the Han came to power, he ranked among the feudal lords. Because Chou Tsao's men were halted by dampness and disease, Chao T'o grew more arrogant than ever. Western Ou and Lo-lo fell to fighting, and Southern Yüeh was filled with unrest until the Han troops appeared on the border and Chao Ying-ch'i was sent to the capital to attend the emperor. The downfall of the state in later days came about through the queen dowager, a daughter of the Chiu family. Lü Chia also, because of his lack of loyalty, caused Chao T'o's line to perish. Yang P'u selfishly chose the best camp site for himself, and his laziness and pride lost him the larger measure of success, but Lu Po-te, though in a difficult position, proved himself a cleverer strategist, turning disaster into good fortune. Thus the shifts of success and failure are entwined like the strands of a rope.[2]

[2] Unlike the remarks of the Grand Historian at the end of other chapters, these do little more than summarize the principal points of the narrative; they are in four-character rhyming phrases, a form much used in later literary and historical works for rhymed "epitomes" at the ends of chapters.

Shih chi 114: The Account of Eastern Yüeh

When Liu P'i, the king of Wu, revolted against the Han, the men of Eastern Ou assassinated him. Later, when they were attacked by Min-yüeh, they guarded Mount Feng-yü as loyal subjects of the Han. Thus I made The Account of Eastern Yüeh.

Wu-chu, the king of Min-yüeh, and Yao, the king of Tung-hai in the region of Yüeh, were both descendants of Kou-chien, king of the state of Yüeh in ancient times.[1] Their family name was Tsou. After the Ch'in dynasty unified the empire both were deprived of their rank as kings and given the title of chieftain. Their lands were made into the province of Min-chung. When the feudal lords rose in revolt against the Ch'in, Tsou Wu-chu and Tsou Yao called out the troops of Yüeh and went to join Wu Jui, the magistrate of P'o-yang (known as the Lord of P'o), taking part with the other feudal lords in the overthrow of the Ch'in dynasty. At that time Hsiang Yü was issuing orders to the other leaders of the revolt, but he failed to make kings of Wu-chu and Yao, and for that reason they refused to give him their support. Instead, when the king of Han attacked Hsiang Yü, they once more called out the troops of Yüeh and aided the Han cause.

In the fifth year of the Han [202 B.C.] Emperor Kao-tsu reestablished Tsou Wu-chu as king of Min-yüeh, ruling over the region that had formerly been the province of Min-chung, with his capital at Tung-yeh. In the third year of Emperor Hui's reign [192 B.C.] the service rendered by the men of Yüeh to Kao-tsu was brought to the emperor's attention. "Tsou Yao, the chief of Min, achieved great merit and his people supported the Han cause," the emperor announced, and set up Tsou Yao as king of Tung-hai, with his capital at Tung-ou or Eastern Ou. For this reason he is popularly known as the king of Eastern Ou.

After the reigns of several Han rulers, in the third year of Emperor Ching's reign [154 B.C.], Liu P'i, the king of Wu, revolted. He tried

[1] Reigned 496–465 B.C.

to persuade the king of Min-yüeh to join him, but the latter refused; only Tsou Yao, the king of Eastern Ou, sided with the rebels. After the armies of Wu had been defeated, the men of Eastern Ou accepted a bribe from the Han government and murdered the king of Wu at Tan-t'u. For this reason the men of Eastern Ou were allowed to return to their homes without punishment.

Liu Tzu-chü, the son of the king of Wu, fled to Min-yüeh, where, deeply angered at Eastern Ou because of his father's murder, he worked constantly to incite Min-yüeh to an attack on Eastern Ou. In the third year of the *chien-yüan* era [138 B.C.] the king of Min-yüeh finally called out his troops and surrounded the city of Eastern Ou. Food supplies in the city were soon exhausted and the defenders in such distress that they were about to surrender, when the king of Eastern Ou dispatched someone to report his plight to the present emperor. The emperor questioned the grand commandant T'ien Fen on what course to follow. T'ien Fen replied, "It is a common occurrence for the men of Yüeh to attack each other. Moreover they have several times proved disloyal to us. There is therefore no reason for China to go to the trouble of rescuing them. It has been the policy since the Ch'in dynasty to let them go their own way and not to attempt to force them into submission!"

The palace counselor Chuang Chu, however, took exception to T'ien Fen's words. "The only thing we should worry about is whether we have strength enough to rescue them and virtue enough to command their loyalty," he said. "If we have, then why should we 'let them go' as you say? As for the Ch'in dynasty, it 'let go' not only Yüeh but the whole empire, including the capital itself! Now a small country has come to report its distress to the Son of Heaven. If he does not save it, to whom can it turn for aid? And how can the Son of Heaven claim that the rulers of all other states are like sons to him if he ignores their pleas?"

"It is obvious," said the emperor, "that T'ien Fen is not worth consulting in these matters! However, since I have just come to the throne, I do not wish to issue the tiger seals and officially call out the troops of all the provinces and kingdoms." He therefore dispatched Chuang Chu with the seals of an envoy to call out only the troops of

K'uai-chi. The governor of K'uai-chi tried to prevent him from carrying out his orders on the grounds that he was not bearing the tiger seals, but Chuang Chu cut off the head of one of the marshals to show that he meant business, and eventually managed to call out the troops and transport them by sea to rescue Eastern Ou. Before they reached their destination, the king of Min-yüeh withdrew his troops and departed. The king of Eastern Ou then requested that he be allowed to move the inhabitants of his state to China. Permission was granted, and he and all his people came and settled in the region between the Yangtze and Huai rivers.

In the sixth year of the era *chien-yüan* [135 B.C.] Min-yüeh attacked Southern Yüeh. The king of Southern Yüeh, abiding by his agreement with the Son of Heaven, did not venture to call out his troops on his own authority, but sent word of his predicament to the emperor. The emperor dispatched the grand messenger Wang Hui from Yü-chang and the minister of agriculture Han An-kuo from K'uai-chi, both of them with the rank of general. Before they had crossed the mountains into the region of Yüeh, however, Tsou Ying, the king of Min-yüeh, sent his troops to block the passes. The king's younger brother, Tsou Yü-shan, began to plot with the prime minister and the other members of his family, saying, "Without requesting permission, the king has arbitrarily sent out his troops to attack Southern Yüeh. Therefore the armies of the Son of Heaven have come to punish us. The Han armies are numerous and powerful, and even if we should somehow succeed in defeating them, more and more would come to follow, until in the end our country would be wiped out. Now if we were to kill the king and apologize to the Son of Heaven, and if he accepted our apology and withdrew his armies, we could preserve the state as it is now. And should he refuse to listen, we could try our luck in battle. If we lose, we can escape to the sea!"

The others all having agreed to this plan, Tsou Yü-shan ran the king through with a spear and dispatched a messenger with his head to Wang Hui.

"My purpose in coming," said Wang Hui, "was simply to punish the king. Now that you have brought his head, the offense has been atoned for. You have surrendered without a fight—I could ask for no greater victory!" He therefore decided to halt his troops, sending word to Han An-kuo of what had happened and dispatching a messenger to hasten back to the capital with the king's head and report to the emperor.

The emperor issued an edict disbanding the armies of the two generals and stating, "Tsou Ying and the others of his party were the chief troublemakers. Only Tsou Wu-chu's grandson Tsou Ch'ou, the chieftain of Yao, refrained from taking any part in the plot." He therefore sent one of his palace attendant generals to set up Tsou Ch'ou as king of Yao in the region of Yüeh so that he could carry on the sacrifices to the former rulers of Min-yüeh.

Tsou Yüeh-shan, having successfully carried out the assassination of his brother Tsou Ying, wielded great power in the kingdom, and the majority of the people favored him. He therefore secretly declared himself king of the region, while the officially recognized king, Tsou Ch'ou, found himself powerless to command his subjects and force obedience to himself. When the emperor received news of this state of affairs, he decided that it was not worth calling out another army to deal with Tsou Yü-shan. Instead he announced, "Although Tsou Yü-shan several times plotted revolt with his brother Tsou Ying, he later took the lead in punishing Tsou Ying, sparing our armies the trouble of attack," and set up Tsou Yü-shan as king of Eastern Yüeh, ruling side by side with Tsou Ch'ou, the king of Yao.

In the fifth year of *yüan-ting* [112 B.C.] the kingdom of Southern Yüeh rebelled against the Han. Tsou Yü-shan, the king of Eastern Yüeh, sent a letter to the throne asking that he be allowed to lead a force of eight thousand men and join Yang P'u, the General of the Towered Ships, in attacking Lü Chia and the other rebels. When he had taken his troops as far as Chieh-yang, however, he halted, claiming that the wind and waves were too high to permit him to embark, and sent an envoy in secret to the rebels in Southern Yüeh, thus maintaining contact with both sides. Even after the Han armies had succeeded in capturing P'an-yü, the capital of Southern Yüeh, he still failed to appear on the scene. Yang P'u sent a letter to the throne asking that he be allowed to lead his troops and attack Eastern Yüeh to punish Tsou Yü-shan for his perfidy, but the emperor replied that the troops were by this time too exhausted for another campaign and refused to grant permission. Instead he disbanded the armies and instructed the officers to garrison Mei-ling in Yü-chang and await further orders.

In the autumn of the sixth year of *yüan-ting* [111 B.C.] Tsou Yü-shan, learning that Yang P'u had requested permission to attack him and seeing that the Han troops were poised on the border ready to invade his territory, finally determined to revolt, calling out his troops to block the roads by which the Han armies might advance. Appointing Tsou Li and others with the title of Generals Who Swallow Up the Han, he invaded Po-sha, Wu-lin, and Mei-ling, and killed three of the Han commanders.

At this time the Han had sent the minister of agriculture Chang Ch'eng and the former marquis of Shan-chou, Liu Ch'ih, to command the garrison, but both of them, not daring to attack the rebels, had instead withdrawn to positions of safety. Both were later tried on charges of cowardice and executed. In the meantime Tsou Yü-shan had a seal carved for himself reading "Emperor Wu" and set himself up with this title, deluding his subjects with all kinds of false assertions.

The emperor dispatched Han Yüeh, the General Who Traverses the Sea, to embark with his troops from Chü-chang and sail around to attack the rebels from the east. Yang P'u marched out of Wu-lin, the military commander Wang Wen-shu advanced from Mei-ling, and the two Yüeh marquises known as the General of the Daggered Ships and the General Who Descends the Torrents proceeded from Jo-yeh and Po-sha. In the winter of the first year of *yüan-feng* [Nov.–Dec., 111 B.C.] [2] all of them invaded Eastern Yüeh.

Eastern Yüeh had earlier dispatched its troops to block the passes and had appointed a General Who Conquers the North to guard Wu-lin, defeating several of Yang P'u's military commanders and murdering the Han officials in the region. One of Yang P'u's subordinates, Yüan Chung-ku of Ch'ien-t'ang, however, defeated and killed the General Who Conquers the North, for which he was made marquis of Yü-erh.

Earlier, before the Han armies had arrived, Wu Yang, the marquis of Yen, a native of Yüeh who made his home in China, had been sent back to Yüeh by the emperor to persuade Tsou Yü-shan to remain

[2] It should be remembered that the official Han year at this time still began with the tenth month, so that although the first year of *yüan-feng* falls largely in 110 B.C., the action described here took place in the last months of 111 B.C.

loyal to the Han. Tsou Yü-shan, however, had refused to listen to his advice, and when Han Yüeh arrived with his troops in the region of Yüeh, Wu Yang, along with seven hundred men of his city, turned against his countrymen and attacked the Yüeh army at Han-yang. Then, joining with Ao, the marquis of Chien-ch'eng, Wu Yang led his troops and placed them under the command of Tsou Chü-ku, the king of Yao. The three of them plotted together, saying, "Tsou Yü-shan is the chief troublemaker and has forced us into defending him. Now the Han armies have come in great strength and number, but if we were to plot together and assassinate Tsou Yü-shan and surrender to the Han general, we might be able to escape punishment." Eventually they joined in murdering Tsou Yü-shan and led his troops to surrender to Han Yüeh. As a result of this action, Tsou Chü-ku, the king of Yao, was enfeoffed as marquis of Eastern Yüeh, with ten thousand households; Ao, the marquis of Chien-ch'eng, was newly enfeoffed as marquis of K'ai-ling; and Wu Yang, the marquis of Yen, was newly enfeoffed as marquis of Pei-shih. Han Yüeh was enfeoffed as marquis of An-tao, and his military commander Liu Fu as marquis of Liao-ying. (Liu Fu was a son of King Kung of Ch'eng-yang. Formerly he had been marquis of Hai-ch'ang, but had been tried for some offense and deprived of his title. He had won no particular distinction in his career with the army but was enfeoffed as a marquis because he was a member of the imperial family.) None of the other Han generals had won any distinction in the campaign and therefore they were not enfeoffed. To Chün, a general of Eastern Yüeh, abandoned his army and surrendered when the Han troops arrived, and was therefore enfeoffed as marquis of Wu-hsi.

With the rebellion at an end, the emperor announced, "The region of Eastern Yüeh is narrow and full of mountain defiles, and the people of Min-yüeh are fickle and have shifted their loyalties numerous times." He therefore commanded the army officials to lead away all the inhabitants of the region and resettle them in the area between the Yangtze and Huai rivers, leaving Eastern Yüeh a deserted land.

The Grand Historian remarks: Although Yüeh is a land of barbarians, its former rulers must have treated the people with great wisdom and virtue. Otherwise how could their line have lasted so long? For generation after generation they held the title of chieftain or king, and Kou-chien even acted for a time as one of the dictator lords of China. And although Tsou Yü-shan, because of his flagrant rebelliousness, brought about the destruction of his kingdom and the resettlement of its inhabitants, yet other descendants of the same line, such as Tsou Chü-ku, the king of Yao, are still enfeoffed as marquises of ten thousand households. The fact that the leaders of Yüeh have for so many generations been great lords is due, no doubt, to the merit which has come down to them from their distant ancestor, the sage Emperor Yü.[3]

[3] The founder of the Hsia dynasty and reputed ancestor of the royal family of Yüeh. The paragraph is a good illustration of Ssu-ma Ch'ien's theory that the virtue and merit of a great man are somehow transmitted to and benefit his descendants, even after the lapse of hundreds or thousands of years.

Tan, the crown prince of Yen, fled to the region of Liao, but later Wei Man gathered together the refugees of Yen and, establishing them in the land of the eastern sea and adding Chen-p'an, guarded the frontier as a foreign vassal of the Han. Thus I made The Account of Ch'ao-hsien.

Wei Man, the king of Ch'ao-hsien [Korea], came originally from the state of Yen. When Yen was at the height of its power, it invaded and conquered the regions of Chen-p'an and Ch'ao-hsien,[1] appointing officials to rule the area and setting up fortifications along the frontier. After the Ch'in dynasty destroyed the state of Yen, the area fell more or less under Ch'in control, bordering as it did the province of Liao-tung. When the Han arose, however, it regarded the region as too far away and difficult to guard, and rebuilt the fortifications at the old border of Liao-tung, leaving the area beyond, as far as the Pei [Yalu] River, to be administered by the king of Yen.

When Lu Wan, the king of Yen, revolted and crossed over into the territory of the Hsiung-nu, Wei Man fled into hiding. He gathered together a band of a thousand or more followers and, adopting the mallet-shaped hairdo and dress of the eastern barbarians, escaped over the eastern border and, crossing the Pei River, settled down in the region formerly administered by the Ch'in, moving back and forth along the old border. Little by little he brought under his control the barbarians and Chinese refugees from Yen and Ch'i who were living in the regions of Chen-p'an and Ch'ao-hsien, and made himself their king, establishing his capital at Wang-hsien [Pyongyang].

During the reigns of Emperor Hui and Empress Lü, because peace

---

[1] Chen-p'an was the region west of the Yalu River; Ch'ao-hsien was that east of the river. Although Ch'ao-hsien is often used as a name for Korea, it is obvious that Chinese influence at this time did not extend very far down the Korean Peninsula.

had only recently been restored to the empire, the governor of Liao-tung Province agreed to regard Wei Man as a "foreign vassal" of the Han if he would guard the frontier against the barbarians and prevent them from raiding the border. In addition, if any of the barbarian chieftains wished to enter China and pay their respects to the emperor, Wei Man was not to hinder them from making the journey. When word of this agreement was reported to the emperor, he gave his approval. As a result, Wei Man was able to acquire considerable wealth and military power, with which he attacked and conquered the smaller settlements in the area until all of Chen-p'an and Lin-t'un were under his control. His territory by this time measured several thousand *li* square.

In time the rule passed to Wei Man's son and then to his grandson Wei Yu-ch'ü, who induced an increasing number of Han subjects to flee to his kingdom. Neither he nor his father or grandfather had ever journeyed to the capital to visit the emperor and, when the chiefs of Chen-p'an or any of the other various states in the area sent a letter to the throne requesting an audience with the Son of Heaven, they blocked the way and refused to let them pass.

In the second year of *yüan-feng* [109 B.C.] the Han dispatched She Ho to rebuke Wei Yu-ch'ü and warn him to mend his ways, but the latter refused to obey the imperial edict. She Ho left the capital of Ch'ao-hsien and began his journey home but, when he reached the border and was about to cross the Pei River, he stabbed and killed Chang, the assistant king of Ch'ao-hsien, who had been sent to escort him out of the kingdom. Then he made a dash across the river and back into Han territory, where he sent a report to the emperor stating that he had killed a general of Ch'ao-hsien. The emperor, pleased by this feat, asked no questions but honored him with the post of chief commandant of the eastern sector of Liao-tung Province. The king of Ch'ao-hsien, angered at this treachery, called out his troops and attacked and killed She Ho, whereupon the emperor gathered together a force of ex-convicts to make an assault on Ch'ao-hsien.

In the autumn Yang P'u, the General of the Towered Ships, embarked from Ch'i and crossed the Gulf of Pohai with a force of five thousand soldiers, while the general of the left Hsün Chih marched out of Liao-tung to aid in punishing Wei Yu-ch'ü. Wei Yu-ch'ü called out his troops and blocked the passes.

One of Hsün Chih's battalion commanders named To took it upon himself to lead a large number of the troops of Liao-tung on ahead of the rest, and as a result suffered a severe defeat. Many of his men were routed and fled back to Liao-tung, and To was tried under military law and executed. As a result Yang P'u and his men from Ch'i succeeded in reaching Wang-hsien, the capital of Ch'ao-hsien, first. Wei Yu-ch'ü had withdrawn into the city, but when he observed that Yang P'u's force was very small, he marched out and attacked, defeating and routing Yang P'u's army. Yang P'u, having lost most of his men, was forced to flee to the mountains, where he spent ten days or more rounding up the remnants of his army, until he had gathered together a sizable force again. Hsün Chih in the meantime was attacking the Ch'ao-hsien army west of the Pei River, but was unable to break their line or advance any farther.

The emperor, seeing that neither of his generals was accomplishing much, dispatched Wei Shan to threaten Wei Yu-ch'ü with further military action if he did not submit. When Wei Yu-ch'ü received the Han envoy, he bowed his head and apologized for his actions: "I wanted to surrender, but I was afraid that the two generals would go back on their promises of safety and kill me. Now that I see you bear the seals of a genuine envoy, I beg to surrender." To make amends, he also agreed to send his son, the crown prince, to the capital to wait on the emperor, and to present a gift of five thousand horses, as well as provisions for the Han armies.

The crown prince set off, accompanied by a force of ten thousand men bearing arms, and was about to cross the Pei River, but the Han envoy and Hsün Chih, suspecting his intentions, told him that, since he had already surrendered, he ought to order his men to lay down their arms. The crown prince in turn began to suspect that the envoy and Hsün Chih were plotting to murder him and so he did not cross the river, but instead turned around and went back to Wang-hsien. The Han envoy Wei Shan then returned to Ch'ang-an and reported to the emperor on his mission. The emperor executed him.

Hsün Chih once more attacked the Ch'ao-hsien army west of the Pei

River and, defeating it, advanced to Wang-hsien, camping in a semi-circle around the northwest corner of the city. Yang P'u arrived at the same time with his forces and took up a position south of the city. Wei Yu-ch'ü, however, guarded his city well, and though several months passed, the Han forces had still not succeeded in taking it.

Hsün Chih had formerly served at court and had enjoyed favor with the emperor. Leading an army made up of men from Yen and Tai, he had plunged forward on a wave of victory and many of his soldiers had grown proud and reckless. Yang P'u, on the other hand, had come by sea with his band from Ch'i and had already suffered a number of times from defeat and desertion. In his earlier encounter with Wei Yu-ch'ü he had been shamefully trounced and had lost many of his men, so that his soldiers were all afraid of the enemy and he himself was deeply mortified. Thus, although he was now taking part in the siege against Wei Yu-ch'ü, he did everything he could to bring about a peaceful settlement.

Hsün Chih in the meantime made a sudden attack on the city, whereupon the high minister of Ch'ao-hsien sent men in secret to discuss plans for a surrender agreement with Yang P'u. Messengers were sent back and forth several times between the two parties, but no final agreement was reached. Hsün Chih repeatedly set a date with Yang P'u for a joint attack on the city, but Yang P'u, anxious to complete arrangements for the surrender as soon as possible, failed each time to put in an appearance. Hsün Chih then began sending envoys of his own to spread discord among the men of Ch'ao-hsien and effect a surrender. The men of Ch'ao-hsien, however, refused to listen to his offers and continued to favor negotiating with Yang P'u. As a result, relations between the two generals became strained. Hsün Chih, considering the fact that Yang P'u had earlier committed the military sin of losing his army and observing that he was now secretly on good terms with the men of Ch'ao-hsien and was making no effort to capture their city, began to suspect that Yang P'u was planning to revolt, but he did not dare at this point to announce his suspicions publicly.

Meanwhile the emperor declared, "Formerly these two generals were unable to make any progress in their campaign, and so I sent Wei Shan as my envoy to persuade Wei Yu-ch'ü to surrender and send the crown prince of Ch'ao-hsien to court. But because Wei Shan was not able to conclude the negotiations on his own, he consulted with Hsün Chih and the two of them acted wrongly and in the end upset the whole agreement. Now Hsün Chih and Yang P'u are besieging the city of Wang-hsien and again there seems to be a clash of opinions. That is the reason the affair has dragged on so long without reaching a settlement!" He then dispatched Kung-sun Sui, the governor of Chi-nan, to go and straighten things out, giving him authority to take what measures might be necessary to clear up the matter.

When Kung-sun Sui arrived on the scene, Hsün Chih said to him, "The men of Ch'ao-hsien should have given in a long time ago. There appears to be some reason why they refuse to capitulate." He then told him how Yang P'u had failed to appear at the times agreed upon for an attack and related in detail all the doubts that he harbored concerning Yang P'u. "If some action is not taken at once, I am afraid a major disaster will result. The emperor will lose not only Yang P'u and his men, but they will take sides with Ch'ao-hsien and wipe out my army as well!"

Kung-sun Sui agreed with him and, using the imperial credentials which he carried, summoned Yang P'u to come to Hsün Chih's camp to plan the next move. Once there, he ordered Hsün Chih's subordinates to arrest Yang P'u and combine the armies of the two generals. When Kung-sun Sui reported his actions to the emperor, the emperor sent back orders to have Kung-sun Sui executed.

With both armies now under his own command, Hsün Chih began to press his attacks on Ch'ao-hsien. At this point the prime ministers of Ch'ao-hsien, Lu-jen, and Han Yin; Ts'an, the prime minister of Ni-ch'i; and a general named Wang Chia, began to plot together, saying, "Originally we had planned to surrender to Yang P'u, but now he has been arrested and Hsün Chih, who is in command of both armies, is pressing his attacks with increasing intensity. It is unlikely that we can win out against him, and at the same time the king refuses to surrender!" Han Yin, Wang Chia, and Lu-jen then fled from the city; Lu-jen was killed on the way, but the others succeeded in surrendering to the Han forces.

In the summer of the third year of *yüan-feng* [108 B.C.] Ts'an, the prime minister of Ni-ch'i, sent men to assassinate Wei Yu-ch'ü, the king of Ch'ao-hsien, and to announce the surrender of the state. The city of Wang-hsien, however, had not yet capitulated, and the former high minister of Wei Yu-ch'ü named Ch'eng I declared the country once more in revolt and sent men to attack the Han officers. Hsün Chih then dispatched Chang, the son of Wei Yu-ch'ü, and Tsui, the son of the prime minister Lu-jen, to persuade the people to submit and to execute Ch'eng I. Thus Ch'ao-hsien was at last conquered and the territory divided into four provinces.

Ts'an, the prime minister of Ni-ch'i, was enfeoffed as marquis of Hua-ch'ing; Han Yin as marquis of Ti-chü; Wang Chia as marquis of P'ing-chou; and Wei Chang as marquis of Chi. Because his father had been killed and because he had rendered signal service, Tsui was made marquis of Nieh-yang. Hsün Chih was recalled to the capital and, on his arrival, tried on charges of inordinate striving for distinction, jealousy of his associates, and betrayal of strategy. He was executed and his corpse exposed in the market place. Yang P'u was also tried on charges of having arbitrarily advanced against the enemy when he reached Lieh-k'ou instead of waiting for the arrival of Hsün Chih, and thereby losing many of his men. He was sentenced to execution but on payment of a fine was allowed to become a commoner.

The Grand Historian remarks: Wei Yu-ch'ü trusted in the natural barriers protecting his land, but brought an end to the sacrifices of the state. She Ho achieved distinction through treachery and became the cause of the bloodshed. Yang P'u, leading a meager army, met with hardship and blame; regretting his failure to win distinction in the siege of P'an-yü some years before, he sought for it this time, but instead aroused suspicion. Hsün Chih contended for glory, but he and Kung-sun Sui suffered execution. Both armies disgraced themselves and none of their leaders were enfeoffed as marquises.[2]

[2] Like the remarks at the end of "The Account of Southern Yüeh," these are in four-character phrases with occasional end rhymes.

After the Han had sent its envoy to open up communications with the state of Ta-hsia [Bactria], all the barbarians of the distant west craned their necks to the east and longed to catch a glimpse of China. Thus I made The Account of Ta-yüan.

Chang Ch'ien was the first person to bring back a clear account of Ta-yüan [Ferghana].[1] He was a native of Han-chung and served as a palace attendant during the *chien-yüan* era [140–135 B.C.]. At this time the emperor questioned various Hsiung-nu who had surrendered to the Han and they all reported that the Hsiung-nu had defeated the king of the Yüeh-chih people [Indo-scythians] and made his skull into a drinking vessel. As a result the Yüeh-chih had fled and bore a constant grudge against the Hsiung-nu, though as yet they had been unable to find anyone to join them in an attack on their enemy.

The Han at this time was engaged in a concerted effort to destroy the Hsiung-nu, and therefore, when the emperor heard this, he decided to try to send an envoy to establish relations with the Yüeh-chih. To reach them, however, an envoy would inevitably have to pass through Hsiung-nu territory. The emperor accordingly sent out a summons for men capable of undertaking such a mission. Chang Ch'ien, who was a palace attendant at the time, answered the summons and was appointed as envoy.

He set out from Lung-hsi, accompanied by Kan-fu, a Hsiung-nu slave who belonged to a family in T'ang-i. They traveled west through the territory of the Hsiung-nu and were captured by the Hsiung-nu and taken before the *Shan-yü*. The *Shan-yü* detained them and refused to let them proceed. "The Yüeh-chih people live north of me," he said. "What does the Han mean by trying to send an envoy to them! Do you

---

[1] As in previous chapters, the better-known western equivalents of Chinese geographical names have been added in brackets where possible. Some of these identifications, however, are still a matter of dispute among scholars.

suppose that if I tried to send an embassy to the kingdom of Yüeh in the southeast the Han would let my men pass through China?"

The Hsiung-nu detained Chang Ch'ien for over ten years and gave him a wife from their own people, by whom he had a son. Chang Ch'ien never once relinquished the imperial credentials that marked him as an envoy of the Han, however, and after he had lived in Hsiung-nu territory for some time and was less closely watched than at first, he and his party finally managed to escape and resume their journey toward the Yüeh-chih.

After hastening west for twenty or thirty days, they reached the kingdom of Ta-yüan. The king of Ta-yüan had heard of the wealth of the Han empire and wished to establish communication with it, though as yet he had been unable to do so. When he met Chang Ch'ien he was overjoyed and asked where Chang Ch'ien wished to go.

"I was dispatched as envoy of the Han to the Yüeh-chih, but the Hsiung-nu blocked my way and I have only just now managed to escape," he replied. "I beg Your Highness to give me some guides to show me the way. If I can reach my destination and return to the Han to make my report, the Han will reward you with countless gifts!"

The king of Ta-yüan trusted his words and sent him on his way, giving him guides and interpreters to take him to the state of K'ang-chü [Trans-Oxiana]. From there he was able to make his way to the land of the Great Yüeh-chih.

Since the king of the Great Yüeh-chih had been killed by the Hsiung-nu, his son had succeeded him as ruler and had forced the kingdom of Ta-hsia [Bactria] to recognize his sovereignty. The region he ruled was rich and fertile and seldom troubled by invaders, and the king thought only of his own enjoyment. He considered the Han too far away to bother with and had no particular intention of avenging his father's death by attacking the Hsiung-nu. From the court of the Yüeh-chih, Chang Ch'ien traveled on to the state of Ta-hsia, but in the end he was never able to interest the Yüeh-chih in his proposals.

After spending a year or so in the area, he began to journey back along the Nan-shan or Southern Mountains, intending to reenter China through the territory of the Ch'iang barbarians, but he was once more captured by the Hsiung-nu and detained for over a year.

Just at this time the *Shan-yü* died and the Lu-li King of the Left attacked the *Shan-yü's* heir and set himself up as the new *Shan-yü* [126 B.C.]. As a result of this the whole Hsiung-nu nation was in turmoil and Chang Ch'ien, along with his Hsiung-nu wife and the former slave Kan-fu, was able to escape and return to China. The emperor honored Chang Ch'ien with the post of palace counselor and awarded Kan-fu the title of "Lord Who Carries Out His Mission."

Chang Ch'ien was a man of great strength, determination, and generosity. He trusted others and in turn was liked by the barbarians. Kan-fu, who was a Hsiung-nu by birth, was good at archery, and whenever he and Chang Ch'ien were short of food he would shoot birds and beasts to keep them supplied. When Chang Ch'ien first set out on his mission, he was accompanied by over a hundred men, but after thirteen years abroad, only he and Kan-fu managed to make their way back to China.

Chang Ch'ien in person visited the lands of Ta-yüan, the Great Yüeh-chih, Ta-hsia, and K'ang-chü, and in addition he gathered reports on five or six other large states in the neighborhood. All of this information he related to the emperor on his return. The substance of his report was as follows:

Ta-yüan lies southwest of the territory of the Hsiung-nu, some ten thousand *li* directly west of China. The people are settled on the land, plowing the fields and growing rice and wheat. They also make wine out of grapes. The region has many fine horses which sweat blood; [2] their forebears are supposed to have been foaled from heavenly horses. The people live in houses in fortified cities, there being some seventy or more cities of various sizes in the region. The population numbers several hundred thousand. The people fight with bows and spears and can shoot from horseback.

Ta-yüan is bordered on the north by K'ang-chü, on the west by the kingdom of the Great Yüeh-chih, on the southwest by Ta-hsia, on the northeast by the land of the Wu-sun, and on the east by Yü-mi and Yü-t'ien [Khotan].

West of Yü-t'ien, all the rivers flow west and empty into the Western Sea, but east of there they flow eastward into the Salt Swamp [Lob

---

[2] The "bloody sweat" was apparently the result of parasites which caused small running sores in the hides of the horses.

Nor]. The waters of the Salt Swamp flow underground and on the south form the source from which the Yellow River rises. There are many precious stones in the region and the rivers flow into China. The Lou-lan and Ku-shih peoples live in fortified cities along the Salt Swamp. The Salt Swamp is some five thousand *li* from Ch'ang-an. The western branch of the Hsiung-nu occupies the region from the Salt Swamp east to a point south of the Great Wall at Lung-hsi, where its territory adjoins that of the Ch'iang barbarians, thus cutting off the road from China to the west.

The Wu-sun live some two thousand *li* northeast of Ta-yüan, moving from place to place in the region with their herds of animals. Their customs are much like those of the Hsiung-nu. They have twenty or thirty thousand skilled archers and are very daring in battle. They were originally subjects of the Hsiung-nu, but later, becoming more powerful, they refused any longer to attend the gatherings of the Hsiung-nu court, though still acknowledging themselves part of the Hsiung-nu nation.

K'ang-chü is situated some two thousand *li* northwest of Ta-yüan. Its people likewise are nomads and resemble the Yüeh-chih in their customs. They have eighty or ninety thousand skilled archer fighters. The country is small, and borders Ta-yüan. It acknowledges nominal sovereignty to the Yüeh-chih people in the south and the Hsiung-nu in the east.

Yen-ts'ai lies some two thousand *li* northwest of K'ang-chü. The people are nomads and their customs are generally similar to those of the people of K'ang-chü. The country has over a hundred thousand archer warriors, and borders a great shoreless lake, perhaps what is known as the Northern Sea [Caspian Sea?].

The Great Yüeh-chih live some two or three thousand *li* west of Ta-yüan, north of the Kuei [Oxus] River. They are bordered on the south by Ta-hsia, on the west by An-hsi [Parthia], and on the north by K'ang-chü. They are a nation of nomads, moving from place to place with their herds, and their customs are like those of the Hsiung-nu. They have some one or two hundred thousand archer warriors. Formerly they were very powerful and despised the Hsiung-nu, but later, when Mo-tun became leader of the Hsiung-nu nation, he attacked and defeated the Yüeh-chih. Some time afterwards his son, the Old *Shan-yü,* killed the king of the Yüeh-chih and made his skull into a drinking cup.

The Yüeh-chih originally lived in the area between the Ch'i-lien or Heavenly Mountains and Tun-huang, but after they were defeated by the Hsiung-nu they moved far away to the west, beyond Ta-yüan, where they attacked and conquered the people of Ta-hsia and set up the court of their king on the northern bank of the Kuei River. A small number of their people who were unable to make the journey west sought refuge among the Ch'iang barbarians in the Southern Mountains, where they are known as the Lesser Yüeh-chih.

An-hsi is situated several thousand *li* west of the region of the Great Yüeh-chih. The people are settled on the land, cultivating the fields and growing rice and wheat. They also make wine out of grapes. They have walled cities like the people of Ta-yüan, the region containing several hundred cities of various sizes. The kingdom, which borders the Kuei River, is very large, measuring several thousand *li* square. Some of the inhabitants are merchants who travel by carts or boats to neighboring countries, sometimes journeying several thousand *li*. The coins of the country are made of silver and bear the face of the king. When the king dies, the currency is immediately changed and new coins issued with the face of his successor. The people keep records by writing horizontally on strips of leather. To the west lies T'iao-chih [Mesopotamia] and to the north Yen-ts'ai and Li-hsüan [Hyrcania].

T'iao-chih is situated several thousand *li* west of An-hsi and borders the Western Sea [Persian Gulf?]. It is hot and damp, and the people live by cultivating the fields and planting rice. In this region live great birds which lay eggs as large as pots. The people are very numerous and are ruled by many petty chiefs. The ruler of An-hsi gives orders to these chiefs and regards them as his vassals. The people are very skillful at performing tricks that amaze the eye. The old men of An-hsi say they have heard that in T'iao-chih are to be found the River of Weak Water and the Queen Mother of the West, though they admit that they have never seen either of them.[3]

[3] The Queen Mother of the West was an immortal spirit who was said to live in some fabulous region of the west. According to later writers the River of Weak Water was so called because it would not float even a goose feather.

Ta-hsia is situated over two thousand *li* southwest of Ta-yüan, south of the Kuei River. Its people cultivate the land and have cities and houses. Their customs are like those of Ta-yüan. It has no great ruler but only a number of petty chiefs ruling the various cities. The people are poor in the use of arms and afraid of battle, but they are clever at commerce. After the Great Yüeh-chih moved west and attacked and conquered Ta-hsia, the entire country came under their sway. The population of the country is large, numbering some million or more persons. The capital is called the city of Lan-shih [Bactra] and has a market where all sorts of goods are bought and sold.

Southeast of Ta-hsia is the kingdom of Shen-tu [India]. "When I was in Ta-hsia," Chang Ch'ien reported, "I saw bamboo canes from Ch'iung and cloth made in the province of Shu. When I asked the people how they had gotten such articles, they replied, 'Our merchants go to buy them in the markets of Shen-tu.' Shen-tu, they told me, lies several thousand *li* southeast of Ta-hsia. The people cultivate the land and live much like the people of Ta-hsia. The region is said to be hot and damp. The inhabitants ride elephants when they go into battle. The kingdom is situated on a great river.

"We know that Ta-hsia is located twelve thousand *li* southwest of China. Now if the kingdom of Shen-tu is situated several thousand *li* southeast of Ta-hsia and obtains goods which are produced in Shu, it seems to me that it must not be very far away from Shu. At present, if we try to send envoys to Ta-hsia by way of the mountain trails that lead through the territory of the Ch'iang people, they will be molested by the Ch'iang, while if we send them a little farther north, they will be captured by the Hsiung-nu. It would seem that the most direct route, as well as the safest, would be that out of Shu."

Thus the emperor learned of Ta-yüan, Ta-hsia, An-hsi, and the others, all great states rich in unusual products whose people cultivated the land and made their living in much the same way as the Chinese. All these states, he was told, were militarily weak and prized Han goods and wealth. He also learned that to the north of them lived the Yüeh-chih and K'ang-chü people who were strong in arms but who could be persuaded by gifts and the prospect of gain to acknowledge allegiance to the Han court. If it were only possible to win over these states by peaceful means, the emperor thought, he could then extend his domain ten thousand *li,* attract to his court men of strange customs who would come translating and retranslating their languages,[4] and his might would become known to all the lands within the four seas.

The emperor was therefore delighted, and approved Chang Ch'ien's suggestion. He ordered Chang Ch'ien to start out from Chien-wei in Shu on a secret mission to search for Ta-hsia. The party broke up into four groups proceeding out of the regions of Mang, Jan, Hsi, and Ch'iung and P'o. All the groups managed to advance one or two thousand *li,* but they were blocked on the north by the Ti and Tso tribes and on the south by the Sui and K'un-ming tribes. The K'un-ming tribes have no rulers but devote themselves to plunder and robbery, and as soon as they seized any of the Han envoys they immediately murdered them. Thus none of the parties were ever able to get through to their destination. They did learn, however, that some one thousand or more *li* to the west there was a state called Tien-yüeh whose people rode elephants and that the merchants from Shu sometimes went there with their goods on unofficial trading missions. In this way the Han, while searching for a route to Ta-hsia, first came into contact with the kingdom of Tien.

Earlier the Han had tried to establish relations with the barbarians of the southwest, but the expense proved too great and no road could be found through the region and so the project was abandoned. After Chang Ch'ien reported that it was possible to reach Ta-hsia by traveling through the region of the southwestern barbarians, the Han once more began efforts to establish relations with the tribes in the area.

Chang Ch'ien was made a subordinate commander and sent to accompany the general in chief Wei Ch'ing on expeditions against the Hsiung-nu. Because he knew where water and pasture were to be found in the Hsiung-nu territory, he was able to save the army from hardship. He was enfeoffed as Po-wang or "Broad Vision" marquis. This occurred in the sixth year of the *yüan-so* era [123 B.C.].

The following year he was appointed colonel of the guard and sent

---

[4] A stock phrase in Han rhetoric meaning that such people come from so far away that they have no knowledge of the Chinese language and their words must therefore be "translated and retranslated" through a number of intermediary languages before being put into Chinese.

with General Li Kuang on an expedition out of Yu-pei-p'ing to attack the Hsiung-nu. The Hsiung-nu surrounded Li Kuang's army and wiped out most of the men. Chang Ch'ien was accused of having arrived late at his rendezvous with Li Kuang and was sentenced to execution, but on payment of a fine he was allowed to become a commoner. This same year the Han sent the swift cavalry general Ho Ch'ü-ping against the Hsiung-nu. He defeated and killed thirty or forty thousand of the Hsiung-nu in the western region [5] and rode as far as the Ch'i-lien Mountains. The following year the Hun-yeh king led his barbarian hordes and surrendered to the Han, and the Hsiung-nu completely disappeared from the region from Chin-ch'eng and Ho-hsi west along the Southern Mountains to the Salt Swamp. Occasionally Hsiung-nu scouts would appear, but even they were rare. Two years later the Han armies attacked the *Shan-yü* and chased him north of the desert.

During this time the emperor occasionally questioned Chang Ch'ien about Ta-hsia and the other states of the west. Chang Ch'ien, who had been deprived of his marquisate, replied, "When I was living among the Hsiung-nu I heard about the king of the Wu-sun people, who is named K'un-mo. K'un-mo's father was the ruler of a small state on the western border of the Hsiung-nu territory. The Hsiung-nu attacked and killed his father, and K'un-mo, then only a baby, was cast out in the wilderness to die. But the birds came and flew over the place where he was, bearing meat in their beaks, and the wolves suckled him, so that he was able to survive. When the *Shan-yü* heard of this, he was filled with wonder and, believing that K'un-mo was a god, he took him in and reared him. When K'un-mo had grown to manhood, the *Shan-yü* put him in command of a band of troops and he several times won merit in battle. The *Shan-yü* then made him the leader of the people whom his father had ruled in former times and ordered him to guard the western forts. K'un-mo gathered together his people, looked after them and led them in attacks on the small settlements in the neighborhood. Soon he had twenty or thirty thousand skilled archers who were trained in aggressive warfare. When the *Shan-yü* died, K'un-mo led his people far away, declared himself an independent

---

[5] Following the reading in *Han shu* 61.

ruler, and refused any longer to journey to the meetings of the Hsiung-nu court. The Hsiung-nu sent surprise parties of troops to attack him, but they were unable to win a victory. In the end the Hsiung-nu decided that he must be a god and left him alone, still claiming that he was a subject of theirs but no longer making any large-scale attacks on him.

"Now the *Shan-yü* is suffering from the recent blow delivered by our armies, and the region formerly occupied by the Hun-yeh king and his people is deserted. The barbarians are well known to be greedy for Han wealth and goods. If we could make use of this opportunity to send rich gifts and bribes to the Wu-sun people and persuade them to move farther east and occupy the region which formerly belonged to the Hun-yeh king, then the Han could conclude an alliance of brotherhood with them and, under the circumstances, they would surely do as we say. If we could get them to obey us, it would be like cutting off the right arm of the Hsiung-nu! Then, once we had established an alliance with the Wu-sun, Ta-hsia and the other countries to the west could all be persuaded to come to court and acknowledge themselves our foreign vassals."

The emperor approved of this suggestion and, appointing Chang Ch'ien as a general of palace attendants, put him in charge of a party of three hundred men, each of which was provided with two horses. In addition the party took along tens of thousands of cattle and sheep and carried gold and silk goods worth a hundred billion cash. Many of the men in the party were given the imperial credentials making them assistant envoys so that they could be sent to neighboring states along the way.

When Chang Ch'ien reached the kingdom of the Wu-sun, the king of the Wu-sun, K'un-mo, tried to treat the Han envoys in the same way that the *Shan-yü* treated them. Chang Ch'ien was greatly outraged and, knowing that the barbarians were greedy, said, "The Son of Heaven has sent me with these gifts, but if you do not prostrate yourself to receive them, I shall have to take them back!"

With this K'un-mo jumped up from his seat and prostrated himself to receive the gifts. The other details of the envoys' reception Chang Ch'ien allowed to remain as before. Chang Ch'ien then delivered his message, saying, "If the Wu-sun will consent to move east and occupy the region of the Hun-yeh king, then the Han will send you a princess of the imperial family to be your wife."

But the Wu-sun people were split into several groups and the king was old. Living far away from China, he had no idea how large the Han empire was. Moreover, his people had for a long time in the past been subjects of the Hsiung-nu and still lived nearer to them than to China. The high ministers of the king were therefore all afraid of the Hsiung-nu and did not wish to move back east. The king alone could not force his will upon his subjects, and Chang Ch'ien was therefore unable to persuade him to listen to his proposal.

K'un-mo had over ten sons, among them one named Ta-lu who was very strong and skillful in leading the people. He lived in a separate part of the realm and had over ten thousand horsemen under his command.

Ta-lu's older brother, who had been designated as heir to K'un-mo, had a son named Ts'en-ch'ü. The heir apparent died early and on his deathbed he begged his father, K'un-mo, to make Ts'en-ch'ü the new heir. "Do not allow anyone to take his position away from him!" he pleaded. K'un-mo, moved by grief, gave his permission and designated his grandson Ts'en-ch'ü as the new heir apparent.

Ta-lu was furious that he himself had not been appointed heir and, persuading his other brothers to join him, led his forces in a revolt, planning to attack Ts'en-ch'ü and K'un-mo. K'un-mo, who was old and lived in constant fear that Ta-lu would attack and kill his grandson, gave Ts'en-ch'ü a force of over ten thousand horsemen and sent him to live in another part of the realm, while he himself kept over ten thousand horsemen for his own protection. Thus it happened that when Chang Ch'ien arrived the Wu-sun people were split into three factions, though the large part of them acknowledged the leadership of K'un-mo. K'un-mo for this reason did not dare make any promises to Chang Ch'ien on his own authority.

Chang Ch'ien dispatched his assistant envoys to Ta-yüan, K'ang-chü, the Great Yüeh-chih, Ta-hsia, An-hsi, Shen-tu, Yü-t'ien, Yü-mo, and the other neighboring states, the Wu-sun providing them with guides and interpreters. Then he returned to China, accompanied by twenty or thirty envoys from the Wu-sun and a similar number of horses which the Wu-sun sent in exchange for the Han gifts. The Wu-sun envoys thus had an opportunity to see with their own eyes the breadth and greatness of the Han empire.

On his return Chang Ch'ien was honored with the post of grand messenger, ranking him among the nine highest ministers of the government. A year or so later he died.

The Wu-sun envoys, having seen how rich and populous the Han was, returned and reported what they had learned to their own people, and after this the Wu-sun regarded the Han with greater respect. A year or so later the envoys whom Chang Ch'ien had sent to Ta-hsia and the other states of the west all returned, accompanied by envoys from those states, and for the first time relations were established between the lands of the northwest and the Han. It was Chang Ch'ien, however, who opened the way for this move, and all the envoys who journeyed to the lands in later times relied upon his reputation to gain them a hearing. As a result of his efforts, the foreign states trusted the Han envoys.

After Chang Ch'ien's death the Hsiung-nu learned that the Han had established relations with the Wu-sun and, infuriated by the news, decided to make an attack on the Wu-sun. By this time the Han had already sent envoys to the Wu-sun, as well as to Ta-yüan, the Great Yüeh-chih, and the other states to the south, and the Wu-sun, frightened by the threat of a Hsiung-nu attack, sent an envoy with a gift of horses to the Han court to ask that a Han princess be granted to the Wu-sun leader and an alliance of brotherhood concluded. The emperor referred the matter to his ministers for debate, and they all replied, "The princess should not be sent until the betrothal gifts have been duly received."

Sometime earlier the emperor had divined by the *Book of Changes* and been told that "divine horses are due to appear from the northwest." When the Wu-sun came with their horses, which were of an excellent breed, he named them "heavenly horses." Later, however, he obtained the blood-sweating horses from Ta-yüan, which were even hardier. He therefore changed the name of the Wu-sun horses, calling them "horses from the western extremity," and used the name "heavenly horses" for the horses of Ta-yüan.

At this time the Han first built fortifications west of the district of Ling-chü and established the province of Chiu-ch'üan in order to provide a safe route to the lands of the northwest, and as a result more and more envoys were sent to An-hsi, Yen-ts'ai, T'iao-chih, and Shen-tu. The emperor was very fond of the Ta-yüan horses and sent a constant stream of envoys to that region to acquire them.

The largest of these embassies to foreign states numbered several hundred persons, while even the smaller parties included over a hundred members, though later, as the envoys became more accustomed to the route, the number was gradually reduced. The credentials and gifts which the envoys bore with them were much like those supplied to the envoys in Chang Ch'ien's time. In the course of one year anywhere from five or six to over ten parties would be sent out. Those traveling to distant lands required eight or nine years to complete their journey, while those visiting nearer regions would return after a few years.

At this time the Han had already overthrown the kingdom of Yüeh in the southeast, and the barbarian tribes living southwest of Shu were all filled with awe and begged to be ruled by Han officials and to be allowed to pay their respects at court. The Han therefore set up the provinces of I-chou, Yüeh-sui, Tsang-ko, Ch'en-li, and Wen-shan, hoping to extend the area under Han control so that a route could be opened to Ta-hsia. The Han sent Po Shih-ch'ang, Lü Yüeh-jen, and others, over ten parties in the space of one year, out of these new provinces to try to get through to Ta-hsia. The parties were all blocked by the K'un-ming barbarians, however, who stole their goods and murdered the envoys, so that none of them were ever able to reach Ta-hsia.

The Han then freed the criminals of the three districts of the capital area and, adding to them twenty or thirty thousand soldiers from Pa and Shu, dispatched them under the command of two generals, Kuo Ch'ang and Wei Kuang, to go and attack the K'un-ming tribes that were blocking the Han envoys. The army succeeded in killing or capturing twenty or thirty thousand of the enemy before departing from the area, but later, when another attempt was made to send envoys to Ta-hsia, the K'un-ming once more fell upon them and none were able to reach their destination. By this time, however, so many envoys had journeyed to Ta-hsia by the northern route out of Chiu-ch'üan that the foreign states in the area had become surfeited with Han goods and no longer regarded them with any esteem.

After Chang Ch'ien achieved honor and position by opening up communications with the lands of the west, all the officials and soldiers who had accompanied him vied with one another in submitting reports to the emperor telling of the wonders and profits to be gained in foreign lands and requesting to become envoys. The emperor considered that, since the lands of the west were so far away, no man would choose to make the journey simply for his own pleasure, and so when he had listened to their stories he immediately presented them with the credentials of an envoy. In addition he called for volunteers from among the people and fitted out with attendants and dispatched anyone who came forward, without inquiring into his background, in an effort to broaden the area that had been opened to communication.

When the envoys returned from a mission, it invariably happened that they had plundered or stolen goods on their way or their reports failed to meet with the approval of the emperor. The emperor, who was very practiced at handling such matters, would then have them summarily investigated and accused of some major offense so that they would be spurred to anger and would volunteer to undertake another mission in order to redeem themselves. Thus there was never any lack of men to act as envoys, and they came to regard it as a trifling matter to break the law. The officials and soldiers who had accompanied them on a mission would in turn start at once enthusiastically describing the wealth to be found in the foreign nations; those who told the most impressive tales were granted the seals of an envoy, while those who spoke more modestly were made assistants. As a result all sorts of worthless men hurried forward with wild tales to imitate their example.

The envoys were all sons of poor families who handled the government gifts and goods that were entrusted to them as though they were private property and looked for opportunities to buy goods at a cheap price in the foreign countries and make a profit on their return to China. The men of the foreign lands soon became disgusted when they found that each of the Han envoys told some different story and, considering that the Han armies were too far away to worry about, refused to supply the envoys with food and provisions, making things very difficult for them. The Han envoys were soon reduced to a state of destitution and distress and, their tempers mounting, fell to quarreling and even attacking each other.

The states of Lou-lan and Ku-shih, though very small, lay right across the path that the envoys traveled, and they attacked and plundered the parties of Wang Hui and other envoys with extreme ferocity. In addition, raiding parties of Hsiung-nu from time to time appeared in the region to swoop down on the envoys to the western states and block their advance. The envoys hastened to the emperor with complaints of all the hardships which they suffered and suggested that, although the inhabitants of the western regions lived in fortified cities, they were poor in combat and could easily be attacked.

As a result of their complaints, the emperor dispatched Chao P'o-nu, the former Ts'ung-p'iao marquis, with a force of twenty or thirty thousand troops recruited from the dependent states and the provinces. He advanced as far as the Hsiung-ho River, hoping to attack the Hsiung-nu, but they withdrew.

The following year an attack was made on Ku-shih. Chao P'o-nu, with a force of seven hundred or more light horsemen, led the attack, captured the king of Lou-lan, and succeeded in conquering Ku-shih. At the same time he used his armies to intimidate the Wu-sun, Ta-yüan, and the other states in the region. On his return Chao P'o-nu was enfeoffed as marquis of Cho-yeh.

Wang Hui, who had several times acted as an envoy and been mistreated by the people of Lou-lan, took his complaint to the emperor. The emperor called out a force of troops and appointed Wang Hui as aide to Chao P'o-nu, in which capacity he attacked and defeated Lou-lan. He was enfeoffed as marquis of Hao. After this a series of defense stations was established from Chiu-ch'üan west to the Jade Gate Pass.

The Wu-sun sent a thousand horses to the Han as a betrothal gift for the Han princess whom they had been promised. The Han then sent a princess of the imperial family, the daughter of the king of Chiang-tu, to be the wife of the Wu-sun leader. K'un-mo, the king of the Wu-sun, made her his Bride of the Right. The Hsiung-nu also sent one of their women to marry K'un-mo, and he made her his Bride of the Left. Later, saying that he was too old, he gave the Han princess to his grandson Ts'en-ch'ü to be his bride. The Wu-sun have a great many horses, the wealthy men among them owning as many as four or five thousand.[6]

When the Han envoys first visited the kingdom of An-hsi, the king of An-hsi dispatched a party of twenty thousand horsemen to meet them on the eastern border of his kingdom. The capital of the kingdom is several thousand *li* from the eastern border, and as the envoys proceeded there they passed through twenty or thirty cities inhabited by great numbers of people. When the Han envoys set out again to return to China, the king of An-hsi dispatched envoys of his own to accompany them, and after the latter had visited China and reported on its great breadth and might, the king sent some of the eggs of the great birds which live in the region, and skilled tricksters of Li-hsüan, to the Han court as gifts. In addition, the smaller states west of Ta-yüan, such as Huan-ch'ien and Ta-i, as well as those east of Ta-yüan, such as Ku-shih, Yü-mi, and Su-hsieh, all sent parties to accompany the Han envoys back to China and present gifts at court. The emperor was delighted at this.

The emperor also sent envoys to trace the Yellow River to its source. They found that it rises in the land of Yü-t'ien among mountains rich in precious stones, many of which they brought back with them. The emperor studied the old maps and books and decided to name these mountains, where the Yellow River has its source, the K'un-lun Mountains.

At this time the emperor made frequent tours east to the seacoast, and at such times he would take all the visitors from foreign lands

---

[6] The purpose of this last statement is no doubt to indicate that a thousand horses was not by any means a very lavish betrothal gift to send in exchange for the Han princess. The parallel passage in *Han shu* 96B gives a much more elaborate account of the princess's attendants and her reception at the Wu-sun court and includes a famous poem supposedly written by her lamenting her exile to a strange and distant land.

along in his party, passing through large and populous cities on the way, scattering gifts of money and silk among the visitors, and supplying them with generous accommodations in order to impress upon them the wealth of the Han empire. He would hold great wrestling matches and displays of unusual skills and all sorts of rare creatures, gathering together large numbers of people to watch. He entertained the foreign visitors with veritable lakes of wine and forests of meat and had them shown around to the various granaries and storehouses to see how much wealth was laid away there, astounding and overwhelming them with the breadth and greatness of the Han empire. After the skills of the foreign magicians and tricksters had been imported into China, the wrestling matches and displays of unusual feats developed and improved with each year, and from this time on entertainments of this type became increasingly popular.

In this way party after party of envoys from the foreign lands of the northwest would arrive in China and, after a while, take their leave. Those from the states west of Ta-yüan, however, believing that their homelands were too far away from China to be in any danger, continued to conduct themselves with great arrogance and self-assurance; it was impossible to make them conform to proper ritual or to compel them to obey the wishes of the Han court.

The lands from that of the Wu-sun on west to An-hsi were situated nearer to the Hsiung-nu than to China, and it was well known that the Hsiung-nu had earlier caused the Yüeh-chih people great suffering. Therefore, whenever a Hsiung-nu envoy appeared in the region carrying credentials from the *Shan-yü,* he was escorted from state to state and provided with food, and no one dared to detain him or cause him any difficulty. In the case of the Han envoys, however, if they did not hand out silks or other goods they were given no food, and unless they purchased animals in the markets they could get no mounts for their riders. This was because the people considered the Han too far away to bother about. They also believed that the Han had plenty of goods and money and it was therefore proper to make the envoys pay for whatever they wanted. As may be seen, they were much more afraid of the Hsiung-nu envoys than of those from the Han.

The regions around Ta-yüan make wine out of grapes, the wealthier inhabitants keeping as much as ten thousand or more piculs stored away. It can be kept for as long as twenty or thirty years without spoiling. The people love their wine and the horses love their alfalfa. The Han envoys brought back grape and alfalfa seeds to China and the emperor for the first time tried growing these plants in areas of rich soil. Later, when the Han acquired large numbers of the "heavenly horses" and the envoys from foreign states began to arrive with their retinues, the lands on all sides of the emperor's summer palaces and pleasure towers were planted with grapes and alfalfa for as far as the eye could see.

Although the states from Ta-yüan west to An-hsi speak rather different languages, their customs are generally similar and their languages mutually intelligible. The men all have deep-set eyes and profuse beards and whiskers. They are skillful at commerce and will haggle over a fraction of a cent. Women are held in great respect, and the men make decisions on the advice of their women. No silk or lacquer is produced anywhere in the region, and the casting of coins and vessels was formerly unknown. Later, however, when some of the Chinese soldiers attached to the Han embassies ran away and surrendered to the people of the area, they taught them how to cast metal and manufacture weapons. Now, whenever the people of the region lay their hands on any Han gold or silver they immediately make it into vessels and do not use it for currency.

By this time a number of embassies had been sent to the west and even the lesser attendants who went along on the expeditions had become accustomed to appearing before the emperor and relating their experiences. "Ta-yüan has some fine horses in the city of Erh-shih [Sutrishna]," they reported, "but the people keep them hidden and refuse to give any to the Han envoys!"

The emperor had already taken a great liking to the horses of Ta-yüan, and when he heard this he was filled with excitement and expectation. He dispatched a party of able young men and carriage masters with a thousand pieces of gold and a golden horse to go to the king of Ta-yüan and ask him for some of the fine horses of Erh-shih.

But Ta-yüan by this time was overflowing with Han goods, and the men of the state therefore plotted together, saying, "The Han is far away from us and on several occasions has lost men in the salt-water wastes between our country and China. Yet if the Han parties go farther north, they will be harassed by the Hsiung-nu, while if they try to go to the south they will suffer from lack of water and fodder. Moreover, there are many places along the route where there are no cities whatsoever and they are apt to run out of provisions. The Han embassies that have come to us are made up of only a few hundred men, and yet they are always short of food and over half the men die on the journey. Under such circumstances how could the Han possibly send a large army against us? What have we to worry about? Furthermore, the horses of Erh-shih are one of the most valuable treasures of our state!"

In the end, therefore, they refused to give the Han envoys any horses. Enraged, the Han envoys cursed the men of Ta-yüan, smashed the golden horse with a mallet, and departed.

The nobles of Ta-yüan were furious, complaining that the Han envoys had treated them with the utmost contempt. After the Han party had left, therefore, they sent orders to the people of Yü-ch'eng on the eastern border of the kingdom to attack and kill the envoys and seize their goods.

When the emperor received word of the fate of the envoys, he was in a rage. Yao Ting-han and others, who had acted as envoys to Ta-yüan in the past, assured the emperor that the kingdom was militarily weak and that it would not require a force of more than three thousand Han soldiers equipped with powerful crossbows to conquer it and take the entire population captive. Earlier, when the emperor had dispatched Chao P'o-nu to attack Lou-lan, Chao had led an advance party of only seven hundred horsemen and had taken the king of Lou-lan prisoner. The emperor therefore believed the assurances of Yao Ting-han and the others and, wishing to have some excuse to enfeoff the relatives of his favorite, Lady Li, he honored her brother Li Kuang-li with the title of Erh-shih General and dispatched him with a force of six thousand horsemen recruited from the dependent states, as well as twenty or thirty thousand young men of bad reputation rounded up from the provinces and kingdoms, to launch an attack on Ta-yüan. The title of

Erh-shih General was given to Li Kuang-li because it was expected that he would reach the city of Erh-shih and capture the fine horses there. Chao Chih-ch'eng was appointed director of martial law for the expedition, and Wang Hui, the former marquis of Hao, was ordered to act as guide. Li Ch'e was made a subordinate commander and put in charge of various military affairs. This was in the first year of the *t'ai-yüan* era [104 B.C.]. At this time great swarms of locusts rose up in the area east of the Pass and flew west as far as Tun-huang.

General Li and his army passed the Salt Swamp and were advancing west when they found that the inhabitants of the small states along the way, terrified by their approach, had all shut themselves up tightly in their walled cities and refused to supply any food to the army. Even attacks on the cities did not always prove successful. The army was able to obtain provisions from some of the cities that submitted, but in the case of others, if a few days of attack did not bring capitulation, the army would move on its way. Thus by the time Li Kuang-li reached Yü-ch'eng he had no more than a few thousand soldiers left, and all of these were suffering from hunger and exhaustion.

He attacked Yü-ch'eng, but was severely beaten and a great many of his men were killed or wounded. General Li then consulted Li Ch'e, Chao Shih-ch'eng, and his other officers and decided that, if they could not even conquer the city of Yü-ch'eng, there was absolutely no hope that they could make a successful attack on Erh-shih, the king's capital, farther to the west. They therefore decided to lead their troops back to China. The journey to Ta-yüan and back had taken them two years, and by the time they reached Tun-huang they had no more than one or two tenths of their original force left.

Li Kuang-li sent a messenger to the emperor explaining that the distance had been so great and he had been so short of provisions that his men, though brave enough in battle, had been defeated by hunger and not enough of them had survived the journey to make an attack on Ta-yüan possible. He asked that the army be disbanded for a while and a larger force recruited for another expedition later on.

When the emperor received word of this, he was enraged and sent an envoy with orders to close the pass at Jade Gate, saying that anyone from General Li's army who attempted to enter the country would be cut down on the spot.

General Li, afraid to move, remained for the time being at Tun-huang. This same summer over twenty thousand Han soldiers under the command of Chao P'o-nu were surrounded by the Hsiung-nu and forced to surrender.

The high ministers and court advisers all wanted the emperor to disband the army that had been sent to attack Ta-yüan and concentrate the strength of the empire on attacking the Hsiung-nu. But the emperor had already undertaken to punish Ta-yüan for its outrage and he was afraid that if his armies could not conquer even a small state like Ta-yüan, then Ta-hsia and the other lands would come to despise the Han. No more fine horses could ever be obtained from Ta-yüan, the Wu-sun and Lun-t'ou people would scorn and mistreat the Han envoys, and China would become a laughingstock among the foreign nations. He therefore had Ten Kuang and the others who were most outspoken in their opposition to the Ta-yüan campaign handed over to the law officials for investigation, freed all the skilled bowmen who were in prison, and called out more young men of bad reputation and horsemen from the border states. By the end of a year or so he had sent sixty thousand new men to Tun-huang to reinforce the army there, not counting porters and personal attendants. The army was provided with a hundred thousand oxen, over thirty thousand horses, and tens of thousands of donkeys, mules, and camels, as well as plentiful provisions and a great number of crossbows and other weapons. The whole empire was thrown into a turmoil, relaying orders and providing men and supplies for the attack on Ta-yüan. Over fifty subordinate commanders were appointed to direct the army.

It was known that there were no wells in the capital city of Ta-yüan, the city drawing its water supply from rivers that flowed outside the walls. The emperor therefore sent water engineers to join the army so that when the time came they could divert the streams which flowed by the city and deprive the inhabitants of their water. A force of a hundred and eighty thousand soldiers was also dispatched to garrison the districts of Chü-yen and Hsiu-t'u, which had been established north of Chiu-ch'üan and Chang-yeh in order to provide greater protection for Chiu-ch'üan. All men in the empire who came in the seven classes of reprobated persons [7] were called out and sent to transport supplies of dried boiled rice to Li Kuang-li's forces. The lines of transport wagons and marching men stretched without a break all the way west to Tun-huang. In addition, two men who were skilled in judging horses were appointed as commanders in charge of steeds so that, when the conquest of Ta-yüan had been accomplished, they would be on hand to select the finest horses to take back to China.

When all of this had been done, Li Kuang-li set off once again. This time he had far more men, and in every little state he came to the inhabitants came out to greet him with gifts of food for his army. When he reached Lun-t'ou, however, the people there refused to submit. He besieged the city for several days and, after taking it, massacred the inhabitants, and from there on west to Erh-shih, the capital of Ta-yüan, his advance was unhindered.

He reached Erh-shih with a force of thirty thousand soldiers. The men of Ta-yüan came forward to attack, but the Han soldiers overwhelmed them with their arrows and forced them to flee into the city, where they mounted the battlements and prepared to defend the city.

General Li's men had wanted to attack Yü-ch'eng on the way, but he was afraid that if he halted his advance it would only give the men of Erh-shih more time to think up plots to save their lives. He therefore pressed on to Erh-shih, where he broke down the banks of the rivers and springs and diverted them from their courses so that they no longer supplied water to the city. This move caused the inhabitants of the city extreme distress and hardship.

After surrounding and besieging the city for over forty days, he managed to break down the outer wall and capture one of the enemy leaders, a noble of Ta-yüan named Chien-mi who was noted for his bravery. The inhabitants were thoroughly terrified and fled within the inner wall, where the nobles of Ta-yüan gathered to plot the next move.

[7] Petty officials who had committed crimes, fugitives, adopted sons-in-law, resident merchants, those formerly registered as merchants, those whose fathers or mothers had been registered as merchants, and those whose grandfathers or grandmothers had been registered as merchants.

"The reason the Han has sent troops to attack us is simply that our king Wu-kua hid his best horses and killed the Han envoys," they said. "Now if we kill the king and hand over the horses, the Han troops will most likely withdraw. Should they refuse, that will be the time to fight to the death for our city!"

All having agreed that this was the best plan, they killed the king and sent one of the nobles to carry his head to General Li and ask for an agreement. "If the Han soldiers do not attack us," the nobleman said, "we will bring out all the finest horses so that you may take your pick, and will supply food to your army. But if you refuse to accept these terms we will slaughter all the best horses. Moreover, rescue troops will soon be coming to aid us from K'ang-chü, and when they arrive the Han will have to fight both our men within the city and their forces on the outside. You had better consider the matter well and decide which course to take!"

At this time scouts from K'ang-chü were keeping a watch on the Han troops, but since the latter were still in good condition, the K'ang-chü forces did not dare to advance against them.

Li Kuang-li consulted with Chao Shih-ch'eng, Li Ch'e, and his other officers on what to do. "I have received word," he said, "that the people within the city have just obtained the services of a Chinese who knows how to dig wells. Moreover, they still seem to have plenty of food. Our purpose in coming here was to punish the chief offender, Wu-kua, and now that we have obtained his head, our task has been accomplished. If under these circumstances we refuse to withdraw our troops, the inhabitants will defend the city to the last man. Meanwhile the scouts from K'ang-chü, seeing our soldiers wearied by the siege, will come with troops to rescue Ta-yüan and the defeat of our army will be inevitable."

His officers all agreed with this opinion, and General Li sent word that he was willing to accept Ta-yüan's proposal. The men of Ta-yüan then brought out their finest horses and allowed the Han officers to choose the ones they wanted. They also produced large stores of provisions to feed the Han army. The Han officers selected twenty or thirty of the choicest horses, as well as over three thousand stallions and mares of less high quality, and set up one of the nobles named

Mi-ts'ai, who had treated the earlier Han envoys with kindness, as the new king of Ta-yüan, promising that they would withdraw their troops. In the end the Han soldiers never entered the inner wall of the city, but withdrew according to their promise and began the journey home.

When Li Kuang-li first started west from Tun-huang, he considered that his army was too numerous to be provided with food by the lands along the way and he therefore divided it up into several parties, some of them taking the northern route and some the southern. One of these separate groups, comprising a thousand or more men and led by the subordinate commander Wang Shen-sheng, the former grand herald Hu Ch'ung-kuo, and others, arrived at Yü-ch'eng. The men of Yü-ch'eng withdrew into the city and refused to provide any food to Wang Shen-sheng's soldiers. Though he was two hundred *li* away from the main army of General Li, Wang Shen-sheng examined the city and, deciding that he had nothing to fear, began to berate the inhabitants for failing to give him any food. The inhabitants could see that Wang Shen-sheng's army was growing smaller day by day, and finally one day at dawn they sent out a force of three thousand men who attacked and killed Wang Shen-sheng and the other commanders and defeated his army. Only a few of the Han soldiers managed to escape and flee to the army of General Li.

General Li thereupon dispatched Shang-kuan Chieh, his chief commandant in charge of requisitioning grain, who attacked and conquered the city of Yü-ch'eng. The king of Yü-ch'eng fled to K'ang-chü, where Shang-kuan Chieh pursued him. When the men of K'ang-chü heard that the Han armies had already conquered Ta-yüan, they handed the king of Yü-ch'eng over to Shang-kuan Chieh. The latter ordered four of his horsemen to bind the king and take him under guard to the headquarters of the commander in chief, General Li.

The four horsemen consulted together, saying, "The king of Yü-ch'eng is the archenemy of the Han. Now we have been given the task of escorting him alive to the general's headquarters, but if he should suddenly escape it would go very badly with us!" They therefore decided to kill the king, but none of them dared to strike the first blow. Finally one of the horsemen from Shang-kuei named Chao Ti, the youngest of the group, drew his sword and cut down the king. Then, bearing the king's head, he and Shang-kuan Chieh and the rest of the group set out after and overtook General Li.

Earlier, when General Li started out on the second expedition against Ta-yüan, the emperor sent envoys to announce the fact to the Wu-sun and ask them to send a large force to cooperate in the attack. The Wu-sun did in fact send two thousand horsemen but, not willing to alienate either party, they held back and refused to join in the attack.

When General Li and his army returned east, the rulers of all the small states they passed through, having heard of the defeat of Ta-yüan, sent their sons or brothers to accompany the army to China, where they presented gifts, were received by the emperor, and remained at the Han court as hostages.

In General Li's campaign against Ta-yüan, the director of martial law Chao Shih-ch'eng achieved the greatest merit. In addition, Shang-kuan Chieh won distinction by daring to venture far into enemy territory and Li Ch'e by his skill in planning. When the army reentered the Jade Gate Pass, it numbered something over ten thousand men, with over a thousand military horses. During General Li's second expedition the army had not suffered from any lack of provisions, nor had many of the soldiers been killed in battle. The generals and other officers, however, were a greedy lot, most of them taking little care of their men but abusing and preying upon them instead. This was the reason for the large number of lives lost.

Nevertheless the emperor, considering that it had been such a long expedition, made no attempt to punish those who were at fault, but enfeoffed Li Kuang-li as marquis of Hai-hsi, and Chao Ti, the horseman who had cut off the head of the king of Yü-ch'eng, as marquis of Hsin-chih. He appointed Chao Shih-ch'eng as superintendent of the imperial household, Shang-kuan Chieh as privy treasurer, and Li Ch'e as governor of Shang-tang. Three of the officers who had gone on the campaign were appointed to posts ranking among the nine highest ministers; over a hundred were enfeoffed as marquises or appointed as chancellors, governors, or two thousand picul officials; and more than a thousand were appointed to posts paying a thousand piculs or less. Those who had volunteered to join the army were given posts which far exceeded their expectations, while the convicts who had been pressed into service were all pardoned and released from penal servitude. The common soldiers were rewarded with gifts valued at forty thousand catties of gold.

The expedition against Ta-yüan required four years to carry out, after which the army was disbanded. A year or so after the Han conquered Ta-yüan and set up Mi-ts'ai as the new king, the nobles of Ta-yüan, considering Mi-ts'ai a servile flatterer who had brought about the destruction of his own country, joined forces and murdered him. In his place they set up Ch'an-feng, the brother of Wu-kua, the former king. Ch'an-feng sent his son as a hostage to the Han court, whereupon the Han dispatched an envoy to Ta-yüan to present gifts to the new ruler and make sure that he restored peace and order to the kingdom. The Han also sent over ten parties of envoys to the various countries west of Ta-yüan to seek for rare objects and at the same time to call attention in a tactful way to the might which the Han had displayed in its conquest of Ta-yüan.

The government set up a chief commandant of Chiu-ch'üan in Tun-huang and established defense stations at various points from Tun-huang west to the Salt Swamp. A force of several hundred agricultural soldiers was sent to set up a garrison at Lun-t'ou, headed by an ambassador who saw to it that the fields were protected and stores of grain laid away to be used to supply the Han envoys who passed through on their way to foreign countries.

The Grand Historian remarks: The *Basic Annals of Emperor Yü* [8] records that the source of the Yellow River is in the K'un-lun Mountains, mountains over twenty-five hundred *li* high where the sun and moon in turn go to hide when they are not shining. It is said that on their heights are to be found the Fountain of Sweet Water and the Pool of Jade. Yet, since Chang Ch'ien and the other envoys have been sent to Ta-hsia, they have traced the Yellow River to its source and found no such K'un-lun Mountains as the *Basic Annals* records. Therefore, what the *Book of Documents* states about the mountains and rivers of the nine ancient provinces of China seems to be nearer the

[8] An ancient text now lost.

truth, while when it comes to the wonders recorded in the *Basic Annals of Emperor Yü* or the *Classic of Hills and Seas*,[9] I cannot accept them.

[9] A geography of ancient China filled with legends and descriptions of fabulous beasts and other wonders. This is the earliest mention of the work. It is from works such as these that Emperor Wu selected the name K'un-lun to apply to the range of mountains discovered by his envoys.

Shih chi 116: The Account of the Southwestern Barbarians

T'ang Meng was sent as imperial envoy to invade the southwest and open up communication with Yeh-lang, and as a result the chiefs of the Ch'iung and Tso peoples begged to become subjects of the Han and to be ruled by Chinese officials. Thus I made The Account of the Southwestern Barbarians.[1]

There are dozens of chiefs ruling among the southwestern barbarians, but the most important is the ruler of Yeh-lang. To the west of Yeh-lang live the chiefs of the Mi-mo, of which the most important is the ruler of Tien. North of Tien live numerous other chiefs, the most important being the ruler of Ch'iung-tu. All of the tribes ruled by these chiefs wear their hair in the mallet-shaped fashion, work the fields, and live in settlements. Beyond them to the west, in the region from T'ung-shih east to Yeh-yü, are the tribes called Sui and K'un-ming, whose people all braid their hair and move from place to place with their herds of domestic animals, having no fixed homes and no chieftains. Their lands measure several thousand *li* square. Northeast of the Sui live twenty or thirty chiefs, the most important being those of Hsi and Tso-tu. Among the numerous chiefs northeast of Tso, those of Jan and Mang are most important. Some of their people live a settled life on the land, while others move about from place to place. Their territory is west of the province of Shu. Northeast of Jan and Mang are numerous other chiefs, the most important being the ruler of Po-ma. All of them belong to the Ti tribe. These are all the barbarian groups living in the area southwest of Pa and Shu.

In earlier times, when King Wei ruled the state of Ch'u [339–328 b.c.], he sent his general Chuang Ch'iao to lead an army along the upper reaches of the Yangtze River and invade Pa, Shu, Ch'ien-chung,

---

[1] The tribes described in this chapter lived in western China in the area of present day Szechwan, Kweichow, and Yünnan Provinces.

and the regions to the west. (Chuang Ch'iao was a descendant of King Chuang, a former ruler of Ch'u.) [2] Chuang Ch'iao advanced as far as Lake Tien, a body of water three hundred *li* in circumference, surrounded by several thousand *li* of rich flatland. Having used his military might to subdue the region and bring it under the rule of Ch'u, he started back to Ch'u to report his success when the armies of Ch'in attacked Ch'u and seized the provinces of Pa and Ch'ien-chung, cutting off his way. Unable to get through to Ch'u, he returned to Lake Tien and with the men under his command made himself ruler of Tien, adopting native dress, following the customs of the people, and acting as their chief.

In the time of the Ch'in dynasty, Ch'ang E invaded the region and opened up the so-called five-foot-wide road. Ch'in officials were set up to administer most of the numerous native states in the area. Some ten years later, however, the Ch'in dynasty was overthrown.

When the Han came to power, it abandoned all relations with these states and reestablished the old frontier defenses along the border of Shu. The people of Pa and Shu often crossed the frontier on unofficial trading expeditions, however, bringing back horses from Tso and slaves and long-haired oxen from P'o. These expeditions brought great wealth to the provinces of Pa and Shu.

In the sixth year of the era *chien-yüan* [135 B.C.] the grand messenger Wang Hui was sent to attack Tsou Ying, the king of Eastern Yüeh, who was in revolt. Shortly afterwards the men of Eastern Yüeh murdered Tsou Ying and reported their willingness to submit to Han rule. Wang Hui, relying upon his military might to bring the region under control, dispatched T'ang Meng, the magistrate of P'o-yang, to visit the king of Southern Yüeh and persuade him to remain loyal to the Han. While T'ang Meng was at the court of Southern Yüeh, he was given some *chü* berry sauce to eat. When he inquired where it came from, he was told, "It is brought down the Tsang-ko River from the northwest. The Tsang-ko is several *li* wide and flows past P'an-yü, the capital of Southern Yüeh." When T'ang Meng returned to Ch'ang-an he questioned a merchant of Shu on the matter and the merchant replied, "Shu is the only place that makes *chü* berry sauce. Large

[2] *Ca.* 600 B.C.

quantities of it are exported in secret to the markets of Yeh-lang, which is situated on the Tsang-ko. The Tsang-ko at that point is over a hundred paces across, wide enough to allow boats to move up and down it. The king of Southern Yüeh sends money and goods in an effort to gain control of Yeh-lang, extending his efforts as far west as T'ung-shih, but so far he has not succeeded in getting Yeh-lang to acknowledge his sovereignty."

T'ang Meng then sent a letter to the throne, saying, "The king of Southern Yüeh rides about in a yellow canopied carriage with plumes on the left side, like the Son of Heaven, ruling a region that measures over ten thousand *li* from east to west. He is referred to as a 'foreign vassal' of the Han, but in fact he is the lord of a whole vast territory. If troops were sent from Ch'ang-sha and Yü-chang to attack him, they would find most of the rivers impassable and would have great difficulty in advancing. I have received information, however, that over a hundred thousand first-rate soldiers could be recruited from the region of Yeh-lang. If these were transported down the Tsang-ko River in ships and deployed against the king of Southern Yüeh while he was still unprepared, it would be an excellent way to bring his territory under control. With the strength of the Han forces and the wealth of Pa and Shu to support the undertaking, it would be an easy task to open up communications with Yeh-lang and establish officials in the region."

The emperor approved of this plan and, appointing T'ang Meng as a general of palace attendants, put him in command of a force of a thousand soldiers and over ten thousand porters. With these he marched out through the Tso Pass in Pa and visited To-t'ung, the marquis of Yeh-lang.

T'ang Meng presented To-t'ung with generous gifts and, describing the might and virtue of the Han dynasty, urged him to permit Han officials to be sent to the area, promising that To-t'ung's son would be appointed as governor. The small towns in the neighborhood of Yeh-lang were all anxious to obtain silk from the Han, and To-t'ung, considering that the road between his territory and China was too steep and perilous to be kept open for long, agreed for the time being to listen to T'ang Meng's demands. T'ang Meng then returned to the capital to report on his mission. As a result, the province of Chien-wei was established in the area and troops from Pa and Shu were sent out to work on the road, extending it through P'o in the direction of the Tsang-ko River.

Ssu-ma Hsiang-ju, a native of Shu, also urged the emperor to set up provinces in the regions of Ch'iung and Tso. The emperor therefore appointed Ssu-ma Hsiang-ju a general of palace attendants and sent him to these regions to negotiate with their rulers. Over ten districts were set up under a chief commandant and attached to the province of Shu, the natives being treated in the same way as the barbarians of the region farther south.

In connection with the building of the road to the lands of the southwestern barbarians, the four provinces in the region of Pa and Shu were obliged at this time to send out men to guard the supply lines and transport provisions to the workmen. But though the work went on for several years, the road was still not completed, while the men engaged in the project, exhausted by starvation and plagued by dampness, died off in great numbers. In addition, the barbarians frequently rebelled against Han rule and forces had to be called out to combat them, using even more money and material and accomplishing little in the way of military success.

The emperor, worried by the way things were going, sent Kung-sun Hung to the region to observe the situation. On his return he advised the emperor that the project was impractical. Shortly afterwards, he was made imperial secretary. By this time the emperor was busy building fortifications in So-fang in an attempt to drive the Hsiung-nu out of the region south of the Yellow River. Kung-sun Hung repeatedly emphasized the dangers involved in attempting to open up communication with the southwestern barbarians and urged the emperor to abandon the project and concentrate his strength on combating the Hsiung-nu. The emperor accordingly gave up the idea, keeping only the two districts of Nan-i and Yeh-lang, with one chief commandant, and leaving the province of Chien-wei more or less to take care of itself.

In the first year of *yüan-shou* [122 B.C.] Chang Ch'ien, the Po-wang marquis, returned from his mission to the land of Ta-hsia [Bactria] and reported that while he was there he had seen cloth produced in Shu and bamboo canes from Ch'iung. On inquiring how they had gotten to Ta-hsia, he was told, "They come from the land of Shen-tu [India], which lies some several thousand *li* southeast of here. We buy them in the shops of the Shu merchants there." He was also told that Shen-tu was situated some two thousand *li* west of Ch'iung. "Ta-hsia, which is situated southwest of our country," Chang Ch'ien reported to the emperor with enthusiasm, "is eager to open relations with China and is much distressed that the Hsiung-nu are blocking the road in between. If we could find a new route from Shu via the land of Shen-tu, however, we would have a short and convenient way to reach Ta-hsia which would avoid the danger of the northern route!"

The emperor therefore ordered Wang Jan-yü, Po Shih-ch'ang, Lü Yüeh-jen, and others to go on a secret expedition through the region of the southwestern barbarians and on to the west to search for the land of Shen-tu. When they got as far as Tien, Ch'ang-ch'iang, the king of Tien, detained them and sent a party of ten or twelve men to the west to find out the way to Shen-tu for them. The Chinese party waited over a year, but all the roads to the west had been closed off by the inhabitants of K'un-ming, so that none of the men who had been sent ahead were able to reach Shen-tu.

In the course of his talks with the Han envoys, the king of Tien asked, "Which is larger, my domain or that of the Han ruler?" and the marquis of Yeh-lang asked the same question. Because there were no roads open between their lands and China, each considered himself the supreme ruler of a vast territory and had no idea of the breadth and greatness of the Han empire.

When the Han envoys returned to the capital, they stressed that Tien was a large state and ought to be bound by closer ties to China. The emperor gave the matter serious consideration.

Some years later, when the kingdom of Southern Yüeh rebelled, the emperor ordered the Marquis Who Hastens to Duty to raise an army among the southwestern barbarians in the province of Chien-wei and aid in the attack on Southern Yüeh. The chief of one of the barbarian states in the region, Ch'ieh-lan, was afraid, however, that if he and his men went on such a distant expedition the inhabitants of neighboring states would invade his territory and seize the old men and boys who had been left behind. He and his people therefore revolted and killed the Han envoys and the governor of Chien-wei. The emperor had ordered a force of released criminals from Pa and Shu to join in the attack on Southern Yüeh, and he now detached eight commanders from this force and sent them to put down the revolt in Ch'ieh-lan. In the meantime the resistance in Southern Yüeh was brought to an end, and the eight commanders, instead of proceeding downriver to the coast, turned back north and on their way executed the chief of T'ou-lan. T'ou-lan was another small state in the region which had constantly been hindering communications with Tien. Thus T'ou-lan and the other tribes of the southwestern barbarians were brought under control and the region made into the province of Tsang-ko.

The marquis of Yeh-lang had originally sided with the king of Southern Yüeh, but when Southern Yüeh was wiped out, he proceeded to execute all those who had advised him to revolt against the Han. Eventually he journeyed to Ch'ang-an to pay his respects to the emperor, who bestowed on him the title of king of Yeh-lang.

After the Han forces had defeated Southern Yüeh, executed the chiefs of Ch'ieh-lan and Ch'iung, and killed the marquis of Tso, all the native rulers in the regions of Jan and Mang were struck with terror and begged to become vassals of the Han, with Chinese officials to govern their lands. The emperor therefore converted Ch'iung-tso into the province of Yüeh-sui, Tso-tu into the province of Ch'en-li, Jan and Mang into the province of Wen-shan, and Po-ma, west of Kuang-han, into the province of Wu-tu.

The emperor also sent Wang Jan-yü to persuade the king of Tien to pay a visit to the capital, pointing out to him the fate that Southern Yüeh and the chiefs of the southwestern barbarians had suffered at the hands of the Han forces. The king of Tien possessed a force of some twenty or thirty thousand men, while to the northeast of him lived the tribes of Lao-chin and Mi-mo which were ruled by members of the same clan as himself and were in a position to aid him. He was therefore not inclined to listen to the threats of the Han envoy. Moreover, the men of Lao-chin and Mi-mo frequently made attacks on the Han envoys and soldiers. In the second year *of yüan-feng* [109

B.C.] the emperor dispatched troops from Pa and Shu to attack and wipe out the Lao-chin and Mi-mo states and take up a position on the border of Tien. Because the king of Tien had originally been friendly toward the Han, they were not ordered to execute him. The king of Tien, Li-nan,[3] then surrendered to the Han forces with all his people, asking that officials be sent to govern his territory and that he be allowed to visit the emperor. His lands were made into the province of I-chou and he was presented with the seals of the king of Tien and restored to the position of leader of the people. Thus, of the hundreds of native rulers among the southwestern barbarians, only those of Yeh-lang and Tien were granted the seals of kings. Tien, although a relatively small fief, still enjoys the highest favor with the emperor.

The Grand Historian remarks: The ancestors of the state of Ch'u must certainly have received the blessing of Heaven! At the founding of the Chou dynasty, one of them served as a general under King Wen and his descendants were enfeoffed in Ch'u. Even when the glory of the Chou had waned, the state of Ch'u still boasted an area of five thousand *li*. The Ch'in dynasty wiped out all of the other feudal families; only the descendants of Ch'u continued to rule as kings of Tien. And although the Han punished many of the barbarians of the southwest and destroyed their states, the ruler of Tien alone was favored and allowed to continue as a king.

The whole affair of Han relations with the southwestern barbarians came about because someone saw some *chü* berry sauce in P'an-yü, and because the people of Ta-hsia carried canes made of Ch'iung bamboo! Later the western barbarians were split up into two groups and their lands made into seven provinces.

[3] The text of the first part of the sentence appears to be corrupt and the translation is highly tentative.

Shih chi 117: The Biography of Ssu-ma Hsiang-ju

Ssu-ma Hsiang-ju's prose poem on The Mighty One and his discussions of Sir Fantasy, although couched in extravagantly rich and exaggerated language, are actually satirical in intent and have their basis in the philosophy of nonaction. Thus I made The Biography of Ssu-ma Hsiang-ju.

Ssu-ma Hsiang-ju was a native of Ch'eng-tu in the province of Shu. His polite name was Ssu-ma Ch'ang-ch'ing. When he was young he loved to read books. He also studied swordsmanship, and for this reason his parents gave him the name of "Dog Boy." [1] In the course of his studies, however, he developed a great admiration for the famous statesman of antiquity, Lin Hsiang-ju,[2] and he accordingly changed his name to Hsiang-ju. Because of the wealth of his family, he was made a palace attendant and served Emperor Ching as a mounted guard. He did not care for this position, but as it happened that Emperor Ching had no liking for literature, he had no alternative.

During this time King Hsiao of Liang came to court to pay his respects to the emperor, bringing with him in his retinue a number of wandering rhetoricians such as Tsou Yang of Ch'i, Mei Sheng of Huai-yin, and Master Chuang Chi of Wu. Hsiang-ju had an opportunity to meet these men and was so delighted with their company that he retired from his post on grounds of illness and journeyed to Liang to become a guest retainer at the king's court. King Hsiao gave orders that Hsiang-ju was to be quartered in the same lodge with the other scholars, so that for several years he was able to live with the scholars and guest rhetoricians of Liang. It was at this time that he wrote his prose poem entitled *Tzu-hsü* or *Sir Fantasy*. With the death of King Hsiao, he left Liang and returned to his home in Ch'eng-tu, but by this

[1] Commentators suggest that the Han pronunciation of the words "dog" and "sword" was sufficiently close to make the name sound like "Sword Boy."

[2] High minister of the state of Chao in pre-Ch'in times who was noted for his bravery. His biography is recorded in *Shih chi* 81.

time his family had grown very poor and he had no means of making a living.

Hsiang-ju had formerly been on close terms with Wang Chi, the magistrate of the district of Lin-ch'iung, and Wang Chi sent word saying, "Since your long journey in search of official position has proved unsuccessful, why don't you come to see me?"

Hsiang-ju accordingly went to Lin-ch'iung and stayed at the officials' lodge in that city. The magistrate made a great show of treating him with respect and honor, going every morning to call upon Hsiang-ju. For the first few times Hsiang-ju received him, but after that he pleaded illness and sent one of the attendants to convey his apologies to Wang Chi. Wang Chi, however, only treated him with greater deference.

There were a number of wealthy men living in Lin-ch'iung, among them Cho Wang-sun, whose household included eight hundred servants and slaves, and Ch'eng Cheng, who also had several hundred servants. These two rich men conferred together and decided, "Since the magistrate seems to have a highly honored guest visiting him, it would be well if we were to give a party for him and invite the magistrate to come along." When the magistrate arrived at the Cho residence on the day of the party, he found it filled with hundreds of guests. As noon approached the host dispatched a messenger inviting Hsiang-ju to join the party, but he sent back word that he was ill and could not come. At this news the magistrate declined to join the feast, but instead went in person to fetch Hsiang-ju. Hsiang-ju, unable to find any further excuse, was forced to appear at the party, and soon all eyes were fixed on him.

When the drinking was at its height the magistrate came forward with a lute and, presenting it to Hsiang-ju, said, "I have heard that you are fond of this instrument. I wonder if you could be persuaded to amuse yourself with a selection?"

Hsiang-ju politely declined, but finally consented to strum a few selections for the company. It happened that Cho Wang-sun had a daughter named Wen-chün who was very fond of music and had only recently been widowed, and although Hsiang-ju pretended to be playing only out of deference to the magistrate, in reality he used the lute to pour out his heart in an effort to win the young girl's attentions. When Hsiang-ju arrived in Lin-ch'iung with his carriage riders, Wen-chün had heard, he had displayed a figure of most elegant poise and refinement, and now that he was in her own home drinking and playing the lute, the young girl secretly peered in through the door at him and her heart was filled with delight; she felt an instant love for him, and her only fear was that she could not have him for her husband.

After the party was over Hsiang-ju sent someone with lavish presents to Wen-chün's ladies in waiting and requested them to inform their mistress of his deep respect. That night Wen-chün ran away from home and joined Hsiang-ju, and the two of them galloped off to Ch'eng-tu. There they took up residence in Hsiang-ju's house, four bare walls with nothing inside.

Her father Cho Wang-sun was in a rage. "What a piece of trash— this daughter of mine!" he exclaimed. "I have not the heart to kill her outright, but I will see to it that she never gets a penny of my money!" A number of people tried to talk him into reason, but he absolutely refused to listen to them.

After a while Wen-chün grew unhappy with her new life and said to her husband, "The only thing for us to do is to go to Lin-ch'iung together. There we can borrow some money from my relatives and find a way to make a living. Why should we force ourselves to live in misery like this?"

She and Hsiang-ju accordingly went to Lin-ch'iung, where they sold their carriage and all their riding equipment and bought a wine-shop. Hsiang-ju left Wen-chün to mind the counter while he himself, dressed in a workman's loincloth, went off on errands with the other hired men or washed the wine vessels at the well in the market place.

When Cho Wang-sun heard the way his daughter was living, he was filled with shame and, shutting his gates, refused to leave the house. His relatives and the other gentlemen of the town once more attempted to reason with him. "You have only one son and two daughters," they said, "so you cannot say that you lack the funds to help your daughter. It is true that she has ruined her reputation by running off with Ssu-ma Hsiang-ju, but he spent a good deal of time in the past traveling about the country, and though he is poor, he surely has the talent and ability to win success eventually. Moreover, he was a guest of the magistrate. Why do you insist upon bringing shame to both him and yourself like this?"

Persuaded that there was no other way out, Cho Wang-sun finally gave his daughter Wen-chün a hundred servants, a million cash, and the clothing, quilts, and other articles that she had received as a dowry at the time of her first marriage. Wen-chün and Hsiang-ju then returned to Ch'eng-tu, where they purchased a house and some fields and lived a life of ease.

Some time after this a man from Shu named Yang Te-i was appointed to serve Emperor Wu as keeper of the imperial hunting dogs. The emperor happened to come into possession of Ssu-ma Hsiang-ju's prose poem, *Sir Fantasy*, which he read with great pleasure, and remarked to Yang Te-i, "What a pity that I could not have lived at the same time as the author of this!"[3]

"There is a man named Ssu-ma Hsiang-ju who comes from the same city as myself," replied Yang Te-i, "and he claims that he himself wrote this prose poem!" The emperor was astonished and, summoning Hsiang-ju to the capital, questioned him about it.

"The poem is mine," said Hsiang-ju, "but it concerns the affairs of the feudal lords and is not worthy of Your Majesty's attention. If I may be permitted, however, I would like to compose a prose poem about the imperial hunt and present it to Your Majesty when it is completed."

The emperor gave his consent and ordered the master of documents to provide Hsiang-ju with the necessary writing tablets. In the poem, Sir Fantasy, so called because his words are all fantasy, is made to praise the state of Ch'u; Master No-such (that is, no such thing ever happened) criticizes the claims of Sir Fantasy and speaks in behalf of the state of Ch'i, while Lord Not-real (not a real person) states the case for the Son of Heaven.[4] Thus the poet utilizes the words of

---

[3] Although the text does not say so, the implication is that Ssu-ma Hsiang-ju had asked Yang Te-i to bring his poem to the emperor's attention.

[4] It would appear that what Ssu-ma Hsiang-ju did was to use the poem, or at least part of it, which he had composed earlier for King Hsiao of Liang, and add a final section on the hunting park of the emperor. The poems in this chap-

these three imaginary characters to describe the hunting parks of the feudal lords of Ch'u and Ch'i and of the Son of Heaven, and at the close makes a plea for greater frugality. The poem as a whole is intended therefore as a satirical reprimand. When it was completed, Ssu-ma Hsiang-ju presented it to the emperor, who was exceedingly pleased. The text reads:

When Ch'u dispatched Sir Fantasy as its envoy to the state of Ch'i, the king of Ch'i called out all the knights within his domain and, providing the party with carriages and horsemen, went out with the envoy on a hunt. After the hunt was over, Sir Fantasy was describing the wonders of the event to Master No-such, while Lord Not-real stood by. When the three of them had taken their seats, Master No-such asked, "Did you enjoy the hunt today?" "Very much!" replied Sir Fantasy. "Did you have a large catch?" Master No-such asked, to which Sir Fantasy answered, "No, the catch was rather meager." "If the catch was small, then what did you find so enjoyable?" he pressed. "What I enjoyed was the way the king of Ch'i was endeavoring to impress me with the great number of carriages and horsemen, while for my part I described to him the hunts which we have at Yün-meng in Ch'u." "Would you perhaps tell us about these hunts of Ch'i and Ch'u?" asked Master No-such, to which Sir Fantasy replied:

---

ter are all in the *fu* or rhyme-prose style, already familiar to the reader from the examples in "The Biographies of Ch'ü Yüan and Chia I" in Volume I. They are composed of rhymed lines of varying lengths and strong rhythmical beat, at times introduced by or interspersed with short passages in prose. Arthur Waley, in his introduction to *The Temple and Other Poems,* a book which has been of great assistance in making these translations, characterizes this type of poetry as a kind of "incantation" or "word-magic" which achieves its effect "not by argument nor even by rhetoric, but by a purely sensuous intoxication of rhythm and language." The reader should keep this apt description in mind in judging what follows. Dr. Waley also remarks, in speaking of this first poem of Ssu-ma Hsiang-ju's, that its "eloquence cannot be described, much less translated." In spite of this warning, I have nevertheless undertaken the task of translation because Ssu-ma Hsiang-ju is such an important figure in the cultural history of the period and because his poetry so well conveys the boundless energy and delight in richness and variety that characterize this era of the Han. I should warn the reader that many of the precious stones, flowers, trees, birds, etc. mentioned in the poems cannot be identified with any certainty and my translations are intended to be no more than rough equivalents. I must beg the indulgence of specialists if in places the translations constitute scientific impossibilities. The poet is obviously less concerned in conveying information than in creating a feeling of lush and exotic language, and for this reason I hope a certain freedom in the translation may be excused.

"Surely!
The king of Ch'i rode forth with a thousand carriages,
Selecting to accompany him ten thousand horsemen,
To hunt on the borders of the sea.
The ranks of men filled the lowlands;
Their nets and snares covered the hills.
They seized the hares and ran down the deer,
Shot the tailed deer with arrows and snared the feet of the unicorns.
They raced along the briny coves,
The new-felled game staining their carriage wheels.
Their arrows found their mark and the catch was plentiful;
The king grew proud and began to boast of his achievements.
He turned in his carriage and said to me,

" 'Does the state of Ch'u also have its hunting lands, its wide plains and stretching lowlands, as rich and joyous as these? Can the hunts of the king of Ch'u rival these of mine?'

"I dismounted from my carriage and replied, 'I am only a humble inhabitant of the land of Ch'u. I have served the king ten years or more, and at times have accompanied him on his travels; I have attended him in the hunting parks of the capital of Ch'u and seen in person what they are like; yet I have not seen all by any means, and I can hardly speak of his hunts in the distant lowlands.'

" 'Be that as it may,' said the king of Ch'i, 'tell me in general what you have seen and heard!' and I replied, 'Of course, of course.

" 'In Ch'u, they say, there are seven lowlands. Of these I have visited only one; the other six I have never seen. The one I have visited is the smallest of them all, called Yün-meng. It is nine hundred *li* square, and in the center there is a mountain.

" 'A mountain which winds and twists upward,
Rearing its lofty crags on high,
Covered with ragged jutting peaks
That blot out the sun and moon
And entangle them in their folds;
Its crest pierces the blue clouds,
Its slopes roll and billow downward,
Reaching to the Yangtze and the rivers around.
Its soil is colored cinnabar and blue, copper and clayey white,
With yellow ochre and white quartz,
Tin and jade, gold and silver,

A mass of hues, glowing and shining,
Sparkling like the scales of a dragon.
Here too are precious stones: carnelians and garnets,
Amethysts, turquoises, and matrices of ore,
Chalcedony, beryl, and basalt for whetstones,
Onyx and figured agate.
To the east stretch fields of gentians and fragrant orchids,
Iris, turmeric, and crow-fans,
Spikenard and sweet flag,
Selinea and angelica,
Sugar cane and ginger.
On the south lie broad plains and wide lowlands,
Rising and falling in gentle slopes,
Secluded hollows and rolling leas,
Hemmed in by the great Yangtze
And bounded by Witch's Mountain.
On the high, dry crests grow
Indigo, broom, and sage,
Basil, sweet fern, and blue artemisia;
In the low, damp places,
Mallows, henbane, cattails, and bulrushes,
Marsh roses and bog rhubarb,
Water lilies, cress and mare's-tail,
Wormwood and swamp cabbage.
All manner of plants are here,
Too numerous to be counted.
To the west, bubbling springs and clear pools
Spread their restless waters,
Lotus and water chestnut blooming on their borders,
Huge rocks and white sand hidden in their depths,
Where live sacred turtles, dragons, and water lizards,
Terrapins and tortoises.
Northward rise dense forests and giant trees—
Medlar, cedar, and camphor,
Cinnamon, prickly ash, and anise tree,
Chinese cork, wild pear, red willow,
Hawthorn, chinaberry, jujube, and chestnut,
Mandarins and citrons, breathing forth their fragrance.
In their branches live apes, gibbons, and langurs,

Phoenixes, peacocks, and pheasants,
Flying lizards and lemurs.
Beneath their shade prowl white tigers and black panthers,
Leopards, lynxes, and jackals.[5]
The king of Ch'u orders his brave warriors
To seize these beasts with their bare hands,
While he mounts behind four piebald horses,
Riding in a carriage of carved jade.
From pliant staffs of whalebone
Stream banners studded with moon-bright pearls.
He grasps his stout lance forged by Kan Chiang.
At his left side hangs the painted bow of the Yellow Emperor;
On his right are strong arrows in a quiver of the Hsia kings.
A companion as wise as Yang-tzu of old stands by his side;
A driver as skilled as Hsien-a holds the reins.
Though the steeds are reined in to an easy pace,
They gain on the wily beasts;
The carriage wheels run down asses,
The steeds kick at onagers,
Spears pierce wild horses, axle points cut down wild mares,
As the hunters behind their powerful steeds shoot at fleeing jackasses.
Swiftly, relentlessly,
Like thunder they move, like the whirlwind they advance,
Streaming like comets, striking like lightning.
No shot leaves their bows in vain
But each must pierce the eye of the game,
Burrow in the breast, strike through the side,
And sever the cords of the heart,
Till the catch becomes a rain of beasts,
Covering the grass and filling the ground.
With this the king of Ch'u slackens his pace and gazes about,
Raising his head with lofty composure;
He looks toward the dark forest,
Observes the fierceness of his brave huntsmen
And the terror of the wild beasts,
Then spurs after the exhausted game, striking those that are spent,
Watching the aspect of every creature.

[5] Two lines, mentioning rhinoceroses and elephants and repeating the name of one of the beasts above, have been omitted, as they appear to be a later addition.

Next come the lovely maidens and fair princesses,
Robed in fine silk cloth
And trailing rich silks and crepes,
Girdled in sheer netting
And draped with scarves like mist,
Beneath which their skirts, gathered in close pleats,
Gently swirl and sway,
Falling in deep and pliant folds,
So long and full
That they must gather up the hems demurely.
With flying beads and dangling pendants,
They bend and sway in their carriages,
Their robes and scarves rustling softly,
Brushing the heads of the orchids below
Or fluttering against the feathered carriage tops,
Tangling in their kingfisher hairpins
Or twining about the jeweled carriage cords.
Lightly and nimbly they come
Like a vision of goddesses.
Together the groups set out to hunt in the fields of marsh orchids;
Scrambling through the thick grasses
And ascending the stout embankments of the river,
They surprise kingfishers
And shoot crow pheasants,
Fix fine cords
To their short arrows
To shoot the white geese
And the wild swans,
Bring down a pair of egrets
Or a black crane.
Tiring of these sports, they embark
To sail upon the clear lake,
And drift over the surface in their pelican-prowed boats.
They lift their cassia oars,
Spread kingfisher curtains,
And raise feathered canopies;
With nets they snare terrapins
And angle for purple mollusks;
They strike golden drums

And sound the wailing flutes,
As the songs of the boatmen
Echo across the water.
The lake insects are startled
By the waves of their wake,
As the bubbling springs gush forth,
A turmoil of water,
And the boulders in the depths grate together
With a dull, reverberating roar
Like the voice of thunder
Resounding a hundred miles.
To signal the huntsmen to rest from their labors,
The sacred drums are sounded
And beacon fires raised;
The carriages draw up in ranks,
The horsemen form in battalions,
And all take their places in proper order,
Range themselves once more in position.
Then the king of Ch'u ascends the Terrace of the Bright Clouds,
Where he rests in perfect repose,
Takes his leisure in perfect ease
And, flavoring his dishes with herbs and spices,
Sits down to feast.
The king of Ch'u is not like Your Highness,
Who counts it a pleasure to race all day,
Never descending from your carriage to rest,
Slashing at game and staining your carriage wheels with blood.
If I may speak from what I have seen,
The hunts of Ch'i cannot match those of Ch'u!' "

"With this the king of Ch'i fell silent and did not answer me."

"How can you speak in such error?" exclaimed Master No-such. "You have not considered a thousand miles too long a journey, but have been gracious enough to visit our state of Ch'i. On this occasion the king of Ch'i, calling out all the knights within his domain and providing them with a multitude of carriages and horsemen, has set forth to the hunt, hoping that by these efforts he might secure a plentiful catch and bring enjoyment to the guests at his court. How can you call it a mere boastful show? When he inquired whether you have such hunting lands in Ch'u, it was his wish to hear of the stalwart customs of your great kingdom and to listen to your discourses. Now, instead of praising the virtues of the king of Ch'u, you lavish your words on the glories of Yün-meng and describe to us in rich phrases the wanton pleasures and reckless extravagances which take place there. For your sake, I cannot help wishing you had not done this. Even if these entertainments are as you describe them, they hardly reflect to the credit of Ch'u. If they exist, for you to speak of them is only to spread abroad the fame of your ruler's faults; and if your reports are false, then you do but injure the trust we bear you. To expose the evils of one's ruler or to place trustworthiness in jeopardy—neither action can be approved. By speaking as you have, you must certainly invite contempt from the king of Ch'i and cause embarrassment to the state of Ch'u.

"As for Ch'i, it is bounded on the east by the vast ocean,
And on the south by the mountains of Lang-ya.
We may take our pleasure upon Mount Ch'eng
And shoot game on the slopes of Chih-fu;
Sail upon the Gulf of Po-hai
And roam the marsh of Meng-chu.
Northeast of us lies the land of the Su-shen,
And east of this we border the Valley of Boiling Water.
In autumn we hunt in the region of the Green Hills,
Sailing far away over the seas;
Our state could swallow eight or nine of your Yün-mengs
And they would never even tickle its throat.
As for the wonders and marvels you speak of,
The strange creatures of other regions,
The rare beasts and odd birds—
All manner of beings are gathered here in Ch'i
In such abundance within our borders
That I could not finish describing them,
Nor could the ancient sage Emperor Yü give them names
Or his minister Hsieh write them all down.
Yet, since the king of Ch'i is but a vassal of the emperor,
He does not consider it right to speak of the joys of travel
Or describe the magnificence of his parks and gardens.
Moreover, you are here as his guest,
And this is why he declined to reply to your words.
How could you think it was because he had no answer?"

Thereupon Lord Not-real broke into a smile and said, "The spokesman for Ch'u has spoken in error, while the case for Ch'i leaves much to be desired.

When the emperor demands that the feudal lords bear their tribute to his court, it is not that he desires the goods and articles they bring, but that his vassals may thereby 'report on the administration of their offices'; [6] and when he causes mounds to be raised on the borders of states and their boundaries to be marked off, these are not for the purpose of defense, but so that the feudal lords may not trespass upon each other's lands. Now, although the king of Ch'i has been enfeoffed in the east to serve as a bastion to the imperial house, he is carrying on secret contacts with the Su-shen and jeopardizing his own state by crossing his borders and sailing over the sea to hunt in the Green Hills, actions which are a violation of his duties. Both of you gentlemen, instead of attempting in your discussions to make clear the duties of lord and subject and striving to rectify the behavior of the feudal lords, vainly dispute with each other over the joys of hunting and the size of parks, each attempting to outdo the other in descriptions of lavish expenditures, each striving for supremacy in wanton delights. This is no way to win fame and gain praise, but will only blacken the names of your rulers and bring ruin to yourselves. Moreover, what do the states of Ch'i and Ch'u possess, that they are worth speaking about? You gentlemen perhaps have never laid eyes upon true splendor. Have you not heard of the Shang-lin Park of the Son of Heaven?

"To the east of it lies Ts'ang-wu,
To the west the land of Hsi-chi;
On its south runs the Cinnabar River,
On its north, the Purple Deeps.
Within the park spring the Pa and Ch'an rivers,
And through it flow the Ching and Wei,
The Feng, the Hao, the Lao, and the Chüeh,
Twisting and turning their way
Through the reaches of the park;
Eight rivers, coursing onward,
Spreading in different directions, each with its own form.
North, south, east, and west
They race and tumble,
Pouring through the chasms of Pepper Hill,
Skirting the banks of the river islets,
Winding through the cinnamon forests
And across the broad meadows.
In wild confusion they swirl

[6] A reference to *Mencius* IB, IV, 5.

Along the bases of the tall hills
And through the mouths of the narrow gorges;
Dashed upon boulders, maddened by winding escarpments,
They writhe in anger,
Leaping and curling upward,
Jostling and eddying in great swells
That surge and batter against each other;
Darting and twisting,
Foaming and tossing,
In a thundering chaos;
Arching into hills, billowing like clouds,
They dash to left and right,
Plunging and breaking in waves
That chatter over the shallows;
Crashing against the cliffs, pounding the embankments.
The waters pile up and reel back again,
Skipping across the rises, swooping into the hollows,
Rumbling and murmuring onward;
Deep and powerful,
Fierce and clamorous,
They froth and churn
Like the boiling waters of a cauldron,
Casting spray from their crests, until,
After their wild race through the gorges,
Their distant journey from afar,
They subside into silence,
Rolling on in peace to their long destination,
Boundless and without end,
Gliding in soundless and solemn procession,
Shimmering and shining in the sun,
To flow through giant lakes of the east
Or spill into the ponds along their banks.
Here horned dragons and red hornless dragons,
Sturgeon and salamanders,
Carp, bream, gudgeon, and dace,
Cowfish, flounder, and sheatfish
Arch their backs and twitch their tails,
Spread their scales and flap their fins,
Diving among the deep crevices;

The waters are loud with fish and turtles,
A multitude of living things.
Here moon-bright pearls
Gleam on the river slopes,
While quartz, chrysoberyl,
And clear crystal in jumbled heaps
Glitter and sparkle,
Catching and throwing back a hundred colors
Where they lie tumbled on the river bottom.
Wild geese and swans, graylags, bustards,
Cranes and mallards,
Loons and spoonbills,
Teals and gadwalls,
Grebes, night herons, and cormorants
Flock and settle upon the waters,
Drifting lightly over the surface,
Buffeted by the wind,
Bobbing and dipping with the waves,
Sporting among the weedy banks,
Gobbling the reeds and duckweed,
Pecking at water chestnuts and lotuses.
Behind them rise the tall mountains,
Lofty crests lifted to the sky;
Clothed in dense forests of giant trees,
Jagged with peaks and crags;
The steep summits of the Nine Pikes,
The towering heights of the Southern Mountains,
Soar dizzily like a stack of cooking pots,
Precipitous and sheer.
Their sides are furrowed with ravines and valleys,
Narrow-mouthed clefts and open glens,
Through which rivulets dart and wind.
About their base, hills and islands
Raise their tall heads;
Ragged knolls and hillocks
Rise and fall,
Twisting and twining
Like the coiled bodies of reptiles;
While from their folds the mountain streams leap and tumble,

Spilling out upon the level plains.
There they flow a thousand miles along smooth beds,
Their banks lined with dikes
Blanketed with green orchids
And hidden beneath selinea,
Mingled with snakemouth
And magnolias;
Planted with yucca,
Sedge of purple dye,
Bittersweet, gentians, and orchis,
Blue flag and crow-fans,
Ginger and turmeric,
Monkshood, wolfbane,
Nightshade, basil,
Mint, ramie, and blue artemisia,
Spreading across the wide swamps,
Rambling over the broad plains,
A vast and unbroken mass of flowers,
Nodding before the wind;
Breathing forth their fragrance,
Pungent and sweet,
A hundred perfumes
Wafted abroad
Upon the scented air.
Gazing about the expanse of the park
At the abundance and variety of its creatures,
One's eyes are dizzied and enraptured
By the boundless horizons,
The borderless vistas.
The sun rises from the eastern ponds
And sets among the slopes of the west;
In the southern part of the park,
Where grasses grow in the dead of winter
And the waters leap, unbound by ice,
Live zebras, yaks, tapirs, and black oxen,
Water buffalo, elk, and antelope,
'Red-crowns' and 'round-heads,'
Aurochs, elephants, and rhinoceroses.
In the north, where in the midst of summer

The ground is cracked and blotched with ice
And one may walk the frozen streams or wade the rivulets,
Roam unicorns and boars,
Wild asses and camels,
Onagers and mares,
Swift stallions, donkeys, and mules.
Here the country palaces and imperial retreats
Cover the hills and span the valleys,
Verandahs surrounding their four sides;
With storied chambers and winding porticos,
Painted rafters and jade-studded corbels,
Interlacing paths for the royal palanquin,
And arcaded walks stretching such distances
That their length cannot be traversed in a single day.
Here the peaks have been leveled for mountain halls,
Terraces raised, story upon story,
And chambers built in the deep grottoes.
Peering down into the caves, one cannot spy their end;
Gazing up at the rafters, one seems to see them brush the heavens;
So lofty are the palaces that comets stream through their portals
And rainbows twine about their balustrades.
Green dragons slither from the eastern pavilion;
Elephant-carved carriages prance from the pure hall of the west,
Bringing immortals to dine in the peaceful towers
And bands of fairies to sun themselves beneath the southern eaves.[7]
Here sweet fountains bubble from clear chambers,
Racing in rivulets through the gardens,
Great stones lining their courses;
Plunging through caves and grottoes,
Past steep and ragged pinnacles,
Horned and pitted as though carved by hand,
Where garnets, green jade,
And pearls abound;
Agate and marble,
Dappled and lined;

[7] In much the same way as the European aristocrats delighted in picturing themselves as rustic shepherds and shepherdesses, their Chinese counterparts loved to imagine that they were carefree immortals riding about on dragons and sipping dew in airy mountain retreats.

Rose quartz of variegated hue,
Spotted among the cliffs;
Rock crystal, opals,
And finest jade.
Here grow citrons with their ripe fruit in summer,
Tangerines, bitter oranges and limes,
Loquats, persimmons,
Wild pears, tamarinds,
Jujubes, arbutus,
Peaches and grapes,
Almonds, damsons,
Mountain plums and litchis,
Shading the quarters of the palace ladies,
Ranged in the northern gardens,
Stretching over the slopes and hillocks
And down into the flat plains;
Lifting leaves of kingfisher hue,
Their purple stems swaying;
Opening their crimson flowers,
Clusters of vermilion blossoms,
A wilderness of trembling flames
Lighting up the broad meadow.
Here crab apple, chestnut and willow,
Birch, maple, sycamore and boxwood,
Pomegranate, date palm,
Betel nut and palmetto,
Sandalwood, magnolia,
Cedar and cypress
Rise a thousand feet,
Their trunks several arm-lengths around,
Stretching forth flowers and branches,
Rich fruit and luxuriant leaves,
Clustered in dense copses,
Their limbs entwined,
Their foliage a thick curtain
Over stiff and bending trunks,
Their branches sweeping to the ground
Amidst a shower of falling petals.
They tremble and sigh

As they sway with the wind,
Creaking and moaning in the breeze
Like the tinkle of chimes
Or the wail of flageolets.
High and low they grow,
Screening the quarters of the palace ladies;
A mass of sylvan darkness,
Blanketing the mountains and edging the valleys,
Ascending the slopes and dipping into the hollows,
Overspreading the horizon,
Outdistancing the eye.
Here black apes and white she-apes,
Drills, baboons, and flying squirrels,
Lemurs and langurs,
Macaques and gibbons,
Dwell among the trees,
Uttering long wails and doleful cries
As they leap nimbly to and fro,
Sporting among the limbs
And clambering haughtily to the treetops.
Off they chase across bridgeless streams
And spring into the depths of a new grove,
Clutching the low-swinging branches,
Hurtling across the open spaces,
Racing and tumbling pell-mell,
Until they scatter from sight in the distance.
Such are the scenes of the imperial park,
A hundred, a thousand settings
To visit in the pursuit of pleasure;
Palaces, inns, villas, and lodges,
Each with its kitchens and pantries,
Its chambers of beautiful women
And staffs of officials.
Here, in late fall and early winter,
The Son of Heaven stakes his palisades and holds his hunts,
Mounted in a carriage of carved ivory
Drawn by six jade-spangled horses, sleek as dragons.
Rainbow pennants stream before him;
Cloud banners trail in the wind.

In the vanguard ride the hide-covered carriages;
Behind, the carriages of his attendants.
A coachman as clever as Sun Shu grasps the reins;
A driver as skillful as the Duke of Wei stands beside him.
His attendants fan out on all sides
As they move into the palisade.
They sound the somber drums
And send the hunters to their posts;
They corner the quarry among the rivers
And spy them from the high hills.
Then the carriages and horsemen thunder forth,
Startling the heavens, shaking the earth;
Vanguard and rear dash in different directions,
Scattering after the prey.
On they race in droves,
Rounding the hills, streaming across the lowlands,
Like enveloping clouds or drenching rain.
Leopards and panthers they take alive;
They strike down jackals and wolves.
With their hands they seize the black and tawny bears,
And with their feet they down the wild sheep.
Wearing pheasant-tailed caps
And breeches of white tiger skin
Under patterned tunics,
They sit astride their wild horses;
They clamber up the steep slopes of the Three Pikes
And descend again to the river shoals,
Galloping over the hillsides and the narrow passes,
Through the valleys and across the rivers.
They fell the 'dragon sparrows'
And sport with the *chieh-ch'ih,*
Strike the *hsia-ko* [8]
And with short spears stab the little bears,
Snare the fabulous *yao-niao* horses
And shoot down the great boars.
No arrow strikes the prey
Without piercing a neck or shattering a skull;

[8] These appear to be mythical beasts. From this point on Ssu-ma Hsiang-ju's
description of the hunt becomes more and more fanciful.

No bow is discharged in vain,
But to the sound of each twang some beast must fall.
Then the imperial carriage signals to slacken pace
While the emperor wheels this way and that,
Gazing afar at the progress of the hunting bands,
Noting the disposition of their leaders.
At a sign, the Son of Heaven and his men resume their pace,
Swooping off again across the distant plains.
They bear down upon the soaring birds;
Their carriage wheels crush the wily beasts.
Their axles strike the white deer;
Deftly they snatch the fleeting hares;
Swifter than a flash
Of scarlet lightning,
They pursue strange creatures
Beyond the borders of heaven.
To bows like the famous Fan-jo
They fit their white-feathered arrows,
To shoot the fleeing goblin-birds
And strike down the griffins.
For their mark they choose the fattest game
And name their prey before they shoot.
No sooner has an arrow left the string
Then the quarry topples to the ground.
Again the signal is raised and they soar aloft,
Sweeping upward upon the gale,
Rising with the whirlwind,
Borne upon the void,
The companions of gods,
To trample upon the black crane
And scatter the flocks of giant pheasants,
Swoop down upon the peacocks
And the golden roc,
Drive aside the five-colored *i* bird
And down the phoenixes,
Snatch the storks of heaven
And the birds of darkness,
Until, exhausting the paths of the sky,
They wheel their carriages and return.

Roaming as the spirit moves them,
Descending to earth in a far corner of the north,
Swift and straight is their course
As they hasten home again.
Then the emperor ascends the Stone Gate
And visits the Great Peak Tower,
Stops at the Magpie Turret
And gazes afar from the Dew Cold Observatory,
Descends to the Wild Plum Palace
And takes his ease in the Palace of Righteous Spring;
To the west he hastens to the Hsüan-ch'ü Palace
And poles in a pelican boat over Ox Head Lake.
He climbs the Dragon Terrace
And rests in the Tower of the Lithe Willows,
Weighing the effort and skill of his attendants
And calculating the catch made by his huntsmen.
He examines the beasts struck down by the carriages,
Those trampled beneath the feet of the horsemen
And trod upon by the beaters;
Those which, from sheer exhaustion
Or the pangs of overwhelming terror,
Fell dead without a single wound,
Where they lie, heaped in confusion,
Tumbled in the gullies and filling the hollows,
Covering the plains and strewn about the swamps.
Then, wearied of the chase,
He orders wine brought forth on the Terrace of Azure Heaven
And music for the still and spacious halls.
His courtiers, sounding the massive bells
That swing from the giant bell rack,
Raising the pennants of kingfisher feathers,
And setting up the drum of sacred lizard skin,
Present for his pleasure the dances of Yao
And the songs of the ancient Emperor Ko;
A thousand voices intone,
Ten thousand join in harmony,
As the mountains and hills rock with echoes
And the valley waters quiver to the sound.
The dances of Pa-yü, of Sung and Ts'ai,

The Yü-che song of Huai-nan,
The airs of Tien and Wen-ch'eng,
One after another in groups they perform,
Sounding in succession the gongs and drums
Whose shrill clash and dull booming
Pierce the heart and startle the ear.
The tunes Ching, Wu, Cheng, and Wei,
The Shao, Huo, Wu, and Hsiang music,
And amorous and carefree ditties
Mingle with the songs of Yen and Ying,
'Onward Ch'u!' and 'The Gripping Wind.'
Then come actors, musicians and trained dwarfs,
And singing girls from the land of Ti-ti,
To delight the ear and eye
And bring mirth to the mind;
On all sides a torrent of gorgeous sounds,
A pageant of enchanting color.
Here are maidens to match
The goddesses Blue Lute and Princess Fu:
Creatures of matchless beauty,
Seductive and fair,
With painted faces and carved hairpins,
Fragile and full of grace,
Lithe and supple,
Of delicate feature and form,
Trailing cloaks of sheerest silk
And long robes that seem as though carved and painted,
Swirling and fluttering about them
Like magic garments;
With them wafts a cloud of scent,
A delicious perfume;
White teeth sparkle
In engaging smiles,
Eyebrows arch delicately,
Eyes cast darting glances,
Until their beauty has seized the soul of the beholder
And his heart in joy hastens to their side.
  "But then, when the wine has flowed freely and the merriment is at its
height, the Son of Heaven becomes lost in contemplation, like one whose

spirit has wandered, and he cries, 'Alas! What is this but a wasteful extravagance? Now that I have found a moment of leisure from the affairs of state, I thought it a shame to cast away the days in idleness and so, in this autumn season, when Heaven itself slays life, I have joined in its slaughter and come to this hunting park to take my ease. And yet I fear that those who follow me in ages to come may grow infatuated with these sports, until they lose themselves in the pursuit of pleasure and forget to return again to their duties. Surely this is no way for one who has inherited the throne to carry on the great task of his forbears and insure the rule of our imperial house!'

"Then he dismisses the revelers, sends away the huntsmen, and instructs his ministers, saying, 'If there are lands here in these suburbs that can be opened for cultivation, let them all be turned into farms in order that my people may receive aid and benefit thereby. Tear down the walls and fill up the moats, that the common folk may come and profit from these hills and lowlands! Stock the lakes with fish and do not prohibit men from taking them! Empty the palaces and towers, and let them no longer be staffed! Open the storehouses and granaries to succor the poor and starving and help those who are in want; pity the widower and widow, protect the orphans and those without families! I would broadcast the name of virtue and lessen punishments and fines; alter the measurements and statutes, change the color of the vestments, reform the calendar and, with all men under heaven, make a new beginning!'

"Then, selecting an auspicious day and fasting in preparation,
He dons his court robes
And mounts the carriage of state,
With its flowery pennants flying
And its jade bells ringing.
He sports now in the Park of the Six Arts,
Races upon the Road of Benevolence and Righteousness,
And scans the Forest of the *Spring and Autumn Annals.*
His archery now is to the stately measures of 'The Fox Head'
And 'The Beast of Virtue'; [9]
His prey is the Dance of the Black Cranes,
Performed with ceremonial shield and battle axe.
Casting the heavenly Cloud Net,[10]
He snares the songs of the *Book of Odes,*

[9] Musical compositions supposed to have been played at the archery contests of the king and the feudal lords respectively in ancient times.

[10] The name of a constellation.

Sighs over 'The Felling of the Sandalwood' [11]
And delights in the ruler who 'shares his joy with all.' [12]
He mends his deportment in the garden of *Rites*
And wanders in the orchard of the *Book of Documents*.
He spreads the teachings of the *Book of Changes,*
Sets free the strange beasts penned in his park,
Ascends the Bright Hall,
And seats himself in the Temple of the Ancestors.

"Then may his ministers freely present before him their proposals for the betterment of the empire, and within the four seas there is no one who does not share in the 'spoils' of this new hunt.[13] Then is the empire filled with great joy; all men turn their faces toward the wind of imperial virtue and harken to its sound. As though borne upon a stream, they are transformed to goodness; with shouts of gladness they set forth upon the Way and journey to righteousness, so that harsh punishments are set aside and no longer used. Finer is this ruler's virtue than that of the Three Sages of antiquity, more plenteous his merits than those of the Five Emperors. When a ruler has achieved such virtue, then may he enjoy himself at the hunt without incurring blame. But to gallop from morn to night in sunshine or rain, exhausting the spirit and tiring the body, wearing out the carriages and horses, draining the energies of the huntsmen and squandering the resources of the treasury; to think only of one's own pleasure before sufficient benefits have been bestowed upon others; to ignore the common people and neglect the government of the nation, merely because one is greedy for a catch of pheasants and hares—this no truly benevolent ruler would do! Thus, from what I can see, the kings of Ch'i and Ch'u merit only pity. Though their domains are no more than a thousand *li* square, their hunting parks occupy nine tenths of the area, so that the land cannot be cleared and the people have no space to grow food. When one who is no more than a feudal prince attempts to indulge in extravagances fit only for the supreme ruler, then I fear it is the common people who will suffer in the end!"

[11] A song from "Airs from the State of Wei," in the *Book of Odes,* said to express censure of a greedy ruler who fails to make use of wise men.

[12] From the song "Sang-hu," "Lesser Odes," *Fu-t'ien* section, in the *Book of Odes.*

[13] In the passage above the poet uses the hunting metaphor to describe the ideal ruler: a student of the Classics and the arts, amusing himself with the stately dances and songs of antiquity and thinking always of the welfare of his people instead of indulging in extravagant pleasures. Thus, after having dazzled the emperor with his rhetoric, the poet delivers his "message."

At these words Sir Fantasy and Master No-such abruptly changed countenance and looked uneasily about, quite at a loss for words. Then, backing off and rising from their places, they replied, "We are uncouth and ignorant men who do not know when to hold our tongues. Fortunately today we have received your instruction, and we shall do our best to abide by it."

When the poem was presented to the emperor, he appointed Ssu-ma Hsiang-ju to the post of palace attendant. To the passages in which Lord Not-real tells of the vastness of the emperor's hunting park at Shang-lin with its hills and valleys and its rivers and countless creatures, as well as Sir Fantasy's description of the great size and richness of Yün-meng in Ch'u, however, it was objected that the extravagant language of the poet had overstepped the bounds of reality and displayed too little respect for the dictates of reason and good sense. As a result only the essential parts of the poem were accepted, and it was discussed in the light of the final passage which shows the ruler returning to just ways of government.[14]

After Ssu-ma Hsiang-ju had been a palace attendant for several years, it happened that T'ang Meng was dispatched to invade the regions of Yeh-lang and Western Pei to the west of China and open up relations with them. To accomplish this, he recruited a thousand officers and men from the provinces of Pa and Shu. In addition, these provinces took it upon themselves to send along a force of ten thousand or more men to transport provisions.[15] When he encountered any difficulties in carrying out his plans, T'ang Meng took advantage of the military supply law to execute the ringleaders of the opposition, a step which threw the people of Pa and Shu into extreme panic. When the emperor got wind of the affair, he dispatched Ssu-ma Hsiang-ju to

[14] Fortunately, Ssu-ma Ch'ien seems to have quoted the entire poem, without omitting the passages that the emperor and his court found objectionable. It should be noted that, although Chinese literature contains many fine works of fantasy, Chinese literary criticism, at least in those periods when it was dominated by Confucian thought, has been suspicious of anything that was too obviously opposed to "reason and good sense," such as the passage in the poem just quoted in which the emperor and his huntsmen mount into the sky and pursue the birds on the wing. The critics tend to regard such flights of fancy as useless and irresponsible, if not actually morally unsound.

[15] With a view, it would seem from what follows, to making a profit from the expedition.

reprimand T'ang Meng and to explain to the inhabitants of Pa and Shu that it had not been his intention to inflict any such penalties upon them. Hsiang-ju issued a proclamation to them which read:

Let this be known to the governors of Pa and Shu. For a long time now the barbarians have been left to conduct themselves as they please and no steps have been taken to punish them; time and again they have invaded and plundered our borders and made trouble for our soldiers and officials. Since His Majesty came to the throne, he has done his best to preserve his people and to bring peace to China. For this purpose he has in recent years raised his armies and called out the troops. To the north he has dispatched them to attack the Hsiung-nu until the *Shan-yü,* filled with terror, has come with clasped hands to receive our orders, with bent knee to beg for peace. K'ang-chü [Trans-Oxiana] and the other regions of the west, translating and retranslating their strange tongues, have come to pay their respects, bowing their heads to the ground and bringing gifts of tribute to our court. Our ruler has dispatched his armies to the east to rescue Eastern Yüeh from the attacks of Min-Yüeh, consenting for the sake of the king of Eastern Yüeh to send them as far as the city of P'an-yü, so that the king in gratitude sent his heir to our court. Thus the princes of the eastern barbarians, as well as the chieftains of the Western Pei, have not dared to be lax in the presentation of their customary tribute and services; standing on tiptoe with necks outstretched, they gasp like little fishes, each striving to outdo the other in the execution of his duties, all begging to become our subjects.

Yet the way to their lands is very far and blocked by precipitous mountains and deep rivers, so that they cannot be trusted to make the journey of themselves. Now His Majesty has already punished those who failed to acknowledge his sovereignty, but he has not yet rewarded those who have acted in good will, and for this reason he has dispatched his general of palace attendants T'ang Meng to journey to these lands and welcome their rulers as guests of China. He has recruited five hundred soldiers from each of the provinces of Pa and Shu and provided them with gifts so that they may act as a bodyguard for his envoy in case of any unforeseen event. There is no reason to believe that this is a matter of open warfare or to fear that the men will become involved in a conflict.

Now it has come to His Majesty's attention that in the calling out of troops and the application of the supply laws the envoy has acted in such a way as to bring panic to the young men and fear and foreboding to the elders. In addition, it appears that the provinces have, on their own initiative, undertaken to transport grain and supplies to the party. None of these actions, I assure you, are in accordance with His Majesty's will. Again, some of those who have been chosen to make the expedition have run away or taken it upon themselves to rob and kill. This, needless to say, is not in accord with the duties of a subject.

The brave men of the other border provinces of our empire, as soon as they see the beacon fires burning or the smoke signals rising, all seize their bows and gallop off, shoulder their weapons and hasten on foot, dashing off in sweaty haste, each fearful only that he will be last. Plunging upon the bare blades of the foe, braving the rain of arrows, they forget all else in the pursuit of duty, nor do they think for a moment to turn aside their steps; each in his breast is burning with anger, as though he were avenging a private wrong. Yet can you say that these men hate life and delight in death? Are they not ordinary citizens like yourselves? Do they serve some other ruler than you men of Pa and Shu? No! It is only that, considering the future and taking deep thought for the dangers which threaten the state, they delight in fulfilling their duty as subjects. Therefore they are rewarded with the split tallies of enfeoffment, the jade emblems of nobility; they take their place among the ranking marquises and reside in the mansions east of the imperial palace; and when their days are ended, they leave a name for later ages to remember, and their lands are handed down to their sons and grandsons. In the execution of their duties they display the utmost fidelity; they dwell in peace and comfort; their fame is sung for endless ages; and the glory of their achievements never fades. This is the reason that wise men and gentlemen do not hesitate at the call to arms, though they may spill their bowels upon the broad plains and drench the wild grasses with their blood.

In contrast to these, however, the men who have now been entrusted with the mission of bearing gifts to the southern barbarians and who rob and kill of their own will, or incur punishment because they run away, will find themselves deprived of both life and fame. Their posthumous name will be "Supreme Stupidity," their shame will reflect upon their fathers and mothers, and they will become the laughing stock of the world. How far apart in wisdom and judgment are these two groups of men!

And yet the fault does not lie wholly with the members of the expedition themselves. You, the elders of Pa and Shu, have failed in your duty to instruct them, and the young men have not been diligent in carrying out your teachings. You are poor in modesty and lacking in shame, and the ways of your people are neither just nor generous. Is it not inevitable, then, that your men should suffer punishment?

His Majesty the emperor is distressed that his envoy T'ang Meng and the other officials have behaved as they have, and he is full of pity for men such as these who have shown themselves to be ignorant and unworthy. He has therefore sent me as his personal messenger to explain to the common people his reasons for calling out the troops, and at the same time to reprimand those who have proved themselves disloyal in the face of death and to censure the elders and mentors of the people for failing to give them proper instruction.

It is now the season when you are most busy in the fields, and I would not add to the burdens of the common people by calling them together to address them. I have been in person to visit the men of the nearby districts, but I am afraid that there are many people living in remote valleys and mountain regions who may not receive word of this. I have therefore issued this proclamation to be delivered with all speed to the districts and marches, so that everyone may be informed of His Majesty's will. Pay heed to what it says!

By the time Ssu-ma Hsiang-ju completed his mission and returned to report to the emperor, T'ang Meng had invaded and opened up communication with the region of Yeh-lang. It was decided to use this opportunity to make contact with the roads in the territory of the barbarians of the southwest. More soldiers were called out from Pa, Shu, and Kuang-han, and a labor force of twenty or thirty thousand men put to work building a road. At the end of two years, however, the road had still not been completed. A number of men died in the course of the construction and the expense reached staggering proportions, so that many of the people of Shu, as well as the Han officials connected with the project, began to complain that it was impractical. At the same time the local chieftains of the regions of Ch'iung and Tso, hearing that the other southern barbarians had entered into relations with the Han empire and were receiving many fine gifts, asked to become subjects of the emperor and requested the officials to grant them the same treatment as the southern barbarians.

The emperor asked Ssu-ma Hsiang-ju's opinion on the question, to which he replied, "The lands of Ch'iung, Tso, Jan, and Mang are situated near Shu and it is an easy task to open up roads to them. In earlier times the Ch'in dynasty was in contact with these regions and divided them up into provinces and districts, but they were abandoned after the rise of the Han. Now if it were actually possible to re-establish these provinces and districts, it would prove of even greater advantage than communications with the southern barbarians."

The emperor approved his opinion and, appointing him a general of palace attendants, sent him with the imperial credentials to act as envoy to these regions. Accompanied by Wang Jan-yü, Hu Ch'ung-kuo, and Lü Yüeh-jen as assistant envoys, he set off in haste by four-horse relay carriage with orders to collect gifts from the officials of Pa and Shu and present them to the western barbarians.

When Hsiang-ju reached Shu, the governor of the province and his subordinates all came out to the suburbs to greet him, and the magistrates of the districts, bearing crossbows and arrows on their backs, rode before his carriage, for the men of Shu considered him a person of great honor. Hsiang-ju's father-in-law Cho Wang-sun, as well as the various distinguished men of Lin-ch'iung, flocked to his gate with presents of meat and wine to express their warmhearted friendship. Cho Wang-sun was filled with remorse that he had been so late in recognizing his daughter's marriage to Hsiang-ju, and to make up for it he presented her with a generous portion of his estate, so that her inheritance equaled that of her brother.

Ssu-ma Hsiang-ju proceeded to carry out his mission of invading and pacifying the lands of the western barbarians, and the chiefs of Ch'iung, Tso, Jan, Mang, and Ssu-yü all begged to become subjects of the Han. He abolished the gates along the old border and moved them farther out, establishing the new frontier at the Mo and Jo rivers in the west and Tsang-ko in the south. In addition he opened up a road through the Ling Pass, built a bridge across the Sun River, and established communication with the capital of Ch'iung. When he returned and reported on his mission, the emperor was overcome with delight.

While Ssu-ma Hsiang-ju was carrying out this mission, he received complaints from many of the elders of Shu that the whole idea of opening up communications with the barbarians of the southwest was a waste of time, and he learned in addition that even one of the high court ministers, Kung-sun Hung, was opposed to the plan. He would have liked to urge the emperor to abandon the idea, but since he was the one who had first suggested it, he did not dare. Instead he composed a letter in which he used the words of the elders of Shu to express his own disapproval of the plan in order to criticize the actions of the emperor, and at the same time explained the purpose of his mission and made known the emperor's wishes in the matter. The letter read as follows:

For seventy-eight years the Han had flourished, its virtue resplendent in the reigns of six sovereigns, glorious in their might and majesty, their deep mercy and blessing spreading far and wide, nourishing all creatures and overflowing beyond the borders of the empire. At that time an envoy [16] was sent by imperial order to carry out an expedition to the west, following the rivers and driving back the enemy, and wherever he went there were none who failed to bow, like grass before the wind, to the word of our sovereign. Thus Jan journeyed to court and Mang followed after; Tso was conquered and Ch'iung pacified; Ssu-yü was invaded and Pao-man forced to its knees. Then the envoy halted his attack, wheeled his carriage about, and headed toward the east to return and make his report to the throne. But when he reached the capital of the province of Shu, a number of elderly statesmen, gentlemen, and teachers, twenty-seven in all, stern and correct in their behavior, came to call upon him. When they had exchanged a word of greeting, the men of Shu came forward and said:

"We have heard it said that the Son of Heaven in his relations with the barbarian tribes should be like one who holds an animal by the halter, merely leading it on without stop. For three years now the men of the provinces of Pa, Shu, and Kuang-han have wearied themselves with the task of building a road to Yeh-lang, and still it is not completed. The soldiers are worn out and the common people are in want, and yet on top of this we are told we must open up communications with the western barbarians. The strength of the people is exhausted, and we fear that the undertaking can never be carried out. The blame for this lies partly with His Majesty's envoy, and we are secretly afraid for the safety of the advisers who urged this plan upon the ruler.

"Moreover, the lands of Ch'iung, Tso, and Western P'o have existed side by side with China for more years than it is possible to reckon, and yet during that period no benevolent ruler has ever succeeded in winning them over by virtue, nor any powerful ruler in annexing them by force. In our

[16] Namely, Ssu-ma Hsiang-ju himself.

opinion the task is next to impossible. The present plan does no more than deprive the common people of China in order to benefit the barbarians, exhausting those who are the support of the nation in the service of worthless foreigners. Ignorant and rustic men that we are, we are unable to comprehend the reasons for such a policy!"

The envoy replied, "How can you make such an assertion? If what you say were true, then the men of Shu as well would be following barbarian customs! [17] Even a man of my own poor capabilities must reject such arguments as these!

"This is a large-scale undertaking, and for that reason it is hardly the kind of thing that mere bystanders like yourselves can comprehend. I am in a hurry to be on my way and I have no leisure to go into details, but I should like at least to give you gentlemen a general outline of the plan.

"In this world there must first be extraordinary men before there can be extraordinary deeds, and there must be extraordinary deeds before extraordinary results can be achieved. Whatever is extraordinary is always regarded with suspicion by ordinary men. Therefore it is said, 'The common folk are terrified by the start of anything extraordinary, but when it has reached completion, the whole world enjoys the benefits thereof.'

"Thus in ancient times a great flood arose, spilling its waters across the whole land; the people were forced to flee over hill and dale in terror, and nowhere could they find refuge. Then Emperor Yü of the house of Hsia, taking pity upon their plight, set about to stem the flood, opening up the rivers and channeling off the streams, dividing and deepening their beds to rescue the people from disaster; he led the waters east to the sea and all the world found peace and safety. Do you suppose that the people accomplished such a task by themselves? The mind of the emperor was fraught with care, and he himself took part in their labors, until his skin was calloused and brown and the hair no longer grew on his body. Thus the glory of his achievements has shone through countless ages and his praises are sung to this very day.

"When a truly wise ruler has ascended the throne, how can you expect him to give his attention only to petty deeds and trifles, to be bound by the letter of custom and led by common ways, to abide only by the stories and traditions of the past, seeking nothing more than the approval and delight of his own generation? Rather will he honor lofty ideals and farsighted proposals, embark upon new undertakings to insure the continuance of

[17] I.e., the region of Shu itself would never have been wrested from the barbarians and made a part of the Chinese empire.

the dynasty, and provide a model for ten thousand ages to admire. Thus will he strive with all his might to bring new lands and people beneath his sway and expend every thought to match the virtue of the life-giving earth, and with earth and heaven to form a triad! Is it not said in the *Odes,*

Beneath all heaven
There is no land that is not the king's;
Throughout the borders of the earth,
None who are not his subjects![18]

"Therefore, within the six directions and beyond the eight corners of the earth, wherever his virtue flows, if there is any creature that is not touched and transformed by his mercy, the wise ruler considers it a source of shame.

"Now, within the borders of the nation, the men of China with their hats and girdles all enjoy the highest blessing, and none are excluded or left out. But in the lands of the strange-mannered barbarians, in the distant regions of the foreigners, where our boats and carriages cannot penetrate and our people seldom set foot, the teachings of our government are as yet unknown and the wind of virtue which issues from our sovereign blows but faintly. Therefore, when they enter our borders they turn their backs upon duty and insult propriety, while within their own lands they commit all manner of wanton evil, banishing or assassinating their leaders. Among them, ruler and subject change places, and honorable and lowly are confounded; fathers and elders suffer for crimes they have not committed, and children and orphans are taken as slaves, bound and weeping. Then do they look toward our land and cry out in anger, saying, 'We have heard that in China there is a ruler of supreme benevolence, whose virtue is manifold and whose mercy is all-embracing, so that under him all beings find their just place. Why are we alone deprived of his blessing?' On tiptoe they stand, gazing longingly like men in drought at a distant rainstorm. Even the cruelest of men would shed tears for them; how much more, then, must a great sage like our ruler be moved to pity by their plight!

"For this reason he sent his armies north to attack the powerful Hsiung-nu, dispatched his envoys to hasten south and reprimand the headstrong rulers of Yüeh, extending his virtue to the lands on every side. Then the chieftains of the west and southwest came to him by the millions, swarming together like fish that battle their way upstream, begging to receive titles from the ruler of China. It was for this reason that he extended the boundaries to the Mo and Jo rivers, moved the frontier to Tsang-ko, opened up a way through Ling Mountain, and bridged the source of the Sun, building a

[18] "Shan-pei," *Ku-feng* Section, "Lesser Odes," in the *Book of Odes.*

new road for justice and virtue and establishing for the sake of posterity a new regime of benevolence and righteousness. Then may his mercy extend far and wide, bringing succor to every foreign land, and the remote regions will no longer be shut up; the dark and inaccessible places will be illumined with a great light of understanding, so that we in China may at last lay down our weapons and the barbarians may find rest from invasion and punishment; near and far will become one body, and China and the lands beyond it will together enjoy good fortune. Will that not be a joyous day indeed?

"To rescue the people from the sea of troubles in which they flounder and to serve the cause of the highest and most beautiful virtue; to turn back a dying age from the course of decay and ruin and to carry on the dynastic labors of the Chou kings which were cut off: these are the urgent tasks which confront the Son of Heaven. Though the execution of them may mean toil for the common people, how can he cease on that account?

"Every task undertaken by a ruler must begin in sorrow and toil, but as surely will it end in ease and joy. The proof that our ruler has received the mandate of Heaven lies in this very undertaking to the west. When it has been completed, he will increase his glory by performing the Feng sacrifice upon Mount T'ai and the Shan sacrifice at Liang-fu; the phoenix bells on his carriage will ring with joy; odes of praise will peal forth in his honor; and he will be acclaimed the equal of the Five Emperors of ancient times and mount to greater heights than the rulers of the Three Dynasties.

"And yet you, the watchers, have not understood his intentions; the listeners do not comprehend his voice. Like a bright swan, he soars to the dome of heaven, but the spreaders of nets still search for him, alas, in the marshy wastes!"

At this the elders of Shu looked about in confusion, forgetting what it was they had come to say and no longer able to make their proposal. With a sigh they replied as in one voice, "Wonderful indeed is the virtue of the Han! This is what we came to hear! Though the common people should be idle in their labors, we beg to lead the way ourselves!"

Then, abashed and at a loss for words, they took their leave and hastily withdrew.

Sometime after this, someone sent a report to the throne accusing Ssu-ma Hsiang-ju of having accepted bribes when he was acting as imperial envoy. As a result, he was dismissed from office, but a year or so later was recalled to the post of palace attendant.

Hsiang-ju stuttered when he spoke, but was very fond of composing works of literature. He also suffered constantly from diabetes. Because of his marriage to the daughter of the Cho family, he enjoyed considerable wealth. Though he was promoted to various offices at court, he never ventured to discuss affairs of state with the high ministers but, pleading ill health, lived a life of retirement. He had no desire for high offices or noble titles.

It was his custom to accompany the emperor on hunting parties to the Palace of Old Poplars. At such times the emperor delighted in shooting down bears and wild boars in person and galloping after the various wild beasts. Hsiang-ju, distressed at this, submitted a memorial reprimanding the emperor for such conduct. It read as follows:

I have heard that even creatures of the same species differ in their abilities. Thus, when we talk of great strength, we mention the famous strong man Niao Hu of Ch'in; for outstanding swiftness we cite Ch'ing Chi of Wu, and for bravery the ancient heroes Meng Pen and Hsia Yü. If this is true of men, may I venture to suggest, then, that it must be true of beasts as well?

Now Your Majesty delights in racing through the dangerous mountain defiles and shooting ferocious beasts. But should you suddenly encounter some creature of extraordinary size and strength, should some startled beast spring out from an unexpected quarter and charge down upon the vehicles of your attendants, your carriages would have no room to wheel about, nor would your men have time to employ their skill and, though they might have the strength of Niao Hu and the skill of the archer Feng Meng, they would be powerless to aid you. Like so many dead limbs or rotten stumps, they would all suffer injury. Were the Hsiung-nu or Yüeh barbarians to spring up from beneath your hubs, or the Ch'iang and I barbarians fling themselves at your crossboard, the situation could not be more perilous. And even if it were absolutely certain that there was no danger involved, it is not the sort of situation in which the Son of Heaven should place himself to begin with!

Even when the roads have been cleared for your passing and your carriage gallops down the middle of the way, there are times when a horse slips the bit or wrenches free of its bridle and runs wild. How much more so, then, when you are racing through the tall grasses or galloping over the hills, with your eyes set only upon the pleasure of the catch before you and your mind forgetful of sudden mishaps that might occur? How easy would it be to meet with misfortune! To make light of the importance of your high position and find no peace in it, but to count it a joy to set out on paths that threaten even a particle of danger is, if I may venture to say so, hardly the way for Your Majesty to act.

An enlightened man sees the end of things while they are still in bud, and a wise man knows how to avoid danger before it has taken shape. Misfortune often lurks in the shadowy darkness and springs forth when men are off their guard. Thus the homely proverb says: "The heir to an estate of a thousand pieces of gold should not sit on the edge of the porch!" This is a trifling remark, and yet it can apply to great affairs. I beg Your Majesty to give it thought and to be kind enough to consider my words!

The emperor was pleased with this memorial. On the way back from the hunt, the emperor stopped for a visit at the Palace of Righteous Spring, nearby which stood the grave mound of the Second Emperor of the Ch'in. Ssu-ma Hsiang-ju thereupon composed a poem in the rhyme-prose style in which he lamented the erroneous ways of the Second Emperor. It read:

I climb the winding face of the long slope
And enter the lofty halls of the many-storied palace;
Looking down upon the banks of the crooked streams
Or gazing far off at the ragged crests of the Southern Mountains,
I see the deep stillness of cliff-bound glens
And the spreading mouths of spacious valleys,
Where the racing torrents endlessly leap and tumble,
Spilling their waters abroad upon the wide plain.
I scan the dark and massive forests,
The dense groves of bamboo;
To the east I gallop up the earthen mound,
To the north, wade across the stony shallows,
And with slackened pace and solemn mien
I pay my respects to the memory of the Second Emperor.
He failed to conduct himself with discretion
And lost his empire and his throne;
He heeded slander and would not wake to truth
And brought destruction to the temples of his ancestors.
Alas, how pitiful
That he went so far astray!

Now his grave mound is untended, a tangle of weeds,
And his spirit wanders homeless and unfed.[19]
With the fleeting years, his tomb falls further into ruin;
With the passing seasons, it sinks deeper into darkness;
While his soul like a shadow wings upward,
Ascending to the nine heavens, to depart from the world forever.
Alas, how pitiful!

After this Ssu-ma Hsiang-ju was honored with the post of keeper of the funerary park of Emperor Wen.

Emperor Wu had earlier expressed admiration for the poet's work on Sir Fantasy. Ssu-ma Hsiang-ju, observing that the emperor was fond of anything dealing with immortal spirits, took occasion to remark, "My description of the Shang-lin Park is hardly deserving of praise. I have something that is still finer. In the past I began a poem in rhyme-prose style on 'The Mighty One.' It is not completed yet, but when I have finished it, I beg to present it to Your Majesty."

The older legends of famous immortals always pictured them as emaciated creatures who dwell among the hills and swamps, but Ssu-ma Hsiang-ju judged that this was not the type of immortal that would take the emperor's fancy. He therefore completed his *"Fu* on The Mighty One," which read as follows:

In this world there lives a Mighty One
Who dwells in the Middle Continent.[20]
Though his mansion stretches ten thousand miles,
He is not content to remain in it a moment
But, saddened by the sordid press of the vulgar world,
Nimbly takes his way aloft and soars far away.
With crimson carriage flags interwoven with crystal rainbows,
He mounts upon the clouds and wanders on high;
He raises his long standard of yellow flame
Tipped with multicolored plumes of shimmering radiance,
Streaming with starry pennants
And banderoles of comets' tails.
Drifting with the wind, he threads his way;
With banners fluttering, he wanders aloft.

[19] Because his descendents are no longer living to offer sacrifices to him.
[20] I.e., China. The Mighty One is of course intended to be Emperor Wu himself.

He snatches a shooting star for a flag
And sheathes his flagstaff in a broken rainbow.
A blaze of vermilion, dazzling the eyes,
He whirls before the gale and drifts upon the clouds.
His elephant-carved chariot is drawn by winged dragons,
With red serpents and green lizards writhing at their sides.
High and low they gallop,
Lifting their heads in lordly pride;
Lithely bending and rearing their backs,
They slither and curl their winding way.
Now they stretch their necks and peer about,
Raising their heads and pausing in passage;
Now with fearless and lofty assurance
They bolt forward in tumultuous flight.
Onward they bound, twisting and turning,
Left side and right leaping in harmony,
Tumbling forward in dauntless array,
Prancing in unison.
Straining at the bridle and uttering strange cries,
They swoop down to tread the earth;
Springing upward in breathless flight,
They careen wildly across the sky.
Pressing forward, chasing after,
They swirl like sparks, they stream like lightning,
Plunging boldly into the mists
And fading out of sight among the clouds.[21]
Thus the Mighty One crosses to the eastern limit and ascends to the
    end of the north,
Searching out other immortal spirits.
Together they wheel about and drive far to the right;
Slanting across the Valley of Leaping Springs, they turn again east.
He summons all the fairies of the Magic Garden
And a host of gods to ride behind him on the Star of Pure Light.
He orders the Emperors of the Five Directions to be his guides,
Beckons to his side the Great Single Star and the immortal Ling Yang.
On his left rides the deity Black Night, on his right, the Thunder
    Bearer,

[21] In this passage, a mass of obscure onomatopoetic compounds, commentators
are able to give only tentative suggestions as to the exact meaning of the words.

While before and behind the gods Lu-li and Yü-huang attend him.
He has the War Earl Ch'iao as his footman, the genie Hsien-men as
his page,
And the physician Ch'i-po to prepare his medicine cup.
The god of fire Chu-jung goes in front to clear the road
And disperse the foul vapors before his coming.
His cortege boasts ten thousand carriages,
Their canopies woven of cloud, their flowered pennants flying.
He calls the god of the east Chü-mang to wait upon him,
Saying, "I would journey south to take my pleasure!"
He visits the sage Emperor Yao on Mount Ch'ung
And Emperor Shun on the Mountain of Nine Peaks.
In endless massive ranks his retinue advances;
Pressing upon each other, they gallop on their way,
Veering and jostling
Amidst a tangle of chariots,
Swooping onward in eternal procession
Like a mighty river rolling by;
Spurring forward in serried ranks,
A host of countless numbers advancing,
Fanning out across the heavens,
Their columns scattered and broken.
Straight they ride into the din and clangor of the Thunder Hall
And swoop through the craggy confines of Devil Valley.
They survey the eight directions and the four outer wastes,
Ford the Nine Rivers and pass over the Five Streams,
Traverse the Flaming Mountain and the River of Weak Waters,
Embark among the floating islets and cross the drifting sands;
They rest upon the Ts'ung-ling Ranges and idle by their waters,
While the goddess Nü-kua strikes the lute and the Lord of the River
dances.
At times, when the sky grows dark and threatening,
They summon P'ing-i, the messenger of the gods,
And send him to chastise the Wind Earl and punish the Rain Master.
They gaze west to the hazy contours of the K'un-lun Mountains,
Then gallop off to the Mountain of the Three Pinnacles.
They batter at the gates of Heaven, enter the palace of the Celestial
Emperor,
And invite the goddess Jade Maiden to return in their chariots.

They roam the slopes of Lang-feng and sit down to rest,
Like ravens that circle on high and come to roost again.
They wander among the Dark Hills,
Winging their way in crooked flight.
"Behold!" cries the Mighty One, "the Queen Mother of the West,[22]
With her hair of silvery white
And her burden of hairpins, living in a cave!
Fortunately she has her three-legged crow to bring her food.
Yet if she must live in this state forever,
Though it be for ten thousand ages, what joy can she find?"
Then he wheels his carriage about and departs from her abode,
Making his way across Mount Pu-chou.
He stops to dine at the Hill of the Somber City;
He sucks up the midnight vapors of the northland
And feasts on golden morning mists;
He nibbles the blossoms of the herb of immortality
And savors the flowers of the Ruby Tree.
Then he rises and resumes his journey,
His chariot dancing wildly towards the heavens.
He threads through the streams of lightning that pour from Heaven's
    portals
And traverses the drenching torrents of the Cloud Master.
With his attendant carriages, he gallops the long road downward,
Racing through the mists and off into the distance.
He presses beyond the borders of the narrow universe
And, with slackened pace, emerges beyond the bounds of the north.
He leaves his attendants behind at the Dark Pass
And rides ahead of them out of the Cold Gate of the North.
Beneath him in the vastness, the earth has disappeared;
Above his head the heavens vanish in endless space.
Gazing about, his eyes swim and grow sightless;
His ears are deafened and discern no sound.
Riding upon the Void, he mounts on high,
Above the world of men, companionless, to dwell alone.

When Ssu-ma Hsiang-ju presented his ode in praise of the Mighty
One, the emperor was overcome with delight, declaring that it made

[22] An immortal spirit whose cult was very popular in Han times, said to dwell
in a cave west of the K'un-lun Mountains. The poet makes fun of her constrained
way of life, contrasting it with the freedom and luxury of The Mighty One.

him feel as though he were already whirling away over the clouds and filled him with a longing to wander about the earth and the heavens.

Hsiang-ju had retired from his post at court sometime earlier because of ill health and was living at his home in Mou-ling. "Hsiang-ju's illness seems to be very serious," the emperor announced to his attendants. "It would be well if someone went to his house and gathered up all of his writings. If it is not done now, they are very likely after his death to become scattered and lost." He dispatched So Chung to carry out the task, but when So Chung reached Mou-ling he discovered that Hsiang-ju was already dead. Finding no manuscripts in the poet's house, he questioned Hsiang-ju's wife, who replied, "My husband never kept any books or writings around the house. From time to time he used to compose pieces, but someone always came and took them away, so that there is nothing left here now. Before he died, however, he did write one piece and told me that if a messenger came from His Majesty looking for books, I was to present it to him. But outside of that there is nothing else!"

She then gave So Chung the manuscript her husband had left behind, written on slips of wood, which dealt with the Feng and Shan sacrifices. So Chung in turn presented it to the emperor, who regarded it very highly. It read: [23]

From the beginnings of highest antiquity, when august Heaven first created the people, until the time of the Ch'in, how many have been the lords who ruled generation after generation! When we survey the records of recent ages and hark back to the legends of far-off times, we find but a vast and shadowy confusion of figures whose names are no longer spoken, their numbers too great to be reckoned. Yet from the reigns of Shun and Yü, among those who were honored with titles and posthumous names, we may still count a total of seventy-two rulers. And of all these, there were none who practiced good and yet failed to prosper; none who wrought evil and yet escaped destruction!

Of those who went before the Yellow Emperor, aeons removed from us today, we can learn nothing in detail; but the history of the Five Emperors and the Three Dynasties has been handed down to us in the Classics and other writings for all to peruse. Thus the *Book of Documents* says:

[23] The purpose of this tiresome piece of rhetoric is to persuade Emperor Wu to perform the Feng and Shan sacrifices. In places the poet uses a pseudo-historical style, as though the emperor had already agreed to perform them.

Enlightened is the Lord of the Multitude!
Good the great ministers, his arms and legs! [24]

From this we may see that among rulers there was none more glorious than Emperor Yao of T'ang, and among ministers, none wiser than his minister Hou Chi, the ancestor of the Chou kings. Hou Chi laid the foundations of their glory in the age of Emperor Yao; Kung Liu increased the power of the family among the western barbarians; and King Wen instituted the changes appropriate to a new dynasty, opening the way for the flourishing might of the Chou. Thus was their great undertaking brought to completion and, though in later ages the power of the Chou lords waned and their virtue declined, yet for a thousand years they ruled without ill repute. Did they not make, as the saying puts it, "a good beginning and a good end"?

There was but one reason for their glory: they were careful to preserve the ways of those who went before them and diligent in handing down their teachings to posterity. Thus their ways were just and easy to follow; their bounty was far-reaching and easily flourished; their laws were manifest and easy to obey; and their method of choosing successors to the throne was logical and easy to maintain. So the dynasty reached its height under King Ch'eng, who came to the throne when he was still in swaddling clothes, and its glory surpassed that of the Hsia and Shang, the two dynasties that had preceded it.

If we examine the origins and survey the later history of the Chou, we find no wonders or extraordinary deeds worthy to compare with those of our present age today. Nevertheless, the Chou kings journeyed to Liang-fu and ascended Mount T'ai, performing the Feng and Shan sacrifices, to publish abroad their glory and proclaim to the world their honor and fame.

The virtue of our great Han, however, is like a mighty fountain of waters, bubbling forth and spreading abroad; to the four borders it extends like a sheltering cloud, an enveloping mist, reaching upwards to the nine levels of the sky, stretching here below to the eight corners of the earth. All living creatures are bathed in its waters. Its harmony flows out in all directions; its might swirls onward to distant lands. Those nearby sport in its springs; those far off swim in its margins. Thus have all evildoers vanished beneath its surface and the dark places have been flooded with light; the very insects and reptiles stir with joy and turn their heads toward the source of this blessing.

[24] *I-chi*, "Documents of Yü."

In response to our ruler's virtue, auspicious creatures such as the fabulous *tsou-yü* [25] come to play in his gardens, and strange beasts like the musk deer appear on his borders. A wonderful variety of grain with six heads growing miraculously out of one stalk is brought to his kitchens and used for offerings, and a beast with a two-pronged horn growing from one base is used for his sacrifices. Marvellous tortoises, still living from the days of the Chou dynasty, have been captured among the rivers of Ch'i, and dragons of blue and gold have been called forth from the lakes. Spirits and gods come to his Garden of Immortals; he receives them as his guests in the Lodge of Leisure. Strange creatures in astonishing profusion, extraordinary occurrences of every description—how manifold are the auspicious signs that come in answer to his virtue! And yet the Son of Heaven protests that he is unworthy and dares not speak of undertaking the Feng and Shan sacrifices. In the days of King Wu of Chou, when a white fish leaped into his boat as he was crossing the Yellow River, he marveled at the wonder and offered it as a burnt offering to Heaven. With only this trifling portent as a sign of his worth, he dared to ascend the great mountain and perform the Feng and Shan sacrifices. Was this not presumptuous of him? How far removed was his presumption from the modesty of our own ruler!

Then the grand marshal came forward and said, "Your Majesty's benevolence has brought succor to all living creatures and your righteousness has punished the evildoers. The clans of China in joy bear tribute to court and the hundred barbarians come with gifts. Your virtue equals that of the rulers of highest antiquity and your achievements are unparalleled. Your goodness and glory have spread far and wide, calling forth a host of auspicious omens; not on one occasion alone have they appeared, but time and again. So it is the opinion of the officials that Your Majesty should order altars erected on Mount T'ai and Liang-fu to await your coming, and there increase the glory of your fame. Then will the Lord on High send down his blessing, and good fortune in abundance to crown your labors!

"So long as Your Majesty modestly declines to take this step, the three deities of Heaven, Earth, and the Mount are robbed of their fulfillment, and the ceremonies proper to a true king are left incomplete, bringing shame to all your ministers.

"Some say that the ways of Heaven are dark and silent, and therefore the auspicious omens, which are the expressions of its will, cannot be ignored. If the rulers of antiquity had similarly declined to heed the mean-

[25] Described by commentators as "a white tiger with black markings" which appears when there is a virtuous ruler in the land.

ing of the omens, then there would be no records of the Feng Sacrifice on the summit of Mount T'ai and none of the Shan Sacrifice at Liang-fu. If each had been content only to enjoy glory in his own time and had thought of nothing but the fulfillment of his days in this world, then what fame would they have enjoyed in generations after, and how could the orators speak of the seventy-two rulers of antiquity? Your Majesty has diligently practiced virtue and been rewarded with these omens from Heaven; if you now respectfully heed them and carry out the measures which they indicate, you will in no sense be overstepping propriety. Thus it was that the sage kings of ancient times did not neglect these steps but carried out their rituals before the Lord of the Earth, manifested their truthfulness to the God of Heaven, and engraved their achievements upon the Central Peak, in order to make known their supreme worth, extend their abundant virtue, spread abroad their fame and honor, and receive generous blessings from above whereby to enrich their people. Ah, how marvelous is this act! The spectacle of the world, the supreme undertaking of a king—it must not be neglected!

"We beg Your Majesty to complete this ritual and make use of the plans drawn up by the officials and court scholars, so that they may be enlightened by the rays of your virtue, which is like the sun and moon, and be warmed by the distant fires of your worth, thereby fulfilling their duties. We beg you at the same time to set forth a true record of the deed, couched in rich and sonorous language, so that it may stand beside the *Spring and Autumn Annals*. Then will a seventh Classic be added to the former six, to be handed down for ages everlasting, that all posterity may be washed by the clear currents of your virtue and lifted upon its spreading waves; that the fame of such virtue may be noised abroad and its precious worth be known to all. The reason the sages of old have for so long maintained their glorious reputations and have constantly been praised as chief among the virtuous was solely that they carried out this ritual. Your Majesty should order the master of ancient affairs to draw up a complete set of rules for the ceremony for you to peruse!"

The Son of Heaven, moved by his words, changed countenance and cried, "You have spoken well. I will try it!" Then he began to consider the matter and to lay his plans, gathering together all the proposals of his high ministers, weighing how best to carry out the Feng and Shan sacrifices, spreading abroad in song his great blessing, and making known to all the wealth of auspicious omens which had appeared. He composed a song of praise which read:

"From the sheltering heavens of my virtue
The clouds come rolling forth,
The sweet dews and seasonable rains fall
To make glad the earth;
What creature lives not succored
By their rich showers and soaking mists?
My harvest is replete
With the auspicious six-headed grain.
I not only send the rain,
But soak the earth with life-giving moisture;
I not only dampen the earth,
But cause the waters to flow abroad!" [26]
All beings in harmony
Turn their thoughts in longing to him;
The great Mount T'ai illumines its heights
And watches expectantly for the coming of its lord.
Oh prince, oh prince!
Why do you tarry?
The dappled *tsou-yü* beast
Sports in our lord's park;
Black markings on its white hide,
Emblems of its auspicious nature;
Gentle and austere,
With the manners of a prince.
It has heard of our lord's virtue
And has come now to observe it;
Over trackless roads it journeyed,
A fair omen sent by Heaven,
As it came before in the time of Emperor Shun,
Heralding his rise to glory.
Likewise the merry unicorn
Was found rambling among the sacred altars
When, in the tenth month, the beginning of winter,
Our lord went to conduct the suburban sacrifice.
It galloped before our lord's carriage
And when he sacrificed to it, the deities of Heaven sent rich blessings.
Even the days before the Three Dynasties

[26] In the first section of this poem the emperor is imagined as speaking in his own words.

Knew no such wonders as these!
The writhing yellow dragon,
Drawn by his virtue, has ascended from the depths,
Shimmering with a dozen hues,
Sparkling like fire,
Showing to all its form and face,
That the people might be awakened to the worth of their lord.
Thus it is written in the ancient records:
"Dragon-drawn is the carriage of the Heaven-ordained ruler"
The will of Heaven is thus made clear;
There is no need for reiterated pronouncements.
By these signs is the commandment conveyed
To carry out the Feng Sacrifice at Mount T'ai!

If we open the Classical texts and study their meaning, we find that, even when the will of Heaven and the deeds of mankind have reached accord and those here below have acted in such a way as to call forth a true response from on high, still the virtue of the sage king is to act with caution and utmost reverence. So the saying has it that "in times of prosperity, one must consider decline; in safety, one must think of danger!" Thus it is said that Kings T'ang and Wu, the founders of the Shang and Chou dynasties, though they held the most honored positions, did not fail to exercise cautious reverence; and Emperor Shun, while carrying out the great rituals, constantly reflected whether he were committing some oversight.

In the fifth year after Ssu-ma Hsiang-ju's death, the Son of Heaven for the first time sacrificed to the Earth Lord, and in the eighth year he proceeded first to the Middle Peak, Mount Sung, to perform rituals there, then to Mount T'ai to carry out the Feng Sacrifice, and finally to Liang-fu to carry out the Shan Sacrifice on the hill called Su-jan. Ssu-ma Hsiang-ju wrote other works besides those which I have quoted here, such as the Letter to Su Chien, the marquis of P'ing-ling, and the Letter to the Five Lords on the relative merits of grasses and trees, but I have not included them here. The only works of his I have quoted are those which are best known among the high officials.

The Grand Historian remarks: The *Spring and Autumn Annals,* by relating matters that are familiar and mundane, manages to convey the most subtle principles. The *Book of Changes,* while dealing with essentially abstruse affairs, is yet perfectly clear in its application. The "Greater Odes" of the *Book of Odes* praise the virtue of kings and powerful men, but nevertheless extend their attention to the virtues of the common people. The "Lesser Odes" criticize the deeds of petty officials, but their criticisms implicate the men in highest office. Thus all these works choose different modes of expression, and yet they are alike in dealing primarily with virtue. Similarly, the works of Ssu-ma Hsiang-ju, although often couched in fantastic and extravagant language, are in the end essentially concerned with moderation and frugality. Can we say, then, that they are any different from the satires and reprimands of the *Book of Odes?* [27] Accordingly, I have selected from among his works those that I consider worthy of discussion and recorded them in this chapter.

[27] The text at this point contains some remarks by Yang Hsiung, a poet who lived some hundred years after Ssu-ma Ch'ien, which have been inserted by later editors. They have been omitted in the translation.

Shih chi 120: The Biographies of Chi An and Cheng Tang-shih

When he donned his formal robes and cap and appeared at court, none of the other officials dared to propound any foolish theories: such was the effect of Chi An's dignity. Fond of recommending others and praised as a worthy man: such was the character of Cheng Tang-shih. Thus I made The Biographies of Chi An and Cheng Tang-shih.

Chi An

Chi An, whose polite name was Chi Ch'ang-ju, was a native of P'u-yang. His ancestors won favor with the rulers of the state of Wei and for seven generations, down to the time of Chi An, served without break as high officials.

During the reign of Emperor Ching, Chi An, on the recommendation of his father, was appointed as a mounted guard to the heir apparent. Because of his stern bearing he was treated with deference. Later, when Emperor Ching passed away and the heir apparent ascended the throne, Chi An was appointed master of guests.

When the tribes of Eastern and Southern Yüeh began to attack each other, the emperor dispatched Chi An to go to the area and observe the situation. He did not journey all the way, however, but went only as far as Wu and then turned around and came back to the capital to make his report. "The Yüeh people have always been in the habit of attacking each other," he said. "There is no reason for the Son of Heaven's envoy to trouble himself about such matters!"

When a great fire broke out in Ho-nei and destroyed over a thousand houses, the emperor once more sent Chi An to observe the situation. On his return he reported, "The roofs of the houses were so close together that the fire spread from one to another; that is why so many homes were burned. It is nothing to worry about. As I passed through Ho-nan on my way, however, I noted that the inhabitants were very poor, and over ten thousand families had suffered so greatly from floods and droughts that fathers and sons were reduced to eating each other. I therefore took it upon myself to use the imperial seals to open the granaries of Ho-nan and relieve the distress of the people. I herewith return the seals and await punishment for overstepping my authority in this fashion."

The emperor, impressed with the wisdom he had shown, overlooked the irregularity of his action and transferred him to the post of governor of Ying-yang. Chi An, however, felt that he was unworthy of a governorship and, pleading illness, retired to his home in the country. When the emperor heard of this, he summoned him to court again and appointed him a palace counselor. But because he sharply criticized the emperor on several occasions, it proved impossible to keep him around the palace for long. The emperor therefore transferred him to the post of governor of Tung-hai.

Chi An studied the doctrines of the Yellow Emperor and Lao Tzu. In executing his duties and governing the people he valued honesty and serenity, selecting worthy assistants and secretaries and leaving them to do as they saw fit. In his administration he demanded only that the general spirit of his directives be carried out and never made a fuss over minor details. He was sick a great deal of the time, confined to his bed and unable to go out, and yet after only a year or so as governor of Tung-hai he had succeeded in setting the affairs of the province in perfect order and winning the acclaim of the people.

The emperor, hearing of his success, summoned him to court and appointed him master of titles chief commandant, promoting him to one of the nine highest offices in the government. In this post, as well, Chi An emphasized a policy of laissez-faire, interpreting his duties very broadly and not bothering with the letter of the law.

Chi An was by nature very haughty and ill-mannered. He could not tolerate the faults of others and would denounce people to their faces. Those who took his fancy he treated very well, but those who didn't he could not even bear to see. For this reason most men gave him a wide berth. On the other hand he was fond of learning and liked to travel about doing daring and generous things for others, and his conduct was always above reproach. He was also fond of outspoken criticism and his words frequently brought scowls to the emperor's face. His constant ambition was to be as direct and outspoken as the Liang general Fu Po and Emperor Ching's minister Yüan Ang. He was on very friendly terms with Kuan Fu, Cheng Tang-shih, and the director of the imperial clan Liu Ch'i. Because of his frank criticisms, however, it was impossible for him to stay in one position for long.

At this time Empress Dowager Wang's younger brother T'ien Fen, the marquis of Wu-an, was serving as chancellor. When officials of the two thousand picul rank would appear before T'ien Fen, they would prostrate themselves in obeisance, but T'ien Fen would never deign to return their greeting. When Chi An went to see T'ien Fen, however, he never prostrated himself, but always just gave a low bow.

The emperor at the time was busy summoning scholars and Confucians to court and telling them, "I want to do thus-and-so, I want to do thus-and-so." Commenting on this, Chi An said to the emperor, "On the surface Your Majesty is practicing benevolence and righteousness, but in your heart you have too many desires. How do you ever expect to imitate the rule of the sage emperors Yao and Shun in this way?"

The emperor sat in silence, his face flushed with anger, and then dismissed the court. The other high officials were all terrified of what would happen to Chi An. After the emperor had left the room, he turned to his attendants and said, "Incredible—the stupidity of that Chi An!"

Later, some of the officials reproached Chi An for his behavior, but he replied, "Since the Son of Heaven has gone to the trouble of appointing us as his officials and aides, what business have we in simply flattering his whims and agreeing with whatever he says, deliberately leading him on to unrighteous deeds? Now that we occupy these posts, no matter how much we may value our own safety, we cannot allow the court to suffer disgrace, can we?"

Chi An was frequently ill, and if it appeared that he would be laid up for as long as three months, the emperor would always grant him a vacation from his duties. This happened several times, but Chi An could never seem to get completely well. When his illness persisted, Chuang Chu, one of the other officials, appeared in his place before the emperor and requested a leave of absence for him.

"What sort of man is Chi An anyway?" the emperor asked, to which Chuang Chu replied, "As long as he is employed in some ordinary post as an official, he will do no better than the average person. But if he were called upon to assist a young ruler or to guard a city against attack, then no temptation could sway him from his duty, no amount of entreaty could make him abandon his post. Even the bravest men of antiquity, Meng Pen and Hsia Yü, could not shake his determination!"

"Yes," said the emperor. "In ancient times there were ministers who were deemed worthy to be called the guardians of the altars of the nation. And men like Chi An come near to deserving the same appellation."

When the general in chief Wei Ch'ing was at court, the emperor would sometimes receive him while lounging informally on the couch, and when the chancellor Kung-sun Hung came to see the emperor on some private affair, the emperor would often not bother to don his hat for the interview. But if Chi An came for an audience, the emperor would never receive him without his hat on.

The emperor was once seated in his curtained armor hall when Chi An appeared to present a memorial on some affair. The emperor caught sight of him from a distance and, because he did not have his hat on at the time, quickly withdrew behind the curtains and sent someone else to accept and approve the memorial. Such was the respect and courtesy that he showed Chi An.

At this time Chang T'ang had just been promoted to the post of commandant of justice because of his services in revising and systematizing the penal code. Chi An several times launched sharp attacks on Chang T'ang in the presence of the emperor. "Here you are, one of the highest officials in the government, and yet you have not succeeded in doing anything to carry on and broaden the accomplishments of the former emperors or to repress the evil desires of the people of the empire. You have not enriched the nation and its inhabitants, nor cleared the jails of malefactors. None of these things have you done, but instead you excel in evil and cruelty and win merit by wantonly destroying the old ways. What right have you to tamper with the old code of laws given to the nation by Emperor Kao-tsu? For such actions you and your family deserve to be wiped out!"

Chi An frequently engaged in arguments with Chang T'ang. Chang T'ang would always base his case on the letter of the law, paying strict attention to the most petty details, while Chi An would fight sternly and stubbornly for general principles, refusing to compromise an inch, and in the end would become so enraged that he would begin cursing Chang T'ang. "People say that petty clerks with their brushes and scrapers have no business becoming high government officials. How right they are! It is men like this Chang T'ang who have gotten the empire into such a state that men are afraid to look each other in the eye or to put one foot down beside the other for fear of breaking the law!"

At this time the dynasty was busy attacking the Hsiung-nu and trying to force the other barbarian tribes surrounding China to acknowledge allegiance to the Han. Chi An did his best to get the government to reduce its activities in this direction, catching the emperor whenever he could in moments of leisure and urging him to make peace with the Hsiung-nu and stop sending out the troops. But the emperor at this time favored Confucian principles and esteemed the advice of Kung-sun Hung. As the number of government undertakings increased, the petty officials and the people grew skillful at evading the law and twisting it around to satisfy their own ends. The emperor himself took a great interest in legal matters, and Chang T'ang and other officials won his favor by frequently submitting memorials to the throne on law cases. Chi An for his part constantly disparaged Confucian teachings and denounced Kung-sun Hung and the others to their faces. "With hearts full of deceit and a façade of learning, all you do is flatter the whims of the ruler! A bunch of brush-and-scraper clerks, intent only on making the laws more severe and thinking up clever ways to ruin people—trapping them into committing some offense, making it impossible for them to tell the truth, and then gloating over your victory!"

The emperor, however, continued to heap greater and greater honor on Kung-sun Hung and Chang T'ang. These two, for their part, had a

profound hatred for Chi An, and even the emperor himself was displeased with Chi An and would have liked to find some excuse to
execute him.

Kung-sun Hung, who was chancellor at this time, one day said to
the emperor, "The area under the jurisdiction of the right prefect
of the capital includes the homes of many prominent men and members of the imperial family and is therefore difficult to govern. Only
an official of longstanding importance is capable of handling the
task. May I suggest that Chi An be transferred to the post of right
prefect?"

Chi An was accordingly appointed to the position and filled it for
several years without a break. By this time the general in chief Wei
Ch'ing enjoyed great honor and his sister had been designated empress, and yet Chi An treated Wei Ch'ing in a very casual manner as
though he were an equal. Someone cautioned him about this, saying,
"It is obviously the emperor's wish that the other officials should all
humble themselves before General Wei Ch'ing. Therefore he keeps
heaping greater honors on him. It is hardly right for you alone to refuse to prostrate yourself before him."

To this Chi An replied, "But the very fact that the general has a
visitor whom he permits to greet him with only a bow—does this not in
itself increase his prestige?"

When Wei Ch'ing heard about this, he was more than ever convinced of Chi An's worth. On various occasions he consulted Chi An
on questions concerning the nation and the court and treated him with
even greater favor than before.

The king of Huai-nan was plotting revolt but was afraid of Chi An.
"A man who is fond of outspoken criticism and willing to die for his
principles is very hard to tempt into doing evil," he commented. "As
for persuading men like Kung-sun Hung to come over to my side,
that is as easy as lifting the lid off a jar or shaking down dry leaves from
a tree!"

By this time the emperor had sent several expeditions against the
Hsiung-nu and won considerable success, so that he paid less attention
than ever to Chi An's recommendations. Formerly, when Chi An held
one of the nine highest posts in the government, Kung-sun Hung and

Chang T'ang were only petty clerks. Later, Kung-sun Hung and Chang T'ang rose step by step until they were equal in rank with Chi An, but Chi An continued to criticize them as before. Finally Kung-sun Hung became chancellor and was enfeoffed as a marquis, and Chang T'ang reached the post of imperial secretary. By this time all of Chi An's former assistants and secretaries had advanced as high as Chi An himself, and some even outranked him. Chi An, rather petty-minded as he was, could not keep from feeling a certain resentment at this, and when he appeared before the emperor one day, he remarked, "Your Majesty appoints officials just the way one stacks firewood—whatever comes to hand last is piled on the top!"

The emperor was silent, and after a little while Chi An retired. When he had gone, the emperor said, "After all, it doesn't do for a man to be without learning! Listening to Chi An's words, I find that they are getting more outrageous every day!"

Shortly afterwards the Hun-yeh king, one of the Hsiung-nu chiefs, led his troops to the border and surrendered to the Han. The Han decided to send twenty thousand carriages to the border to transport them to the capital, but since the government officials had no cash on hand, they were obliged to requisition horses from the common people on promise of future payment. As a result, many people hid their horses and it was impossible to get hold of the necessary number. The emperor was enraged and wanted to execute the governor of Ch'ang-an, but Chi An, who was right prefect of the capital at this time, said, "The governor of Ch'ang-an has done nothing wrong. Since he is under my jurisdiction, it will be enough if I alone am executed. Then I think the people will be willing to bring out their horses. Moreover, we must not forget that these Hsiung-nu have turned against their own ruler in order to surrender to the Han. It should be sufficient if the Han arranges for them to be transported from province to province by easy stages. What need is there to turn the whole empire upside down and exhaust the resources of China merely to accommodate a bunch of barbarians?"

The emperor received his words in silence.

After the Hun-yeh king had arrived in Ch'ang-an some five hundred or more merchants and market traders were condemned to death for having sold contraband goods to the Hsiung-nu. Chi An thereupon asked to speak to the emperor in a moment of leisure and was granted an audience with him in the High Gate Hall of the Eternal Palace. "The Hsiung-nu have attacked the main roads along the border and broken off peaceful relations with us," said Chi An. "Therefore China has called up troops to punish them, suffering innumerable dead and wounded in the process and spending cash by the billions. In my unworthy opinion any Hsiung-nu that Your Majesty captures should be treated as slaves and presented to the families of the men who died in the fighting, along with whatever spoils were taken, in order to repay the empire for the hardships it has borne and gratify the hearts of the common people. Even if that is impossible at the moment, what is the reason, when the Hun-yeh king comes with his thirty or forty thousand followers and surrenders to the Han, for emptying the treasuries and showering gifts on him, and ordering out faithful Chinese subjects to wait on him as though he were a favorite child? Moreover, how are the common people in their ignorance to know that goods which are sold in the markets of Ch'ang-an will be regarded as contraband by the law officials when they are transported to the border and traded to the barbarians? Now, although Your Majesty may not be in a position to distribute the wealth of the Hsiung-nu to the empire in payment for its troubles, do you intend to execute five hundred or more ignorant men simply because of some petty law? This is what is known as protecting the leaves but injuring the branches. If I may say so, I trust Your Majesty will not adopt such a course as this!"

The emperor listened to his words in silence and expressed no approval. Later he said, "It has been a long time since I have heard anything from Chi An, and now he comes to me again with these absurd suggestions!"

Several months later Chi An was tried for some minor infraction of the law; his offense was pardoned, but he was obliged to resign his post. He retired to his home in the country.

After a few years the government put into circulation the new five-*shu* cash currency. Many of the people began minting the coins illegally, the region of Ch'u being particularly notorious for counterfeiting. The emperor, considering that the province of Huai-yang was a key point in Ch'u, summoned Chi An to come to court and receive appointment as governor of Huai-yang. Chi An declined the appointment with great humility and refused to accept the seals of office, but the emperor continued to send edicts urging him to accept until finally he agreed to obey. He was then summoned for an audience, and when he appeared before the emperor, he wept and said, "I expected to die and be tossed into a ditch without ever seeing Your Majesty again. But now, contrary to all my expectations, you have deigned to call me into service once more. However, I am constantly troubled by this miserable illness of mine and have not the strength to undertake the administration of a province. I beg instead to be appointed as a palace attendant so that I may come and go at Your Majesty's side and work to repair defects in government policy. This is my desire!"

"Do you think the governorship of Huai-yang is too insignificant a post?" said the emperor. "Never mind, I will call you back to court in a little while. It is just that the officials and the people of Huai-yang are not getting along well with each other and I thought that, with your weight and prestige, you would be able to straighten things out without having to make any particular effort."

When Chi An had accepted the appointment and was about to leave the capital, he went to visit the grand messenger Li Hsi and remarked, "I am now being cast off and sent to live in the provinces so that I will not be able to take part in the deliberations at court. I should warn you, however, that the imperial secretary Chang T'ang has wisdom enough to block any worthwhile criticism and deceit enough to put a plausible façade on his misdeeds. His only concern is to talk cleverly and ingratiatingly and to argue effectively. He will never consent to speak for the good of the empire, but cares only to flatter the will of the ruler. Whatever the emperor does not desire, he condemns; whatever the emperor wishes to do, he praises. He delights in proposing new undertakings and manipulating the laws to satisfy his ends. With deceit in his heart he bends the emperor to his will, and with his harsh officials supporting him in the provinces he increases his power and authority. Now you occupy one of the nine highest offices. If you do not quickly speak out against him, you yourself will end up by sharing the punishment that is bound to come to him!"

But Li Hsi was too afraid of Chang T'ang and never had the courage to speak out against him. Chi An took up his duties as governor and carried them out as he had in the past in Tung-hai, administering the province of Huai-yang and setting its government to rights again. Later, as Chi An had predicted, Chang T'ang fell from power. When the emperor learned that Chi An had urged Li Hsi to oppose Chang T'ang, he condemned Li Hsi to punishment for having failed to follow the advice. He promoted Chi An to a rank equivalent to that of prime minister to one of the feudal lords and kept him on in Huai-yang. Seven years later, Chi An died.

After his death, and in recognition of his services, the emperor made his younger brother Chi Jen an official and gradually promoted him until he held one of the nine highest offices. Chi An's son Chi Yen also advanced as high as prime minister to one of the feudal lords.

Ssu-ma An, the son of Chi An's father's elder sister, had served in his youth as a mounted guard to the heir apparent along with Chi An. Ssu-ma An was a man of cultured bearing but of cruel disposition and was very clever at getting along in the official world. Four times he advanced to the rank of the nine highest ministers, and he died while holding the office of governor of Ho-nan. Because of Ssu-ma An's influence, ten of his brothers at one time held posts paying two thousand piculs.

Tuan Hung who, like Chi An, also came from P'u-yang, served originally under Wang Hsin, the marquis of Kai and older brother of Empress Dowager Wang. Wang Hsin recommended him to the emperor, and as a result Tuan Hung was twice ranked among the nine highest ministers. All of these other men from the region of Wei who served in the government, however, were terrified of Chi An and never managed to rival his fame.

Cheng Tang-shih

Cheng Tang-shih, whose polite name was Cheng Chuang, was a native of Ch'en. His grandfather Cheng Chün once served as a general under

Hsiang Yü, but after Hsiang Yü was killed he went over to the side of the Han. Emperor Kao-tsu ordered all of Hsiang Yü's former officials to adopt Hsiang Yü's familiar name,[1] Chi, but Cheng Chün alone refused to obey the order. Later, Kao-tsu summoned all men with the familiar name Chi and appointed them as court officials, but Cheng Chün was sent into exile, where he died.

During the reign of Emperor Wen, Cheng Tang-shih amused himself by wandering about and performing daring exploits. After he succeeded in rescuing the Liang general Chang Yü from difficulty, he achieved considerable fame in the area of Liang and Ch'u.

In the time of Emperor Ching, Cheng Tang-shih was made a retainer in the household of the heir apparent. Every five days, when his bath and hair washing day came around,[2] he would order post horses to be held in readiness for him in the suburbs of Ch'ang-an so that he could ride about and visit his friends, or else he would invite guests to his home and entertain them right through the night until dawn, his constant fear being that he would not get around to chatting with them all. He was fond of the teachings of the Yellow Emperor and Lao Tzu, and sought the company of worthy men as though he feared he would never meet enough of them. Although he was still young and held a rather insignificant post, the people he associated with were all of his grandfather's generation and included some of the most famous men of the empire.

After Emperor Wu came to the throne Cheng Tang-shih gradually advanced, holding such posts as palace military commander of Lu, governor of Chi-nan, and prime minister of Chiang-tu, until he ranked with the nine highest officials, being appointed as right prefect of the capital. At the time of the quarrel between T'ien Fen and Tou Ying, he was demoted to the post of steward of the household of the empress and heir apparent, but was later promoted to that of minister of agriculture.

While Cheng Tang-shih was acting as a high official, he instructed his gatekeeper that, whenever visitors came to the house, regardless

---

[1] Presumably so that he could identify them later on.
[2] The periodic holiday of court officials when they were allowed to leave the palace dormitory and return to their homes to "bathe and wash their hair."

of whether they were of high or low rank, he was not to keep them waiting at the gate but to show them in with all due courtesy. This was the way that Cheng Tang-shih, in spite of his high position, humbled himself before others. In addition, he was a man of strict integrity and did nothing to increase the wealth of his family, depending upon his salary and gifts from the emperor to supply the funds needed to entertain his guests. When he sent a present of food to someone, it was never more than a simple dish in a bamboo container.

Every time he appeared at court he would wait until he could catch the emperor in a moment of leisure and then speak to him, always recommending some person of worth in the empire. The ways he used to boost his subordinate officials and assistants into higher positions were truly admirable. When he was recommending someone, he would always take care to show that the person was more worthy than himself. He never addressed his officials by their familiar names, and when he had to speak to one of his subordinates, he took great care not to hurt the man's feelings. If he heard of some worthwhile suggestion that someone else had made, his only thought was to report it to the emperor as quickly as possible. For this reason, gentlemen and men of prominence from east of the mountains all flocked about him and praised him highly.

Once, when the emperor appointed him as envoy to go and observe the break in the dikes of the Yellow River, Cheng Tang-shih requested that he be given five days to prepare for the journey. The emperor replied, "I had always heard that you did not bother to take along provisions even for a journey of a thousand *li*. What do you mean by asking for five days to make preparations?"

Ordinarily, however, when Cheng Tang-shih appeared in court he was always careful to take cognizance of the emperor's wishes and go along with them, and never ventured to argue very forcibly for or against any particular measure.

When he was already well along in years, the Han began to launch attacks on the Hsiung-nu and work to force the submission of the various barbarian tribes, putting the empire to great expense and exhausting the fiscal resources of the government. On Cheng Tang-shih's recommendation one of his friends was appointed as a transportation official in the ministry of agriculture, but the man appropriated large sums of money without making any reparation to the government. When Ssu-ma An became governor of Huai-nan, he brought the affair to light, and Cheng Tang-shih was implicated in the offense. On payment of a fine he was pardoned and reduced to the status of commoner. A short while later he was appointed to act as chief secretary to the chancellor, but the emperor decided that he was too old for this job and appointed him instead as governor of Ju-nan. After a few years he died in office.

Cheng Tang-shih and Chi An at one time ranked among the nine highest officials of the state. They were men of great integrity who always acted with scrupulous honesty. Both men, however, lost their positions in middle age and, their families being poor, their former guests and friends little by little deserted them. Later they went to live in the provinces and died there, leaving no wealth or estate for their sons to inherit. As a result of Cheng Tang-shih's merit, six or seven of his brothers and descendants rose to the position of two thousand picul officials.

The Grand Historian remarks: As long as Chi An and Cheng Tang-shih wielded power, they had friends by the score, but when their power vanished, their friends vanished with it. If even worthy men such as they suffered this fate, how must it be with ordinary people!

Lord Ti of Hsia-kuei tells this story. Formerly, he says, when he was commandant of justice, he had so many guests that they completely filled his gate. Later, however, when he lost his position, he might have spread a sparrow net in front of his gate without fear of anyone stumbling into it. Sometime afterwards, Lord Ti was once more appointed as commandant of justice and all his old visitors wanted to come to see him again, but Lord Ti wrote in large letters over the top of his gate the following inscription:

> When one is dead and the other still living, then you know what kind of friends they were.
> When one is rich and the other poor, then you can see how fast their friendship is.

When one is high and the other low, then it becomes clear what they think of each other!

Alas! Chi An and Cheng Tang-shih might well have said the same thing!

Part III

THE PLOTTERS OF REVOLT

Shih chi 118: The Biographies of the Kings of Huai-nan and Heng-shan

Because Ch'ing Pu rebelled against the throne, Emperor Kao-tsu's son Liu Ch'ang was made ruler of his territory, bringing peace to the region south of the Huai and Yangtze rivers. But his son Liu An robbed the common people of Ch'u. Thus I made The Biographies of the Kings of Huai-nan and Heng-shan.

The King of Huai-nan

Liu Ch'ang, posthumously known as King Li of Huai-nan, was one of the youngest of Emperor Kao-tsu's sons. His mother was originally a concubine of Chang Ao, the king of Chao. In the eighth year of Kao-tsu's reign, when Kao-tsu visited the state of Chao on his way back from Tung-yüan, the king of Chao gave this concubine to him. She won the favor of the emperor and soon became pregnant. After the emperor had gone on his way, the king did not dare to take her back into his own palace, but had a separate palace built to accommodate her.

Shortly afterwards it was discovered that Kuan Kao and the other ministers of Chao were plotting revolt and had intended to assassinate the emperor at Po-jen. They were arrested, along with the king of Chao, and brought to the capital for trial; at the same time the king's mother, his brothers, and his concubines were all seized and taken in chains to Ho-nei. Liu Ch'ang's mother was among those seized. She told the officials, "I have won favor with the emperor and I am pregnant!" but although they reported this to the emperor, he was at the time enraged with the king of Chao and did nothing to rescue her from prison.

Her younger brother Chao Chien managed to get Shen I-chi, the marquis of Pi-yang, to speak to Empress Lü on her behalf, but Empress Lü was jealous and refused to mention the matter to the emperor, while Shen I-chi for his part did nothing to press it.

In due time the lady gave birth to her child, the future King Li, but immediately afterwards committed suicide in rage over the treatment she had received. The officials then took the boy and brought him to the emperor, who regretted his behavior and ordered Empress Lü to raise him as though he were her own child. He also gave instructions for the boy's mother to be buried at her old home in Chen-ting, where her ancestors had lived for generations.

In the tenth month of the eleventh year of Kao-tsu's reign [196 B.C.], after Ch'ing Pu, the king of Huai-nan, had revolted, the emperor appointed his son Liu Ch'ang as king of Huai-nan to rule the territory that had formerly belonged to Ch'ing-pu, four provinces in all. The emperor in person led the troops in attacking and defeating Ch'ing Pu. Thus King Li became ruler of Huai-nan.

Because he had lost his mother at a very early age and had thereafter been constantly cared for by Empress Lü, he enjoyed great favor during the reigns of Emperor Hui and Empress Lü and was able to escape any harm. In his heart he nursed an undying hatred for Shen I-chi, though he did not dare to reveal his feelings.

When Emperor Wen came to the throne Liu Ch'ang, being the only surviving brother of Emperor Wen, considered himself very close to the emperor and began to behave in an arrogant and willful manner, several times failing to obey the law. Because they were brothers, however, the emperor always pardoned him.

In the third year of Emperor Wen's reign [177 B.C.], when Liu Ch'ang journeyed to court to pay his respects, he behaved most presumptuously, joining the emperor on hunts and trips to the pleasure parks, riding in the same carriage with him, and constantly addressing him as "Elder Brother."

Liu Ch'ang was a very powerful man, so strong that he could lift a cauldron. He went to call on Shen I-chi, the marquis of Pi-yang, and requested an interview, and when Shen I-chi appeared, he smashed him over the head with an iron mallet which he had concealed in his sleeve. Then he ordered his attendant Wei Ching to cut off Shen I-chi's head. This done, he mounted his carriage and hurried to the palace gate, where he bared his arms and apologized for his action. "My mother should never have been held guilty along with the others in the Chao affair," he said. "At that time the marquis of Pi-yang exercised great influence with Empress Lü and could have saved her, but he failed to press the matter. This was his first crime. Neither Liu Ju-i, the young king of Chao, nor his mother Lady Ch'i, were guilty of any offense, and yet the marquis of Pi-yang stood by and let Empress Lü murder them without saying a word. This was his second crime. Empress Lü made kings of the members of her own clan, endangering the safety of the Liu family, and yet again the marquis of Pi-yang did not protest. This was his third crime. For the sake of the empire I have respectfully taken upon myself the task of punishing this evil minister and avenging the wrong which my mother suffered. Now with all due respect I bow before the palace gate and beg to receive punishment."

Emperor Wen, moved by the resolution Liu Ch'ang had shown in avenging his mother's death, did not punish him but pardoned his offense. At this time Empress Dowager Po, the heir apparent, and the various high officials were all terrified of Liu Ch'ang. Liu Ch'ang returned to his kingdom and behaved more willfully than ever. He paid no attention to the Han laws but had attendants to cry "Clear the way! Attention!" whenever he went in or out of his palace, called his orders "edicts," and issued whatever decrees he pleased, all in imitation of the Son of Heaven.

In the sixth year of Emperor Wen's reign [174 B.C.], Liu Ch'ang ordered Tan and others, seventy men in all, to join with Ch'ai Ch'i, the heir of Ch'ai Wu, the marquis of Chi-p'u, in plotting a revolt. They set off in forty large carriages and gathered in a place called Valley Mouth to plan their rebellion. Liu Ch'ang also dispatched envoys to negotiate with the Min-yüeh barbarians of the south and the Hsiung-nu. When these actions came to light and steps were taken to punish the offenders, the emperor sent an envoy to summon Liu Ch'ang to the capital.

When Liu Ch'ang arrived in Ch'ang-an, the high ministers presented the following memorial to the throne:

Your servants, the chancellor Chang Ts'ang, the director of guests Feng Ching, the imperial secretary and director of the imperial clan I, the commandant of justice Ho, and Fu, the palace military commander in charge of suppressing rebels, dare to risk death in speaking these words. Liu

Ch'ang, the king of Huai-nan, has cast aside the laws of the former emperors and refused to obey the edicts of the Son of Heaven. He shows no restraint in his manner of living, riding about in a carriage with a yellow canopy and in his comings and goings imitating the prerogatives of the Son of Heaven. He arbitrarily issues his own commands and pays no attention to the laws of the Han. In appointing his officials he has taken it upon himself to elevate his palace counselor Ch'un to the post of chancellor. At his court he has gathered together men from the other fiefs of the Han and fugitives from justice whom he hides from the law, building houses for them and showering them with gifts of wealth, titles, salaries, and lands, even enfeoffing some of them with the title of marquis within the Pass and paying them stipends of two thousand piculs. Though he knows that such actions are not proper for a feudal lord, he persists in them, and would like to do even worse!

In addition, the counselor Tan, the gentleman of the ranks K'ai-chang, and others, seventy men in all, plotted a revolt with Ch'ai Ch'i, the heir of the marquis of Chi-p'u, intending to endanger the ancestral temples and sacred altars of the dynasty. Ch'ai Ch'i sent K'ai-chang in secret to report his plans to the king of Huai-nan, inviting him to join the revolt and to send envoys to the Min-yüeh tribes and the Hsiung-nu to persuade them to send out their troops. When K'ai-chang journeyed to Huai-nan for this purpose and appeared before the king, the king sat feasting and talking with him on numerous occasions and even gave him a house, a bride, and a salary of two thousand piculs. K'ai-chang then sent a man to report to Tan that he had discussed their plans for revolt with the king, and the chancellor Ch'un likewise sent a man to confirm this report to Tan and the other conspirators.

When the officials learned of the affair, they dispatched Ch'i and several other law officers from Ch'ang-an to go to Huai-nan and arrest K'ai-chang. The king, however, refused to hand K'ai-chang over to the authorities, but kept him in hiding and eventually conspired with his former military commander Chien Chi to murder him in order to prevent him from talking. The king put off the officials as long as he could, declaring that he did not know where K'ai-chang was, and then finally buried a coffin and some grave clothes at the city of Fei-ling and attempted to deceive them by constructing a grave mound and setting up a notice saying, "K'ai-chang is buried here."

In addition, Liu Ch'ang himself killed an innocent man in cold blood and got his officials to condemn six other innocent men to death; he sheltered a criminal who had been condemned to die in the market place and arrested an innocent man instead, handing him over to the authorities as the fugitive and letting the real fugitive go without punishment. In the case of fourteen persons he passed arbitrary and unreasonable sentences, carried out punishments without reporting them to the central government, and had them bound and cross-examined and condemned to serve in the men's or women's labor gangs or to worse punishments. He also pardoned criminals without proper authority, including eighteen persons who had been sentenced to death and fifty-eight persons who had been sentenced to the labor gangs or lesser punishments. Finally he handed out titles, honoring ninety-four men with various ranks ranging from marquis within the Pass on down.

Some time earlier, when Liu Ch'ang was ill, Your Majesty, troubled about the state of his health, sent an envoy to him with a letter and gifts of jujubes and dried meat. But Liu Ch'ang was unwilling to accept the presents and refused to receive the envoy and bow before him.

Again, when the tribes living on the border of Lu-chiang Province in Nan-hai revolted and the soldiers of Huai-nan were called out to attack them, Your Majesty, considering that the people of Huai-nan had been put to great hardship and expense by the campaign, dispatched an envoy to present Liu Ch'ang with five thousand rolls of silk which he in turn was to present to the soldiers in recompense for their labors. But Liu Ch'ang again did not wish to accept the gift and put off the envoy, saying, "No one here has suffered any hardship!"

When Chih, the ruler of the people of Nan-hai, sent a letter to the throne accompanied by an offering of jade, Liu Ch'ang's former official Chien Chi arbitrarily intercepted it, burned the letter, and failed to forward any report. The officials asked that Chien Chi be handed over to them for investigation, but Liu Ch'ang refused to send him to them, attempting to deceive them by saying that Chien Chi was ill.

Finally, when Ch'un, the chancellor of Huai-nan, asked the king for permission to journey to the capital for an audience with Your Majesty, Liu Ch'ang flew into a rage and replied, "Do you want to leave me and go over to the side of the Han?"

It is clear from these charges that Liu Ch'ang deserves to be executed and his corpse exposed in the market place. We beg that sentence be passed upon him in accordance with the law.

The emperor replied to their memorial with an edict which read:

I cannot bear to inflict upon the king of Huai-nan the penalty prescribed by law. You must debate the matter further with the feudal lords and the two thousand picul officials.

The ministers responded as follows:

Your servants Ts'ang, Ching, I, Fu, and Ho dare to risk death in speaking these words. We have respectfully discussed the matter with Hsia-hou Ying and the other feudal lords and two thousand picul officials, consulting forty-three persons in all. Their unanimous opinion is that Liu Ch'ang has failed to uphold the laws and obey the edicts of the Son of Heaven. He has secretly gathered together a band of conspirators and revolutionaries, treating fugitives from justice with great generosity in hopes that he may fulfill his ambitions. We and the others therefore recommend that sentence be passed in accordance with the law.

The emperor's edict in reply read:

I cannot bear to inflict the legal penalty upon the king. Let him be pardoned from the death sentence but deprived of his title of king.

The ministers responded once more:

Your servants Ts'ang and the rest risk death in speaking these words. Liu Ch'ang has committed crimes which are eminently deserving of death. Your Majesty, however, cannot bear to enforce the law but would graciously pardon him and deprive him of the position of king. We therefore request that he be exiled to Ch'iung-tu in Yen-tao in the province of Shu. The mothers of his children shall be allowed to accompany him. The district officials shall provide him with the necessary housing and see to his food supplies, providing him with firewood, vegetables, salt, bean preserves, cooking and eating utensils, and mats. We dare risk death to ask that the details of the matter be published throughout the empire.

The emperor replied with an edict which read:

Concerning the food rations of Liu Ch'ang, let him be provided with five catties of meat a day and two measures of wine. Ten of his former palace ladies who have won favor with him shall be allowed to accompany him. The other conditions of his exile shall be as originally proposed. All those who took part with him in the conspiracy shall be executed.

Thus the king of Huai-nan was sent into exile. He was placed in a covered baggage cart and orders were given to the districts along the way to pass him on from one to the other.

At this time Yüan Ang reprimanded Emperor Wen, saying, "The king of Huai-nan has always been willful by nature and yet Your

Majesty failed to appoint strict tutors and chancellors for him. That is the reason things have come to this pass. Moreover, the king is a man of stubborn spirit. Now you have suddenly struck him down, and I fear that, exposed to the dew and damp of the road, he may eventually become ill and die. What would happen if Your Majesty should incur the name of a fratricide?"

But the emperor replied, "I only want to teach him a lesson. Later on I will call him back again."

As the king was passed along from district to district, the attendants were all too terrified of him to break the seals on his prison cart and open it up. "Is it because you fools take me for a man of daring that you are so afraid?" the king said to the attendants. "What have I to do with deeds of bravery? I have come to this because I was too willful to learn my own faults. Who can bear, in the little space of time which is man's life, to suffer such sorrow as this?"

He refused thenceforth to eat any food and died. When his cart reached Yung, the magistrate of Yung broke open the seals and reported his death to the emperor.

The emperor wept with profound grief and said to Yüan Ang, "I would not listen to your advice and now I have lost my brother!"

"There is nothing that can be done about it," replied Yüan Ang. "I beg Your Majesty to take heart and not to be too hard on yourself."

"But what should I do now?" asked the emperor.

"The only thing to do is to execute the chancellor and the imperial secretary in order to make amends to the empire for what they did to the king!"

The emperor did not follow this advice, but instead ordered the chancellor and the imperial secretary to arrest and examine the attendants in the various districts along the king's route who had failed to open up his cart and urge him to eat. All were condemned to be executed and their corpses exposed in the market place. The emperor then had the king buried at Yung with the funeral rites of a feudal lord and established thirty households to act as guardians of his grave mound.

In the eighth year of his reign [172 B.C.] Emperor Wen, out of pity for the king of Huai-nan, enfeoffed his four sons, all of whom were around seven or eight years old at the time. Liu An was enfeoffed as marquis of Fu-ling, Liu Po as marquis of An-yang, Liu Tz'u as marquis of Chou-yang, and Liu Liang as marquis of Tung-ch'eng.

The common people made up a song about the emperor and the king of Huai-nan which went:

> Though it's only a foot of cloth,
>   We can sew it into something;
> Though it's only a peck of grain,
>   We'll grind it together.
> But what of those two brothers,
>   Older and younger,
> Who could not spare
>   A little land for each other? [1]

When Emperor Wen heard of this, he sighed and said, "The ancient rulers Yao and Shun exiled their own kin, and the duke of Chou killed his brothers Kuan and Ts'ai, and yet the whole world calls them sages. This is because, in whatever they did, they did not allow their personal feelings to interfere with the public good. Do the people of the empire now suppose that I acted as I did because I was greedy for my brother's territory?"

Accordingly, in the twelfth year of his reign [168 B.C.], Emperor Wen removed Liu Hsi from his position as king of Ch'eng-yang and made him ruler of the territory that had formerly belonged to the king of Huai-nan. He also awarded the king of Huai-nan the posthumous title of Li, the "Cruel King," and set up a funerary park for him like those of the other deceased feudal lords.

In the sixteenth year [164 B.C.] Emperor Wen, still grieved over the fact that King Li of Huai-nan, by his lawless and wanton behavior, had lost his kingdom and died an early death, moved Liu Hsi back to his former position as king of Ch'eng-yang and, dividing the old territory of Huai-nan into three parts, set up Liu Ch'ang's three sons as rulers there. Liu An, the marquis of Fu-ling, was named king of Huai-nan; Liu Po, the marquis of An-yang, was made king of Heng-

---

[1] Though the wording is deliberately ambiguous, the meaning is that the older brother, Emperor Wen, could not spare a little land for his younger brother to live on in peace, but sent him into exile.

shan; and Liu Tz'u, the marquis of Chou-yang, was made king of Lu-chiang. (Liu Ch'ang's youngest son, Liu Liang, the marquis of Tung-ch'eng, had died earlier and left no heir.)

In the third year of Emperor Ching's reign [154 B.C.] when Wu, Ch'u, and the other members of the conspiracy began the so-called revolt of the Seven Kingdoms, an envoy from Wu came to visit Liu An, the king of Huai-nan. The king decided to call out his troops and join the rebellion, whereupon his prime minister said, "If Your Highness is determined to call out the troops and aid Wu, I beg to be appointed to command them." The king thereupon turned the soldiers over to the prime minister. After the prime minister had gotten command of the troops, however, he guarded the city from the rebels and refused to listen to anything the king said, remaining loyal to the Han government. Meanwhile, the Han dispatched Ch'ung Chieh, the marquis of Ch'ü-ch'eng, with a force of troops to rescue Huai-nan from the rebels. Thus the kingdom of Huai-nan suffered no ill consequences from the revolt.

Envoys from Wu also visited the king of Lu-chiang, but he refused to take part in the conspiracy and instead sent his own envoys back and forth to communicate with the kingdom of Yüeh. The king of Heng-shan likewise remained unshakably loyal to the dynasty and spurned the overtures of the Wu envoys.

In the fourth year of Emperor Ching's reign [153 B.C.], after the rebel states of Wu and Ch'u had been conquered, Liu Po, the king of Heng-shan, journeyed to the capital to pay his respects to the emperor. The emperor wished to do something to repay him for the loyalty he had shown at the time of the revolt. "The region in the south where you rule at present is too damp and unhealthy!" he declared, and transferred Liu Po to the position of king of Chi-pei as a reward. Later, when Liu Po died, the emperor awarded him the posthumous title of Chen, the "Loyal King."

The region of the king of Lu-chiang adjoined the barbarian kingdom of Yüeh, and the king frequently exchanged envoys with Yüeh. The emperor, fearing that such a situation might lead to trouble, transferred him to the position of king of Heng-shan, ruling the territory north of the Yangtze River. The king of Huai-nan remained as before.

Liu An, the king of Huai-nan, was by nature fond of reading books and playing the lute; he took no interest in shooting, hunting, or dashing about with dogs and horses.[2] He hoped to win the support of his people by doing secret favors for them and to achieve a reputation throughout the empire. He would often recall with bitterness the death of his father, King Li, and at times even contemplated revolt, but as yet he had had no opportunity to fulfill his desires.

In the second year of *chien-yüan* [139 B.C.], shortly after Emperor Wu came to the throne, Liu An journeyed to the capital to pay his respects. The king had long been friendly with T'ien Fen, the marquis of Wu-an, who at this time was acting as grand commandant. T'ien Fen came out as far as Pa-shang to meet the king and, in the course of his conversation, remarked, "As you know, the present emperor has no son whom he could designate as heir apparent. Your Highness is a grandson of Emperor Kao-tsu and there is no one who has not heard of your reputation for benevolence and righteous conduct. If some day the empire should be faced with the sorrow of an imperial demise, who but Your Highness would be fit to succeed to the throne?"

The king of Huai-nan was delighted at these words and showered T'ien Fen with lavish gifts of money and goods. He also began to gather a band of followers in secret and to work to win the support of the people in preparation for a revolt.

In the sixth year of *chien-yüan* [135 B.C.] a comet appeared in the sky. The king of Huai-nan was secretly wondering what it portended when someone said to him, "Some years ago, when the armies of Wu rose in revolt, a comet appeared. Its tail was no more than a few feet long, and yet the battles which raged at that time drenched the earth with blood for a thousand miles. Now a comet has appeared which is so long it fills the sky. It must portend a great uprising of the armies of the empire!"

The present emperor has no heir, thought the king to himself, and if there should be a revolt, the feudal lords would be pitted against one another. He therefore began to manufacture the weapons and tools needed for aggressive warfare in ever increasing quantities, set

[2] It was at his court that the *Huai-nan Tzu,* a predominantly Taoist work on philosophy and statecraft, was compiled by scholars whom he had summoned.

aside stores of gold and cash, and sent bribes and gifts to wandering knights and men of unusual ability in the provinces and other feudal kingdoms. The rhetoricians and strategists came forward with the most reckless and absurd pronouncements in order to flatter the king who, delighted with their words, awarded them large sums of money and plunged even deeper into plans for revolt.

The king had a daughter named Liu Ling, an intelligent girl and a clever talker. The king loved her and kept her constantly supplied with money, sending her to Ch'ang-an to spy on the emperor and win supporters for his cause among the emperor's attendants.

In the third year of *yüan-so* [126 B.C.] the emperor granted a stool and cane to the king of Huai-nan, indicating that he was excused because of old age from his obligation to journey to court to pay his respects.

The king's consort was named Queen T'u. She enjoyed great favor with the king and had borne him a son named Liu Ch'ien who was designated crown prince. Liu Ch'ien was married to the granddaughter of Empress Dowager Wang, the mother of the emperor. (His wife was a daughter of Lady Hsiu-ch'eng, the empress dowager's daughter by her first marriage.)

When the king began to lay plans and make preparations for his revolt, he was afraid that the crown prince's wife would find out about them and give away the secret. The king therefore plotted with the crown prince and instructed him to feign indifference toward his wife. For three months the crown prince refused to share the same mat with her, whereupon the king in turn pretended to be angry with the crown prince and shut him up in the same room with his wife for a similar length of time. During the whole time the crown prince would not go near her until finally the girl asked to be allowed to leave the kingdom. The king thereupon wrote a letter of apology to the emperor and sent her back to her own home.

Meanwhile Queen T'u, the crown prince Ch'ien, and the king's daughter Ling, presuming upon the king's favor, began to misuse the power of the state for their own ends, seizing lands and houses from the common people and ordering innocent men to be thrown into prison.

The fifth year of *yüan-so* [124 B.C.]: The crown prince Liu Ch'ien had studied swordsmanship and considered that no one could rival him. When he heard that one of the palace attendants named Lei Pei was skillful with a sword, he summoned him to a fencing match. Lei Pei yielded twice before the thrusts of the crown prince, but in the third encounter he accidentally struck the prince. The prince flew into a rage, and Lei Pei was terrified of what the consequences would be.

At this time there was a ruling that anyone who volunteered for service in the army should be sent immediately to the capital. Lei Pei therefore expressed his wish to take part in the campaigns against the Hsiung-nu. The crown prince meanwhile spoke ill of Lei Pei to the king, until the king ordered the chief of palace attendants to remove Lei Pei from his post and see to it that no one in the future should attempt to imitate his example.

Lei Pei, however, eventually managed to escape from the kingdom and make his way to Ch'ang-an, where he submitted a letter to the throne explaining exactly what had happened. The emperor issued an edict referring the matter to the commandant of justice and the officials of Ho-nan. The officials of Ho-nan conducted an investigation and sent an order for the arrest of the crown prince.

The king and queen plotted what to do next and finally decided not to hand the crown prince over to the authorities, but instead to call out the troops in revolt. They hesitated over their plans, however, and ten days or more passed while they were still trying to reach a decision. Meanwhile, an edict arrived from the emperor ordering the officials to cross-examine the crown prince.

At this time the prime minister of Huai-nan, angry with the law officer of the city of Shou-ch'un for holding up the crown prince's arrest warrant and failing to seize him and turn him over to the authorities, filed charges against the law officer on grounds of failure to respect orders. The king asked the prime minister to drop the charges, but he refused to listen, whereupon the king sent an envoy with a letter to the throne bringing charges against the prime minister. The emperor referred the matter to the commandant of justice for investigation, and it was soon found that the king was deeply involved in the affair. The king then sent another envoy to the capital to determine how the Han ministers stood on the matter. The Han ministers for their part requested the emperor to arrest the king and conduct an investigation.

The king by this time was afraid that the whole plot would come to light, but the crown prince said to him, "If the Han envoys come to arrest you, you should order your men to dress up as bodyguards and station them around the courtyard with spears. Then, if any of the envoys attempts to make a move toward you, they can strike him dead. I myself will at the same time send someone to stab the palace military commander of Huai-nan and it will still not be too late to call out the troops and start a revolt."

At this time the emperor had not followed the recommendation of the high ministers to arrest the king, but instead had sent the Han palace military commander Yin Hung to go to Huai-nan and question the king. Hearing that an envoy had arrived from the capital, the king proceeded to station armed bodyguards in the courtyard as the crown prince had suggested. But when Yin Hung appeared, he addressed the king in a mild and friendly manner and only questioned him about Lei Pei's removal from office. The king therefore assumed that there was nothing to worry about and did not give the order to begin the revolt.

The palace military commander Yin Hung returned to the capital and made his report, whereupon the ministers who were in charge of the investigation announced, "Liu An, the king of Huai-nan, is guilty of having detained Lei Pei and others who volunteered to join in the attacks on the Hsiung-nu, and of defying the imperial command. He deserves to be executed and his corpse exposed in the market place."

When the emperor refused to approve this recommendation, the ministers requested that the king be removed from his position. The emperor refused this request as well, and the ministers then suggested that the king be deprived of five districts of his territory. The emperor reduced the number to two districts and sent the palace military commander Yin Hung to announce to the king that his offense had been pardoned and that he would be punished by being deprived of a part of his lands.

As soon as Yin Hung crossed the border into Huai-nan he began to publish word abroad that the king had been pardoned. The king, however, had heard earlier that the ministers had proposed the death penalty for him, and he did not know that the sentence had been reduced to deprivation of territory. When word reached him that an envoy from the Han was on the way, he was afraid that he was going to be arrested and once more plotted with the crown prince to station assassins in the courtyard as they had done before. When Yin Hung finally arrived, however, he merely congratulated the king on his pardon and the king once more refrained from giving the order to revolt.

After the envoy had gone the king complained bitterly of his fate: "I have practiced benevolence and righteousness and yet I am deprived of territory! What greater shame could I suffer?"

After the two districts had been taken away from him the king plunged deeper and deeper into his plans for revolt. Whenever his envoys returned from the capital, if they spoke only outrageous nonsense, assuring the king that the emperor had no son to be his heir and that the government was in a state of chaos, he was pleased. But if anyone dared to say that the Han government was functioning smoothly and a son had been born to the emperor, the king would fly into a rage and accuse the person of telling wanton lies.

Day and night the king sat over his maps and charts with Tso Wu and his other ministers,[3] deciding how he should dispose his troops for the invasion of Han territory. "Since the emperor has no heir," he said, "if anything happens to him the court ministers will undoubtedly summon one of his half-brothers—either the king of Chiao-tung or the king of Ch'ang-shan—to take the throne. At that time the feudal lords will begin struggling with each other for power, and of course I cannot afford to be unprepared. Moreover, I am a direct grandson of Emperor Kao-tsu and have always practiced benevolence and righteousness. His Majesty has treated me generously, and so I am willing to bear my present situation. But if his years should come to an end, how could I ever bring myself to face north and acknowledge sovereignty to some contemptible child?"

The king one day seated himself in the eastern palace and sum-

[3] Following the reading in *Han shu* 44.

moned his minister Wu Pei to join him in laying plans for the revolt. "Come in, general," he said when Wu Pei appeared.

With an air of grave regret Wu Pei said, "The emperor has graciously pardoned Your Highness's offenses. How is it that you once again employ titles such as 'general' which are reserved for the officers of the central government alone? Such words as these presage the doom of the kingdom!

"I have heard that my namesake in ancient times, Wu Tzu-hsü, admonished the king of Wu, but when the king refused to listen to his advice, Wu Tzu-hsü said, 'I foresee the day when the wild deer will sport over the ruins of the Ku-su Terrace!'[4] Now I too fear that the day will come when weeds and thorns will grow over this palace and the dew will fall through its shattered roof to wet men's robes!"

The king was furious and ordered Wu Pei's father and mother to be bound and thrown into prison for three months. Then he once more summoned Wu Pei. "Now, general, are you ready to go along with me?" he asked.

"No!" replied Wu Pei. "I have come only to try to suggest a plan for Your Highness. I have heard it said that the truly keen-eared man can hear what has not yet made a sound, and the truly keen-eyed can see what has not yet taken form. Therefore, though the sage may launch ten thousand undertakings, he is sure of ten thousand successes. King Wen in ancient times made only one decisive move, the first step towards the founding of the Chou dynasty, and yet his merit brought glory to a thousand generations, and he ranks with the founders of the Hsia and Shang dynasties as one of the three greatest kings of antiquity. This is called moving in accordance with the heart of Heaven. If a move is of this kind, then, though there has been no previous agreement, everyone within the four seas will rise up to

---

[4] Wu Tzu-hsü was a famous warrior and statesman of the late sixth and early fifth centuries B.C. whose biography is the subject of *Shih chi* 66. He aided the king of Wu in conquering the neighboring state of Yüeh. When the king of Yüeh begged for peace, Wu Tzu-hsü urged the king of Wu not to accept the offer, warning him that Yüeh would one day rise again and destroy Wu. The king refused to listen to his warning, which later proved correct, but instead ordered Wu Tzu-hsü to commit suicide. The Ku-su Terrace was a famous pleasure palace of Wu.

follow. This is the example of success we find in the history of a thousand years ago. Now if we look back a hundred years to the defeat of the Ch'in, or a generation ago to the fate of Wu and Ch'u in the revolt of the Seven Kingdoms, we will see where the difference lies between the preservation and the downfall of a state. I am not afraid to suffer the same punishment as Wu Tzu-hsü; I only hope that Your Highness will be better at listening to advice than the king of Wu was!

"In the years before the Han dynasty the First Emperor of the Ch'in abandoned the way of the sages, killed the practitioners of the way, burned the *Odes* and *Documents,* and cast aside the principles of correct behavior, honoring deceit and physical force instead and trusting to harsh punishments. He had grain transported from the seacoast all the way to the upper reaches of the Yellow River, but at that time, although the men worked the fields as hard as they could, they could not scrape together enough to make a meal of chaff and dregs, and though the women wove and spun, they had not enough cloth left to cover their bodies. Then he sent Meng T'ien to build the Great Wall, stretching several thousand *li* from east to west. He exposed his armies to the hardships of the frontier, never keeping less than twenty or thirty thousand in the field, until the dead reached incalculable numbers, the corpses lay strewn for a thousand *li,* and streams of blood soaked the plains. The strength of the comomn people was exhausted, and five families out of every ten longed to revolt.

"Then the First Emperor of the Ch'in sent Hsü Fu to sail over the sea in search of the spirits, and he returned and lied to the emperor, saying, 'In the midst of the sea I met a great spirit who asked me if I were the envoy from the Emperor of the West. When I answered that I was, he asked me what I was seeking for. "I am looking for the medicine which increases one's years and brings long life," I said.

" ' "Your king of Ch'in," replied the spirit, "is too stingy with his courtesy! You may see the medicine, but you cannot take it back with you!"

" 'Then he led me to the southeast, to the mountain of P'eng-lai, where I saw palaces and towers surrounded by lawns of grass. There was a messenger there, copper-colored and shaped like a dragon, with streams of light pouring from his body and lighting up the sky. When I saw him I bowed before him twice and asked, "What sort of offerings should I bring?" and the Sea God (for that was what he was) replied, "If you will bring me the sons of good families, and beautiful maidens, along with the products of your various craftsmen, then you may have the medicine!" '

"When the First Emperor heard this, he was overjoyed and immediately sent Hsü Fu back east again, accompanied by three thousand boys and girls of good families and bearing presents of seeds of the five types of grains and articles produced by the various craftsmen. But when Hsü Fu reached P'ing-yüan and Kuang-tse, he halted his journey, made himself king of the region, and never returned to the Ch'in. With this, the people were filled with sorrow and bitterness and six families out of every ten favored revolt.

"Then the First Emperor sent the military commander Chao T'o south across the Five Ranges to attack the hundred tribes of Yüeh. Chao T'o knew that the people of China had reached the limit of their endurance, and so he stayed where he was and made himself king of the region instead of returning. He dispatched an envoy with a letter asking the emperor to send thirty thousand unmarried women to sew uniforms for his soldiers. The emperor of the Ch'in approved his request and sent half the number, fifteen thousand women of China. With this, the last bit of loyalty in the hearts of the people crumbled away and seven families out of every ten longed for revolt.

"Someone said to the future Emperor Kao-tsu of the Han, 'The hour has come!' but he replied, 'Let us wait. In time a sage shall arise in the southeast!' Before a year had passed, Ch'en She and Wu Kuang began their rebellion.

"Soon afterwards, Kao-tsu raised the cry of revolt in Feng and P'ei and, though there had been no previous arrangement, the whole empire answered his call, flocking about him in countless numbers. This is what is called waiting for an opening and using the mistakes of others as a steppingstone. He waited until the Ch'in was doomed before making a move, and the people longed for his coming as men long for rain in time of drought. Thus he was able to rise from the ranks of the common people and ascend the throne of the Son of

Heaven; his achievements excelled those of the founders of the Three Dynasties and his inexhaustible virtue has been handed down to his descendants.

"Now Your Highness sees that it was easy for Emperor Kao-tsu to win the empire. But have you not also seen what happened to the kings of Wu and Ch'u in more recent years?

"Liu P'i, the king of Wu, was granted the title of master of sacrificial wine for the Liu clan [5] and was not required to journey to the capital to pay his respects at court. He ruled the multitudes of four provinces, and his territory measured several thousand *li* square. He mined copper within his kingdom and melted it down to mint cash, and in the east he boiled the sea water and extracted salt. In the north he cut down the trees of Chiang-ling and made boats, and each one of them could carry as large a load as twenty or thirty of the carts of China. His kingdom was rich and his people numerous and he was able to scatter bribes of pearls and precious stones, gold and silk among the feudal lords, the members of the imperial family, and the high ministers. Only the members of the Tou family refused to accept his gifts.

"When he had completed his plans and made his preparations for revolt, he called out his troops and marched west, but his armies were smashed at Ta-liang; he suffered defeat at Hu-fu and was forced to turn and flee east again. When he reached Tan-t'u, he was taken prisoner by the men of Yüeh. He was killed, the sacrifices of his state were cut off, and he ended as the laughingstock of the world. Why is it that, with all the men of Wu and Yüeh under his command, he could not achieve success? Simply because he violated the way of Heaven and did not understand the times!

"Now Your Highness's troops do not number a tenth of those of Wu and Ch'u, while the empire is ten thousand times more peaceful and contented than it was under the Ch'in. I beg you therefore to listen to my advice. If you do not listen but persist in your plans, I assure you that your undertaking will fail, and indeed the news of

[5] A mark of the highest honor. At feasts and gatherings the person with this title began the proceedings by pouring out a libation of sacrificial wine to the earth god.

your plans will leak out before you even have a chance to put them into action!

"I have heard that when Wei-tzu visited the site of the old Shang capital, he was filled with grief and composed the song called 'The Thick-growing Grain.'[6] He was embittered that Emperor Chou did not listen to the good advice of Prince Pi Kan. Therefore Mencius has said, 'While he lived, Emperor Chou was honored as the Son of Heaven, but once dead, he was less respected than a common farmer!'[7] Emperor Chou did not lose the empire the day he died; he had long before cut himself off from it by his evil deeds!

"Now I too grieve to think that Your Highness may in similar fashion cast away your position as ruler of a state of a thousand chariots. I beg you to bestow upon me the suicide order, as the king of Wu did to Wu Tzu-hsü, so that I may lead the way for the other ministers and die here in the Eastern Palace!"

As he listened the king was overwhelmed with a great sadness that he could not shake off; tears filled his eyes and ran down his cheeks. Wu Pei, when he had finished speaking, rose, descended the stairway with faltering steps, and left the hall.

The king of Huai-nan had a son named Pu-hai whose mother was a concubine. Pu-hai was actually older than the crown prince, but the king had no love for him and neither he, the queen, nor the crown prince treated Pu-hai as a member of the family. Pu-hai had a son named Liu Chien, an able and spirited boy who bore a constant grudge against the crown prince for treating his father with such coldness. He also resented the fact that, although the king of Huai-nan had only two sons, the crown prince and his father, his father had never been made a marquis, although at this time it was customary for all the sons of the feudal lords to be made marquises. Liu Chien plotted in secret with his friends and followers, hoping to bring charges against the crown prince and contrive his downfall so that his father could replace him as heir. The crown prince was aware of this and several times had Liu Chien thrown into prison and flogged.

[6] Wei-tzu was a half-brother of Emperor Chou, the last ruler of the Shang who, by his evil and headstrong ways, brought about the destruction of the dynasty.

[7] No such passage is found in the present text of the *Mencius,* though the sense is much the same as *Mencius* IB, VIII.

Chien knew all about the crown prince's plans to revolt and the fact that he had suggested assassinating the Han palace military commander. In the sixth year of *yüan-so* [123 B.C.] Chien got a friend from Shou-ch'un named Chuang Chih to present a letter to the throne which read:

Bitter medicine burns the mouth but cures the disease; loyal words sting the ears but profit the conduct. Now Liu Chien, the grandson of the king of Huai-nan, is a man of great ability, and yet the king's consort Queen T'u and her son the crown prince Ch'ien constantly treat him with the greatest ill will. Though his father Pu-hai has committed no crime, they have several times arbitrarily arrested Chien and thrown him into prison, hoping to do away with him. Now while Chien is still alive it would be well to summon him for questioning so that all of the secret doings of the kingdom of Huai-nan may be brought to light.

When the emperor received the letter, he referred it to the commandant of justice, who in turn ordered the officials of Ho-nan to take appropriate action.

At this time Shen Ch'ing, the grandson of Shen I-chi, the marquis of Pi-yang, was on close terms with the chancellor Kung-sun Hung. Shen Ch'ing bore a deep grudge against the king of Huai-nan because his father Liu Ch'ang had murdered Shen Ch'ing's grandfather Shen I-chi. He therefore did everything he could to convince Kung-sun Hung that there was something wrong with the affairs of Huai-nan. Kung-sun Hung began to suspect the king of Huai-nan of plotting a revolt and urged the officials to make a thorough investigation.

When the officials of Ho-nan called Liu Chien for questioning, they found that the information he gave implicated the crown prince and his fellow conspirators. The king of Huai-nan, filled with apprehension, decided to call out his troops. He asked Wu Pei, "Would you say that the Han court is well ordered or in a state of confusion?"

"The entire empire is well ordered," replied Wu Pei.

This was not what the king had wanted to hear. "Why do you say that the empire is well ordered?" he demanded.

"From what I have observed of the government of the Han court," replied Wu Pei, "the duties of ruler and subject, the love between father and son, the distinction between husband and wife, and the hierarchical order between senior and junior are all observed in accordance with what is right. In promoting men to office the emperor honors the principles of antiquity, and there is no fault to be found in the customs or administration of the empire. No region is without its roads over which the rich merchants with their heavy loads of goods travel to every part of the empire. Thus the way has been opened up for foreign trade. The people of Southern Yüeh acknowledge their allegiance to the Han, the Ch'iang and P'o tribes come bearing tribute, and the men of Eastern Ou have surrendered. The frontier has been extended to Ch'ang-yü, the province of So-fang opened up, and the Hsiung-nu, their feathers plucked and their wings broken, have lost their allies and cannot rise again. Although ours may not be compared to the era of great peace in ancient times, yet it is worthy to be called a well-ordered age!"

The king was furious and Wu Pei was obliged to apologize, admitting that he deserved death for his words. The king then questioned Wu Pei once more. "If there is an uprising east of the mountains, the Han will surely send the general in chief Wei Ch'ing to attempt to put it down. What sort of man would you say Wei Ch'ing is?"

"One of my friends named Huang I served under Wei Ch'ing in the campaign against the Hsiung-nu," replied Wu Pei, "and when he returned he told me, 'The general in chief treats his officers with great courtesy and is good to his men, so that all of them are happy to serve under him. He dashes up and down the hills on horseback as though he had wings, and his ability far outshines that of other men!' In my opinion, therefore, a man with such capacity, plus the experience gained from numerous campaigns, would be very hard to stand up against!

"Again, when the master of guests Ts'ao Liang returned from a mission to Ch'ang-an, he told me that Wei Ch'ing showed great intelligence in his orders and bravery in the face of the enemy, always leading his men in an attack. When he pitches camp, if the wells that are dug fail to bring up much water, he will wait until all his men have had their fill before he ventures to drink, and when the army is in retreat he will not cross a river until every one of his men has gotten over. All the gifts of gold and silk which the empress dowager has given him he has distributed among his officers. Even the most famous generals of antiquity could not surpass such acts as these!"

The king received these words in silence.

He knew that Liu Chien had already been summoned and questioned by the officials, and he was afraid that all the secrets of the state would soon come to light. He was therefore anxious to begin the revolt, but Wu Pei continued to oppose the move. The king once more summoned Wu Pei and said, "Do you think the king of Wu was right or wrong in starting his uprising some years ago?"

"Wrong!" replied Wu Pei. "The king of Wu enjoyed the greatest possible wealth and honor, and yet he began his uprising and, failing to win success, was killed at Tan-t'u; his head ended up in one place and his feet in another, and every one of his descendants was wiped out. I have heard that the king of Wu regretted very deeply what he had done. I beg Your Highness to consider well so that you too will not have cause to regret like the king of Wu!"

"Once a man has given his word that he will do something," said the king, "there is nothing left for him but to die in the attempt! Moreover, what did the king of Wu know about revolt? He failed to block the pass at Ch'eng-kao, and as a result over forty thousand Han soldiers poured down upon him in one day. Now I have ordered Lou Huan first of all to close the pass at Ch'eng-kao. At the same time Chou Pei will lead down the troops from Ying-ch'uan and block the roads at the Huan-yüan and I passes, and Ch'eng Ting will call out the troops from Nan-yang and guard the Wu Pass. This will leave the governor of Ho-nan in possession of nothing but the city of Lo-yang, so there will be nothing to worry about from him. Of course we will still have the Lin-chin Pass, Ho-tung, Shang-tang, Ho-nei, and the kingdom of Chao in the north to consider. But people say that if you shut off the pass at Ch'eng-kao, the rest of the empire can never get at you. Thus if we hold the strong points of San-ch'uan in this way and then invite all the soldiers east of the mountains to join the uprising, what would you say to the scheme?"

"I can see how it could lead to disaster," replied Wu Pei, "but I cannot see how it could bring good fortune!"

"Tso Wu, Chao Hsien, Chu Chiao, and the others all believe the outcome will be fortunate and consider that we have nine chances out of ten for success!" said the king. "How is it that you alone foresee disaster instead of fortune?"

Wu Pei replied, "Among Your Highness's ministers and advisers, all those who had any ability in leading the people have already been summoned before the emperor's law officials and thrown into prison. Those who are left will be of no use to you."

"In earlier times," said the king, "when Ch'en She and Wu Kuang revolted against the Ch'in, they did not possess enough territory to stick the point of an awl into. With a band of only a thousand men they began their uprising in Ta-tse, but when they raised their arms and sounded the cry of revolt, the whole empire responded, and by the time they had advanced west to Hsi they had a force of one million two hundred thousand men. Now, although my kingdom is small, it can provide over a hundred thousand fighting men, and they are no band of convict laborers armed only with sickles, chisels, and spear handles such as Ch'en She and Wu Kuang commanded. Why then do you say that I will meet with disaster instead of fortune?"

Wu Pei replied, "In former times the Ch'in emperor ruled with utter disregard for principles, plundering and enslaving the empire. He made lavish journeys accompanied by ten thousand carriages, built the huge A-p'ang Palace, demanded over half the people's produce in taxes, and called out the poor in every village to perform forced labor. Fathers could not look after their children nor brothers help each other; the government was harsh, its punishments stern, and the whole empire writhed as though consumed in flame. The people all stretched their necks in search of aid, bent their ears to listen for help, cried out piteously to Heaven and beat their breasts in hatred for their rulers. Therefore Ch'en She was able to sound his cry of revolt and the whole empire rose to answer him.

"Now, however, His Majesty the emperor orders the world and has joined all within the four seas under a single rule; his love embraces the common people, and his virtue and bounty spread abroad. Without uttering a word, his voice goes forth with the swiftness of lightning to all the world; without issuing a command, his virtue transforms the people as though by supernatural power. The thoughts of his innermost mind are translated into a might and majesty which extend ten thousand miles, for the governed respond to their governors like shadows or echoes. Moreover, the abilities of the general in chief Wei Ch'ing are far superior to those of Chang Han and Yang Hsiung, the generals who attempted to defend the Ch'in dynasty against the rebels. Therefore I believe you are mistaken in comparing your own situation to that of Ch'en She and Wu Kuang."

"If it is as you say," said the king, "then do you think there is no chance at all?"

"I have a plan I could suggest," said Wu Pei.

"What is that?"

"At present the feudal lords show no signs of disaffection and the common people have no cause for anger. However, the province of So-fang, which has recently been opened in the north, embraces a large extent of land with fine pastures and good water, and the people who have so far moved there are not sufficient in number to populate it fully. According to my plan, therefore, you could forge a letter from the chancellor and the imperial secretary to the emperor requesting that the powerful and troublesome families from the various kingdoms and provinces, along with men accused of minor offenses, men whose offenses have been pardoned by a general amnesty, and those whose fortunes amount to five hundred thousand cash or over, be resettled in the province of So-fang along with their kin, with a large force of soldiers to be called out to see that those designated for resettlement start on their way as soon as possible. You could also forge letters from the prison officials of the legal offices in the capital and the Shang-lin Park ordering the arrest of the heirs and favorite ministers of the various feudal lords. In this way the people would be enraged, the feudal lords terrified, and you could then send skilled rhetoricians to persuade them to join your cause. In such a case I think you might have one chance in ten of succeeding." [8]

"That would be good, too," said the king, "though I doubt that I will have to go to such lengths."

The king then ordered some of the government slaves to take up

[8] This plan seems so absurd that one must suppose Wu Pei only suggested it to delay the king's preparations for revolt.

residence in his palace and set them to work forging the imperial seal, the seals of the chancellor, the imperial secretary, the general in chief, the army officials, the two thouand picul officials, and the secretaries of the law offices, as well as the seals of the governors and chief commandants of the neighboring provinces, and making imitations of the credentials and hats of the imperial envoys, so that he would be able to put Wu Pei's plan into effect. He also pretended to accuse several men of crimes and then had them escape west to Ch'ang-an; there they were to take service under the general in chief Wei Ch'ing and the chancellor Kung-sun Hung. Whenever the king should call out his troops in revolt, these men were to assassinate Wei Ch'ing and talk Kung-sun Hung into joining the revolt, a task which the king supposed would be as easy as lifting the lid off a jar.

The king wanted to call out his troops, but he was afraid that the prime minister and the two thousand picul officials of the state would not consent to such a move. He therefore plotted with Wu Pei and decided to murder them. He and Wu Pei were to pretend that a fire had broken out in the palace, and when the prime minister and two thousand picul officials arrived on the scene to try to put it out, they would kill them. They had not yet worked out the exact details of the plan, however.

The king also decided to dress some of his men up as thief-seekers [9] and have them come rushing into his capital from the east bearing requests from the local authorities for immediate aid and shouting that the troops of Southern Yüeh were invading the border. In this way he would have an excuse for calling out his army. He therefore sent men to Lu-chiang and K'uai-chi to take office as thief-seekers, but had not yet ordered the plan put into execution.

The king said to Wu Pei, "If I raise my troops and march west, there are sure to be others of the feudal lords who will join my cause. But what shall I do if some of them refuse to join?"

Wu Pei replied, "You must gain control of Heng-shan in the south, attack Lu-chiang and seize the boats at Hsün-yang, guard the city of Hsia-chih, keep the rivers of Chiu-chiang open, block the pass at Yü-chang, and station your strong bowmen along the Yangtze to guard it

[9] Police officials charged with keeping order in the outlying districts.

and prevent the enemy from marching down from Nan Province. Then, if you seize control of Chiang-tu and K'uai-chi in the east, open up communication with the powerful tribes of Yüeh in the south, and keep a firm grip on the region between the Yangtze and Huai rivers, you should be able to hold on for quite a long time."

"Good!" said the king. "I see no reason to depart from this plan. And if the worst comes I can always flee to Yüeh."

Meanwhile, the commandant of justice had reported to the emperor the information which he had received from Liu Chien, the king's grandson, incriminating the crown prince. The emperor then appointed the commandant of justice as military commander of Huai-nan and sent him to Huai-nan to investigate the affair and arrest the crown prince.

When the commandant of justice arrived in Huai-nan, the king, having heard of his mission, consulted with the crown prince on what to do next and decided to summon the prime minister and the two thousand picul officials, kill them, and call out the troops. The prime minister answered the summons and appeared at the palace, but the internal secretary pretended to be out when the summons arrived and the military commander replied that, since he was acting as an envoy from the emperor, he was not allowed to have an audience with the king. The king realized that, so long as the internal secretary and the military commander refused to appear, he would gain nothing by killing the prime minister, and so he sent the prime minister home again. The king hesitated and could not make up his mind what to do.

The crown prince considered that if he were tried it would be on charges of having plotted to kill the Han military commander. Since he had been the one who suggested the plot to the king, he assumed that if he himself were dead there would be no one left to inform against the king. He therefore said to the king, "All of the ministers who might have been of some use to us have already been thrown into prison by the law officials. Now there is no one left who is capable of helping us in our uprising. Moreover, I am afraid that if you attempt to call out the troops when the time is not right you will not be able to succeed. I beg you, therefore, to let me answer the summons for my arrest."

The king was by this time anxious to find some excuse to abandon the whole undertaking, and he therefore gave the crown prince permission to go. Instead, however, the crown prince tried to commit suicide by cutting his throat, but failed in the attempt.

Meanwhile, Wu Pei went to the authorities on his own accord and informed them that he had been plotting revolt with the king, describing to them all the details of the plot. The officials proceeded to arrest the crown prince and the queen and to surround the king's palace. They also arrested all the king's followers throughout the kingdom who had been party to the plot and searched until they had brought to light the weapons which were to be used in the revolt. When the report of their findings was brought to the emperor, he referred the matter to the high officials for action. Several thousand men, including feudal lords, two thousand picul officials, and members of powerful families, were found to be involved in the plot and all were punished according to the gravity of their offenses.

The king of Huai-nan's younger brother Liu Tz'u, the king of Heng-shan, as a member of the immediate family, would ordinarily have been held responsible for the crime along with the king of Huai-nan, but when the authorities asked for permission to arrest Liu Tz'u, the emperor replied, "The feudal lords should all be considered as existing separately in their own territories. They should not be held responsible for each other's offenses. Let the matter be discussed with those among the kings and marquises who have in the past studied legal affairs and precedents with the chancellor!"

Forty-three men, including Liu P'eng-tsu, the king of Chao, Marquis Jang, and others, discussed the matter and unanimously replied, "Liu An, the king of Huai-nan, is guilty of the most treasonable and unprincipled conduct. It is clear that he was plotting revolt and he should therefore be subjected to punishment."

Liu Tuan, the king of Chiao-hsi, after taking part in the discussion, gave his opinion as follows: "Liu An, the king of Huai-nan, has ignored the laws and committed evil, harboring deceit in his heart and attempting to bring chaos to the empire, misleading the common people, turning his back upon the ancestral temples of the dynasty, and uttering all manner of falsehoods. The *Spring and Autumn Annals* says: 'A subject must not even harbor the intention of evil. If he has the intention he should be punished.' [10] Yet Liu An's crime is far more serious than that of mere intention, for he had already completed preparations for revolt. I have seen the letters, credentials, seals, and maps which he prepared, as well as clear evidence of his other treasonable and unprincipled acts, and because of the enormity of his crime it is obvious that he should be punished according to the law. As for the officials of his kingdom who receive a salary of two hundred piculs or more or those of equivalent rank, as well as his favorites and ministers of the imperial family, although legally they may not be guilty of any direct connection with the plot, they have failed in their duty to instruct him and should all be removed from their posts, deprived of their titles, and reduced to the rank of commoners, and should be forbidden to hold office again. All those close to the king who were not officials should be required to pay two catties and eight taels of gold to ransom their lives. In this way Liu An's guilt will be made clear, the empire will understand how a proper subject and son should behave, and no one will again dare to harbor thoughts of evil and rebellion!"

The chancellor Kung-sun Hung, the commandant of justice Chang T'ang, and the other high officials reported these opinions to the emperor, who presented the director of the imperial clan with the seals of an imperial envoy and sent him to deal with the king. Before he had reached Huai-nan, however, the king cut his throat and died. Queen T'u, the crown prince Liu Ch'ien, and all the others who had been involved in the plot were executed, along with the members of their families.

The emperor considered that Wu Pei in his frequent addresses to the king had done a great deal to point out to him the excellence of the Han dynasty, and therefore he did not wish to punish Wu Pei. But the commandant of justice Chang T'ang said, "Wu Pei was one of the leaders in plotting the revolt for the king. His crime cannot be pardoned!" Eventually, therefore, Wu Pei also was executed. The

---

[10] This passage is not found in the *Spring and Autumn Annals* itself, but in the *Kung-yang Commentary* on the *Annals* (Duke Chuang, thirty-second year and Duke Chao, first year), where the wording is slightly different.

kingdom of Huai-nan was abolished and the territory made into the province of Chiu-chiang.

The King of Heng-shan

Liu Tz'u, the king of Heng-shan, had three children by his consort, Queen Ch'eng-shu; the eldest was a boy named Shuang who was designated crown prince, the second a boy named Hsiao, and the third a girl named Wu-ts'ai. The king also had four sons and daughters by a concubine named Hsü-lai and two by a lady in waiting named Chüeh-chi.

The king of Huai-nan and the king of Heng-shan, though brothers, were not on good terms, each angrily accusing the other of failing to behave with the proper respect and courtesy. When the king of Heng-shan heard that his brother was making preparations to start a revolt, he too began to gather a band of followers about him, secretly intending to join in, though he was afraid that his territory might be taken over by his brother.

In the sixth year of *yüan-kuang* [129 B.C.] the king of Heng-shan journeyed to the capital to pay his respects to the emperor. His master of guests Wei Ch'ing, who had some knowledge of medicine, divination, and similar arts, wanted to send a letter offering his services to the emperor, but the king, angry at his intention, accused him of some crime deserving death and beat him into acknowledging his guilt. The internal secretary of Heng-shan, however, considering the charges unjust, dismissed the case. The king then sent a letter to the throne bringing charges against the internal secretary. When an investigation was made, the internal secretary reported the unjust action of the king. It was also found that the king had on various occasions seized lands from his subjects and destroyed grave mounds to make fields for farming. The authorities requested that they be allowed to arrest the king of Heng-shan, but the emperor refused permission, decreeing instead that all officials of the two hundred picul rank or over in the kingdom of Heng-shan should be appointed directly by the central government.[11]

The king of Heng-shan resented this deeply and began to plot with

11 Ordinarily the feudal lords themselves were allowed to appoint all but the highest officials in their states, such as the prime minister, internal secretary, etc.

Hsi Tz'u and Chang Kuang-ch'ang, searching about for men who were skilled in planning military campaigns and predicting the future by observing the stars and clouds. Day and night these men urged the king on, laying secret plans for a revolt.

In time Queen Ch'eng-shu died and the king's concubine Hsü-lai was designated as the new queen. She and Chüeh-chi shared the affections of the king, but they were jealous of each other. Chüeh-chi began to speak ill of Queen Hsü-lai to the crown prince Liu Shuang, saying, "Hsü-lai ordered her maids to put a curse on your mother and kill her and that is why she died!" Because of this the crown prince came to hate Hsü-lai, and when Hsü-lai's older brother visited Heng-shan and was drinking with the crown prince one time, the prince wounded him with his sword. Queen Hsü-lai was furious at this and repeatedly spoke ill of the crown prince to the king.

Liu Wu-ts'ai, the crown prince's younger sister, had formerly been married, but her husband rejected her and sent her back home, where she carried on illicit relations with a slave and with one of the retainers of the house. The crown prince several times reprimanded her, but she only grew angry and refused to have anything more to do with him.

When Queen Hsü-lai heard of this, she immediately began to treat Wu-ts'ai very kindly, and since Wu-ts'ai and her older brother Hsiao had lost their mother at an early age, they soon became quite attached to Queen Hsü-lai. The queen for her part deliberately treated them affectionately so that they would assist her in slandering the crown prince. As a result of their slanders the king on several occasions beat the crown prince.

In the fourth year of *yüan-so* [125 B.C.] someone attacked and injured Queen Hsü-lai's stepmother. The king suspected that the assailant had been employed by the crown prince and proceeded to beat him. Later, when the king fell ill, the crown prince refused to care for him, claiming that he himself was ill. Queen Hsü-lai and the crown prince's younger brother and sister, Hsiao and Wu-ts'ai, again took the opportunity to speak ill of him to the king, saying, "The crown prince is not really ill. He only says he is, but he looks perfectly well and happy!" The king was furious at this and decided to remove the crown prince from his position and set up his younger brother Hsiao as heir instead.

Queen Hsü-lai knew that the king had made up his mind to deprive Liu Shuang of the position of crown prince and give it to his brother Hsiao; her next thought was how she could get him to pass over Hsiao as well. One of the queen's ladies in waiting was a skillful dancer and enjoyed the attentions of the king. She therefore decided to get this girl to commit an indiscretion with Hsiao so as to ruin Hsiao's reputation. In this way she hoped that the king would reject both Shuang and Hsiao and set up her own son Kuang as crown prince instead.

Crown Prince Shuang knew what she was planning and considered that there would be no end to her slanders if he did not do something. He therefore decided to commit adultery with her in order to silence her. One day when the queen was drinking and feasting, the crown prince came forward and proposed a toast to her. Then, pressing up against her thigh, he asked her to go to bed with him. The queen, however, was furious and reported his action to the king.

The king summoned the prince and was preparing to tie him up and beat him when the prince, who knew that the king had long ago decided to deprive him of the position of heir and give it to Hsiao, said, "My brother Hsiao is having an affair with your favorite dancing girl and my sister Wu-ts'ai has been sleeping with a slave! You had better eat hearty and take care of yourself while you can, father—with your leave I intend to report what is going on here to the emperor!" With this he turned his back on the king and walked out.

The king sent someone to stop him, but the prince was not to be detained. The king himself then got into his carriage, dashed after him, and seized him. While the prince cursed and abused his father, the king had him bound and fettered and imprisoned in the royal palace.

From this time on Hsiao enjoyed increasing favor with the king. The king, impressed by his unusual ability, allowed him to wear the seals of a king, addressed him as "general," and gave him a separate house to live in, allotting him large sums of money so that he could attract his own band of followers. The followers who gathered about him had heard rumors that the kings of Huai-nan and Heng-shan were plotting a revolt, and day and night they urged Hsiao to action.

The king ordered Chiu Ho and Ch'en Hsi, two of Hsiao's followers from Chiang-tu, to make armored carriages and barbed arrowheads and to carve forgeries of the imperial seal and the seals of the various generals and officials. Day and night the king sought out men whose daring was like that of Chou Ch'iu,[12] discussed with them the various strategies that had been used at the time of the revolt of Wu and Ch'u, and made them promise to assist him in his rebellion.

The king of Heng-shan did not dare, like his brother the king of Huai-nan, to aspire to the throne of the Son of Heaven. As a matter of fact, he was afraid that if the king of Huai-nan started a revolt, the latter might seize possession of his own kingdom of Heng-shan. He had decided therefore that, if the king of Huai-nan should march west, he would call out his own troops and attempt to seize and maintain possession of the region between the Yangtze and Huai rivers. This was the extent of his ambitions.

In the autumn of the fifth year of *yüan-so* [124 B.C.] the king of Heng-shan was due to visit the capital to pay his respects at court. When the new year came, however, he visited Huai-nan instead, where he talked with his brother, the king of Huai-nan, and the two of them, forgetting their previous differences, agreed to make preparations for a revolt. He then sent a letter to the throne pleading illness and received in reply a letter from the emperor releasing him from his obligation to come to court.

During the sixth year of *yüan-so* [123 B.C.] the king of Heng-shan sent an envoy with a letter to the emperor asking that he be allowed to remove Liu Shuang from the position of crown prince and set up Liu Hsiao instead. When Liu Shuang heard of this, he asked a friend of his named Po Ying to go to Ch'ang-an and present a letter to the throne accusing Hsiao of manufacturing armored chariots and barbed arrowheads and of having illicit relations with one of the king's dancing girls, hoping in this way to bring about Hsiao's downfall.

---

[12] A military adventurer who served the king of Wu at the time of the revolt of the Seven Kingdoms. See "The Biography of Liu P'i," Volume I, p. 480.

Po Ying arrived in Ch'ang-an but had not yet presented the letter when the officials arrested him in connection with the planned revolt of the king of Huai-nan. Meanwhile, the king of Heng-shan, having learning that Liu Shuang had sent Po Ying with a letter to the emperor, was afraid that it contained a report of all the secret doings of the kingdom. He hastily sent a letter of his own, therefore, accusing Liu Shuang of committing crimes of sufficient gravity to deserve execution in the market place. The matter was referred to the officials of P'ei Province for investigation.

In the winter of the seventh year of *yüan-so* [122 b.c.] the authorities and high ministers instructed the officials of P'ei Province to round up and arrest all those who had been plotting revolt with the king of Huai-nan. In the course of their search they arrested Ch'en Hsi in the house of Hsiao, the son of the king of Heng-shan, and accused Hsiao of having taken the lead in concealing Ch'en Hsi from the authorities. Hsiao knew that Ch'en Hsi had repeatedly discussed plans for revolt with the king of Heng-shan, and he was afraid that the whole affair would come to light. He had heard that, according to the law, those who voluntarily confessed and gave information on their crimes would be let off without punishment and, since he suspected that the letter which Liu Shuang had entrusted to Po Ying to give to the emperor would bring everything to light anyway, he took the lead by confessing to the officials that he had plotted revolt with Chiu Ho, Ch'en Hsi, and the others. When the commandant of justice investigated the matter, he found full evidence to support his confession.

The high ministers requested that the king of Heng-shan be arrested and brought to trial, but the emperor forbade his arrest and instead dispatched the palace military commander Ssu-ma An and the grand messenger Li Hsi to go to Heng-shan and question the king. The king gave a full and truthful account of the affair, whereupon the officials of the state were ordered to surround his palace and keep him under guard while Ssu-ma An and Li Hsi returned to the capital to report to the emperor. The high ministers then requested that the director of the imperial clan and the grand messenger be dispatched to pass sentence on the king and, in cooperation with the officials of P'ei Province, on Liu Hsiao as well. When the king heard of this, he cut his throat and died. Liu Hsiao, because he had confessed on his own initiative, was pardoned from the accusation of revolt; instead he was tried on charges of having had illicit relations with one of his father's maids and was executed in the market place. Queen Hsü-lai was also accused of having killed the former queen, Ch'eng-shu, by black magic, while Crown Prince Liu Shuang was accused of having acted contrary to filial piety by reporting on his own father. Both were executed in the market place. All those who had taken part in the planned revolt with the king were executed along with their families. The kingdom of Heng-shan was abolished and the territory taken over by the central government and made into the provice of Heng-shan.

The Grand Historian remarks: How apt are the words of the *Book of Odes:*

> He smote the northern barbarians
> And punished the men of Ching and Shu.[13]

The kings of Huai-nan and Heng-shan were of the same flesh and blood as the emperor and ruled domains a thousand *li* square, ranking among the highest feudal lords of the nation. And yet they did nothing to honor their positions as protector vassals or to aid the Son of Heaven, but gave themselves up wholly to schemes of evil, plotting revolt and treason until father and sons alike had all in turn lost their kingdoms. Each was forced to cut off his life before his allotted days were spent, and ended as the laughingstock of the world!

Yet this was not the fault of the kings alone, for the customs of the region where they lived were corrupt, and their ministers step by step led them into evil. From ancient times the historical records have shown us that the men of Ching and Ch'u are rash and foolhardy, fickle and fond of revolt!

---

[13] From "Pi-kung," the Temple Odes of Lu. Ching and Shu, as well as Ch'u at the end of the passage, are all names for the region in the south occupied in Han times by the kingdoms of Huai-nan and Heng-shan.

Part IV
THE COLLECTIVE BIOGRAPHIES

Shih chi 121: The Biographies of the Confucian Scholars

From the time of Confucius' death there was no one even in the capital who honored the teachings of the ancient schools. Only in the early years of the present emperor's reign did literature once more begin to flourish. Thus I made The Biographies of the Confucian Scholars.

The Grand Historian remarks: Whenever I read over the rules for the educational institutions and see what has been done to encourage and open up the way for official scholars, I never fail to lay aside the book with a sigh. Alas, when the house of Chou declined in ancient time, the song of the "Crying Ospreys" was composed.[1] With Kings Yu and Li, the power of the Chou dynasty began to wane, and rites and music fell into disuse; the feudal lords conducted themselves as they pleased, and the actual rule of the empire passed into the hands of the powerful feudal states. Confucius was saddened that the path of the ancient kings had been abandoned and that evil ways flourished, and therefore he discussed and edited the *Book of Odes* and the *Book of Documents* and worked to revive rites and music. "When he went to Ch'i and heard the ancient Shao music, he did not recognize the taste of meat for three months," and "after he returned to Lu from Wei, the music was reformed and the various sections of the *Book of Odes* were all put in their proper places." [2] But it was an age of confusion and turmoil, and no one was willing to make use of Confucius. Thus, although he sought employment with over seventy different rulers, he could not find a welcome anywhere. "If someone would employ me," he remarked, "I could accomplish something worthwhile in no more than

[1] The first song in the *Book of Odes*. Ssu-ma Ch'ien apparently took it to be a satirical attack on the weak Chou kings, though it is usually regarded as a hymn of praise.
[2] Quoted from *Analects* VII, 13, and IX, 14.

a year!"³ But when a unicorn was captured at the western hunt, he said, "My way is ended!"⁴ Therefore he used the records of the historians to make the *Spring and Autumn Annals,* in order to set forth the laws of a true king. Its words are subtle and its ideas profound; many are the scholars in later times who have written commentaries on it.

After the death of Confucius, his band of seventy disciples broke up and scattered among the feudal lords, the more important ones becoming tutors and high ministers to the rulers, the lesser ones acting as friends and teachers to the lower officials, while some went into retirement and were never seen again. Thus Tzu-lu went to live in Wei, Tzu-chang in Ch'en, Tzu-yü of T'an-t'ai in Ch'u, and Tzu-hsia in Hsi-ho, while Tzu-kung died in Ch'i. T'ien Tzu-fang, Tuan Kan-mu, Wu Ch'i, Ch'in Hua-li, and others of their group all received instruction from Tzu-hsia's companions and became the tutors of kings. Among the feudal lords, however, only Marquis Wen of Wei had any fondness for literature. Conditions continued to deteriorate until the time of the First Emperor of the Ch'in; the empire was divided among a number of states, all warring with each other, and no one had any use for the arts of the Confucians. Only in Ch'i and Lu did scholars appear to carry on the teachings and save them from oblivion. During the reigns of Kings Wei and Hsüan of Ch'i [378–323 B.C.], Mencius and Hsün Ch'ing and their respective groups both honored the doctrines of the Master and worked to expand and enrich them, winning prominence among the men of the time by their learning.

Then followed the twilight days of the Ch'in emperor,⁵ who burned the *Odes* and *Documents* and buried the scholars alive, and from this time on the texts of the Six Classics of the Confucians were damaged and incomplete.

Later, when Ch'en She became a king, the Confucian scholars of Lu

³ *Analects* XIII, 10.
⁴ *Kung-yang Commentary* on the *Spring and Autumn Annals,* Duke Ai, fourteenth year.
⁵ So called because in the opinion of Han writers the evil reign of the Ch'in represented the close of the great cycle of growth and decay that had begun with the founding of the Chou dynasty.

gathered up the ritual vessels that had belonged to Confucius and went to serve under "King Ch'en." Thus K'ung Chia [6] became an erudit under Ch'en She and died with him. Ch'en She rose from among the common people, rounded up a motley band of border guards, and in the space of a month managed to become a king in the region of Ch'u, though before half a year had passed, he and the uprising he led had been completely wiped out. He and his men were of the most humble origin, and yet gentlemen and scholars did not hesitate to take up the vessels of Confucius and journey to his side, where they presented gifts and begged to become his ministers. Why was this? Because they were incensed at the Ch'in dynasty for having burned their books and interrupted their labors, and they hoped that King Ch'en would help them to vent their rage and accomplish their revenge.

Later, when Kao-tsu had defeated Hsiang Yü, he marched north and surrounded the state of Lu with his troops, but the Confucian scholars of Lu went on as always, reciting and discussing their books, practicing rites and music, and never allowing the sound of strings and voices to die out. Is it not because of the teachings and influence which the Sage left behind him that the state of Lu loves rites and music so? Thus, when Confucius was in Ch'en he said, "Let me return! Let me return to Lu! The little children of my school are ambitious and too hasty. They are accomplished and complete so far, but they do not know how to restrict and shape themselves." [7]

Since ancient times the people of the region of Ch'i and Lu have had a natural talent for literature. And when the Han came to power, these scholars were at last allowed to study and teach their Classics freely and to demonstrate the proper rituals for the archery matches and community banquets.

Shu-sun T'ung drew up the ceremonial for the Han court and was rewarded with the post of master of ritual, while all the other scholars who assisted him were likewise given preferential treatment in the government. The emperor sighed over the neglected state of learning

[6] The eighth-generation descendant of Confucius.

[7] *Analects* V, 21. The usual interpretation is that Confucius, while recognizing the faults of his "little children" or disciples in Lu, is anxious to return from his travels so that he may devote his full time to their instruction. This seems to be the way Ssu-ma Ch'ien understood the passage.

and would have done more to encourage its revival, but at the time there was still considerable turmoil within the empire and the region within the four seas had not yet been set at peace. Likewise, during the reigns of Emperor Hui and Empress Lü there was still no leisure to attend to the matter of government schools. Moreover, the high officials at this time were all military men who had won their distinction in battle.

With the accession of Emperor Wen, Confucian scholars began little by little to be summoned and employed in the government, although Emperor Wen himself rather favored the Legalist teachings on personnel organization and control. Emperor Ching made no effort to employ Confucian scholars, and his mother, Empress Dowager Tou, was an advocate of the teachings of the Yellow Emperor and Lao Tzu. Thus various scholars were appointed to fill the posts of court erudit and to answer questions, but they had no prospects of advancement.

When the present emperor came to the throne there were a number of enlightened Confucian scholars such as Chao Wan and Wang Tsang at court. The emperor was much attracted by their ideas and accordingly sent out a summons for scholars of moral worth and literary ability to take service in the government. From this time on we find that all scholars who taught the *Book of Odes* belonged either to the Lu school of Master Shen P'ei, the Ch'i school of Master Yüan Ku, or the Yen school of the grand tutor Han Ying. The teaching of the *Book of Documents* derived from Master Fu of Chi-nan, that of ritual derived from Master Kao T'ang of Lu, and that of the *Book of Changes* from Master T'ien of Tzu-ch'uan. For the *Spring and Autumn Annals* there were the Lu and Ch'i schools deriving from Master Hu-wu, and the Chao school of Tung Chung-shu.

After Empress Dowager Tou passed away, the marquis of Wu-an, T'ien Fen, became chancellor. He rejected the doctrines of the Taoists, the Legalists, and the other philosophical schools, and invited several hundred Confucian scholars and literary men to take service in the government. Among them was Kung-sun Hung who, because of his knowledge of the *Spring and Autumn Annals,* advanced from the rank of commoner to that of one of the three highest ministers in the government and was enfeoffed as marquis of P'ing-chin. Scholars throughout the empire saw which way the wind was blowing and did all they could to follow his example.

As a scholar official, Kung-sun Hung, who held the post of imperial secretary, was disturbed that the teachings of Confucius were being neglected and not put into greater practice and he therefore submitted the following memorial:

The chancellor and the imperial secretary wish to make this statement. Your Majesty has issued an edict which reads:

"I have heard that the people are to be guided by rites and led to the practice of virtue through music, and that the institution of marriage is the basis of the family. Yet at the present time rites have fallen into disuse and music has declined, a fact which grieves me deeply. Therefore I have invited men of outstanding moral worth and wide learning from all over the empire to come and take service at court. Let the officials in charge of ritual encourage learning, hold discussions, and gather all the information they can to encourage the revival of rites in order to act as leaders of the empire. Let the master of ritual consult with the erudits and their students on how to promote the spread of virtue in the countryside and open the way for men of outstanding talent."

In accordance with this edict we have respectfully discussed the matter with the master of ritual K'ung Tsang, the erudit P'ing, and others, and they have told us that, according to their information, it was the custom under the Three Dynasties of antiquity to set up schools for instruction in the villages. In the Hsia dynasty these were called *hsiao,* in the Shang dynasty *hsü,* and in the Chou dynasty *hsiang.* These schools encouraged goodness by making it known to the court and censured evil by applying punishments. Thus it was the officials of the capital who took the initiative in instructing and educating the people, and virtue spread from the court outwards to the provinces.

Now Your Majesty, manifesting supreme virtue and displaying a profound intelligence worthy to rank with that of heaven and earth, has sought to rectify human relations, encourage learning, revive the former rites, promote instruction in goodness, and open the way for men of worth so that the people of the four directions may be swayed to virtue. This is indeed the way to lay the foundations for an era of great peace.

In earlier times, however, the instruction provided by the government was incomplete and the rites were not fully carried out. We therefore beg that the previous official system be utilized to increase the spread of instruction. In order to fill the offices of erudit we suggest that fifty additional students be selected and declared exempt from the usual labor services. The master of ritual shall be charged with the selection of these students from among men of the people who are eighteen years of age or older and who are of good character and upright behavior. In order to supply candidates for the selection, the governors, prime ministers, heads, and magistrates of the various provinces, kingdoms, districts, marches, and feudal cities shall recommend to the two thousand picul officials in their respective regions any men who are fond of learning, show respect for their superiors, adhere to the teachings of the government, and honor the customs of their village, and whose actions in no way reflect discredit upon their reputations. The two thousand picul officials shall in turn make a careful examination of the men recommended; those found worthy shall then be sent in company with the local accounting officials when the latter come to the capital to make their reports, and shall there be presented to the master of ritual. They shall then receive instruction in the same manner as the regular students of the erudits.

At the end of a year, all of them shall be examined. Those who have mastered one or more of the Classics shall be assigned to fill vacancies among the scholar officials in the provinces or among the officers in charge of precedents who serve under the master of ritual. If there are any outstanding students who qualify for the post of palace attendant, the master of ritual shall present their names to the throne. In this way men of exceptional talent and ability will be brought at once to the attention of the ruler. If, on the contrary, there are any who have not applied themselves to their studies, whose ability is inferior, or who have failed to master even one Classic, they shall be summarily dismissed. In addition, if there are any among the recommending officials who have failed to carry out their duties properly, we suggest that they be punished.

We have respectfully examined the edicts and laws which have been handed down to us by Your Majesty and we find that they distinguish clearly the provinces of heaven and man and combine the best principles of ancient and modern times. Their wording is stately and orthodox, their instructions profound, and the bounty displayed in them most beautiful. Nevertheless we, being petty officials of shallow understanding, have been unable to spread them abroad and therefore they have not been fully publicized and understood by those throughout the empire.[8] Now the officials who handle ritual

---

[8] The meaning of this curious burst of humility, it would seem, is that the emperor's edicts and laws are couched in such elegant language that the present

affairs are ranked below those in charge of precedents, and although men may be selected for office because of their knowledge of literature and ritual, they must remain in the same posts and have no opportunity for advancement. We therefore request that men be selected from among those who have a rank of two hundred piculs or over, or those who have a rank of a hundred piculs and who have mastered one Classic or more, to act as secretaries to the left and right prefects of the capital and the grand messenger; and that men be selected from among those who rank below a hundred piculs to act as secretaries to the governors of provinces, two for regular provinces and one for provinces on the border. In the selection, preference shall be given to those who can recite from memory the longest passages from the Classics. If the number of men available should prove insufficient to fill all the posts, selections should be made from among the officials in charge of precedents to fill the secretariats of the prefects and grand messenger, and from these and the scholar officials to fill the offices in the provinces. We request that these provisions be added to the rules for educational institutions, and that in all other matters the present rules remain in effect.

The emperor signified his approval of this proposal, and from this time on the number of literary men who held positions as ministers and high officials in the government increased remarkably.

Master Shen P'ei was a native of Lu. When Kao-tsu visited Lu, Shen P'ei went with his teacher to visit Kao-tsu at the Southern Palace of Lu. During the reign of Empress Lü he journeyed to Ch'ang-an, where both he and Liu Ying, Kao-tsu's nephew, studied under the same teacher. Later, when Liu Ying became king of Ch'u, he summoned Master Shen to act as tutor to his son Liu Mou, the crown prince of Ch'u. But Liu Mou had no taste for learning and hated Master Shen, and when his father died and he suceeded to the throne of Ch'u, he had Master Shen bound and condemned to convict labor. Master Shen, deeply shamed by such treatment, returned to Lu where he lived in retirement at home and spent his time teaching. For the rest of his life he never left his house, nor would he receive guests who came to see him; only a summons from the king of Lu himself

officials on the lower levels are unable to understand them. Therefore Kung-sun Hung recommends that men with special literary training be assigned as secretaries to the prefects and governors. This is also the reason for the emphasis, later on in the paragraph, on familiarity with the Classics, since imperial edicts were often made up largely of difficult and abstruse quotations from the Classics.

could induce him to go out. Men traveled great distances from all directions to become his disciples, and over a hundred students received instruction from him. The only instruction he gave was oral exegesis of the *Book of Odes;* he used no written commentary on the Classic. Any points that he was doubtful about he left unexplained and did not attempt to comment on.

Wang Tsang of Lan-ling received instruction in the *Odes* from Master Shen and was employed by Emperor Ching. He was appointed lesser tutor to the heir apparent for a time, but later retired from the post. When the heir apparent, the present emperor, ascended the throne, Wang Tsang submitted a letter to him and was awarded the post of palace guard. The emperor continued to advance Wang Tsang from one post to another until in the space of a single year he had become chief of palace attendants.

Later, when Chao Wan of Tai, who had also studied the *Odes* under Master Shen, was appointed imperial secretary, he and Wang Tsang joined in urging the emperor to set up a Bright Hall in which to hold audiences with the feudal lords. When their proposal failed to gain acceptance, they recommended their teacher, Master Shen, to the emperor. The emperor thereupon dispatched an envoy with gifts of bolts of silk and jewels and sent a comfortable carriage drawn by four horses to fetch Master Shen. His two disciples Wang Tsang and Chao Wan went along in smaller carriages to accompany their teacher on his journey.

When Master Shen arrived in the capital and appeared before the emperor, the latter questioned him on how to achieve good government. Master Shen was by this time an old man of over eighty, and he replied, "Good government does not require a lot of talk. The only thing to worry about is whether one has the power to carry out one's policies!"

The emperor at this time was very fond of long speeches and fancy phrases and he therefore received Master Shen's answer in silence. But since he had already gone to the trouble of inviting Master Shen to the capital, he appointed him to a post as palace counselor and quartered him at the official residence of the royal family of Lu, where he was to discuss plans for the construction of a Bright Hall.

Empress Dowager Tou, the emperor's grandmother, was very fond of the teachings of Lao Tzu and had no use for Confucian theories. She managed to discover some fault which Chao Wan and Wang Tsang had committed and accused them to the emperor, who accordingly abandoned the Bright Hall project and turned Chao Wan and Wang Tsang over to the law officials for trial. Both of them committed suicide shortly afterwards, and Master Shen, pleading illness, retired from his post and returned to Lu, where he died a few years later.

His disciples included over ten men who became erudits, among them K'ung An-kuo, who became governor of Lin-huai; Chou Pa, who became internal secretary of Chiao-hsi; Hsia K'uan, who became internal secretary of Ch'eng-yang; Lu Tz'u of Tang, who became governor of Tung-hai; Master Miao of Lan-ling, who became internal secretary of Ch'ang-sha; Hsü Yen, who became military commander of Chiao-hsi; and Chüeh-men Ch'ing-chi, a native of Tsou, who became internal secretary of Chiao-tung. All of these men displayed great honesty and integrity in fulfilling the duties of office and governing the people and were renowned for their love of learning.

Among Master Shen's disciples who became scholar officials there were some whose conduct was not always perfect; yet a hundred or more of them advanced to posts of counselor, palace attendant, or officer in charge of precedents. Although they frequently disagreed in their interpretations of the *Odes,* their doctrines were based largely upon the teachings of Master Shen.

Master Yüan Ku, grand tutor to the king of Ch'ing-ho, was a native of Ch'i. Because of his knowledge of the *Book of Odes,* he was appointed an erudit at the court of Emperor Ching. Once he was having an argument with a certain Master Huang[9] in the presence of Emperor Ching. "King T'ang, the founder of the Shang dynasty, and King Wu, the founder of the Chou, did not receive any 'mandate of Heaven' to do what they did," declared Master Huang. "They simply assassinated their sovereigns and set up their own dynasties!"

"That is not so!" protested Master Yüan Ku. "Chieh, the last ruler

[9] A scholar of Taoism. Ssu-ma Ch'ien mentions in his autobiography that his father Ssu-ma T'an "studied the theories of Taoism with Master Huang."

of the Hsia, and Chou, the last ruler of the Shang, were both cruel tyrants, and the people of the empire turned away from them in their hearts and gave their allegiance to T'ang and Wu. T'ang and Wu were acting in accordance with the hearts of the empire when they overthrew and punished Chieh and Chou. The subjects of Chieh and Chou refused to serve them any longer, but gave their allegiance to T'ang and Wu, who had no other choice than to set up their own dynasties. Is this not what it means to receive the mandate of Heaven?"

But Master Huang replied, "A hat, no matter how old, belongs on the head, and shoes, no matter how new, belong on the feet! Why? Because there is a difference between top and bottom! Now, although Chieh and Chou were unprincipled men, they were still sovereigns, and although T'ang and Wu were sages, they were still subjects. When a ruler commits some fault, if his subjects fail to correct his words and reform his actions in order to restore the position of the Son of Heaven to its full dignity, but instead use his errors as an excuse to 'punish' him and set themselves up in his place, facing south and calling themselves the new rulers, what is this but a case of assassination of one's liege lord?"

"If what you say is true," said Master Yüan Ku, "then was Emperor Kao-tsu likewise at fault when he replaced the ruler of the Ch'in dynasty and became Son of Heaven?"

At this point Emperor Ching intervened. "No one accuses a man of lacking good taste in food because he eats other meats but refrains from eating horse liver," he said, "and no one considers a scholar stupid because he discusses other questions but does not discuss the matter of whether or not T'ang and Wu received the mandate of Heaven!" [10]

He thereupon dismissed the two men, and after this scholars no

[10] Horse liver was believed to be deadly poison. Emperor Ching is hinting that the discussions on the question of who has the right to overthrow his sovereign are equally perilous. Mencius had maintained that King Wu was completely justified in overthrowing Chou, the last ruler of the Shang, and setting up his own dynasty, since Chou had by his wicked deeds forfeited the right to be called a true sovereign and King Wu had received the "mandate of Heaven" to punish him. This principle of the "right of revolution" was naturally very useful to men who were attempting to found new dynasties, but could hardly be applauded by rulers such as Emperor Ching who were working to maintain a dynasty that had already been established.

longer dared to engage openly in debates on who had received the mandate and who was guilty of assassinating his sovereign.

Empress Dowager Tou was fond of the writings of Lao Tzu, and she once summoned Master Yüan Ku and asked him what he thought of Lao Tzu's book. "The sayings of a menial, nothing more!" he replied.

Empress Dowager Tou was furious. "And pray tell me, where can I get one of your Confucian books on the Director of Public Works and the convict labor system?" [11] she asked. Then she ordered Yüan Ku to be thrown into the pigpen to fight the pigs.

Emperor Ching knew that she was angry and that Yüan Ku had merely given a frank answer and was guilty of no offense, and he therefore lent Yüan Ku a sharp knife to take with him into the pigpen. Yüan Ku stabbed the pig and pierced it through the heart, bringing it to the ground with one blow. The empress dowager watched in silence, but could think of no excuse to punish him further and was obliged to let him go.

Shortly afterwards Emperor Ching, impressed by Yüan Ku's honesty and directness, appointed him grand tutor to his son Liu Sheng, the king of Ch'ing-ho. After holding this post for a considerable time Yüan Ku retired because of illness.

When the present emperor first came to the throne he summoned Yüan Ku to service in the government again because of his wisdom. Many of the Confucian flatterers at court hated him, however, and did all they could to slander him, complaining that "Yüan Ku is much too old!" until the emperor finally dismissed him and sent him home. By this time Yüan Ku was over ninety.

Summoned at the same time as Yüan Ku was a man from Hsieh named Kung-sun Hung, who was very shy in Yüan Ku's presence and only ventured now and then to cast a glance at him out of the corner of his eye. Yüan Ku said to him, "Master Kung-sun! Always strive

[11] Some of the Confucian works such as the "Institutes of Chou" dealt with the bureaucratic system of the Chou dynasty and its officials, such as the Director of Public Works, etc. The empress dowager is here deriding this attention to bureaucratic and legal details which seems to have absorbed much of the time of Han Confucian scholars. From the Taoist point of view the Confucians were hopelessly concerned with such "artificial" means of government.

to base your words on correct learning. Never twist your learning around in order to flatter the age!"

From this time on the scholars of Ch'i who expounded the *Book of Odes* all derived their interpretations from the teachings of Master Yüan Ku, and all the men of Ch'i who achieved distinction and honor because of their knowledge of the *Odes* were disciples of his.

Master Han Ying was a native of Yen who became an erudit at the court of Emperor Wen. During the reign of Emperor Ching he was made grand tutor to Liu Shun, the king of Ch'ang-shan. Master Han studied the meaning of the *Odes* and compiled an "inner" and an "outer" commentary, running to twenty or thirty thousand words.[12] Although his interpretations very often differed from those of the scholars of Lu and Ch'i, his general approach to the Classic was the same as theirs. Master Pi of Huai-nan carried on his teachings, and from that time on all scholars in the region of Yen and Chao who expounded the *Odes* derived their interpretations from Master Han. Master Han's grandson Han Shang is an erudit at the court of the present emperor.

Master Fu Sheng was a native of Chi-nan and once served as an erudit at the court of the Ch'in emperor. During the reign of Emperor Wen a search was made for someone who had a knowledge of the *Book of Documents,* but no one could be found throughout the whole empire. The emperor then learned that Master Fu had studied the Classic and decided to summon him to court. However, Master Fu was by this time over ninety and was too old to make the journey. The emperor therefore ordered the master of ritual to send Ch'ao Ts'o, one of his officers in charge of precedents, to go to Master Fu's home and receive instruction from him.

During the Ch'in dynasty, when the First Emperor had ordered the burning of the books, Master Fu had hidden his copy of the *Documents* in the wall of his house; later, because of the great military uprisings, he had been forced to flee from his home. After the Han restored peace to the empire, Master Fu looked for his book, but he

---

[12] Only the "outer commentary" is extant today, the *Han-shih wai-chuan,* a collection of anecdotes from earlier works in which a line or two from the *Odes* is used to point the moral of the story.

found that several tens of chapters were missing. All he could recover were twenty-nine chapters, which he taught to the men in the region of Lu and Ch'i. As a result of his efforts, scholars were able to expound the *Book of Documents* in considerable detail, and all the important teachers east of the mountains studied the Classic and included it among their teachings.

Master Fu taught Master Chang and Master Ou-yang of Chi-nan, and Master Ou-yang in turn taught Erh K'uan of Ch'ien-ch'eng. Erh K'uan, after having mastered the *Book of Documents,* was recommended by his province for his ability in literature and was sent to receive instruction under the erudits at court. There he studied under K'ung An-kuo. Erh K'uan was poor and had no money for living expenses. To make up for this he always used to take charge of the preparation of the meals for the other students and occasionally, when he had some free time, would hire himself out as a day laborer in order to earn money for food and clothing. Wherever he went he always carried a volume of the Classics about with him, and if he had a spare moment he would practice reading it over to himself. Because of his good marks in the examination he was appointed as a secretary to Chang T'ang, the commandant of justice.

At this time Chang T'ang favored men of literary ability and treated Erh K'uan with great kindness, appointing him clerk in charge of presenting petitions to the throne so that he could cite the ancient laws in presenting judgments on difficult and important cases.[13]

Erh K'uan was a warmhearted and kind man, honest, wise, and capable of looking out for himself. He was very good at composing memorials and petitions to the throne, being clever at writing, though in speech he could never make his meaning clear. Chang T'ang considered him a man of exceptional worth and often praised him.

When Chang T'ang became imperial secretary he appointed Erh K'uan as his clerk and recommended him to the emperor. The emperor called him in and, after questioning him on various affairs, found him much to his liking. Six years after Chang T'ang died, Erh

---

[13] The *Book of Documents,* it should be noted, includes a section on the ancient penal code of the Chou dynasty, the "Code of Marquis Lü," from which Erh K'uan no doubt quoted in such cases.

K'uan was advanced to the position of imperial secretary; he held the post for nine years and died in office.

Although Erh K'uan held one of the three highest posts in the government, he managed to get along with the emperor because of his gentle and compliant disposition and had no difficulty maintaining his position. But as long as he was in office he did nothing to reform abuses in the government or reprimand the emperor, and the officials who served under him accordingly regarded him with contempt and were unwilling to exert themselves for him.

Master Chang, Master Fu's other disciple, became an erudit, and a grandson of Master Fu was also summoned to court because of his knowledge of the *Book of Documents,* but on examination proved to be unable to explain the work.

From this time on Chou Pa and K'ung An-kuo of Lu and Chia Chia of Lo-yang were noted for their thorough expositions of the *Book of Documents.* The K'ung family possessed a copy of the *Documents* written in archaic characters which K'ung An-kuo would explain in modern characters, and in this way he started his own school of interpretation. The K'ung family text consisted of ten or more chapters from an otherwise lost copy of the work. Thus the number of versions of the *Book of Documents* in circulation was increased.[14]

Many scholars have taught the rites, but among them Master Kao T'ang of Lu was the most eminent. If we look into the history of rites, we find that even in the time of Confucius the texts on ritual were not complete. Later, when the Ch'in dynasty instituted its burning of the books, more of the works on ritual were lost, so that today we have only the rites pertaining to the lower nobility. It was these that Master Kao T'ang expounded.

Master Hsü of Lu was very good at ceremonies, and during the reign

14 "Archaic characters" refers to the type of characters in use before the Ch'in dynasty's standardization of writing. K'ung An-kuo's school, as well as schools devoted to other Classics which used texts written in archaic characters, came to be known as the "Old Text" schools, as opposed to the "New Text" schools which used texts written in the regular Han style characters. Pan Ku (*Han shu* 88) states that Ssu-ma Ch'ien questioned K'ung An-kuo about his text of the *Book of Documents* and incorporated some of the "old text" versions into the early parts of the *Shih chi.*

of Emperor Wen, because of this knowledge, was appointed a palace official in charge of rites. His learning was passed on to his son, and eventually to his grandsons Hsü Yen and Hsü Hsiang. Hsü Hsiang was born with a natural talent for performing the ceremonies well, but he had no understanding of the Classic on ritual, while Hsü Yen had mastered the Classic but was not good at the ceremonies. Because of his ability Hsü Hsiang was appointed a palace official in charge of ritual at the Han court and eventually reached the position of internal secretary of Kuang-ling. Hsü Yen, and Kung-hu Man-i, Master Huan, and Tan Tz'u, who were disciples of the Hsü family, were all appointed ritual officials, while Hsiao Fen of Hsia-ch'iu, because of his familiarity with the ritual texts, was made governor of Huai-yang. From this time on, all those who taught the rites or performed ceremonies derived their knowledge from the Hsü family.

Expositions of the *Book of Changes* began with Shang Chü of Lu, who studied the Classic under Confucius. After Confucius died, Shang Chü's learning was handed down for six generations, until it reached a man of Ch'i named T'ien Ho or T'ien Tzu-chuang.[15] At the beginning of the Han dynasty, T'ien Ho transmitted his learning to a man of Tung-wu named Wang T'ung or Wang Tzu-chung, and Wang Tzu-chung in turn handed it on to Yang Ho of Tzu-ch'uan. In the first year of the era *yüan-kuang* [134 B.C.] Yang Ho was summoned to take service in the government because of his knowledge of the *Book of Changes*, and advanced to the post of palace counselor.

Chi-mo Ch'eng, a scholar of Ch'i, advanced to the post of prime minister of Ch'eng-yang because of his knowledge of the *Changes*, while Meng Tan of Kuang-ch'uan was made a lord of the gate to the heir apparent for the same reason. Heng Hu, a native of Chü, and Chu-fu Yen of Lin-tzu both obtained service because of their knowledge of this Classic and advanced to posts with a salary of two thousand piculs. On the whole, however, all the men who expounded the *Changes* derived their learning from the school of Yang Ho.

Tung Chung-shu was a native of Kuang-ch'uan. He studied the

---

[15] Because it was concerned with divination, the *Book of Changes* was exempted from the Ch'in's burning of the books and its line of transmission was therefore not interrupted.

Spring and Autumn Annals, and in the reign of Emperor Ching was made an erudit. He used to lower the curtains of his room and lecture from within them, and his older disciples would pass on what they had learned to the newer ones, so that some of his students had never seen his face. Three years he taught in this way and never once took the time even to look out into his garden; such was his devotion to his task. In all his activities he never did anything that was not in accord with ritually prescribed behavior, and all the other scholars looked up to him as their teacher.

When the present emperor came to the throne he appointed Tung Chung-shu to the post of prime minister of Chiang-tu. Tung Chung-shu studied the various natural disasters and portentous happenings recorded in the *Spring and Autumn Annals* and on the basis of this study attempted to discover the principles behind the operations and interactions of the yin and yang. Thus he concluded that if one wished rain to fall, one should shut off the yang forces and free those of the yin, while if one wished the rain to cease, one should do the reverse. He put his theories into practice in the kingdom of Chiang-tu and never failed to achieve the results he sought.[16]

In the midst of his career he was removed from the post of prime minister of Chiang-tu and made a palace counselor. He lived in the dormitory for officials and devoted himself to compiling a record of natural disasters and portentous happenings. Shortly before this, the mortuary temple of Emperor Kao-tsu in Liao-tung had burned down. Chu-fu Yen, who hated Tung Chung-shu, managed to get hold of his work on disasters and portents and presented it to the emperor, who summoned the court scholars and showed them the work. Many of them criticized it, among them Lü Pu-shu, a disciple of Tung Chung-shu who, unaware that the book was his teacher's, pronounced it utterly stupid and worthless. Tung Chung-shu was accordingly turned over to the law officials for punishment and was condemned to death, but was

16 Tung Chung-shu's philosophical views are preserved in a work called the *Ch'un-ch'iu fan-lu,* a series of essays by Tung or his disciples on history, ethics, and the metaphysical operations of the yin and yang and the five elements, including a chapter on how to make rain fall. His opinions were extremely influential in moulding Han Confucian thought.

pardoned by imperial edict. After this Tung Chung-shu no longer dared to express his opinions on disasters and portents.[17]

Tung Chung-shu was an honest and forthright man. At this time the Han was busy driving back the barbarian tribes which surrounded its borders. Kung-sun Hung, although no match for Tung Chung-shu in his knowledge of the *Spring and Autumn Annals*, had succeeded, by following the trend of the times and supporting the undertakings of the emperor, in reaching the position of a high minister in the government. Tung Chung-shu for his part considered Kung-sun Hung no more than a servile flatterer. Kung-sun Hung hated Tung Chung-shu for this reason and told the emperor, "Only Tung Chung-shu is worthy to be appointed as prime minister to the king of Chiao-hsi!"[18] The king of Chiao-hsi had long heard of Tung Chung-shu's worthy actions, however, and when Tung Chung-shu was appointed as his prime minister, he treated him very well. Tung Chung-shu was afraid that if he remained in Chiao-hsi for long he would be accused of some crime and so he resigned his post on grounds of illness and lived the rest of his life at home. He never gave any thought to accumulating wealth for his family but devoted himself entirely to studying and writing books. Thus, from the rise of the Han down to the reign of the fifth ruler, only Tung Chung-shu achieved real distinction for his understanding of the *Spring and Autumn Annals*. In interpreting the Classic he followed the *Kung-yang Commentary*.

[17] To understand this incident it should be remembered that, in the Han theory of portents, it was customary to assign some human fault as the cause of all natural disasters or unusual happenings such as fires, earthquakes, droughts, etc. Since the emperor bore the heaviest responsibility in the government, the faults assigned were usually actions of the emperor himself, or at least of his immediate family or high ministers. Most likely Tung Chung-shu had designated some such "error" as the cause of the fire in Liao-tung, and Chu-fu Yen was therefore able to arouse the emperor's enmity by showing him the book. The other court scholars, anxious to save their own skins, would naturally pronounce the book worthless and stupid. "Stupid," *yü*, in Chinese often means simply "imprudent," i.e., behavior which is likely to get one into trouble.

[18] Liu Tuan, the king of Chiao-hsi, was noted for his violent and unruly temperament, and brought about the death of innumerable officials of the central court who were sent to restrain him. (See his biography in Volume I, "Hereditary Houses of the Five Families," p. 454). Kung-sun Hung no doubt thought that this would be a sure way to get rid of Tung Chung-shu.

Master Hu Wu was a native of Ch'i who became an erudit under Emperor Ching. In his old age he returned to his home and devoted himself to teaching. Many of the scholars of Ch'i who expound the *Spring and Autumn Annals* received their instruction from him. Kung-sun Hung also owed a great deal to his teachings. Master Chiang of Hsia-ch'iu studied the *Ku-liang Commentary* on the *Spring and Autumn Annals*.[19] Kung-sun Hung, after taking office in the government, collected the explanations of Master Chiang, along with those of Tung Chung-shu, and compared them, but decided in the end to follow those of Tung Chung-shu.

Among Tung Chung-shu's disciples who achieved fame were Ch'u Ta of Lan-ling, Yin Chung of Kuang-ch'uan, and Lü Pu-shu of Wen. Ch'u Ta became prime minister of Liang, while Lü Pu-shu became a chief secretary. He was given the imperial seals and sent as envoy to settle legal affairs in Huai-nan, where he reprimanded the feudal lords for arbitrarily acting on their own authority and failing to report their actions to the central government, pointing out that such actions were not in accordance with the principles laid down in the *Spring and Autumn Annals*. The emperor highly approved of both Ch'u Ta and Lü Pu-shu. In addition to these some hundred or more disciples of Tung Chung-shu achieved fame as palace counselors and attendants, masters of guests, and officials in charge of precedents. Tung Chung-shu's sons and grandsons all won high office because of their learning.

[19] At this time there were two main commentaries on the *Spring and Autumn Annals*, the *Kung-yang* and the *Ku-liang*, though it is obvious that the former enjoyed wider favor. Ssu-ma Ch'ien himself studied the *Kung-yang* interpretation of the *Annals* under Tung Chung-shu. The third famous commentary, the *Tso chuan*, undoubtedly existed as a separate work at this time but does not seem to have been used as a commentary on the *Annals*.

Shih chi 119: The Biographies of the Reasonable Officials[1]

The officials who upheld the law and carried out their duties in a reasonable fashion did not boast of their accomplishments nor brag of their ability. Though they won no particular praise from the common people, neither did they commit any glaring errors. Thus I made The Biographies of the Reasonable Officials.

The Grand Historian remarks: Laws are made to guide the people and punishments carried out to prevent evil. Both must be adequately attended to if people of good character are not to live in fear. Yet men of truly sound moral conduct will never go wrong no matter what public position they are appointed to. Those who fulfill the duties of their office and behave in a reasonable way are also carrying out the work of government. What need is there for officials to be so stern?

Sun Shu-ao was a gentleman who lived in retirement in the state of Ch'u. Yü Ch'iu, the prime minister, recommended him to King Chuang of Ch'u [ca. 600 B.C.] and suggested that he be appointed prime

[1] In this brief chapter Ssu-ma Ch'ien for a moment seems to forget the harsh realities of life under Emperor Wu as he relates a series of anecdotes about some officials who lived many centuries earlier, during the middle of the Chou dynasty, and were noted for their just and reasonable conduct. But this mask of the garrulous teller of old tales only faintly conceals Ssu-ma Ch'ien's real purpose. As history these anecdotes are practically worthless. Their function here can only be understood when the chapter is read in conjunction with the following one on "Harsh Officials" and the description of Emperor Wu's economic policies in "The Treatise on the Balanced Standard." Not only does Ssu-ma Ch'ien make an over-all satirical point by making all his "reasonable officials" men of the Chou and his "harsh officials" men of his own day; each anecdote in the chapter—the official who objected to the change in currency, the official who would not accept gifts and was so careful not to compete with the occupations of the common people, the law officials whose sense of responsibility drove them to suicide—is calculated to contrast with and satirize some policy or characteristic of official life under Emperor Wu.

minister in his own place. Three months later Sun Shu-ao was made prime minister of Ch'u. He instructed and guided the people so that all ranks of society lived in peace and harmony, and the customs of the people were raised to an admirable level. Though the government was lenient, it was able to prevent evil; the officials did not indulge in corrupt activities, and bandits and robbers disappeared from the kingdom. In autumn and winter Sun Shu-ao encouraged the people to gather wood in the mountains, and in spring and summer to make use of the resources of the rivers and lakes. Thus everyone obtained the benefits of his surroundings and the people delighted in life.

One time King Chuang, deciding that the coins then in use were too light, had them replaced by larger ones, but the people found the new currency inconvenient and all of them abandoned their occupations. The master of the market place came to Sun Shu-ao and said, "The market is in complete confusion! The people are milling around restlessly and no one knows where to set up shop."

"How long has it been this way?" asked Sun Shu-ao.

"For the past three months," replied the master of the market.

"You may go now," said Sun Shu-ao. "I will see that things are put back the way they were."

Five days later Sun Shu-ao appeared at court before the king and said, "Some time ago the currency was changed because it was thought that the old coins were too light, but now the master of the market place comes and tells me that the market is in complete confusion and that the people are milling around restlessly and cannot decide where to set up their shops. I beg that things be put back the way they were before."

The king gave his consent, and three days after the order was issued the market had returned to normal.

The people of Ch'u liked to use very low-slung carriages, but the king did not think that such low carriages were good for the horses and wanted to issue an order forcing the people to use higher ones. Sun Shu-ao said, "If orders are issued too frequently to the people they will not know which ones to obey. It will not do to issue an order. If Your Majesty wishes the people to use high carriages, then I suggest that I instruct the officials to have the thresholds of the community gates made higher. Anyone who rides in a carriage must be a man of some social position, and a gentleman cannot be getting down from his carriage every time he has to go through the community gate."

The king gave his approval, and after half a year had passed all the people had of their own accord made their carriages higher so that they could drive over the threshold without difficulty. In this way, without instructing the people, Sun Shu-ao led them to change their ways. Those near at hand observed his ways and imitated them; those far off in surrounding states heard of them and took them for their model.

Three times Sun Shu-ao was appointed prime minister, but he did not rejoice because he knew that it was no more than the natural result of his ability. Three times he was dismissed from the post, but he had no regrets, for he knew that his dismissal was not due to any fault of his own.

Tzu-ch'an was one of the high ministers of the state of Cheng. When Lord Chao of Cheng [seventh century B.C.] was ruler, he appointed his favorite, Hsü Chih, as prime minister of Cheng, but before long the state was in confusion, superiors and inferiors were at odds with each other, and fathers and sons quarreled. Ta-ming Tzu-ch'i spoke to the ruler about this and had Tzu-ch'an appointed as prime minister. After he had been prime minister one year, the children in the state had ceased their naughty behavior, gray-haired elders were no longer seen carrying heavy burdens, and young boys did not have to work in the fields. After two years, no one overcharged in the markets. After three years, people stopped locking their gates at night and no one ventured to pick up articles that had been left by the roadside. After four years, people did not bother to take home their farm tools when the day's work was finished, and after five years, no more conscription orders were sent out to the knights. As for periods of mourning, people observed them without having to be told to do so. Tzu-ch'an governed Cheng for twenty-six years, and when he died the young men wept and the old men cried like babies, saying, "Has Tzu-ch'an gone away and left us? Who is there for the people to turn to now?"

Kung-i Hsiu was an erudit of Lu. Because of his outstanding ability he was made prime minister. He upheld the law and went about his duties in a reasonable manner, not indulging in needless changes of procedure, so that all the officials under him naturally came to be up-right. He stopped men who were receiving government salaries from scrambling for profit in competition with the common people and prevented those on generous stipends from accepting petty gifts and bribes.

Once one of his retainers sent him a fish, but he refused to accept the gift. "I always heard that you were fond of fish," said another of his retainers. "Now that someone has sent you a fish, why don't you accept it?"

"It is precisely because I am so fond of fish that I do not accept it," replied Kung-i Hsiu. "Now that I am prime minister I can afford to buy all the fish I want. But if I should accept this gift and lose my position as a result, who would ever provide me with fish again? Therefore I have not accepted it."

When he ate some home-grown vegetables and found them very tasty, he immediately pulled up all the vegetables in his garden and threw them away. At the same time, discovering that the cloth being woven by the maids in his house was very fine, he hastily turned them out of the house and burned their looms. "Growing vegetables at home and weaving cloth like this!" he exclaimed. "Do you want to make it so that the farmers and the weaving girls have no place to sell their goods?"

Shih She was prime minister under King Chao of Ch'u [*ca.* 500 B.C.]. He was a man of absolute honesty and integrity and never stooped to favoritism. Once when he was touring the outlying districts, he witnessed a murder on the road, but when he started to pursue the murderer, he discovered that it was his own father. He let his father go and, returning to the capital, had himself put in prison and sent a messenger to report to the king, "I have apprehended a murderer, who turned out to be my father. Now if I administer the legal punishment to my own father, I will be acting contrary to filial piety, while if I disregard the law and pardon him, I will be disloyal. For either offense I deserve the death penalty."

The king replied, "You pursued the murderer but you did not catch him, therefore you need not be punished. Just go about your duties as before!"

But Shih She sent word again, saying, "I would not be a filial son if I did not make an exception in the case of my own father. On the other hand, I would not be a loyal minister if I did not uphold the laws of my sovereign. Your Majesty may bestow mercy upon me by pardoning my offense, but it is still my duty as a subject to submit to punishment and die." In the end he refused to accept the pardon but cut his throat and died.

Li Li was director of prisons under Duke Wen of Chin [late seventh century B.C.]. Once, discovering that an innocent man had been executed because of an error in the investigation conducted at his office, he had himself bound and announced that he deserved the death penalty. Duke Wen said to him, "There are high officials and low officials, and there are light punishments and severe ones. Just because one of the petty clerks in your office made a mistake there is no reason why you should take the blame."

But Li Li replied, "I occupy a position as head of this office and I have made no move to hand the post over to any of my subordinates. I receive a large salary and I have not shared the profits with those under me. Now because of an error in the trial an innocent man has been executed. I have never heard of a man in my position trying to shift the responsibility for such a crime to his subordinate officials!" Thus he declined to accept Duke Wen's suggestion.

"If you insist that, as a superior officer, you yourself are to blame," said Duke Wen, "then do you mean to imply that I too am to blame?"

"The director of prisons," said Li Li, "must abide by the laws which govern his post. If he mistakenly condemns a man to punishment, he himself must suffer punishment; if he mistakenly sentences a man to death, he himself must suffer death. Your Grace appointed me to this post precisely because you believed that I would be able to listen to difficult cases and decide doubtful points of law. But now since I have made a mistake in hearing a case and have executed an innocent man, I naturally deserve to die for my offense." So in the end he refused to listen to the duke's arguments but fell on his sword and died.

The Grand Historian remarks: Sun Shu-ao spoke one word and the markets in the capital of Ch'u were restored to normal. At the death of

Tzu-ch'an the people of Cheng mourned and wept. When Master Kung-i saw the fine cloth the women were weaving, he drove them out of the house. Shih She chose death because he had let his father go, and thus King Chao's fame spread abroad. Li Li fell on his sword because he had mistakenly executed a man, and so Duke Wen was able to maintain the laws of the state without partiality.

Shih chi 122: The Biographies of the Harsh Officials

The people scorned agricultural pursuits and turned more and more to deceit, flouting the regulations and thinking up clever ways to evade the law. Good men could not lead them to a life of virtue; only the sternest and most severe treatment had any effect in controlling them. Thus I made The Biographies of the Harsh Officials.

Confucius says, "If you lead the people with laws and control them with punishments, they will try to avoid the punishments but will have no sense of shame. But if you lead them with virtue and control them with rites, they will have a sense of shame and moreover will become good." [1] Lao Tzu states, "The man of superior virtue does not appear to have any virtue; therefore he keeps his virtue. The man of inferior virtue cannot forget his virtue; therefore he has no virtue." He also says, "The more laws are promulgated, the more thieves and bandits there will be." [2]

The Grand Historian remarks: How true these words are! Laws and regulations are only the tools of government; they are not the spring from which flows the purity of good government or the pollution of bad.

Formerly, in the time of the Ch'in, the net of the law was drawn tightly about the empire and yet evil and deceit sprang up on all sides; in the end men thought of nothing but evading their superiors and no one could do anything to save the situation. At that time the law officials worked to bring about order, battling helplessly as though against fire or boiling water. Only the hardiest and cruelest of them were able to bear the strain of office and derive any satisfaction from the task; those who cared for justice and virtue were left to rot in insignificant posts. Therefore Confucius said, "In hearing litigations, I am

[1] *Analects* II, 3.   [2] Lao Tzu, *Tao-te-ching* 38 and 57.

no better than anyone else. What is necessary is to make it so that there are no more litigations!"[3] And Lao Tzu said, "When the inferior man hears about the Way, he laughs out loud at it."[4] These are no empty words!

When the Han arose, it lopped off the harsh corners of the Ch'in code and returned to an easy roundness, whittled away the embellishments and achieved simplicity; the meshes of the law were spread so far apart that a whale could have passed through. The law officials were honest and simple-hearted and did not indulge in evil, and the common people were orderly and content. So we see that good government depends upon virtue, not harshness.

In the time of Empress Lü we find one instance of a harsh official, a man named Hou Feng who oppressed the members of the imperial family and committed outrages against the high officials, but when the Lü clan was overthrown, he and all his family were arrested and done away with. Again, in the reign of Emperor Ching, we have the case of Ch'ao Ts'o who, combining learning with natural ability, was noted for his sternness. When the leaders of the Seven Kingdoms rose in revolt, however, they used their resentment against Ch'ao Ts'o as an excuse, and in the end Ch'ao Ts'o was executed. After him came such men as Chih Tu and Ning Ch'eng.

Chih Tu

Chih Tu was a native of Yang. He served as a palace attendant under Emperor Wen, and in the time of Emperor Ching was made a general of palace attendants. He had no qualms about voicing his criticisms openly and contradicting the high ministers to their faces at court.

Once he was attending the emperor on an outing to the Shang-lin Park. Madam Chia, one of the emperor's concubines, had retired to the toilet when suddenly a wild boar rushed into the privy. The emperor signaled to Chih Tu to do something, but he refused to move, whereupon the emperor himself seized a weapon and was about to go to her rescue in person. Chih Tu flung himself on the ground before the emperor and said, "If you lose one lady in waiting, we will bring you another! The empire is full of women like Madam Chia. But what

---

[3] *Analects* XII, 13.   [4] *Tao-te-ching* 41.

about Your Majesty? Though you think lightly of your own safety, what will become of the temples of your ancestors and of the empress dowager?"

With this, the emperor turned back, and the boar also withdrew. When the empress dowager heard of the incident, she rewarded Chih Tu with a gift of a hundred catties of gold. From this time on the emperor treated Chih Tu with great respect.

At this time the Chien clan of Chi-nan, consisting of over three hundred households, was notorious for its power and lawlessness, and none of the two thousand picul officials could do anything to control it. Emperor Ching thereupon appointed Chih Tu as governor of Chi-nan. As soon as he reached the province, he executed the worst offenders among the Chien clan, along with the members of their families, and the rest were all overwhelmed with fear. After a year or so under Chih Tu's rule no one in the province dared even to pick up belongings that had been dropped in the road, and the governors of the ten or twelve provinces in the neighborhood looked up to Chih Tu with awe as though he were one of the highest ministers of the court.

Chih Tu was a man of great daring and vigor. He was scrupulously honest and public-minded, and would never deign even to break the seal on letters addressed to him by private individuals. He refused to accept gifts from others or to listen to special requests, but always used to say, "I turned my back on parents and kin when I took office. All that remains for me to do is to fulfill my duties and die, if necessary, to maintain my integrity as an official." To the end of his life he never gave a thought to his wife or family.

Later, Chih Tu was moved to the post of military commander of the capital. The chancellor Chou Ya-fu, the marquis of T'iao, was at the height of his power and behaved with great arrogance, but whenever Chih Tu appeared before Chou Ya-fu, he would only greet Chou Ya-fu with a low bow instead of the customary prostration.

At this time the common people were still simple-hearted and ingenuous; they had a genuine fear of breaking the law and took care to stay out of trouble. Chih Tu alone among the officials put sternness and severity above all other qualities and when it came to applying the letter of the law he made no exception even for the emperor's in-laws.

The feudal lords and members of the imperial family all eyed him askance and nicknamed him "The Green Hawk."

Liu Jung, the king of Lin-chiang, was ordered to come to Ch'ang-an and report to the office of the military commander of the capital to answer a list of charges which Chih Tu had drawn up against him. When he arrived, he asked if he might have a brush and scraper to write a letter of apology to the emperor, but Chih Tu forbade the clerks to give him any writing implements. Tou Ying, the marquis of Wei-ch'i, however, sent someone to slip the writing implements to the king in secret, and so he was able to write his letter of apology, after which he committed suicide.[5] When Empress Dowager Tou heard of this she was furious and managed to have charges brought against Chih Tu. He was obliged to resign his post and retire to his home. Emperor Ching then dispatched an envoy bearing the imperial credentials to honor Chih Tu with the post of governor of Yen-men Province on the northern border. Because of the empress dowager's anger, the emperor did not require Chih Tu to come to the capital to receive the appointment but allowed him to proceed directly from his home to Yen-men and to carry out his new duties as he saw fit.

The Hsiung-nu had long heard of Chih Tu's strict loyalty and integrity, and when he arrived in Yen-men they withdrew their troops from the border; as long as Chih Tu was alive they would not come near the province. The Hsiung-nu leaders even went so far as to fashion a wooden image of Chih Tu which they ordered their mounted archers to use as a target for practice; but none of them were able to hit it, such was the fear that he inspired in them. He was a constant source of worry to the Hsiung-nu.

Empress Dowager Tou, however, finally managed to find some legal pretext for bringing charges against Chih Tu once more. "Chih Tu is a loyal subject," the emperor said to her, "and I would like to pardon

[5] Liu Jung was the oldest son of Emperor Ching. Originally the emperor appointed him as heir apparent, but later removed him from that position because of his annoyance at the prince's mother, Lady Li, and made him king of Lin-chiang instead. From his biography in Volume I, "Hereditary Houses of the Five Families," p. 451, it is obvious that Chih Tu drove the prince to suicide by his threats and accusations. Empress Dowager Tou never forgave Chih Tu for this harsh treatment of her grandson.

him." But the empress dowager replied, "And the king of Lin-chiang—was he not a loyal subject too?" So in the end Chih Tu was executed.

Ning Ch'eng

Ning Ch'eng was a native of Jang. He served under Emperor Ching as a palace attendant and master of guests. He was a man of great spirit. As long as he was a petty official, he thought of nothing but how he could outdo his superiors, and when he himself became a master of others, he treated the men under him like so much soggy firewood to be bound and bundled into shape. By cunning, knavery, and displays of might, he gradually advanced until he had reached the post of chief commandant of Chi-nan.

At this time Chih Tu was the governor of Chi-nan. The men who had previously held the post of chief commandant of Chi-nan had always dismounted from their carriages and entered the governor's office on foot, requesting the clerks to grant them an interview with the governor as though they were no more than magistrates of districts; such was the awe with which they approached Chih Tu. When Ning Ch'eng took over as chief commandant, however, he soon made it clear that he was not only equal to Chih Tu but could outdo him. Chih Tu had long heard of Ning Ch'eng's reputation and was careful to treat him very well, so that the two became fast friends.

Some years later Chih Tu was executed, and the emperor, worried about the large number of outrages and crimes being committed by the members of the imperial family living in the capital, summoned Ning Ch'eng to Ch'ang-an and appointed him as military commander of the capital. In restoring order, he imitated the ways of Chih Tu, though he was no match for Chih Tu in integrity. It was not long, however, before every member of the imperial family and of the other powerful clans was trembling in awe of him.

When Emperor Wu came to the throne he transferred Ning Ch'eng to the post of prefect of the capital. The emperor's in-laws, however, were assiduous in pointing out Ning Ch'eng's faults and finally managed to have him convicted of some crime. His head was shaved and he was forced to wear a convict's collar about his neck. At this time it was customary for any of the high officials who had been accused of a capital offense to commit suicide; very few of them would ever submit to actual punishment. Ning Ch'eng, however, allowed himself to be subjected to the severest punishment. Considering that he would never again be able to hold public office, he contrived to free himself from his convict's collar, forged the credentials needed to get him through the Pass, and escaped to his home in the east.

"An official who can't advance to a salary of two thousand piculs or a merchant who can't make at least ten million cash is not fit to be called a man!" he declared. With this he bought a thousand or so *ch'ing* of hillside farm land on credit and hired several thousand poor families to work it for him. After a few years a general amnesty was issued, absolving him from his former offenses. By this time he had accumulated a fortune of several thousand pieces of gold. He did any sort of daring feat that took his fancy, since he knew all the faults of the officials in the area. Whenever he went out he was accompanied by twenty or thirty mounted attendants, and he ordered the people of the area about with greater authority than the governor of the province.

Chou-yang Yu

Chou-yang Yu's father was originally named Chao Chien. Because he was a maternal uncle of Liu Ch'ang, the king of Huai-nan, he was enfeoffed as marquis of Chou-yang and consequently changed his family name from Chao to Chou-yang. Chou-yang Yu, being related to the imperial family, was employed as a palace attendant and served under Emperors Wen and Ching. During the reign of Emperor Ching he became the governor of a province.

When Emperor Wu first came to the throne, most of the officials still governed with great circumspection and attention to justice, but Chou-yang Yu alone among the two thousand picul officials established a new record for violence, cruelty, and willfulness. In the case of people he liked he would twist the law around to have them set free; in the case of those he hated he would bend the law to any lengths to wipe them out. Whatever province he was appointed to he would not rest until he had brought about the destruction of its powerful families.

If he was acting as governor, he would treat the chief commandant of the province as though he were no more than a district magistrate; and if he was acting as chief commandant, it would not be long before he had gone over the head of the governor and seized the power of government right out of his hands. He was fully as stubborn as Chi An, and as good at utilizing the letter of the law for evil ends as Ssu-ma An; though all three of these men ranked equally as two thousand picul officials, if the other two happened to be riding in the same carriage with Chou-yang Yu, they would never venture to lounge side by side with him on the armrest.

Sometime later, when Chou-yang Yu was acting as chief commandant of Ho-tung, he became involved in a struggle for power with the governor of Ho-tung, Sheng-t'u Kung, each bringing accusations against the other. Sheng-t'u Kung was condemned to suffer punishment, but he cared too much for his honor to undergo the penalty and committed suicide instead. Chou-yang Yu was executed and his corpse exposed in the market place.

From the time of Ning Ch'eng and Chou-yang Yu on, prosecutions became more and more numerous and the people grew very clever at evading the law. The officials for the most part were men of the same type as Ning Ch'eng and Chou-yang Yu.

Chao Yü and Chang T'ang

Chao Yü was a native of T'ai. He served originally as a clerk in his district and was later moved to a post in the capital. Because of his honesty he was appointed a clerk under the master of documents and served the grand commandant Chou Ya-fu. When Chou Ya-fu became chancellor, Chao Yü was made a secretary to the chancellor. Everyone in the chancellor's office praised Chao Yü for his honesty and fairness, but Chou Ya-fu put little trust in him. "I know perfectly well that Chao Yü would never do anything unfair," he remarked. "But he is too severe in applying the letter of the law. It would never do to appoint him to an important post such as chancellor!"

Under the present emperor, Chao Yü continued to work away as a brush-and-scraper clerk, piling up merit and gradually advancing until he became imperial secretary. The emperor considered him a man of ability and even appointed him as a palace counselor, setting him to work with Chang T'ang discussing and drawing up a number of new laws and statutes. They invented the laws that anyone who knowingly allows a criminal act to go unreported is as guilty as the criminal, and that officials may be prosecuted for the offenses of their inferiors or their superiors in the same bureau. From this time on the laws were applied with increasing strictness.

Chang T'ang was a native of Tu. His father worked as an aide in the city government of Ch'ang-an. Once his father went out and left Chang T'ang, who was still a young boy at the time, to mind the house. When he returned he discovered that a rat had stolen a piece of meat. He was furious and beat Chang T'ang for his negligence. Chang T'ang set about digging up the rat's hole, caught the rat, and recovered what was left of the piece of meat. He then proceeded to indict the rat, beat it until it told its story, write out a record of its words, compare them with the evidence, and draw up a proposal for punishment. After this he took the rat and the meat out into the yard, where he held a trial, presented the charges, and crucified the rat. When his father saw what he was doing and examined the documents he had drawn up, he found to his astonishment that the boy had carried out the whole procedure like a seasoned prison official. After this he set his son to writing legal documents.

After his father died, Chang T'ang became a clerk in the Ch'ang-an city government. Some years later it happened that the younger brother of Empress Dowager Wang, T'ien Sheng, who was only an official at the time, was arrested in Ch'ang-an. Chang T'ang did everything in his power to get T'ien Sheng freed and, after his efforts proved successful and T'ien Sheng had been released from prison and enfeoffed as marquis of Chou-yang, T'ien Sheng became fast friends with Chang T'ang and introduced him to all his acquaintances among the nobility.

Chang T'ang served in the office of the prefect of the capital, acting as aide to Ning Ch'eng, who held the post of prefect at that time. Ning Ch'eng, recognizing Chang T'ang's honesty and impartiality, recommended him for a post in one of the higher ministries. On the basis of this recommendation he was promoted to the position of commandant of Mou-ling and was put in charge of the construction work there.[6]

When T'ien Sheng's older brother T'ien Fen, the marquis of Wu-an, became chancellor, he selected Chang T'ang to act as his secretary. From time to time he praised Chang T'ang to the emperor, who appointed Chang T'ang to assist the imperial secretary and take over most of the latter's duties. He was responsible for investigating the charges of sorcery brought against Empress Ch'en and having her deposed, and he worked to root out and bring to justice all the members of her clique. The emperor, impressed by his ability, gradually promoted him until he made him a palace counselor and put him to work with Chao Yü drawing up a number of new statutes. Chang T'ang did his best to make the laws more severe and prevent the government officials from abusing their positions.

Later, Chao Yü was transferred to the post of military commander of the capital and then was appointed privy treasurer, while Chang T'ang was made commandant of justice. The two men were close friends, Chang T'ang treating Chao Yü like an older brother.

Chao Yü was a very parsimonious and arrogant sort of person. From the time he first became an official he never once entertained any guests at his lodgings. Though the other high officials would sometimes go to call on him, he never returned their calls. He did everything he could to prevent his friends and acquaintances from coming to him with requests and sought to act wholly on his own without any advice from others. If he saw that someone was breaking the law, he would have him arrested at once, but he did not extend his investigations or attempt to ferret out the secret faults of his subordinates.

Chang T'ang, on the other hand, was a very deceitful person who knew how to make use of his wisdom to get the better of others. When he was still a petty clerk he tried his hand at making a profit and was secretly friendly with T'ien Chia, Yü Weng-shu, and other wealthy merchants of Ch'ang-an. Later, when he had risen to one of the nine

[6] The construction work was the building of Emperor Wu's mausoleum at Mou-ling, but since Ssu-ma Ch'ien is writing during the reign of Emperor Wu, he avoids direct mention of the gloomy nature of the work.

highest ministerial posts in the government, he attracted some of the most eminent gentlemen in the empire to his side and, though he secretly disliked them, he made a pretense of admiring them.

The emperor at this time showed a great fondness for literature and learning, and Chang T'ang decided that when he was passing judgment in important cases it would be well to back up his decision with references to the Classics. He therefore asked some of the students and court erudits who were familiar with the *Book of Documents* and the *Spring and Autumn Annals* to act as his secretaries in the office of the commandant of justice and help in deciding on doubtful points of law. When he was presenting memorials to the throne concerning difficult cases, he would always inform the emperor beforehand of all the facts of the case. When the emperor had indicated what he thought was the right decision, Chang T'ang would then make a careful record of the emperor's decision and write it down among the statutes of the commandant of justice's office so that it could be used as a precedent in future cases and would make clear to all the wisdom of the ruler.

If the emperor happened to criticize his judgment in some case, he would accept the blame himself and apologize, claiming that he recognized the superior wisdom of the emperor's viewpoint. Then he would invariably mention the name of some worthy man among his aides or secretaries and say, "So-and-so expressed exactly the same opinion as Your Majesty, but I refused to listen to his advice and so I have committed this stupid blunder!" In such cases the emperor would always pardon him. At other times, when the emperor happened to praise him for some judgment, he would say, "I had nothing to do with preparing this memorial. It was drawn up by So-and-so" (mentioning the name of the one of his aides or secretaries). This was the way he worked to advance the officials in his office and make known their good points, at the same time covering up their faults.

In prosecuting cases, if he knew that the emperor was anxious to see the accused man condemned, he would turn the case over to his harshest and cruelest secretaries, but if he knew the emperor wanted the man pardoned, he would turn it over to secretaries who were more lenient and fair-minded. If he was dealing with a member of some rich and powerful family, he would invariably find a way to twist the law around and prove the man's guilt, but if it was someone from a poor and insignificant family, he would say to the emperor, "Although, according to the letter of the law, the man is guilty, I trust that Your Majesty will consider the matter in a generous light." As a result, many of the men whose cases Chang T'ang handled were pardoned.

After Chang T'ang became a high official he was very careful about his conduct.[7] He would entertain guests, dine and drink with his old friends, and look out for their sons and brothers who had become officials or their poor relations with extreme generosity. When it came to paying calls on others, he was not deterred by the hottest or the coldest weather. Thus, although he was severe in legal matters, suspicious and by no means impartial, he managed in this way to win fame and praise. Many of the sternest officials who acted as claws and teeth for him were students of the Classics who were studying under the erudits, and the chancellor Kung-sun Hung, himself a scholar, often praised his virtues.

Later, when Chang T'ang investigated the charges that the kings of Huai-nan, Heng-shan, and Chiang-tu were plotting revolt, he succeeded in ferreting out all the facts of the case. The emperor wished to pardon Chuang Chu [8] and Wu Pei, who were implicated in the case, but Chang T'ang objected, saying, "Wu Pei took the lead in planning the revolt, and Chuang Chu was one of your most trusted ministers, coming and going in the palace itself and carrying out your missions, and yet he engaged in secret doings with one of the feudal lords. If men such as these are not executed, there will be no way to control the officials hereafter!" As a result, the emperor approved the death sentence which Chang T'ang had recommended.

There were many instances like this in which Chang T'ang, in the course of his prosecutions, brought about the downfall of high officials and won merit for himself. Thus he continued to enjoy greater and

---

[7] As opposed to his earlier days, when he associated with merchants and tried to make a profit, conduct which was considered highly degrading for an official.

[8] Chuang Chu has appeared earlier in the accounts of Southern and Eastern Yüeh as the emperor's envoy to those regions. His surname is sometimes written Yen instead of Chuang. He later became a palace counselor and enjoyed great favor with the emperor. He was very friendly with Liu An, the king of Huai-nan, and was therefore implicated when Liu An was accused of plotting revolt.

greater honor and trust and was finally transferred to the post of imperial secretary.

It was at this time that the Hun-yeh king and his followers surrendered to the Han, and the government was busy raising large armies and sending them to attack the Hsiung-nu. The region east of the mountains was suffering from floods and droughts, and the poor and destitute were wandering from place to place, depending entirely upon the district officials for aid and sustenance, until the resources of the government were exhausted. Chang T'ang, acting on the suggestion of the emperor, proposed the minting of white metal coins and five-*shu* cash, and arranged for the government to take complete control of the salt and iron industries, removing them from the hands of the rich merchants and large-scale traders. He also drew up a law making it possible to confiscate the wealth of anyone attempting to evade the *suan* tax on his possessions and used it to bring about the ruin of the powerful families and great landowners, twisting the letter of the law around, devising clever ways to convict others, and patching up loopholes in the statutes. Whenever Chang T'ang would appear at court with some proposal and would begin to discuss the government's fiscal policy, the emperor would listen until sundown in rapt attention, forgetting even to take time out for meals. The chancellor soon became no more than a figurehead, all the affairs of the empire being decided by Chang T'ang.

But the common people continued restless and dissatisfied with their lot, and before the measures taken by the district officials to remedy the situation had had a chance to do any good, corrupt officials began utilizing them to snatch illegal gain. To prevent this, Chang T'ang made the punishments for violation of the law even more severe. Eventually everyone, from the highest officials down to the common people, was pointing an accusing finger at Chang T'ang.

Once, when Chang T'ang was ill, the emperor went in person to his bedside to see how he was: such was the respect and favor that Chang T'ang enjoyed.

When envoys from the Hsiung-nu came to court with requests for a peace alliance, the ministers deliberated their proposal in the presence of the emperor. One of the erudits named Ti Shan suggested that it would be best to conclude a peace alliance and, when the emperor asked him to state his reasons, he replied, "Weapons are the instruments of ill fortune; they cannot be lightly resorted to time and again! Emperor Kao-tsu wanted to attack the Hsiung-nu, but after the extreme difficulties he encountered at P'ing-ch'eng he finally abandoned the idea and concluded a peace alliance. Thus during the reigns of Emperor Hui and Empress Dowager Lü the empire enjoyed peace and security. When Emperor Wen came to the throne he tried again to deal with the Hsiung-nu by force and the northern border was once more thrown into turmoil and forced to suffer the hardships of warfare. In the time of Emperor Ching, when the kings of Wu and Ch'u and the other states raised the Revolt of the Seven Kingdoms, Emperor Ching spent several anxious and fearful months hurrying back and forth between his own palace and that of the empress dowager and planning how to deal with the situation, and once the revolt had finally been put down, Emperor Ching never again mentioned the subject of warfare. Thus under him the empire enjoyed wealth and plenty. Now, since Your Majesty has again called out the armies to attack the Hsiung-nu, the resources of China have become more and more depleted and the people on the border are troubled by severe poverty and hardship. In view of this situation, I believe that it would be better to conclude a peace alliance."

The emperor then asked Chang T'ang what he thought of this statement, and Chang T'ang answered, "This man is only a stupid Confucianist. He knows nothing about such matters!"

"It is quite true that my loyalty is the loyalty of the stupid," replied Ti Shan. "But the loyalty of the imperial secretary Chang T'ang is deceitful and meretricious! Look how he prosecuted the kings of Huai-nan and Chiang-tu, applying the law with the utmost severity and forcing the kings into a position of guilt, bringing about estrangement between the ruler and his own blood relations and filling the other feudal lords with anxiety! This is quite enough to convince me that Chang T'ang's so-called loyalty is meretricious!"

The emperor's face flushed and he said, "Master Ti, if I made you the governor of a province do you think you could keep the barbarian wretches from plundering the region?"

"No, I could not," replied Ti Shan.

"Suppose I made you the magistrate of a district?"

"No," Ti Shan replied again.

"Or the commander of a guard post on the border?"

Ti Shan realized that he could not argue his way out of the situation and that if he did not say yes he would be handed over to the law officials for trial. So he replied, "In that case I could do it."

The emperor then sent Ti Shan to take command of one of the guard posts on the border. A month or so after he arrived there the Hsiung-nu raided the post, cut off Ti Shan's head, and withdrew. After this the other officials were all too terrified to say a word.

Among Chang T'ang's friends was a certain T'ien Chia who, although a merchant, was a man of worth and upright in conduct. When Chang T'ang was still a petty official, he carried on various money dealings with T'ien Chia, but after he became a high minister T'ien Chia scolded Chang T'ang about his behavior and warned him of his faults in the manner of a truly virtuous man.

Chang T'ang's downfall occurred seven years after he assumed the post of imperial secretary and came about in the following way. There was a man from Ho-tung named Li Wen who had once had a falling out with Chang T'ang. Later he became an assistant in the office of the imperial secretary, but he continued to bear a fierce grudge against Chang T'ang and from time to time, whenever he was able to discover some point in the documents handled by the office that would reflect to Chang T'ang's discredit, he saw that it was made known and that Chang T'ang was given no opportunity to escape responsibility. One of Chang T'ang's favorite secretaries, a man named Lu Yeh-chü, knew that Chang T'ang was worried about the situation and therefore got someone to submit an anonymous emergency report to the emperor accusing Li Wen of disaffection and evil-doing. The case was referred to Chang T'ang, who conducted an investigation and ordered Li Wen's execution. Chang T'ang knew quite well that Lu Yeh-chü had engineered the move to relieve him from worry, but when the emperor asked Chang T'ang, "Who do you suppose it was that first brought the charges of disaffection against Li Wen?" Chang T'ang pretended to be completely at a loss and replied, "I suppose it must have been some old acquaintance of Li Wen's who had a grudge against him."

Some time after this Lu Yeh-chü fell ill and was put to bed in the home of a friend in his neighborhood. Chang T'ang went in person to see how he was and even massaged his legs for him.

The kingdom of Chao was the site of an important smelting industry, and the king of Chao on several occasions had brought suit against the iron officials of the central government for the way they were running the industry, but Chang T'ang had always dismissed the complaints. The king of Chao then began to look around for evidence of some secret doings of Chang T'ang that he could use as a weapon against him. In addition, Lu Yeh-chü had in the past once had occasion to draw up charges against the king of Chao, and the king hated him as well. The king therefore submitted a memorial to the throne accusing both Chang T'ang and Lu Yeh-chü and charging that Chang T'ang, although a high minister, had visited his secretary Lu Yeh-chü when the latter was ill and had even gone so far as to massage Lu's legs for him. There were grounds, he suggested, for suspecting that the two were plotting some major crime. The case was referred to the commandant of justice of investigation.

Lu Yeh-chü meanwhile died of his illness, but the investigations implicated his younger brother, who was arrested and imprisoned in the office of the grain selector.[9] Chang T'ang had occasion to cross-examine some other prisoner in the grain selector's office and at that time he saw Lu Yeh-chü's brother but, hoping to find some way to help him secretly, he deliberately pretended not to recognize him. The brother, not realizing this, was deeply resentful and got someone to send a memorial to the throne accusing Chang T'ang and Lu Yeh-chü of conspiring together to bring false charges of dissaffection against Li Wen. The case was referred to Chien Hsüan who, being on bad terms with Chang T'ang, was only too happy to have this opportunity to conduct a thorough investigation.

Before Chien Hsüan had had a chance to submit the results of his investigation to the emperor, however, it was discovered that someone

[9] Chang T'ang had managed to fill all the regular jails to capacity, and it became necessary to use the office of the grain selector to house the overflow.

had broken into the funerary park of Emperor Wen and dug up and stolen the offerings of money that had been buried in the mausoleum. When the chancellor Ch'ing Ti arrived at court, he and Chang T'ang agreed that, as the two highest ministers, they should both present their apologies to the emperor for the crime. After the two men appeared before the emperor, however, Chang T'ang indicated that, since it was the duty of the chancellor to make seasonal inspections of the funerary parks, it was proper for the chancellor alone to make the apologies for the crime. As he himself had nothing to do with such affairs, there was no reason for him to apologize, he said. The chancellor accordingly submitted his apologies and the emperor referred the case to Chang T'ang for investigation. Chang T'ang then set about trying to prove that the chancellor had deliberately failed to report the theft, until the chancellor became concerned about his own safety. The chancellor's three chief secretaries, Chu Mai-ch'en, Wang Ch'ao, and Pien T'ung, all hated Chang T'ang and began looking about for ways to trip him up.

Chu Mai-ch'en was a native of K'uai-chi. He was recommended to the emperor by Chuang Chu because of his knowledge of the *Spring and Autumn Annals;* he and Chuang Chu, who were both from the region of Ch'u and were versed in the *Elegies of Ch'u,*[10] enjoyed great favor with the emperor, serving in the palace and taking part in government affairs as palace counselors. At this time Chang T'ang was still only a petty clerk and used to get down on his knees before Chu Mai-ch'en and the others and take orders from them. Later, when Chang T'ang became commandant of justice and was put in charge of investigating the king of Huai-nan and his fellow conspirators, he brought about the downfall of Chuang Chu, and from that time on Chu Mai-ch'en hated Chang T'ang intensely. When Chang T'ang became imperial secretary, Chu Mai-ch'en, who was governor of K'uai-chi at the time, was made master of titles chief commandant, ranking among the nine highest ministers of the government. A few years later he was tried for some offense and removed from his post and made a chief secretary. Whenever he had occasion to visit Chang T'ang, the

10 The collection of poems by the Ch'u poet Ch'ü Yüan and his disciples and imitators.

latter would receive him perched on a couch, treating Chu Mai-ch'en like a petty clerk and refusing to show him any respect. Chu Mai-ch'en, being a true man of Ch'u, burned with indignation and was constantly looking for some way to bring about Chang T'ang's death.

The second of the chancellor's three chief secretaries was Wang Ch'ao, a native of Ch'i who reached the post of right prefect of the capital because of his knowledge of legal matters. The third was Pien T'ung, a stubborn and violent-tempered man who studied the strategies of the Warring States period and twice served as prime minister of Chi-nan. Thus all three of these men had previously held higher posts than Chang T'ang but had later lost them and become chief secretaries. As a result they were forced to bow and scrape before Chang T'ang who, knowing that they had formerly been highly honored, never lost an opportunity to humiliate them in his frequent dealings with the chancellor's office.

The three of them plotted together and said to the chancellor, "Originally Chang T'ang promised to apologize with you, but later he betrayed his promise. Now he is trying to impeach you for what happened at the grave of Emperor Wen. It is obvious that he simply wants to get you out of the way so that he himself can replace you as chancellor. But we know all about his secret dealings!" Then they sent law officers to arrest T'ien Hsin and others of Chang T'ang's merchant friends, and got them to give evidence against Chang T'ang. "Whenever Chang T'ang was about to present some proposal to the emperor," T'ien Hsin stated, "he would let me know about it beforehand. In that way I was able to buy up whatever goods would be affected by the proposal and hoard them until the price had gone up. Then I would split the profits with Chang T'ang." T'ien Hsin also revealed other corrupt practices of Chang T'ang, all of which were reported to the emperor. The emperor said to Chang T'ang, "Whenever I do something, the merchants always seem to find out about it beforehand and start busily buying up the articles that will be affected. It would almost appear as though someone were deliberately informing them of my plans!" Chang T'ang made no admission of guilt but instead pretended to be completely taken aback and exclaimed, "Why yes, that must be what is happening!"

Meanwhile Chien Hsüan submitted his report to the emperor on Chang T'ang's involvements with Lu Yeh-chü and the other charges which he had investigated. The emperor finally became convinced that Chang T'ang was guilty of deceit and had been cheating him before his very eyes. He dispatched eight envoys with a list of charges to confront Chang T'ang. Chang T'ang denied all of them and refused to make any admission of guilt, whereupon the emperor sent Chao Yü to press the charges once more. When Chao Yü appeared, he began to berate Chang T'ang, saying, "After all the men you have tried and condemned to execution along with their families, don't you even realize what your own position is now? Every charge that people have brought against you is backed up by evidence! The emperor would hate to have to send you to prison. Instead he hopes that you will settle things for yourself! What do you expect to gain by denying the charges?"

Chang T'ang then wrote a letter of apology, saying, "I, though a man of no merit whatsoever, rose from the position of a brush-and-scraper clerk and, through Your Majesty's generosity, became one of the three highest ministers in the government. Though I have failed in my duties, it is the three chief secretaries of the chancellor who have plotted to bring about my ruin." Then he committed suicide [116 B.C.].

After his death it was found that he had no more than five hundred pieces of gold in his home, all of which he had received as salary or gifts from the emperor; outside of this he left no estate whatsoever. His brothers and sons wanted to give him a lavish burial, but his mother objected. "Although T'ang was one of the highest ministers of the emperor, he got a name for corruption and evil and had to kill himself. Why give *him* a lavish burial?" So in the end they carried his coffin to the graveyard in an oxcart and buried him with only an inner coffin and no outer one. When the emperor heard of the incident he remarked, "If she weren't that kind of mother she could never have borne that kind of son!"

The emperor then had charges brought against all three of the chief secretaries and executed them; the chancellor Ch'ing Ti committed suicide. T'ien Hsin was pardoned and released. The emperor felt sorry for what had happened to Chang T'ang and promoted his son Chang An-shih to a higher post in the government.

Chao Yü had once been deprived of his post but was later appointed as commandant of justice. Earlier in his career Chou Ya-fu had refused to trust him, saying that he was much too intent upon harming others and applying the law with severity; later, when Chao Yü became privy treasurer and ranked with the nine highest ministers of the government, he did indeed become one of the harshest of the officials. In his old age, however, as the number of criminal cases continued to increase and the other officials all worked to apply the laws with the greatest possible sternness, Chao Yü became more lenient in his prosecutions and won a reputation for fairness. Later, when men like Wang Wen-shu appeared on the scene, they were much harsher than Chao Yü. In his old age he was transferred to the post of prime minister of Yen, which he held for several years until he became senile and, committing some blunder, was forced to retire to private life. Some ten or more years after Chang T'ang's suicide Chao Yü died of old age in his own home.

I Tsung

I Tsung was a native of Ho-tung. When he was young he and a friend named Chang Tz'u-kung became highwaymen and formed a band of thieves. His older sister I Hsü had won favor with Empress Dowager Wang because of her knowledge of medicine, and one day the empress dowager asked her if she had any brothers who might be appointed to posts in the government. "I have a younger brother," she replied, "but he is worthless and could never be appointed." The empress dowager nevertheless reported her words to the emperor, who made her brother I Tsung a palace attendant and appointed him as magistrate of one of the districts in Shang-tang Province. He governed with great determination and little leniency, and no one in the district was behind time in paying taxes. Having won an outstanding record there, he was transferred to the post of magistrate of Ch'ang-ling and Ch'ang-an. He applied the laws with honesty and directness and made no exceptions even for the emperor's in-laws. When he arrested and tried Chung, the son of Lady Hsiu-ch'eng, Empress Dowager Wang's granddaughter, the emperor concluded that he was a man of ability and transferred him to the post of chief commandant of Ho-nei. When he reached Ho-nei he succeeded in wiping out the powerful Jung family that lived in that province, and the people of Ho-nei were soon too frightened even to pick up objects that had been dropped in the road.

Chang Tz'u-kung was also appointed a palace attendant and, being a brave and reckless man, joined the army and won merit by daring to fight his way deep into the enemy lines. He was enfeoffed as marquis of An-t'ou.

Ning Ch'eng was at this time living in retirement and the emperor wanted to make him the governor of a province, but the imperial secretary Kung-sun Hung said, "When I was still a petty official and living east of the mountains, Ning Ch'eng was serving as chief commandant of Chi-nan. He ruled the inhabitants like a wolf driving a flock of sheep—it would never do to let him govern the people of a province!"

The emperor instead appointed Ning Ch'eng as chief commandant of the Han-ku Pass. After he had been in this post for a year or so, the officials from the provinces and kingdoms east of the Pass who had had occasion to go in or out of the Pass used to say to each other, "Better to face a nursing tigress than the wrath of Ning Ch'eng!"

Later, I Tsung was transferred to the post of governor of Nan-yang. He had heard that Ning Ch'eng had retired and was living at his home, which was in Nan-yang, but when he reached the Pass he found that Ning Ch'eng had very politely come to greet him and escort him on his way. I Tsung, however, treated the matter very lightly and did not deign to return the courtesy. When he got to Nan-yang he proceeded to bring charges against the Ning family and had their houses completely destroyed. Even Ning Ch'eng himself was convicted of some offense. The members of the K'ung, Pao, and other powerful families all fled from the province, and the rest of the officials and people of Nan-yang went around on tiptoe for fear of breaking some law. Chu Ch'iang of P'ing-shih and Tu Chou of Tu-yen served under I Tsung, acting as his teeth and claws in applying the law, and were later transferred and made secretaries in the office of the commandant of justice.

The armies had from time to time marched out of Ting-hsiang Province to attack the Hsiung-nu, and the officials and people of that province had been thrown into turmoil by their presence. The emperor therefore transferred I Tsung to the post of governor of Ting-hsiang. When he reached the province he made a surprise visit to the jail, seized over two hundred prisoners accused of major and minor crimes, along with another two hundred or so of their friends and relatives who had slipped into the jail to visit them, and had the entire group arrested and tried at once. "These men were plotting to free prisoners who deserved to die!" he announced, indicating the friends and relatives of the prisoners, and in one day passed sentence on the entire group of over four hundred and had them all executed. Though the season was warm enough, the entire province shivered and trembled, and the more cunning and rascally among the people hurried forward to make themselves useful to the officials.

At this time Chao Yü and Chang T'ang had advanced to the highest posts in the government through their severe application of the law, but their ways were mild compared with I Tsung's and at least had a legal basis. I Tsung governed like a hawk spreading its wings and swooping down upon its prey.

Sometime later, when the five-*shu* and white metal coins were put into circulation, the people resorted to all sorts of evil practices to make a profit, those living in the capital being among the worst offenders. The emperor therefore appointed I Tsung as right prefect of the capital and Wang Wen-shu as military commander of the capital. Wang Wen-shu was one of the harshest officials. If he did not inform I Tsung in advance of what he was going to do, I Tsung would invariably use his influence to wreck Wang Wen-shu's plans and turn his successes into failures. Between them they executed an extraordinary number of people, but the effect of such measures was only temporary, and the offenders continued to increase until it became impossible to deal with them all. At this time the posts of imperial inquisitor were set up, the officials spent all their time arresting people and cutting off heads, and men like Yen Feng were appointed to office because of their severity. I Tsung was scrupulously honest and in this point resembled Chih Tu.

It was at this time that the emperor was taken ill while visiting Cauldron Lake and was forced to remain there for some time. After he had recovered, he made a sudden trip to the Palace of Sweet Springs and on the way he noticed that the road was in bad repair. "Did I Tsung think I would never have occasion to use this road again?" he remarked angrily, and seemed to be very upset by the incident.

When winter came, Yang K'o was put in charge of hearing accusations against men who had failed to report their possessions for the property tax. I Tsung believed that this procedure would throw the people into turmoil, and he therefore sent out his officials to arrest Yang K'o's agents. When the emperor heard of this, he ordered Tu Shih to investigate the case. I Tsung was convicted of disobeying an imperial edict and impeding the business of the government and was executed and his corpse exposed in the market place. This happened a year before Chang T'ang's death.

Wang Wen-shu

Wang Wen-shu was a native of Yang-ling. In his youth he robbed graves and committed similar evil deeds, but later he was given a trial post as village head in one of the districts. Though he was removed from this position several times, he finally managed to become an official and was made a secretary in the office of the commandant of justice, handling criminal affairs under Chang T'ang. He was transferred to the office of the imperial secretary and put in charge of suppressing robbers and bandits, in which capacity he had occasion to execute an extraordinary number of men. Sometime later, he was transferred to the post of chief commandant of Kuang-p'ing. There he selected some ten or more daring men from the powerful families of the province whom he believed worthy to be employed as his officials and had them act as teeth and claws for him. Meanwhile he ferreted out all of their secret crimes, but overlooked what he had found and put them in charge of capturing the bandits in the region. So long as they did as he wished and brought in the bandits he wanted captured, he did not press charges against them, even though they might be guilty of a hundred crimes. But if they allowed any of the bandits to escape, then he would utilize the information he had gathered to prosecute them and would not rest until he had wiped out their whole families. As a result of this policy, none of the bandits in the region of Ch'i and Chao dared come near Kuang-p'ing, and the province gained a reputation for being so strictly governed that people would not even pick up objects that had been dropped in the road.

The emperor, hearing of this, transferred Wang Wen-shu to the post of governor of Ho-nei. Wang Wen-shu had already learned during his stay in Kuang-p'ing who all the powerful and lawless families of Ho-nei were. When he reached his new post in the ninth month, he got together fifty privately owned horses from the province and had them disposed at the various post stations between Ho-nei and the capital for later use. In appointing his officials he followed the same strategy that he had used in Kuang-p'ing and had soon arrested all the powerful and crafty men in the province. By the time they had been investigated and tried, over a thousand families were implicated in their guilt. He then sent a letter to the throne asking that the major offenders be executed along with the members of their families, the lesser offenders put to death, and all their estates confiscated by the government to compensate for the illegal gains which they had gotten in the past. He forwarded the letter by means of the post horses he had stationed along the way, and in no more than two or three days an answer came back from the emperor approving his proposal. He proceeded to carry out the sentence at once, and the blood flowed for miles around. The whole province was astounded at the supernatural speed with which his proposal had been carried to the capital and approved, and by the time the twelfth month ended no one in the province dared speak a word against him. People no longer ventured out of their houses at night and there was not a single bandit left to set the dogs in the fields to barking. The few offenders who had managed to escape arrest and had fled to neighboring provinces and kingdoms found themselves pursued even there.

When the beginning of spring came Wang Wen-shu stamped his foot and sighed, "Ah! If only I could make the winter last one more month I could finish my work to satisfaction!"[11] Such was his fondness for slaughter and demonstrations of power and his lack of love for others. When the emperor heard of this he concluded that Wang Wen-shu was a man of ability and transferred him to the post of military commander of the capital.

He proceeded the same way in this post as he had in Ho-nei, summoning all of the most notoriously cruel and cunning officials to aid him in his work, such as Yang Chieh and Ma Wu of Ho-nei, and Yang Kung and Ch'eng Hsin from within the Pass. At this time I Tsung was acting as prefect of the capital, and Wang Wen-shu, who was rather afraid of I Tsung, did not dare to do everything he would have liked to do. Later, when I Tsung was executed and Chang T'ang fell from power, Wang Wen-shu was transferred to the post of commandant of justice and Yin Ch'i replaced him as military commander of the capital.

Yin Ch'i was a native of Shih-p'ing in Tung Province. From the position of a brush-and-scraper clerk he gradually advanced until he had become a secretary in the office of Chang T'ang, the imperial secretary. Chang T'ang often praised him for his integrity and fearlessness and put him in charge of suppressing bandits. When it came to ordering executions, Yin Ch'i did not make exceptions even for the emperor's in-laws. He was transferred to the post of chief commandant of the area within the Pass, where his reputation for sternness surpassed that of Ning Ch'eng. The emperor, concluding that he was a man of ability, made him military commander of the capital, and the officials and people under him were driven to even greater exhaustion and destitution.

Yin Ch'i was a boorish man with little refinement or learning. Under his administration the powerful and evil officials all went into hiding, while the good officials were unable to carry out his policies, so that things were continually going wrong in his office and he was even convicted of some fault. With this, the emperor transferred Wang Wen-shu back to the post of military commander of the capital. It was at this time that Yang P'u won the post of master of titles chief commandant because of his harshness and severity.

---

[11] Because capital punishments could not be carried out in the spring months.

Yang P'u was a native of I-yang. By purchasing the military rank of *ch'ien-fu* he managed to become an official and was recommended for his ability by the governor of Ho-nan. He advanced to a post in the office of the imperial secretary and was put in charge of suppressing bandits in the region east of the Pass, where he carried out his duties in the fashion of Yin Ch'i, swooping down upon his victims with the fierceness of a hawk. He continued to advance gradually until he became master of titles chief commandant and ranked among the nine highest officials. The emperor considered him a man of ability and, when the kingdom of Southern Yüeh rebelled, appointed him as General of Towered Ships and sent him to attack the rebels. He won merit in this campaign and was enfeoffed as marquis of Liang. When he was sent on another campaign, this time to Ch'ao-hsien [Korea], he was arrested by his fellow commander Hsün Chih and was reduced to the rank of commoner. He died some time later of illness.

As has been stated above, Wang Wen-shu was once more appointed to the post of military commander of the capital after the failure of Yin Ch'i. Wang Wen-shu was a man of little refinement, and when he appeared in court he acted rather stupid and confused and could never express himself clearly. When he reached the post of military commander of the capital, however, he seemed to find his element and set about suppressing thieves and bandits with great enthusiasm. Since he was a native of the area, he was thoroughly familiar with the customs of the people in the region within the Pass and knew all the powerful and evil officials. The latter for their part did all they could to assist him in carrying out his policies and kept a close watch for thieves, bandits, and young men of bad character. He put out boxes in which people could deposit accusations and reports of crimes, for which the accusers would receive a reward, and set up chiefs in the villages and rural communities to watch for and arrest bandits.

Wang Wen-shu was very much of a toady, playing up to people who had power and treating like so many slaves those who did not. In cases of really powerful families, although they had committed a mountain of crimes he would never bother them, but if he were dealing with people who had no real power, he would invariably impose upon them and insult them, even though they might be in-laws of the emperor himself. He would twist the law around in clever ways and bring about the ruin of all sorts of petty rogues in order to intimidate the more powerful families and show them what he could do if he wanted to. This was the way he carried out his duties as military commander of the capital.

Under his administration knaves and evildoers were subjected to the most thorough investigation; most of them were beaten to a pulp in prison, and none was ever known to have refuted the charges brought against him and gotten out of prison alive. The officials who acted as his teeth and claws were no better than tigers with hats on. In this way he forced all the lesser rogues in the area under his jurisdiction to their knees, while the more powerful ones went around singing his praises and commending the way he governed. During the several years of his administration many of the officials under him were able to utilize his authority to accumulate fortunes.

Later, he was sent to take part in the campaign against the kingdom of Eastern Yüeh, which had rebelled, and on his return the report he made did not entirely meet with the emperor's approval. He was accused of some trifling fault, tried, and dismissed from the post of military commander of the capital.

Just at this time the emperor was planning to construct the Terrace that Reaches to Heaven, but he had not been able to get together enough workmen. Wang Wen-shu then asked to be allowed to round up all the men under the jurisdiction of the military commander of the capital who should have been conscripted for service earlier but who had managed to evade their duty, and was able in this way to get together a force of twenty or thirty thousand men. The emperor was delighted and appointed him to the post of privy treasurer; later he transferred him to that of right prefect of the capital. Wang Wen-shu continued to carry out his duties in the same way as before, doing little to prevent evil and corruption, and was accused of some fault and removed from office. Later he was restored to office as right military commander, carrying out the same duties which he had earlier as military commander of the capital. He continued to behave as before.

A year or so later preparations were begun to send an army against

Ta-yüan [Ferghana] and an imperial edict was issued summoning various powerful officials to take service in the campaign. Wang Wen-shu contrived to hide one of his subordinates named Hua Ch'eng from the conscription. Shortly afterwards, someone sent in a report of disloyalty, accusing Wang of having accepted bribes from the regular members of his cavalry force in exchange for military exemption, and of other corrupt doings. Wang and his three sets of relatives were sentenced to execution; he himself committed suicide. At the same time, Wang's two younger brothers, along with their wives' families, were accused of some other crime and sentenced to execution. The superintendent of the imperial household Hsü Tzu-wei remarked, "Alas! In ancient times men were condemned to die along with their three sets of relatives, but Wang Wen-shu's crime was so great, it seems, that five sets of relatives had to be executed at one time!" [12] After Wang's death it was found that the fortunes of his family were equal in value to some thousand pieces of gold.

A few years later Yin Ch'i died of illness while holding the post of chief commandant of Huai-yang. He left behind him an estate of less than fifty pieces of gold. He had been responsible for the execution of a very large number of people in Huai-yang, and when he died the families which bore grudges against him planned to seize his corpse and burn it. The members of his own family were obliged to conceal the corpse and flee with it to his old home before they could bury it.

From the time when Wang Wen-shu demonstrated the way to rule by harshness, all the governors and chief commandants of the provinces, the feudal lords and two thousand picul officials who wanted to rule effectively began to imitate his ways. The lower officials and people more and more came to regard lawbreaking as a trifling matter, and the number of thieves and bandits continued to increase until there were men like Mei Mien and Po Cheng in Nan-yang, Yin Chung and Tu Shao in Ch'u, Hsü Po in Ch'i, and Chien Lu and Fan Sheng in the region of Yen and Chao. The more powerful of these gathered bands numbering several thousand men, assumed any title they pleased,

---

[12] The three sets of relatives are the families of the father, mother, and wife of the condemned man. In Wang Wen-shu's case two more families, those of his two younger brothers, were executed at the same time.

attacked cities, seized the weapons from the arsenals, freed the convicts, bound and humiliated the governors and chief commandants of the provinces, killed the two thousand picul officials, and circulated proclamations through the districts demanding that they be supplied with food. The lesser ones formed robber bands of a few hundred men, plundering the villages and hamlets in numbers too great to be counted.

The emperor first tried appointing the aides of the imperial secretary and chief secretaries of the chancellor to remedy the situation, but when they failed to achieve any success, he sent out Fan K'un (one of the lords under the superintendent of the imperial household), the military commanders of the capital, and men such as Chang Te, who had formerly been very high officials, dressed in brocade robes and bearing the imperial credentials and the tiger seals, to call out the troops and attack the bandits. They began cutting off heads in great numbers, sometimes as many as ten thousand or more at one time, and when they started arresting people for aiding and giving supplies of food to the bandits, the number of persons involved swelled at times to several thousand, the inhabitants of several provinces being implicated in one investigation.

After a few years of this most of the leaders of the robber bands had been caught and the others had scattered and fled into hiding. It was not long, however, before they began to gather again in the mountain and river fastnesses and to form new bands here and there. At a loss to know how to deal with them, the government promulgated the so-called concealment law, which stated: "If bandits arise and their presence is not reported, or if the full number are not arrested after their presence has been reported, everyone responsible, from the two thousand picul officials down to the lowest clerks, will be executed."

After this the minor officials, terrified of punishment, did not dare to report the presence of bandits, even though they were aware of it, for fear that they would not be able to capture them all and that the investigations would involve them with the provincial office. The provincial offices for their part were only too anxious to have the lower officials remain silent. As a result, the number of bandits began gradually to increase again, but both the higher and lower officials conspired to conceal the fact and sent in false reports to the central government in order to save themselves from involvement with the law.

Chien Hsüan

Chien Hsüan was a native of Yang. Having won a reputation for impartiality as a district secretary, he was promoted to service in the provincial office of Ho-tung. General Wei Ch'ing employed him to purchase horses for him in Ho-tung and, observing that he was very fair in carrying out his duties, recommended him to the emperor. Chien Hsüan was summoned to the capital and made an aide in the imperial stables, where he fulfilled his duties with great competence. He was gradually advanced to the post of secretary and then of aide to the imperial secretary. He was in charge of the prosecution of Chu-fu Yen and, later, of the conspirators involved in the king of Huai-nan's plans for revolt. He paid strict attention to the letter of the law and applied it with great severity, bringing about the death of a very large number of people, and at the same time achieved a reputation for his decisiveness in settling doubtful cases. He was occasionally dismissed from office, but was always reappointed, and served some twenty years as a secretary and aide under the imperial secretary.

When Wang Wen-shu was dismissed from the post of military commander of the capital, Chien Hsüan was appointed left prefect of the capital. He attended to every detail in the area under his jurisdiction down to the very grain and salt consumed; all matters, great and small, passed through his hands. He even doled out the supplies to the various district offices in person in order to prevent the district magistrates and their aides from drawing and handling supplies in any way they wished. He maintained order by applying the law with the utmost severity, and during his several years in office every affair in the province, down to the most trifling, was perfectly arranged. However, only a man like Chien Hsüan could have personally attended to every matter, from the smallest to the largest, in this way. It would be difficult to expect such behavior from all officials.

Later he was removed from his post and appointed supervisor of the right district of the capital. He bore a grudge against one of his subordinate officials named Ch'eng Hsin, who subsequently fled and hid in the Shang-lin Park. Chien Hsüan ordered the district magistrate of Mei to have Ch'eng Hsin sought out and killed, and when the magistrate's guards located him and shot at him, some of their arrows struck the gate of the emperor's garden in the park. Chien Hsüan was charged with the responsibility for the incident and was handed over to the law officials for trial. He was convicted of high treason and was sentenced to die along with the members of his family, but he anticipated the sentence by taking his own life. After this Tu Chou came to power.

Tu Chou

Tu Chou was a native of Tu-yen in Nan-yang. While I Tsung was acting as governor of Nan-yang, he employed Tu Chou as one of his subordinates. Later, Tu Chou was promoted to secretary in the office of the commandant of justice and served under Chang T'ang. Chang T'ang frequently commended him to the emperor for his impartiality, and in time he was appointed to the office of the imperial secretary and put in charge of investigating the losses of men, animals, and supplies that were taking place in the border regions. He was responsible for condemning a very large number of persons to execution. His proposals always won the approval of the emperor, and he enjoyed the same degree of confidence that Chien Hsüan did. He and Chien Hsüan took turns serving as aides to the imperial secretary for over ten years, and Tu Chou imitated Chien Hsüan's ways, though Tu Chou had a much more grave and sedate bearing. On the surface Tu Chou appeared to be tolerant, but at heart he had a severity that cut to the bone.

When Chien Hsüan was appointed left prefect of the capital, Tu Chou was made commandant of justice. He carried out the duties of this office in much the same way that Chang T'ang had, and in addition he was very skillful at divining the ruler's wishes. If the emperor wanted to get rid of someone, Tu Chou would proceed to find some way to trap the victim; if the emperor wanted someone let free, Tu Chou would keep the person bound in prison for an indefinite period awaiting further instructions, meanwhile doing all he could to make it seem that the person had been unjustly accused.

Once one of his guests chided him about this, saying, "You are supposed to be the dispenser of justice for the Son of Heaven, and yet you pay no attention to the statute books, but simply decide cases in any way that will accord with the wishes of the ruler. Do you really think that is the way a law official should be?"

"And where, may I ask, did the statute books come from in the first place?" replied Tu Chou. "Whatever the earlier rulers thought was right they wrote down in the books and made into laws, and whatever the later rulers thought was right they added as new clauses and stipulations. Anything that suits the present age is right. Why bother with the laws of former times?"

After Tu Chou became commandant of justice the flood of cases referred to his office by imperial command grew larger and larger. The number of officials of the two thousand picul class in prison, counting old and new arrests, never fell below a hundred or more men. All cases involving the provincial officials, as well as those of the high ministries in the capital, were referred to the commandant of justice, who handled over a thousand of them a year. In important cases, several hundred men would be arrested or called in to act as witnesses, and even in less important cases the number was twenty or thirty. Men living anywhere from several hundred *li* to several thousand *li* away were summoned to the capital for investigation. When a case was being tried, the prison officials would confront the accused with a list of charges, and if he refused to acknowledge his guilt they would beat him until they had forced a confession. For this reason anyone who heard that he was to be arrested would flee into hiding. Although several amnesties might have been issued in the meantime, men were held in prison for indefinite periods of time and not released. In other cases men who had been in hiding for over ten years were accused when they were found and were almost always tried for immoral conduct or some even more serious charge. In time, the commandant of justice and the other law officials of the capital had succeeded in arresting sixty or seventy thousand persons on imperial order, while the officials found legal grounds for bringing charges against another hundred thousand or more.

Later Tu Chou was dismissed from the post of commandant of

justice and then reappointed as military commander of the capital.[13] He worked to rid the area of thieves, and was responsible for the arrest and prosecution of Sang Hung-yang and the brothers of Empress Wei, whom he prosecuted with great severity. The emperor admired him for his untiring efforts and impartiality and promoted him to the post of imperial secretary. His two sons became governors of the provinces of Ho-nei and Ho-nan on either side of the Yellow River and governed with even greater harshness and cruelty than Wang Wen-shu or the rest.

When Tu Chou was first summoned to serve as a secretary in the office of the commandant of justice, he owned only one horse, and even that was maimed. But by the time he had worked in the government for a number of years and had advanced until he ranked among the three highest ministers, his sons and grandsons all held high offices and the wealth of his family ran to several hundred million cash.

The Grand Historian remarks: These ten men, from Chih Tu to Tu Chou, all won fame for their harshness. Nevertheless, Chih Tu had a certain stubborn frankness and strove to decide between right and wrong in order to provide a basis for justice in the empire. Chang T'ang knew how to be either stern or mild depending upon the will of the ruler, but his decisions on what was fitting and what was not were often of benefit to the nation. Chao Yü stuck to the letter of the law and was careful to be fair, but Tu Chou simply flattered the whims of the ruler and believed that gravity consisted in saying little. From the time of Chang T'ang's death on, the net of the law was drawn tighter and tighter, and harsh penalties became increasingly

---

[13] According to *Han shu* 19B, Tu Chou was relieved of his duties as commandant of justice and made military commander of the capital in the second year of *t'ien-han* (99 B.C.). This was the same year that Ssu-ma Ch'ien, having aroused Emperor Wu's anger by speaking in defense of General Li Ling, was sent to prison and condemned to suffer castration. It is quite possible, therefore, that Ssu-ma Ch'ien's case was handled by Tu Chou, or at least by the officials trained under Tu Chou. Ssu-ma Ch'ien's description of prison methods used at this time may accordingly be based upon personal experience. Certainly, from Ssu-ma Ch'ien's letter to Jen An describing his experience in prison it is obvious that he too was beaten and cowed by the prison officials into acknowledging guilt. See the translation of the letter in *Ssu-ma Ch'ien: Grand Historian of China*, p. 62.

frequent, so that the work of the government officials was gradually hampered and brought to a standstill. The high ministers went about their duties meekly and compliantly, and gave no thought to reforming defects in government policy. Indeed, they were so busy staying out of trouble that they had no time to think of anything but laws and regulations.

Yet among these ten men, those who were honest may serve as an example of conduct, and those who were corrupt may serve as a warning. These men, by their schemes and strategies, their teaching and leadership, worked to prevent evil and block the path of crime. All were men of strong character, combining in themselves both military and civil ability. And although they were known for their cruelty and harshness, it was a reputation that went well with their duties. But when it comes to men like Feng Tang, the governor of Shu, who violently oppressed the people; Li Chen of Kuang-han who tore people limb from limb for his own pleasure; Mi P'u of Tung Province who sawed people's heads off; Lo Pi of T'ien-shui who bludgeoned people into making confessions; Ch'u Kuang of Ho-tung who executed people indiscriminately; Wu Chi of the capital and Yin Chou of Feng-i who ruled like vipers or hawks; or Yen Feng of Shui-heng who beat people to death unless they bribed him for their release—why bother to describe all of them? Why bother to describe all of them?

Shih chi 124: The Biographies of the Wandering Knights [1]

Saving others in distress, helping those who cannot help themselves—is this not what a benevolent man does? Never betraying a trust, never going back on one's word—this is the conduct of a righteous man. Thus I made The Biographies of the Wandering Knights.

Han Fei Tzu has remarked: "The Confucians with their learning pervert the laws; the knights with their contentiousness violate the prohibitions." [2] Thus he condemns both groups.

Yet the Confucian scholars have often been praised by the world. Some of them, by their knowledge of statesmanship, succeeded in becoming prime ministers and high officials and acted as aides to the rulers of the time. Their achievements are fully recorded in the annals of the Chou states, and there is therefore no reason to discuss them here. Others, however, such as Confucius' disciples Chi Tz'u and Yüan Hsien, were simple commoners living in the village lanes. They studied books and cherished independence of action and the virtues of the superior man; in their righteousness they refused to compromise with their age, and their age in turn merely laughed at them. Therefore

[1] The word "knight" here should not be understood as designating any particular formal rank in society. It is used rather to suggest the kind of honorable and self-sacrificing conduct which characterized this group of men at their best. Such self-appointed "bosses" or protectors of others no doubt served a very useful purpose in the chaotic society of the late Chou and early Han. With the restoration of peace and stability, however, they often became a nuisance and the Han government took strict measures to suppress them. Ssu-ma Ch'ien has been severely criticized by later Chinese writers for praising the knights and according them a place in his history. As a historian, however, he could hardly have ignored their existence entirely, while his own bitter experiences at Emperor Wu's court undoubtedly encouraged his admiration for men who "hasten to the side of those who are in trouble." Writers of the Chinese communist regime have praised Ssu-ma Ch'ien for his recognition of the knights, but this is because they regard them as "heroes of the people" who fought against the oppression of the feudalistic system.

[2] *Han Fei Tzu, chuan* 19, "Wu-tu."

they lived all their lives in barren hovels with vine-woven doors, wearing rough clothes, eating coarse food and scarcely enough of that. Yet, though it is over four hundred years since they died, their disciples have never tired of writing about them.

As for the wandering knights, though their actions may not conform to perfect righteousness, yet they are always true to their word. What they undertake they invariably fulfill; what they have promised they invariably carry out. Without thinking of themselves they hasten to the side of those who are in trouble, whether it means survival or destruction, life or death. Yet they never boast of their accomplishments but rather consider it a disgrace to brag of what they have done for others. So there is much about them which is worthy of admiration, particularly when trouble is something that comes to almost everyone some time.

The Grand Historian remarks: In ancient times Emperor Shun was caught in a burning granary and trapped in a well; I Yin was obliged to carry tripods and sacrificial stands; Fu Yüeh served as a convict laborer among the cliffs of Fu; Lü Shang was reduced to selling food at the Chi Ford; Kuan Chung was bound with fetters and handcuffs; Po-li Hsi tended cattle; Confucius was threatened at K'uang, and between Ch'en and Ts'ai he grew pale from hunger. All of these are what scholars call men of benevolence and followers of the Way. If even they encountered such misfortunes, how much more so must men of only ordinary character who are trying to make their way in a discordant and degenerate age? Surely the troubles *they* meet with will be too numerous to recount!

Ignorant people have a saying, "Why bother to understand benevolence and righteousness? Whoever does you some good must be a virtuous man!" Po-i hated the Chou dynasty and chose to starve on Shou-yang Mountain rather than serve under it, but Kings Wen and Wu did not give up their thrones on that account. Chih and Ch'iao were cruel and lawless bandits, yet their own followers never tired of singing their praises. From this we can see that "he who steals a fishhook gets his head chopped off, but he who steals a state becomes a great lord, and when one is a great lord, he automatically acquires benevolence and righteousness." [3] These are no empty words!

[3] *Chuang Tzu, chuan* 4, "Ch'ü-ch'ieh."

Men who stick fast to their doctrines and observe every minute principle of duty, though it means spending all their lives alone in the world, can hardly be discussed in the same breath with those who lower the tone of their discourse to suit the vulgar, bob along with the current of the times, and thereby acquire a glorious name. Yet among the knights of the common people there are men who are fair in their dealings and true to their promises, who will risk death for others without a thought to their own safety, and who are praised for their righteousness a thousand miles around. So they have their good points, too; they do not simply strive to get ahead at any price. Therefore when people find themselves in trouble they turn to these men for help and entrust their lives to them. Is it not just this sort of men that people mean when they talk about the "worthy" and the "eminent"? As a matter of fact, if we speak in terms of actual authority and power and the effect which their actions had *upon their own times,* the knights of the hamlets and villages so far surpass men like Chi Tz'u and Yüan Hsien that there is hardly any basis for comparison. And this is true mainly because their achievements were immediately apparent to everyone and because they were faithful to their word. How then can we say that the righteousness of these knights and retainers is insignificant?

It is no longer possible to discover anything about the knights of the common people in ancient times. In more recent ages there were men like Yen Ling and the princes of Meng-ch'ang, Ch'un-shen, P'ing-yüan, and Hsin-ling.[4] All of these men, because they were related to the ruling families of the time and could rely upon their wealth as landowners and high officials, were able to summon worthy men from all over the empire to be their retainers and thus achieve fame among the feudal lords. This is not to say that they themselves were not worthy men. But it is more like the case of a man "who shouts downwind. The sound of his voice is not necessarily increased in strength";[5] it is the force of the wind that bears it along.

---

[4] Yen Ling was a prince of Wu in the sixth century B.C. The other four men, often referred to as the Four Heroes, were princes of Ch'i, Ch'u, and Chao, and lived in the third century B.C. All were famous for their ability to attract large bands of retainers to their service.

[5] *Hsün Tzu, chuan* I, "Ch'üan-hsüeh."

Yet there were others, knights of the lanes and byways, who, though they had no such advantages, were so upright in conduct and careful of their honor that their reputation was known all over the empire and there was no one who did not praise them as worthy men. This is not quite so easy to do. Nevertheless, the Confucians and Mohists have brushed them all aside and failed to make any mention of them in their writings. As a result, the names of the knights of the common people who lived before the Ch'in have vanished like smoke and can no longer be known. I find this very regrettable indeed!

From what I myself have been able to learn, after the founding of the Han there were men like Chu Chia, T'ien Chung, Wang Kung, Chü Meng, and Kuo Hsieh who, although they sometimes ran afoul of the law in their day, were in their personal relations scrupulously honest and humble. Such qualities are surely worthy of praise. Their reputations were not founded on air and it was not without reason that men gathered about them.

On the other hand, when it comes to those who band together in cliques and powerful family groups, pooling their wealth and making the poor serve them, arrogantly and cruelly oppressing the weak and helpless, giving free rein to their own desires and treating people any way they please—such men the wandering knights despise even as others do. I am grieved that so many people of my day do not take the trouble to examine the intentions of the knights, but foolishly consider Chu Chia, Kuo Hsieh, and the others to be in the same class as these cruel and arrogant men, and so ridicule both groups.

Chu Chia

Chu Chia of Lu was a contemporary of Emperor Kao-tsu, but while most of the men of Lu were teachers of Confucianism, Chu Chia won fame as a knight. He sheltered and concealed hundreds of eminent men in his house, thus saving them from their enemies, while the ordinary men among his followers were too numerous to mention. Yet all his life he never boasted of his abilities nor bragged of the favors he had done for others. On the contrary, his only fear was that the people he had once aided might come to see him and try to repay him. In helping men who were in need, he considered first those who were poor and humble. He and the members of his family had little money, they wore no fine clothes, their food was simple, and their carriage nothing more than an oxcart. He spent all his time hastening to the side of others who were in trouble, considering their well-being more important than his own. Once he concealed General Chi Pu, who was fleeing from the anger of Emperor Kao-tsu, but later, when Chi Pu became honored at the Han court, Chu Chia never made any attempt to see him again. Among the people living east of the Pass there were none who did not stretch forth their necks, longing to become friends with Chu Chia.

T'ien Chung of Ch'u won a reputation as a knight and loved swordsmanship. He looked up to Chu Chia like a father and considered that he himself could never equal Chu Chia's deeds.

Chü Meng

After T'ien Chung died, there was Chü Meng of Lo-yang. The men of the old region of Chou rely mostly on commerce for their livelihood, but Chü Meng won a name among the feudal lords by his daring and chivalrous deeds.

When the kings of Wu and Ch'u began their revolt, Chou Ya-fu, the marquis of T'iao, was made grand commandant of the Han armies and hastened by relay carriage east to Ho-nan, where he met Chü Meng. He was delighted and said, "Wu and Ch'u have embarked on a very serious undertaking, but since they have not sought your services, I am sure they will not be able to accomplish anything!" By this he meant that, at a time when the whole empire was in turmoil, the support of Chü Meng was worth more to him than the conquest of one of the rebel kingdoms. Chü Meng's conduct was much like that of Chu Chia except that he was fond of dice and other amusements of young people. Yet when his mother died, people came from great distances to attend the funeral, their carriages numbering as many as a thousand. When Chü Meng himself died, the wealth of his family did not amount to more than ten catties of gold.

There was also a man of Fu-li named Wang Meng who won fame as a knight in the region between the Yangtze and Huai rivers. At this time the Hsien family of Chi-nan and Chou Yung of Ch'en were both noted for their great power and influence. When Emperor Ching heard of this, he sent an envoy to execute all the members of their group. After this, various members of the Po clan of Tai, as well as Han Wu-pi of Liang, Hsieh K'uang of Yang-ti, and Han Ju of Chia, came to prominence.

Kuo Hsieh

Kuo Hsieh, whose polite name was Kuo Weng-po, was a native of Chih. He was a grandson on his mother's side of the famous physiognomist Hsü Fu, who was skilled at reading people's faces. Kuo Hsieh's father was executed in the time of Emperor Wen because of his activities as a knight.

Kuo Hsieh was short in stature and very quick-tempered; he did not drink wine. In his youth he was sullen, vindictive, and quick to anger when crossed in his will, and this led him to kill a great many people. In addition, he would take it upon himself to avenge the wrongs of his friends and conceal men who were fleeing from the law. He was constantly engaged in some kind of evil, robbing or assaulting people, while it would be impossible to say how many times he was guilty of counterfeiting money or looting graves. He met with extraordinary luck, however, and no matter what difficulties he found himself in, he always managed to escape or was pardoned by a general amnesty.

When he grew older, he had a change of heart and became much more upright in his conduct, rewarding hatred with virtue, giving generously and expecting little in return. In spite of this, he took more and more delight in daring and chivalrous actions. Whenever he had saved someone's life, he would never boast of his achievements. At heart he was still as ill-tempered as ever, however, and his meanness would often flare forth in a sudden angry look. The young men of the time emulated his actions and would often take it upon themselves to avenge his wrongs without telling him.

The son of Kuo Hsieh's elder sister, relying upon Hsieh's power and position, was once drinking with a man and tried to make him drink up all the wine. Though the man protested that it was more than he could do, Hsieh's nephew threatened him and forced him to drain the cup. In anger the man drew his sword, stabbed and killed the nephew, and ran away.

Hsieh's sister was furious. "For all my brother's so-called sense of duty," she exclaimed, "he allows his own nephew to be murdered and won't even go after the culprit!" Then she threw her son's corpse into the street and refused to bury it, hoping to shame Hsieh into action.

Kuo Hsieh sent men to discover where the murderer was hiding and the latter, fearful of the consequences, returned of his own accord and reported to Hsieh exactly what had happened. "You were quite right to kill my nephew," said Hsieh. "He was at fault!" Then he let the murderer go and, laying the blame for the incident entirely on his nephew, took the corpse away and buried it. When men heard of this, they all admired Hsieh's righteousness and flocked about him in increasing numbers.

Whenever Kuo Hsieh came or went, people were careful to get out of his way. Once, however, there was a man who, instead of moving aside, merely sat sprawled by the road and stared at Hsieh. Hsieh sent someone to ask the man's name. Hsieh's retainers wanted to kill the man on the spot, but Hsieh told them, "If I am not respected in the village where I live, it must be that my virtue is insufficient to command respect. What fault has this man committed?" Then he sent secret instructions to the military officials of the district, saying, "This man is very important to me. Whenever his turn comes for military service, see that he is let off!"

As a result, the man was let off from military service every time his turn came, and the officials made no attempt to look for him. The man was baffled by this and asked the reason, whereupon he discovered that Hsieh had instructed that he be excused. The man then went to Hsieh and, baring his arms, humbly apologized for his former disrespect. When the young men of the district heard of this, they admired Hsieh's conduct even more.

In Lo-yang there were two men who were carrying on a feud and, although ten or more of the worthy and eminent residents of the city had tried to act as mediators between them, they refused to listen to talk of a settlement. Someone came to ask Kuo Hsieh to help in the matter and he went at night to visit the hostile families, who finally gave in and agreed to listen to Hsieh's arguments. Then he told them, "I have heard that the gentlemen of Lo-yang have attempted to act as mediators, but that you have refused to listen to any of them. Now, fortunately, you have consented to pay attention to me. However, I would certainly not want it to appear that I came here from another district and tried to steal authority from the virtuous men of your own city!" He therefore went away the same night so that people would not know of his visit, telling the feuding families, "Pay no attention to my advice for a while and wait until I have gone. Then let the eminent men of Lo-yang act as your mediators and do as they say!"

Kuo Hsieh was very respectful in his behavior and would never venture to ride in a carriage when entering the office of his district. He would often journey to neighboring provinces or kingdoms in answer to some request for aid. In such cases, if he thought he could accomplish what had been asked of him, he would undertake to do so, but if he thought the request was impossible, he would go to pains to explain the reasons to the satisfaction of the other party, and only then would he consent to accept food and wine. As a result, people regarded him with great awe and respect and vied with each other in offering him their services. Every night ten or more carriages would arrive at his gate bearing young men of the town or members of the eminent families of neighboring districts who had come begging to be allowed to take some of Hsieh's guests and retainers into their own homes.

When the order went out for powerful and wealthy families in the provinces to be moved to the city of Mou-ling, Kuo Hsieh's family was exempted, since his wealth did not come up to the specified amount.[6] He was so well known, however, that the officials were afraid they would get into trouble if they did not order him to move. General Wei Ch'ing spoke to the emperor on his behalf, explaining that Kuo Hsieh's wealth was not sufficient to require him to move. But the emperor replied, "If this commoner has enough influence to get you to speak

[6] Emperor Wu had established his mausoleum at Mou-ling, and in 127 B.C. he ordered that rich and powerful families (those whose wealth exceeded three million cash) be moved there from other parts of the empire. The purpose of this was to populate the town and at the same time to break the power of the big provincial families and settle them near the capital where they could be more easily watched.

for him, general, he cannot be so very poor!" So in the end Kuo Hsieh's family was ordered to move, and the people who came to see him off presented him with over ten million cash as a farewell gift.

The man who was responsible for originally recommending Kuo Hsieh for transportation to Mou-ling was a district official named Yang, the son of Yang Chi-chu of Chih. In retaliation for this, the son of Kuo Hsieh's elder brother cut off the head of the Yang official, and as a result the Yang and the Kuo families became bitter enemies.

After Kuo Hsieh entered the Pass, the worthy and eminent men within the Pass, both those who had known him before and those who had not, soon learned of his reputation and vied with each other in making friends with him.[7]

Some time after this, Yang Chi-chu, the father of the official who had recommended that Hsieh be moved to Mou-ling, was murdered. The Yang family sent a letter of protest to the throne, but someone murdered the bearer of the letter outside the gate of the imperial palace. When the emperor learned of this, he sent out the law officials to arrest Kuo Hsieh. Hsieh fled and, leaving his mother and the other members of his family at Hsia-yang, escaped to Lin-chin.

Chi Shao-kung, who had charge of the pass at Lin-chin, had never known Kuo Hsieh and therefore, when Hsieh assumed a false name and asked to be allowed to go through the pass, Chi Shao-kung gave him permission. From there Hsieh turned and entered the region of T'ai-yüan. Whenever Hsieh stopped anywhere in his flight, he would make his destination known to his host, so that as a result the law officials were able to trail him without difficulty. When his trail led to Chi Shao-kung, however, Chi Shao-kung committed suicide to keep from having to give any information.

After some time, Kuo Hsieh was captured, and a thorough investigation made of all his crimes. It was found, however, that all the murders he had committed had taken place before the last amnesty.

There was a certain Confucian scholar from Chih who was sitting with the imperial envoys at Kuo Hsieh's investigation. When one of Hsieh's retainers praised Hsieh, the Confucian scholar remarked, "Kuo Hsieh does nothing but commit crimes and break the law! How can

---

[7] The thirteen characters which follow in the text do not belong here and have been omitted in the translation.

anyone call him a worthy man?" The retainer happened to overhear his words and later killed the Confucian scholar and cut out his tongue. The law officials tried to lay the blame on Hsieh, though as a matter of fact he did not know who had committed the murder. The murderer disappeared, and in the end no one ever found out who he was.

The officials finally submitted a report to the throne declaring that Hsieh was innocent of the charges brought against him, but the imperial secretary Kung-sun Hung objected, saying, "Hsieh, although a commoner, has taken the authority of the government into his own hands in his activities as a knight, killing anyone who gave him so much as a cross look. Though he did not know the man who murdered the Confucian scholar, his guilt is greater than if he had done the crime himself. He should be condemned as a treasonable and unprincipled criminal!" In the end Kuo Hsieh and all the members of his family were executed.

After this there were a great many men who acted as knights, but they were an arrogant lot and hardly worth mentioning. In the area within the Pass there was Fan Chung-tzu of Ch'ang-an, Chao Wangsun of Huai-li, Kao Kung-tzu of Ch'ang-ling, Kuo Kung-chung of Hsi-ho, Lu Kung-ju of T'ai-yüan, Erh Ch'ang-ch'ing of Lin-huai, and T'ien Chün-ju of Tung-yang, but although they acted as knights, they were rather timid and retiring and had the manners of gentlemen. Others such as the Yao family of the northern region, the various members of the Tu family of the west, Ch'ou Ching of the southern region, Chao T'o-yü Kung-tzu of the east, and Chao T'iao of Nan-yang, were no more than robbers and brigands of the lowest sort and certainly do not deserve to be treated here. To do so would only be an insult to former men such as Chu Chia.

The Grand Historian remarks: I have seen Kuo Hsieh, and I can report that in looks and bearing he hardly measured up to the average man, while nothing he said was worth remembering. Yet throughout the empire both worthy men and base men, those who knew him and those who did not, all admire his reputation and whenever they talk about the knights, they always cite his name. There is a common saying, "The real looks of a man lie in his reputation, for that will never die!" Alas, that he met with such an end!

Shih chi 125: The Biographies of the Emperors' Male Favorites

Those who served the ruler and succeeded in delighting his ears and eyes, those who caught their lord's fancy and won his favor and intimacy, did so not only through the power of lust and love; each had certain abilities in which he excelled. Thus I made The Biographies of the Emperors' Male Favorites.

The proverb says, "No amount of toiling in the fields can compare to a spell of good weather; no amount of faithful service can compare to being liked by your superiors." This is no idle saying. Yet it is not women alone who can use their looks to attract the eyes of the ruler; courtiers and eunuchs can play at that game as well. Many were the men of ancient times who gained favor in this way.

When the Han arose, Emperor Kao-tsu, for all his coarseness and blunt manners, was won by the charms of a young boy named Chi, and Emperor Hui had a boy favorite named Hung. Neither Chi nor Hung had any particular talent or ability; both won prominence simply by their looks and graces. Day and night they were by the ruler's side, and all the high ministers were obliged to apply to them when they wished to speak to the emperor. As a result all the palace attendants at the court of Emperor Hui took to wearing caps with gaudy feathers and sashes of seashells and to painting their faces, transforming themselves into a veritable host of Chis and Hungs. Both young men were ordered to move from their native places and to take up residence at An-ling, where Emperor Hui had his mausoleum.

The gentlemen who enjoyed favor in the palace under Emperor Wen included a courtier named Teng T'ung and the eunuchs Chao T'an and Pei-kung Po-tzu. Pei-kung Po-tzu was a worthy and affectionate man, while Chao T'an attracted the emperor's attention by his skill in observing the stars and exhalations in the sky; both of them customarily rode about in the same carriage with Emperor Wen. Teng T'ung does not seem to have had any special talent.

Teng T'ung was a native of Nan-an in the province of Shu. Because he knew how to pole a boat he was made a yellow-capped boatman in the grounds of the imperial palace.

Once Emperor Wen dreamed that he was trying to climb to Heaven but could not seem to make his way up. Just then a yellow-capped boatman boosted him from behind and he was able to reach Heaven. When the emperor turned around to look at the man, he noticed that the seam of the boatman's robe was split in the back just below the sash.

After the emperor awoke, he went to the Terrace of Lapping Water, which stood in the middle of the Azure Lake, and began to search furtively for the man who had boosted him up in his dream. There he saw Teng T'ung, who happened to have a tear in the back of his robe exactly like that of the man in the dream. The emperor summoned him and asked his name, and when he learned that the man's family name was Teng [ascend] and his personal name T'ung [reach], the emperor was overjoyed. From this time on, the emperor bestowed ever-increasing favor and honor upon Teng T'ung.

Teng T'ung for his part behaved with great honesty and circumspection in his new position. He cared nothing about mingling with people outside the palace and, though the emperor granted him holidays to return to his home, he was always reluctant to leave. As a result, the emperor showered him with gifts until his fortunes mounted to tens of billions of cash and he had been promoted to the post of superior lord. The emperor from time to time even paid visits to Teng T'ung's home to amuse himself there.

Teng T'ung, however, had no other talent than this of entertaining the emperor and was never able to do anything to advance others at court. Instead he bent all his efforts toward maintaining his own position and ingratiating himself with the emperor.

Once the emperor summoned a man who was skilled at physiognomizing and asked him to examine Teng T'ung's face. "This man will become poor and die of starvation," the physiognomist announced. "But *I* am the one who has made him rich!" exclaimed the emperor. "How could he ever become poor?" With this, he presented Teng

T'ung with the rights to a range of copper-bearing mountains in the Yen region of Shu Province and allowed him to mint copper coins for himself until the so-called Teng family cash were circulating all over the empire. Such was the wealth which Teng T'ung acquired.

Once Emperor Wen was troubled by a tumor, and Teng T'ung made it his duty to keep it sucked clean of infection. The emperor was feeling depressed by his illness and, apropos of nothing in particular, asked Teng T'ung, "In all the empire, who do you think loves me most?"

"Surely no one loves Your Majesty more than the heir apparent!" replied Teng T'ung.

Later, when the heir apparent came to inquire how his father was, the emperor made him suck the tumor. The heir apparent managed to suck it clean, but it was obvious from his expression that he found the task distasteful. Afterward, when he learned that Teng T'ung had been in the habit of sucking the tumor for the emperor, he was secretly filled with shame. From this time on he bore a grudge against Teng T'ung.

After Emperor Wen passed away and the heir apparent, Emperor Ching, came to the throne, Teng T'ung retired from court and returned to his home. He had not been there any time, however, when someone reported to the throne that he was guilty of smuggling cash which he had minted across the border to the barbarians. He was handed over to the law officials for investigation and it was found that the evidence for the most part supported the charges. In the end he was condemned and all of his fortune was confiscated by the government. Even so, it was claimed that his wealth was insufficient to cover the damages and that he still owed the government several hundred million more cash. Emperor Ching's older sister Princess Ch'ang presented Teng T'ung with a gift of money, but the officials immediately seized this as well, until Teng T'ung was not left with so much as a pin to hold his cap on. After this Princess Ch'ang provided him with food and clothing in the form of a loan so that it could not be confiscated. In the end Teng T'ung did not have a single copper cash to call his own, and died as a dependent in someone else's home.

Emperor Ching did not have any particular favorites among the officials at his court. There was one man, a chief of palace attendants named Chou Wen-jen, who enjoyed rather more favor than ordinary men, but even so it was nothing very extraordinary. Among the favorites of the present emperor were the courtier Hann Yen, the great grandson of Hsin, the king of Hann, and the eunuch Li Yen-nien.

Hann Yen was an illegitimate grandson of Hann T'ui-tang, the marquis of Kung-kao. When the present emperor was still king of Chiao-tung, he and Yen studied writing together and the two grew very fond of each other. Later, after the emperor was appointed heir apparent, he became more and more friendly with Yen. Yen was skillful at riding and archery and was also very good at ingratiating himself with the emperor. He was well versed in the fighting techniques of the barbarians and therefore, after the emperor came to the throne and began making plans to open attacks on the Hsiung-nu, he treated Yen with even greater respect and honor. Yen had soon advanced to the rank of superior lord and received as many gifts from the ruler as Teng T'ung had in his days of honor.

At this time Yen was constantly by the emperor's side, both day and night. Once the emperor's younger brother Liu Fei, the king of Chiang-tu, who had come to court to pay his respects, received permission from the emperor to accompany him on a hunt in the Shang-lin Park. The order had already been given to clear the roads for the imperial carriage, but the emperor was not yet ready to depart, and so he sent Yen ahead in one of the attendant carriages, accompanied by fifty or a hundred riders, to gallop through the park and observe the game. The king of Chiang-tu, seeing the party approaching in the distance, supposed it was the emperor and ordered his own attendants off the road while he himself knelt down by the side of the road to greet the emperor. Yen, however, raced by without even noticing him, and after he had passed, when the king of Chiang-tu realized his error, he was enraged and went to the empress dowager in tears. "I beg to return the kingdom which has been granted to me and become a bodyguard in the palace," he said. "Perhaps then I may be accorded as much honor as Hann Yen!" From this time on the empress dowager bore a grudge against Yen.

Because he attended the emperor, Hann Yen was allowed to come and go in the women's quarters of the palace and did not have to observe the customary prohibitions against entering them. Some time later, it was reported to the empress dowager that Yen had had an illicit affair with one of the women there. She was furious and immediately sent a messenger ordering him to take his life. Although the emperor attempted to make apologies for him, he was able to do nothing to change the order, and in the end Yen was forced to die. His younger brother Hann Yüeh, the marquis of An-tao, also managed to win great favor with the emperor.

Li Yen-nien was a native of Chung-shan. His mother and father, as well as he and his brothers and sisters, were all originally singers. Li Yen-nien, having been convicted of some crime and condemned to castration, was made a keeper of the dogs in the palace. Later, the princess of P'ing-yang recommended his younger sister Lady Li to the emperor because of her skill in dancing. When the emperor saw her, he took a liking to her and had her installed in the women's quarters of the palace, at the same time summoning Li Yen-nien to an audience and appointing him to a higher post.

Li Yen-nien was a good singer and knew how to compose new tunes. At this time the emperor wanted some hymns set to music and arranged with string accompaniment to be used in the sacrifices to Heaven and Earth which he had initiated. Li Yen-nien accepted the task and performed it to the emperor's satisfaction, composing melodies and string accompaniments for the new words that had been written. Meanwhile his sister, Lady Li, bore the emperor a son.

Li Yen-nien by this time wore the seals of a two thousand picul official and bore the title of "Harmonizer of Tunes." Day and night he was by the emperor's side and his honor and favor equaled that which Hann Yen had formerly enjoyed.

When some years had passed, his younger brother Li Chi began carrying on an affair with one of the palace ladies and becoming more and more arrogant and careless in his behavior.[1] After the death of Lady Li, the emperor's affection for the Li brothers waned, and he ended by having them arrested and executed.

[1] Following the reading in *Han shu* 93. The *Shih chi* text reads as though Li Yen-nien himself were carrying on the affair, which would hardly be likely.

From this time on, the courtiers who enjoyed special favor with the emperor were for the most part members of the families related to the emperor by marriage, but none of them are worth discussing here. Wei Ch'ing and Ho Ch'ü-ping, who were in-laws of the emperor, also won great honor and favor, but in their case their advancement was due primarily to their talents and abilities.

The Grand Historian remarks: How violent are the seasons of love and hatred! By observing the fate of Mi Tzu-hsia, we can guess what will happen to favorites of later times. "Even the future a hundred ages hence may be foretold!" [2]

[2] The last sentence is a quotation from the *Analects* II, 23. The story of Mi Tzu-hsia is related by Han Fei Tzu and is quoted in Han Fei Tzu's biography in *Shih chi* 63. As it is told there, Mi Tzu-hsia was much loved by the lord of Wei in ancient times. Once when Mi Tzu-hsia heard that his mother was ill, he forged an order from the ruler and went to visit her in the royal carriage of Wei, though he knew that the penalty for such an action was amputation of the feet. The lord of Wei, however, simply praised the young man for his filial piety. Another time Mi Tzu-hsia was strolling in an orchard with the ruler and, biting into a peach and finding it tasty, he offered the remainder to his lord. "How deep is your love for me!" exclaimed the lord of Wei. "You forget your own appetite and think only of me!" Later, however, Mi Tzu-hsia's looks faded, and the ruler ceased to care for him and found some excuse to condemn him to punishment. "After all," said the lord of Wei, "he once stole my carriage, and another time he gave me a half-eaten peach to eat!"

Shih chi 127: The Biographies of the Diviners of Lucky Days

The customs of the diviners of lucky days differ in the regions of Ch'i, Ch'u, Ch'in, and Chao. In order to present a systematic survey of their general methods, I made The Biographies of the Diviners of Lucky Days.[1]

From ancient times the rulers who have received the mandate and become kings always seem to have consulted the tortoise shells or the milfoil stalks in order to determine the will of Heaven. The custom was certainly much in use during the Chou dynasty, and we have evidence that it was continued under the Ch'in. When the king of Tai, who became Emperor Wen, was considering whether or not to journey to the capital to take the throne, he left the decision up to the diviner. The office of court grand diviner originated at the beginning of the Han dynasty.

Ssu-ma Chi-chu[2] was a native of Ch'u who practiced divination in the eastern market of Ch'ang-an. Once Sung Chung, a palace counselor under Emperor Wen, and the erudit Chia I, their bath and hair washing days having fallen on the same day, left the palace together to return to their homes. As they proceeded on their way they began discussing the *Book of Changes,* which they regarded as the embodiment of the wisdom of the ancient kings and sages and the key to an under-

---

[1] This chapter has long been eyed with suspicion. Though Ssu-ma Ch'ien says in his summary that he has discussed the diviners of Ch'i, Ch'u, Ch'in, and Chao, the chapter contains only one account concerning a diviner from Ch'u, supplemented by notes (not translated here) which were added to the chapter by Ch'u Shao-sun some years after Ssu-ma Ch'ien's death. For these reasons many critics have maintained that Ch'ien never got around to writing the chapter he had planned, and that what we have today is from another hand. Regardless of its authorship or reliability as history, it is a fine piece of writing done in the vivid, novelistic style typical of early Chinese philosophical literature.

[2] His personal name, Chi-chu, may be interpreted to mean "Master of the Seasons."

standing of all human affairs, debating its meaning, quoting passages from the Classic, and gazing at each other and sighing.

"I have heard it said," remarked Chia I, "that the sages of antiquity, if they did not hold positions at court, were invariably to be found among the ranks of diviners and doctors. Now I am already acquainted with all the high ministers and court officials and I know what they are like. Let us try searching among the diviners and see what sort of men we can find."

The two men then got into a carriage and drove to the market, where they strolled among the diviners' stalls. It had just begun to rain and there were few people in the street. Ssu-ma Chi-chu was sitting at leisure, attended by three or four of his students, expounding to them the way of heaven and earth, the movements of the sun and moon, and the origin of the good and bad influences of the yin and yang.

Sung Chung and Chia I bowed twice before him and requested an interview. Ssu-ma Chi-chu examined their appearance and, deciding that they looked like intelligent men, greeted them and ordered his students to spread mats for them to sit down. After the two had taken their seats, he repeated his earlier discussion, explaining the cycles of heaven and earth and the movements of the sun, moon, stars, and constellations, distinguishing the signs of good and evil fortune. He spoke at considerable length, and nothing he said was contrary to reason.

Sung Chung and Chia I were struck with wonder and, realizing that he was no ordinary man, they tightened the strings of their hats, arranged their robes, and sat up straight on their mats, saying, "We have observed your appearance, master, and listened to your words and, limited as our experience in the world may be, we have never met anyone like you before! Why, may we ask, do you live in a humble place like this and pursue such a disreputable occupation?"

Ssu-ma Chi-chu clasped his belly and gave an enormous laugh. "From looking at you two gentlemen," he said, "I supposed you must know something about the arts of the Way. But now what stupid things you say! What a barbarous manner of speech! Just what occupation, may I ask, do you consider worthy and what kind of person do you look up to? What do you mean by calling one of your elders humble and disreputable?"

"The world looks up to men who occupy high posts and receive generous stipends," replied the two courtiers, "and therefore men of worth and talent are to be found in such positions. But your present position is certainly quite different, and so we spoke of it as lowly. The words of a diviner cannot be trusted, the value of his actions cannot be verified, and he gets his living by unjust means. Therefore we said that your occupation was disreputable. It is the custom of the world to despise and make light of diviners. People all say, 'Oh, the diviners—all they do is talk exaggerated and imposing nonsense to play on people's feelings, make absurdly glorious predictions about people's fates to delight them, invent stories about disasters to fill their hearts with fear, and babble lies about the spirits to get all their money away from them, demanding generous rewards so they can line their own pockets!' Such actions we consider disgraceful, and therefore we spoke of your occupation as disreputable."

"Gentlemen, make yourselves comfortable and listen a while," said Ssu-ma Chi-chu. "Do you see that little boy there with his hair not yet bound up? When the sun and the moon are shining, he goes out for a walk, but when they are not shining he stays home. But if you were to ask him about the eclipses or the lucky and unlucky seasons of the sun and moon, he could not explain the reasons for them. In the same way, those who can distinguish clearly between worthy and unworthy men are few indeed.

"It is the way of a worthy man to follow what is right and speak out against what he believes to be wrong, but if after admonishing the ruler three times he finds that he is not being heeded, then he will retire from office. When he praises others he has no reward in mind, and when he hates others it is not because of personal grudges; his only concern is what will benefit the nation and profit the mass of people. Therefore, if he is not fitted for a particular post, he will not occupy it, and if he feels that his stipend is greater than he deserves, he will not accept it. He will refuse to respect men who do wrong, no matter how eminent they may be; he will not humble himself before corrupt men, no matter how high their position. He does not rejoice if he is appointed to a post, nor has he any regrets if he must leave it. As long as he himself is not at fault, he will feel no shame no matter what disgraces are heaped upon him.

"But what *you* have called worthy men—they are the ones who ought to be ashamed! Bowing and scraping, they appear before the ruler; fawning and flattering, they speak their piece. Banding together for greater power, leading each other on with promises of profit, they flock together into cliques to drive out honest men. Seeking position and fame, living off the public funds, they devote themselves to private advantage, pervert the ruler's laws, and prey upon the farmers. Using their offices to terrorize others, taking advantage of the power of the law, they seek by every violent and unlawful means to win gain. They are in fact no different from a bunch of bandits who swoop down upon men with drawn swords!

"When they are first put in office for a trial period, they exaggerate their influence with clever deceits and build an imposing façade of achievement with false reports in order to deceive the ruler. They pride themselves upon their high positions and refuse to let worthy men have a try in office. In enumerating their achievements they puff up truth with falsehood, make something out of nothing, and convert little into much, seeking to increase their power and better their positions. While they dash about the countryside feasting and drinking, accompanied by ladies in waiting and singing boys, they disregard the welfare of their parents, break the laws, oppress the people, and waste the resources of the ruling house. They rob without depending upon spears and arrows, plunder without resorting to bows and blades. Though they swindle their parents, they go unpunished; though they assassinate their lords, they are not struck down. How can you look up to such men and call them worthy and talented?

"When bandits appear, such officials are powerless to put them down; though the barbarian tribes are disobedient, they cannot control them. Evil arises and they are incapable of stopping it; corruption and disorder appear among the lower officials and they cannot stamp them out. They are unable to restore harmony to the four seasons, helpless to take proper measures when the harvests are poor. If they are indeed talented and worthy and yet fail to do these things, then they are guilty of disloyalty. And if they are occupying their posts without having any talent or worth, profiting from the ruler's stipends and blocking the way for really worthy men, then they are simply thieves of high office. Recommending others only because of their influence, being polite to men because of their wealth—this is simply hypocrisy. Having you not seen such owls and kites soaring side by side with the phoenixes? [3] Have you not seen the orchid and the spikenard cast out on the broad plain, while the common artemisia flourishes in groves? It is you and your like who cause the truly worthy gentlemen to retire into obscurity!

"It is the business of the gentleman to be 'a transmitter and not a maker.' [4] Now the diviner invariably takes heaven and earth as his pattern and the four seasons as his model. Conforming to benevolence and righteousness, he divides the milfoil stalks and determines the hexagram, revolves the divining instrument and calculates the correct formula. Only then does he venture to discuss what is profitable and unprofitable in heaven and earth or to predict the success or failure of undertakings.

"In ancient times, when the former kings managed the affairs of the state, they invariably consulted the tortoise or the milfoil stalks and observed the sun and moon before undertaking the charge of Heaven. Only after determining the correct hour and day did they come and go. When a child is born to a family, the father divines to see whether its future will be lucky or unlucky before deciding whether to rear it. Ever since Fu Hsi devised the eight trigrams and King Wen of the Chou expanded them with the three hundred and eighty-four explanations of the lines, the world has been well ordered. Kou-chien, the king of Yüeh, by imitating the eight trigrams of King Wen, was able to defeat his enemies and become one of the dictators of China. In view of all this, what fault can you find with the arts of divination?

"Moreover, when the diviner sets to work, he first sweeps a place and spreads his mat, straightens his hat and arranges his sash, and only then does he begin to discuss business. So the diviner has a sense

[3] The owls and kites are metaphors for evil men, the phoenix a metaphor for the man of true worth.

[4] A reference to Confucius' description of himself in *Analects* VII, 1.

of propriety. As a result of his words, offerings are made to the gods and spirits, loyal ministers serve their lords, filial sons look after their parents, and affectionate fathers take care of their sons. These are the virtues the diviner confers. And for all these benefits he is paid with twenty or thirty or a hundred cash!

"As a result of his instructions the sick are somtimes made well, those in mortal danger are saved from death, and those in distress are freed from their worries. Undertakings are brought to a successful conclusion, sons and daughters are happily married off, and people live to a ripe old age. Are such virtues as these worth no more than a handful of coins? This is what Lao Tzu meant when he said, 'The man of superior virtue does not appear to have any virtue; therefore he keeps his virtue.' [5] Now if the diviner confers such great benefits as these and receives such a small recompense, is he any different from the man Lao Tzu is describing?

"Chuang Tzu has said, 'At home the gentleman does not worry about cold and hunger; abroad he has no fear of being robbed. If he is in a superior position he commands respect; if in an inferior one he suffers no harm. This is the way of the gentleman.' [6] Now the diviner in pursuing his profession does not need to gather together a lot of equipment, nor does he require a storehouse to keep his goods. When he travels he does not have to have baggage carts to move the tools of his trade; he may carry them on his back and they are not heavy. He puts them down any place and is ready to start; he uses them as often as he likes and they never give out. Bearing in his hands such inexhaustible tools, traveling the endless reaches of the world— even Chuang Tzu's gentleman could do no better than this! Why then do you tell me that divination is worthless?

"Heaven sags in the northwest, and therefore the stars and constellations move in that direction; earth slumps in the southeast, and so the waters all flow there to form a great lake. The moment the sun reaches the meridian, it begins to move on; as soon as the moon is full, it starts to wane. The way of the ancient kings sometimes flourishes in the world and sometimes is lost. You attack the diviners and demand

[5] Lao Tzu, *Tao-te-ching* 34.
[6] No such passage is found in the present text of the *Chuang Tzu*.

that everything they say must be true, but are you yourselves not de-luded in thinking so?

"Surely, gentlemen, you have observed the rhetoricians and orators. All their plans and schemes are simply the products of their own minds. But if they merely blurted out their own ideas they could never capture the imagination of the ruler. Therefore they always begin their speeches by discussing the kings of antiquity and open their orations with a description of ancient times. In setting forth their schemes and plans they make up elaborate tales about the successes of the former kings or tell about their failures, in order to move the ruler to ad-miration or fear and thereby achieve their objective. When it comes to talking exaggerated and imposing nonsense, as you put it, no one can match them. Yet if one wishes to strengthen the state, insure the success of the ruler, and fulfill his duty as a loyal minister, he must resort to such means or his words will never be heeded.

"It is the diviner's job to guide people who are confused and to teach the ignorant. And when one is dealing with confused and ig-norant people, how can one make them understand in a word or two? Therefore the diviner does not hesitate to speak at length.

"The fleet-footed stallion cannot be harnessed with the worn-out nag; the phoenix does not fly with the flocks of little sparrows. No more so, therefore, does the worthy man stand side by side with the unworthy. Hence the true gentleman hides away in a lowly position in order to avoid the crowd, retires in order to sever his relations with other men, and reveals only a glimmer of his true virtue so as to escape the envy of the masses. In this way he makes clear the heavenly nature of men, assists the governors, and nourishes the governed. He achieves great merit and profit, but does not seek for high position or praise. Men like you with your gaping and gabbling, what do you know about the way of the superior man?"

Sung Chung and Chia I sat listening in bewildered amazement. Their heads swam and the color drained from their faces; their mouths fell open and they could not answer a word. Finally they straightened their robes and, rising from their mats, bowed twice and took their leave. They wandered down the street in a daze, and when they emerged from the gate of the market place they could barely pull themselves up into their carriage. Leaning upon the carriage bar, their heads hanging low, they could not seem to recover their spirits.

Three days later Sung Chung met Chia I outside the gate of the palace. Drawing him aside where they could speak without being overheard, he sighed and said, "The greater one's understanding of the Way, the more security he enjoys; but the greater one's power, the more danger threatens him. When a man enjoys such great power and influence as you and I, the day of his downfall cannot be far off! The diviner, even if he makes a false prediction, does not have his wages taken away from him. But if those who lay plans for the ruler make a mistake, there is no place where they can hide. In this respect we and Ssu-ma Chi-chu are as far apart as the hat that brushes heaven and the shoes that tread the earth. This is what Lao Tzu meant when he said, 'The nameless is the source of all creatures.' [7] Heaven and earth are broad, and the things of creation varied and manifold. At times safe, at times in peril, no one knows where to abide! How can you and I hope to imitate men like Ssu-ma Chi-chu? The longer he lives the greater safety he enjoys. Even Chuang Tzu's gentleman could do no better."

Some time later Sung Chung was sent as envoy to the Hsiung-nu. He returned to the capital without having carried out his mission, however, and was condemned to execution. Chia I was appointed tutor to King Huai of Liang, but when the king one day fell from his horse and was killed, Chia I refused to eat, and died of shame and remorse. So these two men, by striving only for the glory of the world, ended by destroying themselves.

The Grand Historian remarks: The reason I have not said anything here about the diviners of ancient times is that very little material can be found on them in the old books. In the case of Ssu-ma Chi-chu I have been able to gather enough information to write this account.

[7] Lao Tzu, *Tao-te-ching* 1. What Lao Tzu actually said was, "The nameless is the source of heaven and earth." By "nameless," needless to say, he meant the indescribable Tao, not unknown men like Ssu-ma Chi-chi living in humble obscurity, though this is the way Sung Chung and Chia I choose to interpret the passage.

Shih chi 129: The Biographies of the Money-makers [1]

Though only commoners with no special ranks or titles, they were able, without interfering with the government or hindering the activities of the people, to increase their wealth by making the right moves at the right time. Wise men will find something to learn from them. Thus I made The Biographies of the Money-makers.

Lao Tzu has said that under the ideal form of government, "though states exist side by side, so close that they can hear the crowing of each other's cocks and the barking of each other's dogs, the people of each state will savor their own food, admire their own clothing, be content with their own customs, and delight in their own occupations, and will grow old and die without ever wandering abroad." [2] Yet if one were to try to apply this type of government, striving to drag the present age back to the conditions of primitive times and to stop up the eyes and ears of the people, it is doubtful that one would have much chance of success!

The Grand Historian remarks: I know nothing about the times of Shen-nung and before but, judging by what is recorded in the *Odes* and *Documents,* from the age of Emperor Shun and the Hsia dynasty down to the present, ears and eyes have always longed for the ultimate in beautiful sounds and forms, mouths have desired to taste the best in grass-fed and grain-fed animals, bodies have delighted in ease and comfort, and hearts have swelled with pride at the glories of power and ability. So long have these habits been allowed to permeate the lives of the people that, though one were to go from door to door

[1] The title of the chapter, *huo-chih,* literally "wealth increasing," is taken from Confucius' remark about his disciple Tzu-kung (discussed in this chapter): "Ts'e [Tzu-kung] does not acquiesce in his fate and his wealth increases" (*Analects* XI, 17). The chapter, containing as it does a great many technical terms and details of the economic life of the Han, is one of the most difficult in the *Shih chi,* and commentators differ on numerous points of interpretation.

[2] Lao Tzu, *Tao-te-ching* 80.

preaching the subtle arguments of the Taoists, he could never succeed in changing them. Therefore the highest type of ruler accepts the nature of the people, the next best leads the people to what is beneficial, the next gives them moral instruction, the next forces them to be orderly, and the very worst kind enters into competition with them.[3]

The region west of the mountains is rich in timber, paper mulberry, hemp, oxtails for banner tassels, jade and other precious stones. That east of the mountains abounds in fish, salt, lacquer, silk, singers, and beautiful women. The area south of the Yangtze produces camphor wood, catalpa, ginger, cinnamon, gold, tin, lead ore, cinnabar, rhinoceros horns, tortoise shell, pearls of various shapes, and elephant tusks and hides, while that north of Lung-men and Chieh-shih is rich in horses, cattle, sheep, felt, furs, tendons, and horns. Mountains from which copper and iron can be extracted are found scattered here and there over thousands of miles of the empire, like chessmen on a board. In general, these are the products of the empire. All of them are commodities coveted by the people of China, who according to their various customs use them for their bedding, clothing, food, and drink, fashioning from them the goods needed to supply the living and bury the dead.

Society obviously must have farmers before it can eat; foresters, fishermen, miners, etc., before it can make use of natural resources; craftsmen before it can have manufactured goods; and merchants before they can be distributed. But once these exist, what need is there for government directives, mobilizations of labor, or periodic assemblies? Each man has only to be left to utilize his own abilities and exert his strength to obtain what he wishes. Thus, when a commodity is very cheap, it invites a rise in price; when it is very expensive, it invites a reduction. When each person works away at his own occupation and delights in his own business then, like water flowing downward, goods will naturally flow forth ceaselessly day and night without having been summoned, and the people will produce commodities without having been asked. Does this not tally with reason? Is it not a natural result?

[3] A reference to Emperor Wu's economic policies, which put the government officials into competition with the people for profit. This whole chapter must be read in the light of the historian's earlier description of economic measures and conditions in "The Treatise on the Balanced Standard."

The *Book of Chou* says, "If the farmers do not produce, there will be a shortage of food; if the artisans do not produce, there will be a shortage of manufactured goods; if the merchants do not produce, then the three precious things will not circulate; if the foresters, fishermen, miners, etc., do not produce, there will be a shortage of wealth, and if there is a shortage of wealth the resources of the mountains and lakes cannot be exploited." [4] These four classes are the source of the people's clothing and food. When the source is large, there will be plenty for everyone, but when the source is small, there will be scarcity. On the one hand, the state will be enriched, and on the other, powerful families will be enriched. Poverty and wealth are not the sort of things that are arbitrarily handed to men or taken away: the clever have a surplus; the stupid never have enough.

At the beginning of the Chou dynasty, when the Grand Duke Wang was enfeoffed with Ying-ch'iu in the state of Ch'i, where the land was damp and brackish and the inhabitants few, he encouraged the women workers, developed the craft industries to the highest degree, and opened up a trade in fish and salt. As a result, men and goods were reeled into the state like skeins of thread; they converged upon it like spokes about a hub. Soon Ch'i was supplying caps and sashes, clothes and shoes to the whole empire, and the lords of the area between the sea and Mount T'ai adjusted their sleeves and journeyed to its court to pay their respects.

Later, the power of the state of Ch'i fell into decline, but Master Kuan Chung restored it to prosperity by establishing the nine bureaus for controlling the flow of money. As a result Duke Huan of Ch'i [685–643 B.C.] was able to become a dictator; nine times he called together the other feudal lords for conferences and set the empire to rights again. Moreover, Kuan Chung himself, though only a court minister, owned the mansion called the Three Returnings, [5] and his wealth exceeded that of the lord of a great feudal kingdom. Thus the

[4] No such quotation is found in the section of the *Book of Documents* devoted to the Chou dynasty or in the *I-chou-shu*. The "three precious things" are usually identified as the products of the other three classes, i.e., agricultural products, manufactured goods, and the products of mountains, lakes, etc.

[5] On the "Three Returnings" see the biography of the Marquis of P'ing-chin, note 1.

state of Ch'i remained rich and powerful through the reigns of Wei and Hsüan [378–323 B.C.].

Therefore it is said, "Only when the granaries are full can people appreciate rites and obligations; only when they have enough food and clothing do they think about glory and disgrace."[6] Rites are born of plenty and are abandoned in time of want. When superior men become rich, they delight in practicing virtue; but when mean-minded men are rich, they long only to exercise their power. As fish by nature dwell in the deepest pools and wild beasts congregate in the most secluded mountains, so benevolence and righteousness attach themselves to a man of wealth. So long as a rich man wields power, he may win greater and greater eminence, but once his power is gone, his guests and retainers will all desert him and take no more delight in his company. This is even more the case among barbarians.

The proverb says, "The young man with a thousand catties of gold does not meet death in the market place."[7] This is no idle saying. So it is said,

> Jostling and joyous,
> The whole world comes after profit;
> Racing and rioting,
> After profit the whole world goes!

If even the king of a land of a thousand chariots, the lord of ten thousand households, or the master of a hundred dwellings must worry about poverty, how much more so the common peasant whose name is enrolled in the tax collector's list?

In former times when King Kou-chien of Yüeh [496–465 B.C.] was surrounded on Mount K'uai-chi by the armies of the state of Wu and was in great difficulty, he followed the advice of Fan Li and Chi-jan. Chi-jan said, "If you know there is going to be a battle, you must make preparations beforehand, and for ordinary use you must know what goods are needed in each season. When you understand these two

---

[6] The quotation is found in the opening paragraph of the *Kuan Tzu,* a text which purports to represent the sayings and theories of Kuan Chung.

[7] Commentators generally take this to mean that a son of a wealthy family has enough moral training to avoid breaking the law and thus incurring execution in the market place. Obviously, however, it may also be interpreted more cynically to mean that money can buy one's way out of any difficulties.

necessities clearly, then you can perceive how all kinds of goods should be disposed. When Jupiter is in the western portion of the sky, which is dominated by the element metal, there will be good harvests; when it is in the northern portion dominated by water, there will be destruction by floods; when it is in the eastern portion dominated by wood, there will be famine; and when in the southern portion dominated by fire, there will be drought. When there is a drought, that is the time to start laying away a stock of boats; and when there is a flood, that is the time to start buying up carts. This is the principle behind the use of goods.

"Every six years there will be a good harvest, every six years there will be a drought, and every twelve years there will be one great famine. If grain is sold as low as twenty cash a picul, then the farmers will suffer, but if it goes as high as ninety cash, then those in secondary occupations will suffer. If the merchants and others in secondary occupations suffer, then they will produce no goods, while if the farmers suffer they will cease to clear their fields. If, however, the price does not go over eighty cash nor fall below thirty, then both farmers and those in secondary occupations will benefit. If the price of grain is kept level and goods are fairly distributed, then there will be no shortages in the customs barriers and markets. This is the way to govern a country.

"The principle of storing goods is to try to get commodities which can be preserved for a long time without damage or depreciation [8] and can be easily exchanged for other things. Do not store up commodities that are likely to rot or spoil, and do not hoard expensive articles. If you study the surpluses and shortages of the market, you can judge how much a commodity will be worth. When an article has become extremely expensive, it will surely fall in price, and when it has become extremely cheap, then the price will begin to rise. Dispose of expensive goods as though they were so much filth and dirt; buy up cheap goods as though they were pearls and jade. Wealth and currency should be allowed to flow as freely as water!"

King Kou-chien followed this advice for the next ten years until the state of Yüeh became rich and he was able to give generous gifts to

[8] Following the reading in the So-yin and Cheng-i commentaries.

his fighting men. As a result, his soldiers were willing to rush into the face of the arrows and stones of the enemy as though they were thirsty men going to drink their fill; in the end King Kou-chien took his revenge upon the powerful forces of Wu, demonstrated his military might to the other states of China, and came to be known as one of the five dictators.

Fan Li, having helped to wipe out the shame of Yüeh's defeat at K'uai-chi, sighed and said, "Of Chi-jan's seven strategies, Yüeh made use of five and achieved its desires. They have already been put into practice in the state. Now I would like to try using them for my own family."

Then he got into a little boat and sailed down the Yangtze and through the lakes. He changed his family name and personal name and visited Ch'i, where he was known as Ch'ih-i Tzu-p'i, the "Adaptable Old Wine-skin." Later he went to T'ao, where he was called Lord Chu. He observed that T'ao, located in the middle of the empire, with feudal lords passing back and forth in all directions, was a center for the exchange of goods. He therefore established his business there, storing away goods, looking for a profitable time to sell, and not making demands upon others. (Thus one who is good at running a business must know how to select men and take advantage of the times.) In the course of nineteen years Fan Li, or Lord Chu, as he was now called, three times accumulated fortunes of a thousand catties of gold, and twice he gave them away among his poor friends and distant relations. This is what is meant by a rich man who delights in practicing virtue. Later, when he became old and frail, he turned over his affairs to his sons and grandsons, who carried on and improved the business until the family fortune had reached a hundred million cash. Therefore, when people speak of rich men they always mention T'ao Chu-kung, Lord Chu of T'ao.

Tzu-kung, after studying with Confucius, retired and held office in the state of Wei. By buying up, storing, and selling various goods in the region of Ts'ao and Lu, he managed to become the richest among Confucius' seventy disciples. While Yüeh Hsien, another of the Master's disciples, could not get even enough chaff and husks to satisfy his hunger, and lived hidden away in a tiny lane, Tzu-kung rode about with a team of four horses attended by a mounted retinue, bearing gifts of bundles of silk to be presented to the feudal lords, and whatever state he visited the ruler never failed to descend into the courtyard and greet him as an equal. It was due to Tzu-kung's efforts that Confucius' fame was spread over the empire. Is this not what we mean when we say that a man who wields power may win greater and greater eminence?

Po Kuei was a native of Chou. During the time of Marquis Wen of Wei [403–387 B.C.], Li K'o stressed full utilization of the powers of the land, but Po Kuei delighted in watching for opportunities presented by the changes of the times.

> What others throw away, I take;
> What others take, I give away,

he said. "When the year is good and the harvest plentiful, I buy up grain and sell silk and lacquer; when cocoons are on the market, I buy up raw silk and sell grain. When the reverse marker of Jupiter is in the sign *mao*,[9] the harvest will be good, but the following year the crops will do much worse. When it reaches the sign *wu*, there will be a drought, but the next year will be fine. When it reaches the sign *yu*, there will be good harvests, followed the next year by a falling off. When it reaches the sign *tzu*, there will be a great drought. The next year will be fine and later there will be floods. Thus the cycle revolves again to the sign *mao*."

By observing these laws, he was able to approximately double his stores of grain each year. When he wanted to increase his money

[9] Since Jupiter takes approximately twelve years to complete one cycle of the heavens, the years of the cycle were designated by the twelve signs that marked the division of the horizon, depending upon which portion of the sky Jupiter was in. But because Jupiter appeared to revolve counterclockwise through the sky, and the order of the twelve signs ran clockwise, an imaginary marker, called *sui-yin* or *t'ai-yin,* was postulated, which revolved in the opposite direction from Jupiter. As this works out, when the reverse marker was in *mao* (east), Jupiter was in *tzu* (north); when the marker was in *wu* (south), Jupiter was in *yu* (west); when the marker was in *yu* (west), Jupiter was in *wu* (south); and when the marker was in *tzu* (north), Jupiter was in *mao* (east). Hence Po Kuei is saying that when Jupiter is in the north or south, there will be good harvests; when it is in the west there will be drought; and when it is in the east there will be a great drought. The reader may compare this with Chi-jan's laws above.

supply, he bought cheap grain, and when he wanted to increase his stock, he bought up high-grade grain. He ate and drank the simplest fare, controlled his appetites and desires, economized on clothing, and shared the same hardships as his servants and slaves, and when he saw a good opportunity, he pounced on it like a fierce animal or a bird of prey. "As you see," he said, "I manage my business affairs in the same way that the statemen I Yin and Lü Shang planned their policies, the military experts Sun Tzu and Wu Tzu deployed their troops, and the Legalist philosopher Shang Yang carried out his laws. Therefore, if a man does not have wisdom enough to change with the times, courage enough to make decisions, benevolence enough to know how to give and take, and strength enough to stand his ground, though he may wish to learn my methods, I will never teach them to him!"

Hence, when the world talks of managing a business it acknowledges Po Kuei as the ancestor of the art. Po Kuei tried out his theories in practice, and his experiments proved successful. He knew what he was talking about.

I Tun rose to prominence by producing salt in ponds, while Kuo Tsung of Han-tan made a business of smelting iron, and their wealth equaled that of the ruler of a kingdom.

Wu-chih Lo raised domestic animals, and when he had a large number, he sold them and bought rare silks and other articles which he secretly sent as gifts to the king of the Jung barbarians. The king of the Jung repaid him ten times the original cost and sent him domestic animals until Wu-chih Lo had so many herds of horses and cattle he could only estimate their number roughly by the valleyful. The First Emperor of the Ch'in ordered that Wu-chih Lo be granted the same honors as a feudal lord and allowed him to join the ministers in seasonal audiences at court.

There was also the case of a widow named Ch'ing of the region of Pa and Shu. Her ancestors got possession of some cinnabar caves and were able to monopolize the profits from them for several generations until they had acquired an inestimable amount of wealth. Ch'ing, although only a widow, was able to carry on the business and used her wealth to buy protection for herself so that others could not mistreat or impose upon her. The First Emperor of the Ch'in, considering her a virtuous woman, treated her as a guest and built the Nü-huai-ch'ing Terrace in her honor.

Wu-chih Lo was a simple country man who looked after herds, while Ch'ing was only a widow living far off in the provinces, and yet both were treated with as much respect as though they had been the lords of a state of ten thousand chariots, and their fame spread all over the world. Was this not because of their wealth?

After the Han rose to power, the barriers and bridges were opened and the restrictions on the use of the resources of mountains and lakes were relaxed. As a result, the rich traders and great merchants traveled all around the empire distributing their wares to every corner so that everyone could buy what he wanted. At the same time the powerful families of the great provincial clans and former feudal lords were moved to the capital.

The area within the Pass,[10] from the Ch'ien and Yung rivers east to the Yellow River and Mount Hua, is a region of rich and fertile fields stretching a thousand *li*. Judging from the tribute exacted by Emperor Shun and the rulers of the Hsia dynasty, these were already at that time considered to be among the finest fields. Later the ancestor of the house of Chou, Kung Liu, made his home in Pin in the region; his descendants Ta-wang and Wang-chi lived in the area called Ch'i; King Wen built the city of Feng; and King Wu ruled from Hao. Therefore the people of the region still retain traces of the customs they learned under these ancient rulers. They are fond of agriculture, raise the five grains, take good care of their fields, and regard it as a serious matter to do wrong.

Later, Dukes Wen and Mu [11] of Ch'in [765–621 B.C.] fixed the capital of their state at Yung, which was on the main route for goods being brought out of both Lung and Shu and was a center for merchants. Dukes Hsien and Hsiao [384–338 B.C.] moved the Ch'in capital to the city of Yüeh. The city of Yüeh drove back the Jung and Ti barbarians

[10] In the following description of the various geographical areas of the empire and the customs of the people in each, there are no indications of tense and it is not certain whether Ssu-ma Ch'ien is talking about the customs of older times or those of his own day. I have in most cases translated as though he meant the latter.

[11] Omitting the name of Duke Hsiao, which erroneously appears between Wen and Mu in present texts.

in the north and in the east opened up communication with the states that had been created out of the former state of Chin. It too was a center for great merchants. Kings Wu and Chao [310–251 B.C.] made their capital at Hsien-yang, and it was this site that the Han took over and used for its own capital, Ch'ang-an. People poured in from all parts of the empire to congregate in the towns established at the imperial tombs around Ch'ang-an, converging on the capital like the spokes of a wheel. The land area is small and the population numerous, and therefore the people have become more and more sophisticated and crafty and have turned to secondary occupations such as trade to make their living.

South of this region are the provinces of Pa and Shu, which also contain rich fields and produce large quantities of gardenias for making dye, ginger, cinnabar, copper, iron, and bamboo and wooden implements. In the south these provinces control the regions of Tien and P'o, the latter noted for its young slaves. Nearby on the west are the regions of Ch'iung and Tso, the latter famous for its horses and oxtails. Though the area is hemmed in on all four sides by natural barriers, there are plank roadways built along the sides of the mountains for a thousand *li* so that there is no place that cannot be reached. All these roads are squeezed together into one in the narrow defile running between the Pao and Yeh rivers. By means of such roads, areas which have a surplus may exchange their goods for the things which they lack.

North of the capital area are the provinces of T'ien-shui, Lung-hsi, and Shang, whose customs are the same as those of the area within the Pass. To the west there are profits to be gained among the Ch'iang barbarians, while to the north are the herds of the Jung and Ti barbarians, which are one of the riches of the empire. Nevertheless, the region is mountainous and inaccessible and the only route out of it is that which leads to the capital.

Thus the region within the Pass occupies about a third of the area of the empire. The inhabitants represent only three tenths of the total population, but they possess six tenths of the wealth of the nation.

In ancient times the men of the state of Emperor Yao made their capital in Ho-tung, those of the Yin dynasty established their capital in Ho-nei, and those of the Chou dynasty in Ho-nan. These three regions stand like the legs of a tripod in the center of the empire and were used as the sites of their capitals by the successive dynasties, each of which lasted for several hundred or even a thousand years. The region is narrow and constricted and the population large. Since the capitals of the various dynasties served as gathering places for the feudal lords, the people are very thrifty and experienced in the ways of the world.

Yang and P'ing-yang [12] in Ho-tung have customarily traded with the area of Ch'in and the Ti barbarians in the west and with Chung and Tai in the north. Chung and Tai are situated north of the old city of Shih. They border the lands of the Hsiung-nu and are frequently raided by the barbarians. The inhabitants are proud and stubborn, high-spirited and fond of feats of daring and evil, and do not engage in agriculture or trade. Because the region is so close to the territory of the northern barbarians, armies have frequently been sent there, and when supplies were transported to them from the central states, the people were often able to profit from the surplus. The inhabitants have mingled with the barbarians, and their customs are by no means uniform. From the time before the state of Chin was divided into three parts they were already a source of trouble because of their violent temperament. King Wu-ling of Chao [325–299 b.c.] did much to encourage this trait, and the inhabitants today still retain the ways they developed when they were under the rule of Chao. The merchants of Yang and P'ing-yang roam through the region and obtain whatever goods they want.

Wen and Chih in Ho-nei have customarily traded with Shang-tang in the west and Chao and Chung-shan in the north. The soil in Chung-shan is barren and the population large. Even today at Sandy Hill are to be found the descendants of the people who took part in the decadent revels of Emperor Chou, the last ruler of the Yin dynasty, who had his summer palace there. The people are of an impetuous nature and are always looking for some cunning and clever way to make a living. The men gather together to play games, sing sad songs, and lament. When they really put their minds to business, they go out in bands to rob and kill, and in their spare time they loot graves, think up ways to flatter and deceive others or, dressing up in beautiful array, become

[12] Omitting the place name Ch'en, which does not seem to belong here.

singers and actors. The women play upon the large lute and trip about in dancing slippers, visiting the homes of the noble and rich to sell their favors or becoming concubines in the palaces of the feudal lords all over the empire.

Han-tan, situated between the Chang and Yellow rivers, is a city of major importance. In the north it has communications with Yen and Cho, and on the south with the regions of the old states of Cheng and Wei. The customs of Cheng and Wei are similar to those of Chao except that, since they are located nearer to Liang and Lu, the people are somewhat more sedate and take pride in virtuous conduct. The inhabitants of Yeh-wang were moved there from their city on the P'u River when the latter was taken over by the state of Ch'in [207 B.C.]. They are high-spirited and given to feats of daring, traits which mark them as former subjects of the state of Wei.

Yen, situated between the Gulf of Pohai and Chieh-shih, is also a major city. The region of Yen communicates with Ch'i and Chao in the south, borders the lands of the Hsiung-nu in the northeast, and extends as far as Chang-ku and Liao-tung, a distant and remote area, sparsely populated and often subject to barbarian raids. On the whole the customs are similar to those of Chao and Tai, but the people are as fierce as hawks and exercise little forethought. The region is rich in fish, salt, jujubes, and chestnuts. On the north it adjoins the Wu-huan and Fu-yü tribes and on the east it controls the profits derived from trade with the Hui-mo, Ch'ao-hsien, and Chen-p'an peoples.

Lo-yang in the region of Ho-nan trades with Ch'i and Lu to the east and with Liang and Ch'u to the south.

The region south of Mount T'ai is the former state of Lu and that north of the mountain is Ch'i. Ch'i is bounded by mountains and sea, a fertile area stretching a thousand *li,* suitable for growing mulberry and hemp. The population is large and produces beautifully patterned silks and other textiles, fish, and salt. Lin-tzu, the capital, situated between the sea and Mount T'ai, is a city of major importance. The people are by nature generous and easygoing, of considerable intelligence, and fond of debate. They are very attached to the land and dislike turmoil and uprising. They are timid in group warfare but brave in single combat, which accounts for the large number of highway robbers among them. On the whole, however, they have the ways of a great nation. All the five classes of people [scholars, farmers, traveling merchants, artisans, and resident traders] are to be found among them.

Tsou and Lu border the Chu and Ssu rivers and still retain the ways which they learned when they were ruled by the duke of Chou. They are fond of Confucian learning and proficient in matters of ritual, which makes them very punctilious. Mulberries and hemp are grown to some extent, but no resources are to be gained from forests or lakes. Land is scarce and the population numerous, so that the people are very frugal; they are much afraid of committing crimes and give a wide berth to evil. In later days, however, as the state has declined, they have become very fond of trade and are even more assiduous than the men of Chou in pursuing profit.

East of the Hung Canal and north of the Mang and Yang mountains as far as the marsh of Chü-yeh is the region of the old states of Liang and Sung. T'ao and Sui-yang are the most important cities in the area. In ancient times Emperor Yao built his pleasure palace at Ch'eng-yang, Emperor Shun fished in the Lei Marsh, and King T'ang settled in Po, so that the people still retain traces of the customs they learned from these former sage rulers. They are grave in demeanor, devoted to agricultural pursuits, and include a large number of true gentlemen. Though there are no riches to be gained from the mountains and rivers, the people are willing to put up with poor clothing and food and even manage to store up a surplus.

The regions of Yüeh and Ch'u are divided into three areas which differ in their customs. From the Huai River north to P'ei, Ch'en, Ju-nan, and Nan provinces is the area of western Ch'u. The people are very volatile and quickly give vent to their anger. The land is barren and there is little surplus to be stored up. Chiang-ling occupies the site of Ying, the old capital of the state of Ch'u. To the west it communicates with Wu and Pa and in the east draws upon the resources of the Yün-meng lakes. Ch'en is situated on what used to be the border between Ch'u and the old empire of the Hsia dynasty and carries on a trade in fish and salt. The population therefore includes a large number of merchants. The people of the districts of Hsü, T'ung, and Ch'ü-lü are honest and strict and pride themselves on keeping their promises.

From the city of P'eng-ch'eng east to Tung-hai, Wu, and Kuang-ling is the region of eastern Ch'u. The customs are similar to those of Hsü and T'ung. From the districts of Ch'ü and Tseng on north, however, the customs are similar to those of Ch'i, while from the Che and Yangtze rivers on south, they resemble those of Yüeh. Ho-lu, the ancient king of the state of Wu [725–702 B.C.], the lord of Ch'un-shen [third century B.C.], and Liu P'i, the king of Wu in Han times, all did their best to attract wandering scholars and protégés to the city of Wu. The city enjoys the rich salt resources derived from the sea in the east, copper from the Chang Mountains, and the benefits from the three mouths of the Yangtze and the Five Lakes nearby, and is the most important city in the area east of the Yangtze.

Heng-shan, Chiu-chiang, Chiang-nan, Yü-chang, and Ch'ang-sha make up the region of southern Ch'u. The customs of the people are generally similar to those of western Ch'u. Shou-ch'un, which the Ch'u kings used as their capital after they moved from Ying, is the most important city in the area. The district of Ho-fei receives goods transported down both the Huai River in the north and the Yangtze in the south and is a center for the shipping of hides, dried fish, and lumber. The customs of the people have become mixed with those of the Min and Yüeh tribes. Thus the men of southern Ch'u are fond of fancy phrases and clever at talking, but what they say can seldom be trusted. Chiang-nan, the area just south of the Yangtze, is low and damp, and even hardy young men die early there. It produces large quantities of bamboo and timber. Yü-chang produces gold and Ch'ang-sha produces lead ore, but the quantity is so small that, though it exists, it seldom repays the cost of extraction.

From the Nine Peaks and Ts'ang-wu south to Tan-erh the customs are in general similar to those of Chiang-nan, though with a large admixture of the customs of the Yang and Yüeh people. P'an-yü is the most important city in the area, being a center for pearls, rhinoceros horn, tortoise shell, fruit, and cloth.

Ying-ch'uan and Nan-yang were the home of the people of the ancient Hsia dynasty. The Hsia people valued loyalty and simplicity in government, and the influence of the Hsia kings is still to be seen in the ways of the inhabitants of the region, who are warmhearted and sincere. In the latter days of the Ch'in dynasty the government moved large numbers of lawbreakers to the region of Nan-yang. Nan-yang communicates on the west with the area within the Pass through the Wu Pass, and with Han-chung through the Hsün Pass, and from the east and south it receives goods by way of the Han, Yangtze, and Huai rivers. Yüan is the most important city in the region. The customs are rather heterogeneous; the people are fond of business and there are many merchants among them. The local bosses in the area work in cooperation with their counterparts in Ying-ch'an. Even today people refer to the inhabitants of the entire region as "men of Hsia."

Various products are rare in one part of the empire and plentiful in another part. For example, it is the custom of the people east of the mountains to use salt extracted from the sea, while those west of the mountains use rock salt. There are also places in Ling-nan in the far south and in the deserts of the far north which have long produced salt. In general, the same is true of other products as well.

To sum up, the region of Ch'u and Yüeh is broad and sparsely populated, and the people live on rice and fish soups. They burn off the fields and flood them to kill the weeds, and are able to gather all the fruit, berries, and univalve and bivalve shellfish they want without waiting for merchants to come around selling them. Since the land is so rich in edible products, there is no fear of famine, and therefore the people are content to live along from day to day; they do not lay away stores of goods, and many of them are poor. As a result, in the region south of the Yangtze and Huai rivers no one ever freezes or starves to death, but on the other hand there are no very wealthy families.

The region north of the Che and Ssu rivers is suitable for growing the five types of grain, mulberries, and hemp, and for raising the six kinds of domestic animals.[13] Land is scarce and the population dense, and the area often suffers from floods and drought. The people therefore take good care to lay away stores of food. Hence in the regions of Ch'in, Hsia, Liang, and Lu agriculture is favored and the peasants are held in esteem. The same is true of Ho-tung, Ho-nei and Ho-nan, as well as Yüan and Ch'en, though in these regions the people also engage in trade. The people of Ch'i and Chao with their intelligence

[13] Horses, cattle, pigs, goats, dogs, and chickens. Dogs were raised to be eaten.

and cleverness are always on the lookout for a chance to make a profit. Those of Yen and Tai gain their living from their fields and herds of domestic animals, and also raise silkworms.

Judging from all that has been said above, when wise men lay their profound plans in palace chambers or deliberate in audience halls, guard their honor and die for their principles, or when gentlemen retire to dwell in mountain caves and establish a reputation for purity of conduct, what is their ultimate objective? Their objective is simply wealth. So the honest official after years of service attains riches, and the honest merchant in the end becomes wealthy.

The desire for wealth does not need to be taught; it is an integral part of all human nature. Hence, when young men in the army attack cities and scale walls, break through the enemy lines and drive back the foe, cut down the opposing generals and seize their pennants, advance beneath a rain of arrows and stones, and do not turn aside before the horrors of fire and boiling water, it is because they are spurred on by the prospect of rich rewards. Again, when the youths of the lanes and alleys attack passers-by or murder them and hide their bodies, threaten others and commit evil deeds, dig up graves and coin counterfeit money, form gangs to bully others, lend each other a hand in avenging wrongs, and think up secret ways to blackmail people or drive them from the neighborhood, paying no heed to the laws and prohibitions, but rushing headlong to the place of execution, it is in fact all because of the lure of money. In like manner, when the women of Chao and the maidens of Cheng paint their faces and play upon the large lute, flutter their long sleeves and trip about in pointed slippers, invite with their eyes and beckon with their hearts, considering it no distance at all to travel a thousand miles to meet a patron, not caring whether he is old or young, it is because they are after riches. When idle young noblemen ornament their caps and swords and go about with a retinue of carriages and horsemen, it is simply to show off their wealth. Those who go out to shoot birds with stringed arrows, to fish or to hunt, heedless of dawn or nightfall, braving frost and snow, galloping around the animal pits or into ravines without shying from the dangers of wild beasts, do so because they are greedy for the taste of fresh game. The reason that those who indulge in gambling, horse racing, cock fighting, and dog racing turn red in the face, shouting boasts to one another, and invariably quarrel over the victory is that they consider it a very serious matter to lose their wagers. Doctors, magicians, and all those who live by their arts are willing to burn up their spirits and exhaust their talents only because they value the fees they will receive. When officials in the government juggle with phrases and twist the letter of the law, carve fake seals and forge documents, heedless of the mutilating punishments of the knife and saw that await them if they are discovered, it is because they are drowned in bribes and gifts. And when farmers, craftsmen, traders, and merchants lay away stores and work to expand their capital, we may be sure that it is because they are seeking wealth and hope to increase their goods. Thus men apply all their knowledge and use all their abilities simply in accumulating money. They never have any strength left over to consider the question of giving some of it away.

The proverb says, "You don't go a hundred miles to peddle firewood; you don't go a thousand miles to deal in grain. If you are going to be in a place for one year, then seed it with grain. If you are going to be there ten years, plant trees. And if you are going to be there a hundred years, provide for the future by means of virtue." Virtue here means being good to people. Now there are men who receive no ranks or emoluments from the government and who have no revenue from titles or fiefs, and yet they enjoy just as much ease as those who have all these; they may be called the "untitled nobility." A lord who possesses a fief lives off the taxes. Each year he is allowed to collect two hundred cash from each household, so that the lord of a thousand households has an income of two hundred thousand cash. But out of this he has to pay the expenses of his spring and autumn visits to the court and pay for various gifts and presentations. Common people such as farmers, craftsmen, traveling traders, and merchants on the whole may expect a profit of two thousand cash a year on a capital investment of ten thousand. So if a family has a capital investment of a million cash, their income will likewise be two hundred thousand. Out of this they must pay the cost of commutation of labor and military services, as well as property and poll taxes, but with the rest they may buy whatever fine food and clothing they desire.

Thus it is said that those who own pasture lands producing fifty horses a year, or a hundred head of cattle, or five hundred sheep, or five hundred marshland swine; those who own reservoirs stocked with a thousand piculs of fish or mountain lands containing a thousand logs of timber; those who have a thousand jujube trees in An-i, or a thousand chestnut trees in Yen or Ch'in, or a thousand citrus trees in Shu, Han, or Chiang-ling, or a thousand catalpas north of the Huai River or south of Ch'ang-shan in the region of the Yellow and Chi rivers; those who own a thousand *mou* of lacquer trees in Ch'en or Hsia, a thousand *mou* of mulberries or hemp in Ch'i or Lu, or a thousand *mou* of bamboo along the Wei River; those who own farmlands in the suburbs of some famous capital or large city which produce one *chung*[14] of grain per *mou,* or those who own a thousand *mou* of gardenias or madder for dyes, or a thousand beds of ginger or leeks— all these may live just as well as a marquis enfeoffed with a thousand households. Commodities such as these are in fact the sources of considerable wealth. Their owners need not visit the market place or travel about to other cities but may simply sit at home and wait for the money to come in. They may live with all the dignity of retired gentlemen and still enjoy an income.

At the other extreme, when it comes to those impoverished men with aged parents and wives and children too weak or young to help them out, who have nothing to offer their ancestors at the seasonal sacrifices, who must depend upon the gifts and contributions of the community for their food and clothing and are unable to provide for themselves—if men such as these, reduced to such straits, still fail to feel any shame or embarrassment, then they hardly deserve to be called human. Therefore, when men have no wealth at all, they live by their brawn; when they have a little, they struggle to get ahead by their brains; and when they already have plenty of money, they look for an opportunity for a good investment. This in general is the way things work.

When it comes to making a living, the wise man will look around

---

[14] One *chung* is equal to ten *hu,* or about five and a half U.S. bushels. One *mou* at this time was probably about 0.114 acres. The units used in this list are often obscure, and commentators disagree on their interpretation. Throughout the chapter I have followed the interpretations given by Professor Miyazaki Ichisada in his article, in Japanese, "A Price-list in the Biographies of Millionaires in the *Shih-chi,*" *Miscellanea Kiotensia* (Kyoto University, 1956), pp. 451-74.

for some way to gain an income that does not involve any personal danger. Hence the best kind of wealth is that which is based upon agriculture, the next best is that which is derived from secondary occupations, and the worst of all is that which is acquired by evil means. But if a man is not a gentleman of unusual character who has deliberately sought retirement from the world, and if he grows old in poverty and lowliness and still insists upon talking about his "benevolence and righteousness," he ought to be thoroughly ashamed of himself.

As for the ordinary lot of tax-paying commoners, if they are confronted by someone whose wealth is ten times their own, they will behave with humility; if by someone whose wealth is a hundred times their own, they will cringe with fear; if by someone whose wealth is a thousand times their own, they will undertake to work for him; and if by someone whose wealth is ten thousand times their own, they will become his servants. This is the principle of things.

It is said, "If a man is trying to work his way up from poverty to riches, then farming is not as good as handicrafts, and handicrafts are not as good as trade; embroidering lovely patterns at home is not as good as lounging about the market gate." This means that the secondary occupations are the best source of wealth for a poor man.

Anyone who in the market towns or great cities manages in the course of a year to sell the following items: a thousand brewings of liquor; a thousand jars of pickles and sauces; a thousand jars of sirups; a thousand slaughtered cattle, sheep, and swine; a thousand *chung* of grain; a thousand cartloads or a thousand boat-lengths of firewood and stubble for fuel; a thousand logs of timber; ten thousand bamboo poles; a hundred horse carriages; a thousand two-wheeled ox carts; a thousand lacquered wooden vessels; brass utensils weighing thirty thousand catties; a thousand piculs of plain wooden vessels, iron vessels, or gardenia and madder dyes; two hundred horses; five hundred cattle; two thousand sheep or swine; a hundred male or female slaves; a thousand catties of tendons, horns, or cinnabar; thirty thousand catties of silken fabric, raw silk, or other fine fabrics; a thousand rolls of embroidered or patterned silk; a thousand piculs of fabrics made of vegetable fiber or raw or tanned hides; a thousand pecks of lacquer;

a thousand jars of leaven or salted bean relish; a thousand catties of globefish or mullet; a thousand piculs of dried fish; thirty thousand catties of salted fish; three thousand piculs of jujubes or chestnuts; a thousand skins of fox or sable; a thousand piculs of lamb or sheep skins; a thousand felt mats; or a thousand *chung* of fruits or vegetables —such a man may live as well as the master of an estate of a thousand chariots. The same applies for anyone who has a thousand strings of cash [i.e., a million cash] to lend out on interest. Such loans are made through a moneylender, but a greedy merchant who is too anxious for a quick return will only manage to revolve his working capital three times while a less avaricious merchant has revolved his five times. These are the principal ways of making money. There are various other occupations which bring in less than twenty percent profit, but they are not what I would call sources of wealth.

Now I should like to describe briefly the ways in which some of the worthy men of the present age, working within an area of a thousand miles, have managed to acquire wealth, so that later generations may see how they did it and select what may be of benefit to themselves.

The ancestors of the Cho family were natives of Chao who made a fortune by smelting iron. When the Ch'in armies overthrew the state of Chao, the family was ordered to move to another part of the empire for resettlement. Having been taken captive and plundered of all their wealth and servants, the husband and wife were left to make the move alone, pushing their belongings in a cart. All of the other captives who were forced to move and who had a little wealth left vied with each other in bribing the officials to send them to some nearby location, and they were therefore allowed to settle in Chia-meng. But Mr. Cho said, "This region is too narrow and barren. I have heard that at the foot of Mount Min there are fertile plains full of edible tubers so that one may live all his life without suffering from famine. The people there are clever at commerce and make their living by trade." He therefore asked to be sent to a distant region, and was ordered to move to Lin-ch'iung. He was overjoyed, and when he got there and found a mountain which yielded iron ore, he began smelting ore and laying other plans to accumulate wealth until soon he dominated the trade among the people of Tien and Shu. He grew so rich that he owned a thousand young slaves, and the pleasures he indulged in among his fields and lakes and on his bird and animal hunts were like those of a great lord.

Ch'eng Cheng, like Mr. Cho, was one of those taken captive east of the mountains by the Ch'in armies and forced to resettle in the far west. He too engaged in the smelting industry and carried on trade with the barbarians who wear their hair in the mallet-shaped fashion. His wealth equaled that of Mr. Cho, and the two of them lived in Lin-ch'iung.

The ancestors of the K'ung family of Yüan were men of Liang who made their living by smelting iron. When Ch'in overthrew the state of Liang, the K'ung family was moved to Nan-yang, where they began smelting iron with bellows on a large scale and laying out ponds and fields. Soon they were riding about in carriages with a mounted retinue and visiting the feudal lords, and from these contacts they were able to earn large profits in trade. They also won a reputation for handing out lavish gifts in the manner of noblemen of leisure, but at the same time the profits they derived from their business were surprisingly large— far larger, in fact, than those derived by more cautious and tightfisted merchants—and the family fortune eventually reached several thousand catties of gold. Therefore the traders of Nan-yang all imitated the K'ung family's lordly and openhanded ways.

Lu people are customarily cautious and miserly, but the Ping family of Ts'ao were particularly so. They started out by smelting iron and in time accumulated a fortune of a hundred million cash. All the members of the family from the father and elder brothers down to the sons and grandsons, however, made a promise that they would

> Never look down without picking up something useful;
> Never look up without grabbing something of value.

They traveled about to all the provinces and kingdoms, selling goods on credit, lending money and trading. It was because of their influence that so many people in Tsou and Lu abandoned scholarship and turned to the pursuit of profit.

The people of Ch'i generally despise slaves, but Tiao Hsien alone valued them and appreciated their worth. Most men worry in particular about slaves who are too cunning and clever, but Tiao Hsien gladly acquired all he could of this kind and put them to work for him, sending them out to make a profit peddling fish and salt. Though he traveled about in a carriage with a mounted retinue and consorted with governors of provinces and prime ministers of kingdoms, he came to rely more and more upon his slaves, and in the end managed by their labor to acquire a fortune of twenty or thirty million cash. Hence the saying, "Is it better to have a title in the government or to work for Tiao Hsien?" which means that he made it possible for his best slaves to enrich themselves while at the same time he utilized their abilities to the fullest.

The people of the old state of Chou have always been very close in money matters, but Shih Shih was an extreme example. With a couple of hundred cartloads of goods he traveled around to the various provinces and kingdoms peddling his wares; there was absolutely no place he did not go. The city of Lo-yang is situated right in the middle of the old states of Ch'i, Ch'in, Ch'u, and Chao, and even the poor people of the town study to become apprentices to the rich families, boasting to each other about how long they have been in trade and how they have several times passed by their old homes but were too busy to go in the gate. By making use of men like this in his business, Shih Shih was finally able to accumulate a fortune of seventy million cash.

The ancestor of the Jen family of Hsüan-ch'ü was an official in charge of the granary at Tu-tao. When the Ch'in dynasty was overthrown and the leaders of the revolt were all scrambling for gold and jewels, Mr. Jen quietly dug a hole and stored away the grain that had been in his charge. Later, when the armies of Ch'u and Han were stalemated at Jung-yang and the people were unable to plow their fields and plant their crops, the price of grain rose to ten thousand cash a picul, and all the gold and jewels of the great leaders soon found their way into the hands of Mr. Jen. This was the start of the Jen family fortune. But while other rich people were outdoing each other in luxurious living, the Jen family lived very frugally and devoted all their energies to farming and animal raising. And while most people try to buy the cheapest fields and pasture lands, the Jen family bought up only those that were really valuable and of good quality. Thus the family remained wealthy for several generations. Mr. Jen made all the members of the family promise that they would not eat or wear anything that was not produced from their own fields or herds, and that none of them would dare to drink wine or eat meat until their public services had been completed. Because of this rule they became the leaders of the community and, while continuing to be wealthy, enjoyed the respect of the ruler.

When the frontier was expanded and the border regions opened, only Ch'iao T'ao took advantage of the opportunity, acquiring resources calculated at a thousand horses, twice that number of cattle, ten thousand sheep, and ten thousand *chung* of grain.

When Wu, Ch'u, and the other kingdoms, seven in all, raised their revolt in the time of Emperor Ching, the feudal lords in Ch'ang-an made preparations to join the imperial armies in putting down the rebellion and began looking around for ways to borrow money to provide for the expedition. The moneylenders, considering that the fiefs and kingdoms of the feudal lords were all located east of the mountains and that the fate of that region was still a matter of grave doubt, were unwilling to lend them any money. Only one man, a Mr. Wu-yen, consented to lend them a thousand catties of gold at an interest of ten times the amount of the loan. By the end of three months the states of Wu and Ch'u had been brought under control, and within the year Mr. Wu-yen received his tenfold interest. As a result he became one of the richest men in the area within the Pass.

Most of the rich merchants and big traders of the area within the Pass belonged to the T'ien family, such as T'ien Se and T'ien Lan. In addition, the Li family of Wei-chia and the Tu families of An-ling and Tu also had fortunes amounting to a hundred million cash.

These, then, are examples of outstanding and unusually wealthy men. None of them enjoyed any titles or fiefs, gifts, or salaries from the government, nor did they play tricks with the law or commit any crimes to acquire their fortunes. They simply guessed what course conditions were going to take and acted accordingly, kept a sharp eye out for the opportunities of the times, and so were able to capture a fat profit. They gained their wealth in the secondary occupations and held on to it by investing in agriculture; they seized hold of it in times of crisis and maintained it in times of stability. There was a special aptness in the way they adapted to the times, and therefore their stories are worth relating. In addition, there are many other men who exerted themselves at farming, animal raising, crafts, lumbering, merchandising, and trade and seized the opportunities of the moment to make a fortune, the greatest of them dominating a whole province, the next greatest dominating a district, and the smallest dominating a village, but they are too numerous to be described here.

Thrift and hard work are without doubt the proper way to gain a livelihood. And yet it will be found that rich men have invariably employed some unusual scheme or method to get to the top. Plowing the fields is a rather crude way to make a living, and yet Ch'in Yang did so well at it that he became the richest man in his province. Robbing graves is a criminal offense, but T'ien Shu got his start by doing it. Gambling is a wicked pastime, but Huan Fa used it to acquire a fortune. Most fine young men would despise the thought of traveling around peddling goods, yet Yung Lo-ch'eng got rich that way. Many people would consider trading in fats a disgraceful line of business, but Yung Po made a thousand catties of gold at it. Vending sirups is a petty occupation, but the Chang family acquired ten million cash that way. It takes little skill to sharpen knives, but because the Chih family didn't mind doing it, they could eat the best of everything. Dealing in dried sheep stomachs seems like an insignificant enough trade, but thanks to it the Cho family went around with a mounted retinue. The calling of a horse doctor is a rather ignominious profession, but it enabled Chang Li to own a house so large that he had to strike a bell to summon the servants. All of these men got where they did because of their devotion and singleness of purpose.

From this we may see that there is no fixed road to wealth, and money has no permanent master. It finds its way to the man of ability like the spokes of a wheel converging upon the hub, and from the hands of the worthless it falls like shattered tiles. A family with a thousand catties of gold may stand side by side with the lord of a city; the man with a hundred million cash may enjoy the pleasures of a king. Rich men such as these deserve to be called the "untitled nobility," do they not?

FINDING LIST OF CHAPTERS OF THE
SHIH CHI

Biographies and Accounts of Foreign
Peoples (SC 61–130) *Cont.:*

SC 105	Omitted	SC 117	Vol. II, Part II
SC 106	Vol. I, Part X	SC 118	Vol. II, Part III
SC 107	Vol. II, Part II	SC 119	Vol. II, Part IV
SC 108	Vol. II, Part II	SC 120	Vol. II, Part II
SC 109	Vol. II, Part II	SC 121	Vol. II, Part IV
SC 110	Vol. II, Part II	SC 122	Vol. II, Part IV
SC 111	Vol. II, Part II	SC 123	Vol. II, Part II
SC 112	Vol. II, Part II	SC 124	Vol. II, Part IV
SC 113	Vol. II, Part II	SC 125	Vol. II, Part IV
SC 114	Vol. II, Part II	SC 126	Omitted
SC 115	Vol. II, Part II	SC 127	Vol. II, Part IV
SC 116	Vol. II, Part II	SC 128	Omitted
		SC 129	Vol. II, Part IV
		SC 130	Omitted

INDEX

Index